MANAGERIAL AND ORGANIZATIONAL REALITY

MANAGERIAL AND ORGANIZATIONAL REALITY

STORIES OF LIFE AND WORK

Peter J. Frost

University of British Columbia

Walter R. Nord

University of South Florida

Linda A. Krefting

Texas Tech University

PEARSON

Prentice
Hall

UPPER SADDLE RIVER, NEW JERSEY 07458

Library of Congress Cataloging-in-Publication Data

Managerial and organizational reality : stories of life and work / [edited by] Peter Frost, Walter Nord, Linda Krefting.
   p.   cm.
Rev. ed. of: Managerial reality. c1995 and Organizational reality. c1997.
Includes bibliographical references.
ISBN 0-13-142523-4
   1. Management.   2. Industrial management.   3. Organizational behavior.
I. Frost, Peter J.   II. Nord, Walter R.   III. Krefting, Linda A.   IV. Managerial reality.   V. Organizational reality.

HD31.M29394   2003
658.4—dc21   2003045780

Senior Editor: Jennifer Simon
Editor-in-Chief: Jeff Shelstad
Assistant Editor: Melanie Olson
Editorial Assistant: Kelly Wendrychowicz
Marketing Manager: Shannon Moore
Marketing Assistant: Christine Genneken
Managing Editor (Production): John Roberts
Production Editor: Renata Butera
Production Assistant: Joe DeProspero
Permissions Supervisor: Suzanne Grappi
Manufacturing Buyer: Michelle Klein
Cover Design: Bruce Kenselaar
Composition/Full-Service Project Management: BookMasters, Inc./Jennifer Welsch
Printer/Binder: Courier Westford

Credits and acknowledgments borrowed from other sources and reproduced, with permission, in this textbook appear on appropriate page within the text.

Pearson Education LTD.
Pearson Education Singapore, Pte. Ltd
Pearson Education, Canada, Ltd
Pearson Education–Japan

Pearson Education Australia PTY, Limited
Pearson Education North Asia Ltd
Pearson Educación de Mexico, S.A. de C.V.
Pearson Education Malaysia, Pte. Ltd

10 9 8 7 6 5 4 3 2 1
ISBN 0-13-142523-4

PREFACE

Beginning in 1978, two of us, Frost and Nord, working with Vance Mitchell, published the first edition of *Organizational Reality: Reports from the Firing Line.* We created the book because we were troubled by what we saw as a major disconnect between how the contents of the existing textbooks on organizational behavior portrayed organizations and how people who worked in organizations experienced them. It seemed to us that the textbooks made it appear that organizations were reasonably rational and humane places in which to work. On the other hand, from our own experiences in organizations and what we learned informally from conversations with people who worked in organizations and through the popular media, we believed many people did not experience organizations the way the textbooks portrayed them. Consequently, we were determined to compile a set of materials that would help us and our academic colleagues provide a more balanced treatment—one that would complement the traditional textbook by capturing people's experiences in organizations. In this spirit, we began the introduction by writing:

> Suppose that you are a visitor to Earth from the distant planet Utopia. One of your assignments is to bring back printed materials to Utopian scholars who are attempting to understand what Earthlings call formal organizations. You have limited space so you must choose very carefully. One option you have is to bring back one or two of the leading textbooks on organizational behavior. Another option you have is to bring back selections from newspapers, business and general periodicals, and short stories and plays about life in organizations. Which would you choose?
>
> The picture that the Utopian scholars will develop from each of these sets of materials will most likely be very different. If you were to choose the textbooks, the scholars would most likely come to understand organizations as systems that are managed in a rational manner in pursuit of certain stated goals. They would more than likely conclude that people who are committed to achieving these objectives staff organizations. Also, it is probable that the scholars would come to believe that members of organizations are oriented toward cooperation and are sincerely concerned with each other's well-being. Depending on the particular textbook you brought back, however, the scholars might conclude that organizations do not, in fact, operate in these ways, but that through the application of a certain set of procedures, techniques, philosophies, and so on, any organization that is not operating rationally and cooperatively could be made to do so.

By contrast, if you happened to take this book or some other collection of materials from periodicals, newspapers, and other sources that have been less completely filtered by the academic mind, the picture of organizations the scholars derived would be different. They would likely decide that organizations are anything but rational, cooperative systems. They would conclude that members at all levels of the organization frequently pursue their own interests at the expense of others in the organization, as well as at the expense of the achievement of the goals of a total organization. The scholars would see that organizations are frequently inhumane systems. Individuals experience intense stress from task demands as well as intense and often bitter conflict and rivalry with members of their own work group and with members of other work groups and organizations. One also would find that organizational participants often respond aggressively against these pressures and against whatever threatens their own interests. Furthermore, it is unlikely that the scholars would conclude that any discernible set of principles, techniques, and philosophies exists that seem capable of turning most organizations into rational, cooperative systems.

Most students in organizational behavior, introductory business, and even management policy courses are exposed to only the first set of sources. In this book, we plan to provide a ready collection of the second set. We do not offer this collection as evidence that the normative views presented in most academic textbooks are totally irrelevant. In fact, we believe that the normative views are relevant. However, it is ineffective to present them to students without complementary information about how organizations are experienced. Students readily discover that organizations as described in the textbooks are not the same as organizations they actually experience. Consequently, students and managers reject the "whole package" of organizational behavior as "soft," theoretical, or irrelevant without examining the potentially relevant materials. [p. xv – xvi]

Typical textbooks have become somewhat more reality oriented, but in our view, most still do not provide a sufficient treatment of either the "dark side" of organizations or how organizations are experienced by their members. Consequently, we still are editing reality books. Because they are widely adopted in colleges and universities, our colleagues seem to share our view that they are needed.

Clearly, one might suspect that other people would label editors like us, who attempt to present the dark side and to represent the interests of lower-level participants vis-à-vis those of the "establishment," as muckrakers. In this regard, Frost and Nord willingly wear this label—particularly in their younger days. We suspect that Vance Mitchell does too, but following his retirement from the University of British Columbia, he has decided not to participate in further revisions of our earlier books. To try to fill the gap that Vance's decision created, Frost and Nord recruited Linda Krefting to replace him. One might expect that a solid academic and cordial person such as Krefting might lead to moderation of the muckraking tendencies. However reasonable this expectation might seem, it is totally wrong. Much to Frost and Nord's delight, Krefting shares the same critical spirit and has helped to represent the interests of the organizational participants that had been overlooked in our preceding editions;

we hope that with these revisions, this edition provides an even sharper critical edge than the earlier versions did. Thus, this book continues the spirit of its ancestors.

We have made one major change in addition to the change in editorship. In this edition, we merge the *Organizational Reality* book with a parallel series of books we did entitled *Managerial Reality*.

Let us explain our rationale. Following the success of *Organizational Reality*, which was developed to complement textbooks on organizational behavior, we thought that instructors in management courses could benefit from a similarly intended set of counter materials. To this end, we developed two editions of *Managerial Reality: Balancing Technique, Practice, and Values*. As this title suggests, we attempted to maintain a reality focus but move from organizational behavior to management. In making this move, we found the set of reality-oriented materials shifted attention from our somewhat heavy focus on the experiences of lower-level participants to material that captured the experiences of managers and executives, as well.

However, this latter book has proved to be popular in the executive courses in which it is used. The change in focus meant that *Managerial Reality* did not have the same critical edge that the *Organizational Reality* books did. The current book is an effort to combine the previous two sets of books. Specifically, we attempt to preserve the reality orientation while including the realities of executive managerial levels and those of lower-level participants.

We think we have been able to achieve a successful synergy. One way we did this was to make our selections based on our past experiences about what readings worked well in the classroom, many of which were published after our earlier editions. We have used these materials successfully with introductory classes in OB and Management on a variety of levels—Executive MBA, MBA, and undergraduate. We like all the selections but we do not expect to use all of the materials in one class. However, we have found that the readings in previous editions were sufficiently attractive to the students that often, even in the crush of the semester, they read many of the unassigned portions on their own.

Even after our best efforts, revisions of books such as this have mixed consequences. On the positive side, the additions we make keep things current. On the negative side, adding new material requires us to make space by omitting selections from earlier editions. As we have done so in the past, a number of colleagues have chastised us, saying: "You left out reading X, which was one of my favorites. How could you do that?" In response, we have said that we were sorry, but to keep the materials current we needed to open up some space.

As a result of our merger of two books and the substantial number of new selections we have included, we expect even more chastisement for eliminating favorites. In anticipation of it, we apologize in advance if we dropped any of your favorites in this revision, but simultaneously we express our wish that the exciting new selections we have included become new favorites for you.

We enjoy compiling these materials, even though some drudgery is involved. We were extremely fortunate, working on this edition, to have had Michele Walpole assist us. Michele's upbeat personality enhanced our enjoyment, and her competence and diligence helped reduce the drudgery and improve the final product. We gratefully acknowledge her help and also the hard work of Cynthia Ree. We sincerely thank Jennifer Simon, Renata Butera, Suzanne Grappi, and Kelly Wendrychowicz at Prentice

Hall and Jen Welsch at BookMasters for their competence, diligence, and conscientiousness, which were instrumental in publishing this book. In addition, we greatly appreciate the help of Connie Toole in typing portions of our work. Finally, we wish to thank Vance Mitchell for all his work on previous editions and for encouraging us to go forward without him.

Peter J. Frost
Walter R. Nord
Linda A. Krefting

INTRODUCTION

Reiterating a key point from the preface, we believe that most of the teaching materials available for courses in organization behavior and management do not expose students sufficiently to how people in organizations experience the organizations they are in. This book attempts to provide a corrective tool. The word we have chosen to point to these "omitted" experiences is *reality*.

The word *reality* is more problematic than people who use it often acknowledge. Some philosophers tell us there is no reality; these and other philosophers usually use the term *reality* to refer to phenomena that exist independently of the existence of any human being or human experience.

We, on the other hand, use the word to refer to the very experiences of human beings themselves. That is, *when we use* reality *in this book, we are referring to people's experiences*. By qualifying "reality" with the adjective *organizational*, we refer to how people experience life in organizations.

We attempt to capture these experiences as they occur to people at all levels of the organization. Not surprisingly, people at different levels in organizational hierarchies have different experiences. In order to capture this diversity using printed sources, it is necessary to pull from a wide variety of materials. Thus, as you read this book, you'll find a number of readings from a broad range of sources.

Despite the diversity, a very large number come from mainstream publications that are widely read by modern managers—*Harvard Business Review*, the *Wall Street Journal*, and *Fast Company*. Many of these deal with recent changes in the demands placed on organizations that require managers to act in ways that are new to the business world. The readings in the *Harvard Business Review*, in particular, tend to deal with the challenges as they appear to managers and executives; often these articles provide some guidance to help managers deal with these experiences effectively. In short, these materials capture many of the issues that contribute to the experiences managers have today in their decision-making roles and offer some ways to cope with them.

In contrast, to capture the experiences of lower-level participants we need to draw upon a wider variety of sources. To do so, we included a number of essays (some original), some poems, and short stories. Also, we included a speech by a prominent trade union leader and a number of articles from daily newspapers. To some extent, our motivation in offering these materials is to give voice to people whose interests often are not expressed in conventional textbooks. Thus, at least implicitly, we seek to advance their concerns. In addition, some of these diverse sources help the reader gain appreciation of some experiences of high-level participants that often are repressed by the conventional treatments that do not legitimize discourse about such matters. These omitted aspects often make for interesting reading.

Not only does providing a more balanced picture of how people experience organizations make for interesting reading and give voice to neglected concerns, it also is of considerable practical importance to managers because such a picture is more apt to be complete than is a less balanced one. Often, it is the incomplete view that leads to problems because the latent or hidden matters in human affairs are sources of tension and trouble. Developing awareness of these hidden matters before they become problems can help those responsible for coordinating a human system do so more easily and effectively.

If nothing else, however, reading and talking about such hidden aspects of organizations is often fun and produces stimulating discussions.

Putting this all together, we hope you find the results our efforts to place the experiences of organization participants before you to be enlightening, thought provoking, useful, and fun.

Peter J. Frost
Walter R. Nord
Linda A. Krefting

ABOUT THE AUTHORS

Dr. Peter J. Frost is the Edgar F. Kaiser Chair of Organizational Behavior at the University of British Columbia. He is a former associate dean and was a senior editor of the journal *Organization Science*. He is the author/editor of over ten books including *Organizational Reality: Reports from the Firing Line*, 5e (2003); *HRM Reality: Putting Competence in Context*, 2e (2002); and *Reframing Organizational Culture* (1991). Other publications include "Leading in Times of Trauma," in the January 2002 issue of the *Harvard Business Review*; "Why Compassion Counts!" in the *Journal of Management Inquiry;* and "The Toxic Handler: Organizational Hero and Casualty" in the *Harvard Business Review*. Both appeared in 1999. His latest book, *Toxic Emotions at Work*, was published by the Harvard Business School Press (2003). He received the Financial Post Leaders in Management Education Award in 1997 and the prestigious Distinguished Educator Award from the Academy of Management in 1998.

Walter R. Nord (Ph.D., psychology, Washington University, 1967) is Distinguished University Professor and Professor of Management at the University of South Florida. Previously, he was at Washington University–St. Louis (1967 to 1989). His current interests center on developing an agnostic philosophical framework for social science. He has published widely in scholarly journals and edited/authored a number of books. His books include *The Meanings of Occupational Work* (with A. Brief), *Implementing Routine and Radical Innovations* (with S. Tucker), *Organizational Reality: Reports from the Firing Line* and *Managerial Reality* (with P. Frost and V. Mitchell), *Resistance and Power in Organizations* (with J. Jermier and D. Knights), and *HRM Reality: Putting Competence in Context*, 2e (with P. Frost and L. Krefting, 2002). He is currently co-editor of the *Employee Responsibilities and Rights Journal*, past and present book review editor for the *Academy of Management Review*, and is currently a member of the editorial boards of *Organization and Environment* and *Organization*. He has served as consultant on organizational development and change for a variety of groups and organizations. He coedited the *Handbook of Organization Studies* (with S. Clegg and C. Hardy) that received the 1997 George Terry Award.

Linda A. Krefting got her doctorate in industrial relations at the University of Minnesota. She has done research in such areas as human resource policies and practices, equal employment opportunity, and compensation for publications such as *Industrial Relations, Academy of Management Journal, Journal of Management Inquiry,* and *Gender, Work and Organization,* among others. She is coeditor, with Walter Nord and Peter Frost, of *HRM Reality: Putting Competence in Context*, 2e (2002). Her professional affiliations include the Academy of Management and the Society for Human Resource Management. She is currently an associate professor at the Rawls College of Business, Texas Tech University, and teaches survey and advanced courses in human resource management and organizational behavior.

MANAGERIAL AND
ORGANIZATIONAL REALITY

SECTION *1*

CONVERSATIONS ACROSS THE CENTURIES

For literally thousands of years, human beings have conversed about the best way to organize. However, as the nature of organizing has changed, the problems discussed have changed. To try to capture the nature of previous problems and how humans have sought to address them, we begin this section by going well back in history. Although we do not start "In the beginning . . ." with Genesis, we begin with the earliest discussion of delegation and the division of labor that we know of, a selection from Exodus (about Moses). As we will see, matters related to delegation continue to be discussed today, although in the modern context, the terms that appear in the discussions have changed. In modern conversations, concerns about delegation often appear under such new terms as *empowerment*.

We continue with another Old Testament account (an excerpt about King Solomon) that also has surprising modem currency. Although the account of Solomon does not deal as directly with principles of organizing as does the one about Moses, one sees in it evidence of a problem that has long been a source of difficulty for all people who attempt to deal with others. Namely, people are not always truthful, and sometimes they offer false information in pursuing their own interests. People who are leaders and administrators thus need wisdom to make decisions using the information they have available. Solomon's approach was so ingenious that it helped earn him the reputation of being one of history's wisest people.

We then turn from the Holy Bible to a selection from what some say has become the *de facto* bible of capitalism, Adam Smith's 1777 *Wealth of Nations*. This selection contains perhaps the most widely discussed passage in all of the conversations about managing across the ages—the division of labor and the pin factory. These ideas played a major role in improving productivity from the late eighteenth century on. However, as we will see, recently management authorities have come to see the widespread acceptance of Smith's ideas about the division of labor as a source of problems for modern organizations. This concern will be addressed most explicitly by Hammer and Champy later in this section.

In addition to his ideas about the division of labor, Adam Smith is at least equally well-known for his concept of the "invisible hand." According to Smith, operating through the free-market system capitalism provides the invisible hand, induces every individual to employ his or her (although in Smith's writings it was usually "his") capital to promote the public interest, even though the person has no intention to do so, but rather simply intends to promote his/her own security. In the next selection by Chandler, we see that Smith's idea of the invisible hand, even though it is still proclaimed loudly by most economists and many politicians, also has been challenged in *some* ways by management practice over time. Whereas traditionally, the "invisible hand" was thought to be the best mechanism for guiding a firm's operations along its value adding chain, the famous business historian Alfred Chandler found that in the early twentieth century, many businesses discovered a superior way—in some ways, they substituted a "visible hand" of organization structure for the invisible hand. This substitution was associated with developing much more complex organizations. These organizations, in turn, contributed to some of the problems Hammer and Champy address in the next selection. In essence, the visible hand helped make businesses into large bureaucratic organizations.

Hammer and Champy tell us that the visible hand of the early and mid-twentieth century helped create organizations that seemed to be too bureaucratic and rigid to be effective in the dynamic/rapid-change environment of the late 1900s. It appears that the changes Chandler considered followed the age of Adam Smith but preceded the demands for flexible organizations that arose in the late 1900s and that continue to pressure today's organizations to change.

The selection, from Hammer and Champy's *Reengineering the Corporation* (1993), suggests not only that we need to revise our thinking about Adam Smith's division of labor, but because recent changes demanded that organizations respond flexibly to the somewhat unique and customer-specific demands they faced in the latter part of the twentieth century, we also need to rethink ways for managing the large structures Chandler described.

Hammer and Champy signal how the organizations portrayed by Chandler need to be readjusted to become the more flexible, empowering organizations that the late twentieth and early twenty-first century seemed to demand. Interestingly, the challenges such changes present to modern managers are related to the challenge Moses faced. They demand that managers find ways to move decisions and power into the hands of lower-level participants.

Implementing such changes requires managers to think and act differently toward their people. In the next selection, Pfeffer and Veiga capture the gist of such changes nicely; specifically managers must "put people first." The authors articulate some of the specific things managers must do to actualize this new priority. Not surprisingly, these changes seem provocative because they often call for actions and policies that negate many of the ideas of Chandler's times that had become almost "givens" in modern thinking about how to manage. Among other things, Pfeffer and Veiga show nicely how to be customer sensitive in the ways suggested by Hammer and Champy; organizations need to make major changes in how they approach people. However, implicit in Pfeffer and Veiga's piece is the view that some people still have not gotten this message despite its clear importance.

As conversations about managing evolved across the ages, knowledge began to be systemized and disseminated in institutions of higher education, often in prestigious, expensive MBA programs. Exposure to these conversations was associated with success in business, although why so is a matter of debate. Thus, many recent conversations were about the value of MBA degrees themselves. Many of these conversations have a distinctly cynical tone. For example, Russell Ackoff a leading scholar in the study of twentieth-century business, was quoted by Detrick (2002) as follows:

> When I retired from Wharton, I wrote an article that endeared me to the faculty. The question was, "What are the contributions of business education?" I said there were three. The first was to equip students with a vocabulary that enables them to talk authoritatively about subjects they do not understand. The second was to give students principles that would demonstrate their ability to withstand any amount of disconfirming evidence. The third was to give students a ticket of admission to a job where they could learn something about management.("Russell L. Ackoff: Interview by Glenn Detrick Educational Benchmarking, Inc." *Academy of Management Learning and Education,* 2002, Vol. 1, No. 1, p. 56)

If Ackoff had it right, as some believe he did, it seems strange that so many intelligent young people continue to spend thousands of dollars and two years or more of their lives to get an MBA degree. What does the evidence say about the educational benefits of MBA degrees? In the next selection, Jeffrey Pfeffer and Christina Fong examine the evidence, and as the subtitle of their article. ("The End of Business Schools? Less Success Than Meets the Eye") implies, the evidence provided reasonable support for Ackoff's skeptical observations.

Clearly, in the selections we have considered so far, we see that through the ages people who manage organizations have needed to change how they managed in ways that they often experienced as radical. One of the problems humans have in attempting to behave in radically new ways is that at the time, it is not always clear exactly what they need to do. Things appear especially uncertain in comparison to how clear the things that they have been doing recently have come to appear. Consequently, when they attempt to make these changes, they experience uncertainty. In responding to great uncertainty, people often combine their old and new approaches in strange ways. In doing so, they act in ways that appear to others to be confused, contradictory, and self-defeating. Such behavior makes them grist for the satirist's mill. In fact, today we can pick up almost any major daily newspaper and find the cartoon strip Dilbert portraying self-contradictory actions by managers. Such actions are so common that many employees describe them as typical of their daily realities. Thus, no portrayal of conversations about management would be complete without including the voice of the satirist. Dave Barry is an exceptionally effective satirist, so we include a short piece by him describing how a motivational consultant to Burger King attempted to enhance motivation within the firm by having people walk on hot coals during a retreat.

Another human response to uncertainty is to blindly follow what other people seem to be doing. Foss's "The Calf Path" points to this tendency and should be kept in mind later in the book when we consider the frequency of fads in management.

No summary of conversations across the ages would be complete without giving some voice to the human spirit of compassion and human desires to make their world better. Accordingly, we conclude this section with a piece that speaks with this voice — an anonymous piece titled "The Cracked Water Pot."

Conclusion

This chapter explores a number of things that human beings have said about their experiences in and management of organizations across the ages. After study of these materials, it should be clear that whatever constancies there might be in human nature, the ways organizations attempt to deal with humans has not remained constant. Perhaps the best conclusion to come to is that people must keep an open mind about what is appropriate and, in order to decide what is appropriate, have an in-depth understanding of the times in which they are functioning and the experiences that people are having during those times.

It is in this context that the following sections in this book should be useful. Basically, they reveal the pressures that organizational participants experience in modern times and how people in the organizations experience them. We suggest that awareness of and sensitivity to these matters are essential inputs to help people manage today's organizations and those of the future.

I-1: Exodus
Chapter 18

. . . 13: And it came to pass on the morrow, that Moses sat to judge the people and the people stood by Moses from the morning unto the evening. 14: And when Moses' father in law saw all that he did to the people, he said, What is this thing that thou doest to the people? why sittest thou thyself alone, and all the people stand by thee from morning unto even? 15: And Moses said unto his father in law, Because the people come unto me to inquire of God: 16: When they have a matter, they come unto me; and I judge between one and another, and I do make them know the statutes of God, and his laws. 17: And Moses' father in law said unto him, The thing that thou doest is not good. 18: Thou wilt surely wear away, both thou, and this people that is with thee; for this thing is too heavy for thee; thou art not able to perform it thyself alone. 19: Hearken now unto my voice, I will give thee counsel, and God shall be with thee: Be thou for the people to Godward, that thou mayest bring the causes unto God: 20: And thou shalt teach them ordinances and laws, and shalt shew them the way wherein they must walk, and the work that they must do. 21: Moreover thou shalt provide out of all the people able men, such as fear God, men of truth, hating covetousness; and place such over them, to be rulers of thousands, and rulers of hundreds, rulers of fifties, and rulers of tens: 22: And let them judge the people at all seasons: and it shall be, that every great matter they shall bring unto thee, but every small matter they shall judge: so shall it be easier for thyself, and they shall bear the burden with thee. 23: If thou shalt do this thing, and God command thee so, then thou shalt be able to endure, and all this people shall also go to their place in peace. 24: So Moses hearkened to the voice of his father in law, and did all that he had said. . . .

From Holy Bible: King James Version. World Bible Publishing Company, 1989.

I-2: 1 Kings
Chapter 3

. . . 16: Then came there two women, that were harlots, unto the king, and stood before him. 17: And the one woman said, O my lord, I and this woman dwell in one house; and I was delivered of a child with her in the house. 18: And it came to pass the third day after that I was delivered, that this woman was delivered also: and we were together; there was no stranger with us in the house, save we two in the house. 19: And this woman's child died in the night; because she overlaid it. 20: And she arose at midnight, and took my son from beside me, while thine handmaid slept, and laid it in her bosom, and laid her dead child in my bosom. 21: And when I rose in the morning to give my child suck, behold, it was dead: but when I had considered it in the morning, behold, it was not my son, which I did bear. 22: And the other woman said, Nay; but the living is my son, and the dead is thy son. And this said, No; but the dead is thy son, and the living is my son. Thus they spake before the king. 23: Then said the king, The one saith, This is my son that liveth, and thy son is the dead: and the other saith, Nay; but thy son is

From Holy Bible: King James Version. World Bible Publishing Company, 1989.

the dead, and my son is the living. 24: And the king said, Bring me a sword. And they brought a sword before the king. 25: And the king said, Divide the living child in two, and give half to the one, and half to the other. 26: Then spake the woman whose the living child was unto the king, for her bowels yearned upon her son, and she said, O my lord, give her the living child, and in no wise slay it. But the other said. Let it be neither mine nor thine, but divide it. 27: Then the king answered and said, Give her the living child, and in no wise slay it: she is the mother thereof. . . .

I-3: An Inquiry into the Nature and Causes of the Wealth of Nations

Adam Smith

[6] ● ● ● ● ● ● ●
BOOK I

Of the Causes of Improvement in the productive Powers of Labour, and of the Order according to which its Produce is naturally distributed among the different Ranks of the People

● ● ● ● ● ● ● ● ● ●
CHAPTER I

OF THE DIVISION OF LABOUR

1 The greatest *a*improvement*a* in the productive powers of labour, and the greater part of the skill, dexterity, and judgment with which it is any where directed, or applied, seem to have been the effects of the division of labour.[1]

2   The effects of the division of labour, in the general business of society, will be more easily understood, by considering in what manner it operates in some particular manufactures. It is commonly supposed to be carried furthest in some very trifling ones; not perhaps that it really is carried further in them than in other of more importance: but in those trifling manufactures which are destined to supply the small wants of but a small number of people, the whole number of workmen must necessarily be small; and those employed in every different branch of the work can often be collected into the same workhouse, and placed at once under the view of the spectator. In those great

---

"Of the Division of Labor" from *An Inquiry into the Nature and Causes of the Wealth of Nations* by Adam Smith, editors R. H. Campbell and A. S. Skinner. Oxford University Press, pp. 6–20. Reprinted by permission of Oxford University Press.
*a–a*improvements *I*
[1]The first considered exposition of the term division of labour by a modern writer was probably by Sir William Petty: "Those who have the command of the Sea Trade, may Work at easier Freight with more profit, than others at greater: for as Cloth must be cheaper made, when one Cards, another Spins, another Weaves, another Draws, another Dresses, another Presses and Packs; than when all the Operations above-mentioned, were clumsily performed by the same hand; so those who command the Trade of Shipping, can build long slight Ships for carrying Masts, Fir-Timber, Boards, Balks, etc." (*Political Arithmetick* (London, 1690), 19 in C.H. Hull, *The Economic Writings of Sir William Petty* (Cambridge, 1899), i. 260). "For in so vast a City *Manufactures* will beget one another, and each *Manufacture* will be divided into as many parts as possible, whereby the work of each *Artisan* will be simple and easie: As for Example. In the making of a *Watch*, If one Man shall make the *Wheels*, another the *Spring*, another shall Engrave the *Dial-plate*, and another shall make the *Cases*, then the *Watch* will be better and cheaper, than

manufactures, on the contrary, which are destined to supply the great wants of the great body of the people, every different branch of the work employs so great a number of workmen, that it is impossible to collect them all into the same workhouse. We can seldom see more, at one time, than those employed in one single branch. Though *b*in such manufactures*b*, therefore, the work may really be divided into a much greater number of parts, than in those of a more trifling nature, the division is not near so obvious, and has accordingly been much less observed.

3   To take an example, therefore, from a very trifling manufacture; but one in which the division of labour has been very often taken notice of, the trade of the pin-maker; a workman not educated to this business (which the division of labour has rendered a distinct trade), not acquainted with the use of the machinery employed in it (to the invention of which the same division of labour has probably given occasion), could scarce, perhaps, with his utmost industry, make one pin in a day, and certainly could not make twenty. But in the way in which this business is now carried on, not only the whole work is a peculiar trade, but it is divided into a number of branches, of which the greater part are likewise peculiar trades. One man draws out the wire, another

straights it, a third cuts it, a fourth points it, a fifth grinds it at the top for receiving the head; to make the head requires two or three distinct operations; to put it on, is a peculiar business, to whiten the pins is another; it is even a trade by itself to put them into the paper; and the important business of making a pin is, in this manner, divided into about eighteen distinct operations, which, in some manufactories, are all performed by distinct hands, though in others the same man will sometimes perform two or three of them. I have seen a small manufactory of this kind where ten men only were employed, and where some of them consequently performed two or three distinct operations. But though they were very poor, and therefore but indifferently accommodated with the necessary machinery, they could, when they exerted themselves, make among them about twelve pounds of pins in a day. There are in a pound upwards of four thousand pins of a middling size. Those ten persons, therefore, could make among them upwards of forty-eight thousand pins in a day. Each person, therefore, making a tenth part of forty-eight thousand pins, might be considered as making four thousand eight hundred pins in a day. But if they had all wrought separately and independently, and without any of them having been educated to this peculiar

---

if the whole Work be put upon any one Man." (*Another Essay in Political Arithmetick, concerning the Growth of the City of London* (London, 1683), 36-7, in C.H. Hull, ii.473.)

Later use was by Mandeville and Harris: "There are many Sets of Hands in the Nation, that, not wanting proper Materials, would be able in less than half a Year to produce, fit out, and navigate a First-Rate [Man of War]: yet it is certain, that this Task would be impracticable, if it was not divided and subdivided into a great Variety of different Labours; and it is as certain that none of these Labours require any other, than working Men of ordinary Capacities." (B. Mandeville, *The Fable of the Bees*, pt. ii.149, ed. F. B. Kaye (Oxford, 1924), ii.142.) "No number of Men, when once they enjoy Quiet, and no Man needs to fear his Neighbour, will be long without learning to divide and subdivide

their Labour." (Ibid., pt. ii.335, ed. Kaye ii.284.) "The advantages accruing to mankind from their betaking themselves severally to different occupations, are very great and obvious: For thereby, each becoming expert and skilful in his own particular art; they are enabled to furnish one another with the products of their respective labours, performed in a much better manner, and with much less toil, than any one of them could do of himself.(J. U. Harris, *An Essay upon Money and Coins* (London, 1757), i. 16.)

The advantages of the division of labour are also emphasized by Turgot in sections III and IV of his *Reflections on the Formation and Distribution of Riches* (1766). The translation used is by R. L. Meek and included in his *Turgot on Progress, Sociology and Economics* (Cambridge, 1973).
*b–b*in them *I*

business, they certainly could not each of them have made twenty, perhaps not one pin in a day; that is, certainly, not the two hundred and fortieth, perhaps not the four thousand eight hundredth part of what they are at present capable of performing, in consequence of a proper division and combination of their different operations.

4   In every other art and manufacture, the effects of the division of labour are similar to what they are in this very trifling one; though, in many of them, the labour can neither be so much subdivided, nor reduced to so great a simplicity of operation. The division of labour, however, so far as it can be introduced, occasions, in every art, a proportionable increase of the productive powers of labour. The separation of different trades and employments from one another, seems to have taken place, in consequence of this advantage. This separation too is generally carried furthest in those countries which enjoy the highest degree of industry and improvement; what is the work of one man, in a rude state of society, being generally that of several in an improved one. In every improved society, the farmer is generally nothing but a farmer; the manufacturer, nothing but a manufacturer. The labour too which is necessary to produce any one complete manufacture, is almost always divided among a great number of hands. How many different trades are employed in each branch of the linen and woollen manufacturers, from the growers of the flax and the wool, to the bleachers and smoothers of the linen, or to the dyers and dressers of the cloth. The nature of agriculture, indeed, does not admit of so many subdivisions of labour, nor of so complete a separation of one business from another, as manufactures. It is impossible to separate so entirely, the business of the grazier from that of the corn-farmer, as the trade of the carpenter is commonly separated from that of the smith. The spinner is almost always a

distinct person from the weaver; but the ploughman, the harrower, the sower of the seed, and the reaper of the corn, are often the same. The occasions for those different sorts of labour returing with the different seasons of the year, it is impossible that one man should be constantly employed in any one of them. This impossibility of making so complete and entire a separation of all the different branches of labour employed in agriculture, is perhaps the reason why the improvement of the productive powers of labour in this art, does not always keep pace with their improvement in manufactures. The most opulent nations, indeed, generally excel all their neighbours in agriculture as well as in manufactures; but they are commonly more distinguished by their superiority in the latter than in the former. Their lands are in general better cultivated, and having more labour and expence bestowed upon them, produce more, in proportion to the extent and natural fertility of the ground. But ^{c}this^c superiority of produce is seldom much more than in proportion to the superiority of labour and expence. In agriculture, the labour of the rich country is not always much more productive than that of the poor; or, at least, it is never so much more productive, as it commonly is in manufactures. The corn of the rich country, therefore, will not always, in the same degree of goodness, come cheaper to market than that of the poor. The corn of Poland, in the same degree of goodness, is as cheap as that of France, notwithstanding the superior opulence and improvement of the latter country. The corn of France is, in the corn provinces, fully as good, and in most years nearly about the same price with the corn of England, though, in opulence and improvement, France is perhaps inferior to England. The ^{d}corn-lands^d of England, however, are

---

$^{c-c}$the *I* $^{d-d}$lands *I*

better cultivated than those of France, and the ^ecorn-lands^e of France are said to be much better cultivated than those of Poland. But though the poor country, notwithstanding the inferiority of its cultivation, can, in some measure, rival the rich in the cheapness and goodness of its corn, it can pretend to no such competition in its manufactures; at least if those manufactures suit the soil, climate, and situation of the rich country. The silks of France are better and cheaper than those of England, because the silk manufacture, ^fat least under the present high duties upon the importation of raw silk,^f does not ^gso well^g suit the climate of England as ^hthat of France^h. But the hardware and the coarse woollens of England are beyond all comparison superior to those of France, and much cheaper too in the same degree of goodness. In Poland there are said to be scarce any manufactures of any kind, a few of those coarser household manufactures excepted, without which no country can well subsist.

5   This great increase ⁱofⁱ the quantity of work, which, ^jin consequence of the division of labour^j, the same under of people are capable of performing^k, is owing to three different circumstances; first, to the increase of dexterity in every particular workman; secondly, to the saving of the time which is commonly lost in passing from one species of work to another; and lastly, to the invention of a great number of machines which facilitate and abridge labour, and enable one man to do the work of many.

6   First, the improvement of the dexterity of the workman necessarily increases the quantity of the work he can perform, and the division of labour, by reducing every man's business to some one simple opera-

tion, and by making this operation the sole employment of his life, necessarily increases very much the dexterity of the workman. A common smith, who, though accustomed to handle the hammer, has never been used to make nails, if upon some particular occasion he is obliged to attempt it, will scarce, I am assured, be able to make above two or three hundred nails in a day, and those too very bad ones. A smith who has been accustomed to make nails, but whose sole or principal business has not been that of a nailer, can seldom with his utmost diligence make more than eight hundred or a thousand nails in a day. I have seen several boys under twenty years of age who had never exercised any other trade but that of making nails, and who, when they exerted themselves, could make, each of them, upwards of two thousand three hundred nails in a day. The making of a nail, however, is by no means one of the simplest operations. The same person blows the bellows, stirs or mends the fire as there is occasion, heats the iron, and forges every part of the nail: In forging the head too he is obliged to change his tools. The different operations into which the making of a pin, or of a metal button, is subdivided, are all of them much more simple, and the dexterity of the person, of whose life it has been the sole business to perform them, is usually much greater. The rapidity with which some of the operations of those manufactures are performed, exceeds what the human hand could, by those who had never seen them, be supposed capable of acquiring.

7   Secondly, the advantage which is gained by saving the time commonly lost in passing from one sort of work to another, is much greater than we should at first view be apt to imagine it. It is impossible to pass very quickly from one kind of work to another, that is carried on in a different place, and with quite different tools. A country weaver, who cultivates a small farm, must lose a

---

^{e–e}lands *I*   ^{f–f}2–6
^{g–g}2-6   ^{h–h}2–6
^{i–i}in 6   ^{j–j}2–6
^kin consequence of the division of labour, *I*

good deal of time in passing from his loom to the field, and from the field to his loom. When the two trades can be carried on in the same workhouse, the loss of time is no doubt much less. It is even in this case, however, very considerable. A man commonly saunters a little in turning his hand from one sort of employment to another. When he first begins the new work he is seldom very keen and hearty; his mind, as they say, does not go to it, and for some time he rather trifles than applies to good purpose. The habit of sauntering and of indolent careless application, which is naturally, or rather necessarily acquired by every country workman who is obliged to change his work and his tools every half hour, and to apply his hand in twenty different ways almost every day of his life; renders him almost always slothful and lazy, and incapable of any vigorous application even on the most pressing occasions. Independent, therefore, of his deficiency in point of dexterity, this cause alone must always reduce considerably the quantity of work which he is capable of performing.

8   Thirdly, and lastly, every body must be sensible how much labour is facilitated and abridged by the application of proper machinery. It is unnecessary to give any example^l. I shall ^{l}only observe, ^{m}therefore^m, that the invention of all those machines by which labour is so much facilitated and abridged, seems to have been originally owing to the division of labour. Men are much more likely to discover easier and readier methods of attaining any object, when the whole attention of their minds is directed towards that single object, than when it is dissipated among a great variety of things. But in consequence of the division of labour, the whole of every man's attention comes naturally to be directed towards some one very simple object. It is naturally to be expected, therefore, that some one or other of those who are employed in each particular branch of labour should soon find out easier and readier methods of performing their own particular work, wherever the nature of it admits of such improvement. A great part of the machines ^{n}made use of^n in those manufactures in which labour is most subdivided, were originally the inventions of common workmen, who, being each of them employed in some very simple operation, naturally turned their thoughts towards finding out easier and readier methods of performing it. Whoever has been much accustomed to visit such manufactures, must frequently have been shewn very pretty machines, which were the inventions of ^{o}such^o workmen, in order to facilitate and quicken their own particular part of the work. In the first fire-engines, a boy was constantly employed to open and shut alternately the communication between the boiler and the cylinder, according as the piston either ascended or descended. One of those boys, who loved to play with his companions, observed that, by tying a string from the handle of the valve, which opened this communication, to another part of the machine, the valve would open and shut without his assistance, and leave him at liberty to divert himself with his play-fellows.

$^{l-l}$therefore, *I* $^{m-m}$2-6 $^{n-n}$employed *I* $^{o-o}$common *I*

I-4: The Visible Hand
The Managerial Revolution in American Business

Alfred D. Chandler, Jr.

● ● ● ● ● ● ● ● ● ● ● ● ● ● ● ● ● ● ●
INTRODUCTION: THE VISIBLE HAND

The title of this book indicates its theme but not its focus or purpose. Its purpose is to examine the changing processes of production and distribution in the United States and the ways in which they have been managed. To achieve this end it focuses on the business enterprise that carried out these processes. Because the large enterprise administered by salaried managers replaced the small traditional family firm as the primary instrument for managing production and distribution, the book concentrates specifically on the rise of modern business enterprise and its managers. It is a history of a business institution and a business class.

The theme propounded here is that modern business enterprise took the place of market mechanisms in coordinating the activities of the economy and allocating its resources. In many sectors of the economy the visible hand of management replaced what Adam Smith referred to as the invisible hand of market forces. The market remained the generator of demand for goods and services, but modern business enterprise took over the functions of coordi-

Introduction of *The Visible Hand* by Alfred D. Chandler, Jr. Harvard University Press, 1977, pp. 1–12.

nating flows of goods through existing processes of production and distribution, and of allocating funds and personnel for future production and distribution. As modern business enterprise acquired functions hitherto carried out by the market, it became the most powerful institution in the American economy and its managers the most influential group of economic decision makers. The rise of modern business enterprise in the United States, therefore, brought with it managerial capitalism.

MODERN BUSINESS ENTERPRISE DEFINED

Modern business enterprise is easily defined. As Figure 1-1 indicates, it has two specific characteristics: it contains many distinct operating units and it is managed by a hierarchy of salaried executives.

Each unit within the modern multiunit enterprise has its own administrative office. Each is administered by a full-time salaried manager. Each has its own set of books and accounts which can be audited separately from those of the large enterprise. Each could theoretically operate as an independent business enterprise.

In contrast, the traditional American business firm was a single-unit business enterprise. In such an enterprise an individual or a small number of owners operated a

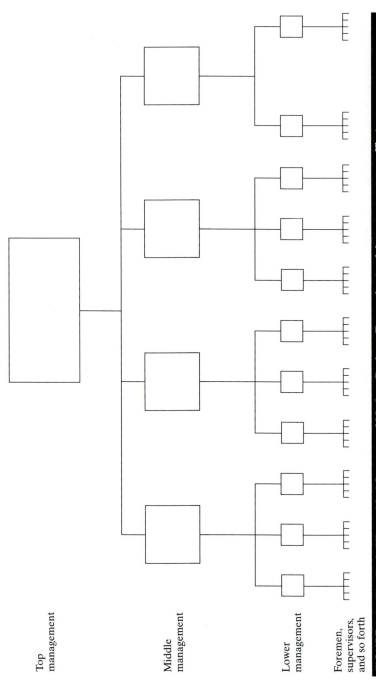

FIGURE 1-1 The Basic Hierarchical Structure of Modern Business Enterprise (each box represents an office)

Top
management

Middle
management

Lower
management

Foremen,
supervisors,
and so forth

shop, factory, bank, or transportation line out of a single office. Normally this type of firm handled only a single economic function, dealt in a single product line, and operated in one geographic area. Before the rise of the modern firm, the activities of one of these small, personally owned and managed enterprises were coordinated and monitored by market and price mechanisms.

Modern enterprise, by bringing many units under its control, began to operate in different locations, often carrying on different types of economic activities and handling different lines of goods and services. The activities of these units and the transactions between them thus became internalized. They became monitored and coordinated by salaried employees rather than market mechanisms.

Modern business enterprise, therefore, employs a hierarchy of middle and top salaried managers to monitor and coordinate the work of the units under its control. Such middle and top managers form an entirely new class of businessmen. Some traditional single-unit enterprises employed managers whose activities were similar to those of the lowest level managers in a modern business enterprise. Owners of plantations, mills, shops, and banks hired salaried employees to administer or assist them in administering the unit. As the work within single operating units increased, these managers employed subordinates—foremen, drivers, and mates—to supervise the work force. But as late as 1840 there were no middle managers in the United States—that is, there were no managers who supervised the work of other managers and in turn reported to senior executives who themselves were salaried managers. At that time nearly all top managers were owners; they were either partners or major stockholders in the enterprise they managed.

The multiunit enterprise administered by a set of salaried middle and top managers can then properly be termed modern.

Such enterprises did not exist in the United States in 1840. By World War I this type of firm had become the dominant business institution in many sectors of the American economy. By the middle of the twentieth century, these enterprises employed hundreds and even thousands of middle and top managers who supervised the work of dozens and often hundreds of operating units employing tens and often hundreds of thousands of workers. These enterprises were owned by tens or hundreds of thousands of shareholders and carried out billions of dollars of business annually. Even a relatively small business enterprise operating in local or regional markets had its top and middle managers. Rarely in the history of the world has an institution grown to be so important and so pervasive in so short a period of time.

Describing and analyzing the rise of an institution and a class of such immense historical and current significance provides a fascinating challenge to a historian of the American economy. Because this institution is so easy to define and because it came into being so recently, the scholar has little difficulty in answering the historian's special questions of when, where, and how. He can record with precision at what dates, in what areas, and in what ways the new institution first appeared and then continued to grow. In so doing, he can document the rise of the new subspecies of economic man—the salaried manager—and record the development of practices and procedures that have become standard in the management of American production and distribution. Once he has answered the historical questions of when, where, and how, he can begin to suggest the reasons why this institution first appeared and then became so powerful.

The challenge is particularly attractive because it has not yet been taken up. For all its significance, the history of this institution has not been told. Scholars have paid surprisingly little attention to its historical development. Before the 1930 economists only grudgingly acknowledged its existence, and since then they have looked on large-scale business enterprise with deep suspicion. Much basic economic theory is still grounded on the assumption that the processes of production and distribution are managed, or at least should be managed, by small traditional enterprises regulated by the invisible hand of the market. According to such theory, perfect competition can only exist between such single-unit enterprises, and such competition remains the most efficient way to coordinate economic activities and allocate economic resources. The modern, multiunit enterprise, by its very act of administrative coordination, brings imperfect competition and misallocation of resources. Since many economists have for so long considered the modern business enterprise as an aberration, and an evil one at that, few have taken the trouble to examine its origins. For them the desire for monopoly power has provided an adequate causal explanation.

Until recently historians as well have concentrated little systematic attention on the rise of modern business enterprise and the managerial class that came to administer it. They have preferred to study individuals, not institutions. In fact, few businessmen have appeared in general American histories except those who founded modern business enterprises. Historians have been attracted by entrepreneurs, but they have rarely looked closely at the new institution these entrepreneurs created, at how it was managed, what functions it carried out, and how the enterprise continued to compete and grow after the founders had left the scene. Instead they have argued as to whether these founding fathers were robber barons or industrial statesmen, that is, bad fellows or good fellows. Most historians, as distrustful as the economists about the enterprises these men built, agreed that they were bad. These same historians, however, made few value judgments either way about

the new class of managers whose actions were so influential in the continuing development of the American economy.

In recent years economists and historians have increasingly turned their attention to modern economic institutions. Economists such as Edward S. Mason, A.D.H. Kaplan, John Kenneth Galbraith, Oliver E. Williamson, William J. Baumol, Robin L. Marris, Edith T. Penrose, and Robert T. Averitt, following the pioneering work of Adolph A. Berle, Jr., and Gardiner C. Means, have studied more closely the operations and actions of modern business enterprise. They have not attempted, however, to examine its historical development, nor has their work yet had a major impact on economic theory. The firm remains essentially a unit of production, and the theory of the firm a theory of production.

Economists with a historical bent have only just begun to study institutional change and its impact on industrial organization. Douglass C. North has been the innovator here.[1] In his work with Lance E. Davis he outlined a most useful theory of institutional change and applied it to American economic growth. In his study with Robert Paul Thomas he demonstrated how the changing industrial organization affected the rise of the west. The works of North and his colleagues use this sweeping panorama of history to test, buttress, and refine their theory. They have not yet focused on a detailed analysis of the historical development of any specific economic institution.

Historians of the American experience have also moved to the study of institutions. Such scholars as Robert H. Wiebe, Morton Keller, Samuel Hays, and Lee Benson have taken a close look at the changing nature of political, social, and economic organizations. They have pioneered in what one analyst of recent writing in American history has called the "new institutionalism."[2] Few historians, however, have tried to trace the story of a single institution from its beginnings to its full growth. None have written about the rise of modern business enterprise and the brand of managerial capitalism that accompanied it.

This study is an attempt to fill that void by concentrating on a specific time period and a specific set of concerns. It centers on the years between the 1840s and the 1920s—when the agrarian, rural economy of the United States became industrial and urban. These decades witnessed revolutionary changes in the processes of production and distribution in the United States. Within this time period I examine the ways in which the units carrying out these changing processes of production and distribution—including transportation, communication, and finance—were administered and coordinated. I have not tried to describe the work done by the labor force in these units or the organization and aspirations of the workers. Nor do I attempt to assess the impact of modern business enterprise on existing political and social arrangements. I deal with broad political, demographic, and social developments only as they impinge directly on the ways in which the enterprise carried out the processes of production and distribution.

SOME GENERAL PROPOSITIONS

This study is a history. It moves chronologically. It is filled with details about men and events, about specific processes, policies, and procedures, and about changing technologies and markets. It attempts to carry out the historian's basic responsibility for setting the record straight. That record, in turn, provides the basis for the generalizations presented. The data have not been selected to rest and validate hypotheses or general theories. I hope that these facts may also be useful to scholars with other questions and concerns other than those relevant to the generalizations presented here.

Before I enter the complexities of the historical experience, it seems wise to out-line a list of general propositions to make more precise the primary concerns of the study. They give some indication at the outset of the nature of modern business enterprise and suggest why the visible hand of management replaced the invisible hand of market mechanisms. I set these forth as a guide through the intricate history of inter-related institutional changes that follows.

The first proposition is that modern multiunit business enterprise replaced small traditional enterprise when administrative coordination permitted greater productivity, lower costs, and higher profits than coordination by market mechanisms.

This proposition is derived directly from the definition of a modern business enterprise. Such an enterprise came into being and continued to grow by setting up or purchasing business units that were theoretically able to operate as independent enterprises—in other words, by internalizing the activities that had been or could be carried on by several business units and the transactions that had been or could be carried on between them.

Such an internalization gave the enlarged enterprise many advantages.[3] By routinizing the transactions between units, the costs of these transactions were lowered. By linking the administration of producing units with buying and distributing units, costs for information on markets and sources of supply were reduced. Of much greater significance, the internalization of many units permitted the flow of goods from one unit to another to be administratively coordinated. More effective scheduling of flows achieved a more intensive use of facilities and personnel employed in the processes of production and distribution and so increased productivity and reduced costs. In addition, administrative coordination provided a more certain cash flow and more rapid payment for services rendered. The savings resulting from such coordination were much greater than those resulting from lower information and transactions costs.

The second proposition is simply that the advantages of internalizing the activities of many business units within a single enterprise could not be realized until a managerial hierarchy had been created.

Such advantages could be achieved only when a group of managers had been assembled to carry out the functions formerly handled by price and market mechanisms. Whereas the activities of single-unit traditional enterprises were monitored and coordinated by market mechanisms, the producing and distributing units within a modern business enterprise are monitored and coordinated by middle managers. Top managers, in addition to evaluating and coordinating the work of middle managers, took the place of the market in allocating resources for future production and distribution. In order to carry out these functions, the managers had to invent new practices and procedures which in time became standard operating methods in managing American production and distribution.

Thus the existence of a managerial hierarchy is a defining characteristic of the modern business enterprise. A multiunit enterprise without such managers remains little more than a federation of autonomous offices. Such federations were formed to control competition between units or to assure enterprises of sources of raw materials or outlets for finished goods and services. The owners and managers of the autonomous units agreed on common buying, pricing, production, and marketing policies. If there were no managers, these policies were determined and enforced by legislative and judicial rather than administrative means. Such federations were often able to bring small reductions in information and transactions costs, but they could not lower costs through increased productivity. They could not provide the administrative coordination that became the central function of modern business enterprise.

The third proposition is that modern business enterprise appeared for the first time in history when the volume of economic activities reached a level that made administrative coordination more efficient and more profitable than market coordination.

Such an increase in volume of activity came with new technology and expanding markets. New technology made possible an unprecedented output and movement of goods. Enlarged markets were essential to absorb such output. Therefore modern business enterprise first appeared, grew, and continued to flourish in those sectors and industries characterized by new and advancing technology and by expanding markers. Conversely in those sectors and industries where technology did not bring a sharp increase in output and where markets remained small and specialized, administrative coordination was rarely more profitable than market coordination. In those areas modern business enterprise was late in appearing and slow in spreading.

The fourth proposition is that once a managerial hierarchy had been formed and had successfully carried out its function of administrative coordination, the hierarchy itself became a source of permanence, power, and continued growth.

In Werner Sombart's phrase, the modern business enterprise took on "a life of its own."[4] Traditional enterprises were normally short-lived. They were almost always partnerships which were reconstituted or disbanded at the death or retirement of a partner. If a son carried on the father's business, he found new partners. Often the partnership was disbanded when one partner decided he wanted to work with another businessman. On the other hand, the hierarchies that came to manage the new multiunit enterprises had a permanence beyond that of any individual or group of individuals who worked in them. When a manager died, retired, was promoted, or left an office, another was ready and trained to take his place. Men came and went. The institution and its offices remained.

The fifth proposition is that the careers of the salaried managers who directed these hierarchies became increasingly technical and professional.

In these new business bureaucracies, as in other administrative hierarchies requiring specialized skills, selection and promotion became increasingly based on training, experience, and performance rather than on family relationship or money. With the coming of modern business enterprise, the businessman, for the first time, could conceive of a lifetime career involving a climb up the hierarchical ladder. In such enterprises, managerial training became increasingly longer and more formalized. Managers carrying out similar activities in different enterprises often had the same type of training and attended the same types of schools. They read the same journals and joined the same associations. They had an approach to their work that was closer to that of lawyers, doctors, and ministers than that of the owners and managers of small traditional business enterprises.

The sixth proposition is that as the multiunit business enterprise grew in size and diversity and as its managers became more professional, the management of the enterprise became separated from its ownership.

The rise of modern business enterprise brought a new definition of the relationship between ownership and management and therefore a new type of capitalism to the American economy. Before the appearance of the multiunit firm, owners managed and managers owned. Even when partnerships began to incorporate, their capital stock stayed in the hands of a few individuals or families. These corporations remained single-unit enterprises which rarely hired more than two or three managers. The traditional capitalist firm can, therefore, be properly termed a personal enterprise.

From its very beginning, however, modern business enterprise required more managers than a family or its associates could provide. In some firms the entrepreneur and his close associates (and their families) who built the enterprise continued to hold the majority of stock. They maintained a close personal relationship with their managers, and they retained a major say in top management decisions, particularly those concerning financial policies, allocation of resources, and the selection of senior managers. Such a modern business enterprise may be termed an entrepreneurial or family one, and an economy or sectors of an economy dominated by such firms may be considered a system of entrepreneurial or family capitalism.

Where the creation and growth of an enterprise required large sums of outside capital, the relationship between ownership and management differed. The financial institutions providing the funds normally placed part-time representatives on the firm's board. In such enterprises, salaried managers had to share top management decisions, particularly those involving the raising and spending of large sums of capital, with representatives of banks and other financial institutions. An economy or sector controlled by such firms has often been termed one of financial capitalism.

In many modern business enterprises neither bankers nor families were in control. Ownership became widely scattered. The stockholders did not have the influence, knowledge, experience, or commitment to take part in the high command. Salaried managers determined long-term policy as well as managing short-term operating activities. They dominated top as well as lower and middle management. Such an enterprise controlled by its managers can properly be identified as managerial, and a system dominated by such firms is called managerial capitalism.

As family- and financier-controlled enterprises grew in size and age they became managerial. Unless the owners or representatives of financial houses became full-time career managers within the enterprise itself, they did not have the information, the time, or the experience to play a dominant role in top-level decisions. As members of the boards of directors they did hold veto power. They could say no, and they could replace the senior managers with other career managers; but they were rarely in a position to propose positive alternative solutions. In time, the part-time owners and financiers on the board normally looked on the enterprise in the same way as did ordinary stockholders. It became a source of income and not a business to be managed. Of necessity, they left current operations and future plans to the career administrators. In many industries and sectors of the American economy, managerial capitalism soon replaced family or financial capitalism.

The seventh proposition is that in making administrative decisions, career managers preferred policies that favored the long-term stability and growth of their enterprises to those that maximized current profits.

For salaried managers the continuing existence of their enterprises was essential to their lifetime careers. Their primary goal was to assure continuing use of and therefore continuing flow of material to their facilities. They were far more willing than were the owners (the stockholders) to reduce or even forego current dividends in order to maintain the long-term viability of their organizations. They sought to protect their sources of supplies and their outlets. They took on new products and services in order to make more complete use of exist-

ing facilities and personnel. Such expansion, in turn, led to the addition of still more workers and equipment. If profits were high, they preferred to reinvest them in the enterprise rather than pay them out in dividends. In this way the desire of the managers to keep the organization fully employed became a continuing force for its further growth.

The eighth and final proposition is that as the large enterprises grew and dominated major sectors of the economy, they altered the basic structure of these sectors and of the economy as a whole.

The new bureaucratic enterprises did not, it must be emphasized, replace the market as the primary force in generating goods and services. The current decisions as to flows and the long-term ones as to allocating resources were based on estimates of current and long-term market demand. What the new enterprises did do was take over from the market the coordination and integration of the flow of goods and services from the production of the raw materials through the several processes of production to the sale to the ultimate consumer. Where they did so, production and distribution came to be concentrated in the hands of a few large enterprises. At first this occurred in only a few sectors or industries where technological innovation and market growth created high-speed and high-volume throughput. As technology became more sophisticated and as markets expanded, administrative coordination replaced market coordination in an increasingly larger portion of the economy. By the middle of the twentieth century the salaried managers of a relatively small number of large mass producing, large mass retailing, and large mass transporting enterprises coordinated current flows of goods through the processes of production and distribution and allocated the resources to be used for future production and distribution in major sectors of the American economy. By then, the managerial revolution in American business had been carried out.[5]

These basic propositions fall into two parts. The first three help to explain the initial appearance of modern business enterprise: why it began when it did, where it did, and in the way it did. The remaining five concern its continuing growth: where, how, and why an enterprise once started continued to grow and to maintain its position of dominance. This institution appeared when managerial hierarchies were able to monitor and coordinate the activities of a number of business units more efficiently than did market mechanisms. It continued to grow so that these hierarchies of increasingly professional managers might remain fully employed. It emerged and spread, however, only in those industries and sectors whose technology and markets permitted administrative coordination to be more profitable than market coordination. Because these areas were at the center of the American economy and because professional managers replaced families, financiers, or their representatives as decision makers in these areas, modern American capitalism became managerial capitalism.

Historical realities are, of course, far more complicated than these general propositions suggest. Modern business enterprise and the new business class that managed it appeared, grew, and flourished in different ways even in the different sectors and in the different industries they came to dominate. Varying needs and opportunities meant that the specific substance of managerial tasks differed from one sector to another and from one industry to another. So too did the specific relationships between managers and owners. And once a managerial hierarchy was fully established, the sequence of its development varied from industry to industry and from sector to sector.

Nevertheless, these differences can be viewed as variations on a single theme. The visible hand of management replaced the invisible hand of market forces where and when new technology and expanded markets permitted a historically unprecedented high volume and speed of materials through the processes of production and distribution. Modern business enterprise was thus the institutional response to the rapid pace of technological innovation and increasing consumer demand in the United States during the second half of the nineteenth century.

Notes

1. Lance E. Davis and Douglass C. North, *Institutional Change and American Economic Growth* (Cambridge, Eng., 1971) and Douglass C. North and Robert Paul Thomas, The Rise of the Western World (Cambridge, Eng., 1973).
2. John Higham, with Leonard Kreiger and Felix Gilbert, *History* (Englewood Cliffs, N.J., 1965), pp. 231–232.
3. Richard Coase, "The Nature of the Firm," *Economica*, n.s., 4:386–405 (1937) provides a pioneering analysis of the reasons for internalizing of operating units. His work is expanded upon by Oliver Williamson, particularly in his *Corporate Control and Business Behaviour* (Englewood Cliffs, N.J., 1970), p. 7. Useful articles on coordination and allocation within the enterprise are Kenneth J. Arrow, "Control in Large Organization," *Management Science*, 10:397–408 (April 1964); H. Leibenstein, "Allocative Efficiency Versus X-Efficiency," *American Economic Review*, 56:392–415 (June 1966); A. A. Alechian and H. Demsetz, "Production, Information Costs, and Economic Organization," *American Economic Review* 62:777–795 (December 1972); and G. B. Richardson, "The Organization of Industry," *Economic Journal*, 83:883–896 (Sept. 1972).
4. Werner Sombart, "Capitalism," *Encyclopedia of Social Sciences* (New York, 1930), III, 200. Though there is very little written on the nature of coordination and allocation

of resources and activities within the firm, there is a vast literature on the bureaucratic nature of modern business enterprise and on the goals and motives of business managers. Almost none of this literature, however, looks at the historical development of managerial hierarchies or the role and functions of managers over a period of time.

5. James Burnham, who in his *Managerial Revolution* (New York, 1941) was the first to describe and analyze that phenomenon, gives in chap. 7 a definition of the managerial class in American business but makes no attempt to describe the history of that class or the institution that brought it to power.

I-5: Reengineering the Corporation

M. Hammer and J. Champy

Most companies today—no matter what business they are in, how technologically sophisticated their product or service, or what their national origin—can trace their work styles and organizational roots back to the prototypical pin factory that Adam Smith described in *The Wealth of Nations*, published in 1776. Smith, a philosopher and economist, recognized that the technology of the industrial revolution had created unprecedented opportunities for manufacturers to increase worker productivity and thus reduce the cost of goods, not by small percentages, which one might achieve by persuading an artisan to work a little faster, but by orders of magnitude. In *The Wealth of Nations*, this forebear of the business consultant, a radical thinker in his time, explained what he called the principle of the division of labor.

Smith's principle embodied his observations that some number of specialized workers, each performing a single step in the manufacture of a pin, could make far more pins in a day than the same number of generalists, each engaged in making whole pins. "One man, "Smith wrote, "draws out the wire, another straightens it, a third cuts

it, a fourth points it, a fifth grinds it at the top for receiving the head; to make the head requires two or three distinct operations; to put it on is a peculiar business, to whiten the pins is another; it is even a trade by itself to put them into the paper." Smith reported that he had visited a small factory, employing only ten people, each of whom was doing just one or two of the 18 specialized tasks involved in making a pin. "These ten persons could make among them upwards of forty-eight thousand pins in a day. But if they had all wrought separately and independently, and without any of them having been educated to this peculiar business, they certainly could not each of them have made twenty, perhaps not one pin in a day."

The division of labor increased the productivity of pin makers by a factor of hundreds. The advantage, Smith wrote, "is owing to three different circumstances; first, to the increase of dexterity in every particular workman; secondly, to the saving of the time which is commonly lost in passing from one species of work to another; and lastly, to the invention of a great number of machines which facilitate and abridge labor, and enable one man to do the work of many."

Today's airlines, steel mills, accounting firms, and computer chip makers have all

Reengineering the Corporation: A Manifesto for Business Revolution by Michael Hammer & James Champy. New York: Harper Business, 1993.

been built around Smith's central idea—the division or specialization of labor and the consequent fragmentation of work. The larger the organization, the more specialized is the worker and the more separate steps into which the work is fragmented. This rule applies not only to manufacturing jobs. Insurance companies, for instance, typically assign separate clerks to process each line of a standardized form. They then pass the form to another clerk, who processes the next line. These workers never complete a job; they just perform piecemeal tasks.

Over time, American companies became the best in the world at translating Smith's organizing principles into working business organizations, even though, when Smith first published his ideas in 1776, not much of a domestic market existed for American-made goods. Americans, who numbered only 3.9 million, were separated from one another by bad roads and poor communications. Philadelphia, with 45,000 residents, was the fledgling nation's largest city.

Over the next half century, though, the population exploded and the domestic market expanded accordingly. The population of Philadelphia, for example, quadrupled, though New York was now the largest city with 313,000 people. Manufacturing facilities sprouted around the country.

Part of this growth occurred because of innovative changes in the ways in which goods could be shipped. In the 1820s, Americans began building railroads, which not only extended and accelerated economic development, but also moved the evolution of business management technology forward. It was railroad companies that invented the modern business bureaucracy—a significant innovation then and an essential one if industrial organizations were going to grow larger than the span of one person's control.

To prevent collisions on single-track lines that carried trains in both directions, railroad companies invented formalized operating procedures and the organizational structure and mechanisms required to carry them out. Management created a rule for every contingency they could imagine, and lines of authority and reporting were clearly drawn. The railroad companies literally programmed their workers to act only in accordance with the rules, which was the only way management knew to make their one-track systems predictable, workable, and safe. Programming people to conform to established procedures remains the essence of bureaucracy even now. The command-and-control systems in place in most companies today embody the same principles the railroads introduced a hundred and fifty years ago.

The next large evolutionary steps in the development of today's business organization came early in the twentieth century from two automobile pioneers: Henry Ford and Alfred Sloan.

Ford improved on Smith's concept of dividing work into tiny, repeatable tasks. Instead of having skilled assemblers build entire cars from parts they would fit together, Ford reduced each worker's job to installing a single part in a prescribed manner. Initially, workers walked from one assembly stand to the next, taking themselves to the work. The moving assembly line, the innovation for which Ford is best remembered, simply brought the work to the worker.

In breaking down car assembling into a series of uncomplicated tasks, Ford made the jobs themselves infinitely simpler, but he made the process of coordinating the people performing those jobs and of combining the results of their tasks into a whole car far more complex.

Then Alfred Sloan stepped in. Sloan, the successor to General Motor's founder William Durant, created the prototype of the management system that Ford's immensely more efficient factory system demanded.

Neither Henry Ford nor Durant ever learned how to manage the huge, sprawling organizations that their success with assembly-line production both necessitated and made possible—the engineering, manufacturing, assembly, and marketing operations. Durant, especially, with GM's far greater mix of cars and models, was constantly finding that the company had produced too many of one model for current market conditions or that production had to be suspended because not enough raw materials had been procured. After Sloan took over at GM, he made the system Ford had pioneered complete, and it is this total system to which the term mass production applies today.

Sloan created smaller, decentralized divisions that managers could oversee from a small corporate headquarters simply by monitoring production and financial numbers. Sloan set up one division for each car model—Chevrolet, Pontiac, Buick, Oldsmobile, and Cadillac—plus others making components such as generators (Delco) and steering gears (Saginaw).

Sloan was applying Adam Smith's principle of the division of labor to management just as Ford had applied it to production. In Sloan's view, corporate executives did not need specific expertise in engineering or manufacturing; specialists could oversee those functional areas. Instead, executives needed financial expertise. They had only to look at "the numbers"—sales, profit and loss, inventory levels, market share, and so forth—generated by the company's various divisions to see if those divisions were performing well; if not, they could demand appropriate corrective action.

Sloan's management innovations saved General Motors from early oblivion and, what's more, also solved the problems that had kept other companies from expanding. The new marketing specialists and financial managers that Sloan's system required complemented the company's engineering professionals. GM's head firmly established the division of professional labor in parallel with the division of manual labor that had already taken place on the factory floor.

The final evolutionary step in the development of corporations as we know them today came about in the United States between the end of World War II and the 1960s, a period of enormous economic expansion. The regimes of Robert McNamara at Ford, Harold Geneen at ITT, and Reginald Jones at General Electric epitomized management of that era. Through elaborate planning exercises, senior managers determined the businesses in which they wanted to be, how much capital they should allocate to each, and what returns they would expect the operating managers of these businesses to deliver to the company. Large staffs of corporate controllers, planners, and auditors acted as the executives' eyes and ears, ferreting out data about divisional performance, and intervening to adjust the plans and activities of operating managers.

The organizational model developed in the United States spread rapidly into Europe and then to Japan after World War II. Designed for a period of heavy and growing demand and therefore accelerating growth, this form of corporate organization suited the circumstances of the postwar times perfectly.

An unrelenting demand for goods and services, at home and abroad, shaped the economic environment of the time. Deprived of material goods, first by the Depression, then by the war, customers were more than happy to buy whatever companies offered them. Rarely did they demand high quality and service. Any house, any car, any refrigerator were infinitely better than none at all.

In the 1950s and 1960s, the chief operational concern of company executives was capacity—that is, being able to keep up with ever-increasing demand. If a company built too much productive capacity too soon, it could go deep in the red financing its new plants. But if it built too little capacity or built it too late, the company could lose market share from its inability to produce. To solve these problems, companies developed ever more complex systems for budgeting, planning, and control.

The standard, pyramidal organizational structure of most organizations was well suited to a high-growth environment because it was scalable. When a company needed to grow, it could simply add workers as needed at the bottom of the chart and then fill in the management layers above.

This kind of organizational structure was also ideally suited for control and planning. By breaking work down into pieces, supervisors could ensure consistent and accurate worker performance, and the supervisors' supervisors could do the same. Budgets were easily approved and monitored department by department, and plans were generated and pursued on the same basis.

This organizational form also made for short training periods, since few production tasks were complicated or difficult. Moreover, as new office technology became available in the 1960s, companies were encouraged to break down even more of their white-collar work into small, repeatable tasks, which could also be mechanized or automated.

As the number of tasks grew, however, the overall processes of producing a product or delivering a service inevitably became increasingly complicated, and managing such process became more difficult. The growing number of people in the middle of the corporate organization chart—the functional or middle managers—was one of the prices companies paid for the benefits of fragmenting their work into simple, repetitive steps and organizing themselves hierarchically.

Another cost was the increasing distance that separated senior management from users of their product or service.

Customers and their responses to the company's strategy became a set of faceless numbers that bubbled up through the layers.

These, then, are the roots of today's corporation, the principles, forged by necessity, on which today's companies have structured themselves. If modern companies thin slice work into meaningless tasks, it is because that is how efficiency was once achieved. If they diffuse power and responsibility through massive bureaucracies, it is because that was the way they learned to control sprawling enterprises. If they resist suggestions that they change the way they operate, it is because these organizing principles and the structures to which they gave birth have worked well for decades.

The reality that organizations have to confront, however, is that the old ways of doing business—the division of labor around which companies have been organized since Adam Smith first articulated the principle—simply don't work anymore. Suddenly, the world is a different place. The here-and-now crisis of competitiveness that American corporations face today is not the result of a temporary economic downturn or of a low point in the business cycle. Indeed, we can no longer even count on a predictable business cycle—prosperity, followed by recession, followed by renewed prosperity—as we once did. In today's environment, nothing is constant or predictable—not market growth, customer demand, product life cycles, the rate of technological change, or the nature of competition. Adam Smith's world and its way of doing business are yesterday's paradigm.

Three forces, separately and in combination, are driving today's companies deeper and deeper into territory that most of their executives and managers find frighteningly unfamiliar. We call these forces the three Cs: Customers, Competition, and Change. Their names are hardly new, but the characteristics of the three Cs are remarkably different from what they were in the past.

Let's look at the three Cs and how they have changed, beginning with customers.

● ● ● ● ● ● ● ● ● ● ● ● ● ● ● ● ● ●
CUSTOMERS TAKE CHARGE

Since the early 1980s, in the United States and other developed countries, the dominant force in the seller-customer relationship has shifted. Sellers no longer have the upper hand; customers do. Customers now tell suppliers what they want, when they want it, how they want it, and what they will pay. This new situation is unsettling to companies that have known life only in the mass market.

In reality, a mass market never existed, but for most of this century the idea of the mass market provided manufacturers and service providers—from Henry Ford's car company to Thomas Watson's computer company—with the useful fiction that their customers were more or less alike. If that were true, or if buyers behaved as if it were true, then companies could assume that a standard product or service—a black car or a big blue computer—would satisfy most of them. Even those that weren't satisfied would buy what was offered, because they had little choice. Mass market suppliers in the United States had relatively few competitors, most of which offered very similar products and services. In fact, most consumers weren't dissatisfied. They didn't know that anything better or different was available.

Now that they have choices, though, customers no longer behave as if they are all cast in the same mold. Customers—consumers and corporations alike—demand products and services designed for their unique and particular needs. There is no longer any such notion as *the* customer; there is only *this* customer, the one with whom a seller is dealing at the moment and who now has the capacity to indulge his or her own personal tastes. The mass market has broken into pieces, some as small as a single customer.

Individual customers—whether consumers or industrial firms—demand that they be treated individually. They expect products that are configured to their needs, delivery schedules that match their manufacturing plans or work hours, and payment terms that are convenient for them. Individually and in combination, a number of factors have contributed to shifting the balance of market power from producer to consumer.

Consumer expectations soared in the United States when competitors—many of them Japanese—burst upon the market with lower prices combined with higher quality goods. Then the Japanese introduced new products that established American producers had not had time to bring to market—or may be hadn't even thought of yet. What's more, the Japanese did it all with levels of service that traditional companies could not match. This was mass production *plus*—plus quality, price, selection, and service.

In the service sector, consumers expect and demand more, because they know they can get more. Technology, in the form of sophisticated, easily accessible databases, allows service providers and retailers of all kinds to track not only basic information about their customers, but their preferences and requirements, thereby laying a new foundation for competitiveness.

In Houston, if a customer calls Pizza Hut to order a pepperoni and mushroom pie, the same kind of pizza that the customer ordered last week, the clerk asks if the caller would like to try a new combination. If the person says "yes," the clerk mails him or her discount coupons with offerings customized to that individual's tastes. When a consumer calls Whirlpool's service line, the call is automatically routed to the same service representative with whom the consumer spoke last time, creating a sense of personal relationship and intimacy in a world of 800 numbers. Mail-order retailers, which have the capability of collecting enormous amounts of data about their customers, have perfected an even higher targeted level of service. Once customers experience this superior service, they do not happily return to accepting less.

The incredible consolidation of customers in some markets—the growth of megadealers in the automobile business, the handful of fast-food franchises replacing thousands of independent eateries, and the mall-sized discounters that have emptied Main Street store fronts—has also profoundly changed the terms of the seller-customer relationship. If the sign out front now reads "Joe Smith's Oldsmobile, Nissan, Isuzu, Mercedes, Jeep, Honda, and Saturn," then Joe Smith, not General Motors, has the upper hand in their negotiations. With so many other brands available to him, Joe needs General Motors less than GM needs him.

The threat of backward integration has also helped to shift power from producers to consumers. Often, customers now can do for themselves what suppliers used to do for them. Companies may not want to, but they can buy the same machines and hire the same people as their vendors. "Do it my way," they can say, "or I will do it myself." Inexpensive and easy-to-learn desktop publishing technology, for instance, gives companies the choice of doing for themselves jobs for which they used to rely on printers.

What holds true for industrial customers also holds true for consumers. When individual depositors realized that they could themselves purchase the same high-grade, short-term government securities and commercial paper that the banks were buying with their deposit money, many of them reduced their balances in those low interest-bearing accounts, depriving the banks of an important source of revenue.

Customers have gained the upper hand in their relationships with sellers, in part, because customers now have easy access to enormously more data. The information-rich world made possible by new communications technologies doesn't even require the consumer to have a computer at home. Anyone can, for instance, pick up a daily newspaper and compare rates on CDs from banks all around the country. Publishers collect that data electronically and pass it on to readers, who now know positively if their local bank is offering a good deal and if not, who is. An auto dealer today has to assume that any customer has read the appropriate issue of *Consumer Reports* and is well aware of what the dealer paid the manufacturer for the car. This makes the negotiation process decidedly trickier for the dealer.

For companies that grew up with a mass market mentality, the hardest new reality to accept about customers is that each one counts. Lose a customer today and another doesn't just appear. For thirty years after World War II, consumer goods were in chronically short supply. Manufacturers could not produce enough of them at prices sufficiently low to satisfy every possible buyer. The effect of insatiable demand was to give producers the advantage over buyers. In a mass market, to paraphrase the movie, *Field of Dreams*, if you build it they will buy.

Consumer goods shortages no longer exist. On the supply side of the equation, more producers now operate around the world. On the demand side, developed countries now have lower population growths. Also, many product markets have matured. Almost everyone who wants one now owns a refrigerator, a videocassette recorder, and even a personal computer. Those industries are in a replacement mode. Consequently, consumers wield a great deal of power. They can, in other words, be very choosy.

In short, in place of the expanding mass markets of the 1950s, 1960s, and 1970s, companies today have customers—business customers and individual consumers—who know what they want, what they want to pay for it, and how to get it on the terms they demand. Customers such as these don't need to deal with companies that don't understand and appreciate this startling change in the customer-buyer relationship.

COMPETITION INTENSIFIES

The second C is competition. It used to be so simple: The company that could get to market with an acceptable product or service at the best price would get a sale. Now, not only does more competition exist, it's of many different kinds.

Niche competitors have changed the face of practically every market. Similar goods sell in different markets on entirely disparate competitive bases: in one market on the basis of price, in another on selection, somewhere else on quality, and elsewhere on service before, during, or after the sale. With trade barriers falling, no company's national turf is protected from overseas competition. When the Japanese—or Germans, French, Koreans, Taiwanese, and so forth—are free to compete in the same markets, just one superior performer can raise the competitive threshold for companies around the world. Caterpillar competes with Komatsu, Dupont with Hoechst, Chase Manhattan with Barclays. Good performers drive out the inferior, because the lowest price, the highest quality, the best service available from any one of them soon becomes the standard for all competitors. Adequate is no longer good enough. If a company can't stand shoulder to shoulder with the world's best in a competitive category, it soon has no place to stand at all.

Start-up companies that carry no organizational baggage and are not constrained by their histories can enter a market with the next product or service generation before existing companies can even recoup their development costs on the last one. Big is no longer impregnable, and every established company today needs to post a lookout for start-ups–those that are brand new and those that have been around for a while but still operate on their founders' principles. By that definition, Sun Microsystems is still a start-up, and so is Wal-Mart. Sun's workstation innovation changed the course of history for every computer maker in the world. Wal-Mart reinvented retailing.

Start-ups do not play by the rules. They write new rules about how to run a business. Wal-Mart did not create itself in the image of Sears. Unburdened by Sears's past, it conceived new ways of working that produce better results. Sears's apparent assets—lots of stores employing well-trained salespeople, established supplier relationships, smoothly tuned operating and administrative systems—have turned into liabilities in that they cannot produce the results that Wal-Mart has established as the new competitive standards.

Technology changes the nature of competition in ways companies don't expect. In retailing, for instance, it has allowed manufacturers and retailers, such as Procter & Gamble and Wal-Mart, to merge their distribution and inventory systems in ways that are mutually beneficial. In after-sales service, technology allows innovators to devise entirely new service techniques. Otis Elevator Company, for example, has developed an ingenious computer system for managing the Byzantine task of servicing ninety-three thousand elevators and escalators in North America around the clock. Repair technicians arrive at the scene already briefed on the nature of the problem and the particular machine's maintenance history. By innovating with technology in order to streamline the interaction between themselves and their customers, companies such as Otis expand the limits of the possible, thereby raising customer expectations for all the companies in a market.

CHANGE BECOMES CONSTANT

Change is the third C. We already know that customers and competition have changed, but so, too, has the nature of change itself. Foremost, change has become both pervasive and persistent. It is normality.

Not long ago, for example, life insurance companies offered only two products: term and whole life. Today, they supply a constantly changing smorgasbord of products, and the competitive pressure on insurance companies to create new products is constantly increasing.

Moreover, the pace of change has accelerated. With globalization of the economy, companies face a greater number of competitors, each one of which may introduce product and service innovations to the market. The rapidity of technological change also promotes innovation. Product life cycles have gone from years to months. Ford produced the Model T for an entire human generation. The life cycle of a computer product introduced today might stretch to two years, but probably won't. A company in the pension business recently developed a service to take advantage of a quirk in the tax laws and interest rates. Its anticipated market life was exactly three months. Coming to this market late by just thirty days would have cut the company's selling time for the service by a third.

The point is that not only have product and service life cycles diminished, but so has the time available to develop new products and introduce them. Today, companies must move fast, or they won't be moving at all.

Moreover, they have to be looking in many directions at once. Executives *think* their companies are equipped with effective change-sensing radars, but most of them aren't. Mostly what they detect are the changes they expect. The brand managers at a consumer goods manufacturer we know assiduously tracked consumer attitudes in order to detect shifts that might affect their products. Their surveys kept giving them good news, but market share took a sudden drop. They did more surveys. Customers loved the products, but market share kept tumbling. It turned out the problem was that the company's sloppy order fulfillment process was infuriating its retailers, who responded by cutting its shelf space, but neither the brand managers not anyone else at the company had a broad enough perspective to detect and deal with this problem.

The changes that will put a company out of business are those that happen outside the light of its current expectations, and that is the source of most change in today's business environment.

The three Cs — customers, competition, and change — have created a new world for business, and it is becoming increasingly apparent that organizations designed to operate in one environment cannot be fixed to work well in another. Companies created to thrive on mass production, stability, and growth can't be fixed to succeed in a world where customers, competition, and change demand flexibility and quick response.

Some people blame corporate America's problems on factors beyond management's control — closed foreign markets, the low cost of Japanese capital, and predatory pricing by foreign companies subsidized by their governments. They blame the federal government's mishandling of the economy, its regulations, and its poor husbandry of natural and human resources. They blame unions or poorly educated and unmotivated American workers.

But if these reasons accounted for our dilemma, nearly all American companies would be in decline. But they aren't. Sears may be losing its market, but Wal-Mart and The Gap are thriving. GM has trouble making world-class cars in America, but Honda doesn't. The insurance industry, as a whole, may be hemorrhaging money, but some companies, such as Progressive Insurance, earn outstanding returns. Bethlehem Steel has shrunk to a tenth of its former size, but Nucor and other minimills perform well in the global market. In almost every industry, under the same rules and with the same players, the successes of a few companies rebut the excuses of the many.

If American managers can't decide why their companies are in trouble, neither do they agree on what to do about it. Some people think American companies would bounce back if only they had the right products and services for the times. We reject that thinking, because products have limited lifespans, and even the best soon become obsolete. It is not products but the processes that create products that bring companies long-term success. Good products don't make winners; winners make good products.

Some people think companies could cure what ails them by changing their corporate strategies. They should sell one division and buy another, change their markets, get into a different business. They should juggle assets or restructure with a leveraged buyout (LBO). But this kind of thinking distracts companies from making basic changes in the real work they actually do. It also bespeaks a profound contempt for the daily operations of business. Companies are not asset portfolios, but people working together to invent, make, sell, and provide service. If they are not succeeding in the businesses that they are in, it is because their people are not inventing, making, selling, and servicing as well as they should. Playing tycoon might be more exciting for senior managers than dirtying their hands in the mundane details of operations, but it is not more important. "God," said the architect Mies van der Rohe, "is in the details." Van der Rohe was speaking of buildings, but his observation applies equally well to running a business.

Some people, including many managers, blame corporate problems on management deficiencies. If companies were only managed differently and better, they would thrive. But none of the management fads of the last twenty years—not management by objectives, diversification, Theory Z, zero-based budgeting, value chain analysis, decentralization, quality circles, "excellence," restructuring, portfolio management, management by walking around, matrix management, intrapreneuring, or one-minute managing—has reversed the deterioration of America's corporate competitive performance. They have only distracted managers from the real task at hand.

Some people think that automation is the answer to business problems. True, computers can speed work up, and in the past forty years businesses have spent billions of dollars to automate tasks that people once did by hand. Automating does get some jobs done faster. But fundamentally the same jobs are being done, and that means no fundamental improvements in performance.

Our diagnosis of America's business problems is simple, but the corrective action that it demands is not as easy to implement as the solutions that have already been tried. Our diagnosis goes to the very heart of what a company does. It rests on the premise that a company that is better than others at the meat and potatoes of its business—inventing products and services, manufacturing or providing them, selling them, filling orders, and serving customers—will beat the competition in the marketplace. We believe that, in general, the difference between winning companies and losers is that winning companies know how to do their work better. If

American companies want to become winners again, they will have to look to how they get their work done. It is as simple and as formidable as that.

To illustrate what we mean when we talk about a company getting its work done, let's look at a common process found in practically every company in America. Order fulfillment begins when a customer places an order, ends when the goods are delivered, and includes everything in between. Typically, the process involves a dozen or so steps performed by different people in different departments. Someone in customer service receives the order, logs it in, and checks it for completeness and accuracy. Then the order goes to finance, where someone else runs a credit check on the customer. Next, someone in sales operations determines the price to charge. Then the order travels to inventory control, where someone checks to see if the goods are on hand. If not, the order gets routed to production planning, which issues a back order. Eventually, warehouse operations develops a shipment schedule. Traffic determines the shipment method—rail, truck, air, or water—and picks the route and carrier. Product handling picks the products from the warehouse, verifies the accuracy of the order, assembles the pickings, and loads them. Traffic releases the goods to the carrier, which takes responsibility for delivering them to the customer.

This process may be complex, but, when viewed from the perspective of Adam Smith's division of labor priniciple and Alfred Sloan's principles of management control and accountability, it does have certain advantages. First, companies don't have to hire people with advanced degrees to get it done. Every person involved in the process has specific responsibility for performing one simple task. Second, everyone in the process is accountable through the bureaucratic chain of command.

Companies must accept trade-offs, however, for keeping the tasks simple and maintaining tight control of employee actions. First, because no one in the company overseas the whole process and its result, no *one* person is responsible for it. No one involved in the process can tell a customer where the order is and when it will arrive. Many people are involved in order fulfillment, but it is no single person's job or the job of any *one* functional unit.

Second, the process is error prone. Errors are inevitable with so many people having to handle and act separately on the same order.

Preaching quality won't help. Even if every person involved in order fulfillment did his or her job perfectly and in exactly the time allotted, the process would still be slow and error prone. Too many handoffs exist—nine at least, and more if the order is placed on back order. Each handoff entails queues, batches, and wait times.

Furthermore, classical order fulfillment involves no element of customer service at all. Complex processes involving a dozen people working across departmental lines can't be made flexible enough to deal with special requests or to respond to inquiries. No one is empowered to answer a question or solve a problem. Once an order enters the process, it might as well be lost until it emerges at the other end—whenever that might turn out to be.

Merely fixing the pieces of the order fulfillment process won't solve the larger problem. Companies that try to improve their performance by working on the pieces of the process miss this point. In fact, trying to fix what's wrong with American companies by tinkering with the individual process pieces is the best way we know to *guarantee* continued bad business performance. Yet, in company after company we have seen, management works at fixing the pieces instead of redesigning the processes by which the company's work gets done.

The core message of our book, then, is this: It is no longer necessary or desirable for companies to organize their work around Adam Smith's division of labor. Task-oriented jobs in today's world of customers, competition, and change are obsolete. Instead, companies must organize work around *process*.

This is an assertion as radical and as far-reaching today as Adam Smith's was in his time. Managers who understand and accept this concept of process-based work will help their companies leap ahead. Those who don't will stay behind.

We write about "processes" throughout the rest of this book, but already it should be apparent why a process perspective is so important to any company that would find its way out of the dilemma that currently confounds American business. It should already be possible to see why American companies can't be fixed but have to be reinvented.

In most companies today, no one is in charge of the processes. In fact, hardly anyone is even aware of them. Does any company have a vice president in charge of order fulfillment, of getting products to customers? Probably not. Who is in *charge* of developing new products? Everyone—R&D, marketing, finance, manufacturing, and so on—is involved, but no one is in charge.

Companies today consist of functional silos, or stovepipes, vertical structures built on narrow pieces of a process. The person checking the customer's credit is part of the credit department, which is probably part of the finance organization. Inventory picking is performed by workers in the warehouse, who may report to the vice president of manufacturing. Shipping, on the other hand, is part of logistics. People involved in a process look *inward* toward their department and *upward* toward their boss, but no one looks *outward* toward the customer. The contemporary performance problems that companies experience are the inevitable consequences of process fragmentation.

Classical business structures that specialize work and fragment processes are self-perpetuating because they stifle innovation and creativity in an organization. If someone in a functional department actually has a new idea—a better way of filling customer orders, for instance—he or she first has to sell it to the boss, who has to sell it to his or her boss, and so on up the corporate hierarchy. For an idea to win acceptance, everyone along the way must say yes, but killing an idea requires only one no. From the point of view of its designers, this built-in innovation damper is not a flaw in the classic structure but a safeguard against change that might introduce unwarranted risk.

The fragmented processes and specialized structures of companies bred for an earlier day also are unresponsive to large changes in the external environment—the market. Existing process design embodies the assumption that conditions will vary only within narrow, predictable limits. By removing management from operations and fracturing those operations among specialized departments, today's organizations ensure that no one will be in a position to recognize significant change or, if he or she should happen to recognize it, to do anything about it.

Today, fragmented organizations display appalling diseconomies of scale, quite the opposite of what Adam Smith envisioned. The diseconomies show up not in direct labor, but in overhead. If, for instance, an organization does 100 units of work an hour, and each of its workers can do 10 units an hour, the company would need 11 people: 10 workers and 1 supervisor. But if demand for the company's output grew tenfold to 1,000 units of work an hour, the company wouldn't need just 10 times the number of workers plus one manager for each 10 new workers. It would need something like 196 people; 100 workers, 10 supervisors, 1 manager, 3 assistant managers, 18 people in a human resources organization, 19 people in long-range planning, 22 in audit and control, and 23 in facilitation and expediting.

This diseconomy of scale is not just bureaucratic proliferation and empire-building, although some of that may be at work too. Rather, it is a consequence of what we call the Humpty Dumpty School of Organizational Management. Companies take a natural process, such as order fulfillment, and break it into lots of little pieces—the individual tasks that people in the functional departments do. Then, the company has to hire all the king's horses and all the king's men to paste the fragmented work back together again. These king's horses and king's men have titles such as auditor, expediter, controller, liaison, supervisor, manager, and vice president. They are simply the glue that holds together the people who do the real work—the credit checkers, the inventory pickers, the package shippers. In many companies, direct labor costs may be down, but overhead costs are up—way up. Most companies today, in other words, are paying more for the glue than for the real work—a recipe for trouble.

Inflexibility, unresponsiveness, the absence of customer focus, an obsession with activity rather than result, bureaucratic paralysis, lack of innovation, high overhead—these are the legacies of one hundred years of American industrial leadership. These characteristics are not new; they have not suddenly appeared. They have been present all along. It is just that until recently, American companies didn't have to worry much about them. If costs were high, they could be passed on to customers. If customers were dissatisfied, they had nowhere else to turn. If new products were slow in coming, customers would wait. The important managerial job was to manage growth, and the rest didn't matter. Now that growth has flattened out, the rest matters a great deal.

America's business problem is that it is entering the twenty-first century with companies designed during the nineteenth century to work well in the twentieth.

We need something entirely different.

I-6: Putting People First for Organizational Success

Jeffrey Pfeffer and John F. Veiga

Executive Overview

There's a disturbing disconnect in organizational management. Research, experience, and common sense all increasingly point to a direct relationship between a company's financial success and its commitment to management practices that treat people as assets. Yet trends in management practice are actually moving away from these very

(continued)

Academy of Management by Jeffrey Pfeffer and John F. Veiga. Copyright 1999 by Academy of Management. Reproduced with permission of Academy of Management in the format Textbook via Copyright Clearance Center.

(*continued*)

principles. Why is common sense so remarkably uncommon when it comes to managing people? Why do organizations habitually overlook readily available opportunities to boost their financial performance? Drawing on extensive empirical research, an irrefutable business case can be made that the culture and capabilities of an organization—derived from the way it manages its people—are the real and enduring sources of competitive advantage. Managers today must begin to take seriously the often heard, yet frequently ignored, adage that "people are our most important asset."

Over the past decade or so, numerous rigorous studies conducted both within specific industries and in samples of organizations that cross industries have demonstrated the enormous economic returns obtained through the implementation of what are variously called high involvement, high performance, or high commitment management practices. Furthermore, much of this research serves to validate earlier writing on participative management and employee involvement. But even as these research results pile up, trends in actual management practice are, in many instances, moving in a direction exactly opposite to what this growing body of evidence prescribes. Moreover, this disjuncture between knowledge and management practice is occurring at the same time that organizations, confronted with a very competitive environment, are frantically looking for some magic elixir that will provide sustained success, at least over some reasonable period of time.

Rather than putting their people first, numerous firms have sought solutions to competitive challenges in places and means that have not been very productive—treating their businesses as portfolios of assets to be bought and sold in an effort to find the right competitive niche, downsizing and outsourcing in a futile attempt to shrink or transact their way to profit, and doing a myriad other things that weaken or destroy

their organizational culture in efforts to minimize labor costs.

SHOW ME THE EVIDENCE

Though we could go on at length about a company like Apple as a case in point (see "The Apple Story"), executives frequently say, "don't just give me anecdotes specifically selected to make some point. Show me the evidence!" Fortunately, there is a substantial and rapidly expanding body of evidence, some of it quite methodologically sophisticated, that speaks to the strong connection between how firms manage their people and the economic results achieved. This evidence is drawn from studies of the five-year survival rates of initial public offerings; studies of profitability and stock price in large samples of companies from multiple industries; and detailed research on the automobile, apparel, semiconductor, steel manufacturing, oil refining, and service industries. It shows that substantial gains, on the order of 40 percent, can be obtained by implementing high performance management practices.[1]

According to an award-winning study of the high performance work practices of 968 firms representing all major industries, "a one standard deviation increase in use of such practices is associated with a . . .

7.05 percent decrease in turnover and, on a per employee basis, $27,044 more in sales and $18,641 and $3,814 more in market value and profits, respectively."[2] Yes, you read those results correctly. That's an $18,000 increase in stock market value *per employee*! A subsequent study conducted on 702 firms in 1996 found even larger economic benefits: "A one standard deviation improvement in the human resources system was associated with an increase in shareholder wealth of $41,000 per employee"[3]—about a 14 percent market value premium.

> *A one standard deviation improvement in the human resources system was associated with an increase in shareholder wealth of $41,000 per employee.*

Are these results unique to firms operating in the United States? No. Similar results were obtained in a study of more than one hundred German companies operating in ten industrial sectors. The study found "a strong link between investing in employees and stock market performance. Companies which place workers at the core of their strategies produce higher long-term returns to shareholders than their industry peers."[4]

One of the clearest demonstrations of the causal effect of management practices on performance comes from a study of the five-year survival rate of 136 non-financial companies that initiated their public offering in the U.S. stock market in 1988[5]. By 1993, some five years later, only 60 percent of these companies were still in existence. The empirical analysis demonstrated that with other factors such as size, industry, and even profits statistically controlled, both the value the firm placed on human resources—such as whether the company cited employees as a source of competitive advantage—and how the organization

rewarded people—such as stock options for all employees and profit sharing—were significantly related to the probability of survival. Moreover, the results were substantively important. As shown in Figure 1-2, the difference in survival probability for firms one standard deviation above and one standard deviation below the mean (in the upper 16 percent and the lower 16 percent of all firms in the sample) on valuing human resource was almost 20 percent. The difference in survival depending on where the firm scored on rewards was even more dramatic, with a difference in five-year survival probability of 42 percent between firms in the upper and lower tails of the distribution.

How can such substantial benefits in profits, quality, and productivity occur? Essentially, these tremendous gains come about because high performance management practices provide a number of important sources for enhanced organizational performance. Simply put, people work harder because of the increased involvement and commitment that comes from having more control and say in their work; people work smarter because they are encouraged to build skills and competence; and people work more responsibly because more responsibility is placed in hands of employees farther down in the organization. These practices work not because of some mystical process, but because they are grounded in sound social science principles that have been shown to be effective by a great deal of evidence. And, they make sense.

. . . .
SEVEN PRACTICES OF SUCCESSFUL ORGANIZATIONS

Based on these various studies, related literature, and personal observation and experience, a set of seven dimensions emerge that seem to characterize most, if not all, of the systems producing profits

The Apple Story

Most accounts of Apple Computer's history have stressed either strategic mistakes, such as not licensing the Macintosh operating system, or leadership issues, such as the succession to CEO by John Sculley and others. However, the Apple story also illustrates rather poignantly the negative case of what happens when a firm whose success derives fundamentally from its people fails to put people first.

Apple was founded in 1976 by Stephen Wozniak and Stephen Jobs in Jobs's garage. Their vision was to bring the power of the computer to the individual user. The Macintosh operating system, introduced in 1984, was (and many would maintain, still is) a leading technology in terms of ease of use. Apple launched the desktop publishing movement, and the company's emphasis on networks and connectivity among machines was also ahead of its time.

Apple was a company largely built on a unique culture. The Macintosh design team worked in a separate building with a pirate flag flying over it. The company built a cult-like commitment among its employees. People were recruited to Apple with the idea that they would be helping to change the world. Apple was more than a company; it was a cause. Its strategy of being an innovator in designing user-friendly personal computers that would make people more productive required a highly talented, creative, and innovative work force. When it took actions that resulted in the loss of that work force, its ability to implement its business strategy and to regain market leadership was irreparably harmed.

Not all of Apple's problems can be traced to how it handled its people. Even though its competitive advantage lay in its operating system, employing a mouse and a graphical user interface, the company consistently failed to license the operating system to other manufacturers, thereby limiting its share of the personal computer market. Because its culture emphasized technological innovation, Apple would occasionally introduce products, such as the Newton personal digital assistant that were either far ahead of their time or had some remaining hardware or software bugs, or both, thus occasionally suffering commer-

cial flops. But, a case can be made that its handling of its people made both its technical and market problems and its recovery from them much worse.

In the beginning, the *Apple Employee Handbook* espoused the importance of people to the firm's success and spelled out many of the company's cherished cultural traditions, such as management accessibility and open communication, mementos of significant company events, celebrations of important life events of employees, and bagels and cream cheese on Friday mornings. After John Sculley laid off 20 percent of its work force to cut costs when sales did not meet expectations in 1985, Apple maintained that its responsibility to its employees was not to give them any security or a career with a progression of jobs, but rather simply to provide a series of challenging job assignments that would permit them to learn and develop so as to be readily employable. In a booming local job market, this encouraged people to develop talent and skills at Apple and then to use them elsewhere. Apple's shift in emphasis to an individualistic culture could also be seen in the language used to talk about employees, who were characterized as A, B, or C players. Apple wanted to attract and retain more As and get rid of the Cs.

In 1991, about 10 percent of the work force was laid off. In 1993, Michael Spindler replaced Sculley and continued the cost cutting by laying off 2,500 people, about 14 percent of the work force. In 1997, another round of layoffs affected almost a third of the remaining people. More damaging than the layoffs themselves was the way they occurred in waves over time, making people unsure of their futures and tempting the best people to leave. Salaries, which had been excellent to attract the best people, were cut, as were many of the amenities that had made working at the company special. Because they feared losing jobs when a project was over, many people slowed their progress substantially. The loss of key technical and marketing personnel made the firm's prospects even worse.

More damaging than the layoffs themselves was the way they occurred in waves over time, making people unsure of their futures and tempting the best people to leave.

(continued)

(*continued*)

The pathologies of Apple Computer are all too common. A company initially having problems with its profits, costs, or share price, takes quick action to raise profits and lower costs. Since employee costs are typically the most quickly and easily changed, the following actions are common: training is curtailed; pay may be frozen or cut; promotions are held up; the use of part-time or temporary help increases; and people are laid off or forced to work reduced hours. These measures logically and inevitably reduce motivation, satisfaction, and loyalty to the company. Rather than focus on their jobs, employees spend time discussing rumors and sharing complaints with coworkers. Cutting training cuts skill and knowledge development and dissemination. Attention focused on unhappiness at work can create a climate in which accidents and poor customer service

flourish. Poor service, high accident rates, and increased turnover and absenteeism adversely affect sales, profits, and costs. So the cycle continues.

In the short run, some firms may be able to cut costs and thereby increase profits. In some cases, cuts can be made in ways that do not damage the viability of the organization. And, of course, Apple's obituary has yet to be written. While employees admit that Apple was in a death spiral, the recent return of Stephen Jobs and Apple's introduction of the iMac suggest to some that a rebirth is possible.

Indeed, as Stephen Jobs told *Fortune*,[a] "Innovation has nothing to do with how many R&D dollars you have. . . . It's not about money. It's about the people you have, how you're led, and how much you get it."

---

[a]Kirkpatrick, D. 1998. The second coming of Apple. *Fortune*, 138:90.

FIGURE 1-2   Probability of an Initial Public Offering Firm's Surviving Five Years

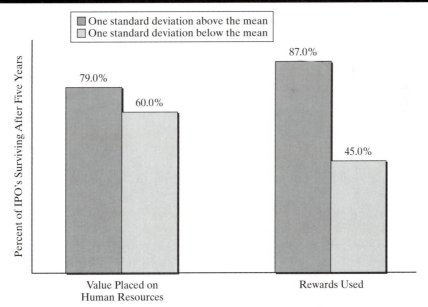

Source: Based on Information from Theresa Welbourne and Alice Andrews, 1996. "Predicting Performance of Initial Public Offering Firms: Should HRM Be in the Equation?" *Academy of Management Journal*, 39: 910–911.

through people emerge. Let's take a look at each one briefly.

EMPLOYMENT SECURITY

Most research on the effects of high performance management systems has incorporated employment security as an important dimension. Indeed, "one of the most widely accepted propositions . . . is that innovations in work practices or other forms of worker-management cooperation or productivity improvement are not likely to be sustained over time when workers fear that by increasing productivity they will work themselves out of their jobs."[6]

The idea of providing employment security in today's competitive world seems somehow anachronistic or impossible and very much at odds with what most firms seem to be doing. But employment security is fundamental to the implementation of most other high performance management practices. For example, when General Motors wanted to implement new work arrangements in its innovative Saturn plant in the 1990s, it guaranteed its people job security except in the most extreme circumstances. When New United Motors Manufacturing, Inc. (NUMMI) was formed to operate the Fremont automobile assembly plant, it offered its people job security. How else could it ask for flexibility and cooperation in becoming more efficient and productive?

Many additional benefits follow from employment assurances besides workers' free contribution of knowledge and their efforts to enhance productivity. One advantage to firms is the decreased likelihood that they will lay off employees during downturns. How is this a benefit to the firm? In the absence of some way of building commitment to retaining the work force—either through pledges about employment security or through employment obligations contractually negotiated with a union—firms may lay off employees too quickly and too read-

ily at the first sign of financial difficulty. This constitutes a cost for firms that have done a good job selecting, training, and developing their work force, because layoffs put important strategic assets on the street for the competition to employ. Herb Kelleher, the CEO of Southwest Airlines, summarized this argument best when he wrote:

> Our most important tools for building employee partnership are job security and a stimulating work environment . . . Certainly there were times when we could have made substantially more profits in the short-term if we had furloughed people, but we didn't. We were looking at our employees' and our company's longer-term interests . . . [A]s it turns out, providing job security imposes additional discipline, because if your goal is to avoid layoffs, then you hire very sparingly. So our commitment to job security has actually helped us keep our labor force smaller and more productive than our competitors'.[7]

SELECTIVE HIRING

Companies serious about obtaining profits through people will expend the effort needed to ensure that they recruit the right people in the first place. This requires several things. First, the organization needs to have a large applicant pool from which to select. In 1993, for example, Southwest Airlines received about 98,000 job applications, interviewed 16,000 people, and hired 2,700. In 1994, applications increased to more than 125,000 for 4,000 hires. Some organizations see processing this many job inquiries as an unnecessary expense. Southwest sees it as a necessary first step.

Second, the organization needs to be clear about what are the most critical skills and attributes needed in its applicant pool. At Southwest, applicants for flight attendant positions are evaluated on the basis of initiative, judgment, adaptability, and their ability to learn. These attributes are assessed in part from interview questions that evoke specific instances of these attributes. For instance, to assess adaptability, interviewers ask, "Give an example of working with a difficult co-worker. How did you handle it?".[8] To measure initiative, one question asks, "Describe a time when a co-worker failed to pull their weight and what you did about it."

Third, the skills and abilities sought need to be carefully considered and consistent with the particular job requirements and the organization's approach to its market. Enterprise Rent-A-Car is today the largest car rental company in the United States, and it has expanded at a rate of between 25 and 30 percent a year for the past 11 years. It has grown by pursuing a high customer service strategy and emphasizing sales of rental car services to repair garage customers. In a low-wage, often unionized, and seemingly low-employee-skill industry, virtually all of Enterprise's people are college graduates. But these people are hired primarily for their sales skills and personality and for their willingness to provide good service, not for their academic performance. Brian O'Reilly interpolates Enterprise's reasoning:

> The social directors make good
> sales people, able to chat up service
> managers and calm down someone
> who has just been in a car wreck . . .
> The Enterprise employees hired
> from the caboose end of the class
> have something else going for
> them . . . a chilling realization of
> how unforgiving the job market
> can be.[9]

Fourth, organizations should screen primarily on important attributes that are difficult to change through training and should emphasize qualities that actually differentiate among those in the applicant pool. Southwest rejected a top pilot from another airline who did stunt work for movie studios because he was rude to a receptionist. Southwest believes that technical skills are easier to acquire than a teamwork and service attitude. Ironically, many firms select for specific, job-relevant skills that, while important, are easily acquired. Meanwhile, they fail to find people with the right attitudes, values, and cultural fit—attributes that are harder to train or change and that are quite predictive of turnover and performance.

One MBA job applicant reported that interviewers at PeopleSoft, a producer of human resource management software, asked very little about personal or academic background, except about learning experiences from school and work. Rather, the interviews focused mostly on whether she saw herself as team-oriented or as an individual achiever, what she liked to do outside school and work, and her philosophy on life. The specific question was "Do you have a personal mission statement? If you don't, what would it be if you were to write it today?" Moreover, the people interviewing the applicant presented a consistent picture of the values that were shared among employees at PeopleSoft. Such a selection process is more likely to produce cultural fit. A great deal of research evidence shows that the degree of cultural fit and value congruence between job applicants and their organizations significantly predicts both subsequent turnover and job performance.[10]

SELF-MANAGED TEAMS AND DECENTRALIZATION AS BASIC ELEMENTS OF ORGANIZATIONAL DESIGN

Numerous articles and case examples, as well as rigorous, systematic studies, attest to the effectiveness of teams as a principle of organization design. For example, Honeywell's defense avionics plant credits improved on-time delivery—reaching 99 percent in the first quarter of 1996 as compared with below 40 percent in the late 1980s—to the implementation of teams.[11] Perhaps one of the greatest payoffs from team-based organizations is that teams substitute peer-based control for hierarchical control of work. Team-based organizations also are largely successful in having all of the people in the firm feel accountable and responsible for the operation and success of the enterprise, not just a few people in senior management positions. This increased sense of responsibility stimulates more initiative and effort on the part of everyone involved. In addition, and perhaps most importantly, by substituting peer for hierarchical control, teams permit removal of layers of hierarchy and absorption of administrative tasks previously performed by specialists, avoiding the enormous costs of having people whose sole job it is to watch people who watch other people do the work.

> *Perhaps one of the greatest payoffs from team-based organizations is that teams substitute peer-based control for hierarchical control of work.*

The tremendously successful natural foods grocery store chain. Whole Foods Markets, organized on the basis of teams, attributes much of its success to that arrangement. Between 1991 and 1996. the company enjoyed sales growth of 864 percent and net income growth of 438 percent as it expanded, in part through acquisitions as well as through internal growth, from 10 to 68 stores. In its 1995 annual report, the company's team-oriented philosophy is clearly stated.

> Our growing information systems capability is fully aligned with our

goal of creating a more intelligent organization—one which is less bureaucratic, elitist, hierarchical, and authoritarian and more communicative, participatory, and empowered. The ultimate goal is to have all team members contributing their full intelligence, creativity, and skills to continuously improving the company . . . Everyone who works at Whole Foods Market is a team member. This reflects our philosophy that we are all partners in the shared mission of giving our customers the very best in products and services. We invest in and believe in the collective wisdom of our team members. The stores are organized into self-managing work teams that are responsible and accountable for their own performance.[12]

Teams also permit employees to pool their ideas to come up with better and more creative solutions to problems. Teams at Saturn and at the Chrysler Corporation's Jefferson North plant, for example, provide a framework in which workers more readily help one another and more freely share their production knowledge—the innumerable 'tricks of the trade' that are vital in any manufacturing process."[13]

Team-based organizations are not simply a made-only-in-America phenomenon. Consider, for example. Vancom Zuid-Limburg, a joint venture in the Netherlands that operates a public bus company. This company has enjoyed very rapid growth in ridership and has been able to win transport concessions by offering more services at the same price as its competitors. The key to this success lies in its use of self-managed teams and the consequent savings in management overhead.

> Vancom is able to [win transport contracts] mainly because of its

very low overhead costs . . . [O]ne manager supervises around forty bus drivers . . . This management-driver ratio of 1 in 40 substantially differs from the norm in this sector. At best, competitors achieve a ratio of 1 in 8. Most of this difference can be attributed to the self-managed teams. Vancom . . . has two teams of around twenty drivers. Each team has its own bus lines and budgeting responsibilities . . . Vancom also expects each individual driver to assume more responsibilities when on the road. This includes customer service (e.g., helping elderly persons board the bus), identifying problems (e.g., reporting damage to a bus stop), and active contributions (e.g., making suggestions for improvement of the services).[14]

COMPARATIVELY HIGH COMPENSATION CONTINGENT ON ORGANIZATIONAL PERFORMANCE

It is often argued that high compensation is a consequence of organizational success, rather than its progenitor, and that high compensation (compared with the average) is possible only in certain industries that either face less competition or have particularly highly educated employees. But neither of these statements is correct. Obviously, successful firms can afford to pay more, and frequently do so, but high pay can also produce economic success.

When John Whitney assumed the leadership of Pathmark, a large grocery store chain in the eastern United States in 1972, the company had about 90 days to live, according to its banks, and was in desperate financial shape. Whitney looked at the situation and discovered that 120 store managers in the chain were paid terribly. Many of them made less than the butchers, who were

unionized. He decided that the store managers were vital to the chain's success and its ability to accomplish a turnaround. Consequently, he gave the store managers a substantial raise—about 40 to 50 percent. Whitney attributes the subsequent success of the chain to the store managers' focusing on improving performance instead of worrying and complaining about their pay.

The idea that only certain jobs or industries can or should pay high wages is belied by the example of many firms. Home Depot has been successful and profitable, and its stock price has shown exceptional returns. Even though the chain emphasizes everyday low pricing as an important part of its business strategy and operates in a highly competitive environment, it pays its staff comparatively well for the retail industry, hires more experienced people with building industry experience, and expects its sales associates to provide a higher level of individual customer service.

Contingent compensation also figures importantly in most high performance work systems. Such compensation can take a number of different forms, including gain sharing, profit sharing, stock ownership, pay for skill, or various forms of individual or team incentives. Wal-Mart, AES Corporation, Southwest Airlines, Whole Foods Markets, Microsoft, and many other successful organizations encourage share ownership. When employees are owners, they act and think like owners. However, little evidence suggests that employee ownership, by itself, affects organizational performance. Rather, employee ownership works best as part of a broader philosophy or culture that incorporates other practices. Merely putting in ownership schemes without providing training, information sharing, and delegation of responsibility will have little effect on performance. Even if people are more motivated by their share ownership, they don't necessarily have the skills, information, or power to do anything with that motivation.

EXTENSIVE TRAINING

Training is often seen as a frill in many U.S. organizations, something to be reduced to make profit goals in times of economic stringency. Studies of firms in the United States and the United Kingdom consistently provide evidence of inadequate levels of training and training focused on the wrong things: specialist skills rather than generalist competence and organizational culture. This is the case in a world in which we are constantly told that knowledge and intellectual capital are critical for success. Knowledge and skill are critical—and too few organizations act on this insight. Training is an essential component of high performance work systems because these systems rely on front-line employee skill and initiative to identify and resolve problems, to initiate changes in work methods, and to take responsibility for quality. All of this requires a skilled and motivated work force that has the knowledge and capability to perform the requisite tasks.

> *Training is an essential component of high performance work systems because these systems rely on front-line employee skill and initiative to identify and resolve problems, to initiate changes in work methods, and to take responsibility for quality.*

Training can be a source of competitive advantage in numerous industries for firms with the wisdom to use it. The Men's Wearhouse, an off-price specialty retailer of men's tailored business attire and accessories, went public in 1991. Its 1995 annual report noted that it had achieved compounded annual growth rates in revenues and net earnings of 32 and 41 percent, respectively, and that the value of its stock had increased by approximately 400 percent. The company attributes its success to how it treats its people and particularly to

the emphasis it has placed on training, an approach that separates it from many of its competitors. The company built a 35,000 square foot training center in Fremont, California, its headquarters. In 1994, some 600 "clothing consultants" went through Suits University, and that year the company added Suits High and Selling Accessories U.[15] During the winter, experienced store personnel come back to headquarters in groups of about 30 for a three-or four-day retraining program.

While training is an investment in the organization's staff, in the current business milieu it virtually begs for some sort of return-on-investment calculations. But such analyses are difficult, if not impossible, to carry out. Successful firms that emphasize training do so almost as a matter of faith and because of their belief in the connection between people and profits. Even Motorola does a poor job of measuring its return on training. Although the company has been mentioned as reporting a $3 return for every $1 invested in training, an official from Motorola's training group said that she did not know where these numbers came from and that the company is notoriously poor at evaluating its $170 million investment in training. The firm mandates forty hours of training per employee per year, and believes that the effects of training are both difficult to measure and expensive to evaluate. Training is part and parcel of an overall management process and is evaluated in that light.

REDUCTION OF STATUS DIFFERENCES

The fundamental premise of high performance management systems is that organizations perform at a higher level when they are able to tap the ideas, skill, and effort of all of their people. In order to help make all organizational members feel important and committed, most high commitment management systems attempt to reduce the status distinctions that separate individuals and groups and cause some to feel less valued. This is accomplished in two principle ways—symbolically, through the use of language and labels, physical space, and dress, and substantively, in the reduction of the organization's degree of wage inequality, particularly across levels.

At NUMMI, everyone wears the same colored smock; executive dining rooms and reserved parking don't exist. At Kingston Technology, a private firm manufacturing add-on memory modules for personal computers, the two cofounders sit in open cubicles and do not have private secretaries.[16] Status differences are also reduced, and a sense of common fate developed, by limiting the difference in compensation between senior management and other employees. Herb Kelleher, who earns about $500,000 per year as the CEO of Southwest, including base and bonus, has been on the cover of *Fortune* magazine with the headline, "Is he America's best CEO?" In 1985, when Southwest negotiated a five-year wage freeze with its pilots in exchange for stock options and occasional profitability bonuses, Kelleher agreed to freeze his base salary at $395,000 for four years. Sam Walton, the founder and chairman of Wal-Mart, was one of the most underpaid CEOs in the U.S. Kelleher and Walton weren't poor; each owned stock in his company. But stock ownership was also encouraged for their employees. Having an executive's fortune rise and fall together with those of the other employees differs dramatically from providing large bonuses and substantial salaries for executives even as the stock price languishes and people are being laid off.

SHARING INFORMATION

Information sharing is an essential component of high performance work systems. The sharing of information on such things as

financial performance, strategy, and operational measures conveys to the organization's people that they are trusted. John Mackey, the chief executive of Whole Foods Markets, states, "If you're trying to create a high-trust organization . . . an organization where people are all-for-one and one-for-all, you can't have secrets.[17] "Whole Foods shares detailed financial and performance information with every employee, including individual salary information. Every Whole Foods store has a book that lists the previous year's salary and bonus of all 6,500 employees.[18]

Every Whole Foods store has a book that lists the previous year's salary and bonus of all 6,500 employees.

Even motivated and trained people cannot contribute to enhancing organizational performance if they don't have information on important dimensions of performance and training on how to use and interpret that information. The now famous case of Springfield ReManufacturing Corporation (SRC) illustrates this point. On February 1, 1983, SRC was created when the plant's management and employees purchased an old International Harvester plant in a financial transaction that consisted of about $100,000 in equity and $8.9 million in debt, an 89-1 debt to equity ratio that has to make this one of the most leveraged of all buyouts. Jack Stack, the former plant manager and now chief executive, knew that if the plant was to succeed, all employees had to do their best, and had to share all their wisdom and ideas for enhancing the plant's performance. Stack came up with a system called "open-book management," that has become so popular that SRC now makes money by running seminars on it. When General Motors canceled an order in 1986 that represented about 40 percent of Springfield's business for the coming year, the firm averted a layoff by providing its people with information on what had happened and letting them figure out how to grow the company and achieve the productivity improvements that would obviate layoffs. SRC has since enjoyed tremendous financial success. In 1983, its first year of operation, sales were about $13 million. By 1992, sales had increased to $70 million and the number of employees had grown from 119 to 700. The original equity investment of $100,000 was worth more than $23 million by 1993. No one who knows the company, and certainly not Jack Stack or the other managers, believes this economic performance could have been achieved without a set of practices that enlisted the cooperation and ingenuity of all of the firm's people. The system and philosophy of open-book management took a failing International Harvester plant and transformed it into a highly successful, growing business.

IT ALL SEEMS SO EASY

How difficult can it be to increase the level of training, to share information and plans with people, to reorganize work into teams, to upgrade hiring practices, and to do all the other things described above? It is easy to form the ideas that are the foundation for people-centered management. But, if it were actually easy to implement those ideas, other airlines would have been able to copy Southwest, other grocery stores would be as successful as Whole Foods Markets, other power producers would be as profitable and efficient as AES, other retailers would have achieved the same record of growth and profitability as the Men's Wearhouse. Implementing these ideas in a systematic, consistent fashion remains rare enough to be an important source of competitive advantage

for firms in a number of industries. Why is this so?

MANAGERS ARE ENSLAVED BY SHORT-TERM PRESSURES

Because achieving profits through people takes time to accomplish, an emphasis on short-term financial results will not be helpful in getting organizations to do the right thing. Short-term financial pressures and measurements abound. Many organizations provide raises and bonuses based on annual results. Ask senior managers how long it takes to change an organization's culture, and it's extremely unlikely that you will hear, "a year or less." But that is the time horizon of the evaluation process. Taking actions with payoffs that will occur beyond the time for which you will be measured on your performance is difficult and risky.

A second pressure occurs when organizations seek to create shareholder value by increasing stock price. The time horizon for evaluating stock market returns is again often quite short, often a year or less. Mutual fund and other institutional money managers are themselves frequently evaluated on a quarterly or at most an annual basis; they often invest in stocks for only a short time and have high portfolio turnover, so it is little surprise that they, in turn, put pressure on organizations for short-term, quick results.

A third pressure is that the immediate drives out the long-term. Today's pressing problems make it difficult to focus on actions aimed at building a better organization for the future. Managerial career processes contribute to this short-term pressure. When and where managers are hired for an indefinite period and careers are embedded in a single organization, it makes sense for those individuals to take a long-term view. But movements by managers across organizations have increased dramatically at nearly all organizational levels. Individuals trying to build a track record that will look good on the external labor market aren't likely to take a longer-term view of building organizational competence and capabilities. Stephen Smith has argued that the typical career system facing managers today encourages "managerial opportunism." He suggests that "managers are rewarded . . . for appropriating the ideas of their subordinates or for improving the bottom line in the short run and then moving on to other positions before the long-term implications of the strategies they have adopted make themselves felt".[19]

ORGANIZATIONS TEND TO DESTROY COMPETENCE

Organizations often inadvertently destroy wisdom and competence or make it impossible for wisdom, knowledge, and experience to benefit the firm. Management practices that require programs and ideas to be explained and reviewed in groups are a major culprit.

Organizations often inadvertently destroy wisdom and competence or make it impossible for wisdom, knowledge, and experience to benefit the firm.

That formal planning and evaluation, and particularly the use of financial criteria, destroy competence is consistent with the results of research on innovation. Experts on organizational management have acquired the ability to see and understand things that are not evident to novices. An expert advertising executive moves quickly and creatively to come up with a good advertising campaign; an expert in production management understands the dynamics of both the human and mechanical elements of the production system and can accurately and quickly diagnose problems and figure out appropriate action; an expert in management or leadership has a good grasp of the principles of human motivation, great intuition, and the ability to read people and situations. But in any domain of expertise, by definition, some portion of the expert's knowledge and competence must be tacit, not readily articulated or explainable, irreducible to a formula or recipe. If that were not the case, then the expert knowledge would be codified and novices could do about as well as experts at the task in question, given access to the same formulas or insights.

But if expert knowledge has a substantial component of tacit knowledge, it will be impossible for experts to present the real basis of their judgements and decisions. Experts are more likely to rely on those factors and evidence that are available and accessible to all. In so doing, they lose virtually all the benefits of their expertise. Forced to explain decisions to a wider audience, the experts will have to rely on the same data and decision processes as anyone else. Thus, the organization will have created a decision process in which its experts behave like novices, and will have lost the benefits of the expert's wisdom and competence.

Consider the following example. Bob Scott, associate director of the Center for Advanced Study in the Behavioral Sciences at Stanford, had to give a talk about the Center's management to an outside group interested in establishing an interdisciplinary, social-science research center. As he was giving the talk, he recalled thinking, "If we actually managed the center this way, it would be a disaster." It was not possible for him to articulate his expertise, to explain his tacit knowledge. Suppose that instead of a group of curious outsiders, his audience had been a governing board or oversight body that would hold Scott and his colleagues accountable for following and implementing the ideas he expressed? They might have been forced to manage in ways that could seriously degrade the organization's operations.

MANAGERS DON'T DELEGATE ENOUGH

Relying on the tacit knowledge and expertise of others requires trust and the willingness to let them do what they know how to do. Using self managing teams as an organizing principle requires permitting the teams to actually manage themselves. At NUMMI, teams were given real responsibility and were listened to, while at the General Motors Van Nuys, California, plant, a culture of hierarchical control meant that team members were frequently told to be quiet and supervisors exercised the same control they had before the institution of teams.

Even though employee participation is associated with enhanced economic performance, organizations frequently fail to introduce it, and it remains fragile even when it is implemented. At least some of this resistance derives from two social psychological processes: first, belief in the efficacy of leadership, that is, the "faith in supervision" effect; and second, a self-enhancement bias. The faith in supervision effect means that observers tend to believe that the greater the degree of supervisor involvement and control, the better the work produced. In one study, for instance, identical company performance was evaluated more positively when the leadership factors accounting for the performance were made more apparent,[20] The self-enhancement bias is a pervasive social psychological phenomenon. Researchers have found that "one of the most widely documented effects in social psychology is the preference of most people to see themselves in a self-enhancing fashion. As a consequence, they regard themselves as more intelligent, skilled, ethical, honest, persistent,

original, friendly, reliable, attractive, and fair-minded than their peers or the average person. . . . On the job, approximately 90 percent of managers and workers rate their performances as superior to their peers."[21] It is no wonder then that such a bias would lead supervisors to evaluate more positively the work they have been evolved in creating.

Both of these processes contribute to the same prediction: work performed under more oversight and control will be perceived as better than the identical work performed with less oversight. This effect will be particularly strong for the person doing the supervision. In a real work setting, these social psychological processes would, of course, be counterbalanced by pressures to achieve results and by the knowledge that participation and empowerment may be helpful in improving performance. Nonetheless, these beliefs may be significant factors hindering the use of high performance work practices and the participation and delegation they imply.

PERVERSE NORMS ABOUT WHAT CONSTITUTES GOOD MANAGEMENT

Two norms about what constitutes good management are simultaneously growing in acceptance and are enormously perverse in their implications. The first is the idea that good managers are mean or tough, able to make such difficult choices as laying off thousands of people and acting decisively. The second is that good management is mostly a matter of good analysis, a confusion between math and management. The two views are actually related, since an emphasis on analysis takes one away from such issues as motivation, commitment, and morale, and makes it more likely that one can and will act in a tough fashion.

An article in Newsweek stated that "firing people has gotten to be trendy in corporate America . . . Now you fire workers—

especially white collar workers—to make your corporate bones . . . Wall Street and Big Business have been in perfect harmony about how in-your-face capitalism is making America great."[22] Fortune magazine regularly runs an article entitled "America's Toughest Bosses. "Does one want to appear on that list, especially since many of those on it do not last very long in their jobs, having been "fired —in part, for being too mean"?[23] Little evidence exists that being a mean or tough boss is necessarily associated with business success. "Financial results from these bosses' companies vary from superb to pathetic. The medium return on shareholder's equity over the past five years for seven of the ten companies for which data are available ranged from 7.3 percent . . . to 18.1 percent . . . That compares with the median for the *Fortune* 500 of 13.8 percent."[24] Nonetheless, *Fortune* predicts that "toughness . . . will probably become more prevalent. Most nominees for this list rose to prominence in industries shaken by rapid change . . . As global competition heats up and turmoil rocks more industries, tough management should spread. So look for more bosses who are steely, super demanding, unrelenting, sometimes abusive, sometimes unreasonable, impatient, driven, stubborn, and combative."[25]

> *Little evidence exists that being a mean or tough boss is necessarily associated with business success.*

The belief that the good manager is a skilled analyst also has questionable merit and validity. The belief first arose after World War II with the emergence of Robert McNamara and systems analysis in the Defense Department. It spread to operations research and mathematical analysis in such business schools as Carnegie Mellon and such businesses as the Ford Motor Company. The emphasis on mathematical elegance and analysis as cornerstones for effective management implicitly derogates the importance of emotion, leadership, and building a vision. It represents an attempt to substitute data and analytical methods for judgment and common sense. Emphasizing analytical skills over interpersonal, negotiating, political, and leadership skills inevitably leads to errors in selection, development, and emphasis on what is important to an organization.

A ONE-IN-EIGHT CHANCE

Firms often attempt piecemeal innovations. It is difficult enough to change some aspect of the compensation system without having to also be concerned about training, recruitment and selection, and how work is organized. Implementing practices in isolation may not have much effect, however, and, can actually be counterproductive. Increasing the firm's commitment to training activities won't accomplish much unless changes in work organization permit these more skilled people to actually implement their knowledge. If wages are comparatively low and incentives are lacking, the better-trained people may simply depart for the competition. Employment security can be counterproductive unless the firm hires people who fit the culture and unless incentives reward outstanding performance. Implementing work teams will not accomplish much unless the teams receive training in specific technical skills and team processes, and are given financial and operating performance goals and information.

Implementing and seeing results from many of these practices takes time. It takes time to train and upgrade workers' skills and even more time to see the economic benefits of this training in reduced turnover and enhanced performance. It takes time to share operating and financial information with people, and to be sure that they understand

and know how to use it. Even more time is needed before suggestions and insights can provide business results. It certainly requires time for employees to believe in employment security and for that belief to generate trust and produce higher levels of innovation and effort. Consequently, a long-term view of a company's development and growth is at least useful, if not absolutely essential, to implementation of high performance organizational arrangements.

One must bear in mind that one-half of organizations won't believe the connection between how they manage their people and the profits they earn. One-half of those who do see the connection will do what many organizations have done—try to make a single change to solve their problems, not realizing that the effective management of people requires a more comprehensive and systematic approach. Of the firms that make comprehensive changes, probably only about one-half will persist with their practices long enough to actually derive economic benefits. Since one-half times one-half times one-half equals one-eighth, at best 12 percent of organizations will actually do what is required to build profits by putting people first. Don't like these odds? well, consider this: almost every other source of organizational success—technology, financial structure, competitive strategy—can be initiated in a short period of time. How many other sources of competitive advantage have a one-in-eight chance of success?

In the end, the key to managing people in ways that lead to profits, productivity, innovation, and real organizational learning ultimately lies in the manager's perspective. When managers look at their people, do they see costs to be reduced? Do they see recalcitrant employees prone to opportunism, shirking, and free riding, who can't be trusted and who need to be closely controlled through monitoring, rewards, and sanctions? Do they see people performing activities that can and should be contracted out to save on labor costs? Or, do they see intelligent, motivated, trustworthy individuals—the most critical and valuable strategic assets their organizations can have? When they look at their people, do they see them as the fundamental resources on which their success rests and the primary means of differentiating themselves from the competition? With the right perspective, anything is possible. With the wrong one, change efforts and new programs become gimmicks, and no army of consultants, seminars, and slogans will help.

Notes

1. Pfeffer, J. *The Human Equation: Building Profits by Putting People First*, Harvard Business School Press: Boston, MA, 1998, Chapter 2.
2. Huselid, M. A. 1995. The impact of human resource management practices on turnover, productivity, and corporate financial performance. *Academy of Management Journal*, 38:647.
3. Huselid, M. A. & Becker. B. E. 1997. The impact of high performance work systems, implementation effectiveness, and alignment with strategy on shareholder wealth. Unpublished paper. Rutgers University, New Brunswick, NJ: 18–19.
4. Blimes, L., Wetzker, K., & Xhonneux, P. 1997. Value in human resources. *Financial Times,* February: 10.
5. Welbourne, T., & Andrews, A. 1996. Predicting performance of initial public offering firms: Should HRM be in the equation? *Academy of Management Journal,* 39:891–919.
6. Locke, R. M. 1995. The transformation of industrial relations? A cross-national review, in *The Comparative Political Economy of Industrial Relations*, eds. Kirsten S. Wever and Lowell Turner, Madison, WI: Industrial Relations Research Association: 18–19.
7. Kelleher, H. 1997. A culture of commitment. *Leader to Leader.* 1:23.
8. Southwest Airlines. 1994. Case S-OB-28, Paio Alto, CA: Graduate School of Business, Standard University: 29.

9. O'Reilly, B. 1996. The rent-a-car jocks who made Enterprise #1. *Fortune* 28: 128.

10. See, for instance, O'Reilly, C. A., Chatman. J. A., & Caldwell, D. F. 1991. People and organizational culture: A profile comparison approach to assessing person-organization fit. *Academy of Management Journal.* 34:487–516; and Chatman, J. A. 1991. Managing people and organizations: Selection and socialization in public accounting firms. *Administrative Science Quarterly*, 36:459–484.

11. Work Week. 1996. *The Wall Street Journal*, 28 May: Al.

12. Whole Foods Market, Inc. 1995 *Annual Report*, Austin, TX:3.17.

13. Shaiken, H., Lopez S., & Mankita, I. 1997. Two routes to team production: Saturn and Chrysler compared. Industrial Relations. 36:31.

14. Van Beusekom, Mark. 1996. *Participation Pays! Cases of Successful Companies with Employee Participation.* The Hague: Netherlands Participation Institute: 7.

15. Men's Wearhouse, *1994 Annual Report*, Fremont, CA:3.

16. Doing the right thing. 1995. *The Economist*, 20: 64.

17. Fishman, C. 1996. Whole Foods teams. *Fast Company,* April May: 106.

18. Ibid., 105.

19. Appelbaum, E., & Batt, R. 1994. *The New American Workplace*. Ithaca, NY: ILR Press: 147.

20. Meindl, I. R., & Ehrlich, S. B. 1987. The romance of leadership and the evaluation of organizational performance. *Academy of Management Journal* 30: 91–109.

21. Ibid.

22. Sloan, A. 1996. The hit men. *Newsweek*, 28: 44–45.

23. Dumaine, B. 1993. America's toughest bosses. *Fortune.* 18:39.

24. Flax, S. 1984. The toughest bosses in America. *Fortune* 6:19.

25. Nully, P. 1989. America's toughest bosses. *Fortune* 27:54.

Jeffrey Pfeffer is the Thomas D. Dee Professor of Organizational Behavior at Stanford Business School. He is the author of more than 100 articles and nine books, including *Managing with power, The human equation and The knowing-doing gap: How smart companies turn, knowledge into action.* He has made numerous presentations to companies and industry associations in the U.S. and in 22 other countries.

John F. (Jack) Velga is the Airbus Industrie International Scholar, professor, and head of the Department of Management at the University of Connecticut. He has a BS and MA from Gannon University and a DBA from Kent State University: His work has appeared in the *Academy of Management Journal, Journal of Applied Psychology, Organization Science, Strategic Management Journal, Human Relations*, and *Harvard Business Review.*

I-7: The End of Business Schools? Less Success Than Meets the Eye

Jeffrey Pfeffer and Christina T. Fong

Although business school enrollments have soared and business education has become big business, surprisingly little evaluation of the impact of business schools on either their graduates or the profession of management exists. What data there are

(continued)

(continued)

suggest that business schools are not very effective: Neither possessing an MBA degree nor grades earned in courses correlate with career success, results that question the effectiveness of schools in preparing their students. And, there is little evidence that business school research is influential on management practice, calling into question the professional relevance of management scholarship.

At first blush, business schools are the success story of late twentieth-century education. Both undergraduate and graduate business administration enrollments in degree-granting colleges and universities have soared. For instance, "in 1955–56, graduate business education was virtually nonexistent, with only 3,200 MBA degrees awarded in the U.S. By 1997–98, this number had grown to over 102,000" (Zimmerman, 2001: 3). By the fall of 2000, there were 341 accredited master's programs in business in the United States (*U.S. News and World Report, 2002*), 900 American universities offered a master's in business (Leonhardt, 2000: 18), and in the spring of 2001, some 1,292 schools, or 92% of all accredited colleges and universities, offered an undergraduate major in business (*U.S. News and World Report, 2002*). In 1996-1997, more than a quarter million undergraduate degrees in business were awarded (AACSB Newsline, 1999). New business education programs have started, and existing programs have expanded in the U.S. even as business education has grown around the world. For instance, "the number of business schools in Britain has risen from 20 in the early 1980s to 120" (*The Economist, 1996: 54*), while

business education has spread throughout Asia and continental Europe. Within the United States, an informal study conducted by the Graduate Management Admissions Council indicated that 93% of business schools surveyed intended to either increase or maintain their target class size (GMAC Application Trends Survey, 2001).

There is little doubt that business education is big business and for many, including business schools and their professors, a lucrative business at that. "Since the mid-1980s, 36 Americans have each given more than $10m to business schools" (*The Economist, 1996: 53*). One study estimated that even in the United Kingdom, certainly not the largest or earliest participant in the business education market, business schools "are among the United Kingdom's top fifty exporters, attracting over . . . $640 million a year from other countries" (Crainer & Dearlove, 1999: 4). In the United States, business schools have rapidly expanded their money-making executive education activities. A McKinsey-Harvard report from 1995 estimated that nondegree executive education "generated around $3.3 billion and was growing at rate of 10 percent to 12 percent annually" (Crainer & Dearlove, 1999: 6).

Does this past market success mean that business schools have provided important value and that their future success is also assured? Here the evidence is much more equivocal. Although business schools and business education have been commercial successes, there are substantial ques-

Academy of Management Learning and Education by Jeffrey Pfeffer and Christina T. Fong. Copyright 2002 by Academy of Management. Reproduced with permission of Academy of Management in the format Textbook via Copyright Clearance Center.

We gratefully acknowledge the comments of Charles O'Reilly and James Bailey, the assistance of Darrell Rigby, and the analyses so generously provided by Ronald Burt and Charles O'Reilly.

tions about the relevance of their educational product and doubts about their effects on both the careers of their graduates and on management practice. These concerns, coupled with the rise of many competitors including consulting and training companies, e-learning and company in-house programs, as well as the fact that according to Robert Hamada, ex-dean of the University of Chicago's business school, "the [MBA] industry is overbuilt" (Gaddis, 2000: 52) mean that business schools may soon confront some substantial challenges.

Note that throughout the modern history of business schools, there have been criticisms of their educational product, although the specifics of these criticisms have changed dramatically over time. In the 1950s, the Gordon and Howell report (1959) "described American business education as a collection of trade schools lacking a strong scientific foundation" (Zimmerman, 2001: 2). The Gordon and Howell report and funding from the Ford Foundation and the Carnegie Council (Pierson, 1959) started business schools on their continuing trajectory to achieve academic respectability and legitimacy on their campuses by becoming social science departments, or perhaps, *applied* social science departments. In the process of achieving academic legitimacy, business schools took "on the traditions and ways of mainstream academia" (Crainer & Dearlove, 1999: 40). Quantitative, statistical analyses gained prominence, as did the study of the science of decision making. In both their teaching and research activities, business schools "enthusiastically seized on and applied a scientific paradigm that applies criteria of precision, control, and testable models" (Bailey & Ford, 1996: 8).

However, adopting the ways of other academic social science departments has produced a new set of problems, including concerns about the relevance and centrality of business schools and business education to the world of management. In an update

and revisiting of the Gordon and Howell report, Porter and McKibbin (1988: 64–65) noted that business school curricula were seen as too focused on analytics, with insufficient emphasis on problem finding as contrasted with problem solving and implementation (Leavitt, 1986), and as insufficiently integrative across the various functional areas. More than a decade later, these criticisms remain relevant. The themes—an overemphasis on analysis at the expense of both integration and developing wisdom as well as leadership and interpersonal skills, or teaching the wrong things in the wrong ways (and perhaps to the wrong people, or at least at the wrong time in their careers)-have been picked up and expanded upon by others, including Henry Mintzberg, who may have emerged as the most articulate critic of business school curricula (e.g., Mintzberg, 1996; Mintzberg & Gosling, 2002; Mintzberg & Lampel, 2001), and Harold Leavitt (1989). Leavitt asserted that "we have built a weird, almost unimaginable design for MBA-level education" that distorts those subjected to it into "critters with lopsided brains, icy hearts, and shrunken souls" (1989: 39).

Recent criticisms of business schools have seldom been confronted with much systematic evidence. Mintzberg and Lampel (2001) for instance, noted that of the four CEOs people most often named when asked who had accomplished great things, none had a business school degree (and two, Galvin of Motorola and Gates of Microsoft didn't even finish college). They also reported that 40% of U.S. CEOs mentioned in the *Fortune* article "Why CEOs Fail," had MBAs (Charan & Colvin, 1999). The implication of their observations is that possessing an MBA neither guarantees business success nor prevents business failure. Speaking at a conference, Gary Hamel claimed that most of the best ideas in management over the past decade or so did not originate in business schools (Crainer & Dearlove, 1999: xx), although he did not provide any data to buttress that assertion. Others also complain about the relevance of business school research: "Richard R. West, writing 10 years ago as dean of New York University's graduate school of business, applied the stinging terms 'fuzzy, irrelevant, and pretentious' to management school research" (Gaddis, 2000: 55). Bailey and Ford asserted that "business schools appeal to one another as scholarly communities through a plethora of academic journals that are utterly divorced from the challenges of everyday management" (1996: 8). These observations are interesting anecdotally and certainly suggestive of a problem, but they do not provide convincing evidence about the effects of business schools on their graduates or of the impact of their research on management practice.

Therefore, our first task in this article is to review the empirical evidence — as well as offering some of our own — on what business schools actually do and what their effects are. When we examine the actual effects of business schools on the two outcomes of most relevance and importance, the careers of their graduates and the knowledge they produce, the picture is reasonably bleak. There is little evidence that mastery of the knowledge acquired in business schools enhances people's careers, or that even attaining the MBA credential itself has much effect on graduates' salaries or career attainment. Similarly, the impact of business school research, judged by a number of different criteria, appears to be quite small, and this is true even when research produced by business school professors is compared with business research conducted by writers not in business schools.

There is little evidence that mastery of the knowledge acquired in business schools enhances people's careers, or that even attaining the

MBA credential itself has much effect on graduates' salaries or career attainment.

We first review the evidence on what business schools don't do, consider some reasons why, and then argue that prospects for change and reform are not particularly good, especially for established, elite schools, for some very understandable reasons. Business education does not have to be in this condition. Medical and other professional schools offer some interesting contrasts, and there are some innovative business schools and business school programs that actually embody a model that overcomes many of the problems we enumerate.

To focus the argument and for reasons of space, we don't try to cover all aspects of business education in this article, but concentrate our analysis of research impact on management research and its effects, although there is some indication that the data and conclusions would be similar for many of the other subjects taught. Our analysis of the effects of business schools on careers concentrates on the MBA degree. Even though executive education is an increasingly large proportion of teaching at some schools, such as Harvard, Columbia, and Wharton, we know of no published studies, or even informal but systematic data, that would enable us to assess the effects of executive education on either the individuals who receive it or their organizations. In fact the absence of much assessment of any kind is one of the defining characteristics of contemporary business education, and one reason that problems are likely to persist. Finally, we focus our argument on the formal goals of a business school, to impart knowledge and influence the practice of management, rather than examining some of the more informal benefits of attending business school, such as building useful social networks.

● ●

MBA EDUCATION AND CAREER OUTCOMES

If an MBA education is useful training for business, then the following should be true as a matter of logic: (1) having an MBA degree should, other things being equal, be related to various measures of career success and attainment, such as salary; and (2) if what someone learns in business school helps that person be better prepared for the business world and more competent in that domain—in other words, if business schools convey professionally useful knowledge— then a measure of how much one has learned or mastered the material, such as grades in course work, should be at least somewhat predictive of various outcomes that index success in business. Consider some evidence on each of these questions and some reasons that may help explain why business education has such a small effect on career outcomes.

THE EFFECTS OF THE MBA DEGREE

In the late 1990s, consulting firms found it difficult to compete with high-technology start-ups for talent. Consultants had always hired some people without MBA degrees, but now they increased the pace. For instance, the Boston Consulting Group hired 20% of its consultants without MBAs in 2000, Booz Allen and Hamilton planned to hire one third of its people without graduate business degrees, and "more than half of the consultants at McKinsey and Company do not have a Master of Business Administration degree" (Leonhardt, 2000:1). If there is a job that ought to be connected to the MBA degree, it is management con-

sulting. Consulting has typically been the destination for a large fraction of graduates, particularly from the elite programs. In 1995, for instance, 38% of Harvard Business School graduates went into consulting (Norris, 1997: C23).

Consulting firms who hired people without business degrees—some of them lawyers, doctors, and philosophers—obviously had to provide some training so these individuals could go out and give advice to companies using business language and business knowledge. Many of the companies started or expanded relatively short, 3-week programs in which "new hires" learned the basics of business. Apart from the fact that apparently it took only 3 or 4 weeks for people to cover what business schools take 2 years to teach, is the more interesting question: How did the hires without graduate business degrees perform? Internal studies conducted by the firms found that the non-MBAs did no worse and, in some cases, better than their business school counterparts. The London office of the Boston Consulting Group (BCG) reported that the "non-MBAs were receiving better evaluations, on average, than their peers who had gone to business school," (Leonhardt. 2000: 18) while a study at McKinsey of people on the job 1, 3, and 7 years found that at all three points, the people without MBAs were as successful as those with the degree. Similarly, an internal study by Monitor Consulting "had determined that the people . . . hired from high-end business schools were no better at integrative thinking than the undergraduates . . . hired from top-notch liberal-arts programs" (Lieber, 1999: 262).

Internal studies conducted by the firms found that the non-MBAs did no worse and, in some cases, better than their business school counterparts.

Investment banking is another major destination for graduates of MBA programs (Norris, 1997), and another occupation where one might think that having a graduate business degree is important and useful. Ronald Burt did a private consulting study of the careers and career success of its employees for an investment bank, and concluded that because getting a degree takes time, people with an MBA were, on average, a year older than those without the degree (R. Burt, personal communication, Nov. 26, 2001). "With respect to pay" however, "more education has no association with total compensation . . . but has a negative association when it matters at all." Bur, who has also done follow-up studies of University of Chicago alumni, concluded: "I have never found benefits for the MBA degree—usually it just makes you a couple of years older than non-MBA peers" (Burt, personal communication, Nov. 26, 2001).

Livingston (1971), comparing Harvard MBA graduates and attendees at an advanced management course with similar years of work experience, reported that the senior managers earned more than the Harvard Business School graduates. Two studies compared the salaries of graduates from MBA and undergraduate business programs, in one instance from the University of California at Berkeley, and in the second case from three business schools in the Midwest. Both studies reported that, although there was an effect of having the graduate MBA degree on starting salary, there was no effect of having an MBA on current salary, except for students from lower socioeconomic status backgrounds (Dreher, Dougherty, & Whitely, 1985; Pfeffer, 1977).

Even those studies that have found a positive effect of the MBA degree are open to the alternative interpretation that what is being assessed is the quality of the student body rather than the effects of acquiring some specific skills or knowledge. A study by the Graduate Management Admissions Council of people who registered for the GMAT (Graduate Management Admissions Test) found that 7 years later those who had graduated from business school had higher earnings than those who had either never attended business school or who had started a program but did not finish (Dugan, Grady, Payne, & Johnson, 1999). But the benefits accrued mostly to graduates of the more prestigious programs; individuals coming from unaccredited or less competitive schools earned amounts that were more similar to people who either did not attend business school at all or who did not graduate. These findings echo those of others who have observed there are almost no economic gains from an MBA degree unless one graduates from a top-ranked program (e.g., *The Economist, 1994*).

Even those studies that have found a positive effect of the MBA degree are open to the alternative interpretation that what is being assessed is the quality of the student body rather than the effects of acquiring some specific skills or knowledge.

A straightforward interpretation of these results is that it is not education in business but selectivity that is being assessed. As Dugan et al. noted, the fact that graduates from the most competitive, elite programs achieved the greatest earnings is scarcely surprising as these people "were selected by their programs on the basis of their much higher than average capabilities and credentials" (1999: 23). This interpretation, that what matters are the personal attributes of the attendees not what they learn while in attendance, is consistent with the fact that the course of study, and even the textbooks used, are remarkably similar across schools of different degrees of selectivity, so it is hard to argue that there are important differences in the knowledge being provided in the different schools. Studies conducted by the Educational Testing Services in 1982, as well as Porter and McKibbin's (1988) investigations of curriculum across business schools have emphasized that the curriculum is quite similar across schools.

The fact that graduate business programs may be as much networking, screening, or recruiting services as educational institutions is an observation made by numerous others. For instance, Jill Rupple, a partner at the consulting firm Diamond Technology Partners in response to the question of why companies recruit MBAs, replied, "It is a prescreened pool" (Leonhardt, 2000: 18). Similarly, Seth Godin, a journalist from *Fast Company* who attended Stanford's Graduate School of Business, argued that the core curriculum taught at business schools is irrelevant, and that the utility of a business school degree is to provide a pedigree rather than learning (Godin, 2000: 322).

DO HIGHER GRADES—MORE MASTERY OF THE SUBJECT MATTER—HAVE ANY EFFECT?

One reason that having an MBA degree may show no effect is that mere possession of the credential may not be strongly related to the individual's mastery of business knowledge. Recently, an investment bank was horrified to find that an MBA graduate it hired from a leading business school, an individual who had apparently taken a number of courses in finance, could not calculate the net present value of a future stream of payments. Crainer and Dearlove (1999), in their critical overview of business education, described the "Wharton Walk"—a drinking ritual in which the students at the University of Pennsylvania business school visit 10 bars in one night. They concluded, "This is what happens in business schools. Most students simply get drunk. MBA stu-

dents bond and network" (Crainer & Dearlove, 1999: xix). Robinson's (1994) description of his life at the Stanford Business School is illustrative of many students' perspective. "Learning is not an explicit goal. Nowhere does Robinson address the issue of *what he wants to learn*" (Armstrong, 1995: 102, emphasis in original). Obviously this is not a generalization that applies to all students in all schools all of the time, but to the extent this depiction of what goes on in business schools has some validity, it can help explain why the credential, in and of itself, may not have a lot of economic value.

If the credential itself could potentially mean nothing in terms of mastery of the subject matter, then perhaps we need to examine the effects of some measures of knowledge acquired. Although grades are certainly not a perfect measure of subject matter mastery, they have the advantage of being available in some studies and, moreover, are likely to be at least somewhat related to how much one has learned in courses. The empirical evidence on the effects of business school grade point average (GPA) is mixed. Neither Pfeffer (1977) nor Dreher, Dougherty, and Whiteley (1985) found any effect of grade point average on either starting or current salaries. O'Reilly (2001), at our request, reanalyzed data from his study with Chatman on the effects of personality and intelligence on MBA graduates' subsequent career outcomes (O'Reilly & Chatman, 1994). He reported that U.C. Berkeley MBA graduates' GPA was unrelated to (a) salary increases over 3 to 4 years after graduation, (b) average salary of the job accepted, (c) the number of jobs held since graduation, (d) the number of promotions since graduation, (e) the number of job offers received upon graduation, (f) either job or career satisfaction, and (g) the person's fit with his or her current job. Burt (personal communication, Nov. 26, 2001) reported that data from a survey of women who graduated from the University of Chicago Business School showed that GPA had no effect on either income or the probability of reaching senior rank.

Williams and Harrell (1964) found that GPA in required courses was unrelated to earnings for Stanford MBA graduates, but that grades from second-year electives were correlated with compensation (see also Harrell & Harrell, 1974). Harrell interpreted this difference in the effects of core versus elective grades as reflecting the consequences of strong work motivation and working hard, rather than as an advantage from what was learned. The logic is that grades in elective courses reveal more about a person's willingness to expend discretionary effort. Weinstein and Srinivasan (1974), however, did find a statistically significant effect of GPA on compensation for their subsample of line managers. Srinivasan and Hanson (1984) also reported an effect of MBA's GPA on compensation, regardless of whether the MBA was computed on core or elective classes. Their analysis also demonstrated that this effect was not driven by the relationship between GPA and prior work experience.

This evidence, at best mixed, does not provide a lot of support for the contention that mastery of the subject matter of business schools, at least as assessed by grades, is related to subsequent performance in business. If the subject matter of business schools were directly tied to business success, there should be more consistent and stronger connections between business success and mastery of the relevant content.

· · · · · · · · · · · · · · · · · ·
WHY IS THERE SO LITTLE EFFECT OF THE MBA ON THE GRADUATES?

For a number of reasons the empirical observation of little effect of either the MBA credential or grades on the subse-quent careers of MBA graduates is not surprising. First, there are economic reasons for why the MBA provides little advantage. The supply of MBAs has, as already noted, expanded rapidly. Because business education is a "cash cow" at many universities, programs have proliferated, including, more recently, part-time, evening, and weekend programs; executive MBAs; and expansion of existing programs. Although fewer than half of the schools offering an MBA degree are accredited, the fact of rising supply remains. At the same time, demand for MBAs may be falling: "In Britain, the demand for MBA graduates has fallen by a fifth since 1991 (*The Economist, 1996: 54*). More supply and about the same or less demand would translate into less advantage in terms of salary or other career outcomes for MBA graduates. Moreover, unlike other professions such as law, medicine, accounting, architecture, and some branches of engineering, the practice of business management is not restricted to people who possess a formal credential or certificate of training. Thus, with no barriers to entry into the profession—and with no entry point controlled by business schools—it is not surprising that there is a smaller effect of the credential on various economic outcomes (e.g., Pfeffer, 1974).

Second, neither grades in business school nor completion of the program may provide much evidence of learning. Grade inflation is pervasive in American higher education, and business schools are no exception (Kuh & Shouping, 1999; Muuka, 1998; Redding, 1998). As a consequence, almost no one fails out of MBA programs, which means the credential does not serve as a screen or an enforcement of minimum competency standards. If the MBA degree doesn't really distinguish among people then it is no surprise that it doesn't have much effect on career outcomes. As Armstrong, a professor who has taught MBAs for more than 30 years, observed:

In today's prestigious business schools, students have to demonstrate competence to get in, but not to get out. Every student who wants to (and who avoids financial and emotional distress) will graduate. At Wharton, for example, less than one percent of the students fail any given course, on average. . . . the probability of failing more than one course is almost zero. In effect, business schools have developed elaborate and expensive grading systems to ensure that even the least competent and least interested get credit (1995: 104).

Next, a large body of evidence suggests that the curriculum taught in business schools has only a small relationship to what is important for succeeding in business. Porter and McKibbin (1988: 65) noted that many critics felt that quantitatively based analytical techniques received too much attention, while there was too little attention given to developing leadership and interpersonal skills, and too little emphasis on communication skills. Not surprisingly, a survey conducted in 1982 by the Graduate Management Admissions Council came to the same conclusions regarding "perceived weaknesses in personal skills" (Jenkins & Reizenstein, 1984: 21). Mintzberg and Gosling (2002) noted that "contemporary business education focuses on the functions of business more than the practice of managing" (p. 28).

> *[A] large body of evidence suggests that the curriculum taught in business schools has only a small relationship to what is important for succeeding in business.*

Another GMAC survey of first-year graduate students in business from 91 schools asked what attributes they believed were important in business and which attributes they thought were enhanced by the curricula business schools teach. Of 10 traits, only one, communication skills, was perceived by more than 50% of the respondents as being both important and something that business schools improved (Stolzenberg, Abowd, & Giarrusso, 1986: 12). Many inconsistencies arose between what skills students thought were important and what they perceived business schools as proficient at developing. "The ability to apply theories to practical situations is ranked seventh . . . in its importance for successful management but is ranked *first* . . . in the extent to which it is believed to be enhanced by the business school experience" (Stolzenberg et al., 1986: 13). "For those who see business schools as academies of leadership skills, these may be disappointing results" (Stolzenberg et al., 1986: 13). If students see little connection between what is important and what is being taught, small wonder that they are occasionally cavalier about their classroom performance. And if there is, in fact, only a slight connection between the skills needed in business and what is taught in graduate business programs, then the absence of an effect of the MBA or mastery of the subject matter on the careers of graduates is understandable.

An interesting paradox occurs in the list of attributes or skills taught by business schools and what students and others believe to be the most important. Much of what business schools impart—theory and analytical techniques of various sorts—is readily learned and imitated, at least by intelligent people. Communication ability, leadership, interpersonal skills, and wisdom—"the ability to weave together and make use of different kinds of knowledge" (Mintzberg & Gosling. 2002: 28)—are at once less easily taught or transferred to others but, at the same time, because they are less easily imitated, have more value in the competition for leadership positions that occur in organizations. There are some alternative models of business education and, for that matter, leadership development that can do a better job imparting these qualities, and we discuss some of them presently. But we need to be cognizant of the trade-off between what schools can and do readily teach and what might be required to differentiate oneself and succeed in the world of management.

In spite of these long-standing issues about the curriculum, and lest one be concerned about the age of some of the surveys and studies, there is evidence that curricula have changed little over time. "Course materials have been upgraded and some class offerings have changed, but the 1960s product is still quite recognizable . . . in the 1990s" (Davis & Botkin, 1994: 90). Delivering essentially the same material over the Internet is an innovation in access and delivery, not in content, and the same holds true for programs held in remote locations or under different—for instance part-time or evening—schedules. As Mintzberg and Gosling (2002) commented, "curricula for so-called executive MBA programs, or educational programs for working managers, are organized in much the same fashion" (p. 28) as regular MBA programs. This is not to say that curricula haven't changed to incorporate new knowledge—obviously they have. But the basic structure of courses and the basic concepts have remained remarkably similar.

ISSUES WITH THE TEACHING PROCESS

Two other issues can further help us understand the limited effects of MBA education. The first is that many programs operate on the basis of some incorrect assumptions about learning, thereby doing things that contribute to poorer learning outcomes. One such assumption is that good teaching equals more learning, and that good teaching is best assessed by the

students in end-of-quarter (or midquarter) evaluations. Partly in response to the ratings game and the accompanying emphasis on student satisfaction with MBA programs, for instance in the *Business Week* ratings, and partly because for many business schools, attracting students is an issue, most schools have made courses more "student friendly." Students now routinely expect summaries of course readings and materials. For instance, at Stanford and many other business schools, it is now customary to pass out copies of overheads at the end of each class session summarizing the main points and ideas of the class, in response to student demands for "structure" and "take-aways."

The problem is that when students are relieved of any sense of responsibility for their learning and much involvement in the learning process, the evidence is that they learn much less. Tough (1982), studying self-reported learning by adults, found that few learning experiences occurred in groups with a teacher. Armstrong maintained that "when teachers direct and evaluate learning, students feel less responsibility" (1995: 102). Interestingly, the evidence shows there is little relationship between students' satisfaction with their teachers and what they learn (Attiyeh & Lumsden, 1972), calling into question the emphasis on course ratings. Teaching and learning are fundamentally different in their orientations: "The focus on teaching incorporates an input orientation. A focus on learning requires an output orientation" (Boyatzis, Cowen, & Kolb, 1995a: 9).

The second incorrect assumption is that external incentives are important and that by grading students' performance, the motivation problems previously enumerated can be overcome, either by providing positive recognition or by threatening academic difficulty. There are two problems with this assumption. First, as already noted, few sanctions are actually administered for poor performance in classes. Moreover, although schools can offer various forms of recognition for academic achievement, in the business schools, unlike law schools, where class standing has a real effect on job prospects, there is little evidence that course grades or class standing, even when available, are given much weight by employers in their applicant screening. Second, as reviewed extensively by Kohn (1993), the evidence, particularly in education, is that the use of external incentives, such as grading, impedes, rather than enhances, learning outcomes.

The final issue is the method of instruction. Some schools lecture, others teach by the case method, some use a combination. But in relatively few instances in established business schools is there much clinical training or learning by doing—experiential learning where "concrete experience is the basis for observation and reflection" (Kolb, 1976: 21). Students learn to talk about business, but it is not clear they learn business. "Unfortunately you cannot replicate true managing in the classroom. The case study is a case in point: Students with little or no management experience are presented with 20 pages on a company they do not know and told to pronounce on its strategy the next day" (Mintzberg & Lampel, 2001:244). As Bailey and Ford argued, although a scientific approach may be useful for the study of management, it is not at all clear that it helps in teaching management: "The practice of management is best taught as a craft, rich in lessons derived from experience and oriented toward taking and responding to action" (1996: 9). But as Leavitt noted, "business schools have been designed without practice fields" (1989: 40).

> *But as Leavitt noted, "business schools have been designed without practice fields."*

A method of instruction stressing language and concepts, not wisdom or mastery

of practice, explains how consulting firms can, in 3 weeks, replicate a 2-year business school experience: "The three-week program was helping them learn the vocabulary of corporate America . . . It's a question of learning the jargon" (Leonhardt, 2000: 18). But as Mintzberg (1996) has argued, management is a practice craft, and the typical business school experience is too far removed from the context of business. Schon (1983, 1987) has noted that "practice is characterized by indeterminacy, and what distinguishes the excellent practitioner from the merely adequate one is the ability to render indeterminate situations determinate. Professional artistry, then, requires transcending the rules and plans of technical rationality to 'reflect in action' (Bailey, Saparito, Kressel, Christensen, & Hooijberg, 1997: 157). The importance of practice and experience is why studies of leadership development (e.g., McCall, 1998) consistently find that the best way of developing leaders is to provide people with opportunities to lead. The importance of clinical experience is also one reason why on-the-job training is so effective—it avoids the transfer of training problem, or generalizing what is learned in the classroom to the work setting, that to some extent bedevils other education modalities. Without a larger clinical or practice component, it is not clear that business schools ever will impart much lasting knowledge that affects graduates' performance.

THE IMPACT OF BUSINESS SCHOOL RESEARCH

At the outset we should note that one goal of business school research is to enhance the prestige of the business school where the research is done. There is evidence that research does achieve that goal, as "research has, historically, been regarded as the primary determinant of a school's prestige" (Armstrong, 1995: 103). Armstrong and Sperry (1994) observed a significant correlation between the prestige of a business school and a measure of research impact for each school. Armstrong also found a relationship between research impact and a measure of the tax-adjusted net present value of graduating from a particular school: "The most obvious answer to the question, 'Why does research correlate with students' earnings?' is ...in reference to its effect on a school's prestige" (1995: 103). *Business Week* has now added a research influence measure to its ratings of business schools, so to the extent a school scores highly on that measure, it will enhance its overall prestige ranking. Most deans' ratings of business schools, which are incorporated in rankings such as that produced by *U.S. News and World Report* respond, at least partly, to the research prestige of the schools.

The second goal of research—and the focus of our examination—is to influence, either proximately or remotely, the practice of management. Here the evidence indicates considerably more modest results than is the case for the impact of research on prestige. One piece of evidence comes from the innovative study by Barley, Meyer, and Gash (1988) in which they used constructs from academics' and practitioners' writing about organizational culture over time to study patterns of mutual influence. Barley et al. concluded that "the pragmatics of academic discourse came to resemble more closely that of the practitioners' subculture" (1988: 52). The practitioner conceptualizations stayed constant while the academics' changed in a direction to become more similar to the practitioners. This suggests that although academics are influenced by practitioners, little influence flows from academics to industry. Future research, perhaps using other operationalizations of influence, such as diffusion of ideas, methods of analysis or data, or language, could examine the

direction of influence between academia and management practice. This would provide useful generalizations of Barley et al.'s work and potentially help us understand the conditions under which there is comparatively more influence from academics to practitioners and vice versa.

> *This suggests that although academics are influenced by practitioners, little influence flows from academics to industry.*

To further explore the impact of academic research on management, we collected two data sets to shed some light on this question. The first data examined *Business Week*'s lists of the best business books in 2001, 1991, and 1984 (the first year that such a list was published), to find out what percentage of the best business books were written by people teaching at business schools. The underlying assumption is that the books listed by *Business Week* on this best books list are, in general, more influential than other books in affecting management thought, language, and practice. Our interest was in exploring the extent to which these influential books came out of academia, specifically business schools, or from other nonacademic sources. We also wanted to see if there had been any change in the origins of these books over time—in other words, if there was any evidence that business schools were increasing or decreasing their influence on management thought.

These data show that only a very small fraction of business books that presumably influence management are actually written by academics. In 2001, only 2 of the Top 10 Best Business Books were written by academics, with the remainder of these books authored by journalists or businesspeople. One of those two books was written by Jim Collins, who does not have a PhD, was once a lecturer at Stanford, and is now an independent consultant and researcher. Therefore, it could be argued that only one book, just 10% of the list, was written by someone currently in a business school. In 1991, again only 1 of the top 10 books was authored by an academic, and in 1984, just 4 of the Top 10 Best Business Books came from academic authors. The data suggest little change over time in the origins of influential management books, but if there is a trend, it is in the direction of having fewer of the best business books authored by academics. This is consistent with the observation that the connection between business schools and the profession of management has diminished over time.

We also examined *Business Week*'s lists of the business best-sellers. The list of the best books reflects *Business Week*'s judgment, while the best-seller list reflects the judgments of the market. As far as we know, this is the only national best-seller list devoted solely to business books. Since 1995, the first year that these lists appeared, a maximum of 2 of the top 15 best-selling business books came out of academia in any year. Again the data suggest that business schools are not a major source of books that directly influence management thought, whether measured by sales or by more subjective assessments of the value of the books.

Some people will object to using the origins of the best or best-selling business books as a measure of the relative influence of business schools compared with other sources of business ideas. After all, academic research does not necessarily have a *direct* influence on business practice or thinking, but possibly there is an indirect influence as this research is cited and used by others, including those writing more popular and accessible texts. This is a reasonable argument, so we collected a second set of data to explore whether this argument has much face validity. We did this by comparing the citations earned by a selected list of academic business books against the citations to books listed as the best

business books by *Business Week*. Note that this procedure overstates the influence of the academic books, as they can be highly cited within the academic community even if they do not influence business thought or practice at all. Nonetheless, the data are informative.

The academic management books we selected were those that had won the George R. Terry Book Award, given annually by the Academy of Management. These are academic books that presumably should have a lot of influence on the discipline of management because they have won a prize given by that discipline. From 1991 to 2001, there have been 10 Terry Book Award winners. On average, these books received 39.9 total citations. Adjusting for the number of years since publication, on average the Terry Award winners received 6.80 citations per year. When we considered citations to books on the *Business Week* list of the 10 best business books, the average citations per year were 2.49. Although the academic books were cited, on average, more than twice as much per year as the business books, as already noted, these citations reflect impact on both other academics and more general writing, so the influence on management practice is undoubtedly overestimated by this comparison. Although the difference between the two sets of books in percentage terms is great, remember that the absolute difference is only 4 citations per year, on average, distinguishing Terry Award winners from the books on the *Business Week* list.

We also compared the average number of citations of books written by academics versus others within the best business books from 1991 to 2001. Out of the 107 books that have been listed in the past 11 years, just 19 (17.76%) were authored by academics. These books have been cited an average of 27.36 times. Books authored by journalists, CEOs, and other nonacademics were cited an average of 13.48 times, about half as often. However, as shown in Figure 1-3,

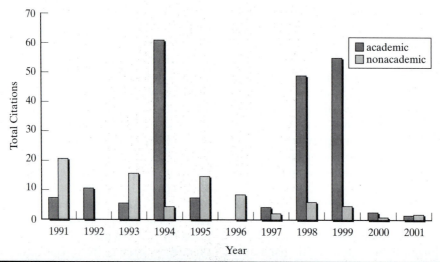

FIGURE 1-3 Total Number of Citations for Academic and Nonacademic Authors, *Business Week's Best Business Books*, 1991–2001

nonacademic books were cited more often than academic books in 5 out of the 11 years we examined.

The three most-cited books were authored by academics: *Competing for the Future* by Gary Hamel and C. K. Prahalad (121 total citations), *Development as Freedom* by Amartya Sen (91 total citations), and *The Corrosion of Character* by sociologist Richard Sennett (84 citations). Only one of these books came out of a business school; the others were written by an economist and a sociologist. When these three books are removed from the analysis, nonacademic books are cited an average of 1.62 times more often than the academic books on the *Business Week* list.

Yet another way of looking at the influence of business school research on management practice is to consider the source of ideas and techniques used in management consulting, things that businesses actually pay money to implement. Rigby (2001) has done a survey of management tools for the past 7 or 8 years, beginning when he noticed that there were consumer ratings on cereal but no rating of techniques and approaches

that companies were spending tens of millions of dollars on. "The term 'management tool' can mean many things, but often involves a set of concepts, processes, exercises, and analytic frameworks" (Rigby, 2001: 139). Rigby gets his list from (1) a literature search on Dow Jones Interactive pulling off generic terms, (2) interviews with 10–15 business school professors, and (3) interviews with about 30 senior executives in companies. This list does change somewhat from year to year.

The 1999 survey results, reported by Rigby (2001), covered some 25 management ideas and tools. We interviewed Rigby to get his definitions of the tools and ideas as well as to jointly determine where the ideas originated. Seven of the 25 management tools came out of academia, and 18 came out of either corporations, consulting firms, or some combination. The survey asks about satisfaction with the tools, their utilization, and gives estimates of a defection rate, or the proportion of companies that stopped using a tool. The tools that came out of consulting firms and companies had a higher utilization rate than the tools from academia (49.7% vs.

33.6, $p > 10$), had a higher level of satisfaction (3.79 vs. 3.71, n.s.), and a lower defection rate (11.9% vs. 20.6%, $p > 10$). Rigby's data suggest that less than one third of the tools and ideas that companies are paying money to implement came out of academia and those that originated in universities were used less often and were abandoned more often.

Considering the evidence, the data suggest that the research done in business schools is making a modest contribution to management practice and management thought, even when compared to research produced by nonacademics such as journalists, consultants, and people working in companies.

EXPLAINING THE RELATIVELY SMALL IMPACT OF BUSINESS SCHOOL RESEARCH

Why has there been such a modest effect of business school scholarship on practice, in spite of the tremendous expenditure of resources by intelligent and motivated people? One possible answer comes from a reflective essay by Paul Lawrence. Lawrence argued that "the better work in our field has come from problem-oriented research, rather than from theory-oriented research," (1992: 140) but that many institutional pressures conspired to ensure that there was not very much problem-oriented research being done. Sutton and Staw questioned whether theory in the organizational sciences was useful and wrote that "the field first needs more descriptive narratives about organizational life" (1995: 378). Pfeffer (1997), in a similar vein, argued that research should be anchored in important phenomena. So, perhaps the emphasis on theory rather than observation, problems, or phenomena explains part of the problem.

Another issue is whether research is actually oriented toward being used and useful and whether research proceeds from an intimate knowledge and concern with organizations and the people in them. For instance, Lawrence (1992) argued that whether the research "is in fact used by practitioners is the first quality test" (p. 141) to be applied, and suggested listening "for our subjects' voices identifying important problems where knowledge is needed" (p. 142). In a similar vein, "Argyris argues that for scholars to produce knowledge that is 'actionable,' they must capture in their research the conditions experienced by the practitioner" (Bailey & Eastman, 1996: 354).

Yet another, complementary answer about why organizational research has less effect on management thought and practice comes from Weick's (1989) analysis of theory construction. Using an evolutionary or selection logic, Weick argued that "heterogeneous thought trials are more likely than homogeneous thought trials to solve theoretical problems" (1989: 522). One implication of this argument is that there is a research benefit to generalists and generalism. That is because to the extent theories and theorists are increasingly narrowly focused and constrained, achieving the requisite heterogeneity or variety to solve interesting theoretical puzzles or to generate important theory is less likely. Therefore, to the extent that business school research increasingly resembles that of more paradigmatically developed social sciences, with the accompanying strictures, business school research is inadvertently disadvantaged: "Theorists often write trivial theories because their process of theory construction is hemmed in by methodological strictures that favor validation rather than usefulness" (Weick, 1989: 516). Moreover, Weick's argument suggests that the very generalism of training in the organization sciences provides an advantage in theory development, but this is an advantage that is lost as recruiting increasingly focuses on disciplinary specialists and as the career system rewards a narrowing of focus.

Although one may quarrel with the prescriptive wisdom of these various insights, there is little doubt that the arguments help us understand something about why research efforts in business schools do not invariably produce the impact one might like, given both the talent and resources expended. Following the recommendations—to be more problem or phenomenon focused, to pay attention to observation, to listen to our subjects, to occasionally hire and reward generalism and conceptual diversity, and to be concerned with applicability as well as other aspects of theory—although seldom implemented in the world of academic business schools, would probably produce research that has at least the potential of being more useful as well as more theoretically interesting.

A DIFFERENT PERSPECTIVE AND APPROACH TO BUSINESS SCHOOL EDUCATION

Although much of the foregoing argument may at first glance appear to be controversial or provocative, in fact it is neither—the problems are at once well recognized and simply not frequently acknowledged or discussed. For instance, Donald Hambrick, in his 1993 presidential address to the Academy of Management, bemoaned the lack of impact of the work of its members on the larger society because of the "incestuous, closed loop" nature of the research and writing (Hambrick, 1994: 13). More than 2 decades ago, Hayes and Abernathy complained about the "preference for . . . analytic detachment rather than the insight that comes from 'hands on' experience" (1980: 68).

Business schools are relatively unique among professional schools such as law, social work, medicine, education, architec-

ture, and engineering in the degree of separation from the profession that they supposedly serve. This is not to say that business school faculty don't consult for businesses or teach in company executive programs, or that students from business school don't go on to practice management—obviously all of this occurs. But, what is unique is the degree of separation that differentiates business from other professional schools—differences in terms of the proportion of faculty who move in and out of the profession or who practice it regularly, and the extent to which curricula in the various professions are or are not linked to the concerns of the profession and directly oriented toward preparing the students to practice that profession, including in many instances incorporating a clinical component.

A number of programs have begun to address the issue of relevance, and most share the following features:

1. *They concentrate on more experienced students*, often practicing managers who attend classes episodically and then return to their work environments to confront their learning with their everyday experiences, and vice versa. Teaching working adults assists in the transfer of training between the classroom and the workplace. Teaching working adults also helps with the readiness-to-learn issue, as for the most part, people with jobs are interested in learning things that will make them more effective on their jobs and are less concerned simply with acquiring a credential so they can find a job. And third, teaching working adults addresses the relevance problem, as pressures from these students will tend to ensure more connection between what is taught and what is needed.

2. *Their design is multidisciplinary.* These programs tend not to have the conventional set of functional courses, but instead recognize the interdisciplinary, interrelated world of modern business. This design element

leaves them more veridical with the problems people face in actual management situations, where issues do not arrive to be solved segmented by discipline.

3. *They focus not only on learning concepts and techniques, but also on changing how people think about business issues.* This is an important dimension because many people who teach in business schools note how small the effect sometimes is on those who pass through the school. Changing how people think is an essential element in changing what they do and how they manage, as it is philosophy that underlies many management perspectives and approaches, such as total quality management (e.g., Pfeffer & Sutton, 2000).

4. *They have a clinical or action component.* Learning is coupled with the application of that learning, sometimes in groups, and invariably in ways relevant to the individual's current job and company.

These are a few examples of different models of business education. At the Duxx Graduates School of Business Leadership in Mexico, 35 courses are offered in three core areas: "business reasoning, social knowledge, and personal and interpersonal skills" (Ransdell, 1999: 48). The courses are taught by part-time faculty who fly in for short periods and spend time interacting on an intense basis with students. At the Rotman School at the University of Toronto, there is an increased emphasis on interdisciplinary training (Lieber, 1999: 262). One of the most ambitious and innovative business school education models is the International Masters in Practicing Management (IMPM), founded by Henry Mintzberg (Reingold, 2000: 286). The program consists of 2-week modules spread over 16 months and across five continents—there is no home campus. Students must be practicing managers and must be sponsored by their companies. When students return from their learning modules to work, "they must write a reflec-

tion paper describing how what they learned relates to their job" (Reingold, 2000: 286). The program is focused on changing how students think, rather than on a set of specific analytical constructs. It consists of five modules: "Managing Self, the reflective mind-set: Managing Relationships, the collaborative mind-set; Managing Organizations, the analytic mind-set; Managing Context, the worldly mind-set; and Managing Change, the action mind-set" (Reingold, 2000: 286). Mintzberg's philosophy is that good management education will help people "learn to ask the right questions, to reflect, and to avoid the traditional manager's trap of reacting to one crisis after another" (Reingold, 2000: 286). Classes are structured to leave 50% of the time for students to talk to other students in the class, and are much less professor-centric than traditional MBA classes.

Boyatzis, Cowen, and Kolb (1995b) described the redesign of the MBA program at the Weatherhead School at Case Western Reserve University, notable in that it was shaped by an underlying philosophy, not just the typical political horse trading among functional groups for places in the curriculum as well as by conscious and systematic efforts to evaluate the consequences of the curriculum redesign. Outcome evaluation—the analysis of the effects of various educational program interventions—is more frequently seen in public elementary and high school education, and indeed evaluation research and methodology is a component of training in educational schools. However, evaluating results or curricula is extremely rare, if not nonexistent in university graduate programs and business school programs in particular. The Association to Advance Collegiate Schools of Business (AACSB) for a time advocated evaluating programs, courses, and their effects (Boyatzis et al., 1995b), but such efforts never went very far and have not penetrated the day-to-day design and management of business school programs. The MBA program the Weatherhead School developed "has six key elements: the managerial assessment and development course, the Learning Plan, the core courses, Executive Action Teams, perspectives courses, and advanced electives" (Boyatzis et al., 1995b: 37).

We have not tried to cover every new or different model of business education here, but to provide some representative examples of what is being done and what is possible. As business school training and research have become less problem-centered and more self-referential, problems of relevance and impact have arisen. Therefore it is understandable that recent innovations in business education incorporate more clinical work, more connection between concepts and practice, and a less-fragmented view of the subject matter.

BARRIERS TO CHANGING THE CURRENT MBA EDUCATION MODEL

There are several, seemingly insurmountable barriers to fundamentally altering MBA programs in the ways just described, and the existence of these barriers helps us understand why so little has changed in spite of the evidence. First and foremost is cost. The shortage of business school faculty is severe and growing. Zimmerman (2001: 15) noted that the top ten PhD-producing schools have reduced by one-third the number of students produced each year, and the forecast is for the next decade to graduate only half as many PhDs as in the 1990s. This shortage has resulted in two inexorable trends— increasing salaries, including providing more summer support, research support, and higher 9-month salaries—and reduced teaching loads, particularly at the more competitive

business schools, although the salary pressures exist almost everywhere. Both of these trends increase costs, as more highly paid faculty (who also cost more because of increased support) teach fewer classes.

The way many schools have coped is to increase the size of sections, to increase average class size and reduce the number of smaller classes, or at a minimum, to hold class sizes constant. At Stanford, some classrooms were retrofitted a few years ago, much like airplanes, to place more seats into the existing space. At many schools, utilization of facilities and of classes is measured and managed. With MBA tuition covering at most one half the cost of educating students, business schools face budget pressures that show no sign of diminishing. But these financial pressures, met, in part, by having each professor teach more students in a given classroom encounter, almost preclude the type of clinical instruction that one sees in medical schools or in some of the newer MBA programs described above. The Center for Creative Leadership limits its leadership programs to enrollments in the mid-20s. Many business schools would cancel programs, including executive programs, if they consistently ran at that size.

The second barrier to fundamentally altering MBA programs is that few if any of the current business school faculty are particularly well equipped to staff new models of business education that link education to practice. Unlike other professions such as medicine, law, architecture, and even business schools of the distant past (and a few today that employ more clinical faculty), many full-time faculty have not practiced the profession or craft of management. The shortage of faculty means more business schools are hiring from social science departments such as economics, psychology, or sociology. These faculty, who derive power from their scarcity, are able to focus importance on disciplinary-based research and publication in traditional scholarly journals, rather than emphasizing managerial concerns. Therefore, faculty who have been hired and promoted for their theoretical and analytical skills and for their ability to generate and, one might hope, impart knowledge are not as able to apply the knowledge that they teach.

Third, as with any status-based system, it is scarcely in the interests of those schools winning the competitive war for status to change the rules of the game that have put them on top. Therefore, it is not surprising that much of the innovation in business education and in MBA programs comes from either new schools or programs that are not so much in the status mainstream, such as Case Western Reserve, or from corporations that are not in the MBA status contest at all. As Podolny (1994) has argued, status is achieved partly through the status of the organizations with which one associates. So, although schools can start innovative educational programs, their ability to compete successfully for status and prestige—and recall that prestige does have a real effect on MBA salaries—will be limited.

In other words, we have a self-reinforcing system that will be difficult to change. The most prestigious schools attract the best students who have the best job opportunities and the highest salaries and attract the highest status recruiters. Because the status of the schools derives in part from the achievements of their graduates, those that obtain the best students retain their prestige. Schools that win in this status-based competition, and for that matter, their students, have little incentive to change. Schools that have an incentive to innovate, the ones that are newer or for other reasons are interested in experimenting with different models of MBA education, begin with the disadvantage of not necessarily being able to attract

the most applicants or the best students, and therefore, are not as attractive to corporate recruiters. Mintzberg's (Reingold, 2000) new program is insightful in this regard, as by focusing on people already working in companies, the competition for the best jobs and the best students is nicely avoided.

[As] with any status-based system, it is scarcely in the interests of those schools winning the competitive war for status to change the rules of the game that have put them on top.

And finally, the status quo is maintained by the taken-for-granted aspect of so much of business education, the fact that what we do and how we do it has become truly institutionalized. Institutionalization of existing practices and models legitimates them and insulates them from both competition and change and even from serious questioning. "Every treatment of institutions emphasizes their contribution to social stability" (Scott, 1995: 49). Accrediting organizations such as the AACSB and the various disciplinary professional associations constitute the institutional field of business schools and business education and act, in a mutually reinforcing way, to maintain the status quo. Moreover, most business school faculty are too busy doing their work of teaching and research to consider the broader environment in which they are working, and even if and when they do so, their ability to change that environment is severely constrained.

Consequently, the likelihood of profound change or reform in contemporary management education, at least in the United States and at least as practiced by university-based business schools, seems limited. We do not foresee the appearance of forces or actors that can reasonably be expected to overcome the inertia that derives from the factors discussed in this article, and others, that maintain the current model of business education and research.

● ● ● ● ● ● ● ● ● ● ● ● ● ● ● ● ● ● ●

WHERE DO BUSINESS SCHOOLS GO FROM HERE?

Our depiction of business education, its evolution over time, and the problems that have emerged, shares features with other studies of schools that have emphasized their institutionalized elements (e.g., Meyer & Rowan, 1977). Institutionalization leads to ritualized practices that assume a taken-for-granted quality and little attempt to connect technical rationality to actual structures and policies. In particular, it is striking that business education and business schools can be so large and so prominent for such a long time without attracting much outcome evaluation or assessment. At a minimum, much more research is needed to address the various questions posed here, as well as other questions that speak to the organization and effects of business school curricula, faculty staffing patterns, and research practices.

The studies of business education in the 1950s (e.g., Gordon & Howell, 1959) and the accompanying foundation support to "improve" business education, came to define a normative structure for what business education should be—research-based, analytical, and founded in economics and other social sciences, teaching people general knowledge that they could use throughout their working lives. The best business schools thus attracted people from social science departments and had faculty that won awards in the social sciences, including the Nobel Prize in Economics.

In implicitly or explicitly rejecting the so-called trade-school model, business schools gained respectability and approval on their campuses by conforming to the norms and behaviors of arts and sciences departments. Just as institutional theory

would suggest, this evolving model of business education soon assumed a taken-for-granted quality that came to be valued in and for itself, and is seldom, if ever, confronted with data about its actual effects. However, every so often, the lack of connection between institutionalized organizational practices and the activities they are expected to enhance forces us to examine whether business schools are doing their jobs of enhancing MBA careers and providing useful knowledge.

Our review of the evidence suggests potential problems for business schools. For the most part, there is scant evidence that the MBA credential, particularly from non-elite schools, or the grades earned in business courses—a measure of the mastery of the material—are related to either salary or the attainment of higher level positions in organizations. These data, at a minimum, suggest that the training or education component of business education is only loosely coupled to the world of managing organizations. A similar disconnection is observed when we consider research. Again, the small amount of available evidence suggests a modest effect and limited linkage between the research on management and management practice.

But as this situation is scarcely new, why should we suddenly anticipate problems that could threaten the existing order? For several reasons. First, management has become the subject of popular books and popular discourse. Decades ago, biographies of business leaders were seldom written and were even scarcer on best-seller lists. Special business publications, business media, and business magazines have proliferated. In short, business, not just the stock market, has become a spectator sport in the United States. So, business, business education, and by extension, business schools are coming under increasing scrutiny.

Second, management and managerial skill has been identified as a core competence required for economic prosperity and possibly even economic development. In an increasingly knowledge-based economy, the ability to mobilize and use knowledge is a critical skill. With the privatization of industries and companies all over the world, the ability to manage large-scale private sector organizations effectively is a sine qua non for economic well-being. So, business and business education are increasingly the topic of conversation, and managerial skills are accordingly important for society. In this environment, the fact that business schools apparently have not done a better job in either the educational or research missions leaves them more vulnerable to focused criticism, attack, and competition.

Yes, competition. The demands for better managers and more and better leaders, and the demands for business knowledge are inexorable, and these demands have already generated numerous alternative sources of supply. Greater numbers of educational and research organizations exist separately from business schools (e.g., Gaddis, 2000). Indeed, one can view the short courses offered by consulting companies as alternative business schools, and the research conducted and published by various professional service firms as alternative sources of business research. Executive education is now offered not only by business schools but also by consulting companies and various training and education firms. In every domain in which they operate, business schools face competitors that, for the most part, are not necessarily playing by the same rules because they don't operate in the same normative environment with the same history as most business schools (Gaddis, 2000).

For business schools to lose this coming competition would be unfortunate and unnecessary. The research capabilities, and particularly the rigorous thinking and theoretical grounding that characterizes business school scholars and their research, actually offer an advantage over the casual empiricism and hyping of the latest fad that characterizes much, although not all, of the research that comes out of nonacademic sources. And business school faculty have spent years honing the craft of preparing and delivering educational material in ways that are at once accessible and intellectually sound. There is no reason that, in a world seeking both knowledge and training, business schools can't succeed in doing both well.

> *There is no reason that, in a world seeking both knowledge and training, business schools can't succeed in doing both well.*

To do so, all that is required is for business schools to model themselves more closely on their other professional school counterparts and less on arts and sciences departments. This entails focusing research on phenomena and problems of enduring importance, and building curricula that are evaluated, in part, by how well they actually prepare students to be effective in practicing the profession. At a minimum, it would seem to require systematic assessments of business school products and more attention to the competitive environment. If business schools don't change in this way, competitive institutions may pose a substantial and growing threat to their continued prosperity, if not to their very existence.

References

AACSB Newsline, 1999. Number of undergraduate business degrees continue downward plunge, while MBA degrees awarded skyrocket; Doctoral degrees on the decline. [online], Available: www.cacsb.edu.

Applications Trends Survey 2001, 2001. Graduate Management Admissions Council. [online], Available: www.amac.com.

Armstrong, J. S. 1995. The devil's advocate responds to an MBA student's claim that research harms learning. *Journal of Marketing*, 59: 101–106.

Armstrong, J. S., & Sperry, T. 1994. Business school prestige—Research versus teaching. *Interfaces*, 24: 13–43.

Attiyeh, R. & Lumaden, K. G. 1972. Some modern myths in teaching economics: The U.K. experience. *American Economic Review*, 62: 429–433.

Bailey, J. R., & Eastman, W. N. 1996. Tensions between science and service in organizational scholarship. *Journal of Applied Behavioral Science*, 32: 350–355.

Bailey, J., & Ford, C. 1996. Management as science versus management as practice in postgraduate business education. *Business Strategy Review*, 7(4): 7–12.

Bailey, J. R., Saparito, P., Kressel, K., Christensen, E., & Hooijberg, R. 1997. A model for reflective pedagogy. *Journal of Management Education*, 21:155–167.

Barley, S. R., Meyer, G. W., & Gash, D. C. 1988. Cultures of culture: Academics, practitioners, and the pragmatics of normative control. *Administrative Science Quarterly*, 33:24–60.

Boyatzis, R. E., Cowen, S. S., & Kolb, D. A. 1995a. Introduction: Taking the path toward learning. In R. E. Boyatzis. S. S. Cowen, D. A. Kolb, & Associates (Eds.), *Innovation in professional education: Steps on a journey from teaching to learning*: 1–11. San Francisco: Jossey-Bass.

Boyatzis, R. E., Cowen, S. S., & Kolb, D. A. 1995b. Management of knowledge: Redesigning the weatherhead MBA program. In R. E., Boyatzis, S. S. Cowen, D. A. Kolb & Associates (Eds.). *Innovation in professional education: Steps on a journey from teaching to learning*: 32–49. San Francisco: Jossey-Bass.

Charan, R., & Colvin, G. 1998. Why CEOs fail. *Fortune*, 139: June 21, 69.

Crainer, S., & Dearlove, D. 1999. *Gravy training: Inside the business of business schools*. San Francisco: Jossey-Bass.

Davis, S., & Botkia, J. 1994. The monster under the bed: *How business is mastering the opportunity of knowledge for profit*, New York: Simon and Schuster.

Dreher, G. F., Dougherty, T. W., & Whitely, B. 1985. Generalizability of MBA degree and socioeconomic effects on business school graduates' salaries. *Journal of Applied Psychology*, 70: 769–773.

Dugan, M. K., Grady, W. R., Payne, B., & Johnson, T. R. 1999. The benefits of an MBA: A comparison of graduates and non-graduates. *Selections*, 1: 18–24.

The Economist, 1994. The MBA cost-benefit analysis. *The Economist*, August 6, 1994: 58.

The Economist, 1998. Dona and Dollars. *The Economist*, July 20, 1996: 53–54.

Gaddis, P. O. 2000. Business schools: Fighting the enemy within. *Strategy and Business*. 21(4): 51–57.

Godin, S. (September 2000). Change agent. *Fast Company*, 38: 322.

Gordon, R., & Howell, J. 1959. *Higher education for business*. New York: Columbia University Press.

Hambrick, D. C. 1994. What if the academy actually mattered? *Academy of Management Review*, 19: 11–16.

Harrell, T. W., & Harrell, M. S. 1974. Predictors of management success. Technical Report No. 3 to the Office of the Naval Research, Palo Alto, CA: Stanford University, Graduate School of Business.

Hayes, R. H., & Abernathy, W. J. 1980. Managing our way to economic decline. *Harvard Business Review*, 58(4): 67–77.

Jenkins, R. L., & Reizenstein, R. C. 1984. Insights into the MBA: Its contents, output, and relevance. *Selections*, 2: 19–24.

Kohn, A. 1993. Punished by rewards. Boston: Houghton Mifflin.

Kolb, D. A. 1976. Management and the learning process. *California Management Review*, 18: 21–31.

Kuh, G. D., & Shouping, S. 1999. Unraveling the complexity of the increase in college grades from the mid-1980s to the mid-1990s. *Educational Evaluation & Policy Analysis*, 21: 297–300.

Lawrence, P. R. 1992. The challenge of problem-oriented research. *Journal of Management Inquiry*, 1: 139–142.

Leavitt, H. J. 1986. *Corporate pathfinders.* Homewood, IL: DowJones-Irwin.

Leavitt, H. J. 1989. Educating our MBAs: On teaching what we haven't taught. *California Management Review*, 31(3): 38–50.

Leonhardt, D. 2000. A matter of degree? Not for consultants, *New York Times*, October 1, 2000, Section 31: 1–18.

Lieber, R. December 1999. Learning and change: Roger Martin. *Fast Company*, 30: 262.

Livingston, J. S. 1971. The myth of the well-educated manager. *Harvard Business Review*, 49: 79–89.

McCall, M. W., Jr. 1998. *High flyers: Developing the next generation of leaders.* Boston: Harvard Business School Press.

Meyer. J. W., & Rowan, B. 1977. Institutionalized organizations: Formal structure as myth and ceremony. *American Journal of Sociology*, 83: 340–363.

Mintzberg, H. 1996. Ten ideas designed to rile everyone who cares about management. *Harvard Business Review.* July–August: 61–68.

Mintzberg, H., & Gosling, J. R. 2002. Reality programming for MBAs. *Strategy and Business*, 26(1): 28–31.

Mintzberg, H., & Lampel, J. 2001. Matter of degrees: Do MBAs make better CEOs? *Fortune*, February 19, 2001: 244.

Muuka, G. N. 1998. One business professor's experience with the diversity issue and pressure to raise students' grades. *Journal of Education for Business*, 73: 184–189.

Norris, F. H. 1997. The crimson crop is plenty green. *New York Times.* January 2, 1997: C23.

O'Reily, C. A., III. 2001. Personal communication. November 15, 2001.

O'Reilly, C. A., III, & Chatman, J. 1994. Working smarter and harder: A longitudinal study of managerial success. *Administrative Science Quarterly*, 39: 603–627.

Pfeffer, J. 1974. Administrative regulation and licensing: *Social problem* or solution? *Social Problems*, 21: 469–479.

Pfeffer, J. 1977. Effects of an MBA and socioeconomic origins on business school graduates salaries. *Journal of Applied Psychology*, 62: 609–705.

Pfeffer, J. 1997. *New directions for organization theory.* New York: Oxford University Press.

Pfeffer, J., & Sutton, R. I. 2000. *The knowing-doing gap.* Boston: Harvard Business School Press.

Pierson, R. C. 1959. *The education of American businessmen.* New York: McGraw-Hill.

Podolny, J. M. 1994. Market uncertainty and the social character of economic exchange. *Administrative Science Quarterly*, 39: 458–483.

Porter, L. W., & McKibbin, L. E. 1988. *Management education and development: Drift or thrust into the 21st century.* New York: McGraw-Hill.

Ransdell, E. April. 1999. School for leaders. *Fast Company*, 23:48.

Redding, R. E. 1998. Students' evaluations of teaching fuel grade inflation. *American Psychologist*, 53: 1227–1229.

Reingold, J. November. 2000. You can't create a leader in a classroom. *Fast Company,* 40: 286.

Rigby, D. 2001. Management tools and techniques: A survey. *California Management Review*, 43(2): 139–160.

Robinson, P. 1994. *Snapshots from Hell.* New York: Warner Books.

Schon, D. 1983. *The reflective practitioner.* New York: Basic Books.

Schon, D. 1987. *Educating the reflective practitioner.* San Francisco: Jossey-Bass.

Scott, W. R. 1995. *Institutions and organizations.* Thousand Oaks, CA: Sage.

Srinivasan, V., & Hanson, B. A. 1984. Decision aids for MBA program admissions: Predicting management potential. Unpublished manuscript, Stanford Graduate School of Business.

Stolzenberg, R. M., Abowd, J., & Giarrusso, R. 1986. Abandoning the myth of the modern MBA student. *Selections*, 3 (Autumn): 9–21.

Sutton, R. L., & Staw, B. M. 1995. What theory is not. *Administrative Science Quarterly*, 40: 37–384.

Tough, A. 1982. *Intentional changes.* Chicago: Follet.

U.S. News and World Report: 2002 Top Business Schools. 2002. *U.S. News and World Report* [online]. Available: usnews.com.

Weick, K. E. 1989. Theory construction as disciplined imagination. *Academy of Management Review*, 14: 516–531.

Weinstein, A. G., & Srinivasan, V. 1974. Predicting managerial success of master of business administration (MBA) graduates. *Journal of Applied Psychology*, 59: 207–212.

Williams, F. J., & Harrell, T. W. 1964. Predicting success in business. *Journal of Applied Psychology*, 48: 164–167.

Zimmerman, J. L. 2001. Can American business schools survive? Rochester, NY: Unpublished manuscript. Simon Graduate School of Business Administration.

I-8: Company Puts Employees' Feet to the Fire

Dave Barry

I read a fascinating business-related article in my newspaper, *The Miami Herald* (official motto: "The Person Who Was Supposed To Think Up Our Motto Got Laid Off"). This article, which was written by Elaine Walker, concerned an incident wherein employees of the Burger King marketing department walked barefoot over hot coals.

If you're unfamiliar with modern American corporate culture, you're probably assuming that somebody spiked the Burger King coffee machine with LSD. Nope. The fire walking was a planned activity on a corporate motivational retreat, supervised by a professional fire walking consultant to whom Burger King paid thousands of actual U.S. dollars.

According to the Herald article, the consultant also had the Burger King marketing people bend spoons, break boards, smash bricks, bend steel bars with their throats and walk over a bed of sharp nails. American corporate employees are required to do this kind of thing all the time, and for a sound business reason. Their management has lint for brains.

No, seriously, these are motivational activities that make employees self-confident and unafraid to tackle tough business challenges. The employees think: "Hey, if I can bend a steel bar with my throat, there's no reason why I can't change the toner cartridge in the printer!"

The Burger King people got off easy. Some corporations motivate their employees by shipping them off to rugged wilderness survival programs, where they learn vital lessons that help them excel in the business world. Like, if they need to impress an important client, they could use their survival training to, I don't know, catch him a squirrel.

The point is that subjecting employees to physical abuse is a standard corporate motivational technique that has proved, in study after study, to be a highly effective means of transferring money to consultants. Still, you might think that employees would draw the line at walking on hot coals, on the grounds that they could, theoretically, burn their feet. This would seem to be especially obvious to employees of Burger King, a company whose main product is a graphic example of what happens to flesh that is exposed to high temperatures.

Nevertheless, at the Burger King marketing retreat, more than 100 employees walked across an 8-foot strip of white-hot coals, and—in an inspirational triumph of mind over matter that shows the amazing miracles that the human spirit, when freed of self-doubt, can accomplish—about a dozen of them burned their feet. One woman had to be taken to the hospital. Several people were in wheelchairs the next day.

Now, you may feel that an employee-motivation event that actually injured some employees could not be described as a total success. That is why you are not a marketing executive. The Herald article quotes Burger King's vice president of product marketing, Dana Frydman—whose personal feet were among those burned—as saying: "It was a great experience for everyone."

The article also quotes the firewalking consultant, Robert "Cork" Kallen, as saying: "The majority of the people get through it without a nick or a blister. When you see over 100 people and only 10 to 15 people have blisters, I don't term that unusual. Some people just have incredibly sensitive feet."

There you have the REAL problem: Employees with sensitive feet. It's high time that corporations did something about this problem.

Here's my proposal: When you apply for a job, at the end of your interview, you would be required to take off your shoes and socks, and the interviewer would snap the bottoms of your feet sharply with a rubber band. For particularly important jobs, the interviewer might staple a document to your insole, to see if you truly have the foot toughness it takes to succeed in the modern corporate environment.

What do you think? I think it's a great idea. In fact, I think I would be an excellent motivational consultant. You can be my first client! Here's what you do: (1) Tear this column out of the newspaper. (2) Wad it into a ball. (3) Insert the ball into your left nostril and jam it in there as far as you can with a pencil. (4) Send me thousands of dollars.

Ha ha! I'm just kidding, of course. I know you're not THAT stupid. Hardly anybody is!

NOTE TO MARKETING EXECUTIVES: I would prefer cash.

Dave Barry is a humor columnist for The Miami Herald.

I-9: The Calf Path

Samuel Foss

One day thru the primeval wood
A calf walked home, as good calves
   should;
But made a trail, all bent askew,
A crooked trail, as all calves do.

Since then 300 years have fled,
And I infer the calf is dead.
But still, he left behind his trail
And thereby hangs my mortal tale.

Source: "The Calf Path" from *Poems That Live Forever*, by Samuel Foss. Copyright © 1965 Samuel Foss.

The trail was taken up next day
By a lone dog, that passed that way.
And then a wise bell weathered sheep
Pursued the trail, o'er vale and steep
And drew the flocks behind him too
As good bell weathers always do.
And from that day, o'er hill and glade
Thru those old woods, a path was made.

And many men wound in and out,
And dodged, and turned, and bent
   about,
And uttered words of righteous wrath

Because 'twas such a crooked path.
But still they followed, do not laugh
The first migrations of that calf.
And thru the winding woods they
    stalked
Because he wobbled when he walked.

This forest path became a lane
That bent, and turned, and turned
    again.

This crooked lane became a road
Where many a poor horse with his load
Toiled on beneath the burning sun
And traveled some three miles in one.
And thus a century and a half
They trod the footsteps of that calf.

I-10: The Cracked Water Pot

Author Unknown

A water bearer in India had two large water pots. They hung on opposite ends of a pole which he carried across his neck. One of the pots had a crack in it and while the other pot was perfect and always delivered a full portion of water at the end of the long walk from the stream to the master's house, the cracked pot always arrived only half full.

For a full two years this went on daily, with the water bearer delivering only one and a half pots full of water in his master's house. Of course, the perfect pot was proud of its accomplishments, perfect to the end for which it was made. But the poor cracked pot was ashamed of its imperfection, miserable that it could accomplish only half of what it had been made to do.

After two years of what it perceived to be a bitter failure, it spoke to the water bearer one day by the stream. "I am ashamed of myself and I want to apologize to you."

"Why?" asked the water bearer. "What are you ashamed of?"

"I have been able, for these past two years, to deliver only half my load because this crack in my side causes water to leak out all the way back to your master's house. Because of my flaws, you have to do all of this work and you don't get full value from your efforts," the pot said.

The water bearer felt sorry for the old cracked pot and in his compassion he said, "As we return to the master's house, I want you to notice the beautiful flowers along the path."

Indeed, as they went up the hill, the cracked pot took notice of the sun warming beautiful flowers on the side of the path and this cheered it. But at the end of the trail, it still felt bad because it had leaked out half its load, and so again it apologized to the water bearer for its failure.

The water bearer said to the pot, "Did you notice that there were flowers only on your side of your path, but not on the other pot's side? That's because I have always known about your flaw and I took advantage of it. I planted flower seeds on your side of the path and everyday while we have walked back from the stream, you've watered them. For two years I have been able to pick these beautiful flowers to decorate my master's table. Without you being just the way you are, he would not have this beauty to grace his house."

MORAL: Each of us has our own unique flaws. We're all cracked pots. But it's the cracks and flaws we each have that make our lives together so very interesting and rewarding. We need to take each person for what they are and look for the good in them. There is a lot of good out there. Every day we look in the mirror we can wonder what flowers we'll unknowingly be watering that day.

SECTION

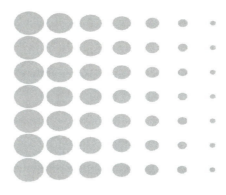

ISSUES OF SUCCESSFUL ENGAGEMENT

The active engagement of organizational members is crucial to the success of organizations and individuals. In this section, we focus on several themes fundamental to successful engagement: Getting in tune with the organization, being adaptive in rapidly changing environments, reading clues and signals to make sense of the organizational environment, the tensions of being different, and successfully making it in the organization. The readings selected to illustrate each theme describe often hard-won insight.

GETTING IN TUNE

U.S. organizations typically are described as goal-seeking meritocracies where organizational effectiveness in meeting stated goals and the real contributions individuals make toward that end are all that matter. This might be the ideal, but reports from the firing line attest that organizational reality often differs substantially from this ideal. Getting in tune with what life is like in organizations requires sensitivity to factors that might systematically alter or undermine organizational ideals of meritocracy and effectiveness.

"Maxwell's Warning" by David Halberstam provides interesting insights into the operation of the American automobile industry in the 1970s. Major firms of that time were structured such that they were unable to even consider the possibility that serious change was necessary. Organizational routines associated with the existing systems of power and privilege pushed information about possible change to low management ranks.

John Paulos argues that "An Excess of Excellence" poses problems for discerning the true state of affairs in organizations. If only excellence is acceptable, then the pressure is on to characterize everything as "excellent." As a result the information about actual performance can become seriously distorted. Perhaps the perceived need to appear excellent may have contributed to the business scandals concerning accounting practices and "cooking the books" that came to light during 2001–2002.

Finally, the realization that style can overwhelm substance is an important step in "The Journey from Novice to Master Manager." Important individuals in an organization might have little information on actual performance and so base judgments, probably unwittingly, on appearances.

BEING ADAPTIVE

Being Adaptive is advantageous in a rapidly changing corporate world. "Killer Results Without Killing Yourself" suggests some of the hazards of a high-stress job and explores a strategy for getting beyond them. The role age and experience play in the implicit social order at work has been upset by younger workers' greater familiarity with technology and their skills in their meeting the technological demands of the information age. "Junior mentors" notes a creative adaptation to this change in the traditional order. Zander and Zander recount how granting rewards in advance can successfully encourage high levels of performance when command-and-control styles of management might be inappropriate.

READING CLUES AND SIGNALS

The selections in Reading Clues and Signals focus on factors important to making sense of organizational reality. Although communication is widely recognized as essential to effective organizations, numerous impediments affect the flow of valid and timely information. Issues of power are particularly important to the first four selections. Those with power may intimidate others with less power, inhibiting the flow of information necessary for organizational performance. "Expertise in Nursing Practice" and Scott's response present two perspectives on the nuances of information flow between nurses and doctors in hospital settings. The initial piece is written from the point of view of nurses. As a doctor, Scott sees the issues somewhat differently. "Criticizing Your Boss" offers specifies to consider when facing the delicate task of delivering potentially disruptive information upward in organizations. On the other hand, Peck deals honestly with his tardy realization that his own preferences for consensus-based management weren't shared by subordinates who wanted more structure.

The next two readings move beyond issues of power. "On That Fateful Day" reviews what United and American Airlines faced on September 11, 2001, as the tragic events unfolded and they struggled to discern what was happening and how to respond. Learning to read oneself is at least as important as reading others and situations. Many today find themselves torn between the adrenaline-induced "highs" of work and their responsibilities and opportunities at home. In "Weighing the Fast Track Against Family Values," sensitivity to emotional clues and signals was important to the balance devised by one family, a solution that other families also are adopting.

Language and symbols are vital tools for the exercise of influence in our society. Successful organizational engagement depends on marshalling efforts of members toward organizationally desired ends. Two selections provide examples of the persuasive use of language from contexts many will find familiar. The Reverend Martin Luther King's 1963 "I Have a Dream" speech is among the most frequently reprinted

American texts for its succinct and effective articulation of a vision for civil rights with which most Americans agree. "The 2,988 Words That Changed a Presidency" makes the case that speeches composed in response to the tragedy of September 11, 2001 significantly impacted President Bush's standing.

BEING DIFFERENT

Being Different in organizations—or in any human group—probably always is associated with a certain degree of tension. However, the sources of difference and the ways that organizations respond to them are apt to be changing continually. Some of the tensions and dynamics of difference are captured in the selections of this section and related selections elsewhere in the book.

The initial three selections detail the organizational experiences of those who are different. Gail Dawson recounts the frustrations of African-Americans in the 1960s and 1970s, who encountered career obstacles rather than the equal employment opportunity promised by the Civil Rights Act of 1964. The experiences of Natalie Kramer and Ana Ibarra at a 1990's Information Age firm include not only difficulties but successes.

"Constructing Carly Fiorina" emphasizes the importance of everyday language and activity in our understanding of differences. Language used in business press coverage of Fiorina, Hewlett Packard CEO and first woman to head a Dow 30 company in the United States, mirrors commonly discussed concerns about the competence and likability of women in executive roles, constructing and circulating a problematic, mediated identity by which Fiorina is primarily known.

"Looking Like America???" takes a somewhat different tack to issues of diversity. The Reverend Martin Luther King (see "Learning the Language of Influence") dreamed of a world in which individuals were judged by criteria more important than visible demographic characteristics. However, demographic diversity is now sometimes advocated as an important gauge of the diverse skills and abilities needed for organizational success. This represents a substantial shift with implications for compliance with legal requirements and—even more importantly—the way diversity is engaged by organizations.

Finally, Bell and Nkomo's study of white women and women of color finds that they view each other with some misgiving. The authors offer fruitful suggestions for positive engagement among diverse individuals.

MAKING IT

"Making It" in the world of work has always been a concern. Nowadays, success requires more than simply competence and hard work. Success is, after all, a judgment call. Many elements contributing to the assessment of an individual's success involve social, political, and personal attributes that might have little to do with the technical aspects of work but in actuality might have a great deal to do with what an individual accomplishes. Moreover, appearances—and the manipulation of appearances—often play an important role in determining an individual's success.

In the first reading, Josefowitz reminds us that because we constantly are faced with competing demands, we simply "Can't Do It All." The other two selections examine how competing demands play out when someone works at home, an increasingly popular work arrangement. To be successful, alternative claims on time must be negotiated realistically at home, and an identity as a valuable employee must be negotiated at work among bosses and coworkers who are not seen regularly. "Making It" as an at-home worker requires attention to appearances in two locations, as well as personal attributes beyond mere technical competence.

II-1: Maxwell's Warning

David Halberstam

There had been plenty of warnings. Some experts had pointed out that the sources of oil were not limitless, that consumption was rising faster than production. Some noted that certain of the oil-producing countries were politically unstable and hostile to the United States. The men of the auto industry had not heeded the warnings. They dismissed them as veiled criticisms of the cars they were making. In June 1973 a young man named Charley Maxwell flew from New York to Detroit to talk to the top executives of the three main auto companies. A decade later astute observers would mark that particular time, mid-1973, as the last moment of the old order in the industrialized world. It was a time when energy was still remarkably cheap and in steady supply, a time when the great business captains could still make their annual forecasts with some degree of certainty. Detroit was still Detroit in those heady days. It regularly sold eight million cars a year, and in a good year, a boomer's year, the kind loved by everyone in the business from the president of a company to the lowliest dealer, it sold ten or eleven million. More, these were precisely the kind and size of cars Detroit wanted to sell—big heavy cars loaded with expensive options. In those days no one talked about energy conservation except a few scholarly types. The average American car got about thirteen miles per gallon then, a figure far below that expected of cars in most other modern countries. Detroit's cars were large, weighty, and powerful. Comfort and power, rather than economy, seemed important in the marketplace. Americans were a big people, and they liked to drive long distances. If the

cars were no longer of quite the quality many of the company engineers and manufacturing men wanted, this was deemed a matter of no great consequence, for they still sold. Anyone who complained about the quality of the cars was a quibbler, more than likely an egghead who subscribed to *Consumer Reports*. After all, a car need last no more than the three years before the owner turned it in for a brand-new model, which would be equally large, or, given the American presumption of rising social status, even larger. As the new car reflected the owner's climb, so the old car now began its own journey down the social scale, ending up an owner or two later in some ghetto inhabited by members of the American underclass. There, patched and repatched, it would consume even greater quantities of gas.

The intelligentsia of America, much given to driving small, fuel-efficient, rather cramped foreign cars, often mocked Detroit for the grossness and gaudiness of its product. To many liberal intellectuals Detroit symbolized all that was excessive in the materialism of American life (just as to many small-town American conservatives, the companies' partner, the United Auto Workers, symbolized everything that was excessive about the post-New Deal liberal society). None of this carping bothered Detroit. It was a given that Americans preferred big cars—and only Detroit made big cars. There was a seldom-spoken corollary to this axiom: Big cars meant big profits, and small cars meant small profits. In early 1973 the fact that Detroit was selling what it wanted to sell was considered proof that Detroit, rather than its critics, truly understood the American customer. The future looked brighter than ever. An ugly war in

From *The Reckoning* by David Halberstam, pp. 43–8. Copyright © 1986 by David Halberstam.

Southeast Asia which had sapped the nation's strength and resources was finally ending, and Detroit was bullish about the auto economy just ahead. That bullishness seemed to be based on good reason. For if there was one benign economic certainty as far as American industrialists and American consumers were concerned, it was the low price of gas and oil, a price that seemed almost inflation-proof in the postwar era. In 1950 the price of a gallon of gas at the pump had been 27 cents, 20 cents of it for the gas itself and the rest for taxes. Twenty years later, the price of virtually every other basic consumer commodity had approximately doubled, but the price of gas had remained, tantalizingly, almost the same. At the moment that Charley Maxwell set out for Detroit in 1973, a gallon of gas cost 37 cents at the pump, 26 of it for the gas itself. The price seemed a blessing so constant that everyone had come to take it for granted.

That was the premise of the city to which Charley Maxwell was traveling. He was thirty-five years old and had spent all of his adult life in the oil business, mostly with Mobil in the Middle East and Nigeria. He was by nature scholarly, and those long years in the field had added practical experience to his theoretical expertise, a rare combination. In the late sixties, when Mobil had started replacing its American overseas employees with foreign nationals, Maxwell had been sent back to the United States. It seemed to him that his career opportunities in the oil industry had been drastically reduced, and, looking for a way to exploit his knowledge, he had become an oil analyst for a Wall Street firm called Cyrus Lawrence.

Every field has its awesome experts, but there was something about Charley Maxwell's professional authority that was almost chilling. Part of it was his appearance, the hair plastered down over his forehead and parted in the middle, the old-fashioned, almost prim wire-rimmed glasses, the

slightly stooped posture, the pre-occupied manner; he looked like the sort of person who as a sixth-grader had been doted upon by his teachers because he had always gotten the right answer to every question, who had been good at what his teachers wanted rather than at what mattered to his peers....

In those June days of 1973, however, he was not yet well known outside his field, and his field was not yet a hot one. Americans believed that their own domestic supplies of oil were plentiful and that there were virtually limitless sources in the Persian Gulf. What Charley Maxwell intended to tell the top-level auto executives he believed he would meet in Detroit was what he had been telling his superiors for some time now—that there would soon be dramatic, indeed revolutionary, changes in the price of energy. The assumption of the past, that energy would remain cheap because it had always been cheap and its price would increase only at small, acceptable, noninflationary increments, had to be discarded. America's own resources were rapidly proving inadequate, and the nation would thus become far more dependent upon the oil-producing nations of the Middle East. But the American oil companies would no longer be able to control the prices set for Arab oil, as they had so easily in the past. The Arabs would set the prices themselves. Since oil was in those days significantly underpriced in terms of its true market value, the loss of that control would have serious consequences for American heavy industry in general and Detroit in particular.

Maxwell had seen all this coming for a number of years. As early as 1970 he had started using the phrase "energy crisis"— apparently his coinage. He used it to refer to a crucial, ominous shift in the supply and demand of oil. He calculated that worldwide oil consumption was climbing 5 to 6 percent annually, and there was no reason to believe the surge would abate. If anything, it was likely to accelerate. New nations, recently graduated from their colonial past, were fast becoming both industrialized and urbanized and demanding far greater amounts of energy. Throughout the underdeveloped world, people were leaving their tribal huts and moving into cities, and, as they did, they took new jobs in factories which required energy, they lived in apartments which required energy, and to get to work they used transportation, which also required energy. It was a revolution taking place, a revolution of people who were changing their way of life and of nations that were expanding and modernizing their economies. The world, Maxwell concluded, had changed dramatically and was going to continue to change as more and more nations moved toward industrial economies. Ten and sometimes fifteen additional countries were leaving the preindustrial age each year and coming into the mechanical age. But there had not as yet been any reflection of this trend in the price of the ingredient most precious to the modern industrialized state, oil. There was going to be one terrible moment, Maxwell was sure, when the price would simply shoot up, out of anyone's control, the oil seeking its true market value. . . .

Maxwell knew that he was not alone in his pessimism, that a number of other energy experts, using much the same research, had come to similar conclusions. But most of these experts worked for the large oil companies, where the darker view had not yet been accepted. Maxwell's own superiors at the Wall Street investment firm of Cyrus Lawrence, however, had been greatly impressed by his estimates and the dispassionate way in which he presented his evidence. Both as a courtesy and also out of their own self-interest, for it would not hurt to lend out so brilliant a man with such original and important perceptions, they decided to send him to Detroit. There, the Cyrus Lawrence people proposed, he would talk to executives at the highest level, who surely would be more than anxious to hear these findings that had such fateful implications for their companies.

Maxwell himself was not so sure. He knew Detroit and he knew it well. He had grown up there, his stepfather had been employed at a middle level by Ford, he himself had even gone to Cranbrook, the city's elite prep school, where many of his classmates were sons of auto titans. Maxwell knew how stratified the city was, how isolated and insular. It was, he believed, a place of bedrock beliefs, a place where new truths did not seep easily from the bottom to the top. In Detroit, truth moved from the top to the bottom.

Maxwell had been promised meetings with the high auto executives, people who operated at the ultimate level of power. He was dubious about that. He might be well known in the world of oil, but he was young, and Detroit did not readily listen to junior people. Detroit believed in hierarchy and seniority rather than in individual brilliance. One advanced in Detroit not necessarily by being brilliant—brilliance meant that someone might be *different* and implied a threat—but by accommodating oneself with attitudes of those above one. Maxwell, because of his age and the nature of his message, would almost surely be looked upon as impertinent. These men would have their own sources of information, among them the men who headed the great oil companies, the men still resistant to the pessimistic vision of Maxwell and his kind. Powerful, successful, and conventional, typical of the corporate class, they believed that tomorrow would be like today because it had always been like today and because they wanted it to be like today. In their view, if the price of oil went up, it would go up slowly over many decades. They had controlled the oil world—and thus the price of energy—in the past. They would control that world and the price of energy in the future. So Charley Maxwell had been skeptical from the start that he would get the very top people as promised. If his supporters thought so, he knew better, and he had automatically translated his prospects downward. He would be lucky, he decided, to meet people at the 65 percent level of power. That, he soon learned, was too sanguine an expectation.

He did not do badly at the start. He went first to Chrysler, where Tom Killefer, the senior financial officer, had assembled a group of upper-middle-level executives. They listened quietly as Maxwell made his solemn little speech, saying in effect that all their estimates about what kind of cars Americans could and would drive were about to fly out the window. Killefer himself had been pleasant; he was a Rhodes scholar, different from the average Detroit executive, less narrow, in better touch with the outside world. When Maxwell finished, Killefer thanked him and said, "Well, what you say is very, very impressive, very impressive indeed, and of course if it's true, then we're going to have to give it a hard, hard look." There were questions, and bright young men in the group, perhaps less complacent because Chrysler was already a shaky company, were clearly interested. But even as he was finishing his presentation, Maxwell had a sense that it was all to no end, that these men would leave the meeting and shake their heads and say how interesting it had been, what a bright fellow Maxwell was, maybe a bit rash, something of an alarmist, didn't they think, but bright and interesting nonetheless. Worth thinking about. That would be it, Maxwell thought, possibly a letter or two thanking him, but no real penetration of the process.

Chrysler, unfortunately, turned out to be by far the best of the three meetings. He had been taken seriously there, and Killefer was, whatever else, a representative of top management. Ford was a good deal worse. At Ford he met two people at the lower planning level. They were junior executives, making, he suspected, about $25,000 a year, which

was a very small salary in executive Detroit. They were, he knew instantly, completely without power, and they had been sent there because a steadily descending series of Ford executives had told their immediate subordinates that someone had to go and cover the meeting, until finally, far down the line, there had been two men so unimportant that they had no subordinates to send. These two were there precisely because they were powerless. Maxwell felt a bit odd, standing in that room saying that Detroit was going to have to change its whole line of cars and that an entire era had ended, and saying this to men who could not change the design of an ashtray. Somehow that thought made his presentation more impassioned than ever.

General Motors, of course, was the worst. There were no high-level meetings scheduled. In fact, there were no meetings scheduled at all. Someone very junior asked Maxwell if he would like to drive out to the testing grounds and meet with some GM people there. He did, encountering no one in any position of responsibility, though for his troubles he was able to see some of GM's new models. They looked rather large to him, cars that would surely use a great deal of gas.

Such was Charley Maxwell's trip to Detroit. He had not even gotten across the moat. Detroit was Detroit, and more than most business centers it was a city that listened only to its own voice. But he left town worried about what he was sure was going to happen to a vital American industry. Maxwell did not think that the coming change in price would necessarily be so great that even a Detroit that was prepared for change would be severely damaged. Rather, he was worried because Detroit was unprepared—because no one in America seemed willing to practice even the most nominal kind of conservation, which suggested that the country was physically unready for major increases. A big jump in price might trigger a panic, which would compound the difficulty of entering a new economic order. Those who were set up for change could deal with it, he suspected; those who were not were likely to come apart. Detroit, he feared, was going to have to learn its new truths the hard way.

A few months later, on October 6, 1973, on the eve of Yom Kippur, the holiest of Jewish holy days, Egypt tried a military strike on Israel. Eventually Israel struck back and once again, for the third time since World War II, defeated the Egyptians. To the Arab world this humiliation was one more demonstration of its powerlessness. The Arabs blamed Israel's existence on its American sponsorship. Thwarted both militarily and politically, the Arabs now turned at last to their real strength, their economic leverage. They began an oil embargo on the West. Before it was over, the price of oil had rocketed from $3 a barrel to $12 a barrel. The United States, long accustomed to cheap energy, was completely unprepared to respond to the Arab move. Unwilling to increase the taxes on gasoline and oil and thus at least partially stabilize the price of energy, it had in effect permitted the Arabs to place a tax not just on the American oil consumer but on the entire country. The effects on the American economy at every level were dramatic. The era of the cheap energy upon which so much of America's dynamism and its broad middle-class prosperity was premised was beginning to end. A new era with profound implications for the industrial core of America, the great Middle Atlantic and Midwestern foundry of the nation, had arrived. Occasionally in later years Charley Maxwell would run into Tom Killefer, who by then had left Chrysler to become the chairman of the United States Trust Company, and when he did, Killefer would shake his head and say, "You—you're the one man I hate to see. God, I still remember that warning...."

II-2: An Excess of Excellence

John Allen Paulos

These days, it seems, all must have prizes.

The Army announced last week that the beret, which for decades has been the mark of elite units, will now become standard issue. Gen. Eric Shinseki, the Army's chief of staff, said that the change, which will take effect on June 14, the Army's birthday, is intended to show that American troops are "soldiers of the world's best army."

It should be noted that "soldiers of the best army" are not at all the same as the "best soldiers of the Army." The change in fashion seems to be a pointless devaluation of the beret and those who now wear it.

On a related note, Al Gore recently declared that "most schools are excellent but we've got to make sure that all of them are." But if all or even most schools are excellent, what exactly would it be that they were excelling? Even if by "excellent school" Mr. Gore meant "one doing an adequate job," it's not clear that most schools are excellent, and calling them so devalues those schools that are. (In a spirit of non–partisanship, I must add that George Bush's pledge to leave no child behind is comparably hyperbolic.)

Similarly, American students often do poorly on international tests but seldom score poorly on measures of self-confidence. They sometimes seem to be saying. "We are the most bestest." Parents heaping encomiums on their preschool youngsters for coloring more or less within the lines, and teachers handling out ever-higher grades in high schools and colleges, are related evidence of this mania to declare us all extraordinary in every way.

AVERAGE ISN'T GOOD ENOUGH

These are only the most recent manifestations of the infamous Lake Wobegon syndrome, whereby everybody, or almost everybody, is deemed to be above average. Studies repeatedly show, for example, that the vast majority of us think we have a better-than-average sense of humor and possess a better-than-average empathy for others. (Technically, of course, almost everybody can be above average; in fact, almost everybody has two arms, which is slightly more than the average number of arms.)

The Wobegon syndrome extends to the supposedly hard-headed world of business. If one frequents online business sites, one will discover that almost all the stocks they are writing about are "buys" or "strong buys," with occasional "holds." Where are the "sells" and "strong sells"? Maybe only companies that manufacture solar-powered flashlights qualify.

Pick any social dimension along which people can differ and their attitude toward it often demonstrates some trace of Wobegonism. In most communities, for example, if one asks about crime, one will hear something like: "It's awful in general, but we don't really have any problems around here." This might be literally true in a few places, but not, by definition, in most.

STARS EVERYWHERE

The case can be made that reviews of movies, books and restaurants are similarly skewed upward, with only real dogs receiv-

ing the dreaded one star, or none. William Grimes, of the New York Times, got in trouble with local chefs last year when he took over the restaurant-reviewing position at the paper: He was seen to be stingy, compared with his generous predecessor, Ruth Reichl, about handing out two- and three-star ratings. He explained, to anyone who would listen, that he was merely trying to restore some standards. Naturally, the restaurateurs around town still preferred a starrier atmosphere in the *Times'* food columns.

Of course, I intend no offense to the underachievers of this world, most of whom seem to possess the same need for compliments as everyone else. Sharing this natural desire, I don't think that praise for others should always be stinging or that the social niceties of harmless exaggeration should be discouraged. What does make inflationary commendation worrisome is that by diminishing real achievements it can weaken our ability to discern quality and make distinctions.

A recent study suggests that most incompetent (in various senses of the word) people do not know that they are incompetent. Dr. David Dunning, a psychology professor at Cornell, found that people who do badly at different tasks are unaware of their incompetence because the skills needed to evaluate how well they're doing are often the same as those needed to do the job in the first place.

Thus people who insist on telling one lame joke after another are not only unable to make us laugh, they're unlikely to recognize that we're not laughing. And when the subjects in the study were asked to evaluate the logic of an argument or the grammar of an article, those who scored the lowest often rated themselves the highest at the very skill they could not judge.

In short, some minimal skill and judgment are needed to recognize that we have little skill or judgment and that we may be, horrors, average or even below average. If most of us see ourselves as extraordinary, excellent, well above average and forever donning our stylish berets to buy strong stocks that only move up, the meaning of superlatives will begin to fade behind clouds of self-esteem, and critical evaluation will gradually become empty congratulation.

I could be wrong, but I think that would be a below-average development.

Mr. Paulos, a professor of mathematics at Temple University, writes the "Who's Counting" column for ABCNews.com. He is the author of *Innumeracy* and *A Mathematician Reads the Newspaper.*

II-3: The Journey from Novice to Master Manager

Bob Quinn

As I listened to the man sitting in front of me, my mind ran backwards across the interviews that I had just completed. His subordinates and peers had given him glowing reviews: "Born to manage." "A great role model." "He is one person I am glad to work for."

As I tried to ask him questions that would unlock the mystery behind his success, an interesting story began to unfold. It seemed to involve both a crisis and a transformation.

After graduating from a five-year engineering program in four years, he had taken a job with his current organization. He had made a brilliant start and was promoted four times in eight years. He had the ability to take a complex technical problem and come up with a better answer than anyone else could. Initially he was seen as an innovative, action-oriented person with a bright future.

After his last promotion, however, everything started to change. He went through several very difficult years. For the first time he received serious negative feedback about his performance. His ideas and

proposals were regularly rejected, and he was even passed over for a promotion. In reflecting on those days, he said:

> It was awful. Everything was always changing and nothing ever seemed to happen. The people above me would sit around forever and talk about things. The technically right answer didn't matter. They were always making what I thought were wrong decisions, and when I insisted on doing what was right, they got pissed off and would ignore what I was saying. Everything was suddenly political. They would worry about what everyone was going to think about every issue. How you looked, attending cocktail parties—that stuff to me was unreal and unimportant. . . .

On several occasions, the engineer's boss commented that he was very impressed with one of the engineer's subordinates. Finding the comment somewhat curious, the engineer finally asked for an explanation. The boss indicated that no matter how early he himself arrived at work, the subordinate's car was always there.

"The Journey from Novice to Master Manager" by Bob Quinn. *Beyond Rational Management,* © 1988 Jossey Bass. This material is used by permission of John Wiley & Sons, Inc.

The engineer went to visit the subordinate and relayed that he had noticed that the subordinate always arrived at work before he did. The subordinate nodded his head and explained: "I have four teen-agers who wake up at dawn. The mornings at my house are chaotic. So I come in early. I read for awhile, then I write in my personal journal, read the paper, have some coffee, and then I start work at eight."

When the engineer left his subordinate's office, he was at first furious. But after a couple of minutes, he sat down and started to laugh. He later told me, "That is when I discovered perception." He went on to say that from that moment everything started to change. He became more patient. He began to experiment with participative decision making. His relationships with superiors gradually improved. Eventually he actually came to appreciate the need to think and operate in more complex ways at the higher levels of the organization. . . .

In the end, the frustration and pain turned out to be a positive thing because it forced me to consider some alternative perspectives. I eventually learned that there were other realities besides the technical reality.

I discovered perception and long time lines. At higher levels what matters is how people see the world, and everyone sees it a little differently. Technical facts are not as available or as important. Things are changing more rapidly at higher levels, you are no longer buffered from the outside world. Things are more complex, and it takes longer to get people on board. I decided I had to be a lot more receptive and a lot more patient. It was an enormous adjustment, but then things started to change. I think I became a heck of a lot better manager.

II-4: Killer Results Without Killing Yourself

Michael B. Malone

"As far as I'm concerned," says David B. Marsing, "having to change your life when you arrive at work each morning is tantamount to slavery."

Revolutionary words from a professor or labor organizer? Not exactly. Dave Marsing, 41, sits in one of the highest pressure jobs in U.S. industry: plant manager of Intel Corp.'s $2 billion Fab 11 near Albuquerque, New Mexico, the largest microprocessor fabrica-

tion plant of the most successful electronics company in the world.

Marsing is an agent provocateur—he calls himself a "transformational virus"—in a company legendary for long hours and "creative confrontation." Marsing knows that "if I'm too aggressive, the corporate immune system will kick in" and consume him. He also knows that if he can successfully infect Intel, he will save it.

The medical analogy is no accident. Five years ago, at age 36, while trying to pull an Intel fabrication plant out of a crisis, Marsing suffered a near fatal heart attack. Lying on a gurney in the hospital, he remembers thinking. "How can I live my life

"Killer Results Without Killing Yourself" by Michael B. Malone, *US News and World Report*, October 30, 1995. Reprinted by permission.

as meaningfully as possible?" To this day, he visits cardiac units every six months, "just to look at the gray faces and remember."

It's tough to be a rebel in any business. But this is the semiconductor industry, a take-no-prisoners battle among silicon killers, hardly the kind of place to find a soft-spoken nice guy—especially one who's using a multibillion-dollar facility to experiment with new management theories.

Intel corporate knows only a little about the intensity of Marsing's views. But it does know the bottom line—and here Marsing excels. According to Marsing's boss Mike Splinter, 45, vice president and general manager of the company's components-manufacturing group, Marsing is one of Intel's best fab managers. Throughout his career, he's surpassed every target and quota set for him; every plant Marsing has run has ranked number one on the company's productivity charts.

That's why Intel's management has selected Marsing to help train its next generation of fab managers as the company prepares to spring-board off the success of the Pentium chip into the greatest expansion in its history. By the end of the decade, Intel will have at least 10 giant new fabs directed by as many as 300 newly trained managers. Intel also expects to be the most profitable company in the world.

By placing Dave Marsing in charge of its next generation of leaders, Intel, long known for its business brains, may unwittingly have made its smartest move yet. And if Marsing succeeds, be may not only transform his own company but also set the model for the new breed of manager who will lead U.S. industry into the next century.

● ● ● ● ● ● ● ● ● ● ● ●
THE ROAD TO DAMASCUS

Like most apostles of change, Dave Marsing had an awakening on his own road to Damascus.

Until five years ago, his had been a typical career for a young manager in high tech. After earning a degree in physics from the University of Oregon in 1976, Marsing followed his interest in thin-film technology and solar power to Texas Instruments to work with industry legend Jack Kilby on that company's then-secret solar-panel project. Marsing got the job he wanted, only to see the project collapse a year later.

But that was long enough for Kilby to be impressed by the young man and to recommend him to his Intel counterpart (and integrated circuit coinventor) Robert Noyce, who sent Marsing to work in development at the company's plant in Portland, Oregon. By 1986, at just 32, Marsing became the product engineering manager at Intel's Fab 3 in Livermore. California. Fab 3 was an older plant with established production levels, but by the time he was done, the plant was the company's leading manufacturer of the 80386, setting new standards for productivity.

Tired of the pressure of fab life, Marsing took a three-month sabbatical at the end of 1989. When he returned, he accepted an assignment as director of the company's Chandler, Arizona, factory automation group—only to find a new kind of pressure, learn a new kind of lesson. "I saw how fab treats support," he recalls. "Now I was the enemy. And it was obvious neither group knew how to deal with the other." In the world of semiconductors, where the construction of a single chip is as complex as the Manhattan Project, processes developed in the lab must be copied exactly on the factory floor. What were the odds of making mistakes if the two sides were locked in combat?

The more conflicts Marsing saw between department and department, between employee and company, and between employee and supervisor, the more conflicted he became. Without realizing it. Marsing internalized Intel's civil war. But to others it was obvious. As Mike Splinter later noted, during this period Marsing was summed up by the car he drove: a nondescript Volvo, "very meek on the outside, but with a big monster engine under the hood." Marsing even suffered the requisite divorce, brought on in part, he admits, by the stresses he was feeling on the job.

Still, if the work was frustrating, Marsing's career remained meteoric. On July 1, 1990 he returned to running a fab, this time Intel's seven-year-old Fab 9-1 (now part of Fab 9) in Rio Rancho, a suburb of Albuquerque.

He was now halfway through the worst year of his life. And it was about to get worse. Fab 9-1 was in turmoil. Marsing had been parachuted in to save the plant, and surveying the scene, he saw it had all the earmarks of a suicide mission. The new Intel microprocessor, the 80486, the company's hope for the future, depended on this plant more than on any other and Fab 9-1 couldn't get the chips out the door. Yield rates were disastrous: a failure in the plant's diffusion furnaces, a critical piece of equipment in the processing of silicon wafers, was turning half of the plant's chip production into worthless scrap each day. And it was growing streadily worse. Two weeks after Marsing arrived, the plant had wasted $50 million worth of chips.

Intel headquarters demanded an immediate end to the red ink; employees at the plant confronted Marsing with their frustration and fear. Caught in between, Marsing found himself crushed under pressure like he'd never known. Being diabetic didn't help. He'd drag himself home late at night barely able to sleep from worry. Even his morning exercise, which had always renewed him in the past, couldn't calm him. In fact, all Marsing was getting for his morning efforts was a stiff neck.

That was Monday. On Tuesday the stiff neck came back again. By Wednesday his neck hurt even when he walked fast between buildings. But the urgency of putting the fab back on its feet obscured a little physical discomfort.

Then at 5:26 A.M. on August 11, 1990, 36-year-old Dave Marsing found himself on a hospital gurney suffering a heart attack. Coronaries at that age are usually fatal, but Marsing was lucky. He had made it to the hospital in time. Within hours he was out of bypass surgery and on his way to recovery.

● ● ● ● ● ● ● ● ● ● ● ●
THE BIG LIE

In the weeks of recuperation that followed, Marsing had time to think. The heart attack had not permanently damaged his heart, but Marsing knew he could no longer live as he had.

He began to take stock. The first and most obvious question was whether he should continue working for Intel. After all, this was a company that prided itself on demanding superhuman contributions from its employees. Back in 1986, during a severe industry recession, Intel had become famous (and notorious) for instituting the "125% Solution," a six-month program in which employees were asked to work an extra two hours each day without pay—"voluntarily."

As Marsing thought about the people with whom he worked, he realized that he wasn't alone: "It hit me that most of the people around me were also exhibiting stress-related or stress-enhanced problems, either physically or emotionally." They were living a kind of lie, caught between who they were and who they had to be. And it was destroying their lives.

Every morning, Marsing realized, he and most of the people around him put on their work faces in the parking lot and played their roles as employees all day. The long hours, in which overtime often became a goal in itself, meant that most of each day was spent trapped in this fraud. And when they finally got home, the sheer intensity of the day—the disappearing edges between work and play, and the inevitable late-night and weekend crisis calls—sealed off any chance of escape into their true selves.

Intel, as much as any high-tech company, sought to create and enforce a homogeneous employee personality. The company had long recruited engineers right out of college, who wouldn't be tainted by having worked at other companies. And, fulfilling CEO and president Andy Grove's famous words, "Only the paranoid survive," the company promulgated a siege mentality among its people. Changing this attitude could mean challenging what lay at the heart of Intel's phenomenal success.

Yet in the face of those reasons to run away, Marsing chose to stay. He realized that he was committed to Intel and proud of its achievements. His mission, he saw, was to help the company prepare for a new century: "I wanted to try to develop the next generation of fab managers so that they could create an operating environment where balance exists. There had to be a way to work in this environment without being killed by it."

But what was that way? Marsing had no idea; he'd never heard of any alternative management model. So he turned to philosophers and some of the most outre management thinkers. He started with the economist and philosopher Joseph Schumpeter. Then on to Zen Buddhism. Next, physicist David Bohm.

He was still looking for answers when, in early 1992, he got the call: Marsing was named plant manager of the soon-to-be-constructed Fab 11, the largest capital investment any chip company had ever made. The pressure to succeed would be immense. But this was the chance that Marsing had been waiting for.

He would go out in the hot sun and sit in the middle of the vacant field where the plant would stand and dream: "The people who worked for me thought I was going crazy," Marsing recalls. "But I could just imagine that building rising up around me."

Now he could conduct his experiment in the greatest laboratory on earth.

THE HUMAN TEST

In the world of fabs, the ultimate test comes at startup, when the fab is trying to convert diagrams and flow charts into real-life mass production. And this is also the ultimate test of Marsing's management philosophy. The product is an eight-inch silicon wafer covered with a grid of several hundred integrated circuit chips (ICs)—each worth as much as $1,000. One mistake on a wafer can cost $250,000 or more. And mistakes are easy: each of those hundreds of ICs contains millions of individual circuits, none much larger than bacteria. Billions of them must be made correctly each day.

With so much that can go wrong, nerves are frayed, tempers explosive.

So we visit Marsing just two days after Fab 11 "went to silicon."

Almost everything—meetings, telephone calls, interviews—seems to take place in a subdued tone. Marsing moves through the day calmly, his voice sometimes so soft as to be unintelligible. It's only later that it hits you: in one of the toughest manufacturing environments anywhere, in the center of its most stressful period, there are no raised voices, no barely controlled outbursts. The man whose heart once exploded over bad yield rates now navigates a far tougher management challenge without breaking a sweat.

Marsing, in a job that once nearly destroyed him, has made the day look effortless. He is not a philosopher but an extraordinarily adept businessman; his vision is his actions.

WHAT CAN I DO FOR YOU?

It's a hot summer New Mexico morning as Marsing sips the last of his coffee. He's already spent a half hour meditating, as he did before going to bed last night. Marsing's youngest child, one-year-old Hannah, is still asleep, but three-year-old Elliot is up and wandering grumpily through the house. He is ushered into the kitchen for breakfast by Marsing's wife, Vicki, who is also on her way to work at Intel, where she is an engineering manager. The atmosphere is casual and relaxed.

So is Marsing. He's wearing chinos and a work shirt. Combined with a shock of unruly brown hair and wire-rimmed glasses, he looks less like a high-tech executive and more like a high school civics teacher who also coaches the wrestling team.

At 7:40 A.M. he climbs into the family's new Toyota Land Cruiser and starts down the hill to the wide plateau below. Even from here, 10 miles away, it's hard to miss the Intel plant. The two giant fabs, along with a third, Fab 7, stretch across a ridge above Rio Rancho, dominating the view.

At 7:56 A.M. Marsing pulls into a non-reserved parking place. He looks up at the immense white building, and it's clear that he's still in awe of Fab 11: five stories and 170,000 square feet of clean room, the ultrapure area where chips are made; 1,400 employees with nearly 500 more soon to be added; equipment that can draw lines on silicon wafers just 1,500,000th of an inch across; the potential to generate revenues in excess of $5 billion per year. And it all works.

Marsing sprints up the five flights of stairs to his office to start the day. He had assumed that running such a facility had no precedent. Then a few months ago he taped a documentary on cable about life on an aircraft carrier: an immense structure costing billions of dollars, filled with a couple thousand highly trained specialists focused on a vital mission, with no room for error. The similarities were stunning. The only difference Marsing could see was that the captain of the carrier had to cope with a 40% annual turnover from completed enlistments, retirements and transfers. And then I struck

Marsing that, given Intel's expansion plans for the next few years, the change among his employees would be just as dramatic.

He watched the tape over and over and showed it to his subordinates. He even used a company meeting in San Diego as an excuse to tour a U.S. Navy carrier. The result was a subtle shift in command to imitate the Navy captain/executive officer model. Marsing took on a more external, strategic role, and his assistant, factory manager Brian I. Harrison, moved into position as the internal, executive officer, a role roughly equivalent to a full plant manager in the rest of the industry.

"Marsing just thinks differently from other fab managers," Harrison says. "There is a mold for fab managers. They're hired as engineers and then pass through a series of filters as they come up. Somehow Marsing went through those filters, got to this level, and still sees things from a different perspective: more holistically, I guess, where others think in discrete details."

Marsing's morning is spent in one-on-one meetings with his direct reports, discussing various plant activities. After each presentation, Marsing asks, "OK, now what can I do for *you*?"

The late morning is spent in a teleconference with other Intel plant managers around the country, planning how to deal with upcoming products and expansion plans. During this hour, little of the rebel is on display. Still, there are moments when Marsing frowns, runs a hand through his hair, and looks like he's ready to cut loose. But in this meeting, at least, he never does. The Zen training helps.

Later there's a meeting with a new hire, a retired military safety officer, who's been brought on board to set up a crisis management program at the plant. The man is visibly nervous and expects a grilling. But Marsing puts him at ease by turning the tables and asking what he can do to help. The new safety officer looks relieved. Not only has he been put at ease; without knowing it, he's been given a first glimpse of the Marsing style.

At 5 P.M. the day comes to an early finish: Marsing returns phone calls: and reads and writes e-mail messages. In between, he tries to explain his management philosophy—something, he admits, he's never really been asked to do.

"Look," Marsing says, pushing his glasses back onto the bridge of his nose, "if you had equipment running at only 10% efficiency, you'd apply engineering to get that performance up. It's the same with people. If your employees are showing up at work with only a fraction of their possible efficiency, then you need to ask yourself: What is it about their job, their attitude, and their work environment that's doing that to them?"

To Marsing, the point is not only productivity but also diversity: the more disparate the experiences and skills of team members, the more adaptable and dynamic the organization. But that's not the way most companies look at it. "What most companies want is homogeneity," Marsing says. "They want 150 trumpets playing in unison. But homogeneous teams have blind spots; they move like a herd and often in the wrong direction. What's needed instead is complexity, the team as a jazz band that both harmonizes and improvises."

But what prevents this "true-to-yourself" model from producing as much stress as the "two-faced" model it replaces? One answer can be found in Marsing's own career. After all, he had to learn to balance his own maverick streak with the greater benefits of becoming a team player. And that is precisely the attitude he tries to convey to those around him. They are free to be themselves on the job, to work regular hours, to spend time with their families and their community. But the bottom line is Intel's competitive success. And if that means they have to compromise to

deal with workmates, they know that those workmates are also bending halfway to meet them.

It's neither an elegant model nor an empirical one. It doesn't even have a name though "Middle Path" conveys Marsing's belief that the organizational solution for the future is one that steers between Taylor's model of employees as identical cogs in a machine and the anarchy of rampant individualism in a Balkanized company in which people have no sense of common cause.

Here's how Marsing looks at it: "If the goal is to maximize profits, then it seems obvious to me that the best way to get there is to have happy people who are motivated to work. And the way you do that is to bring together different types of people, allow them to be themselves, get them behind the larger corporate vision, and then give them room to create. Above all, if you want breakthrough thinking and innovation—and you definitely do in this business to survive—then you have to cultivate those aspects of each employee's personality where it will come out."

● ● ● ● ● ● ● ● ● ● ● ● ● ●
DAVE MARSING'S DANCE

It's early evening when Marsing pulls into the carport of his home. As he stands on the driveway amid Elliot's scattered toys, he reflects on the path he's taken since those terrible days in the hospital.

For the first time, his voice betrays excitement: "Imagine if you could build a company that was capable of learning from *all* its experiences, as well as from other companies' experiences. What you'd get is a new kind of asset: corporate wisdom. Now, combine that with the kind of compassion that accepts employees for who they really are, that motivates them to reach their potential, and you'd have something truly extraordinary. Just think what a company like Intel, 35,000 highly intelligent people, could do if it ever reached that combination."

Is Marsing the model for the future of Intel? "Well, I'm not sure if it's possible for everybody to be like him," Mike Splinter says. "But I will say that if he keeps challenging the way we do things, he will have a large influence on future management methods at Intel."

For his part, Marsing has no doubt he will succeed. "This is the perfect place to do all this because the risks are so great. I think of it as an interesting dance. If you sit on the sidelines, you don't do anything. But once you're on the dance floor, you have a chance to change the steps."

And no one is better motivated than Dave Marsing to practice the dance, to find and follow the Middle Path. For him it is a matter of life and death.

II-5: Junior Mentors
"Cross-Pollination" Benefits Old-Economy Companies

Diane E. Lewis

Jay Pomeroy, a GE Plastics executive, knew familiarity with the Web was fast becoming an essential part of his job. So to help him get up to speed, his company paired him with Amelia Burkhart, a tech-savvy thirty something at the Pittsfield, Mass., firm who used her online experience to show the 46-year-old senior manager the ropes.

"I brought him knowledge of the Internet realm," said Burkhart, global manager of e-plastics.com, GE Plastics' online division. "He has to deal with people from other regions and countries. We actually conducted a virtual meeting so that he would understand how to participate in meetings online." She said that before their mentoring sessions, Pomeroy didn't partici-

pate in online chats. "Now he is on a lot and he's become a pretty avid Internet user," she added.

Call it reverse mentoring—a form of one-on-one coaching that gives younger techies a chance to teach senior executives how to surf the Net, use instant messaging, collaborate with a team in real time, find new business applications or explore the ins and outs of buying products online.

The relationship is a two-way street: it also allows corporate greenhorns to seek advice from seasoned executives to help hone the managerial skills and relationships they need to advance in the workplace.

Specialists say reverse mentoring is one way established companies such as GE are embracing the Internet in order to survive—and thrive—in a technology-driven world. The practice, which began in Europe, is taking hold in the United States as young workers bring newfound energy and skills to old-economy companies once labeled slow-moving monoliths.

Joel Kurtzman, co-author of a new book titled *Radical E: From GE to Enron— Lessons on How to Rule the Web*, says the interchange between mentoring pairs is a form of cross-pollination: Students gain new knowledge. Mentors gain valuable institutional information from veterans whose political astuteness and management savvy helped them succeed.

Burkhart, for example, said the program helped her develop a relationship with Pomeroy, who returned the favor by providing tips on managing her career at GE. He also shared some of his institutional knowledge, and he remains a close contact at the firm.

"We now have a relationship that has blossomed," Burkhart said. "It's also been good exposure for me."

Glenn Rifkin, co-author of *Radical E*, says the trend is a positive result of the dot-com boom. "For the first time, entrenched business people and companies have had their eyes opened to the fact that there are now some really smart young people in their corporate settings who can teach them new things," he said.

Rifkin and Kurtzman, who spent months interviewing people at mature companies with well-known brands, are convinced the future will be shaped by old economy "hybrids"—companies that combine the best practices from e-commerce and older brick-and-mortar firms. This, they say, is a more radical form of reverse mentoring in which Net companies with little business knowledge are paired with established firms, or young employees at mature companies find new ways to do business online.

Some of those companies include General Motors, Procter & Gamble, GE and Houston-based Enron, a global energy company. GE, the first U.S. old-economy firm to endorse and use reverse mentoring, began a formal program two years ago after CEO Jack Welch introduced the concept. The company has paired dozens of workers in a push to bring key people into the computer age and expand the company's market to include cyberspace.

Procter & Gamble began encouraging information-technology employees to participate in an informal reverse-mentoring program last year. "Because technology changes so rapidly, individuals pair up with people who seem to be more adept at the latest application," said P&G spokeswoman Vicky Mayer.

Meanwhile, in Philadelphia, the Wharton School has implemented a program that helps top executives from around the world bring new-economy practices into old-economy firms. One feature of the e-fellows program: Mentoring sessions staffed by MBA students in their 20s who share their knowledge with seasoned corporate leaders.

Wharton e-fellows learn how to use the Internet to reshape their firms. Over the course of three weeks, e-fellows spend time at the business school's Philadelphia campus, in Silicon Valley and at an international site. The program began in September.

"The goal is to show senior executives how the landscape will change at their firms with this technology," said Neil Neveras, director of e-business at Wharton's e-fellows program.

Executives are paired one-on-one with MBA students. "Typically, these students are Internet-savvy and they live in a world where e-business and business are synonymous," said Neveras. "There is no distinction for them; it's not new."

II-6: Giving an A

Rosamund Stone Zander and Benjamin Zander

At the University of Southern California, a leadership course was taught each year to fifty of the most outstanding students out of twenty-seven thousand in the school, hand-picked by each department. At the end of the semester, the grader for the course was instructed to give one-third of the students A's, one-third B's and one-third C's—even though the work of any member of this class was likely to surpass that of any other student in the university. Imagine the blow to the morale of the eager and hardworking student who received the requisite C.

Not just in this case, but in most cases, grades say little about the work done. When you reflect to a student that he has misconstrued a concept or has taken a false step in a math problem, you are indicating something real about his performance, but when you give him a B+, you are saying nothing at all about his mastery of the material, you are only matching him up against other students. Most would recognize at core that the main purpose of grades is to compare one student against another. Most people are also aware that competition puts a strain on friendships and too often consigns students to a solitary journey.

Michelangelo is often quoted as having said that inside every block of stone or marble dwells a beautiful statue; one need only remove the excess material to reveal the work of art within. If we were to apply this visionary concept to education, it would be pointless to compare one child to another. Instead, all the energy would be focused on chipping away at the stone, getting rid of whatever is in the way of each child's developing skills, mastery, and self-expression.

We call this practice *giving an A*. It is an enlivening way of approaching people that promises to transform you as well as them. It is a shift in attitude that makes it possible for you to speak freely about your own thoughts and feelings while, at the same time, you support others to be all they dream of being. The practice of *giving an A* transports your relationships from the world of measurement into the universe of possibility.

An A can be given to anyone in any walk of life—to a waitress, to your employer, to your mother-in-law, to the members of the opposite team, and to the other drivers in traffic. When you give an A, you find yourself speaking to people not from a place of measuring how they stack up against your standards, but from a place of respect that gives them room to realize themselves. Your eye is on the statue within the roughness of the uncut stone.

This A is not an expectation to live up to, but a possibility to live into.

● ● ● ● ● ● ● ● ● ● ● ● ● ● ●
BRIGHT FUTURES

BEN: THIRTY GRADUATE STUDENTS ARE GATHERED AT THE NEW ENGLAND CONSERVATORY FOR THE FIRST CLASS OF THE YEAR ON A FRIDAY AFTERNOON IN SEPTEMBER. THE STUDENTS, ALL INSTRUMENTALISTS AND SINGERS, ARE ABOUT TO UNDERTAKE A TWO-SEMESTER EXPLORATION INTO THE ART OF MUSICAL PERFORMANCE, INCLUDING THE PSYCHOLOGICAL AND EMOTIONAL FACTORS THAT CAN STAND IN THE WAY OF GREAT MUSIC-MAKING. I PROMISE THEM THAT IF

THEY ATTEND MY INTERPRETATION CLASS REGULARLY AND APPLY THEMSELVES TO MASTERING THE DISTINCTIONS THAT ARE PUT FORWARD IN THE COURSE, THEY WILL MAKE MAJOR BREAKTHROUGHS BOTH IN THEIR MUSIC-MAKING AND IN THEIR LIVES.

YET, AFTER TWENTY-FIVE YEARS OF TEACHING, I STILL CAME UP AGAINST THE SAME OBSTACLE. CLASS AFTER CLASS, THE STUDENTS WOULD BE IN SUCH A CHRONIC STATE OF ANXIETY OVER THE MEASUREMENT OF THEIR PERFORMANCE THAT THEY WOULD BE RELUCTANT TO TAKE RISKS WITH THEIR PLAYING. ONE EVENING I SETTLED DOWN WITH ROZ TO SEE IF WE COULD THINK OF SOMETHING THAT WOULD DISPEL THEIR ANTICIPATION OF FAILURE.

WHAT WOULD HAPPEN IF ONE WERE TO HAND AN A TO EVERY STUDENT FROM THE START?

ROZ AND I PREDICTED THAT ABOLISHING GRADES ALTOGETHER WOULD ONLY MAKE MATTERS WORSE, EVEN IF THE CONSERVATORY COULD BE PERSUADED TO SUPPORT SUCH A PLAN. THE STUDENTS WOULD FEEL CHEATED OF THE OPPORTUNITY FOR STARDOM AND WOULD STILL BE FOCUSED ON THEIR PLACE IN THE LINEUP. SO WE CAME UP WITH THE IDEA OF GIVING THEM ALL THE ONLY GRADE THAT WOULD PUT THEM AT EASE, NOT AS A MEASUREMENT TOOL, BUT AS AN INSTRUMENT TO OPEN THEM UP TO POSSIBILITY.

"EACH STUDENT IN THIS CLASS WILL GET AN A FOR THE COURSE," I ANNOUNCE. "HOWEVER, THERE IS ONE REQUIREMENT THAT YOU MUST FULFILL TO EARN THIS GRADE: SOMETIME DURING THE NEXT TWO WEEKS, YOU MUST WRITE ME A LETTER DATED NEXT MAY, WHICH BEGINS WITH THE WORDS, 'DEAR MR. ZANDER, I GOT MY A BECAUSE . . . ,' AND IN THIS LETTER YOU ARE TO TELL, IN AS MUCH DETAIL AS YOU CAN, THE

STORY OF WHAT WILL HAVE HAPPENED TO YOU BY NEXT MAY THAT IS IN LINE WITH THIS EXTRAORDINARY GRADE."

IN WRITING THEIR LETTERS, I SAY TO THEM, THEY ARE TO PLACE THEMSELVES IN THE FUTURE, LOOKING BACK, AND TO REPORT ON ALL THE INSIGHTS THEY ACQUIRED AND MILESTONES THEY ATTAINED DURING THE YEAR AS IF THOSE ACCOMPLISHMENTS WERE ALREADY IN THE PAST. EVERYTHING MUST BE WRITTEN IN THE PAST TENSE. PHRASES SUCH AS "I INTEND," OR "I WILL" MUST NOT APPEAR. THE STUDENTS MAY, IF THEY WISH, MENTION SPECIFIC GOALS REACHED OR COMPETITIONS WON. "BUT," I TELL THEM, "I AM ESPECIALLY INTERESTED IN THE PERSON YOU WILL HAVE BECOME BY NEXT MAY. I AM INTERESTED IN THE ATTITUDE, FEELINGS, AND WORLDVIEW OF THAT PERSON WHO WILL HAVE DONE ALL SHE WISHED TO DO OR BECOME EVERYTHING HE WANTED TO BE." I TELL THEM I WANT THEM TO FALL PASSIONATELY IN LOVE WITH THE PERSON THEY ARE DESCRIBING IN THEIR LETTER.

HERE IS ONE LETTER FROM A YOUNG TROMBONIST WHO TOOK THAT INSTRUCTION TO HEART AND DISCOVERED THE POETRY OF SELF-INVENTION.

Thursday 15 May, nighttime

Dear Mr. Z

Today the world knows me. That drive of energy and intense emotion that you saw twisting and dormant inside me, yet, alas, I could not show in performance or conversation, was freed tonight in a program of new music composed for me, . . . The concert ended and no one stirred. A pregnant quiet. Sighs; and then applause that drowned my heart's throbbing.

I might have bowed—I cannot remember now. The clapping

sustained such that I thought I
might make my debut complete
and celebrate the shedding of

> the mask and skin
> that I had constructed
> to hide within,
> by improvising on my own melody
>   as an
> encore–unaccompanied. What fol-
>   lowed is
> something of a blur. I forgot
>   technique,
> pretension, tradition, schooling,
>   history–
> truly even the audience.
> What came from my trombone
> I wholly believe, was my own
> Voice.
> Laughter, smiles,
> a frown, weeping
> Tuckerspirit
> did sing.

Tucker Dulin

And here is another one of the A letters written by a young Korean flute player who entered wholeheartedly into the game, capturing perfectly its playfulness, while addressing in the process some of the most serious issues facing performers in a culture of measurement and competition.

Next May

Dearest Teacher Mr. Zander;

I received my grade A because I worked hard and thought hard about myself taking your class, and the result was absolutely tremendous. I became a new person. I used to be so negative person for almost everything even before trying. Now I find myself happier person than before. I couldn't accept my mistakes about a year ago, and after every mistake I blamed myself, but now, I enjoy making mistakes and I really learn from these mistakes. In my playing I have more depth than before. I used to play just notes, but, now, I found out about the real meaning of every pieces, and I could play with more imagination. Also I found out my value. I found myself so special person, because I found out that if I believe myself I can do everything. Thank you for all the lessons and lectures because that made me realize how important person I am and also the clear reason why I play music. Thank you,

Sincerely,
Esther Lee

In this letter, the young performer focuses her gaze on the person she wants to be, momentarily silencing the voice in her head that tells her that she will fail. She emerges like the graceful statue from within Michelangelo's marble block. The person that I teach each Friday afternoon is the person described in the letter. The student reveals her true self and also identifies much of the stone that blocks her expression. Chipping away at the stone that encases her becomes our task in the class. Our job is to remove the extraneous debris that stands between her and her expression in the world.

Next May

Dear Mr. Zander,

I got my A because I had the courage to examine my fears and I realized that they have no place in my life. I changed from someone who was scored to make a mistake in case she was noticed to someone who knows that she has a contribution to make to other people, musically and personally. . . . Thus all diffidence and lack of belief in myself are gone. So too is the belief that I only exist as a reflection in other people's eyes and the resulting desire to please everyone. . . . I understand that trying and achieving are the some thing when you are your own master—and I am.

I have found a desire to convey music to other people, which is stronger than the worries I had about myself. I have changed from desiring inconsequentiality and anonymity to accepting the joy that comes from knowing that my music changes the world.

—Giselle Hillyer

Small wonder that I approach each class with the greatest eagerness, for this is a class consisting entirely of A students and what is more delightful than spending an afternoon among the stars? Most members of the class share this experience, and some even report that as they walk down the corridor toward the classroom each Friday afternoon, the clouds of anxiety and despair that frequently shadow a hothouse American music academy perceptibly lift.

When I come to your class, Ben, I feel the glow coming as I walk down the corridor, and by the time I've arrived—I've arrived happy and excited and ready to go.

—Carina

We in the music profession train young musicians with utmost care from early childhood, urging them to achieve extraordinary technical mastery and encouraging them to develop good practice habits and performance values. We support them to attend fine summer programs and travel abroad to gain firsthand experience of different cultures, and then, after all this, we throw them into a maelstrom of competition, survival, backbiting, subservience, and status seeking.

And from this arena we expect them to perform the great works of the musical literature that call upon, among other things, warmth, nobility, playfulness, generosity, reverence, sensitivity, and love!

It is dangerous to have our musicians so obsessed with competition because they will find it difficult to take the necessary risks with themselves to be great performers. The art of music, since it can only be conveyed through its interpreters, depends on expressive performance for its lifeblood. Yet it is only when we make mistakes in performance that we can really begin to notice what needs attention. In fact, I actively train my students that when they make a mistake, they are to lift their arms in the air, smile, and say, "How fascinating!" I recommend that everyone try this.

Not only mistakes, but even those experiences we ordinarily define as "negative" can be treated in this way. For instance, I once had a distraught young tenor ask to speak to me after class. He told me he'd lost his girlfriend and was in such despair that he was almost unable to function. I consoled him, but the teacher in me was secretly delighted. Now he would be able to fully express the heartrending passion of the song in Schubert's *Die Winterreise* about the loss of the beloved. That song had completely eluded him the previous week because up to then, the only object of affection he had ever lost was a pet goldfish.

My teacher, the great cellist Gaspar Cassado, used to say to us as students, "I'm so sorry for you; your lives have been so easy. You can't play great music unless your heart's been broken."

Dear Mr. Zander,

I got my "A" because I became a great gardener to build my own garden of life. Till last year I was intimidated, judgmental, negative, lonely, lost, no energy to do what-so-ever, loveless, spiritless, hopeless, emotionless . . . endless. What I thought so miserably was actually what really made me to become what I am today, who loves myself, therefore music, life, people, my work, and even miseries. I love my weeds as much as my unblossomed roses. I can't wait for tomorrow because I'm in love with today, hard work, and reward . . . what can be better?

Sincerely,
Soyan Kim

● ● ● ● ● ● ● ● ● ● ● ● ● ● ● ● ● ●
THE SECRET OF LIFE

A few weeks into the first year of the giving the A experiment, I asked the class how it had felt to them to start the semester off with an A, before they had had to prove themselves in any way. To my surprise, a Taiwanese student put up his hand. Apart from a natural diffidence to speak up in a foreign language, it is rare for students from Asia, often among our most accomplished performers, to volunteers to speak in class. A few of the Asian students have tried to explain to me why this is so. In some Asian cultures, a high premium is traditionally put on being right. The teacher is always right, and the best way for students to avoid being wrong is not to say anything at all. So when this young student raised up his hand quite enthusiastically, of course I called on him.

"In Taiwan," he explained,

I was Number 68 out of 70 student. I come to Boston and Mr. Zander says I am an A. Very confusing. I walk about, three weeks, very confused. I am Number 68, but Mr. Zander says I am an A student . . . I am Number 68, but Mr. Zander says I am an A. One day I discover

much happier A than Number 68. So I decide I am an A.

This student, in a brilliant flash, had hit upon the "secret of life." He had realized that it's all invented, it's all a game. The Number 68 is invented and the A is invented, so we might as well choose to invent something that brightens our life and the lives of the people around us.

OFTEN PEOPLE ARE quite uncomfortable with the idea of granting the unearned A because it seems to deny the actual differences between one person's accomplishments and another's. We are not suggesting that people be blind to accomplishment. Nobody wants to hear a violinist who cannot play the notes or to be treated by a doctor who has not passed the course. Standards can help us by defining the range of knowledge a student must master to be competent in his field.

It is not in the context of measuring people's performance against standards that we propose giving the A, despite the reference to measurement the A implies. We give the A to finesse the stranglehold of judgment that grades have over our consciousness from our earliest days. The A is an invention that creates possibility for both mentor and student, manager and employee, or for any human interaction.

The practice of giving the A allows the teacher to line up with her students in their efforts to produce the outcome, rather than lining up with the standards against these students. In the first instance, the instructor and the student, or the manager and the employee, become a team for accomplishing the possible; in the second, the disparity in power between them can become a distraction and an inhibitor, drawing energy away from productivity and development.

One of the complications of working with standards is that those in charge—be they teachers, school systems, CEOs, or management teams—often fall into the trap of identifying their own agendas with the standards. How often in a business situation does a manager find himself at his wit's end when he discovers that work has not been done by others the way he would have done it himself? A common response is to deliver the ultimatum, whether explicitly or implicitly. "Do it the right way—my way."

Not only does this latter message tend to squelch innovation and creativity, but it also trains students and employees to focus solely on what they need to do to please their teachers or their bosses, and on how much they can get away with. The mentor's disappointment with a student whose style and interests vary from her own is often what is measured in the grade she gives. Instead of providing real information to a student on his learning, it tells him by how much, in the eyes of the authority, he has fallen short.

II-7: Expertise in Nursing Practice
Caring, Clinical Judgement, and Ethics

Patricia Benner, RN, PhD, FAAN, Christine A. Tanner, RN, PhD, FAAN and Catherine A. Chesla, RN, DNSc

THE ROLE OF EXPERIENCE

Most advocates of collaboration between physicians and nurses, and many of the critics of the extant nurse-physician relationship, seem to assume that there is an ideal kind of relationship. This assumption, of course, requires that all physicians and nurses are equally competent and equally knowledgeable about a particular patient's situation; clearly, however, a renowned attending physician and a clinical nurse specialist with years of experience do not function in the same way as a resident or a new graduate nurse. It is ludicrous to assume, for example, that the physician is always in the most knowledgeable position when, for example, the physician is a relatively inexperienced resident working with an experienced and well-educated clinical nurse spe-

cialist. It is also ludicrous for a physician to assume that all nurses are equally skilled in recognizing salient aspects of a situation and in recommending appropriate treatment. It is, of course, difficult for the new resident, unfamiliar with any of the nurses on the unit, to sort out the nurses who can be trusted for reasonable advice. As nurses in this discussion point out:

> It really makes me nervous when I see interns and residents asking inexperienced nurses for the same kind of input and they haven't got it to give. They do tend to look at all nurses as being the same. It is hard for them because they are here for 1 month and there are 100 and some of us. There is no way they're going to know who knows what they're doing and who doesn't. So you really get it from both ends. You have some intern trying to teach you your business and you just want to punch his lights out. Then you have another one who's going to a new grad

Excerpt from *Expertise in Nursing Practice* by Benner, Tanner, and Chesla. Springer Publishing Company, pp. 294–305. Copyright © 1996. Used by permission by Springer Publishing Company, Inc. New York 10012.

saying, "What do you think I should do about this?"

In our data, we found that the classic nurse-doctor game was far more likely to occur between the inexperienced resident and the expert nurse. The more enlightened and liberated exchanges occurred between expert nurse clinicians and clinically expert attending physicians. With clinical expertise, the dialogue is a lively discussion of qualitative distinctions situated by the concerns of the particular patient. The exchange does not deteriorate into a confused power play with the decision resting on rank, but rather the decision is weighted by the clinical issues at hand.

Physicians may develop some expectations about the kind and quality of information they receive from nurses. An expert nurse provides clinical data to the physician, ordering it according to relevance, salience, and the interrelatedness of the facts. Moreover, the expert nurse knows by the physician's response whether she or he has "heard" the clinical story with the correct weighting and significance. If the nurse is surprised by the physician's response, he or she can ask directly why the physician is not worried about the same thing that he or she is worried about.

In the following excerpt, a breakdown occurs because expected communication patterns were not followed. A beginning nurse, working nights, is assigned to the care of a man dying of AIDS with multiple system problems including DIC, ARDS, septicemia, a pneumothorax, bladder infection and renal failure. He was bucking the ventilator, so had been pavulonized. The family had wanted everything done.

> It was a lack of knowledge on my part. When I got his blood gas back, even though it looked similar to the previous ones, I should have noted that this man was in metabolic acidosis. As the night went on, I felt really uncomfortable with him. Just looking at him, saying this man just looks like he's going to die any moment now. You know, his heart was taching at 150s. His blood pressure was OK. He was breathing real fast in the 28–30s, and I guess they had done gases before that and they had said that was fine, satisfactory. Well, I was uncomfortable. So by 5:00 AM I had done gases and I called and told the doctor that I was really uncomfortable, that this man didn't look good. I gave him the gases and I gave him my assessment. And he didn't want anything done about it. His neuro status, he was getting a little more lethargic, his blood pressure was dropping, his urinary output was real low, his gases were not looking so good. I guess they were the same. The 7:00 crew came on and the nurse who had come on had taken care of this patient now for a couple days, so she knew him too. And he was being dialyzed and she pointed out, "Yes, he's in metabolic acidosis. He should have been dialyzed a lot sooner than he's going to be." You know dialysis, usually they come at 6:00. He should have been dialyzed a lot earlier.
>
> But I gave the little scenario to the doctor, two of them, and they didn't do anything about it . . . the head nurse who later counseled the nurse about this incident said that the doctor had felt that I hadn't given him enough information when I had called and I had stressed something different . . . than the metabolic acidosis. So he didn't catch it.

The physician received a report from an inexperienced nurse, and being accustomed to a nurse's report shaped by the subtleties of sequencing and which points out saliences, he missed the relevant points. The inexperienced nurse does not know how or when to present the most salient clinical facts to the physician because he or she has not yet learned to weigh the clinical issues. Thus, an inexperienced nurse's report to the physician will most often be factual with almost equal weight given to all the "facts." The inexperienced nurse, unsure of her own clinical knowledge, and feeling dependent on the authority of the physician, doesn't recognize when the report has been misunderstood. In the above example, the inexperienced nurse was unable to read from the physician's response that he had not picked up on the abnormal blood gas report; instead, she doubted her own judgement that something should have been done, and so didn't push the issue. This breakdown in expected communication patterns resulted in the patient not receiving timely treatment.

Inexperience on the part of the physician also contributes significantly to conflicts between disciplines. Nurses in the study repeatedly discussed situations in which their own clinical knowledge was overlooked or ignored by inexperienced physicians who wanted to claim superior status by virtue of greater education and presumed social mandate.

> I think one thing they don't realize is that I've been in the NICU for 10 years and I'm there for at least 40 hours a week. They come once a year for 6–10 stints, 3 years in a row. When I was in graduate school, I spent 17 weeks with a resident during my internship, making calls with the doctors, so I also know some of that aspect. And so, then to have them tell me in so many words that I don't know what I'm talking about can sometimes make one irate.

In the following clinical episode, the frustration of the nurse in working with inexperienced physicians is apparent:

> I was taking care of a 39-year-old Samoan lady who had a renal transplant, then rejected it, and then got a huge necrotizing fasciitis in her wound. She was on the ventilator and developed pneumos [*pneumothoraxes*] and had chest tubes. The residents came in one afternoon and wanted to pull the chest tubes on one side and proceeded to get ready to do it without any warning, didn't allow me to give her any pain medicine. And then, because it was early July. I don't remember exactly, they were teaching. They were doing it because there were new residents there, they were describing it in the most graphic terms. They might as well have said they were going to pull the garden hose out of this lady's chest, because that's what it sounded like. It made me squeamish, and I've seen hundreds of tubes pulled out. So I finally interrupted them and said, "When can I give her some pain medication? When are you going to do this; she really needs it." "Oh, she doesn't need any pain medication." It really irritated me; they were both young, probably younger than me and probably never had a chest tube pulled out. They probably had no idea that it hurt, and it was like, why don't you realize this is a person laying in this bed. You shouldn't be standing beside her bed and describing in graphic detail what you're going to do to pull this chest tube out, much less not give her any pain medicine. This lady was very stoic. You had

to anticipate her pain. In a Samoan culture, that's a culturally based thing, so she never would have said if she needed something anyway. This was a lady who was getting 300 micrograms of fentanyl for every dressing change. So she needed a lot of pain medication. And she would lay there and not say a word. Some patients will stiffen up; she wouldn't even do that. Finally, I got them to tell me when they were going to do it. So I gave her the pain medication. Then I proceeded to get ready to do her dressing change after they pulled the chest tube, and they were going to do it with no sterile gloves, no nothing. And she had this huge wound. And true, it wasn't clean per se; it wasn't like it was sterile, but I felt like pulling gloves out of a box on the other side of the room. She had very resistant Pseudomonas in her lungs that could have contaminated those gloves. At least they could have used sterile gloves. The difference between clean and sterile in that room might have been significant.

The nurse wasn't successful in getting young residents to stop talking in the room. She gave pain medication, without "asking their permission." When asked how she convinced them that they needed to use sterile gloves the nurse responded . . .

I think I said, "What size gloves do you need so you can do [it right]?"

In this situation, the nurse knew the patient, knew her usual response to pain, and knew what was needed to try to control the pain. She showed a grasp of the patient's situation that was overlooked and ignored by the medical staff. Because of the power

afforded even beginning residents, they could decide to proceed to do the painful procedure despite the advice of the nurse who knew this patient and knew what she needed. The nurse also understood the risks involved in contaminating an open wound of this person who already had compromised immune function. Through an indirect approach ("What size gloves would you like?") the nurse was able to assure the patient some protection from further contamination. In these circumstances, the nurse covers over her well-founded rationale for suggesting an appropriate course of action. To expound on the reason for her suggestions may call too much attention to the fact that she's making a suggestion. However, this covering over may contribute to the continuing perception of physicians that nurses have little role in decision making, and little scientific basis for their suggestions. In this situation, the doctor-nurse game continues, due, in part, to the extreme breakdown caused by the physician's inexperience.

The inexperienced physician who has been socialized is medical school to believe that she or he is the "captain of the ship" and must have the leadership authority cannot tell when he or she is being harassed by trivial suggestions or when she or he is missing the boat, overlooking important details, or paying too much attention to the abstract, general science and not enough to this particular patient's responses. In her response to Stein et al. (1990), expresses well the dilemmas of the new physician trying to assert the authority of the role based upon formal education.

As a young female physician, perhaps I am more sensitive to this issue of hierarchy. Some nurses resent receiving orders from a younger colleague and offer resistance at every turn. I am tired of defending literally every order I write. Question me when it is warranted, show me my mistakes when I have made them but give me credit for my years of college, medical school, and postgraduate and residency training. Also, remember in the eye of the patient and my colleagues. I am ultimately responsible for your actions as well as my own. In return, I will value your ideas and listen when you have a grievance. I will view you as an ally. (p. 201)

No doubt fledgling physicians and nurses receive more than their share of advice. Once credibility is lost in the clinical situation, it is hard to regain it. But the way out is not to insist on authority based on education and credentials alone, but rather to be a clinical learner open to the issues in the particular situation. Physician and nurse allies are needed in order for fledglings from both disciplines to learn from experience. The grim truth is that there is no real designation of responsibility in a patient's death, or when a terrible clinical mistake is made. No professional can morally or legally shrug off the human responsibility to use their knowledge to the best of their ability in the situation. The worth and dignity of the work require that the nurse and physician draw on their own and other's clinical wisdom, expertise and science when a patient's life is at stake, regardless of the social conflict that may ensue.

COVERING OVER THE HUMAN SIDE OF DISEASE, SUFFERING, PAIN, FEAR, AND CONFLICT

As Stein et al. (1990) and response letters indicate it is a mistake to assign all the caring and compassion function to nurses and all the instrumental functions of cure to physicians. The current commodification of health care serves to diminish the relationship between providers and clients to a mere economic exchange. The healing function of all health care workers breaks down without care and compassion. There is no cure without care. But the culturally and socially mandated healing roles of nurses and physicians are, in fact, different. Nurses are culturally expected to attend to alleviation of vulnerability and to coaching patients toward recovery of social and physical integrity. Patients seek help from nurses in practicing their "medical questions" and in framing their complaints prior to asking physicians. Nurses are socially and culturally more approachable than physicians.

In this project, for example, we found that nurses frequently assumed the role of translator for families once the physician left the scene. They coached family questions in the presence of the medical team, and/or interpreted into medical terms the family's concerns:

A lot of the attending physicians have a kind of abrupt manner. "Well, this is the way it is and I think you should do this," and the families say "Well, OK, you're the doctor and I won't question your judgement." But they do have questions, and I ask them, "Are you wondering about anything?" A lot of the time, they do not know the questions to ask. So when the families come in, it's very important to discuss what is going on. And what these tubes are, and these lines, and it's OK to touch them. By having the family get close to the patient physically, then they start asking more and more questions. . . . When the doctor is around, I'll say, Oh excuse me, they have questions here. And if they can't ask it . . . then you facilitate that. "Well, are you referring to this?" They'll say, "Yes, this is what I'm talking about." Getting them to communicate is the hard thing to do. But then they feel like they are participating and they care, too, which is important.

This social and cultural distinction usually works well as long as the healing role does not drop out of either profession and as long as the communication between nurses and physicians works.

Physicians and medical students alike are willing to grant decision-making authority to nurses in certain aspects of care: psychosocial aspects of care, discharge planning, assessing what a patient can or can't do physically, dealing with the family, and evaluating a patient's abilities to perform life functions (Prescott et al., 1987; Webster, 1985). Prescott et al. (1987) reported that there was a general lack of value accorded to decisions within the domain of nursing. One physician reflected a view, apparently echoed by others, that "in something like how to feed or manage a depressed patient, if I don't think it makes a difference, I think it is important to let a nurse choose, to give her respect in the management" (p. 39). The view is that nurses have decision-making authority over aspects of care that don't matter.

Nursing judgment, in the view of these physicians, then relates to the impact of the illness and treatment on the patient's daily life, his psychological state, and his personal values. Referred to medicine's selective inattention to these aspects of illness, or the redefining of patients' complaints only into biophysical derangements, as "medicocentrism." Of medicocentrism, Bernard (1988) writes:

This tendency to view the world of health care through the providers' eyes is not surprising. Medicine and its allied disciplines in the humanities and social sciences have long been afflicted with this disturbance of vision. For most of medicine's modern history. Physicians have distrusted patients' views of their own experience. The scientific physician's goal has been to replace the patient's subjective language of distress with data from the laboratory; to translate idiosyncratic or culture-bound expressions of discomfort into the supposedly universal categories of biomedicine. (pp. 89-90)

Given this understanding of the assumption underlying medical practice and the physician's interpretation of what constituies the domain of nursing practice, it is not surprising that nurses find themselves at odds with physicians when there is conflict between the medical plan of care and the nursing plan of care. Nurses can do what they wish, as long as it does not cross the boundaries of or interfere with medical practice.

Both professions suffer to some degree from medicocentrism and from the Cartesian suspicion that seeks to determine the "validity" of the patient's complaint. Are the complaints related to "real pathology? If they are not "real," then the respect and attention to the suffering may be withheld or relegated to psychiatrists or alternative health care practitioners (Benner & Wrubel, 1989; Cassel, 1989; Lock & Gordon, 1988; Lowenberg, 1989).

● ● ● ● ● ● ● ● ● ● ● ●
THE SKILL OF NEGOTIATION

Negotiation between physicians and nurses is a skill acquired through experience. From nurses' accounts, negotiation clearly rests on: (1) having a strong clinical grasp and the judgment that this situation needs to be attended to; (2) knowing the physician and having developed a relationship of trust, and (3) skill in making the case.

CLINICAL GRASP

Nurses learn through experience, often in difficult circumstances of extreme breakdown, that they should trust their clinical sense and be more aggressive in negotiating with the physician for a different management plan. They also learn from experience what situations require immediate attention, which can wait, how long they can wait, and what the risks are of either pursuing physican intervention or not. Here is a conversation among a group of nurses about weighing the pros and cons of pushing through the line of authority to get medical action.

NURSE 1: YOU'RE ALWAYS CONFRONTING PEOPLE, WHETHER IT BE OTHER NURSES OR PHYSICIANS EVEN. IT SEEMS LIKE THAT'S ACCEPTABLE HERE. YOU CERTAINLY GET THE PEOPLE WHO SAY, "DO IT BECAUSE I TOLD YOU TO DO IT." THE HIERARCHY OF THE AUTHORITY LINE HERE IS CERTAINLY MORE OPEN TO COMMUNICATION THAN IS SOME OTHER AREAS. ONCE AGAIN, YOU GET TO THE SITUATION WHERE IF YOU QUESTION A PHYSICIAN WHY THEY'RE DOING THAT, THEY ALWAYS HAVE THE OUT OF SAYING "BECAUSE I'M WRITING THE ORDERS, AND YOU FOLLOW THE ORDERS. "THAT'S THE WAY THE OLD STRUCTURE WAS, AND IT'S GOING TO BE A LONG TIME BEFORE IT CHANGES.

NURSE 2: BUT IF YOU DO THAT, AND YOU GET THAT KIND OF RESPONSE, YOU ALWAYS HAVE THE OPPORTUNITY TO ASK YOUR COLLEAGUE OR YOUR CHARGE NURSE, "IS THIS IMPORTANT ENOUGH THAT I SHOULD CARRY IT ANY FURTHER? OR IS THIS SOMETHING THAT I SHOULD JUST DO?"

NURSE 1: DO YOU HAVE ENOUGH ENERGY TO PURSUE IT? I THINK IT IS SELF-MOTIVATED.

NURSE 3: I ALWAYS THINK YOU PICK YOUR BATTLES, THOUGH. AND IF YOU'RE ARGUMENTATIVE AND YOU'RE RESISTIVE TO EVERYTHING WHAT'S THE POINT?

Choosing one's battles is an important judgment on the part of nurses. They must balance the immediate risk to the patient, and the possibilities they have for being successful in making the case. There are also long-term risks; if not for this particular patient, then for the nurse's relationship with the physician and her credibility when future issues surface.

Sometimes it is obvious to the nurse that when the risk for the patient of doing what the physician wants is not great, and the likelihood of successfully making a case is not good, it is better not to pursue it further. The nurse in the following excerpt describes her disagreement with the physician that a newborn needed bili lights. Her assessment of the physician was that his primary concern wasn't about the baby, but rather that it was a "power thing"

NURSE 1: THIS PHYSICIAN FELT [THAT THE BILI LIGHTS COULD NOT BE TURNED OFF SINCE THE BILI'S NOT BELOW 5.] I LEFT THE BILI LIGHTS ON BECAUSE IT WASN'T WORTH FIGHTING ABOUT.

NURSE 2: IT DOES DEPEND ON WHAT THE ISSUE IS. YOU KNOW IF THEY [THE PHYSICIANS] ARE JUST BEING A STINKER.

NURSE 1: YEAH, YOU KNOW. IN THAT CASE, IT DIDN'T MATTER WITH ME. IT WASN'T ANY BIG DEAL THAT THE BILI LIGHTS WERE LEFT ON; IT CLINICALLY ISN'T GOING TO AFFECT THE BABY TREMENDOUSLY IN ANY WAY OTHER THAN HE HAS TO WEAR LITTLE EYE PATCHES AND PRETEND HE'S LAYING IN MAZATIAN, BUT THERE ARE OTHER SITUATIONS WHERE THE IMPACT WILL BE MUCH GREATER.

NURSE 2: IT TAKES JUDGMENT, THOUGH,
AND TIME TO FIGURE OUT WHAT ARGU-
MENT IS WORTH FIGHTING FOR AND
WHAT ARGUMENT ISN'T WORTH FIGHT-
ING OVER IN THE LONG RUN.

KNOWING THE PHYSICIAN

Negotiating with a physician also rests on a firm relationship between the nurse and physician, in which communication patterns have been established, there is at least tacit recognition of one another's abilities, and there is a sense of mutual trust and respect. In teaching hospitals, where physician turnover is rapid, particularly among first and second-year residents, the possibilities for developing this kind of relationship are limited. In these circumstances, nurses express great frustration when they have to prove themselves competent before physicians will take their recommendations seriously. While they don't necessarily expect that the physicians will just do what they suggest, they do wish for a serious discussion in which their clinical understanding of the particular situation can be explored, and different treatment options examined.

In contrast, when experienced nurses and attending physicians have worked together for extended periods of time, negotiating clinical knowledge is a challenge. The following excerpt is particularly rich in its illustration of nursing judgment in indeterminate clinical situations. The nurse is describing a premature baby who began to show early signs of deterioration. She describes how she recognized the signs, and how she attempted, unsuccessfully, to get medical attention for the infant. Finally, a more experienced nurse knew exactly how to make the case with this physician. Here's how the story unfolds:

NURSE 1: I HAD A BABY WHO WAS ABOUT
26 OR 27 WEEKS, WHO HAD BEEN DOING
WELL FOR ABOUT 2 WEEKS. HE HAD

OPEN DUCTUS. THE DIFFERENCE
BETWEEN THE WAY HE LOOKED AT 9:00
AND THE WAY HE LOOKED AT 11:00 WAS
VERY DRAMATIC. I WAS AT THAT POINT
REALLY CONCERNED ABOUT WHAT WAS
GOING TO HAPPEN NEXT. THERE ARE A
LOT OF COMPLICATIONS WITH PATENT
DUCTUS. IT IS NOT JUST IN ITSELF, BUT
THE FACT THAT IT CAUSES A LOT OF
OTHER THINGS. I WAS REALLY CON-
CERNED THAT THE BABY WAS STARTING
TO SHOW SYMPTOMS OF ALL OF THEM.

INT: JUST FOR 2 HOURS?

NURSE 1: YES, YOU LOOK AT THIS KID
BECAUSE YOU KNOW THIS KID AND YOU
KNOW WHAT HE LOOKED LIKE 2 HOURS
AGO. IT IS A DRAMATIC DIFFERENCE TO
YOU, BUT IT'S HARD TO DESCRIBE THAT
TO SOMEONE IN WORDS. THERE ARE
CLUSTERS OF THINGS THAT GO WRONG . . .
THE KID IS MORE LETHARGIC, PALER,
HIS STOMACH IN BIGGER, HE'S NOT TOL-
ERATING HIS FEEDINGS, HIS CHEM STRIP
MIGHT BE A LITTLE STRANGE. THE
BABY'S URINE OUTPUT GOES DOWN,
THEY SOUND LIKE THEY'RE MORE IN
FAILURE. AT THIS TIME I THINK I HAD
BEEN IN THE UNIT 2 OR 3 YEARS. I WAS
REALLY STARTING TO FEEL LIKE I KNEW
WHAT WAS GOING ON BUT I WASN'T AS
GOOD AT THROWING MY WEIGHT IN A
SITUATION LIKE THAT. AND I TALKED TO
A WOMAN I KNEW WHO HAS MORE EXPE-
RIENCE AND I SAID, "LOOK AT THIS
ADD" AND I TOLD HER ANY STORY AND
SHE GOES "OK." ROUNDS STARTED
SHORTLY AFTER THAT AND SHE WALKS
UP TO THE ATTENDING AND VERY QUI-
ETLY SIDLES-UP AND SAYS, "YOU KNOW,
CAROL'S REALLY WORRIED ABOUT THIS
KID." SHE TOLD HIM THE STORY, AND
SAID "REMINDS ME ABOUT THIS KID WE
HAD 3 WEEKS AGO," AND HE SAID "OH."
EVERYTHING STOPS, HE GETS OUT THE
STETHOSCOPE AND LISTENS TO THE KID,
EXAMINES THE KID AND HE SAYS, "CALL
THE SURGEONS." IT'S THAT KIND OF

THING WHERE WE KNEW WHAT HAD TO BE DONE. THERE WAS NO TIME TO BE WAITING AROUND. HE IS THE ONLY ONE THAT CAN MAKE THAT DECISION. IT WAS A CASE THAT WE HAD PRESENTED TO OTHER PHYSICIANS WHO SHOULD HAVE MADE THE CASE, BUT DIDN'T. WE ARE ABLE IN JUST TWO SENTENCES TO MAKE THAT CASE TO THE ATTENDING BECAUSE HE KNEW EXACTLY WHAT WE WERE TALKING ABOUT. . . . AND THIS PHYSI-CIAN RELIES AT LEAST HALF THE TIME ON ANECDOTAL MEDICINE. SO THAT WAS ONE THING. THE OTHER THING WAS THAT THIS PARTICULAR NURSE KNEW WHAT SHE WAS DOING. HE KNEW THAT SHE KNEW WHAT SHE WAS DOING AND SHE ALSO PRACTICED A LOT OF ANECDOTAL MEDICINE. SO BETWEEN THE TWO OF THEM SHE KNEW WHAT BUTTON TO PUSH.

Here the nurse was contrasting a scientific rational approach to "anecdotal medicine." While in many instances, nurses may be criticized for this practice, in this situation it may have been the only approach that would have worked with this attending physician. By providing an exemplar from their shared practice, the nurse helped the physician to immediately grasp the current situation in the same way that the nurse did. Stein and associates (1990) have suggested that using anecdotes is a way of avoiding direct suggestions in order to maintain the rules of the game. In this situation, it appears that the use of an anecdote was a deliberate effort to provide a frame of reference for the physician.

SKILL IN MAKING A CASE

Expert nurses take on as their responsibility the task of making a case—for example, persuading the physician that a change in therapy is needed. In actual practice, this is not framed in a quest for more power, or to usurp the physician's legally and socially mandated role to provide medical diagnoses and treat-

ment, but rather in terms of getting adequate attention paid to patients' responses to treatment and adequate changes made in therapies that are not working well for the patient. Making a case can be a particularly difficult task in situations that call for indeterminate clinical knowledge, where the quest for certainty in medical decisions cannot be attained through objective medical data, and where the judgement call is based on knowing the particular patient's responses to therapy rather then on abstract scientific facts about the properties of the drug. Nurses frequently talk about avoiding open conflict that may deteriorate into power plays and interfere with making clear and accurate judgments about patient needs.

There are circumstances, of course, where the physician recognizes the nurse's expertise, and the nurse can say, simply and directly, "I believe that this patient needs something different medically. "But there are many other circumstances in which the nurse must find other ways to capture the physician's attention or in some way alter his or her perception of the situation. Expert nurses recognize this as an important part of their practice and feel that they have failed the patient when they are unsuccessful in making a case.

A variety of approaches for making a case have been described in the literature (Damrosch, Sullivan, & Haldeman, 1987) and appear in our data. The first approach is coaching the physician by asking questions. For example:

> Sometimes you are saying "Explain your reasoning behind this to me" without saying "This is a dumb order," which is tempting to say sometimes.

The question prompts a perceptive physician to reconsider his or her choice, and it may also provide information to the experienced nurse about whether she or he should pursue the problem further, picking this as a battle, or going up the ladder. The second approach involves coaching the physician by pointing out facts that contradict or contraindicate a chosen plan, or that will lead to an obvious plan of treatment for example:

> When I came in on Saturday night, they weren't giving enough osmotic diuretics. This is not a nursing judgement call, but it's certainly something that a nurse who would take care of these patients would know, that the serum osmolarily is only 280 and you can bump it up to 310 or 320. And you can't say "I'm going to give 25 more grams of Manitol" but you can certainly tell the physician "the CO_2 is 19 and his osmolarity is only 200, maybe we should do something else here."

The third approach is to frequently remind the physician of the continuing changes in the patient condition. For example, one nurse referred to this practice as "nudging:"

> And it's that kind of nudging that you do all day long every day, if you have the experience to do it. And it's just that exact situation that I think is the difference between people who have the experience and know exactly what you need to do and how you need to nudge it and who you need to nudge, and people who say "She told me that in this case you know you give the Maritol and we're giving it." And you're going to go back 3 or 4 or 5 times until you get the answer you want.

When all else fails in persuading the primary physician that the patient needs a change in medical therapy or in altering his or her perception of the situation, nurses may resort to going up the ladder—in teaching hospitals from the first year resident, to the senior resident to the attending; in private hospitals, from the attending to the chief of the service or director of the unit. Expert nurses again see this practice as part of their responsibility; one nurse explains:

> If you don't get a good answer, you're expected to do that. Sometimes the intern or the junior, whoever you jump over, gets a little upset. But if it's serious enough, I'll go to the top.

Another nurse expresses a common view when discussing her decision to go up the ladder:

> It's a balance—just not wanting to step on toes, yet wanting to be sure that the patient gets the adequate treatment. It's something that you kind of get a feel for. It's like "I can wait" or "I can't wait" or "I'll step on toes. I'm sorry but my goal is the care of this patient and it needs to be addressed. And if your toes get stepped on, too bad.

As described by nurses in our study, finding ways to negotiate with the physician does not rest on a context-free set of strategies, but rather on a deep understanding of the clinical situation, the physician's likely response, and the physician's usual pattern of responses; moreover, the skillful negotiation requires reading the physician's demeanor and responses, and modifying the approach accordingly, all in an effort to help the physician share the same perspective, and enter into a discussion of the best treatment options.

References and Bibliography

Bernard, D. (1988). "Ship? What ship? I thought I was going to the doctor!" Patient centered perspectives on the health care team. In N. M. P. King, L. R. Churchill, & A. W. Cross

(Eds.), *The physician as captain of the ship: A critical reappraisal* (pp. 89–111). Boston: D. Reidel Publishing Company.

Benner, P., &Wrubel, J. (1909). *The primary of caring: Stress and coping in health and illness.* Menlo Park, CA: Addison-Wesley.

Cassel, E. J. (1909). *The nature of suffering and the goals of medicine.* Oxford: Oxford University Press.

Damrosch, S. P., Sullivan, P. A., &Haldeman, L. L. (1987). How nurses get their way: Power strategies in nursing. *Journal of Advanced Nursing*, 13, 284–290.

Lock, M., &Gordon, D. R. (Eds). (1988). *Biomedicine examined.* Dordrecht, The Netherlands: Kluwer Press.

Lowenberg, J. S. (1989). *Caring and responsibility*, Philadelphia: University of Pennsylvania Press.

Prescott, P. A., Dennis, K. E. & Jaeox, A. K. (1987). Chemical decision making of staff nurses, Image: *The Journal of Nursing Scholarship*, 19, 56–62.

Stein, L. I., Watts, D. T., & Howell, T. (1990). The doctor-nurse game revisited. *New England Journal of Medicine*, 322, 546–549.

Webster, D. (1905). Medical students' views of the nurse. *Nursing Research*, 34, 313–317.

II-8: A Physician View of the Nurse-Physician Relationship

Jack Douglas Scott, MD

The nurse-physician relationship is discussed at length in the *Expertise in Nursing Practice* excerpt on The Nurse-Physician Relationship. Many salient points are reviewed, primarily in relation to the level of experience of each health care provider participating in the "game" of communicating about patient care. While I agree with the concepts presented, I would like to offer a physician perspective of the nurse-physician relationship.

Physicians are the "Captain of the Ship" regarding patient care, and the medico-legal consequences of this responsibility have never been greater. Health care has undergone tremendous reform in the last decade, some for the better, some not. In the hospital setting, much more emphasis has been give to the team approach to patient care,

implying all input from the team members should be weighed into the decision-making process. Nurses are being taught and encouraged to become more assertive in their advocate role for patients, questioning treatment modalities they do not understand or appear, in certain circumstances, to be contraindicated. But this role has taken on a life of its own, particularly in teaching hospitals, where a bureaucratic ladder has evolved to subrogate the decision of the physician. This movement to empower the nursing staff has occurred without a concomitant increase in education or risk-sharing, while at the same time nurses are spending less time at the bedside and more time with documentation, regulatory, and administrative requirements.

The physician continues to shoulder high-risk, medico-legal responsibility for patient care in an environment where the communication game has become much

"A Physician View of the Nurse-Physician Relationship" by Jack Douglas Scott, MD, February 2002. Reprinted by permission of the author.

more complicated, and in some instances, adversarial. The nurse-physician communication dynamics have changed, but the liability still rests with the member of the health care team who has the widest view and most depth of education and training, the physician. These observations are in no way meant to demean or diminish the tremendous contribution to health care by the nursing profession. Nurses and physicians need to work on communication strategies that relay essential data to each other about patient care within the paradigm to whom the medico-legal risks of outcome currently fall. No one advocates silence to the detriment of patients, but energy could be expended in other areas of medicine that may reap greater benefits.

II-9: Criticizing Your Boss

Hendrie Weisinger and Norman M. Lobsenz

"Criticize my boss?" "I don't have the right to."

"I'd get fired."

"It's his company, not mine."

Many executives recognize that it's important to encourage criticism from their subordinates. Walking about United Airlines, Ed Carlson solicited criticism, both as a source of information and as a way of conveying respect to middle managers. At ITT, Harold Geneen was well-known for the way he bawled out subordinates, but he also structured the organization to encourage criticism of superiors, including himself. Mr. Geneen felt that criticism of superiors would enable problems to surface more quickly, so they could be nipped in the bud. Konosuke Matsushita build his namesake company with a philosophy stressing criticism as a form of self-discipline necessary to the growth of the individual and the company.

Unfortunately, not everyone has the good fortune to work in such companies. George Steinbrenner, owner of the New York Yankees, is said to have given manager Billy Martin a contract specifically prohibiting him from criticizing his superiors. And the business sections of newspapers and magazines are filled with example of criticism of top executives with the source consciously being kept anonymous.

If you think things could be improved in your company, but aren't quite sure how your boss will respond to criticism, the following guidelines may be helpful:

1. Make sure it is appropriate to criticize your boss. You must have direct line of communication to him, and his work must affect your job or the job of your subordinates. It is inappropriate to criticize your superior if his decisions or action have nothing to do with you.

2. Acknowledge that the boss is the boss, that you are not claiming to be right while he or she is wrong. Any criticism that sets up a power struggle will make your superior more intent on defending his position. Phrase your remarks in a two-sided solution. Summarize the situation you believe should be changed; present your criticism as a productive alternative. By offering both sides of the situation you are in effect, acknowledging your superior's view and defusing his need to defined it. The decision—to make a change or not—is left with the boss.

3. Build the validity of your criticism. By offering it as information you want to share for the common good, you maximize its importance. Cite authoritative sources, submit supporting data from objective and reliable sources. While Mr. Geneen welcomed criticism, he did not suffer fools. He demanded that his people have what he called "unshakable facts." Thus, instead of having to accept or reject a "criticism," your superior is in a position of evaluating material you supplied.

4. Ask for your superior's help in a resolving the problem you are calling to his attention. By doing so you will not be "criticizing" your superior but seeming to criticize yourself by taking responsibility for the "problem." You are making your superior your ally. For example, if your boss is chronically late in providing you with data you need to function effectively, you can say. "I'm having trouble running my department when I don't have the necessary data on time. Can you give me some suggestions for improving this situation?" If your criticism is valid, chances are your superior will "solve the problem"—and resolve the criticism—by meeting his or her deadlines more promptly.

There also may be ways to determine how receptive your superior is to criticism. If he interacts with you outside of structured meetings, and if he is flexible enough to make changes in organizational policy from time to time, he probably tends to see criticism as a source of information rather than as an emotional attack. If your boss keeps to himself and seldom encourages change, criticism will probably not be acceptable despite its constructive intent, and you will likely be seen as a complainer.

What about those impossible bosses—the ones with short tempers, the ones who "never listen"? Can or should you attempt to offer criticism to them? Only if you can be clever and creative. Gear you strategy to this fundamental question: "How can I communicate this information so that my superior perceives it as being useful?"

II-10: Civility Rediscovered

M. Scott Peck

After completing my psychiatry residency training in mid-1967, I owed the army three years of "payback" time. To fulfill this obligation I was assigned, at the age of thirty-one, to be the director of psychiatry at the U.S. Army Medical Center in Okinawa. In this position I was to manage a department of approximately forty. One senior sergeant was considerably older than I. The three other psychiatrists were approximately my age. Two junior officers were in the late twenties. The remaining thirty-five personnel were enlisted men and women in their late teens or early twenties.

Until that time I had never managed anybody. Through college, medical school, internship, and residency, I had always been at the very bottom of the hierarchy. Nor, typical of such schooling, had I ever received anything faintly resembling management training. Yet from the moment I took over the department. I was perfectly clear in my own mind about what my management style would be: I was going to be just as different from every authoritarian boss who had ever been in charge of me as I could possible be.

I had no idea how to define consensus, but I was going to strive for it. Certainly my model was a highly consultative one. Not only did I never make an administrative decision without consulting everyone involved; I did my very best to see that, within the constraints of professional competence, the people under me made their own decisions wherever possible about the matters that affected their own lives. Because ours was a medical, "professional" department, I felt we could ignore the matter of rank. I discouraged them from addressing me as "Major Peck." Soon everyone was calling me Scotty. I was "Mr. Nice Guy." And it worked. The mood was euphoric. Everybody spoke glowingly of what of good leader I was and how relieved they were to be free of that stupid old lieutenant colonel, their previous commander. The work ran smoothly. The department morale was superb.

After just about six months, however, things began to go sour. It was almost imperceptible at first. The euphoria was gone. The men stopped talking about what a great place it was to work. "All right," I told myself. "the honeymoon's over. What else could you expect? Now it's work as usual, but nothing's wrong." But by the nine-month mark it began to get worse. While the work went on, petty bickering started. I wondered whether there might be a problem, but I could see nothing to account for it. Certainly it had nothing to do with me, for hadn't I shown myself to be a born leader? By the year mark, however, it was clear there was a problem. The bickering had escalated and the work was beginning to suffer. Little things were being left undone. At this point fate seemed to come to my rescue. A major new outpatient medical complex was in the final stages of construction, and the hospital commander told me that the clinic, the largest part of our department, would move there. Our current offices

were cramped, cold, and gloomy. The new ones would be modern and airy, with view out over the Pacific and wall-to-wall carpeting. Surely the morale would improve at the prospect of such a pleasant move.

Only it didn't. It got worse. As moving day approached the entire staff grew ever more irritable. They began to squabble with each other over who would get which office in the new building. The packing of the files fell way behind schedule. It was now finally obvious it was my responsibility to do something. But what? I announced to the staff that we were going to meet over in the new conference room for the entirely of the next morning. And that we would continue to meet in that way every successive morning—even though it meant working in the evenings—until we got to the bottom of the problem.

The two four-hour meetings we had were two of the stormiest I have ever attended. Everyone took potshots at me and at each other. Everyone was angry. Everyone had something to complain about. Yet all the complaints were picky, superficial, and seemingly unreasonable. It was unrelieved chaos. But toward the end of the second morning one of the enlisted men said, "I feel I don't know where I stand." I asked him if he would elaborate. He couldn't. He became inarticulate and the group continued with its random conflict. But the young man's words reverberated through my mind. Earlier that morning someone else had said, "Everything's vague around here." And the day before another young men had voiced the complaint: "It's like we're at sea." I told the group that I needed time to think, that they should get back to work, and that we would not have any more of these meetings for the foreseeable future.

We returned to the old building, and I sat in my office staring at the ceiling, my lunch on the desk beside me, uneaten. Was it possible the department needed more structure than I had provided it? What kind of structure? A clearer sense of rank? What did they want me to do—boss them around like a bunch of children? That was totally against my nature. But then most of them were rather young, after all. Could it be that they wanted me to be some kind of father figure? Yet if I find started ordering them around like an autocrat, wouldn't they hate me? I wanted to be Mr. Nice Guy. But come to think of it, it was not my job to be popular; it was my job to run the best possible department I could. Maybe they did need a stronger kind of leadership from me.

I called the noncommissioned officer in charge (NCOIC) of the department, asked him to find the plans for the new building, and bring them to me as soon as possible. When he arrived, we unrolled the floor plan for the psychiatry outpatient clinic onto my desk. I pointed to the larger corner office. "That will be mine," I announced. Then, intermittently pausing just long enough for him to write each assignment, I proceeded along the blueprint through the smaller offices: "We'll put Captain Ames here, you here, Sergeant Ryan there, Lieutenant Hobson here, Private Coopermen there, Captain Marshall here, Sergeant Mosely here, Private Enowitch there," and so on down the map. "Now please go inform each of them of the office I've assigned him to."

You could practically hear the howls of dismay across the island. But by evening the morale had begun to improve. The next day I watched it escalate. By the end of the week it was back to where it had been at its best. They still called me Scotty and my overall style of leadership continued to be relatively—although no longer rigidly—nonauthoritarian. Yet the moral stayed high for the remaining year of my tour of duty.

You could think of this as a success story. I did eventually acknowledge that there was a problem and that it was my responsibility. I finally took the correct steps to diagnose it. I was able to readjust my

behaviors to meet the needs of the organization. Indeed, the story is used in part precisely because it is such a dramatic example of how a system can be successfully changed by a singly simple intervention.

I prefer, however, to regard it as a story of failure. For the fact of the matter is that the department—the organization and the individuals within it—suffered for over six months on account of my poor leadership. It was indelibly clear that we had a significant morale problem at least six months before I took corrective action. Why did I take so long?

One reason was my self-esteem. I simply did not want to believe that there was anything wrong with Scott Peck or that his leadership was anything other than perfect.

Fueling that conceit, however, were my needs; my need to offer the department a simplistically compassionate, nonauthoritarian style of supervision, and my need to receive back the constant affection and gratitude of my subordinates. Until that final day I never even stopped to ask whether my needs were in consonance with those of the organization. It almost required a vertible revelation for me to realize that it was not necessarily my job—my role in the organization—to be popular.

It also never occurred to me that there was anything other than one best way to run any organization. I had never heard of contingency theory. My group consciousness was so limited I gave no thought to how remarkably young the members of the department were, and hence no thought to the possibility that the department might require a different style of leadership than an organization whose personnel were more mature. So it was that we suffered needlessly for months.

Would it have been different had I received some management training before being assigned to Okinawa? Would Lily and I have suffered substantially less, I wonder, had we had the benefit of some instruction on marriage before the fact? These questions are too hypothetical to answer with certainty, but at the very least, the response should be guarded yes.

It must be a guarded response since, being different, individuals have different styles of learning. Some children learn better in open classrooms while others do best in more structured situations. Some young adults benefit far more from formal instruction than from experience, while others do far better with experiential learning. Moreover, certain types of instruction are more or less suitable depending on the type of material being presented. Contingency theory again! I cannot be sure how much I could have benefited from management training until I actually became a manager. Or how much a course in marriage would have meant before I had an actual marriage to deal with.

II-11: On That Fateful Day, Two Airlines Faced Their Darkest Scenario
American, United Watched and Worked in Horror as Hijackings Unfolded

Scott McCartney and Susan Carey

We Didn't Have Time to Cry

Across America skies were clear, a beautiful day for flying everywhere but in Atlanta, where low clouds draped a summery landscape.

Early in the business day, American Airlines and United Airlines each had more than 100 flights in the air, a fraction of the more than 2,000 flights they had scheduled. Their top executives were digging through paperwork, meeting with other managers and answering e-mail from home.

Then, at 7:27 A.M. CDT. Craig Marquis got a mind-boggling emergency phone call.

Mr. Marquis, manager-on-duty at American's sprawling System Operations Control center in Fort Worth, Texas, heard a reservations supervisor explain that an airborne flight attendant, hysterical with fear, was on the phone and needed to talk to the operations center. In the background, Mr. Marquis could hear the flight attendant shrieking and grasping for air.

"She said two fight attendants had been stabbed, one was on oxygen. A passenger had his throat slashed and looked dead, and they had gotten into the cockpit," Mr. Marquis recalls.

● ● ● ● ● ● ● ● ● ● ● ● ● ● ● ●
THE UNTHINKABLE UNFOLDS

In 22 years at American's operations center. Mr. Marquis has made split-second, multi-million-dollar decisions to cancel flights during storms, separate threats from hoaxes and set in motion the airtime's response to a crash. But none of that could have prepared him for the morning of Sept. 11. When all he and other American and United Airlines officials could do was listen and watch as the system they control spun gruesomely out of control.

"I felt so helpless," says Mr. Marquis. "I was along for the ride."

A little more than 20 minutes later, inside United System Operations Control center in suburban Chicago, Rich "Doc" Miles, the DOC duty manger, received equally starting news: air traffic controllers had lost contact with United Flight 175 from Boston's Logan Airport, and a flight attendant on that plane had called in word that the plane had been hijacked.

The televised events of Sept. 11 are etched on the world's memory. But this is the story, recalled in detail in extensive interviews with senior executives and front-line managers, of what happened that day inside the command centers of American and United, each of which lost two jets to the terrorist attacks. It was there that normally unflappable aviation experts first started to unravel the puzzle of horror that at first seemed too diabolical to be real. Hijackers were supposed to coerse pilots to land someplace that the hijackers wanted to go. Never had Hijackers murdered pilots, taken control of planes and used them as giant suicide missiles.

Jim Goodwin, United's chairman and chief executive, knew instantly that the ramifications went well beyond his airline and American. "The enormity of this is going to change everyone's life profoundly," he recalls thinking to himself.

● ● ● ● ● ● ● ● ● ● ● ● ● ● ● ●

LOSING CONTACT

As American and United lost communications, one by one, with a total of four hijacked planes, confusion set in. Managers couldn't tell right away which particular plane had been ensnared in the catastrophes that unfolded on TV sets all around

them. There was an unprecedented flurry of intercompany calls; even the two chief executives spoke by phone.

Quickly, people at the football-field-sized command centers began executing the biggest shutdown in commercial aviation's 50-year history, orders that pre-empted even the Federal Aviation Administration's grounding of planes and may have prevented other hijackings. Beyond that, UAL Corp.'s United and AMR Corp.'s American also had to attend to victims' relatives, secure hundreds of stranded airplanes and accommodate tens of thousands of stranded passengers and crew.

"I remember thinking. I'm in one of those B-movies, with a script so bizarre no one would believe it. It cannot be happening," says Donald J. Carty, American's chairman and chief executive officer.

Sitting in the middle of a horseshoe of desks surrounded by screens, phones and computers when his hotline began blinking, from a woman who identified herself as Betty Ong, an attendant aboard Flight 11, a Boeing 767 wide-body that had left Boston 30 minutes earlier. Fearing a hoax, he called up her personnel record and asked her to verify her employee number and nickname.

She did. This was real.

"Is there a doctor on board?" Mr. Marquis remembers asking.

"No. No doctor," Ms. Ong said.

The plane had been headed to Los Angeles, but it turned south over Albany, N.Y., and began flying erratically; most likely when hijackers were killing the plane's two pilots. FAA air-traffic controllers told American's operation center that they could hear arguing over the plane's radio. Ms. Ong, screaming but still coherent, said the four hijackers had come from first-class seats 2A, 2B, 9A and 9B. The fatally injured passenger was in 10B. The hijackers had hit people with some sort of spray that made her eyes burn. She was having trouble breathing. Mr. Marquis recalls her saying.

"Is the plane descending?" Mr. Marquis asked.

"We're starting to descend," Ms. Ong said. "We're starting to descend."

Air-traffic controllers couldn't get a response to frantic voice and text messages to the cockpit. Hijackers had turned off the plane's transponder, which identifies an airplane among hundreds of other blips on a radar, but Mr. Marquis had an aide tell the FAA that American had confirmed a hijacking.

"They're going to New York!" Mr. Marquis remembers shouting out, "Call Newark and JFX and tell them to expect a hijacking," he ordered, assuming the hijackers would land the plane. "In my wildest dreams, I was not thinking the plane was going to run into a building," Mr. Marquis says.

● ● ● ● ● ● ● ● ● ● ●
A SHOCKING ANNOUNCEMENT

Even as the line to Fight 11 was still open, American's executives were rushing to the operations center to deal with the crisis. Geard Arpey, American's executive vice president of operations, had been in Boston the day before for his grandmother's funeral, and had arrived at his desk in Fort Worth at 7:15 A.M. CDT to work through a pile of issues that needed attention. The 43-year-old executive called American's operations center to say he couldn't participate in the daily 7:45 A.M. system-wide operations call.

Joe Bertapelle, the manager at American's operations center, told him of Ms. Ong's phone call that had just come in. Mr. Arpey slumped back in his chair and sat stunned for 30 seconds. "Something inside me said this had the ring of truth to it," Mr. Arpey recalls. He called the office of Mr. Carty, who was at home answering e-mails, and left word of a possible hijack-ing, then hurried to the operations center a few miles west.

As he walked in, he was met immediately by Mr. Bertapelle and Craig Parfitt, manager of American's dispatch operations, a 29-year American veteran nicknamed "Ice Man" for his even keel. Mr. Marquis had confirmed the hijacking, they had to open American's crisis command center, a room perched one floor up in the operations center. The facility is used in the event of crashes, military troop movements and other emergencies.

A page went out to American's top executives and operations personnel: "Confirmed hijacking Flight 11." The regular 7:45 CDT conference call started, but was almost immediately interrupted: "Gentlemen, I have some information here I need to relay," Mr. Bertapelle announced.

The FAA had tagged the radar blip that Flight 11 had become, and it was now isolated on an Aircraft Situation Display, a big radar-tracking screen. All eyes watched as the plane headed south. On the screen, the plane showed a squiggly line after its turn near Albany, then it straightened. "All we knew for sure was that he's not going to LAX," said Mr. Bertapelle.

Big centers deal almost daily with unusual events, from bomb scares to blizzards to unruly passengers, and they hold frequent crisis drills. In those few minutes of uncertainly, American's operations experts were trying to anticipate the plane's next move. But they were in new territory here.

At 7:48 A.M. CDT, the radar image stopped moving and showed Flight 11 "frozen" over New York. A blink more, the plane simply vanished from the screen.

Three minutes later, a ramp supervisor at Kennedy airport in New York called to say a plane had flown into a World Trade Center tower. Someone shouted to turn on CNN but workers realized they didn't get CNN, so they switched to ABC.

Mr. Arpey was on the phone with Mr. Carty. "The press is reporting an airplane hit the World Trade Center. Is that our plane?" Mr. Carty remembers asking.

"I don't know, Don. We confirmed it was hijacked, and was headed south from Boston," Mr. Arpey told him.

Mr. Carty had a bad feeling that it was indeed his plane that had hit the north tower. But when his wife asked him point blank, he replied: "No, it couldn't be . . . In my brain, I knew. But I couldn't say it," Mr. Carty recalls.

TENSION IN CHICAGO

Outside Chicago, at United's SOC, Mike Barber, the dispatch manager, had his eye on a large overhead screen that happened to be tuned on CNN. "My God, the World Trade Center's on fire," Mr. Barber remembers blurting out.

Bill Roy, United's SOC director, wheeled to look at the pictures. "It looks like a small airplane," he said to the others. "Maybe they veered off the La Guardia flight path?" But within minutes, United got a call from the FAA saying it was an American Airlines jet.

Mr. Roy called over to the adjacent headquarters building, where Mr. Goodwin. United's chairman and chief executive, was having his morning session with senior officers. Today, he was sitting with Andy Studdert, 45, the chief operating officer, Rono Dutta. United's president, and three or four others.

Maryann Irving, Mr. Studdert's secretary, took Mr. Roy's call and ran to Mr. Goodwin's second-floor office, knocked and burst into the room. "Andy," she said. "Call the SOC. An American plane just went into the World Trade Center."

Mr. Goodwin remembers thinking. "This is rather bizarre," and flipped on the TV.

Mr. Studdert, a former banker who joined united only six years ago, ran across the bridge between the two buildings and entered the SOC, thinking about American: "My God, what are they going to go through?" Upon reaching the command post, he barked out. "Confirm—American into World Trade Center."

A manager at the post had other news: "Boss, we've lost contact with one of our airplanes."

A few minutes later, DOC Miles, the SOC shift manager, heard from United's maintenance center in San Francisco, which has a system to take in-flight calls from flight attendants about cabin items that need repairs. The mechanic had gotten a call from a female flight attendant on Flight 175, who had said, "Oh my God, the crew has been killed, a flight attendant has been stabbed. We've been hijacked." Then, the line from the plane want dead.

"No, the information we're getting is that it was an American 757," Mr. Miles recalls protesting.

The mechanic insisted, "No, we got a call from a flight attendant on 175."

The dispatcher monitoring Flight 175, a Boeing 767 from Boston to Los Angeles, sent messages by radio and to the cockpit computer, and got no response. At 8:03 CDT, the group—now assembling in the crisis room off the SOC under Mr. Studdert's command—watched as a large, dark jet slammed into the second tower of the World Trade Center.

While United was trying to understand what happened to Flight 175, American's operations experts received a call from the FAA saying that a second American plane, Flight 77 out of Washington-Dulles, had turned off its transponder and turned around. Controllers had lost radio communications with the plane. Without hearing from anyone on the plane, American didn't know its location.

That raised the disaster to a whole new level. Mr. Arpey looked across the crisis room at Ralph Richard, a vice president in charge of operations planning, and saw his eyes widen in horror. "That was the first time we realized this was something other than a hijacking," Mr. Richardi says.

Mr. Arpey instantly gave an order to ground every American plane in the Northeast that hadn't yet taken off. Within minutes, American got word that United also had an airliner missing and out of contact.

"The minute we heard that, we all agreed we needed to ground-stop the whole airline," Mr. Arpey said. At 8:15 A.M. CDT, the order went out on the command center's loudspeaker: no new takeoffs. The decision, though it clearly would lead to monstrous logistical headaches, could save lives. "I never sensed any fear or panic. We were too shell-shocked," says Mr. Aprey.

Meanwhile, United was making similar decisions Mr. Studdet ordered all international flights frozen on the ground at 8:20. Ten minutes later, United began diverting its domestic flights and putting them on the ground.

Just as these orders were being given, the American command center heard television reports of a plane hitting the south tower of the trade center. Many in the room instantly assumed it was American Flight 77, the missing plane from Washington.

"How did 77 get to New York and we didn't know it?" Mr. Bertapelle recalls shouting.

Mr. Aprey looked at Mr. Carty, who had just arrived. "I said, 'I think we better get everything on the deck'" and shut down the whole airline.

Mr. Carty replied: "Do it."

● ● ● ● ● ● ● ● ● ● ● ● ● ● ● ● ●
BRINGING THEM DOWN QUICKLY

American ordered planes to land at the nearest suitable airport. It activated crash teams to deal with the accidents and the

families of passengers and began beefing up security at American's headquarters and major stations. Mr. Carty called his counterpart at United, Mr. Goodwin. Each man told the other he thought he had a second missing plane. "We focused entirely on what was transpiring—the physical takeover of our planes," recalls Mr. Goodwin.

Mr. Carty and Mr. Goodwin also were taking on the phone with Secretary of Transportation Norman Mineta, who was in a government command bunker with Vice President Dick Cheney. Mr. Carty told Mr. Mineta that American was ordering all 162 of its planes out of the sky: United already had ordered its 122 planes down. About five minutes later, the FAA shut down the skies over the U.S. completely to all but military aircraft.

At 8:45 A.M. CDT, American lost contact with a third flight, a Boston-to-Seattle trip. Everyone in the room was convinced it was a third hijacking. But it turned out to be a radio glitch, and the panic ended when radio contact was restored in 10 minutes.

Soon, reports began pouring in that a plane had crashed into the Pentagon. Maybe it was the missing United plane? American still believed its Flight 77 had gone into the second World Trade Center tower. The command center ordered a plane readied to take crisis response teams to New York to assist investigators and relatives of passengers.

Capt. Ed Soliday, United's vice president of safety and security, talked to AMR Vice Chairman Bob Baker trying to sort out the confusion. "We did not want to mislead families and loved ones," said Capt. Soliday. "American was really pressing us. They thought our airplane had crashed in Washington and that both their planes had crashed at the World Trade Center. We weren't sure." Finally, he and Mr. Baker agreed the government should make the final confirmation.

Mr. Carty recalls quizzing Mr. Mineta for confirmation of which plane had hit the

Pentagon. "I was frustrated. I remember saying. 'For God's sake, it's in the Pentagon. Can't somebody go look at it and see whose plane it is?'"

"They have," Mr. Mineta responded, according to Mr. Carty's recollection. The problem, Mr. Mineta told him: "You can't tell."

At about 8:30 CDT, air-traffic controllers and United lost contact with United Flight 83, a 757 bound from Newark to San Francisco. The dispatcher who had handled Flight 175 had been sending messages to all 23 of his assigned flights that were airborne, instructing them to land at the nearest United station because of two World Trade Center crashes. One flight didn't answer: Flight 93.

The dispatcher, a 42-year veteran of United still so shaken by the tragedy he asked that his name not be used, kept firing off messages, but there was no response.

In the United crisis center, mangers isolated Flight 93 on the big Aircraft Situation Display screen. The plane had made a wide U-turn over Ohio and seemed to be heading toward Washington. Everyone in the room by now knew that a flight attendant on board had called the mechanics desk to report that one hijacker had a bomb strapped on and another was holding a knife on the crew. There also were reports that passengers were calling their families from cell phones and seatback air phones.

"This was worse because we watched it until the end of the radar track . . . and then, poof," says Mr. Roy, director of system operations control. "We didn't have time to cry." That was at 9:03 A.M. CDT.

After Flight 93 crashed, Mr. Studdert dispatched Pete McDonald, United's senior vice president of airport services, to Pennsylvania. Mr. McDonald had himself been in the air on a flight that was diverted from Washington's National Airport to Dulles. Because the no-fly order made flying to the crash site uncertain,

Mr. McDonald recruited 40 United volunteers at Dulles, all trained in humanitarian relief duties, rounded up eight vans and cars, and set off at noon. In Pennsylvania, two state trooper squad cars met the caravan to give it a speedy escort.

After reaching the site, Mr. McDonald went up in a helicopter to take a look and all he could see was "very small pieces" of debris, since the plane itself was deep in the trench it created when it crashed.

With each twist and turn, airline officials also had the grisly task of trying to understand who was on board and who the hijackers were. Early on, American officials pulled up computerized passenger lists from Flights 11 and 77. With seat numbers from their flight attendant's call, they quickly identified suspects. United, working with the FBI, did the same. Other Middle Eastern names jumped out, and as calls poured in from worried relatives, they quickly realized that they hadn't gotten calls for those very passengers.

The tally: 19 suspected hijackers, 213 passengers, eight pilots and 25 flight attendants.

"BITING OUR NAILS"

Within two hours, all of United's and American's domestic flights were on the ground and accounted for. Late in the afternoon, however, United still had some planes over the Pacific. These were nerve-racking times. United said it had to press hard on Canadian authorities and even Alaskan airport officials who initially refused to let the planes land. "Until we got the last airplanes on the ground, we were biting our fingers," CEO Mr. Goodwin recalls. "By then, we were spooked. Every time we got an unusual communication from an airplane, we thought, 'my God, is there another one?'"

Once all planes were safely on the ground, the airlines sat stunned at the logistical quagmire before them. They would have to figure out where each of their hundreds of planes were and how to get tens of thousands of stranded passengers back to their destinations. They had to instantly create new security procedures. The days would turn into a blur of conference calls to regulators. Plans constantly changed. There was no time to go home and watch TV reports, no time to reflect.

For many in the command center that day, grief was delayed for days, if not weeks, by the workload. "Some of the reality of what happened both to our country and our company didn't set in until much later," says Mr. Arpey, who stayed in the crisis center all through the night.

For most, going home brought the first real emotional shock. "It hit me when I first looked in my kids' faces," pictures of shock and sorrow, says Kyle Phelps, manager of administration for the operations center and a 27-year veteran with American.

Mr. Prafitt, the "Ice Man," says it didn't hit him until much later, when he began to realize that his son in the Army might be headed to war. "The grief for the people on the airplanes, for the crews, for the people of New York in the World Trade Center is all-encompassing," Mr. Prafitt says.

Mr. Bertapelle says that when he is home how he craves the Comedy Channel, hungry for a laugh. On the Friday after the hijacking, Mr. Carty came on American's intercom system, piped through its headquarters, operations center, flight academy and other facilities, to observe a moment of silence. "That's the first time I remember just stopping to think about it," Mr. Bertapelle said. "Any moment of silence is hell."

Some now are angry. Others say their emotions are frozen much like the radar image of the plane flying over New York, only to disappear.

Mr. Marquis, who talked with flight attendant Betty Ong, says he's met twice with a psychologist. He hasn't had a real night of sleep since. "It's still like a dream," he says, "I've been through lots of stuff before, but nothing like this."

The United dispatcher who handled both Flight 175 and Flight 23 stayed at his post on Sept. 11 and helped the remaining planes under his watch land. Then, he says, "I went home and got drunk," after running several red lights in the stress of the moment. He took three days off and availed himself of a company counselor. When the counselor said, "It's OK to cry, I broke down" the man says.

It's been touch and go since. The dispatcher says he won't watch TV, "My wife had a dream she was seated on an airplane with her wrists bound, along with all of the other passengers," he says, weeping. "The hijackers were walking down the aisle, slashing throats."

The dispatcher, who has worked some days and taken off some, says he takes solace in talking to colleagues who have lost friends in wartime. "When we're busy, I like it," he says. But then he is reminded again of what happened, like when a United pilot recently told him. "Your name is all over this airline," as word spread of who handled both doomed flights.

The man wept again in the interview. "Something inside me died," he said.

Mr. Studdert, United's chief operating officer, got a call three days after the terrorist attacks from an old friend. "How you doing, kid?" the friend asked. "There is no kid left in me anymore," Mr. Studdert replied. "I'll never be the same person. We'll never be the same company or the same country."

II-12: Weighing the Fast Track Against Family Values

Deirdre Fanning

Susan Lawley seemed to have it all. As a vice president at Goldman, Sachs & Company, Mrs. Lawley earned $250,000 a year in 1988 supervising the administration of the firm's mortgage securities department. She and her husband, Robert, then a vice president at Bankers Trust Company, owned a four-bedroom house in New Jersey, drove to work in a Mercedes-Benz and a Lincoln Continental, tooled around the waters off their Long Island beach house in a sleek new motorboat and even wore matching Rolex watches. At least once a year, they whisked their son, Greg, now 11 years old, away on a European vacation.

So why give up this world of power, prestige and wealth? "I was driving home from work around 10 o'clock one night and as I crossed into New Jersey I suddenly burst into tears," recalled Mrs. Lawley. "I couldn't see the road I was crying so hard. I realized that tonight, like almost every night, I would miss seeing my son because he was already in bed. I realized that life is too short to live like that."

A few weeks later, in early 1989, Mrs. Lawley quit her job to set up her own human resources consulting firm closer to home. She adjusted her work schedule to jibe with Greg's school hours and set out to find the things she felt she had missed while struggling up the corporate ladder.

The professional world is littered with executives who complain about the per-

sonal sacrifices required by their fast-track careers. But Mrs. Lawley is among the few who have actually made a dramatic change.

Along the way, she hoped she could instill in her son the same middle-class values that were the source of her own drive and ambition. "My parents were Depression people and I saw how hard they worked, for how little," said Mrs. Lawley. "One day my dad was visiting and my son Greg had his wallet out. Greg counted his money and had more in his wallet than my dad did. My father was appalled. I realized that all my son had ever seen was a life where everyone made a lot of money. As far as he was concerned, there was nothing he couldn't have."

Her own childhood was very different. Mrs. Lawley grew up in Greenwich Village in New York City. Her mother ran the household while her father operated a profitable but small manufacturing business.

Mrs. Lawley went to a Catholic girls high school and quickly established herself as a straight-A student. She won a scholarship to the City University of New York, finished college in three years and took an entry-level management position with the American Telephone and Telegraph Company. By 1980, she was in charge of all non-management staffing and was earning $38,000 a year.

She left for Bankers Trust, ultimately to become vice president in charge of administration for the company's burgeoning investment banking department. "I loved my job," she said. " I had power, responsibility and influence. I was surrounded by small people." And money. Her first bonus at the bank was $25,000. "It was more than my dad earned in his best year," she said.

Those bonuses increased as the division grew until by 1987 she was earning a total of about $225,000 a year. She negotiated an even sweeter deal from Goldman Sachs, at $250,000 in salary and various bonuses.

Her husband, meanwhile, whom she had married in 1978, was now vice president in charge of Bankers Trust's telecommunications. Between the two of them, they had annual income of more that half a million dollars.

Yet the more she earned, the more competitive she became. She says she was sometimes jealous of the bigger bonuses some investment bankers in her department earned. "There was a feeling of entitlement there that was contagious," she said.

Worse, her son Greg "was turning into a demanding brat." As she recalled it, "He got every toy and went to every movie he wanted because I wanted to make him happy. His teachers called me from school to say he was disruptive and doing badly in class. How could he know any better? We didn't give him a value system—no one was there to teach him at home. He really believed all of this money happened automatically."

That is when Mrs. Lawley started her own firm, Cameron Consulting Group Inc., giving up a private secretary to share one with eight others in her office, once the building's coffee room. At about the same time, her husband decided to leave Bankers Trust and start his own telecommunications firm, Gain Communication. The two companies now share office space in Parsippany, N.J.

For the Lawleys, it has been an eye-opening transition. As with new ventures in general, business did not take off instantly; the Lawleys now make do with an annual income of less than $100,000.

"Sometimes I still worry," said Robert, the son of a British coal miner. "I think, 'Gee, I walked away from all that money.' But we think now before going out and blowing $1,000 and that's the way it should be."

Greg also seems positively contented, according to his mother. He is making A's at school instead of C's. Now, when he can't choose between toys at the store, he picks one or gets none. He says he even plays with the old, but little-used toys in his toy box. For the first time, his spending money is limited—to a weekly allowance of $5, for which he does chores.

Mrs. Lawley feels proud of the way she and her family now live. "I wanted Greg to see me struggle, like my parents did," she said, "I wanted him to see me worrying about writing bills, so he could appreciate the real, hard work that goes into making money."

II-13: I Have a Dream

Martin Luther King, Jr.

Delivered on the steps at the Lincoln Memorial in Washington, D.C., on August 28, 1963

Five score years ago, a great American, in whose symbolic shadow we stand signed the Emancipation Proclamation. This momentous decree came as a great beacon light of hope to millions of Negro slaves who had been seared in the flames of withering injustice. It came as a joyous daybreak to end the long night of captivity.

But one hundred years later, we must face the tragic fact that the Negro is still not free. One hundred years later, the life of the Negro is still sadly crippled by the manacles of segregation and the chains of discrimination. One hundred years later, the Negro lives on a lonely island of poverty in the midst of a vast ocean of material prosperity. One hundred years later, the Negro is still languishing in the corners of American society and finds himself an exile in his own land. So we have come here today to dramatize an appalling condition.

In a sense we have come to our nation's capital to cash a check. When the architects of our republic wrote the magnificent words of the Constitution and the declaration of Independence, they were signing a promissory note to which every American was to fall heir. This note was a promise that all men would be guaranteed the inalienable rights of life, liberty, and the pursuit of happiness.

It is obvious today that America has defaulted on this promissory note insofar as her citizens of color are concerned. Instead of honoring this sacred obligation, America has given the Negro people a bad check which has come back marked "insufficient funds." But we refuse to believe that the bank of justice is bankrupt. We refuse to believe that there are insufficient funds in the great vaults of opportunity of this nation. So we have come to cash this check—a check that will give us upon demand the riches of freedom and the security of justice. We have also come to this hallowed spot to remind America of the fierce urgency of now. This is no time to engage in the luxury of cooling off or to take the tranquilizing drug of gradualism. Now is the time to rise from the dark and desolate valley of segregation to the sunlit path of racial justice. Now is the time to open the doors of opportunity to all of God's children. Now is the time to lift our nation from the quicksands of racial injustice to the solid rock of brotherhood.

It would be fatal for the nation to overlook the urgency of the moment and to underestimate the determination of the Negro. This sweltering summer of the Negro's legitimate discontent will not pass until there is an invigorating autumn of freedom and equality. Nineteen sixty-three is not an end, but a beginning. Those who hope that the Negro needed to blow off steam and will now be content will have a rude awakening if the nation returns to business as usual. There will be neither rest nor tranquility in America until the Negro is granted his citizenship rights. The whirlwinds of revolt will continue to shake the foundations of our nation until the bright day of justice emerges.

But there is something that I must say to my people who stand on the warm threshold which leads into the palace of justice. In the process of gaining our rightful place we must not be guilty of wrongful deeds. Let us not seek to satisfy our thirst for freedom by drinking from the cup of bitterness and hatred.

We must forever conduct our struggle on the high plane of dignity and discipline. We must not allow our creative protest to degenerate into physical violence. Again and again we must rise to the majestic heights of meeting physical force with soul force. The marvelous new militancy which has engulfed the Negro community must not lead us to distrust of all white people, for many of our white brothers, as evidenced by their presence here today, have come to realize that their destiny is tied up with our destiny and their freedom is inextricably bound to our freedom. We cannot walk alone.

And as we walk, we must make the pledge that we shall march ahead. We cannot turn back. There are those who are asking the devotees of civil rights, "When will you be satisfied?" We can never be satisfied as long as our bodies, heavy with the fatigue of travel, cannot gain lodging in the motels of the highways and the hotels of the cities. We cannot be satisfied as long as the Negro's basic mobility is from a smaller ghetto to a larger one. We can never be satisfied as long as a Negro in Mississippi cannot vote and a Negro in New York believes he has nothing for which to vote. No, no, we are not satisfied, and we will not be satisfied until justice rolls down like waters and righteousness like a mighty stream.

I am not unmindful that some of you have come here out of great trials and tribulations. Some of you have come fresh from narrow cells. Some of you have come from areas where your quest for freedom left you battered by the storms of persecution and staggered by the winds of police brutality. You have been the veterans of creative suffering. Continue to work with the faith that unearned suffering is redemptive.

Go back to Mississippi, go back to Alabama, go back to Georgia, go back to Louisiana, go back to the slums and ghettos of our northern cities, knowing that somehow this situation can and will be changed. Let us not wallow in the valley of despair.

I say to you today, my friends that in spite of the difficulties and frustrations of the moment, I still have a dream. It is a dream deeply rooted in the American dream.

I have a dream that one day this nation will rise up and live out the true meaning of its creed: "We hold these truths to be self-evident: that all men are created equal."

I have a dream that one day on the red hills of Georgia the sons of former slaves and the sons of former slave owners will be able to sit down together at a table of brotherhood.

I have a dream that one day even the state of Mississippi, a desert state, sweltering with the heat of injustice and oppression, will be transformed into an oasis of freedom and justice.

I have a dream that my four children will one day live in a nation where they will not be judged by the color of their skin but by the content of their character.

I have a dream today.

I have a dream that one day the state of Alabama, whose governor's lips are presently dripping with the words of interposition and nullification, will be transformed into a situation where little black boys and black girls will be able to join hands with little white boys and white girls and walk together as sisters and brothers.

I have a dream today.

I have a dream that one day every valley shall be exalted, every hill and mountain shall be made low, the rough places will be made plain, and the crooked places will be made straight, and the glory of the Lord shall be revealed, and all flesh shall see it together.

This is our hope. This is the faith with which I return to the South. With this faith we will be able to hew out of the mountain of despair a stone of hope. With this faith we will be able to transform the jangling discords of our nation into a beautiful symphony of brotherhood. With this faith we will be able to work together, to pray together, to struggle together, to go to jail together, to stand up for freedom together, knowing that we will be free one day.

This will be the day when all of God's children will be able to sing with a new meaning, "My country, 'tis of thee, sweet land of liberty, of thee I sing. Land where my fathers died, land of the pilgrim's pride, from every mountainside, let freedom ring."

And if America is to be a great nation this must become true. So let freedom ring from the prodigious hilltops of New Hampshire. Let freedom ring from the mighty mountains of New York. Let freedom ring from the heightening Alleghenies of Pennsylvania!

Let freedom ring from the snowcapped Rockies of Colorado!

Let freedom ring from the curvaceous peaks of California!

But not only that; let freedom ring from Stone Mountain of Georgia!

Let freedom ring from Lookout Mountain of Tennessee!

Let freedom ring from every hill and every molehill of Mississippi. From every mountainside, let freedom ring.

When we let freedom ring, when we let it ring from every village and every hamlet, from every state and every city, we will be able to speed up that day when all of God's

children, black men and white men, Jews and Gentiles, Protestants and Catholics, will be able to join hands and sing in the words of the old Negro spiritual, "Free at last! free at last! thank God Almighty, we are free at last!"

II-14: The 2,988 Words That Changed a Presidency: An Etymology

D. T. MAX

The president could not find the right words. Soon after the World Trade Center and the Pentagon were attacked on Sept. 11, he tried to articulate his response. In one week he gave more than a dozen speeches and remarks to comfort, rally and then—when he'd rallied too much—calm the country. To some, his language seemed undisciplined. He called the terrorists "folks" and referred to the coming battle as a "crusade." He called for "revenge," called Osama bin Laden the "prime suspect" and asked for him "dead or alive." He said "make no mistake" at least eight times in public remarks. When Bush didn't seem lost, he often seemed scared. When he didn't seem scared, he often seemed angry. None of this soothed the public. "It was beginning to look like 'Bring Me the Head of Osama bin Laden,' starring Ronald Colman," one White House official remembered.

In a time of national crisis, words are key to the presidency. Too many and people tune out; too few and they think he is hiding. The president knew he had not yet said the right things. He returned from Camp David the weekend after the attacks with an

intense desire to make a major speech. His aides agreed. The president needed to reassure Americans while conveying a message of resolve to the world.

Shaping a successful speech wouldn't be easy. Karen P. Hughes, the counselor to the president, helped write the straightforward statement the president gave on the night of the attack. The speech, delivered from the Oval Office, was poorly received; it felt too slight, too brief for the great events. Three days later, the president's speechwriting team, led by Michael Gerson, came up with an eloquent meditation on grief and resolution, which the president read at the National Cathedral. "We are in the middle hour of our grief," it began. But the beautiful speech sounded borrowed coming from Bush's mouth. The tone was too literary. The president's next speech had to be grand—but it also had to sound more like him.

The White House also had to decide where to give it. Among the choices the president and his advisers had was an address to Congress, which had invited him to speak before a joint session. There is no greater backdrop for a president. But some advisers were reluctant. The president couldn't march up Pennsylvania Avenue without something new to say. And according to his advisers, Bush wasn't sure yet what the administration's response to the attack would be. Some advisers suggested a second Oval Office speech, which would be more intimate and controlled than an address to Congress. Others suggested speaking at a war college. He would look strong there.

Karl Rove, the president's chief political adviser, felt strongly that the president did better with a big audience. Applause revved him up. Congress, he thought, was ideal: it would build a sense of national unity. That was important. The speech was a huge political opportunity for Bush. War had given the president a second chance to define himself, an accidental shot at rebirth. Bush's first eight months had been middling. To many, he seemed a little slight for the job. His tax cut had gone through, but the education initiative, the defense transformation and the faith-based initiative were not moving forward well. Americans had still not embraced him as a leader. A strong speech could revive Bush's presidency.

The president decided to speak to Congress. But he wasn't sure yet what to say. The main focus of the speech was tricky to define. "He had to speak to multiple audiences," his national security adviser, Condoleezza Rice, later told me. "He was speaking to the American people, foreign leaders, to the Congress and to the Taliban."

Karen Hughes met Bush at the White House residence Sunday afternoon to discuss what ground the speech might cover. She jotted down notes: *Who are they? Why they hate us? What victory means? How will it be won?* On Monday morning, Bush talked to Hughes again. According to Hughes, he told her how to deal with the fact that military action might come anytime. "If we've done something, discuss what we have done, "he told Hughes. "If not, tell people to get ready." He told her he wanted a draft quickly. Hughes called Michael Gerson and told him that he had until 7 p.m. to come up with something.

Gerson does not write alone. He has five other writers, two of whom he works closely with, Matt Scully and John McConnell. Scully is wiry and ironic, like a comedy writer. McConnell is more earnest. They help bring Gerson down to earth. Gerson, 37, is an owlish man who fills yellow pads with doodles when you ask him a question. He says he believes that social justice must be central in Republican thought. "The great stories of our time," he told me, "are moral stories and moral commitments: the civil rights movement, the War on Poverty." He and the president get along well. The president calls Gerson "the scribe." They share an intensely felt Christianity.

Gerson had written speeches with Scully and McConnell during the campaign. They worked well together. Since then, Gerson has moved up a notch: he now has an office in the basement of the West Wing. The office is prestigious but not great for writing. It is claustrophobic and illuminated by artificial light. McConnell and Scully were in the Old Executive Office Building. If the West Wing, with its plush carpeting and secretaries in heels, resembles a Sun Belt office suite, the O.E.O.B. is by comparision a funky hotel. Every office, no matter how small, had its own couch, yet no office had a matching set of chairs. It was a good place to brainstorm.

So Gerson crossed West Executive Avenue to see McConnell and Scully. The three writers sat around the computer in McConnell's office, Gerson in one of the gray suits he wears, bouncing nervously, Scully's feet up on the couch. They began to write, adopting the magisterial tone of presidential speechwriting. These were great events. They deserved great sentiments, a lofty style that Don Baer, a communications director in the Clinton administration, called "reaching for the marble." The three wrote as a team, trying out sentences on each other: "Tonight we are a country awakened to danger. . . ." They went quickly. They knew there would be time to change things and plenty of hands to do it. They assumed that one of the widows of the heroes of United Airlines Flight 93 would be there, so they put in Lyzbeth Glick, the widow of Jeremy Glick, one of the men who apparently fought with hijackers. (In fact it would be Lisa Beamer, whose husband, Todd, had also been on the plane.) They knew little for certain, and knowing little increased their natural tendency to sound like Churchill, whose writing they all liked. Gerson tried out: "In the long term, terrorism is not answered by higher walls and deeper bunkers." The team kept going: "Whether we bring our enemies to justice or justice to our enemies, justice will be done." The computer screen filled with rolling triads. "This is the world's fight; this is civilization's fight; this is the fight of all who believe in progress and pluralism, tolerance and freedom." Words tumbled out.

"They were just sitting there, jamming," said Juleuna Glover Weiss, the vice president's press secretary, whose office is next door. "There was a sort of one-upsmanship to it." Gerson wrote, "Freedom is at war with fear." Together, they tweaked it: "Freedom and fear are at war." They worked steadily, getting meals from the White House mess to keep them going.

The patriotic riffs were falling in place. But what, and how much, could they tell the country about the administration's plans for bin Laden and Afghanistan? They received some help from John Gibson, another speechwriter. Gibson writes foreign-policy speeches for the president and the National Security Council and regularly attends meetings with Condoleezza Rice, the national security adviser, and Stephen Hadley, her deputy. Gibson has the odd job of writing public words about the government's most private decisions. He has top-secret security clearance; his hard drive is stored in a safe.

Getting good information is always a problem for White House speechwriters.

The most important officials keep it away from them for the obvious reason that they are writers: they have friends at newspapers; they eventually write memoirs. When sensitive policy is made, the principals close the door. Since the attack, information, as they say in the intelligence community, had become "stovepiped." Gibson's meeting with Rice and Hadley was canceled, and he couldn't get through to them.

Fortunately, Gibson had made contact with Richard A. Clarke, the counterterrorism director for the N.S.C. Clarke is a white-haired, stocky man who has been in the job for nearly a decade. He speaks very loudly. "even his e-mails are blustery," one White House employee told me. Whatever the meetings were, he was still going to them. Gibson e-mailed Clarke questions that unintentionally echoed Hughes's original discussion with Bush: *Who is our enemy? What do they want?*

The e-mailed answer came in a bulleted memo. *Who is our enemy?* "Al Qaeda." *What do they want*? "That all Christians and Jews must be driven out of a vast area of the world," and "that existing governments in Islamic countries like Egypt and Saudi Arabia should be toppled. They have issued phony religious rulings calling for the deaths of all Americans, including women and children." Gibson liked the tone and authority of the response. He handed over an edited version to Gerson.

Using Gibson's edit, Gerson, Scully and McConnell began on the Taliban. Scully started: "We're not deceived by their pretenses to piety." Gerson wrote: "They're the heirs of all the murderous ideologies of the 20th century. By sacrificing human life to serve their radical visions, by abandoning every value except the will to power, they follow in the path of Fascism and Nazism and imperial Communism." Scully added, "And they will follow that path all the way to where it ends." They paused. Where would it end? They didn't know. But there were plenty of ready-made phrases around. McConnell threw out five or six, like crumbs from his pocket. They liked the idea of predicting the end of Taliban's reign of terror. "You know, history's unmarked grave," McConnell said. The group bounced the phrase around until McConnell came up with: "It will end in discarded lies." Gerson liked that, too. So the line read, "history's unmarked grave of discarded lies."

But if the Taliban were going to wind up on the ash heap of history, then someone had to suggest how this would be accomplished. Would we attack tomorrow? Would we mount a land invasion of Afganistan? Would we take on Iraq as well? No one knew. Policy and prose work their way on separate tracks at the White House, only meeting at higher levels. Speechwriters sometimes sit around with finished speeches, waiting for the policy person to call and let them know what the whole thing is for. Not knowing what the president was going to announce, Gerson and his team couldn't come up with the right tone for an ending. But they had done what they could, written a joint-session speech in a day. They sent it off to Hughes.

Late Monday night, Karen Hughes told Gerson that the president found the draft promising but thought it needed a lot of work. Hughes herself was already considering changes. Like Bush, she is a Texan who looks to the heartland. She is the person who reads with the president's eyes. "I can hear his voice," she said, "the way he likes to inflect and speak and the rhythm of his words."

Gerson and his team gave Hughes notes for a suggested ending. Hughes gave the draft a critical read. Speechwriters like beautiful phrases, the "marble." But this president stumbles over ornate writing. It makes him seem small. When he has time to edit, he cuts adjectives. "I've always described the president's style as eloquent simplicity," Hughes said. "There's a poetry, but it's a minimalist poetry." Some of this

was image and some was reality and some was reality imitating image. The walls of the West Wing are lined with pictures of the president on the range in his jeans, pulling out trees by their roots. After two years of national exposure, the public had a certain expectation.

The way Hughes saw it, the speech needed to be vivid. "I felt strongly the need for new images to replace the horrible images we'd all seen," she said. It had to have sound bites. That was also her department: she had at one point been a TV reporter before going to work for Bush's first gubernatorial campaign. The White House press secretary, Ari Fleischer, would distribute a summary of the speech to the press beforehand so it could alert their listeners what to listen for. And the language couldn't be too flowery. Hughes felt the way to reach the vast middle ground was to explain things as if you were talking to a friend. The speechwriters were writing for history, but she just wanted it to be an informative conversation. She began making additions to the text: "Al Qaeda is to terror what the Mafia is to crime."

Meanwhile, the answer to what America was going to do next had been decided. Meeting at Camp David, the president's war cabinet among them Rice; Secretary of Defense Donald Rumsfeld; Rumsfeld's deputy, Paul Wolfowitz; and Secretary of State Colin Powell—spread out maps and charts of Central Asia before they began discussing strategy. Not everyone had a firm sense of the geography of places like Tajikistan. One question was how the United States would define victory. Obviously, capturing bin Laden wasn't enough. But should the United States go after every state that had ever harbored terrorism in the Middle East? Syria, Iraq and Iran were all on the State Department's state-sponsored terrorism list. Powell argued for a narrow targeting of the terrorists; Wolfowitz argued for a broader statement, one that would include Iraq. Powell prevailed. The president subsequently sided with him at a National Security Council meeting. "We decided we'd start with O.B.L., his lieutenants and Al Qaeda and then take it from there," a senior administration official recalled. For a president who had surprised many Americans in his first eight months with his hard-line conservatism, it was a turn toward the center.

At the same time, it was agreed that the speech would have flexible language that would give the military free license to win a war. There would be no pledge made not to bomb Kabul or Baghdad.

Under Powell's guidance, the State Department drafted the language of the goals. Condoleezza Rice walked them into the Oval Office. There, Bush was saying that he liked the speech but the ending wasn't right; the speechwriters and Hughes scribbled notes as he spoke. Bush was enormously excited, Hughes recalled. The speech shouldn't end reflectively, he said. It should end with him leading. Rice then read aloud the demands Powell sent over: deliver the leaders of Al Qaeda to the United States; release detained foreign nationals and protect those in Afghanistan; close the terrorist camps. Give the United States full inspection access. Bush liked the points. Calling on the Taliban to give up bin Laden in front of Congress would be a moment of some power. He told the speechwriters to translate them from bureaucratese. Rice left her notes with the speechwriters.

Bush still wasn't sure whether to give the speech or not. Andrew Card, his chief of staff, told Bush that Congress was eager for a decision. Bush said he still needed time.

The speechwriters went back to work. They laid more marble: "This is not, however, just America's fight. And what is at stake is not just America's freedom. This is the world's fight. This is civilization's fight."

Meanwhile, Rice and Hughes wondered if the speech conveyed the Taliban's evil well enough. Rice sent Dick Clarke and Zalmay Khalilzad, another N.S.C. member, who is Afghan born, to Hughes to help punch up the section. Clarke and Khalilzad told her how men could be punished if their beards were too short, how women weren't allowed to go to school, how movies were illegal. Hughes took notes and put them into her copy of the speech. She was thinking domestically: these were wrongs Americans could understand. Hughes also amplified language that Gerson's team had written expressing compassion for the Afghan people. What had helped Bush become president were the overtures of compassion in his conservatism. In the days after the attack, he'd been so bellicose that his father called to tell him to tone it down. It was time to bring back the candidate.

Gerson, Scully, McConnell and Hughes sat down in Hughes's office on Wednesday at 11 A.M. They grouped around Hughes's computer. In front of her was a little plaque quoting Churchill: "I was not the lion, but it fell to me to give the lion's roar." New material kept coming in. Vice President Dick Cheney sent up a short text with McConnell defining the new cabinet position, director of homeland security. Hughes felt that the speech didn't make the point clearly enough about America's respect for Muslim Americans. The president's rush visit to a mosque had gotten a good response on Monday; it was important to highlight that theme. Hughes changes the phrase "Tonight I also have a message for Muslims in America" to "I also want to speak tonight directly to Muslims throughout the world. We respect your faith." She helped write the sentence "The United States respects the people of Afghanistan." Hughes was taking the speech out of marble and making it concrete. She added "I ask you to live your lives and hug your children." Rove stopped by; as a result of his input, the speechwriters added the line "I know many citizens have fears tonight, and I ask you to be calm and resolute." Rice's deputy, Stephen Hadley, who had to worry about more terrorism, suggested reminding people that there might be more terrorism to come. "Even in the face of a continuing threat" was added to the sentence.

All week, the president worked on the speech at night in the residence. He likes his speeches to make a point and for the point to be clear. He hates redundancies. He took a course in American oratory at Yale and remembers how a speech divides into an introduction, main body, peroration. (He once annotated a speech with phrases like "tugs at heartstrings" and "emotional call to arms.") Bush writes his notes with a black Sharpie pen. His edits tend to simplify. He is a parer. "Bush favors active verbs and short sentences," Rove said.

The president had strong feelings about the speech's ending. Although they had not yet found a place for it, the writers had suggested including a quote from Franklin Delano Roosevelt in the speech's conclusion: "We defend and we build a way of life, not for America alone, but for all mankind." The president didn't want to quote anyone else. He'd said this to them in emphatic terms at a meeting the day before, explaining that he saw this as a chance to lead. "I was scribbling notes as fast as I could," Gerson said.

The team worked on an ending that would be all Bush. They revisited the phrase "freedom and fear are at war" and gave it a providential spin: "We know that God is not neutral between them." Without hitting it too hard, a religious note would be sounded.

At 1 p.m., Gerson's team met with Bush and Hughes. They pulled up their chairs around the desk in the Oval Office. "You all have smiles on your faces; that's good," Bush said. Then, wearing his glasses, he began reading the speech aloud, stopping only for a few edits. He read the new ending aloud. "It is my hope that in the months and years ahead, life will return almost to normal," it said. "Even grief recedes with time

and grace." But these comforting words were not all. "I will not forget the wound to our country and those who inflicted it," the speech went on. "I will not yield. I will not rest. I will not relent in waging this struggle for freedom and security for the American people." It echoed William Lloyd Garrison ("And I will be heard!"), but it was his own. Here was his peroration, and it tugged on your heartstrings and called you to arms. The final "freedom and fear" image worked, too. The president said: "Great speech, team. Let's call the Congress." He would give the speech the next night, on Thursday the 20th.

Although the main building blocks of the speech were in place and the speech would definitely be given, a lot had still to be nailed down. Other agencies had yet to be heard from. Speeches are sent out for comment to all the interested parties in the administration. Sometimes this encompasses much of the executive branch, speeches being like a ligament that binds together the administration. "The process of writing the speech forces the policy decisions to be finalized," Hughes said. In the case of a speech as big as a joint-session address, nearly everyone in involved, from the secretary of state to the chief of staff. People drop by and read a draft late in the process to make sure nothing has changed. They call with suggestions and send their emissaries.

Predictably, the State Department wanted emphasis on the coalition building that Powell was working on. Language went in. Defense was worried that the speech would focus on the wrong things. "Their point of view," one official remembered, "was that you could put a concrete dome over every stadium in the country and we still wouldn't be safe. The best defense is a good offense." These jostlings were the last echo of the arguments over the map at Camp David. They were an attempt to affect policy through minute changes in the text. Motivating it was the fact that a president's words receive enormous scrutiny overseas. Bin Laden had already thrown back some of Bush's most ill-chosen remarks, promising his Jihad would beat Bush's "crusade." As Karl Rove told me: "In a crisis there's a gravity to each sentence. It's an awesome time and an awesome responsibility."

So the text got an extraordinary going-over. Language suggesting that Islamic organizations in the Unites States should be more aggressive in denouncing terrorism had earlier been tabled. Now "imperial Communism" was deleted from the list of ideologies that McConnell had put on the unmarked grave of discarded lies. According to one participant, the worry was about offending Russia, whom the alliance was courting. (The generic "totalitarianism" replaced it.) Some things that were in the text for no reason anyone could understand were cut. At one point, Hughes had put in that in Afghanistan you could be jailed for watching "movies like 'Gone with the Wind.'" It seemed odd to everyone, including Hughes, so it went out. Surprisingly to some, Hughes's Mafia line was not cut by Rove, who expended much effort courting American Catholics. Fact checking led to more changes. Someone realized that it was not true, as the speech asserted, that "Americans have known wars. But for the past 136 years they have been wars on foreign soil." What about Pearl Harbor? Pearl Harbor was added. History was history. But "sneak attack" became a "surprise attack." We were friends of the Japanese now and hoped to remain so. The staff collated the changes.

It was amazing how many countries you had to be nice to. The phrase "there are thousands of these terrorists concealed in more than 60 countries" lost the word "concealed." The terrorist organizations linked to Osama bin Laden were limited strategically to the Egyptian Islamic Jihad and the Islamic Movement of Uzbekistan—two, as one White House official noted, "of the most obscure terrorist organizations in the world." The Hezbollah, the Fatah and the Muslim Brotherhood never got in. The Middle East was a fragile place. Still, that wasn't enough. An N.S.C. official flagged the phrasing of a sentence that read, "Any nation that harbors or supports terrorism will be regarded by the United States as "hostile." What about Syria? The wording became "any nation that continues to harbor," giving the country, as one official said, "another chance to straighten up and fly right." Such softening was inevitable, but America still had to stand strong. Bush needed one hard phrase to lean on. It became this: "You're either with us, or with the terrorists."

Rice got one last look at the speech. If something misguided slipped in, it would be her problem first. She signed off. Policy and prose were now in place.

The president had to rehearse. It was the first thing he'd thought of after deciding to do the speech. The more time he practices, the better his speeches come off. The downward furl of his mouth relaxes. His tendency to end every phrase with an upward cadence diminishes. The first teleprompter rehearsal was at 6:30 Wednesday night. The president came out in his blue track suit with his baseball cap on. His dog, Spot, ran around the room, nuzzling the writers as they sat listening. The president weighed the sounds in his mouth. He came to lines about the administration's domestic legislative agenda, lines that had been slowly piling up—the energy plan, the faith-based initiative, the patients' bill of rights. "This isn't the time," he said and cut them. Hughes agreed. This was the time for Bush to assert his credentials on foreign policy and not retreat into the domestic sphere.

The president made more cuts. When he saw how many billions of bailout dollars the speech promised for the airline industry, he insisted the line be deleted. "We're still negotiating that," he said. He put in little things for sound. After "The United States respects the people of Afghanistan" he inserted the phrase "After all" to begin the next sentence, "We are currently its largest source of humanitarian aid." It would give him a chance to breathe. Hughes coached him: "Give the ear time to catch up," she advised.

Thursday morning, the day of the speech, Bush rehearsed again. He didn't like the clunky paragraph that contained the list of our allies: the Organization of American States and the European Union, among others. It was too much of a mouthful. They would no longer hear their names spoken. State lost that round.

The president took a nap at 4:30, was awakened by an aide and rehearsed one more time. At 5:15 Hughes told Gerson the name of the new director of homeland security. It was Bush's old friend, the governor of Pennsylvania, Tom Ridge. The news had been held back so it wouldn't leak. Tony Blair, the British prime minister, was late arriving for dinner, and the president was offered a chance to rehearse again but said he was ready. The communications office prepared a list of sound bites and distributed them to the press: "The enemy of America is not our many Muslim friends." "Be ready." "Freedom and fear are at war."

The president got into his motorcade and went to the Capitol. The vice president stayed behind so they would not be in the Capitol together. It was an unprecedented security move. It meant that every time the camera showed Bush, you would think about the meaning of Cheney's absence. You would remember the crisis. Bush walked into the Capitol, a president in wartime. He wore a pale blue tie. He began: "Mr. Speaker, Mr. President pro tempore, members of Congress and fellow Americans." He was interrupted for applause 31 times.

A week after the speech, the flag at the White House was back at full mast, waving in the wind. Karen Hughes wore a metal American flag on her lapel, upward streaming too. Was the speech a success? For the president, yes. "He told me he felt very comfortable," Hughes said. "I told him he was phenomenal." Bush had wanted to steady the boat, and he had done it. He had shown leadership. The Congress felt included. "The president's speech was exactly what the nation needed—a message of determination and hope, strength and compassion," Ted Kennedy said. For the writers, there was catharsis: Gerson felt that by working on the speech, he had become connected to "the men digging with shovels in New York." Pundits wrote that the president had said just the right thing in a time of crisis. The Uzbeks were pleased. The Syrians were not enraged. Only the Canadians, of all people, were piqued: their mention, as part of O.A.S., had been cut so the speech wouldn't sag. Even professional speechwriters, tough critics of one another, were impressed. "It was a good, strong speech," said Ted Sorensen, who wrote speeches for John F. Kennedy. "I'm not sure 'freedom versus fear' means much. But it had a nice ring to it, and you can be sure we're on the side of freedom."

Hughes quoted to me an e-mail message she had gotten from a journalist, saying that after the speech he'd been able to sleep again. It made sense. The speech reassured, even in the way it alternated its soaring Gersonian moments and its Hughesian explanations. America was mad but not too mad, mindful and not weak. Courage, compassion, civility and character were all there too—the values that Bush ran on and that Gerson helped articulate in all the campaign. After months of placating the right wing and days of disarray, the president had returned to the political and emotional center.

The very act of the speech suggested that civilized life would continue. The president had just sat around a big war map at

Camp David—but instead of first doing something violent, he turned to words. Some of those words were bland. Many were vague. Other than the demands to the Taliban, there was little policy in it. "This was a strategic speech, not tactical," admitted a senior White House official.

This wasn't a State of the Union address. It wasn't a moment to look ahead.

Bad news could wait. New presidents are terrified of looking indecisive, but this one realized it would be worse to be rash. Who are they? Where are they? How can we strike back? The coming challenge is enormous. By delivering a speech that emphasized reason over wrath, Bush bought himself some time until someone could draw a real map for the first war of the 21st century.

II-15: African American Experiences in Corporate America

Gail A. Dawson

The passage of the Civil Rights Act of 1964 and the affirmative action programs that followed opened the doors of corporate America to a large number of African American managers and professionals. However, most of these affirmative action programs focused only on changing the demographic profile of organizations; they did not attempt to change the culture within the organizations or the attitudes and beliefs of their workers. As a result, African American managers and professionals entered challenging and sometimes hostile corporate environments in which legislation mandated admittance, but not acceptance. Although African Americans were no longer excluded from corporate America, they were not welcomed and faced many obstacles in pursuit of careers in corporate America.

What was life like for them? This paper summarizes the types of obstacles some of these people expressed in interviews I conducted of a sample of these African American managers and professionals who entered corporate America during the 1960s and 1970s. Within corporate America, African American professionals were often frustrated because of inequities in starting positions, constraints that limited their ability to adequately perform their jobs, constantly having to prove themselves, and being passed over for promotions. In addition, they faced challenges in adapting to the corporate environment.

DIFFERENCES IN ENTRY-LEVEL POSITIONS

The actual entry-level positions, in some cases, were different for African Americans than for White employees with the same qualifications. Joe illustrated this point by recanting the practices at the Western Electric facility where he was employed:

> What happened was, when Blacks were employed at Western Electric, we had to go through the house services department—that's the cleaning department. Wherein a

Specially prepared for *Management and Organizational Reality* by Gail A. Dawson, Assistant Professor, University of Tennessee at Chattanooga. Copyright © 2003, Gail A. Dawson.

White employee would just come in and automatically go into the shop, you know, they wouldn't have to go through that house services thing.

Joe rebelled against this practice and refused to go into the house services department, which delayed the start of his employment by nearly a year (about the same amount of time other African Amercians spent in house services before being brought into the shop). Then, when he entered the corporation, he went directly to the shop floor—the same way White entry-level employees did.

John told of a very similar situation at a GE facility in which he worked as a technician until he completed his engineering degree and became an electrical engineer. Prior to his employment with GE, White applicants with a certificate from a local vocational technical school had been hired as technicians while African Americans with certificates from local vocational technical schools had to start as third-shift custodians, and they had to apply for positions as technicians as the jobs became available. In some cases, employees worked as custodians for a year before they were able to transfer to technician jobs for which they had been trained.

● ● ● ● ● ● ● ● ● ● ● ● ● ●
CONSTRAINED

Many African Americans found themselves in racially segmented jobs where they only dealt with ethnic markets, the African American community, or EEO and affirmative action programs. Bob, who started in a sales position with the Seagram Corporation and worked his way up to regional vice president of operations for the southeast region, spending the last three of his 31 years with Seagram in the area of diversity, considered himself fortunate not to have been limited by racially segmented markets, but commented on the prevalence

of this strategy, which he saw in action all around him.

> Most of the Black people who were hired were hired to serve Black people. Whether they call it Black-market, special-markets, urban, whatever—it still meant the same thing. It was almost like being on the police force but you dealt only with Black folks—you weren't allowed to arrest White people. Well, that's the way it was back in those days. There may have been minor exceptions, but for the most part, that's what Black people were hired to do.

Nick, who for a time during the mid-70s worked in marketing for Schlitz Brewery where the market was racially segmented, touched on an even more serious issue surrounding racially segmented jobs:

> They were moving more to the ethnic market as opposed to the general market . . . I was in marketing advertisement in the Black sector more so than I was dealing with my other counterparts. It was mostly relegated to that, which didn't give you a broader scope as to which way the company was going—it wasn't in high finance, it wasn't in distribution, and all of that. So, it was segment marketing, that's what it really was.

Nick pointed out that he and others who held segmented jobs were not exposed to a broad range of skills and knowledge or given opportunities to learn other areas of the corporation that would allow them to adequately perform their jobs and develop the skills necessary to advance in the corporation.

African Americans in EEO positions had similar complaints about constraints limiting their ability to perform their jobs. Jim, the director of EEO and affirmative action for Jim Walters Corporation, complained that he was not given adequate authority and resources to make real changes as far as hiring more minority employees. Reflecting on his position and that of others who worked in EEO and affirmative action, Jim says:

> Some of them had less staff than I had. And, so therefore you weren't expected to do but so much.
> Because you didn't have a big staff, a lot of people working, you can't do but so much [sic.].

Jim was frustrated being in a position were he hoped to make a difference by hiring more minority workers, but found that his hands were tied. He believed that most organizations wanted to give the appearance that they were changing their discriminatory practices, but in actuality they had no real desire to change.

African American managers and professionals also often complained that they did not always have access to the same information and training opportunities as their White counterparts. Inside corporate America, African Americans often found that information regarding the job, training, and opportunities for promotion were withheld. Some perceived this as intentional sabotage. Nick complained,

> It [information] was not shared amongst us. And some of it is still not shared. . . . Information is always power—the more you have, the more power you have.

John, an electrical engineer, explained that some of his coworkers had a tendency to withhold information; he believed this was because they were insecure and considered him a threat.

> [Y]ou can come across technicians and engineers sometimes who see you as a threat and they're insecure, they will withhold informa-

tion that they know. They are very careful not to tell you anything—it's like if I tell you this, then you might get the promotion next time.

Similarly, Nick reported that information regarding training necessary to adequately perform his job was sometimes withheld.

> The working conditions were feasible; however, being a Black man in an all-White organization, in an all-White department, certainly there was some reluctance about training you to the fullest. They would give you limited training, and you'd have to sort of pick up the remaining training on your own or through networking with other Black people.

Some African American professionals felt that they were at an unfair disadvantage because they were denied the same information and training their White counterparts received. Their struggle to succeed was made more difficult without the information and training. They were expected to perform the same jobs at the same level as their White counterparts but were not given the same training and information to perform the job. Under these conditions, the end product would undoubtedly be different. Therefore, people who looked only at the end product would be likely to consider the performance of these African Americans inferior to that of their White counterparts who had been better equipped with both skills and information.

● ● ● ● ● ● ● ● ● ● ● ●
CONSTANTLY PROVING THEMSELVES

In addition to not always having the same information, some African American employees observed that they did not receive equitable treatment in comparison with their White counterparts. Most felt they always had to work harder than and perform better than their White counterparts in order to maintain their positions. This, they assured me, was not because they lacked the ability or the confidence to do the job, but rather that their jobs were often made more difficult due to inequitable treatment within the corporation. They perceived that they were more highly scrutinized and subjected to double standards, were not respected for their abilities and contributions, and were not promoted in the same ways as their counterparts.

African Americans reported that they were often given heavier workloads than their White counterparts and experienced enormous pressure associated with constantly having to prove themselves. Perceiving that the odds were stacked against them in almost every conceivable way, these African American managers and professionals felt a great deal of pressure to perform despite the odds. Some felt that obstacles were intentionally placed in their way in order for them to prove themselves.

This burden of having to prove themselves over and over again began to wear on some of them. Carlos, a project manager in the pharmaceutical industry, explained that as a new project manager he was given a much heavier workload than more experienced project managers and had to prove himself.

> The fact of the matter is that I was always given more to do. It was always like, we are going to load you up and you've got to prove [yourself]—and even after you prove you can do it, they just keep loading you up.

Some African Americans felt that no matter how well they performed or how much they accomplished, they were never viewed as being good enough and never received the respect they felt they were due

in the workplace. This was a source of frustration and tension for some of the African American professionals. Al, who worked his way up through General Foods, Mars, and Campbell's Corporation to the position of vice president, stated:

> No matter how good you were at something, the tension that is there on the basis of the person not giving you respect, not respecting what you have done in the sense of acknowledging it . . . That's this tension that I'm talking about-that we're held to a different standard. Even when you are "kick-ass," it's almost like, so what?

African American managers also suffered the indignation of not having their position and authority acknowledged as White coworkers would bypass them in the organizational hierarchy by addressing White subordinates of the African American managers rather than communicating with the African American manager.

● ● ● ● ● ● ● ● ● ● ● ● ● ● ● ● ● ● ●
BEING PASSED OVER

Many African Americans perceived that their advancement was restricted by the existence of a glass ceiling, reporting that there was a noticeable lack of advancement of African Americans within most organizations. Bob described a situation in his organization in which African Americans were consistently among the top performers, but still failed to see this performance translate into promotions:

> They had a tradition that was continued, opening up every national meeting by mentioning all the various promotions that had taken place in the previous year. I found that it really was great because it said to everyone that, "There's opportunity here, with all the

moves that we've had in the last year, since the last time we met." And so, they did that but they also had a ceremony where they gave out awards to the top state manager within each division or region. And, out of the five or six or seven regions that they had—because of the different configurations in different companies—that out of the five, six, or seven, maybe three or four of them were Black who were awarded whatever the prize was for being outstanding state manager. And yet, when you named people who were promoted, none of them were Black.

In situations where one would reasonably assume that performing well and being recognized and even rewarded for that performance would lead to promotion, African Americans were still being denied promotions they believed they deserved. There seemed to be no logical explanations other than that they were denied promotion on the basis of their race. Some African Americans felt that no matter how well they performed in corporate America, they could still be denied promotional opportunities. Bob described the thinking of some of his superiors as "rigid," leading them to refuse to accept African Americans in certain roles.

The guy who had the division in Chicago . . . I now think did not want me out there. And, I do believe part of it was race. I don't mean it to say that he was anti-Black, because I don't believe that was really the reason. I just think he was one of those guys that had rigid thoughts and ideas about the place of Black people. And, he just could not see a Black person in that role, because when you walked in to deal with your wholesalers, as the boss and in this case the assis-

tant; he just couldn't see—he had just never seen something like this before and I don't think his mind could expand to the point where he could see a Black person in that role.

Despite the exemplary records of performance and high achievement of African Americans, some people just could not conceive of them in certain positions and seemingly denied them promotions, not based on the abilities the individuals demonstrated, but based on the stereotypes and limiting perceptions they held about African Americans.

Even in situations where the African Americans were better educated and more qualified for the job or had specific skills that made them more suitable for a particular position, they were passed over in favor of other applicants. Carlos, who had a B.S. degree in biology and chemistry, an M.S. in chemistry, an M.B.A., and ten years of experience, expressed his frustration when the research administration position within his corporation for which he applied was given to a White woman who had a BS degree and about three years of experience. He was angry that they had chosen a less-educated, less-experienced person, but he was even more angry that they had not even given him the courtesy of interviewing him for the position. Believing that he had been discriminated against, Carlos filed a claim with EEOC. He was told that he had a good case but that it would be difficult to prove, and the best they could do was to send a letter to personnel informing them that a claim had been filed and that they would be monitored for discriminatory practices.

About a year later, when he applied for a position as a project manager within the corporation, he was at least interviewed for the position, but he sensed that he was not being seriously considered. As a result, he made an appointment to have lunch with the senior vice president over that department. Over lunch, Carlos explained his concerns about the interview and was told point blank that he was considered a troublemaker, stemming from the earlier EEOC claim. Carlos explained that he had only fought for what he thought was right and that if that made him a troublemaker, he conceded, then he was indeed a troublemaker. After an exchange of words with the vice president and standing up for himself, Carlos was offered the position of project manager. A few years later, the company laid off over 2000 people. Despite the fact that one of the products he submitted to the firm made over $100 million a year, he was one of the first to be laid off. He perceived that the layoff provided an opportunity for his superiors to get rid of him in such a way that he could not claim that it was due to discrimination.

After working four years in project management at another firm where his supervisor resented the fact that Carlos was more highly educated and experienced than he, Carlos decided to leave that situation and went to work as an associate director for SmithKline and Beecham and eventually worked his way up to senior director. At the time he was hired as an associate director, he noted that a White woman whom he had trained at Hoffman La Roche—who was not as highly educated and had no experience in project management—was also hired, as a director. When a layoff came, Carlos was among the people laid off, but the White female director was not.

ADAPTING TO THE CORPORATE ENVIRONMENT

While perceiving constraints on their abilities to perform their jobs, constantly having to prove themselves, and being passed over for promotions were difficult, African

American professionals also felt they were expected to assimilate or blend into the corporate environment. They perceived that blending into the corporate environment included learning the environment and adjusting enough to be at least marginally acceptable in corporate America without losing their sense of their identity as African Americans or turning their backs on the African American community as a whole.

Learning the rules and decoding the symbols. In order to adapt to corporate America, African American managers and professionals first had to learn what was acceptable. They were usually the only one or one of very few African Americans in managerial and professional positions within their corporations and, in most cases, they did not have social connections within corporate America. Without having the social connections and specific knowledge about corporate America prior to gaining entrance, some African Americans felt ill prepared for what they faced as far as adjusting to corporate America.

> Initially, it was a shock, a culture shock, not being in the business sector, I didn't know what to expect.
>
> Nick

Some of the adjustments were as simple as adhering to certain dress codes and standards. Others involved changing their speech, mannerisms—their whole way of life to "fit in" in corporate America. One corporate executive described his early years in corporate America and his realization of the importance of how you are perceived:

> I showed up at General Foods, I made a big point, and this was the '70s, I made a big point that I wanted to be able to wear my jumpsuits and my beads. I used to have a big' fro then. And the guy who was my mentor said, "Yeah,

you can wear all that stuff, yes."
And I did. And I kicked butt the
way I told you, but I was seen as
this "super hip dude" who had
done all this stuff, but in year two
this guy said, "Now, if you really
want to go any further, you gotta
take all that stuff off."

And I started to consider that,
"Hey, I want the top job, and I'm
now prepared." . . . I bought those
suits with the vests . . . and I went
and put my "uniform" on and I cut
my 'fro and I got the Allen
Edmonds wing tips and I did what I
had to do. So, I changed my uniform because it was about winning,
and it wasn't about, "I want to
wear . . ." I could still wear the
jumpsuit, but it wasn't about the
jumpsuit.

He went further to explain that African
Americans had to be conscious of their
mannerisms—that even the way a person
walked could be perceived in a way in which
it was not intended.

While we think walking down the
hall bopping and walking very
smooth is the way to be in control
of yourself, they saw that as weird,
goofing off—that we don't walk
with purpose.

Al learned that his style of dress, hair,
and mannerisms were important cues that
indicated to others within the organization
and that he was capable of functioning
within a certain organizational role. Certainly, he had shown that he was capable of
performing the work, but in order to move
up the corporate ladder it was also necessary
for him to demonstrate that he could wear
the corporate "uniform" and act within the
corporate role. On the surface these adjustments may seen relatively minor, but when

you consider that this generation of African
Americans was faced with deciphering these
cues as well as constantly being conscious of
their actions and how they might be perceived, the task was more formidable. Not
only were they being scrutinized for their
work-related performance, but also for their
appearance, speech, and mannerisms—they
felt as if they were constantly being viewed
under a microscope. This was a very stressful
situation, which added to the pressure they
felt within corporate America.

Dealing with isolation. Another major
drawback of being one of very few African
Americans in corporate America was a
feeling of isolation and loneliness that some
African American professionals expressed.

In mid-town Manhattan where I
worked, it was possible to move
around during the day and not see
another single Black person. Which
means, there were no Black secretaries and clerks. Maybe, in the
evening, you might see, when the
cleaning staff came on, maybe the
women might be African American
but, for the most part, you could go
from day-to-day and see almost no
one. And when you went out to
lunch it was the same thing. More
than likely you would be the only
Black person in the restaurant. So,
that was the atmosphere. It was
very, very unfortunate.

Bob

At that time, the company had, I
would say, 36,000 employees—
there was one Black vice president
and two senior directors, I was one
of the directors in the company . . .

I didn't like it, because, you
know, you meet with all these
people—assistant vice presidents,
vice presidents—and I look at them

and I'd say to myself, "I know Black people just as smart as them." You start asking yourself, "Why aren't they here?" You see them out there, and you know them, and you keep asking yourself why they're not there. The answer comes pretty quickly—they aren't there because they don't want them there. It was lonely.

Carlos

Being the only one or one of a few African Americans in the workplace was a lonely experience, in part due to the lack of acceptance and the lack of social and informal contact with coworkers, which might have led to better information, mentor relationships, and potentially career-enhancing networking opportunities.

Social isolation, lack of access to the informal networks, and social connections left some African American professionals out of the organizational information flow and impacted their opportunity to build supportive work relationships. Surprisingly, however, some African American professionals revealed that their lack of social contact with their White coworkers was, to some extent, due to their own conscious and intentional actions. In some cases, they simply had no desire to interact with White coworkers outside of the workplace. The choice to limit social interaction with their coworkers seemed to stem from their own personal preferences—they chose to interact socially with people among whom they felt more comfortable. In some cases, this choice almost seemed to be a form of resistance or defiance in the sense that they did not have a choice concerning their interactions with White coworkers in the work setting, but could control whom they socialized with on their own time. Although they were fully aware that they were "missing out" on the social connections that might have helped advance their careers, they

often chose not to interact with their coworkers during off-hours including some social gatherings sponsored by their employers.

There were a couple of times that they had a picnic on the premises, where they had a cookout Friday night, and Saturday they had an all-day picnic-type thing. And what I would do in cases like that, I may show my face Friday night, but then on Saturday I wouldn't go because I just . . . it wasn't that I wasn't comfortable . . . I just chose not to participate.

John

John perceived the social contact simply as something that he didn't want to do. In contrast, Carlos had stronger feelings and viewed social contact as something that he didn't feel he should have to do. He expressed his indignation at the fact that in corporate America he was not evaluated and appropriately rewarded based on his demonstrated skills, abilities, and knowledge, but on more subjective criteria of whom he had ingratiated himself to.

I knew I was supposed to do it— not that I was supposed to do it— but I knew that other people in the department did it and I knew why they were doing it. Because they were getting these contacts, they were making these connections; they would go to all those different parties and so forth . . . Yes, it probably held me back because I didn't and I knew it would, but it was my choice not to. Yes, I remember coming out of the laboratory as a research scientist, everything that I did as a research scientist was based on the result of my research, not on whether or not I kissed somebody's behind. . . . That was a conscious choice and basically I just figured that they really don't like me that much anyway and I'm not going to kowtow to any of them, because I always had the feeling that even if I did it wouldn't matter. Because of who I was and the color I was, I felt that if I did the same thing I wouldn't get the same results. So why do it?

Similarly, Al noted that initially he avoided social contact with coworkers, but worked hard to compensate for the benefits he was missing out on. As he rose in the organization, however, he found it almost impossible to avoid social contact.

> You had to understand their culture. I did not feel comfortable in thinking that I had to assimilate, because I chose not to. My life outside the office was with "my folks," my crew, and I agonized over the learning and the communication that took place in their social situations. I didn't even eat lunch with them. So, I was conscious even during that period of time that if I'm not sitting with them, if I'm not drinking with them, if I'm not hanging with them, I'm not going to get the benefits of those things. So, what happened to compensate? I busted my ass, excuse my profanity, but that's how it went . . . I busted my ass.
>
> It was a conscious trade-off. And as I got older and in more direct contact in the management roles— you wind up not having the choice because then the positions and privileges that come with the rank put you into the dinners, puts you into the "Let's go see the Yankees in the World Series," "Let's go to

the golf course," and let's do these things. And you suddenly are thrust into that environment and if you choose not to participate, you don't deal. I came to the realization that the decision of who got the senior jobs had to do with who was comfortable with you.

The reality of the how business was conducted sank in and Al recognized that socializing with his White colleagues outside of work was necessary in order to advance in the corporate world, but it did not detract from his "Blackness" or change him in any way. The concern with their racial identity contributed to yet another tension.

Leading two lives. The issue of their "Blackness" or their racial identity was prominent for many African American professionals. Some expressed it in terms of maintaining connection with other African Americans and keeping their work relationships separate from personal relationships:

> I kept all my Black friends there. Even though I had lunch with the vice presidents, after work we'd go out, have a drink or something, have a beer. It would always be with the Black people, the people that I knew. You see, I'd talk to these other people—the assistant vice presidents—but they were never my friends. I never once brought any of them home. When I left work, I wanted to be with my friends. They used to invite me to their houses and receptions or whatever and basically 95 percent of the time I would make an excuse and wouldn't go, because I didn't want to deal with them after work. I felt, okay, you pay me well and I come to work, but when I leave I

don't want to see you. That's another thing that went against me. When you get into a position like that, they actually expected you to show up at all these functions. If they invite you to dinner at their house, they expected you to show up. And I'm very adamant about things like that, when I left, I wanted to be with my wife and my own friends. Basically what I tried to do was leave—it was like having two lives. I would just leave that life, and go to my own life and the next morning I'd go back to that life.

Carlos

Carlos alluded to trying to maintain the difficult balance between life in the corporate world, which required him to act and interact with people in a different way, and his personal life as "like having two lives." One marked difference between the two lives was in the types of people with whom he interacted; others were in the mannerisms and ways of interacting with people, which required African Americans to, in essence, set aside a part of themselves for the sake of succeeding in corporate America. However, on his own time he wanted to interact with people in a manner in which he felt more comfortable.

Nick expressed a different aspect of the feeling of leading two lives. He was particularly annoyed at the treatment he received outside the office.

As soon as you step outside of this office, you're still a Black man. I don't care if you're making a million dollars a year or 15 dollars a day, when you step outside, nobody can differentiate between me and the person up on the corporate ladder.

Nick pointed out that regardless of his status within the corporate world, society as a whole still held a very narrow and somewhat negative view of African Americans. Even if he could somehow gain the respect and fair treatment he felt he deserved within the corporate world, he still had to face the disrespect and indignities of society outside the corporation.

Dealing with threats, fear, and hostility in the workplace. Even in the corporation where they hoped for a chance to prove themselves, African American professionals still had to deal with the threats, fear, and hostility that were common in society. Some African American professionals expressed tension in the workplace in mild terms as an underlying influence that permeated daily life by simply stating that "race was always an issue" or that they never felt fully accepted by their coworkers. Others illustrated threats, fear, and hostility more graphically in their depiction of what day-to-day interactions were like and the extreme tension they felt.

Well, remember I said that I grew up in the projects, I grew up where I carried a knife; I carried a six-inch blade, until 1979. That's four years into General Foods [four years after he received his M.B.A. from Harvard and started working for General Foods]. So, in my first working environment, I still approached the work environment as a very, very distrustful one. At any moment, you'd have that much tension that while you're negotiating and navigating this thing, at any moment "the shit is on" and I was not about to be caught unable to defend myself. So, what I'm really dealing with, and expressing this to you, is—I'm talking about having a sense of being on guard all that time.

Al

For Al, the threats and fears in corporate America were just as real and just as dangerous as the ones he faced growing up in the inner city. Initially, he equated the threats, fear, and hostility to physical danger—he did not want "to be caught unable to defend" himself. He later realized that it "wasn't about the blade"—the attacks he faced in corporate America were not physical, but in a sense they were equally painful. Dealing with the threats, fear, and hostility, for him, meant constantly being on guard, always expecting some kind of confrontation.

In some respects, the experience of distance was shown in subtle, everyday events. For Carlos, it was the fear that, no matter how much he had done for the company and how much profit had resulted from his efforts, he would be the first to get laid off in times of economic downturn. Despite all of his accomplishments, he was never able to find a sense of security within corporate America. For Nick, it was demeaning things, like his colleagues being careful not to use the same bathroom stall after he did—as if that would contaminate them. Their actions made him feel like he was less than human or like he had some kind of communicable disease. For Thomas, it was having coworkers recheck his work because they did not trust his ability to perform the work to their standards or not being acknowledge by colleagues as the person in charge.

Responses

African American professionals recognized that these matters were parts of the work environment that they did not have control over. They were on guard for these dangers, but refused to let these obstacles impede their achievement and, instead, focused on succeeding despite the odds.

Some African American professionals grew weary of having to deal with corporate America, constantly being on guard, and overcoming the obstacles. After being overlooked, passed over, and laid off in corporate America, Carlos decided to go into business for himself. Similarly, Al decided to start his own business to realize his goal of becoming CEO. Not that either of them gave up on business or doubted their ability to succeed in business, but they did grow tired of the corporate games and the rules that were usually stacked against them.

II-16: LINK.COM
A Silicon Valley Legend

Joanne Martin and Debra Meyerson

Link.Com is a supplier of high performance computer products—part of an industry that has expanded dramatically in the last decade. The company's hardware and software products provide an essential function in an era of personal computers.

Professor Joanne Martin and Visiting Professor Debra Meyerson, of the Graduate School of Business, Stanford University, prepared this case as the basis for class discussion rather than to illustrate either effective or ineffective handling of an administrative situation. The organizational name, the people involved, and some details of the case have been disguised to protect anonymity and for teaching purposes. The preparers thank the individuals who have contributed from their experience to build this case. The case was made possible by the generous support of the BankAmerica Foundation. Copyright © 1996 by the Board of Trustees of the Leland Stanford Junior University. All rights reserved. Used with permission from the Stanford University Graduate School of Business.

Within this lucrative market, the firm's triumphs have been legendary, even in Silicon Valley, California, where skyrocketing entrepreneurial success stories are not rare. In 1989, its net income was $4,000 million on sales of $27,000 million. By 1993, the net income was $172,000 million on sales of $650,000 million. And by 1995, the net income was $421,000 million on sales of $1,979,000,000.

These achievements were reflected in the firm's stock price. After its Initial Public Offering in 1990, the stock's value increased 75-fold and by 1995 it had split four times. David Unsworth, the Chairman of the Board when the company went public, was the renowned venture capitalist responsible for Link.Com's first and only round of outside financing. He described the firm's record in these terms: "Nothing compares to this. Nothing." All Link.Com employees have stock options and by now, hundreds have become millionaires and, in a few cases, multi-millionaires. That includes some of the protagonists in the Link.Com series of cases.

Figure 2-1 shows an organizational chart for the Link.Com top management team in 1989, the year that Natalie Kramer joined the company as Vice President of Marketing and a Corporate officer. Figure 2-2 is a similar chart for 1993, the year Natalie left the company. Figure 2-3 shows the top management team two years later, with entries for the other top executives profiled in the Link.Com case series (case protagonists who were not top executives are not included in these exhibits). Table 2-1 shows the numbers of employees, and the percentages of women, at various levels of the hierarchy in 1989, 1993, and 1995. In 1989, women were scarce throughout the top ranks of the company, as is typical of the industry. Before Natalie joined Link.Com, for example, there were only two employees, no women, in Marketing and no women in Sales. At that time, at least one Vice President took pride in the fact that there were no women in his department—"no skirts." Although the company had a woman on the founding team, none of the corporate officers between 1989 and 1993 hired high ranking women as direct reports—except Jim Nelson, the President and C.E.O., who hired Natalie Kramer, and Natalie herself, who hired several women. But that is getting ahead of the story.

• • • • • • • • • • • • • • • • • • •

NATALIE KRAMER'S STORY

When Jim Nelson moved from being President and C.E.O. to Chairman of the Board of Link.Com, his wife, Susan, organized a "repotting" party. Jim gave a speech and had plaques made for some of the original corporate officers. including me. My plaque was inscribed with letters that said, "Natalie Kramer, Building Gender Awareness at Link.Com, 1989–1993." I felt some ambivalence about this plaque. On the one hand I had worked hard to be the best I could be in my job. I wanted to be recognized for my professional contributions to the success of the company. I believed that Nelson's intent was to acknowledge the impact I had on his own development and his awareness of gender issues in the workplace. He thought he was recognizing me for something that was important to me, and it was. I believed it was also important to him. Still, I would rather have had him say. "Natalie, she was a great marketer."

Natalie was hired in 1989 as Vice President of Marketing, employee #114 at

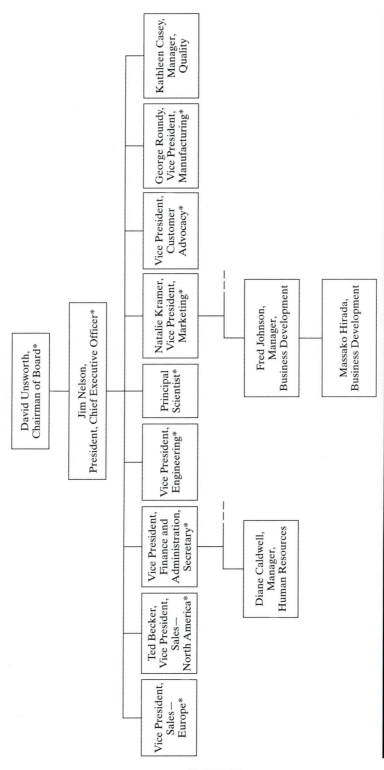

FIGURE 2-1 LINK.COM Top Executive Organizational Chart—September, 1989[a]

[a]An * indicates a Corporate Officer; Dashed lines indicate other reporting relationships not included on this chart.

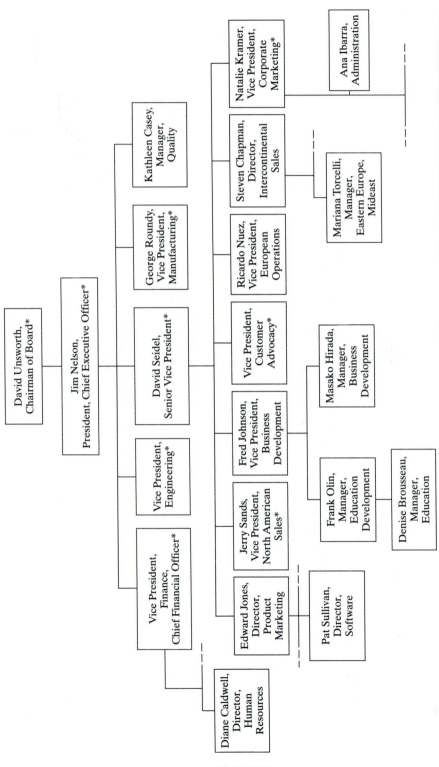

FIGURE 2-2   LINK.COM Top Executive Organizational Chart — September, 1993[a]

[a] An * indicates a Corporate Officer; Dashed lines indicate other reporting relationships not included on this chart.

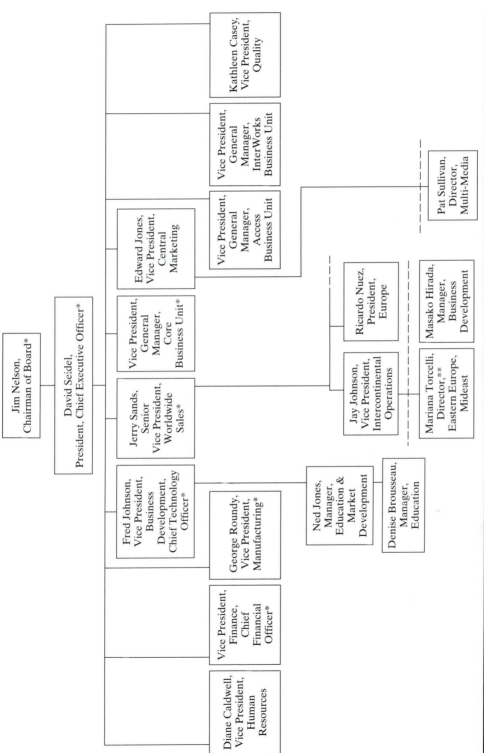

FIGURE 2-3 LINK.COM Top Executive Organizational Chart—September, 1995[a]

[a] An * indicates a Corporate Officer; Dashed lines indicate other reporting relationships not included on this chart.

** Mariana was promoted to Director in November, 1995.

Note: Ana Ibarra does not appear on this chart, but was employed at LINK.COM.

TABLE 2-1 Women Managers at LINK.COM: Domestic Employees

Positions	September 1989		September 1993		September 1995	
	# Women	% Women	# Women	% Women	# Women	% Women
Board Members	0	0	0	0	1	14
Corporate Officers	2	22	1	11	0	0
Senior or Executive Vice Presidents	n/a	n/a	0	0	0	0
Non-Officer Vice Presidents	0	0	0	0	2	8
General Managers	n/a	n/a	n/a	n/a	0	0
Directors	1	20	8	22	14	15
Managers	4	19	43	25	90	21
Total Employees	36	29	421	27	1123	28

	9/88 – 9/89	9/92 – 9/93	9/94 – 9/95
Turnover Rate: Men	4.80%	3.00%	5.17%
Turnover Rate: Women	1.60%	1.24%	2.37%

Note: n/a = position did not exist

Link.Com. She was well qualified for the position. She had earned an MBA from Stanford and had gone on to hold Vice President and corporate officer-level positions at two other highly successful companies in the computer industry. She was not hired for any gender-related reasons and she was not expected to incorporate such concerns into her responsibilities:

> It was not in my job description to be a change agent on any issue other than the fundamental economics of running a business and making the company successful. I did not come to the company with an agenda about being a change agent for women. I came to the company with an agenda about being a marketing person with a job to do.

AN INAUSPICIOUS START

On her first day on the job at Link.Com Natalie arrived a little after nine A.M. Jim Nelson, her boss, greeted her by saying, "What have we here—the Mommy Track?" Natalie turned to Jim's secretary and said, "How do you say 'Go to hell' to your new boss?" Natalie immediately saw, from Jim's reaction, that this was hardly an auspicious start, and she made a conscious effort to seek a better fit between her behavior and Jim's preferences:

> I could see I had made him uncomfortable. When I said "Go to hell" it was clear he didn't like women using that kind of language. He didn't like aggressiveness in women—"pushy broads." I changed my language. I did not swear or use foul language at Link.Com. And I rarely expressed anger to him, although others did. Fortunately, there were a lot of

things about me that were compatible with him. We shared similar values—work, education, contributing to community, business ethics. And although I was the mother of a young child (later two children), I worked full-time, long hours, and traveled for the company.

PAY EQUITY PROBLEMS

Soon after she arrived, Natalie received a department budget prepared in advance of her coming by her predecessor, who had been fired. In it she saw that her predecessor's salary was 6% higher than hers. Her first reaction was rapid and emotional, but she took her time confronting the problem:

> Here was a guy who had been fired. I was replacing him. I had more industry knowledge, more relevant business and functional experience, and better educational credentials. And, he had made more money than I was making. So I had to think, "This is not right. What should I do about this?" Within weeks I talked to Jim Nelson about it. Eventually, in the course of the discussion, Jim said, "Well, maybe I could have paid you more." But he was not going to do anything about it right away; he wanted to think about it. He never got back to me and I did not pursue it because I didn't want to cause trouble. I could see he felt uncomfortable. I had an empathetic response. I imagined the scenario: He would have had to go back to the Board of Directors and say, "We need to pay her more money." This would probably be difficult and embarrassing for him.

Natalie took away from this experience the conviction that she should watch out for others who might face similar problems:

> I tried to be vigilant about pay equity. I tried to find the best economics for people who worked for me, especially where I thought there might be potential injustice. I tried to make sure people got what they deserved. For example, I noticed in our technical documentation department that we had a male manager and a female manager; the male manager was making more money. She was hired more recently, she was younger, but nonetheless, she had the same job as the man. I brought it to the attention of the director and he took care of it. I'd be just as vigilant with a male manager's salary, but other people would notice that kind of problem. Other people might not be attuned to picking up salary inequity for a woman, so I was watchful.

THE DANGERS OF BECOMING A SINGLE-ISSUE PERSON

Other gender-related problems surfaced in seemingly minor ways as part of the normal flow of communication in an organizational culture defined by men. Natalie thought these issues were important, although others disagreed or did not understand some of the strength of her reaction. For example:

> An executive staff meeting was starting off with casual conversation and informal banter. Jim Nelson came in and said, "Natalie, you and your women (political) candidates . . ." I felt I was becoming a caricature. What do you mean "my women candidates." Like I was responsible for or associated with all women political candidates.

On a different occasion, one of the Executive staff members used the expression: "We will extra 'rape and pillage' the competition." A Vice President who worked for him started using the same expression—and English was not his native language. At that point, Natalie asked people not to use the expression:

> It evokes images of arbitrary violence against women. There are other ways to express competitive ambition in the marketplace. I found rape offensive in this context.

Natalie had a good sense of humor and was inclined to agree that sometimes she went too far in her remarks:

> There is a risk run by people who are trying to influence others. You can become a single-issue person or a caricature of the cause. People don't think of you as the marketing person or the sales person. They think of you as the teacher who is always correcting them and telling them how to behave. Who wants to be around a person like that? There certainly were times when I let things pass but, in general, I did speak up. I would make an issue of things that I thought were inappropriate or unjust. I think that cost me. I paid a price for being an internal advocate for women in the company.

MARGINALITY AND AUTHENTICITY

Natalie did not see these subtle or not so subtle problems as intentional attempts to discriminate:

> Theoretically, we all worked in an "equal opportunity employment" situation. We were trying to obey the

law. But a lot of the barriers that women and minorities face are cultural. It is a question of norms, acceptance, and marginality—whether you fit in with the dominant culture and the people who work there or not. This is true especially at the executive staff level, where the tendency is toward conformity. Senior executives prefer to surround themselves with people they are comfortable with and can trust, whether that trust is based on personal loyalty, commonalty of values and experience, or career dependence.

Link.Com had a clearly defined dominant culture. It was an environment where people felt comfortable expressing some emotions—anger, for example. They raised their voices when they disagreed or were upset and they engaged, regularly and with enthusiasm, in corporate intrigues. Employees and the business press described this rough and tumble atmosphere with strong words. The Executive Committee, for example, included one person who was described as "power-focused, a control freak, with a very strong temper; a disturbed person." Another employee, labeled by other employees simply as "difficult," was described as "hating" some of the other Executive Committee members, not being supportive of many of the others, and generally having "a tremendous amount of anger." Natalie saw this atmosphere as pathological. She characterized the executive staff, in these early days of the company's history, as having an "intense disequilibrium. It was not a team. It was the Link.Com dysfunctional family."

Perhaps in recognition of some of these problems, Jim Nelson brought in Marvin Greenberg, an industrial psychologist who worked with the executive staff, administered a battery of tests, and interviewed executive staff candidates and eventually many of the company's new senior hires. Natalie called Marvin the "company shrink," because she felt the company needed a therapist; people would "Yell at each other in the halls" and behave in ways she considered crazy:

> I was not really a good fit with the organization in many respects. The culture was, in its early days, kind of pathological and in its later days, very "old boy." So, the dominant culture was one in which I was marginal. There were people in the organization who were threatened by me. I challenged behavior and tried to set an alternative example.

Natalie was known as a highly creative marketing executive. She attributed some of her success in this regard to her inability to fit easily within the culture:

> Sometimes if you are marginalized, or an outsider, or a dual insider/outsider, you have a borderline identity that permits you to think outside the usual paradigms and make creative contributions. I really liked and understood our customers. I understood how to use symbols to communicate with them. Maybe what I was able to do in marketing, and in positioning the company was seen as creative because I didn't share the usual paradigms. I wasn't an engineer. I wasn't a man. I was drawn to and identified with our customers partly because I was an iconoclast like them.

Some people counseled Natalie, encouraging her to fit in with the dominant culture. For example, Marvin, the industrial psychologist, advised Natalie to change her behavior:

> Marvin told me that as an open, participative, and collaborative

person, it would be hard for me to survive at the company. In this environment, these characteristics would be perceived as weakness and put me at a disadvantage. They were not qualities valued by this culture. So, very early in my career at Link.Com, I was directly confronted with a problem. I had come to believe that one has to be authentic to be an effective manager. It takes too much energy to pretend to be someone other than who you are. Now here was somebody advising me to be less open, less participative, less cooperative—to be not the way I am. It was a real dilemma for me. I had enemies at the company and I was hurt in this environment, but I did stick to being myself.

Natalie thought Marvin, at this stage, was trying to counsel her in a helpful way. Later on, however, another woman manager told Natalie that Marvin had warned her, "Natalie is too confrontational," implying she would not be an appropriate role model. Natalie was ambivalent about this criticism. On one hand, she knew she was a potential role model:

Some people saw me as a leader. I was visible because I was (after the female founder left) the most senior woman in the company and the only woman officer. So, there were reasons why people throughout the organization, especially women, might have modeled certain aspects of my behavior and looked to me for leadership.

On the other hand, she understood why her outspoken ways and marginal status sometimes made her a less than desirable role model for some of her co-workers:

I tried to treat people with respect (unlike others). I didn't throw

tantrums. I didn't yell and scream. I didn't stab people in the back, capitalize on their mistakes, or engage in turf wars or political maneuvering. This was not the way I was going to build a power base at the company. The behavior I was modeling was not behavior that my male colleagues on the executive staff were going to emulate.

THE INVISIBLE JOB

Natalie invested a lot of time being accessible to women throughout the company who came to her for support and counsel:

It seemed like almost every woman manager in the whole company came to see me at one point or another for feedback and advice about her career. They would come if they had a specific issue with their boss or colleague or if they wanted some general advice or just someone to listen. They would say "I didn't have anywhere else to go." I gave my time and cared about the outcomes.

Occasionally men in the company would seek out Natalie for her input on a "woman's issue." She was the resident expert because she was one of so few women managers. This aspect of Natalie's work is not uncommon for women or minorities. It has been called the shadow job or the invisible job—because those who do not do it regularly, do not see the time and energy it takes, have not experienced the negative effects of refusing to do it, and do not generally take it into account when performance is being evaluated.

SUBTLE BARRIERS

The invisible job, insofar as it was a handicap with respect to Natalie's other responsibilities, presented a relatively subtle barrier to her advancement, albeit one that was easy to describe. Other subtle barriers were more difficult to articulate, often because they were communicated with silences and omissions, rather than overt acts. Natalie found it useful to describe these kinds of problems with a "half empty, half full" metaphor used by one of her MBA classmates who was an investment banker:

> She described how something would happen—maybe she wouldn't get a promotion—and she would think, "I must not have had this quality" or "I hadn't done this or that" She was always saying, "What am I lacking?" It wasn't until 15 years later that she realized, "Wait a minute. Why is my glass half empty and not half full?"

As Natalie thought about it, she understood that this was part of her experience too. The half full, half empty metaphor captured the subjective nature of perceptions that influenced performance evaluations. For example, she thought about the decision to hire a young man as Vice President—a decision she had supported:

> He was young, smart, focused, ambitious, and immature. He had poor people skills and needed a lot of attention. He could be a bit too quick "on the draw" and had made some bad judgment calls. However, his glass was half full; his boss said. "He has great potential. He lacks some sensitivity to organizational needs and to people. Natalie, you could help him develop these skills." All managers have both strengths and weaknesses. Everyone makes mistakes. In this case, the young Vice President had a mentor and boss who shaped the perception that his glass was half

full. In my case, there must have been times when Jim Nelson supported me, in a similar fashion, in private. But I don't recall any conversation about my potential.

COPING WITH ISOLATION

Natalie spent time giving advice to other women, but she had no female colleagues at her level in the corporation to talk to about career issues. She missed having a colleague, male or female, to whom she could confide on a regular basis:

> I never felt that I could ask for help because I had been so influenced by the early days of the company—you didn't want to appear weak. And Marvin (the industrial psychologist) had advised me, "Don't be open, don't be yourself, don't ask for help." I didn't feel that I had someone who was truly interested in my development and my career, an advocate or a mentor. It was lonely and difficult.

When she stopped to think about her isolation, Natalie realized that her most important confidante had been her administrative assistant, Ana Ibarra:

> Ana really helped me because she listened and was supportive. She could see a lot of what I was experiencing and I could talk to her. I could be totally honest because I trusted her. She was respected by the other Executive Administrative Assistants. She would learn things and share information with me.

Natalie sought information from her MBA classmates, wondering how they coped with similar problems of isolation. She recalled how she had listened to Diane Mitchell, who was then Chief Financial Officer at a large corporation. Diane had found out that the other corporate executives at her rank were being awarded additional stock option grants. After "peeling herself off the ceiling," Diane called up her management coach, an outside expert she had been working with for years. He knew her general situation and personal history. He listened carefully and together they worked out a plan. The next morning Diane spoke to the C.E.O. of the corporation, calmly and reasonably, and said. "I think there has been a mistake in my compensation that you probably want to correct at the next board meeting." He did just that. Natalie listened to such stories with a bit of envy:

> I didn't have a resource like that. It's one of my regrets because I really could have benefited from having a management coach— someone from outside Link.Com who could advise and support me.

Natalie partially compensated for her isolation by seeking out professional women outside the company:

> While I was still with Link.Com, I became a trustee at a woman's liberal arts college. I was interested in women's education. The Board members were lawyers, professors, doctors—all accomplished women in their respective fields. It was a sustaining experience to work with them. It provided a balance, an alternative to the environment at Link.Com, where I felt isolated and lonely.

In her search for potential confidantes coping with similar issues at work, Natalie attended a small dinner of MBA women who had graduated between 1975 and 1978, the first relatively large cohort of women at the university she attended:

> There were 15 of us sitting around the table. I realized that I was the only woman there who had a job in a company. The others had left corporations to work on their own as consultants, or in the non-profit sector, or as entrepreneurs. Each had a story. Some of the women had husbands who weren't up to the task of a dual career marriage, so they couldn't rely on their partners the way one needs to with a demanding career. One had an alcoholic husband and left him. Another had been fired because she got pregnant. Someone else had been blatantly discriminated against and had quit her job. Another had hit the glass ceiling. There was one woman who had a career at a large corporation. She had been laid off and was now looking for another job. And there was one who was a born entrepreneur. But I was the only one who had a career in a company and had worked up the usual ladder to a high ranking executive position. I wondered, "How did this happen? What happened to all these competent and educated women who chose not to pursue careers in corporations?" I had assumed that more and more women would enter and transform companies. At this dinner I looked around and said. "The women are not there." I felt a real sadness.

THE NUMBERS GAME

Natalie tried to ignore her loneliness and isolation, throwing herself into her work and home life. The company was growing very rapidly, Marketing was expanding, and they needed to hire people. Unlike most of her colleagues, Natalie was hiring women. Natalie felt she had not deliberately set out to increase the numbers of women at the company, but jobs were a resource she could control, and she had thought about the issue for some time:

> I didn't set out to hire a cadre of women to change Link.Com as a company. Rather, I was someone who was open to hiring women. People will naturally gravitate toward hiring people like themselves if left to their own devices. I had read Rosabeth Moss Kanter's book (Men and Women of the Corporation) when it first came out and I was influenced by her main conclusion: that sheer numbers of women matter. The book had a conceptual impact on my thinking about organizational change and women. I recognized the value and importance of numbers—representatives—as a way of influencing an organization's culture. I had learned how culture includes, excludes, and defines many things and how it drives behavior. If there were more than one or two women on an executive staff, for example, their presence could influence behavior. One woman is not sufficient because she is too different from the norm.

Natalie started hiring women right away and, fairly soon, there were signs that once again she perhaps had gone too far. It was a delicate balancing act, trying to respond with authenticity when her fundamental beliefs were threatened, while simultaneously conforming enough to garner the support and respect she needed to do her job well:

> At one point, Jim Nelson asked me "Natalie, do you only hire women?" He was telling me I was out of line. It was later in the same conversation, I think, that he said. "You know, some men don't like reporting to women." I said, "That's their problem." I was surprised that people still held belief systems like this. It was another one of these times when I thought. "I'm becoming a little too single issue here."

Natalie contradicted herself regularly when she spoke of hiring women. Sometimes it appeared to be something she did without planning, simply because she was "left to her own devices." Other times, it appeared that increasing the sheer numbers of women hired was a key part of her deliberate strategy to change the dominant culture of the firm. Whether this strategy was deliberate or not, it was not seen by others as being central to the economic success of the firm.

> The company was one of the most phenomenal success stories that Silicon Valley had ever seen. Whether we treated women equally—or not—had absolutely nothing to do with the fundamental factors that make a company successful. These social issues were not even on the screen. It wasn't like the situation of the new mayor, who appointed an Asian man the head of the police force, and appointed an African American to be head fire-fighter. The mayor brought these minority

leaders into his administration because they represented significant constituencies who vote and have a say. It's different in the private sector where issues of diversity and social equity are not perceived as having anything to do with the company's financial success.

A QUESTION OF LONG-TERM IMPACT

Looking back on her years with the company, and her attempts to create culture and climate that valued women, Natalie gave herself mixed reviews.

> My influence as an advocate for social equity was dependent upon the power of my personality and my presence. Any legacy was the influence I may have had on other individuals. When there is systematic discrimination, single individuals cannot make systemic change. At best, individuals operate at the margin, affecting small incremental changes. Since I left the company, no women of executive rank have become officers. Two women were promoted to Vice President (Figure 2-3) but they were not in operating positions in the company. More women were promoted to Director. One woman was elected to the Board of Directors. The measurable results did not point to major structural or institutional change.

Moving from the structural level to the individual level, however, Natalie did see changes that she felt she could take partial credit for:

> I was able to help, in small ways, some other women's careers in the company. I think, in certain cases, that I influenced a few of them to help other women.

Natalie also felt that her efforts had influenced some men, most importantly the man who had hired her and had helped her throughout her career at Link.Com, Jim Nelson. They had often jointly prepared presentations for investors and users of the company's products. She worked for him in various capacities and continued to have a working relationship after she left the company and he moved on to become Chairman of the Board. Natalie took pride in having had some impact on Jim with regard to gender issues. She told one story that, she said:

> . . . capped his transformation and his education as a man who was more aware of gender issues. One time, after I left Link.Com, we had breakfast with some people from another organization which we were trying to influence, through philanthropic donations, to be more receptive to women. Jim concluded the meeting with a remark about their organization's "totally dismal record of hiring women." I felt embarrassed by what he said. It was confrontative about gender issues, and socially a bit inappropriate. He was behaving in a radical way. He reminded me of myself.

II-17: LINK.COM
Ana Ibarra's Story

Joanne Martin and Debra Meyerson

I've always had so much self-doubt. I never went to college. Being Mexican-American and having grown up the way I did, I've always tried not to make waves. Here in California, I have not experienced the kind of prejudice that I encountered in Texas where I was born and grew up. Whenever we went to the movies, because we were Mexican, we had to sit in the balcony or in the back of the theater. When I graduated from high school, I could type 100 words a minute, I could take shorthand at 120 words a minute, and I couldn't get a job. So I've always tried to be invisible and not to have high expectations.

When my son, Carl, finally graduated from college, he got a job and left home. Two months after he left, on my birthday, he called me at work and said "Mom, I left you a birthday present. When you go into my room, it's behind my bed—all wrapped up." I went into his room that night and I opened it up. It was a frame containing his college diploma. In the middle was a little picture of the two of us taken at my surprise 50th birthday four years ago. At the bottom of the frame was a letter giving me his diploma because, the letter said, we had both earned it and if it hadn't been for me, he would have never finished college. The letter went on to say, "Some people are star athletes, some make millions of dollars, and while you are none of the above, you are my role model in life. I hope one day I can be the kind of parent you were." I cannot tell you what that did for me. It was the most beautiful letter. I just felt, "I can do anything."

I'm very excited at this point in my life. Two years ago I thought if I never work again, I would be so happy. Now I want to see What I can do. I didn't have that feeling before. And it's amazing, I'm 54 years old and I'm starting a career, which is something I had never even thought of. A job to me was survival.

Professor Joanne Martin and Visiting Professor Debra Meyerson, of the Graduate School of Business, Stanford University, prepared this case as a basis for class discussion rather than to illustrate either or ineffective handling of an administrative situation. The organizational name, the people involved, and some details of the case have been disguised to protect anonymity and for teaching purposes. The preparers thank the individuals who contributed from their experience to build this case. The case was made possible by the generous support of the BankAmerica Foundation. Copyright © 1996 by the Graduate School of Business, Stanford University. All rights reserved. Used with permission from the Stanford University Graduate School of Business.

Before she joined Link.Com, Ana had been working as an Executive Assistant to a President (who was also C.E.O. and Chairman of the Board) of a small company. The firm had been having financial difficulties and had been laying people off for three years. In the last round of layoffs, Ana had lost her job. When she searched for a new position, she wanted a company with financial stability, so she would never have to go through the trauma of layoffs again. She also wanted to avoid a long commute. She went to the library, researched the financial history of several companies, and found a financially solid young company located, at that time, near her home. The company was Link.Com.

They had only one position open at that time—an Administrative Assistant reporting to a Director in the Marketing Department. When she went for her interview, a person in Human Resources looked at her resume, decided she was overqualified, and suggested that she interview with Natalie Kramer, the Vice President of Marketing and a Corporate Officer.

I had never worked for a woman before. All I'd heard about working for women was horrendous—how bad women are with women. But a Vice President is higher than a Director and it was closer to the position I had held before. I wanted at least to meet her, so I made an appointment with her that same afternoon. Natalie was very direct, very open, and very set in her ways. But, there was something about the two of us. In 45 minutes I knew I wanted to work for her and she knew she wanted to hire me. I walked out of there saying want "I want this job; I want this job." I was so jazzed. It wasn't really anything she had done because she had just said, "This is what I want." But for

me, if you give me the parameters of what you want, I can tell you whether I can work within those boundaries or not. She was so up front—nothing was hidden. I thought, "I can do this." She offered me the job and I accepted, based on the salary figure she had given me. It felt great.

When Human Resources called me back a few days later, they said, "I'm really sorry, but the salary that Natalie offered you, she can't offer you. This is what the salary is for this position." I thought about it, and I said, "I can't accept it." Then I called Natalie and I said, I can't do this. "Even at the figure she'd cited to me, I had taken a cut from what I earned before. Natalia said, "Let me see if there is anything I can do." She called me back about a week later and she asked me, "Are you still interested? I've talked to Human Resources and they can't revise the entry level salary for that position, according to their guidelines, but they will do something unheard of at Link.Com: a sign-on bonus for an Administrative Assistant." She said, "It's not the salary figure I gave you before, but I know that within a year, I will get you up to the figure I initially cited. At least this lets you know that we're really trying to do something about this." So then I accepted. True to her word, Natalie was marvelous and within a year, I had the raise she promised. But that's another story.

Ana worked hard, long hours for Natalie. For example, one time Maria, a manager from another department, came to Ana with a huge presentation she had prepared for Natalie. It was all "last minute" and the request arrived just as Ana was getting ready to go home.

> I just took it and said, "No problem. Just tell me when you want it." She said, "We really need it for tomorrow morning at ten o'clock." I canceled what I was going to do and I stayed and I got it ready. If it was for Natalie, that was all there was to it; she was going to have this presentation. Maria came to me later the following day. She said, "I wanted to tell you that I was very impressed with how you handled this. I know you were stressed. I know you were trying to leave, but you were totally professional. You didn't even blink. You performed so well under pressure, I wanted to thank you."

Issues of personal loyalty were crucial to Ana, and she felt strong loyalty to Natalie.

> Natalie called me in her office about six months before she left. She said that she was going to be leaving Link. Com on a certain date; she didn't want anyone else to know, but she wanted to tell me so I could start looking within the company for another position. I told her, "I won't look until you leave. When you make it official, then I'll start. If my staying here is meant to be, then something will happen and if it's not, I can always find a job because I'm a hard worker." That's how we left it.

When Natalie did announce she was leaving, Ana's situation changed rapidly. Three of Natalie's direct reports came to her and asked if they could approach Ana about a position. And David Seidel went to Ana and said, "I don't want you to worry or be uncomfortable. You will have a job here with Link.Com. We will be bringing some other executives in here and you could report to one of them."

Within a few weeks, Ana had seven job offers. Six of them were Administrative Assistant positions. But what really surprised Ana was the seventh offer: a job in Marketing. Maria, the same woman who had been so impressed with Ana's work on the last-minute presentation for Natalie, came to talk to Ana. She had openings in her seminar group. This wasn't an Administrative Assistant position; it was a promotion "across the line." This presented a dilemma for Ana.

> In a way, I'd been demoted three times. I'd started with a President of a company, who was also C.E.O. and Chairman of the Board. Then I went to Link.Com and worked for Natalie, who was both a Vice President and Corporate Officer. Now if I took one of these administrative job offers, I would working for just a Vice President. But a lot of the Administrative Assistants looked at my choices and said "Are you crazy? You should work for another Vice President." It was very hard because if I took the Marketing job I would be going into the totally unknown—farther down the ranks, into an area where I had no training. But I took it because the money was better and I wanted to learn something new. Even though it looked to me like it was a demotion, financially it was an improvement; I would get better stock options. I felt, "Oh, my god, what am I doing?" But I was always motivated because I had to raise a child. If I didn't bring the money in, it wasn't going to happen at my house. So I thought, "It's

never too late to learn. I'll just jump in with both feet." The one thing that I've always known about myself is that I have a lot of pride in the work that I do. I would give everything I had because it would not only reflect on others; it would reflect on me.

Ana was successful in her new Marketing position.

The seminar group was phenomenal. I have never worked with a team like that. Maria's group was well managed — total professionals. No one said, "I did this." It was, "We did this." The job required taking technical presentations on the road, coaching speakers, and arranging room setups and handout materials. I went on the road with one of my teammates for a week, to learn what I would be doing on my own. She said, "You tell me when you think you can do this." On Thursday, in the first week I said, "OK, you can go home now." She said, "Really?" I said to her, "Yes, I can do this myself. I'm fine." So she left and I did it by myself. Everything worked well. The following week, she canceled her trip, and I was on my own. When I left that Monday, I had voice messages from three of the team members saying, "Don't worry; this is going to be great. You're going to love it. If you need any help call me; page me any time." When I returned to the office at the end of the week there were flowers and balloons in my office with a card saying, "Congratulations on your first solo seminar."

Ana worked with the seminar group for a year and a half. Gradually the grueling travel schedule began to take a toll. Although Ana's son was in college by then, and not living at home, she lost touch with her friends because she was away three weeks out of four. When Ana's son graduated from college and came home to look for a job, Ana was feeling burned out:

I would come home, take a shower, and go to bed. Then I would get up and start my week over again. Most of the time I was out of town. I think I saw my son two times in the two months he had been home. Then one night I had just taken a shower and was sitting in the family room. He said "Mom, let's go out to dinner." I said, "Oh, honey, I'm so tired right now. Maybe tomorrow." He looked at me and said "Mom, get a life." I thought about that all week. I decided, "He's absolutely right; I have no life."

This conversation encouraged Ana to start looking for another type of job at Link.Com. Soon she heard of an opening in Travel for a contracts manager, a job which involved less time on the road. Ana knew little if anything about hotel contracts, but when she approached Winnie, the Travel group's manager, the position was hers — no interviews necessary because everyone knew her and was delighted she was interested. The new job involved developing a different set of skills.

Travel was a woman-managed operation too. For a woman who wasn't sure that she wanted to work for a woman, I ended up working for three women in succession. It wasn't a team job, which was something that I really missed. I was an individual contributor. I had been working for Winnie about a year, and she had given me no feedback on my performance. I assumed I was doing OK, but at first it was a real struggle for me to negotiate contracts. I took contract negotiations classes, but dealing with suppliers was still uncomfortable. I asked for a one-on-one with Winnie. We sat down and I said, "I'd like to know how I am doing. I'm going to have a formal review in a few months and if there is something that is not going to be favorable in that review, I'd like to know now, so I can work toward correcting it." She said, "I think you guys walk on water." I was so happy. I said, "Winnie, why didn't you say this? I have been going through such—there were times when I didn't want to go to work in the morning because I was worried." Winnie had left me dangling. She was new at being a manager.

As Ana moved from working on as an Administrative Assistant to Vice Presidents, into "unknown" lower levels of the firm, her increased responsibilities and compensation were indications that she had earned a new kind of respect and status.

● ● ● ● ● ● ● ● ● ● ● ●

THE LINK.COM CULTURE: WATCHING NATALIE'S STRUGGLE TO SURVIVE

When Ana described the Link.Com culture, she saw it through Natalie's eyes. Shortly before Ana went to work for Natalie, David Seidel was hired as the heir apparent to Jim Nelson. David immediately had been given a lot of responsibility, including the Marketing group, which meant that Natalie reported to David, not Jim Nelson.

It seemed to me that Natalie was not David's favorite person. If a man was talking, David would not interrupt. He would wait until the man finished speaking, even if he was struggling to find the right words. But if Natalie was speaking, David would just cut her off and turn to someone else. The men saw how he was treating Natalie and there was a gradual, uncalled—for change in how they treated her. After a while, Natalie became really good about saying, "I'm not finished yet." She really stood up for herself.

Ana had many stories about how Natalie stood up for herself. One of the most dramatic involved Ted Becker, a man who had done his share of contributing to Link.Com's "yelling and screaming" work norms.

I remember sitting in my cube outside Natalie's office one day. Ted was in her office and they were having some kind of a meeting. You could hear him shout throughout our half of the building. I remember thinking, "My god, isn't she going to say anything? What can she say?" I turned around and I saw her—it was so wonderful and it's so vivid in my mind. There were four chairs. She just sat back in her chair. She put her hands behind her head, started rocking back in her chair, and then all of a sudden looked at him very calmly and said, "Ted, go to hell." I turned away. I was so happy. I just kept right on working, but I was just ecstatic seeing that.

Although it was clear that Natalie had dared to speak up to defend herself, and Ana admired her for this, Ana was convinced that some of Natalie's co-workers were not so approving.

Natalie was very outspoken when she thought the company was not going in the right direction. (In contrast) the men would go with the trend—with the consensus. Or if they were going to disagree, they would do it in a softer way so they weren't really being confrontational, for example, with Seidel. The men didn't like her outspokenness. It was as if they were saying, "You are going to be put in your place. And this is not your place." I think a lot of it was because she was a woman. I think they would have taken that style from a man.

Ana watched Natalie with admiration, and with sympathy, as she saw the costs entailed in dealing with so much opposition and disdain.

So Natalie did fight for herself. It was so hard to watch it, week after week, month after month. And to see the toll it took on her. I would think, "This is going to destroy her." I didn't see how she could come in every day. I would never have done that. You couldn't pay me enough to put up with that. There were some weekends when I would go home on Friday, and I didn't know if on Monday she would be there.

Slowly, Ana and Natalie developed a close relationship. They did what they could to make each other's work lives easier. From Ana's perspective:

It was the strangest relationship because she was so highly educated and I wasn't. But I think I was more worldly—maybe that was not the right word. For example, when I started working at Link.Com, some people would ask me, "My god, how can you work for Natalie?" She was very tough. She

didn't mince words. You always knew where you stood.

She was very demanding. She was very exact in how she wanted her work done, how you should comport yourself—that kind of thing. We just hit it off. It wasn't like we immediately knew each other. I didn't know for a long time that she was married. She didn't know my situation; she just didn't ask about that kind of thing. If she didn't ask, I wasn't going to volunteer. The personal sharing started very gradually.

Although their friendship developed slowly, it grew deep and became important to both Ana and Natalie.

Natalie said there were times when I was the only person she had to talk to. She would get very quiet. I would just go in her office, close the door, and ask her if she wanted to talk about it. And she would start talking. I think that the only thing that I ever reiterated was her value. I'd say, "Don't forget, Natalie, you are so good at what you do. It's because of their jealousy, because it's such a male-dominated environment. But don't let them do this to you. Remember your worth. You have so much to give to all of us." I would sit and listen to her. I saw what she went through daily.

Few were surprised when Natalie announced she would be leaving the company. According to Ana, the reactions and interpretations of her co-workers reflected their ideas of gender-appropriate behavior.

Unfortunately, there was this unspoken thing. The men felt that the professional women at Link. Com were not serious. When

Natalie said she going to retire, one of the men said, "Oh, you're going to go home and take care of the children now." Because she was a woman, they assumed that this was what she was going to retire to do. The men didn't see women in the same light, regardless of whether they were totally committed. So the children thing was just an excuse.

● ● ● ● ● ● ● ● ● ● ● ● ● ●

SEARCHING FOR FEMALE ROLE MODELS

Ana kept an eye on the women executives, watching their styles of behavior to see what worked, and what didn't, in the Link.Com environment. Her strongest role model was Natalie, who in spite of her own difficulties, had consistently managed to help Ana, as well as others. Ana attributed much of her career success at Link.Com to Natalie:

> She taught me so much, without realizing that she was teaching me. I would watch her handling things. I don't think she realized that I was soaking it in like a sponge. She was so very central in my life. Natalie would go and fight for all of us. She was the only female in that kind of position who would do that. How different her style was from the others. None of the other women would speak up, take an issue up the ladder, or fight for someone in their group. So Natalie probably got some bad feelings for that from the men, but the women loved that she did that.

Ana knew the story about how Patricia Sullivan's promotion to Director had been delayed. Ana attributed Patricia's final victory in part, to Natalie's efforts:

> There were three other managers at the same level, all men. Each of

them got promoted to Director but Patricia did not. The reason given was that Patricia was a rookie—she had just come on board and had to grow a bit more. But the men hadn't been there more than a couple of months longer than Patricia. Natalie fought for her for six months, at every Executive Staff meeting. She fought and fought. She would not let the issue die.

Ana thought that other women executives were less outspoken than Natalie. For example, Diane Caldwell was feminine, beautiful, nice, and seemed reluctant to challenge her boss.

> If he said, "Maybe we should do this," she would follow that path. If he changed his mind, she would change direction too. Even if he was just playing with ideas, she would change direction twenty times, or try to cover all the bases, rather than just say, "Well, you know realistically that if we do this, it isn't going to work. If we try this, it may work—but this last alternative should not be an option." Instead, she tried to make any and all options work. And in the process, she drove everybody totally crazy.

There was one high ranking woman, however, who was not as outspoken as Natalie, and not as eager to please as Diane. This was Masako Hirada, the Director of Business Development. Ana was interested to see if her intermediate style would be more effective:

> Masako was very bright, very intelligent. But when I was in executive row one time, I heard a few male Vice Presidents talking. The Senior Vice President said, "I don't want her presenting. It wouldn't send out the

right message to the people in the audience because she is a woman."

Ana had begun to wonder if there were any style—independent, forthright, eager to please, unwilling to disagree—that was effective for women at Link.Com. One success story was Mariana Torcelli. She was a Regional Sales Manager. Unlike Patricia, who had Natalie fighting for her, Mariana was an independent operator.

> Mariana was looking for a way to grow. I think Mariana asked for her particular region. They gave it to her because they didn't want her where she was. In the new job, she reported to a different line of command. They didn't think she was going to succeed. They did not give her staff or any kind of help. Instead they said, "You go out there and show us you can do the job and then we'll help you." She started developing the market almost immediately. Her first year's growth was phenomenal. With all those accounts coming in, did they give her staff? Even after the first year, no. Mariana was mistreated. With a man, this would not have happened.

Ana watched a variety of women executives, but even the most obviously competent women, like Masako, Patricia, and Mariana, were facing obstacles that were not visible to many others. Female role models, for whom success came easily, were hard to find.

BECOMING HERSELF

Although she had a hard time finding female models of success, Ana had been of inspiration, support, and information for other people in a variety of positions at Link.Com. Ana was committed to listening to and helping others because of difficulties she had experienced earlier in her life:

> Everybody at Link.Com talked to me. They confided in me because they knew that I would keep a confidence and that I would try to help if I could. I did this because, when I was going through my divorce, I had no one to talk with. I was in so much pain. My mother turned away from me. We were Catholic and we were supposed to marry for life. I had a four-year son who was crying every day. I had to work it out myself. There was no one to turn to for help. I swore that if I got through it, I would never turn anyone away who wanted to talk. Never.

As the company grew, the Human Resources staff came to the conclusion that mentoring should be done within departments. Recognizing Ana's skills, Winnie made her the official mentor for the travel department. Ana was pleased, but not surprised:

> Even back when I was in the seminar group, Maria said to me, in one of our one-on-one conversations, "I just want you to know that it is OK if you need to take extra time to spend with your team when they have problems. I really value your maturity. And I want you to know that you will get extra points on your review for this."

Ana was an equal opportunity mentor, helping men as well as women.

> I was fighting for them emotionally. Some of the young guys in the mailroom came to me. They felt their reviews were unfair and wanted me to help them write a response. I said, "Yes, absolutely, I

will help you. Tell me what you think is unjust—what you disagree with—and we will put it into words." I wanted it to be in their words, not my words.

Although Ana found being a confidante and mentor important and rewarding, it was also emotionally draining and time consuming. She worked long extra hours to make up for time spent on this supportive work. It was, in a sense, an "invisible job."

Whenever I dealt with Elizabeth's problems, we would go out to dinner—that's how long it would take for her to unload. In an average month, I'd spend maybe 10–12 hours, give or take, on these kinds of things. The night after one person got fired, I couldn't sleep. I asked her to come stay with me. And I used to keep all these feelings about these relationships inside. Now I know I can't do that; there is only so much I can do. The rest is not my responsibility.

● ● ● ● ● ● ● ● ● ● ● ●
PAY EQUITY

Ana's performance reviews had always been excellent, but that had not always translated into excellent pay raises.

Once, when Natalie was discussing my review with me, she gave me by mistake her copy of the form. I could see that the percentage of my raise had been changed—three times. I said "Natalie, what is this?" She was very honest. She said "I didn't mean to give you that copy, but this first percentage is what I proposed giving you after your performance review. David Seidel said no, and proposed a ten percent increase. I said no, and so we com-

promised." I said "If you value the work I do for you at a certain level, why didn't he agree with that?" Natalie answered, "David felt you shouldn't make more than his Administrative Assistant." I said, "If he wants his Assistant to make more money than I do, then give her more money, but don't penalize me." Every year the same thing happened. The percentage increase was only adequate; it was not what it should have been, given Natalie's high evaluation of my performance. I think my fate was tied to hers. I reported to Natalie, so rewarding me would be like rewarding her.

It would have been easy for Ana to blame Natalie for these problems. Instead, Ana continued to praise Natalie's efforts to find other ways to help her financial situation:

I had taken a $15,000 pay cut to join Link.Com. Natalie would give me projects at the start of a quarter and then arrange for bonuses if I could complete the projects within a three-month time limit. One day, she said "Have you received your first certificate from the stock purchase plan?" When I said, "I'm not participating," she objected strenuously. I said, "I can't have any more money taken out of my paycheck and still feed my child and pay rent." She didn't say anything; she just looked at me. She came back the following week and she said "Ana, come in here." I went into her office, we closed the door, and she said "How much would you need for six month's stock purchase?" She wrote me a check to make up for what would be deducted from my paycheck to pay for the stock. She would not take any interest. She said, "Pay it back whenever you feel that you are in a position to pay it back." She didn't want anyone to know. I had enough to pay her back in six months. It made all the difference in the world. I've never felt this kind of gratitude or loyalty to an employer.

Ana continued to have problems getting pay raises commensurate with her high performance reviews in subsequent jobs, but by then she had become adept at negotiating for herself.

When I got my formal offer letter for the contracts job from Human Resources (HR), the starting salary was much lower than the initial figure that Winnie, who would be my new manager, had quoted. I had been through this before. I said to Winnie, "This isn't what you and I talked about." She said "Well, no, but this is what HR is willing to offer." Anyone who has been with the company a while knows that you need to be very firm with HR. Was she not used to fighting? I said, "I want the amount we first discussed. I'm really happy where I am. I love the people I work with. Yes, I'm burned out from the travel, but I can take a week or two off. The real reason I'm making this move is because of the money. If the money isn't there, then I can stay where I am." Winnie went back to HR and the next offer was slightly improved, but it was still short of the initial offer. Winnie said, "This is January and your review will be in April. If your performance is as high as in the past, HR says you'll get a very good increase." I said, "No, I'm sorry. This isn't how it works. The issue is:

what is the position worth now? I'll worry about April in April." Winnie finally called me up and said "Get in here and sign this letter." I went into her office. Finally—the letter matched the original salary offer, but I noticed something was missing, "Where are my stock options?" Winnie laughed, "Ana, if you negotiate like this with hotels, you're going to ace this job."

Ana had learned how to negotiate and fend for herself. She also was teaching her managers and peers what she had learned about how to work the system. In this way, Ana's early experiences with Natalie, and what she had learned, had repercussions beyond the two of them.

ANA'S FUTURE PLANS

Ana was older than many of her co-workers, and her approach to working was like that of many women of her generation and background:

I was born in an age when you were raised to get married. I thought I would be taken care of and would be happy forever after. It didn't work out that way. I've been divorced for 23 years, so I've had to get out in the workforce. I took pride in what I did, but I always thought I would rather not work, so I never really thought about having a career. When my son graduated and left home, I found that a lot of people respected me. I've had to solve a lot of my own problems. I'd love to be in a position where I wouldn't have to work, but I'm not. So all of a sudden I find myself thinking, "Where can I go from here?"

Ana was not one to sit on a good idea. She asked for an appointment "to talk about the future" with her boss, Winnie.

Winnie got right to the point, "What are you looking for in your future?" I answered, "Frankly, I'd like to be two grade levels higher. Since you say you are very happy with my work, I'd like to speak to you about what we need to do, to make this happen. It's a brand new department so we can be entrepreneurial." Winnie said, "Funny you should say that. I've been thinking about how I've got to do something with you and Donna. I know you can't report to her or her to you." She was right about that. Donna and I are so different. I would leave if I had to report to Donna. Winnie said she was thinking of reorganizing the groups in April so that she could validate a two-grade promotion for me. That would mean I would be a manager. I have a manager's title now, but at Link.Com if you are an individual contributor, like I am now, it's just a title. But if you have people reporting to you, then you really are a manager.

As she waited for April to come around, Ana was full of optimism and excitement about her future at Link.Com.

I am very interested to see what Winnie comes up with in April. It's certainly going to be a different avenue. I can do a good job of this. There's nothing holding me back. Before, I never wanted a job which required me to be gone. I wanted to be there for my son. I had to be a good parent because for a long time I felt so much guilt for having deprived him of a father figure. Now I have worked out so many things; it's amazing that I came out of it the way I did. I'm still living, I'm still learning, and I'm still growing. What's exciting is at this age — in two days I'll be 54, an age when most people are at the point where they are feeling, "OK, it's half way over" — I'm excited about what I can do. My glass is not half empty; it's almost full.

II-18: Constructing Carly Fiorina: Gender and the Business Press

Linda A. Krefting

In March 2002, Hewlett-Packard's 750,000+ shareholders sided with HP management by narrowly approving a merger with Compaq. The merger was controversial and unusual because it was actively opposed by HP board member Walter Hewlett, son of an HP founder, who was joined by other founding family members and their foundations. The business press played a prominent role in the six months between the announcement of the proposed merger and the shareholder vote. Both HP management and Walter Hewlett used full-page ads to help communicate their positions to shareholders and other constituencies. There was also a steady stream of stories in the *Wall Street Journal, Business*

Week, Fortune, Forbes, industry publications, and the business pages of daily newspapers. Approval was portrayed as hinging on shareholder belief in HP CEO Carly Fiorina's ability to integrate the two companies. A few publications (e.g., *NY Times, Fast Company*) questioned whether a male CEO would be covered by the press comparably to Fiorina, the first woman to head a Dow 30 company. Recognizing that she is primarily "known" to most through media coverage, this paper examines how Carly Fiorina has been portrayed in the business press as HP's CEO and the salience of these representations to the merger controversy.

MEDIA AND GENDER

As the first woman to head a Dow 30 company, Fiorina has been the subject of regular coverage since her appointment as CEO in July 1999. Media accounts are often considered to be objective representations of fact but are more realistically viewed as social constructions shaped by a variety of editorial decisions. Through the inclusion—or omission—of facts or sources and their arrangement, stories are framed in ways that convey value-laden messages (Byerly, 1999). News accounts are very brief and tend to be constructed from commonly shared understandings of relevant issues to make them comprehensible. News media wish to appear consistent in coverage so early coverage of an emerging issue is likely to structure subsequent coverage of the event. Thus, initial coverage of Fiorina as HP CEO would tend to set the terms for stories about the subsequent merger controversy.

"Newsworthiness" arises from threats to social order; departures from established custom or changes in power structure make a story worthy of attention. Fiorina downplayed issues of gender at the time of her appointment as HP CEO. However, her selection marked a significant change in power relations and departure from custom, which sparked a flood of stories on gender and management. Doubts about women in executive roles remain common (Powell, 1999). "Women experience a double bind when it comes to their perceived competence: either it is questioned, or it is acknowledged but at the cost of losing likability and influence" (Carli & Eagly, 1999, 212). Business press coverage of women executives and business cartoons both portray women in executive roles as problematic, reflecting reservations about women's competence, about whether powerful women are likable, and about the implications of women's changing roles for the social order (Krefting, 2001, forthcoming). Women executives are often posed as a woman's issue, not an issue of relevance to management. These familiar concerns might affect the way news accounts about Fiorina are framed by editors and writers or understood by readers.

COVERAGE OF FIORINA

Carly Fiorina is principally "known" through media coverage by all but the few large institutional investors and employees who have direct access to her. U.S. business press coverage of Fiorina examined in this paper includes the *Wall Street Journal (WSJ), Business Week (BW), Fortune, Forbes*, plus business pages of some local newspapers and other business sources. The analysis looks first at coverage prior to announcement of the HP-Compaq merger, the initial coverage, and then examines how terms of initial coverage carried forward into accounts of the controversy about the proposed merger.

INITIAL COVERAGE

Fascination with the unconventional aspects of Fiorina's career and "accidental" path into technology follows the theme "you've come a long way, baby" but entails tensions about her competence as well. Firoina is scrutinized as an oddity. There is more attention to her undergraduate major in medieval history and philosophy than her more relevant MBA in marketing. Early accounts tend to refer to her as Carleton S. Fiorina, but later accounts use the more familiar and feminine Carly, "what most everyone inside and outside HP has taken to calling her" (*Fortune*, Jan. 10, 00). Fiorina comes across as superficial and interested in appearances. "Flashy" and well-dressed (Armani suits), she flies in a private jet met by a chauffer-driven Lincoln (unlike her predecessor), and worries about spinning financials. "Leadership is performance," she says in a *Forbes* cover story. "You have to be conscious about your behavior because everyone else is" (Dec. 13, 99, 138).

At the time of her selection by HP, the *WSJ* characterized her as a "Lucent star" with "high marks as a decision-maker" and "integral to the spinoff" from AT &T. "She works relentlessly" with a "quick wit" and "a warm way of asserting herself" (July 20 &22, 99). Credit for her success is diluted with references to help received from others and the depiction that she came "almost accidentally" to her career, having worked at HP as a secretary and dropped out of law school before seeking an MBA and joining AT&T's Network Systems, an "unconventional" career move to the periphery of the organization where she and other women thrived in part because "it was considered the company's ugly duckling." She owes her career not to skill and effort but to luck and the help of many—her parents, previous superiors, and her husband who took early retirement and now serves as househusband.

This pattern of shared credit for success continues in accounts of Fiorina's role at HP. Her staff plays a prominent role in accounts because "Carly . . . herself can't do it alone" (*Fortune*, Jan. 10, 00). The *WSJ* front-page review of her first year at HP

gives "Kudos to Ann Amazon" in a subtitle (Aug. 22, 00). *BW*'s "The Radical" (Feb. 19, 01) closes with the foregrounded photo captioned: "New Deal: After Fiorina embraced Mancuso's team-based ideas, sales to top-customers jumped more than 30%."

Fiorina is posed alone when downsides and risks of her HP reorganization plan are the issue. Demands for improved performance took a personal toll on subordinates, indicative of too much change, too fast (*WSJ*, Aug. 22, 00). Her "approach is so radical that experts say it has never been tried before at a company of HP's size and complexity" (*BW*, Feb. 19, 01). Highlighted text warns "Fiorina is overhauling HP at Net speed, ordering up changes before fine-tuning them" (74), "Fiorina holds quarterly marathons to determine how to cast HP's financials in the best light" (76), and HP is "careening." *Forbes* and *Fortune* ran similar stories on dissension at HP, "Backstabbing Carly" and "Open Season on Carly Fiorina" (June 11, July 23, 01).

Some coverage of Fiorina is consistent with the stereotype of traditional women: if they are likable (quick wit, warm way), their competence is uncertain. Like women in general, she may have come a long way, but she required luck and much help. Her initiatives are "radical" and problematic. Along with her undergraduate major in medieval history and philosophy, Fiorina's background in sales is regularly noted. [Representing Fiorina as *career salesperson*, flashy and interested in appearances, emphasizes the seductive, unsavory side of management rather than leadership (Calas & Smircich, 1991).] In a *BW* photo caption Fiorina "Won Over" (seduced?) engineers (who "know they have to perform") as a *career salesperson*, not through authenticity or leadership (*BW*, Feb. 19, 01, 76).

Other aspects of coverage emphasize the tension in the stereotype of career women, women who may be competent but perhaps not likable. A stern photo of a Fiorina with crossed arms is captioned

"Carly to HP: Snap to It" (*BW*, Feb. 19, 01, 74). Photos and graphics were flattering and artsy (e.g., a full page with 9 reproductions of Fiorina's face in *Forbes*, Dec. 13, 99) in the initial coverage, but are less becoming in later, less positive accounts like the "snap to it" photo in *BW*'s "The Radical." Foregrounded elements, such as headlines and highlighted text, are often more negative than the text of news accounts.

Emphasis on Fiorina's "accidental" career in technology, the help she has received from numerous others across her career, sales/seduction—not leadership—as her expertise, and the risks in her "radical" efforts to transform HP are consistent with widely-circulating concerns about women's competence in executive roles. Language, photos and graphics expose uneasiness about women with power and women's changing social position.

COVERAGE OF THE MERGER CONTROVERSY

Consistency over time is important for media credibility. A CEO's ability to ride out controversy or negative performance depends on images constructed previously (Chen & Meindl, 1991). By the time the proposed HP-Compaq merger was announced in Sept. 2001, images of Fiorina were already conflicted. Issues that emerged in early coverage carry forward to accounts of the proposed merger. For example, the business editor for a Texas paper recaps her "accidental career" in conjunction with the merger:

> Carly Fiorina . . . must be sitting on top of the world having undoubtedly had a hand [in the merger]. Fiorina, the first woman ever to lead a Dow 30 company, will be the center of attention again in the weeks and months ahead as she attempts to sell the deal . . . It has to be pleasing to women across the U.S. with eyes on other CEO posts to see how this one-time reception-

ist, who holds a degree in medieval history and philosophy from Stanford, has worked her way to the head of the PC industry class . . . Fiorina can at least bask in the fact that's [sic] she's been on top of a man's world for some time now . . . They were swallowing their pride in Houston, the home of 20-year old Compaq (Van Wagenen, Lubbock Avalanche-Journal, Sept. 9, 01).

While touting women's progress, Fiorina's success is an issue for social order, a change in a man's world, and her accomplishments a source of celebration *for women*. Those in Houston are left swallowing their pride.

Jim Collins, author of the leadership best-seller *Good to Great* casts Fiorina skeptically as a self-promoting publicity hound in a *WSJ* commentary (Nov. 26, 01, A18) based on a previous *Forbes* cover story (Dec. 13, 99). He argues self-promoting male CEOs are also suspect but advances the late Katherine Graham as an alternative.

> Katie and Carly. One took a good company and made it great, the other has thus far taken a great company and made it good . . . One saw the purpose of it all beyond herself, the other has acted as if the supreme purpose is herself.

Graham is an interesting choice of comparison. Her success came with relatively little challenge to the traditional gender order: a housewife and mother, she took over the Washington Post, a business that had been in her family, after her husband's suicide and generously credited the advice of men on whom she relied.

Collins' source, the prior *Forbes* cover story, can be interpreted in multiple ways. Nine artful reproductions of Fiorina's face might "read" as narcissism but are a *Forbes* decision, not Fiorina's. Her concern for communication can be seen as legitimate as easily as self-promotion. The first outsider to head HP, how else but via communication could she develop a constituency? That "everyone is watching" might be a literal exaggeration, but it was (and remains) realistic for Fiorina to be aware of scrutiny. Like the Texas business editor, Collins' source is secondary, not direct knowledge,

Fortune continued to rank Fiorina the most powerful woman in business (a process separating women from men) in Oct. 01. However the article, "Patient but Not Passive," highlights women who have moved to power with less fanfare than Fiorina. The graphic in *BW*'s first merger story is a pigeon-toed, knock-kneed Fiorina with a worried expression on an oversized, cocked head trying to balance the two companies as a barbell. The stern "snap to it" photo from *BW*'s "The Radical" (Feb. 19, 01) re-emerges on the cover for "Carly's Last Stand" (Dec. 24, 01), which characterizes the HP-Compaq merger as a "soap opera of historic proportions."

A *WSJ* headline (Dec. 21) declared the "teetering" merger the "sales challenge of [Fiorina's] career." The "beauty" of the merger "differ[ed] in the eyes of HP holders" (*WSJ*, Dec. 3), and the benefit of the doubt depended on whether shareholders believed Fiorina could successfully combine the two companies (*BW*, Dec. 24). An undergraduate major in medieval history and philosophy with a preference for Armani suits who consistently needed both help and luck in a *sales* career seemed an unlikely choice to integrate two large technology firms, a feat no one had previously accomplished. *WSJ* commentary suggested HP abandon the merger and instead return to its roots in innovative technology or become a printer company (Dec. 17 & 19, 01).

Coverage of Firoina in early 2002 again emphasized others, particularly the HP board, and the merger as a soap opera. The board chair instrumental in hiring her, not Fiorina, was held responsible for difficulties

at HP. HP's strategy for winning shareholder support depended on Institutional Shareholder Services' endorsement (*BW*, Dec. 24, 01); yet when it was secured, no credit was given to Fiorina or HP. "Institutional Shareholder Services may have done what millions of dollars in ads and related proxy-fight expenses couldn't do: tip the scales in favor of Hewlett-Packard Co.'s contested purchase of Compaq Computer Corp" (*BW*, March 18, 02).

Ultimately, shareholders approved the HP-Compaq merger by a narrow margin in March 2002. Walter Hewlett raised legal questions but was unable to overturn the vote. In reporting the approval, *BW* focused on the cost of the shareholder campaign, "What Price Victory?" and reiterated concerns of "The Radical" (Feb. 19, 01) in "Why a Bold Management Plan Didn't Work" (April 1, 02). Detailed merger planning by HP and Compaq was ascribed to the controversy (necessity as the mother of invention) rather than to leadership, foresight or effort. "What's in Store for This Happy Couple" warned "the star may not last long … Fiorina and Capellas [Compaq's CEO] need to roll up their sleeves, because their merger faces huge challenges" (*BW*, May 20, 02).

Concerns apparent in initial coverage of Fiorina as CEO are also apparent in accounts of the merger. Posed early on as an oddity, a radical with reorganization plans so mysterious and confusing as to be beyond the realm of expert knowledge, accounts of the merger reflect skepticism about the wisdom of the merger and Fiorina's ability to successfully complete the integration.

RE-READING FOR GENDER

The role of gender in accounts of Fiorina can be assessed by re-reading with a male subject. The following phrases from accounts of

Fiorina are unlikely to have been written, or surely would have different effects, had the subject been a male executive:

- In this family, she's the CEO and he's home (*WSJ* headline, July 22, 99)
- I hope I've reached the point where my gender is interesting, but not the main point here. (*WSJ*, July 22, 99)
- The Boss (*BW* cover, Aug. 2, 99)
- Why she always looks so sharp. Two words: Giorgio Armani (*BW*, Aug. 2, 99)
- . . . until Carly moves a few steps in the Madeleine Albright direction of sensible shoes and damn the mascara (*BW*, March 19, 01)
- These Women Rule (Fortune, Oct. 25, 99)
- As Leaders, Women Rule (*BW*, Nov. 20, 00)
- Approach . . . so radical that experts say it has never been tried before at a company of HP's size and complexity (*BW*, Feb. 19, 01).
- Williams and other engineers quickly warmed to career salesperson Fiorina (*BW*, Feb. 19, 01)
- Carly couldn't miss a quarter without the death watch starting (*WSJ*, Mar. 13, 01)
- What's in Store for This Happy Couple? (*BW*, May 20, 02)

Reading effects reveal that Fiorina's newsworthiness derives from her relevance for the social order. A male becoming "The Boss" or being among men who rule would not be sufficient for a business press cover story. Marriage metaphors, common in describing mergers, have different effects with photos of a heterosexual "Happy Couple."

Fiorina minimized gender when appointed to HP, ["My gender is interesting, but not the point here"] and "I hope that we are at a point where we have figured out that there is not a glass ceiling" (*WSJ*, July 20 & 22, 99). Her appointment has,

however, been the occasion for others to comment on gender and the social order. *Fortune* poses her as the most powerful *woman* in U.S. business today. The *Wall Street Journal*'s follow-up piece two days after her appointment was announced is titled "In this family, she's the CEO and he's home," a title which clearly notes the unusualness of this social arrangement (*WSJ*, July 22, 1999). *Business Week* refutes Fiorina's contention that there is no longer a glass ceiling (Nov. 22, 99). That she and other women "pioneers" in the executive suite seem to be subject to extraordinary scrutiny has also been noted (*WSJ*, Mar. 13, 01).

Conclusions

From her selection as HP CEO through the shareholder vote on the HP-Compaq merger, issues of gender have been apparent in U.S. business press coverage of Carly Fiorina. Her role at HP is portrayed as problematic in ways consistent with other research on gender and media. She is a woman executive and concerns about her competence, her likability, and the implications for the social order are evident. Business press publications maintained consistency by using issues raised in early coverage to frame coverage of the merger controversy. Language, photos, and whole stories from earlier accounts reappear in subsequent coverage.

But should we be surprised? Gender is salient from a very early age—even infants show sensitivity to gender-appropriate dress. Gender has always played an important part in defining the social order circulated and sustained through everyday language and activity. Portrayals of Fiorina constructed by the business press reflect the tensions her role as CEO pose for the social order—her low gender status inconsistent with the high status of her executive position. Attributions crediting others for her success and emphasizing risks of her radical change initiative and merger are typical of those made about low-status individuals. As a status marker, gender continues to be a salient issue in management, and the business press plays a significant role in sustaining and circulating reservations about women as executives.

References

Byerly, Carolyn M. 1999. News, feminism, and the dialectics of gender relations. In M. Meyers (ed.), *Mediated women: Representations in popular culture*, 383–404. Cresskill, NY: Hampton Press.

Calas, Marta & Smircich, Linda 1991. Voicing seduction to silence leadership. *Organization Studies*, 12 (4), 567–602.

Carli, Linda L. & Eagly, Alice H. 1999. Gender effects on social influence and emergent leadership. In G. N. Powell (ed.), *Handbook of gender&work*, 203–222. Thousand Oaks, CA: Sage.

Chen, Chao C. & Meindl, James R. 1991. The construction of leadership images in the popular press: The case of Donald Burr and People Express. *Administrative Science Quarterly*, 36, 521–551.

Krefting, Linda A., 2001. Problematics of gender and place: Evidence from the business cartoons of the *Wall Street Journal* and New Yorker. Paper presented at Critical Management Studies II, Manchester England, July.

Krefting, Linda A., forthcoming. Re-presenting women executives: Valorization and devalorization in the US business press. *Women in Management Review*.

Powell, Gary N. 1999. Reflections on the glass ceiling: Recent trends and future prospects. In G. N. Powell (ed.), *Handbook of gender &work*, 325–346. Thousand Oaks, CA: Sage.

II-19: Looking Like America???

Linda A. Krefting

If we don't have people of diverse backgrounds in back, how in the world can we satisfy the diversity of people coming through the front door?
(former J.C. Penny chairman William R. Howell, quoted in *Business Week,* Feb. 17, 1997, 64)

Diverse marketing drives diverse recruiting.
(Minneapolis Star-Tribune, Aug. 17, 1999)

Our audience is growing more diverse, so communities we serve benefit if our employees are racially and ethnically diverse.
(Granite Broadcasting Corp. CEO W. Don Cornwell, quoted in *Business Week,* March 11, 2002, 56)

It has become commonplace for executives in the U.S., like those quoted above, to explain the importance of workforce diversity with references to diversity of customers, communities or the population. President Clinton established "looking like America" as a goal for the Cabinet selected for his first term as president. Metaphorically linking diversity of employees with that of different constituencies seems to have become taken-for-granted and accepted with little need for reflection. It is popularized as obvious "business sense," an opportunity for doing well by doing good.

However, using demographics of customers or neighbors to guide selection of employees is a substantial departure from the principles of the earlier days of the civil rights movement. Martin Luther King's classic 1963 "I Have a Dream" speech (see "Learning the Language of Influence") frames a very different view. Delivered to a Washington, D.C., rally supporting passage of the Civil Rights Act (eventually passed in 1964), he envisioned a world in which his children would be judged on the content of their character, not on the color of their skin. Equal employment opportunity regulations prohibited discrimination in terms, conditions or privileges of employment based on demographics. Regulations sought to replace employment decisions based on presumptions about an individual derived from group stereotypes (e.g., women aren't interested in management) with decisions based on the unique, job-relevant qualifications of an individual.

Employers have been successfully challenged under existing equal opportunity regulations by qualified individuals who were bypassed in efforts to meet "looking like" diversity goals (for more detail, see "Suggestions for Further Reading"). Potential for legal problems aside, the terms on which employment decisions are based merit careful consideration. What is our ultimate goal? A world in which individuals are employed based on superficial demographic characteristics or based on qualifications without regard to demographics?

Suggestions for Further Reading

Brief, A. P., Buttram, R. T., Reizenstein, R. M., Pugh, S. D., Callahan, J. D., McCline, R. L., &Vaslow, J. B., 1997. Beyond good intentions: The next steps toward racial equality in the American workplace. *Academy of Management Executive*, 11, 59–72.

Krefting, L. A., Kirby, S. L., &Krzystofiak, F. J., 1997. Managing diversity as a proxy for requisite variety: Risks in identity-conscious inclusion and pressures to conform. *Journal of Management Inquiry*, 6, 376–389.

McMorris, F. A., 1999 (Sept. 10). Race-based jobs stir new debate in workplace. *Wall Street Extra Journal*, B1, 8.

II-20: Our Separate Ways
Black and White Women and the Struggle for Professional Identity

Ella L. J. Edmondson Bell and Stella M. Nkomo

We plead to each other
We all come from the same rock

We all come from the same rock
Ignoring the fact that we bend
at different temperatures
that each of us is malleable
up to a point.
Yes, fusion is possible
But only if things get hot enough—

All else is temporary adhesion,
   patching up.
—CHERRIE MORAGA, THE WELDER

OUR SEPARATE WAYS began as a vision of three African-American women: Stella Nkomo, Ella L. J. Edmondson Bell, and Toni Denton. We dreamed of telling the stories of the women who walked, talked, and fought their way up the corporate ladder of some of the most prestigious companies in America. These women were the first generation of their race to hold managerial or executive positions. Yet their stories remained untold.

. . . [W]e can help readers think through the broader implications of our research, by offering the following guidance.

• *Black women do not neatly fit into either of the two groups in which they are usually placed: women professionals or black professionals.* Nor should companies try to make them fit into one group or the other. Black women face both racism and sexism in their corporate life. Companies should not assume that programs and initiatives addressing gender issues will solve all of the problems black women face. Conversely, policies and practices aimed at enhancing racial diversity may also miss issues unique to black women. We have a simple suggestion for CEOs and others who ask: "Who are they? Where do they fit?" Ask the black women in your company about their lives, their goals, and their particular concerns. Few will have qualms about telling you of their experiences in the face of earnest interest.

• *While colleagues should sponsor and support black women.* They must learn to both understand black women and he advocates for their development and advancement. If anything, the narratives of the black women in this study have been a cry to be accepted for who they are, not for who people think they are or who they want them to be. The narratives indicated that many worked for white supervisors who did not fully understand their talents or who were not willing to give them meaningful assignments. This happened despite their outstanding educational backgrounds and proven competence. The black women in our study experienced more demotions and lateral moves than their white women counterparts. Many felt it was difficult for them to get credit for excellent work or for colleagues to get past the stereotypes of black women being incompetent.

• *Black women want deeply to be themselves and be able to express their cultural identity.* This identity has been a source of strength in their lives—allowing them to withstand and prevail in spite of the obstacles encountered in their careers. Companies need to sensitize and train majority group managers, both male and female, about the unique challenges facing black women—a complex web of pressures emanating from both racism and sexism in the workplace and from the extra burden they carry in their communities. When black women end up as the conscience of their company, championing the cause of others who feel oppressed or excluded, their own needs can suffer.

• *Companies must support black and white women's networks.* This will help to alleviate the isolation all women feel—especially black women, or other women of color who are few in number in the managerial ranks in their companies. It will also enable the women to build constructive collegial bonds with one another. While a company may take pride in placing a lone black woman in a prominent position, it must also be keenly aware of the ways in which it is making her vulnerable to the extreme pressures brought by performance anxiety, tokenism, and demanding communities. We are not suggesting that black women not be promoted to showcase a company's commitment to affirmative action, but white colleagues must understand the pressures this places on them. Companies must find ways to offer concrete support and enable the women's success. Indeed, since black women have been taught from early life to "armor" themselves, many are reluctant to reveal their pain. So they put on extra armor. Overarmoring can end up immobilizing them to the point they feel they have no way out.

• *Companies must build upon black women's talents and institute policies and practices that incorporate their concerns and special challenges.* We have discussed the extent to which black women withhold fully committing to their organizations. Company leaders must not use this as justification for not making an effort to recruit and retain black women. When black women feel fully accepted and embraced, they will fully vest themselves in their companies.

• *One way to attract and retain black women managers is to show them that you are prepared to assist their communities and the causes important to them.* This can only be a win-win situation. The ethics of giving back is a significant part of how black women make sense of their work and lives. Giving to their communities in various ways such as through recruitment, training, or philanthropy will strengthen black women's connections to the company. It will reap benefits for the company in both retention and good community relations.

BLACK AND WHITE WOMEN TOGETHER

For trusting, authentic relationships between black and white women to develop, black women must know that if they are not represented, their white sisters will speak for them and will be advocates for ending both racism and sexism in the companies where they work. Black and white women managers in corporate America are often trapped in a mutual perceptual illiteracy about one another. The fragile bond of gender is not enough to overcome the divisiveness of race. Black women often lament that while white women may speak out against sexism they do not bring the same energy to confronting racism.

For many white women, confronting the possibility of their racism is not only agonizing but also often incomprehensible. Before coming together with black women, white women should seek out other white women to talk about their apprehensions and confusion about race, including their own racial membership. Many white women spoke of their disappointment over not connecting to other white women at work. They felt unsupported by their female colleagues. White women can get caught up in assimilating white male models of behavior at work, becoming competitive, instrumental, and individualistic. Added to this is their belief that gender does not matter at work. Such behavior sabotages any chance of connecting with or supporting other women.

Black women need safe spaces in their lives to take off the armor that they have been wearing since childhood. Armor left on for too long can make a spirit heavy and burdened. It can cause a black woman to become emotionally brittle. When this happens, she is not open to constructive feedback or support from others and she maintains a defensive stance toward her colleagues and her loved ones. This is the beginning of a downward spiral that can affect black women's performance at work, as well as their personal relationships. As sociologist Kesho Scott suggests, "The habits of surviving that we mistakenly thought made us whole make no sense to us now.[4]

We suggest that black women, when feeling out of control or overwhelmed, seek out a qualified therapist, spiritual counselor, mentor, or coach who can help them learn how to effectively cope and to create fulfilling lives.

One truth raised in this book is the dark side of women's relationships with each other, especially across racial lines. Women are expected to be nurturing, supportive, caring, and loving in their relationships with other women. Women bond. Women make good friends. We are thought of as naturally building and attending to relationships. Men and women alike reinforce the good behaviors associated with females being the ideal caretakers within our society. Women who break this conventional wisdom of femininity, those who act within the dark side of negative emotions, are often called any number of nasty names. So it is extremely difficult for women to publicly acknowledge the the dark side of their relationships. Competition, envy, jealousy, pettiness, rage, and scorn remain hidden and repressed for the sake of maintaining the ideal feminine self. Infusing race into the situation only serves to make matters worse.

Coming face to face with the racial undercurrents that exist in black and white women's relationships hurts deeply, forcing each to own the disfigured image she has constructed of the other. By not attending to this racial shadow, all the hurt, frustration, guilt, and ambivalence continues to fester. The seed of hope for changing this situation is for us as women to struggle through the darkness. We cannot change our tarnished history, but we can begin to build sturdy bridges today. We can establish positive, healthy relationships between one another. Yes, it takes courage, it takes reaching out, it takes forgiving, it takes listening, and it takes accepting, but it is possible. Our reward for doing so is creating a new energy that allows us to be our true selves, to become more authentic in our relationships, and to grow into women who will make a difference in the companies where we work, in our families, and in the communities we live in.

Notes

4. Scott, *Habit of Surviving,* 187.

II-21: Can't Do It All

Natasha Josefowitz

If I do this
I won't get that done
If I do that
this will slip by

If I do both
neither will be perfect.

Not everything worth doing
is worth doing well.

From *Is This Where I Was Going?* by Natasha Josefowitz, 1983. New York: Warner Books. Reprinted by permission.

II-22: Work at Home? First, Get Real

Susan B. Garland

Often, visions of time and freedom are quickly dashed

Drains
*   A big mistake is underestimating the time it takes to do housework and run errands—which cut into income-producing time.*

No Blame
*   Whatever you do, you'll still face occasional conflicts between work and family that will cause one or the other to suffer.*

Every day, moms and dads quit their jobs in the hope of becoming part of that popular image of the work-at-home parent, the one where they are smiling at the computer while their adorable little baby crawls underfoot. I wish I could tell you that this picture squares with reality. But it doesn't. In fact, it's pure fantasy. Last November, after 12 years as a full-time Washington correspondent for *Business Week*, I resigned to become a freelance writer, setting up shop in my basement. I wanted to spend more time with my daughter, Kristina, who was then 5. But like many who had made this move before me, I had unrealistic expectations about how much I could accomplish with only a carpet commute.

Of the 37.8 million households with dependent children, there are 11.6 million that have at least one parent who works from home, says International Data Corp., based in Framingham, Mass., which provides market data on information technology. For parents out there who are thinking

of trading in their power suits for sweatsuits, managing expectations is critical.

Figure out at the start how you can spend more time with your child. Will you need a reduced workload? Are you also looking for a better quality of life, with a spectrum of other activities, such as more time at the gym? Or do you simply plan to transfer a full-time workload to a home office? To help you plan, here are 10 tips for the prospective at-home working parent:

• *No work, no pay*. If you telecommute with a regular salary, you may have time to play with your child, get a haircut, and putter in your garden. But if you plan to be a free agent, remember. Money coming in depends directly on doing the work. Yes, you can put in a load of wash while your PC is booting up. But every hour you spend running errands means lost income.

• *Beware the 24–7 week*. The great advantage of working at home is that you can work at 3 A.M. if necessary. That's the disadvantage, too—work is always there. It's hard to turn down jobs that will bring in money, and it's hard to pit your child's needs against those of your clients. But if you don't set limits, there's no point being home. "When my daughter was 12, she wrote a message on my [computer] screen because she knew that's where I looked: 'Can you please pick me up?' That's when I knew it was bad," recalls Lisa Roberts, who runs www.en-parent.com.

• *Establish a routine*. Thought you were leaving behind scheduled meetings and set hours? The choices that come with being home can be overwhelming, so set regular hours. That could mean working from 9 A.M. to noon, taking the rest of the day off to go to the gym and care for kids, then working again from 9 A.M. to midnight. Or work from 9 A.M. to 3 P.M. and take Fridays off for chores and downtime. Your life can turn chaotic unless you stick to a schedule that's as predictable as the office was.

• *Allow for emergencies.* Routines are great, but they can easily fall apart. Plan for the unplanned—such as a child's illness. I had daydreamed that if my child fell ill, I would read aloud by her bedside and feed her chicken soup. But when Kristina was sick on the same day a work assignment was due, she had to spend several hours upstairs by herself, miserable. If you pace your work, you can keep mini-disasters to a minimum.

• *Be realistic about money.* Whatever your lowball earnings projections are, deduct 20% just to be safe. Unless you're telecommuting for an employer, you're probably forgoing health insurance, retirement-plan contributions, paid vacations, and expense accounts. Calculate conservatively the time you can put in. I thought I could easily work 25 hours a week—9 A.M. to 3 P.M., with an hour off a day for errands. I underestimated the time it took for chores, doctors' visits, and other responsibilities.

• *Just say no.* So you want to be president of the PTA? Becoming an integral part of your child's school may seem alluring from the distance of your downtown office. But volunteering can eat into your paid hours. Valerie Finberg, a Boulder (Colo.) mother of two—who, until recently, worked at home full time as a management consultant—ran a book program for her child's class. "I was a miserable failure at it," she says. "It required constant attention." So volunteer for an occasional field trip, but be careful not to overcommit.

• *Don't fire the nanny.* If you have a baby or toddler, you may be able to get some work done during nap time, but not much. The best bet is to hire a part-time sitter if you have young children and want to get in extra hours without working at 3 A.M. I set my office hours while my daughter is in school, giving her my full attention at other times. But that doesn't always work. I recently had to schedule a phone interview while my daughter was home with a play date. The six-year-olds promised not to

---

Advice from the Front

Online
Web sites that offer guidance to work-at-home parents, plus links to other sites.
EN-PARENT.COM for "the entrepreneurial parent"
WAHM.COM for "work-at-home moms"
IVILLAGE.COM/WORK for "stay-at-home parents"
SLOWLANE.COM for "stay-at-home dads"

Books
How to Raise a Family and a Career Under One Roof by Lisa Roberts
The Work at Home Balancing Act: The Professional Resource Guide for Managing Yourself, Your Work, and Your Family at Home by Sandy Anderson
Working at Home While the Kids Are There, Too by Loriann Hoff Oberlin
Mompreneur: A Mother's Practical Step-By-Step Guide to Work-at-Home Success by Ellen Parlapiano and Patricia Cobe

interrupt unless there was an emergency. The emergency? They wanted candy NOW.

• *Get even more reinforcements.* When I left my full-time job, I let the nanny go without realizing how much housework I would have to take on. Besides caring for Kristina, she had folded my daughter's laundry, cleaned her room, and straightened the family room. I spent the first hour of every workday on those chores. But I could earn more—and reduce my stress—by adding a second day for a cleaning person. As Roberts writes in *How to Raise a Family and a Career Under One Roof:* "Take the time you would have spent, say, cleaning the house or mowing the lawn, and earn money at something you are really good at."

• *Give yourself a break.* You would think that Jeralyna Burke, 42, would know something about stress reduction. Burke, of Des Plaires, Ill., runs E-scent-ials, a Web site that sells aromatherapy products. A year ago, she suffered from palpitations, shortness of breath, and chest pains. Between caring for two preschoolers, running her house, and setting up her home business, she hadn't taken a day off from work for eight months. "Now, I'm taking some time off each day," she says, "even if it's 15 minutes sitting on the porch with a cup of tea."

• *Get out and about.* For me, the first few weeks of working at home were euphoric. Without the distractions of the office, my productivity soared. But then I started talking to myself for prolonged periods. I was suffering from isolation—a common affliction of the at-home worker. So, despite the pressures, see a friend for lunch. Meet a client face-to-face even if it would be quicker to do business by phone.

Most important: Don't forget why you wanted to become a work-at-home parent. The chance to test new skills, build a business, and assert more control over your life are all important goals. But strengthening bonds with your children tops the list. As long as you're prepared, you can find that right balance.

II-23: Telecommuters Learn to Put Bosses at Ease and Get Promoted, Too

Joann S. Lublin

Remember "Face Time"? It used to be critical for advancement. Without frequent personal interaction with your boss, you rarely moved ahead. Out of sight, out of mind.

No longer.

A growing number of "teleworkers" toil full time from home or offices far from their supervisors. Some even receive performance reviews by phone. Remote work has surged in popularity since the Sept. 11 terrorist attacks as more Americans choose to stay close to their families, avoid potential targets or deal with lost office space.

With the right mix of ingredients, working a significant distance from your boss can even be a recipe for career success. "You have to do your own PR . . . and in a broad sense, you have to manage your boss," advises Caela Farren, a principal of Mastery-Works, career-development consultants in Annandale, Va.

That's the winning formula for Eileen Luhta McFarlane. The EDS senior business analyst has worked from a basement office in her Chagrin Falls, Ohio, home since late 1995. She is one of about 2,500 full-time telecommuters at the big computer-services company based in Plano, Texas.

Her Five Immediate bosses over the past six years have been as far away as Singapore and no closer than Troy, Mich., a three-hour drive from her home. Despite her isolation, she has been promoted twice during the past two years.

"You have to have a leader who is comfortable not seeing you," plus "a proven track record and results working with this [remote] arrangement," explains the 45-year-old Ms. McFarlane, who joined EDS in 1985. Keenly aware that certain supervisors of telecommuters feel uncomfortable with their lack of visual oversight, she tries to start off right with each new boss.

Dennis Walters, a business-support manager, hired Ms. McFarlane in June as his first full-time telecommuter after a telephone job interview. They had their initial face-to-face encounter weeks later. They have only met twice.

In her present post, Ms. McFarlane gives sales teams the knowledge required to sell services tailored to customers' specific needs. Mr. Walters is pleased with her performance so far. "She volunteers to do [extra] things and sees them through," he reports. "She has taken leadership on projects and delivers as promised."

Ms. McFarlane also regularly checks during work projects to make sure she is meeting sales teams' needs. Afterward, she asks whether they would recommend her to others within EDS—all part of her strategy to become more visible there.

Constant feedback "is especially important when you're working virtually," she says.

Arlyn Imberman, a principal at Emerging Image, a New York executive-coaching firm, suggests Ms. McFarlane make it even easier for satisfied internal customers to pass along praise. She urges writing recommendations for them to sign and forward to her manager.

Ms. McFarlane says she also builds rapport with co-workers by paying attention to their vocal inflections on the phone and keeping notes about their personal lives. She knows who has a Siamese cat and whose daughter plays soccer. Such "relationship management" requires more effort when you're virtual, "but it's worth it," she says.

A former EDS boss helped Ms. McFarlane land her latest promotion. Eleanor Stryker sent Mr. Walker an unsolicited recommendation for Ms. McFarlane without her knowledge. "I just wanted him to know that while she was in our organization, [telecommuting] never presented a problem," the business-development manager recalls.

Ms. Stryker, who oversaw Ms. McFarlane between 1997 and 1999, recollects her frequent updates and eagerness to accept additional tasks. "Not everyone does [networking] as well as Eileen does," she says.

Strong networking skills are especially crucial for telecommuters in a complex and constantly changing company like EDS. Ms. McFarlane maintains ties with EDS staffers outside her area through visits, calls, e-mail and Christmas cards. "I hear about potential opportunities within their teams or maybe others that they've heard about," she continues. "So as people move about the company, I stay in the loop."

The ambitious analyst may have to tap these EDS contacts to achieve her goal of becoming an account manager, which she would also try to do through telecommuting. Ms. Farren suggests Ms. McFarlane devise informal ways to assist account managers whose customers she'd like to serve.

Other career coaches say the telecommuter could increase her visibility by volunteering for corporate task forces and asking her boss to arrange face-to-face meetings with influential higher-ups.

Yet even at EDS, telecommuters don't easily gain managerial promotions. "It's so easy to walk around the corner and give Johnny all the extra tasks because he's in my line of sight," concedes Darrell Heinrichs, an EDS account manager in Plano.

He gave a telecommuter supervisory responsibilities for the first time last April—after resisting the idea for more than six months. Michelle Kupperman Ott, the promoted project manager, now supervises two staffers. Like her, they work from home.

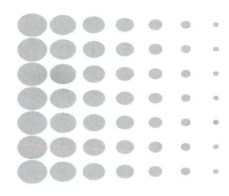

SECTION III

ISSUES OF EFFECTIVE LEADERSHIP

These days, only a few subjects in the management literature get as much attention and draw as much debate as does the question of what effective leadership looks like and how it can be developed and practiced. Writing about leadership is a growth industry in the academic and the popular press, and countless books and courses are devoted to understanding leadership and to showing how it can be done better. At the same time, most of us seem to be dissatisfied with the leaders we have or we argue that the days of great leadership are long gone. Others believe that leadership does not make "a dime's worth of difference." They may be right, but few if any of them would leave the choice of leaders in their organizations to chance or let the behavior of their leaders go unchallenged.

Many people say that effective leadership is essential as a means to guiding our work teams, our organizations, and our society to more productive and humane futures. In a time of great change and uncertainty, we cannot rely on routines and programs to figure out visions for the future, responses to crises, ways to reinvigorate those who are slogging it out in the firing line. Effective leading is a critical factor here.

In this section of the book, we have chosen some provocative pieces to illustrate the many facets of effective leadership and its practice. You will notice that our take on leadership is that it does not reside in one single individual (at the top of some structure or entity) but can be found in the actions of many different people in the organization. We take seriously, also, the notion that leadership is as much about leading oneself as it is about leading others. Self-knowledge is an important ingredient of good leadership. Finding ways to use self-insight and self-discipline to create breathing space for oneself and for others can add to the tone and the resilience of the relationships among leaders and followers. Therefore, our selections on leadership focus on leading oneself and on leading others.

PRACTICING THE POLITICS
OF ACCOMPLISHMENTS

Our opening chapter, "Practicing the Politics of Accomplishments," deals with an aspect of leadership frequently overlooked in discussions of what makes for good leadership, namely the practice of politics. Not only is it soft-pedaled in many texts, but it also is avoided or treated with disdain by many practicing leaders. We think this is a mistake, and when it is discussed in terms of having influence, building coalitions, lobbying for needed resources, "asking for forgiveness rather than seeking permission," and framing one's message from the *listener's* point of view, resistance melts away to the idea that there is a political aspect to effective leadership. In fact, a leader can be superbly organized and help the team stay on track. She can be warm and supportive to members of the team—a great listener. But leaders also need to attend to the larger games going on in the organization, of resource allocation, of future directions of the company, and so on. Leaders also need to work at creating understanding in the minds of other managers and leaders of what their team or division is accomplishing. (Remember, those other players typically have different agendas and takes on the world and need to be "educated" and reminded about what we are doing to help the organization, and them, prosper.) This political work does not have to be dramatic. In the article "We Don't Need Another Hero," Joseph Badaracco describes how effective leaders work unobtrusively behind the scenes for success. He states, "Before they take stands or tackle tough problems, the quiet leaders calculate how much political capital they are putting at risk and what they can expect in return."

Leaders who practice the politics of their craft need to maintain a good sense of their own grounds for action or, in time, they will lose their way and become cynical actors in the game. Sam Culbert and John McDonough address this balance issue in their discussion of "alignment" in "The Invisible War: Pursuing Self-Interest at Work." According to them, alignment involves "what an individual goes through in attempting to relate his or her subjective and self-centered interests to what he or she perceives as the objective requirements of the job." Many psychologists tell us that when people achieve effective alignments (i.e., synergistic relationships between internal and external demands), they are happier and more energized and, in our view, their political interventions are more authentic and enduring.

Colin Powell has achieved remarkable success as a leader in many different arenas. Among the practices that appear linked to his high competence is his political acumen. This becomes evident in Oren Harari's discussion of Powell's uses of power ("Behind Open Doors: Colin Powell's Seven Laws of Power"). Simply listing some of these principles makes aspects of his political leadership clear; for example: Dare to be a skunk! That is, ask the hard questions that no one else is willing to address (a bold and brave form of leadership.) Share the Power! Wise leaders think of power that they use to forge the relationships and alliances between the leader and other key players in the organization so that they can create opportunities and remove roadblocks for their team and for their organization. It is a resource to be shared, lifting others up and giving them space and the confidence to perform.

Organization and empathy are not enough to meet the requirements of good leadership. Without a willingness to exercise power and the skills to do so, that hardworking, happy group of employees will not survive. If their leader is willing and able to do the political work necessary to keep them in resources and in the organizational game, they have a much better long-term future and they and their organization are the winners.

FOSTERING COURAGE

"Fostering Courage" is our next chapter in this section on leadership issues. It certainly can take an act of courage to work thoughtfully with power. Good leadership draws upon courage in other ways, too. In fact, we often say that "if it's safe, it's not leadership!" and to the extent that this is true, then one of the qualities that leaders need to attend to is courage—theirs and others. Dick Daft and Robert Lengel tell the poignant story of the young eaglet who lived among chickens. We won't spoil the story for you but urge you to think about the messages it conveys and how they might relate to your own aspirations for leadership. The chapter that follows their story, "Courage," provides some useful ways to think about courage (e.g., as fighting for what you believe) and about the role of fear and failure in the development of courage. They make an important point that the ability to say "no" and the ability to say "yes" are each illustrations of courage, depending on the merits of the situation.

The courageous exploits of Sir Ernest Shackleton in the early twentieth century are receiving a great deal of attention at the present time. Movies, books, and traveling exhibitions of the amazing journey of survival to the Antarctic of Shackleton and his team attest to the current interest in the courage and capacity of leaders. In the *National Geographic* article, "Epic of Survival," the details of his and his men's heroism make for inspiring reading.

The trouble with courage is like the trouble with compassion. We are all in awe of it, especially the stories of the incredible feats of a Shackleton (or of a Mother Theresa, when thinking about compassion). If this is our only perspective on the phenomenon, we are apt to marvel and to move on. "Wonderful," we say, "but this is not about us. It's not something we can or ever do!" Monica Worline ("Creating Courageous Organizations") helps us get out of this trap. Writing about life inside organizations (where we spend so much of our time), she points out that courage is something that "involves a sense of action that is deliberately directed toward what is right rather than what is expedient." Not all of leadership is about being political, although it often takes courage to work constructively with power. She says later in her article that a key aspect of leadership is the way in which the actions of the leader give voice to the courage in others, and that he or she releases this capacity in others. She also carefully distinguishes between reckless behavior and courage that is a "reasoned pursuit of what is good, regardless of the fear, yet heedful of risk."

WINNING WITH OTHERS

How do leaders get things done well through others? Not well if you believe the amusing but somewhat accurate messages in "The Creation," a poem about the way plans for action are created and communicated. One of the issues that leaders have to deal with is conflict, and one tried and relatively true approach to the disagreements is for the leader to act as a facilitator to the conflict process and to guide the warring parties toward a consensual decision. Another possibility is to preside over the battle and to let them fight it out. This is the advice of Kathleen Eisenhardt and her colleagues in "How Management Teams Can Have a Good Fight." In Eisenhardt's view, the absence of conflict is not harmony but apathy, and it is in management teams in which "members challenge one another's thinking" that a richer array of options and decisions emerges. She and her coauthors provide useful guidelines for making needed battles productive and invigorating for those who are involved. In this era of continuous change and of increasingly diversified workforces, the leader who can relate to and harness the talents of many different people in the organization has an edge. This premise also is picked up in the short piece by Del Jones in the *USA Today* article featuring leaders who have come to the job with nonbusiness education ("Offbeat Majors Help CEO's Think Outside the Box").

We find many cogent suggestions for leaders about winning with others in the *Fast Company* interview with Ronald Heifetz ("The Leader of the Future") Heifetz touches on the need for leaders to have the courage to face the hard realities they encounter and to help others face up to mistakes and failures in the organization. He identifies the need for leaders to assist people as they struggle to keep their balance and to focus in times of change. Heifetz makes a comment that carries with it a compelling image. "Most leaders die with their mouths open," he says. What they need to do, he argues, is to listen with empathy and curiosity so that we get a realistic picture of how an issue looks and feels to our staff. We can then derive some of their actions from this knowledge and understanding.

Leadership is a dangerous enterprise, says Heifetz, and he gives us some sense in the interview of why this is so. He suggests that some of the danger comes from trying to ripen issues that are not yet ready for direct attention but that must be confronted at some point. He gives us the example of Lyndon Johnson doing this work to help get civil rights to the top of the agenda during his tenure as president of the United States of America. He also addresses some strategies that leaders can use to protect and rejuvenate themselves, given the heavy demands that they carry. He advises us to "not take things personally" when we find ourselves under attack but to understand that others attack the position we represent, not us personally. He suggests also that we find a daily sanctuary from the rigors of leadership. These are useful strategies for managing our roles as leaders, and they provide a clear bridge to our next section, which deals with how we can lead ourselves effectively.

LEADING ONESELF

We said at the outset of this discussion of leadership issues that a key element in effective leadership is how we lead ourselves. The opening short story, "Sharpening Saws," underscores the importance and the value of this assumption. The hermit who neglects to sharpen his saw (invest in himself) finds that when the going gets tough, he cannot cope with the tasks he must do in order to survive. What are the essentials of self-leadership? We don't really know yet, as this is relatively new territory in the leadership literature. (It is an issue that was given attention in a special issue on leadership in the December 2001 issue of the *Harvard Business Review*). Wayne Muller's questions about the meaning of who we are and what we do with our lives "Questions That Matter" give us a place to start in exploring our progress as leaders. "Who am I and what do I love?" he asks. In trying to answer these questions, we can begin to identify what passions we bring to the leadership table. "How shall I live, knowing I will die?" and "What is my gift to the family of the earth?" are questions that push us to think beyond the day-to-day triumphs and tragedies to think about the larger contributions we might want to make as leaders. Consultant and author Jim Collins ("The Learning Executive") provides illustrations of the issues that Wayne Muller addresses—and raises some questions of his own for us to ponder.

Stephen Covey, author of *The Seven Habits of Highly Effective People* suggests that leaders treat their employees the way they would want employees to treat their customers. This is cogent advice. In the context of this discussion on self-leadership, we might add "Always treat yourself as you would want to treat your best employees," that is, with respect and kindness while setting the bar high for attention and effort.

Finally, as an antidote to the often all-encompassing demands and the often lonely experiences of being a leader, we have the words of the late Harry Chapin's song "The Cat's in the Cradle" about the lament for lost time with his son. We also have the poetry of 85-year-old Nadine Satir, "If I Had My Life to Live Over," to remind us to take time for ourselves and those we love so that we nourish others and take time to feed ourselves.

● ● ● ● ● ● ● ● ● ● ● ● ● ● ● ●

LEADING OTHERS

One of the myths of leadership is that it resides only in specific individuals, notably those who are at the top of organizations. Leadership can come from anywhere in the organization, and the more this role and set of practices is distributed throughout the system, the healthier that system is likely to be. In "Leading from Any Chair," Benjamin Zander discusses the effect on his role as an orchestra conductor when he recognized that his power came from his ability to make other people feel powerful. Leadership resided everywhere in the orchestra, and when he sought and acknowledged feedback from the musicians on his own leadership behavior, orchestra performance was enhanced. He found also that the orchestra played much better and its members felt more satisfied and inspired when he was able to draw on their insights about the music being played for his own contribution as conductor. His vivid examples of how this played out (pun intended) are instructive and inspiring.

Phil Jackson, fabled coach of two basketball dynasties (the Chicago Bulls and the LA Lakers) characterizes his own leadership style as value based—as striving to reach and motivate his players through inclusion and participation, rather than by adopting a top-down approach to his coaching ("The Invisible Leader"). He talks eloquently about applying *skillful means* to disciplinary decisions involving people, by which he means addressing them from a basis of compassion and humanity, regardless of the issue or infringement. "A person who packs a kid off to bed for spilling milk instead of handing the child a sponge is not practicing skillful means," he observes.

Organizations need leaders with vision, daring, and energy to help them survive and prosper in the challenging world of the present. One breed of leaders who do this well are those Michael Maccoby calls narcissists (*Narcissistic Leaders: The Incredible Pros, the Inevitable Cons*). These leaders are larger-than-life personalities who inspire others to act and to join them in ventures that challenge and change the direction and impact of their organizations. However, as Maccoby argues, these same leaders need others to keep their egotism and drive in check, or their virtues eventually become liabilities for themselves and their organizations. They give us the best and worst of times, and it is as much in the contributions of these other leaders that we find the modification and partial containment of the narcissistic effects.

III-1: We Don't Need Another Hero

Joseph L. Badaracco, Jr.

The most effective moral leadership, it turns out, is provided by people who work behind the scenes for quiet victories.

Everybody loves the stories of great leaders, especially great moral leaders. Think of Martin Luther King, Jr., Mother Teresa, and Gandhi. We exalt these individuals as role models and celebrate their achievements. They represent, we proclaim, the gold standard of ethical behavior.

Or do they? I don't ask this because I question the value of ethical behavior—far from it. I ask because over the course of my career as a specialist in business ethics, I have observed that the most effective moral leaders in the corporate world often sever the connection between morality and public heroism. These men and women aren't high-profile champions of right over wrong and don't want to be. They don't spearhead large-scale ethical crusades. They move patiently, carefully, and incrementally. They right—or prevent—moral wrongs in the workplace inconspicuously and usually without casualties. I have come to call these people quiet leaders because their modesty and restraint are in large measure responsible for their extraordinary achievements. And since many big problems can only be resolved by a long series of small efforts, quiet leadership, despite its seemingly slow pace, often turns out to be the quickest way to make the corporation—and the world—a better place.

In this article, I explore the findings of my four-year effort to understand how quiet leaders see themselves, think about ethical problems, and make effective decisions. Although all names have been changed, the anecdotes below are based on more than 150 case studies that I gathered from several sources, including direct observation, participation in situations as an adviser, and papers and accounts by many of my older MBA students who came from corporate positions with serious management responsibilities. The stories have convinced me that while certain ethical challenges require direct, public action, quiet leadership is the best way to do the right thing in many cases. That's because quiet leadership is practical, effective, and sustainable. Quiet leaders prefer to pick their battles and fight them carefully rather than go down in a blaze of glory for a single, dramatic effort.

TWO ETHICAL APPROACHES

To understand why quiet moral leadership works so well, consider what can result from a public display of heroism. Rebecca Waide was a manager at a small regional bank. Convinced that a set of lending policies was exploitative, she made an appointment with her boss and quickly launched into a made-for-Hollywood speech about the rights of the poor. "I can almost swear that while I was talking, there was inspirational music in the background," she says. "I must have sounded like Sally Field in *Norma Rae*. I wanted to defend the oppressed."

It didn't work. Waide's emotionalism and lack of careful preparation undermined her credibility. The company thought its policies were sound, particularly for riskier customers, and her boss didn't appreciate the lecture. Not surprisingly, the company's lending policies remained unchanged.

Now consider Barry Nelan, another banker whose case I studied. He was going through files one day when he discovered that a company had been charged too little interest on a bank loan for more than five years. He wondered if the bank's executives, some of whom were good friends with the borrower's managers, knew about the problem but were conveniently overlooking it. He feared that his boss, who had authorized the loan, might be scapegoated if the problem came to the attention of others.

At first, Nelan saw only two choices. He could report the error through official channels and let the chips fall where they might, or he could leave things alone. But then he came up with an alternative: He took the matter directly to his boss. His boss's first instinct was to rebury the problem, but Nelan said that if they couldn't find an answer, he would be forced to inform bank executives about the mistake. They sat down with the client and restructured the loan, then reported the problem and the solution to the executives. Nelan was careful, patient, and politically astute throughout the process. He managed to benefit himself and the organization while protecting his colleague's job. He was the quintessential quiet leader.

● ● ● ● ● ● ● ● ● ●

OPERATING INSTRUCTIONS

My research suggests that quiet moral leaders follow four basic rules in meeting ethical challenges and making decisions. Although not always used together, the rules constitute an indispensable tool kit that can help quiet leaders work out the dilemmas they face. Some tactics may seem a little too clever or even ethically dubious. Certainly, few people would want to work at jobs where such moves constitute business as usual. Nevertheless, these guidelines often

prove critical when leaders have real responsibilities to meet.

The rules serve another purpose, too. By offering insight into how an organization's unknown soldiers achieve their moral victories, the guidelines can help top executives foster the development of quiet leaders among middle managers. Tactics they can use include setting examples of quiet leadership in meetings; going out of the way to praise and reward individuals who take quiet, sustained, effective approaches to problems; and appointing top managers who are themselves quiet leaders. Such actions send powerful messages about the right way to deal with difficult, messy problems.

Put Things Off Till Tomorrow   When ethical dilemmas heat up, quiet leaders often look for ways to buy time. Careful execution of this tactic can spell the difference between success and failure. The passage of time allows turbulent waters to calm. It also lets leaders analyze the subtle way in which individuals and events interact—lets them look for patterns and watch for opportunities to arise from the flow of events. More important, sound moral instincts have a chance to emerge. Of course, there are situations—such as when a defective product is about to be shipped or a new leading financial report is about to be released—that call for immediate action. But the drama of do-or-die situation can lead us to exaggerate the frequency with which they arise. The vast majority of practical ethical challenges facing most managers are mundane and subtle, calling for unglamorous virtues of patience and staying power.

To see how quiet leaders create buffer zones that permit them to put their unglamorous virtues to use, let's look at a quiet leader who succeeded in thinking clearly and moving at a deliberate pace, even though top management was breathing down his neck. Kyle Williams had recently become a branch president for a small regional bank in Maine.

He was excited about a job that gave him visibility and profit-and-loss responsibility. The only drawback to the promotion was the intense financial pressure on the bank and its senior executives. Williams was told that if the stock price didn't rise quickly, the bank was likely to be bought and dismantled by a larger bank.

Among the 55 employees Williams inherited were four chronic underperformers, including a 56-year-old teller who was notoriously rude to customers and raised the issue of age discrimination whenever her performance was questioned. Another of the four was a widow who had been at the bank 30 years. She was recovering from cancer surgery but was reluctant to go on disability. Finally, there were the two lead loan officers: One lacked initiative and imagination; he did everything by the book. The other had more potential, but even the promise of a performance bonus didn't fire her up.

Williams was eager to reduce expenses, but he wanted to avoid shortsighted cost-cutting measures and to be fair to longtime employees. He thought firing the four underperformers, as was tacitly but clearly expected of him, might embroil the company in legal problems. He needed time to persuade his boss to take a different approach, such as transferring the underperformers or encouraging them to take early retirement. If there had been less stress on the bank, Williams would have openly argued for moving slowly. But given the pressures, a request for more time could have prompted the bank management to replace him with someone willing to clean house more quickly. So he took steps to divert attention while he postponed action. Call it game playing if you will, but Williams's games were hardly trivial amusements. They were tactics that allowed him to find a "good enough" solution to the bank's problems.

There are two kinds of time buying: quick fixes and strategic stalling. Everyday dodges such as, "I've got someone on the other line—can I get back to you on that?" can buy a few hours or a couple of days; such gambits have helped countless managers whose backs were against the wall. But Williams needed weeks to rectify the situation he inherited. His situation called for strategic stalling.

The fundamental line of attack in strategic stalling is to dot all the i's and cross all the t's. As a first step, Williams tossed his boss a bone by cutting a few unnecessary expenses (badly managed operations often have plenty of those). He then sought legal advice on his personnel issues—after all, one employee had already raised the issue of age discrimination. He also got human resources involved, a move that gained him weeks. Then he began to raise strategic questions: Do we have the appropriate contingency plans in place? Are there more options we should evaluate?

Strategic stalling gave Williams time to resolve all the issues he faced. He never caught the teller being rude, but he fired her for leaving large amounts of cash unattended. The widow went on permanent disability. After pep talks, quotas, and incentives failed to motivate the two loan officers, Williams threatened to fire them. One quit; the other, galvanized into action, became a first-rate loan officer.

Before they take stands or tackle tough problems, quiet leaders calculate how much political capital they are putting at risk and what they can expect in return.

PICK YOUR BATTLES

Political capital is the hard currency of organizational life. You earn it by establishing a reputation for getting things done and by having a network of people who can appreciate and reward your efforts. Political capital is hard to accumulate and devilishly easy to dissipate. That's why quiet leaders invest it astutely and use it with care. Before they take stands or tackle tough problems, quiet leaders calculate how much political capital they are putting at risk and what they can expect in return. In other words, they pick their battles wisely.

For an example of how not to squander political capital, consider Michele Petryni, the public relations manager at a large Washington, D.C. law firm. Petryni stood in astonishment one day as she was refused admittance to a meeting with several law partners. The purpose of the meeting was to deal with a very sensitive problem in the firm, and for several weeks Petryni had been working with one of the partners on a solution. Now the partner was telling her that a "nonpartner female" would stir up the brew.

Petryni was shocked and furious. Her first impulse was to threaten a discrimination lawsuit. But Petryni was also shrewd. She understood that most of the time, getting on a white horse and leading a charge does little good. If she forced her way into the meeting, no one would be openly sympathetic and a few partners would be overtly hostile. Besides, she liked her job. She had been promoted rapidly and was widely respected in the firm. She didn't want to be labeled a troublemaker. So Petryni decided not to waste her hard-earned political capital. She opted for pointed humor instead.

"You know," she said to the partner she had been working with, "I've never been told I couldn't play ball because I didn't have the right equipment!" He appreciated her effort to smooth over the rupture and later told the senior partner what happened. The senior partner sought out Petryni and apologized for the firm. He acknowledged there were sexists in the firm but said they were an aging minority. He asked Petryni for her patience and support.

How well did Petryni handle this situation? Her tactics didn't fit the standard model of heroic leadership. She didn't tell the first partner that he was doing something obnoxious, insulting, and perhaps illegal. She didn't go to the meeting, even though she belonged there. Many people would argue that she surrendered her interests. But Petryni made a prudent investment. Her restrained approach enabled her to make her case to the partner she had worked with and the senior partner without offending either. Of course, her efforts didn't change the firm's culture, but she was able to get management to acknowledge that there was a problem. Most important, Petryni added untold riches to her political capital for the occasions when she really wants to fight.

BEND THE RULES, DON'T BREAK THEM

Most of us don't associate bending the rules with moral leadership. But following the rules can be a moral cop-out. If a friend asks if you like her new shoes, and you think they look ridiculous, you don't tell the truth. And when the Gestapo demanded to know who was hiding Jews, some people lied. Between the trivial and the tragic are many everyday situations in which responsible people work hard to find ways to maneuver within the boundaries set by the rules. Instead of acting like moral bookkeepers, they bend the rules and own up to their deeper responsibilities.

Consider Jonathan Balint, a consultant who was working on a large project for a manufacturing company. Balint's brother-in-law happened to work for the client and was trying to decide whether to take an offer from another company or stay in his present job. Balint had learned that the client was three weeks away from announcing a major layoff; Balint's brother-in-law would likely lose his job. Should Balint tip him off to the danger of staying at the company?

Balint didn't want to betray the confidentiality of his client or his firm; doing so, he knew, would be wrong, and it could severely hurt his career. So he spent several days searching for wiggle room. He took the rules seriously but didn't treat them as a

Ordinary People

The quiet moral leaders in my study typically work in the middle of organizations where they look for modest but effective solutions to the problems they face. They don't aspire to perfection. In fact, their thinking is distinguished by two characteristics that would almost certainly disqualify them for sainthood: Their motivations are decidedly mixed, and their worldviews are unabashedly realistic. Let's take a closer look at each of these traits.

MIXED MOTIVES

According to the heroic model of moral leadership, true leaders make great sacrifices for the benefit of others. In truth, however, very few people would sacrifice their lives for a cause (which is why we revere the handful of people who do and why we call them saints and heroes). Most people, most of the time, act out of mixed and complex motives. They want to help others, but they also care about themselves. They have lives, interests, and commitments that they are unwilling to risk. Because they need to put food on the table, crusades and martyrdom are not options.

Consider John Ayer, an experienced sales rep at a major pharmaceutical company that had been selling physicians a very popular drug for treating depression. Although federal laws forbade it, the company started discreetly promoting the drug to doctors whose patients wanted to lose weight or stop smoking. Ayer didn't want to limit his pay or promotion prospects, but he didn't want to break the law or contribute to patients suffering side effects from unapproved uses. So he tried to walk a fine line: He talked about unapproved uses of the drug only if doctors asked him. But as more and more of his sales came from those uses, he became increasingly troubled and decided to stop answering questions about unapproved uses. He also visited doctors who were prescribing the drug for problems other than depression and discussed the risks and side effects with them. Then he went a step further: He told his manager and a few other sales reps what he was doing and why, in part to protect himself against future liability.

By any standard of moral purity, Ayer doesn't measure up very well. His motives for doing the right thing are unmistakably self-serving. As he puts it: "My decision was made as much out of fear as anything else. I was scared of finding out that a patient had died because one of my clients had prescribed the drug at a high dose. I also suspected that my company would not stand behind me if something horrible happened."

Although Ayer's motives were hardly unadulterated, they nonetheless gave him the strength to persevere. Indeed, when there is a tough moral challenge, the degree of a person's, motivation can matter more than the purity of the motives. That's because real leaders draw strength from a multitude of motives—high and low, conscious and unconscious, altruistic and self-serving. The challenge is not to suppress self-interest or low motives but to harness, channel, and direct them. If Ayer had been motivated by empathy alone, I believe he would have been far less likely to act.

Of course, mixed motives can leave people in Ayer's position feeling bewildered and frustrated, but that's not all bad. Confusion in complex situations can prompt people to pause, look around, reflect, and learn before they plunge into action. Soldiers who clear minefields move slowly and methodically, but their deliberate pace takes nothing away from their valor and adds greatly to their effectiveness. Indeed, my research shows that when quiet leaders succeed, it is usually *because* of their complicated and ambivalent motives, not despite them.

CLINGING TO REALITY

Ayer's quiet approach to leadership raises important questions. Should he have done more? Should he have taken the issue to senior management? Should he have blown the whistle and alerted federal regulators?

I believe the answer is no. All too often, whistle-blowing is career suicide. Torpedoing your career might be fine if you end up changing your company—or the world—for the better. But dramatic action seldom leads to such

(continued)

(*continued*)

impressive results. Quiet leaders pay close attention to the limits of their power. They don't overestimate how much influence they have over other people or how well they can control events in an uncertain world. Each quiet leader realizes that, in most situations, he or she is only one piece on a chessboard.

Such realism is often confused with cynicism. But realists aren't cynics; they merely see things in Technicolor, whereas cynics see black and white. Quiet leaders' expansive vision of reality in all its colors helps them avoid acts of heroic self-immolation.

Consider Ben Waterhouse, the head of marketing at a medium-sized company. His boss asked him to drop a high-performing ad firm and replace it with a six-month-old agency. Waterhouse was flabbergasted, especially when he discovered that the owner of the new agency was a good friend of his boss. Waterhouse's immediate instinct was to dash off a strong memo or call a meeting with his boss's superior. But after he calmed down, Waterhouse recognized that he didn't have the clout to override his boss on this issue. So he developed a prag-matic plan. He gave the new ad agency a couple of very challenging assignments, which they handled poorly. He documented the failures to his boss, who opted to stick with the veteran agency.

From the perspective of heroism, Waterhouse's story seems more like a cop-out than a profile in courage. He didn't take a stand on principle; in fact, he engaged in subterfuge. But Waterhouse's realism was not a moral handicap—far from it. It gave him a sense of proportion and a degree of modesty and caution that helped him move wisely across a hazardous landscape. In the process, he managed to preserve one of the company's most valued relationships. He also kept his company from incurring unnecessary expenses. This made much more sense—realistically and ethically—than flaming out in a single heroic, but futile, act.

Taken together, the traits of mixed motives and hard-boiled realism describe the working assumptions of quiet moral leaders. A moral compass points these individuals in the right direction, but the guidelines for quiet leadership help them get to their destinations—in one piece.

paint-by-numbers exercise. Eventually he decided he could send signals to his brother-in-law without revealing everything he knew. For example, he reminded him that no one is indispensable, that anyone can be laid off; Balint also said he had heard rumors about impending layoffs at local manufacturers. His brother-in-law took the hint.

Balint's choice perfectly illustrates the way quiet leaders work. They know that breaking the rules is wrong—and in some cases illegal. They also want to protect their reputations, networks, and career prospects. So they don't break the rules. But when situations are complicated, they typically search for ways to bend the rules imaginatively.

Quiet leaders don't view such tactics as ideal ways to handle problems, but sometimes situations give them no choice. Balint, for example, had competing obligations to his client and his family. In complex ethical situations such as these, bending the rules is never easy and certainly not fun. Indeed, bending the rules—as opposed to breaking them—is hard work. It requires imagination, discipline, and restraint, along with flexibility and entrepreneurship.

Instead of acting like moral bookkeepers, they bend the rules and own up to their deeper responsibilities.

FIND A COMPROMISE

Compromise has a bad reputation in some circles. For some people, compromise is what politicians and lobbyists do in smoke-filled rooms. Many of us believe that good people—moral people—refuse to compromise. They tell the truth, the whole truth, and nothing but the truth, and they are always fair. Quiet leaders understand this view of moral principles, but they don't find it particularly useful in most situations. They reject the idea that moral principles can be treated like salami and sacrificed slice by slice, but they try not to see situations as black-and-white tests of ethical principles. For this reason, crafting responsible, workable compromises is not just something that quiet leaders occasionally do. It defines who they are.

Take Roger Darco, for example. Darco was a hardworking, successful sales rep who learned he wouldn't be able to sell a long-time customer a new server it needed. The servers were in limited supply, and his company was saving them for "premier" customers. Roger raised the issue with his boss and got lots of sympathy—but no assistance. Instead, his boss reminded him of the importance of making quota.

On the face of it, Darco had only two options. He could refuse to give his client the server, or he could violate company policy and sell the server by faking documents, as some reps were doing. But somewhere between extremes there is often a compromise solution. Darco found it by discovering that if his client was willing to be a test site, it could get the server early. The client agreed and got the machine it needed.

Darco may not look like much of a moral hero, but he did take on a complicated ethical issue and get it right. He didn't start a revolution—the situation didn't call for a revolution. Yet by finding a workable compromise, Darco uncovered a middle that was "good enough"—responsible enough and workable enough—to satisfy his customer, his company, and himself.

THE SILENCE BETWEEN THE WAVES

The quiet approach to leadership is easy to misunderstand and mock. It doesn't inspire or thrill. It focuses on small things, careful moves, controlled and measured efforts. It doesn't provide story lines for uplifting TV shows. In contrast to heroic leadership, quiet leadership doesn't show us the heights that the human spirit can reach. What, then, do the imperfect, unglamorous, everyday efforts of quiet leaders amount to? Almost everything. The vast majority of difficult human problems are not solved by the dramatic efforts of people at the top but by the consistent striving of people working far from the limelight.

This was the view of Albert Schweitzer, a hero if ever there was one. After he won the 1952 Nobel Peace Prize for working with the poor in central Africa, Schweitzer used the money to build a facility for treating leprosy. He changed many lives and inspired countless others. Yet he was unromantic about the role of great moral heroes in shaping the world: "Of all the will toward the ideal in mankind only a small part can manifest itself in public action," he wrote. "All the rest of this force must be content with small and obscure deeds. The sum of these, however, is a thousand times stronger than the acts of those who receive wide public recognition. The latter, compared to the former, are like the foam on the waves of a deep ocean."

Joseph L. Badaracco, Jr., is the John Shad Professor of Business Ethics at Harvard Business School in Boston. He has taught courses on strategy, general management, and business ethics in the school's MBA and execu- tive programs. He is the author of *Leading Quietly: An Unorthodox Guide to Doing the Right Thing*, published by Harvard Business School Press in February 2002.

III-2: The Invisible War
Pursuing Self-Interest at Work
Samuel A. Culbert and John J. McDonough

Each time people enter a new work situation they engage in the implicit process of *aligning* personal values, interests, and skills with what they perceive to be the task requirements of their job. They seek an orientation that maximizes self-pursuits and organizational contribution. *Alignment* is our term for the orientation that results from such an effort, however implicitly this takes place. Once such an orientation has been evolved, it becomes a self-convenient lens through which all organizational happenings are viewed. That is, once people hit on an alignment—an orientation that lines self-interests up with the task-requirements of their jobs—this alignment serves to alert them to meanings they can use in promoting and supporting their personal and organizational endeavors, and to meanings put forth by others which threaten the credibility and relevance of what they are pursuing.

Not all alignments are effective. That is, the orientation some people use is too far removed either from the needs and obligations of their jobs or from expressing the inner themes that can make their jobs personally meaningful. We say an individual possesses an "effective" alignment when the orientation directing that person's actions and view of reality allows him or her to represent important self-interests while making a contribution to the organization. We say an individual lacks an effective alignment when important discrepancies exist between what that person inwardly values, endeavors to express, does well, and needs to do in order to satisfy what he or she perceives to be the task requirements of the job.

Now we can return to the questions raised at the beginning of this chapter. [in original—eds.]

- Why do people with the same job perform their assignments so differently?

Easy, they have unique interests, values, and competencies to bootleg into their jobs at every opportunity.

- Why do people with comparable organizational goals see the same situation differently and fight unyieldingly over which interpretation is correct?

Easy, while they may be striving to attain comparable organizational objectives, what they are striving to attain in their lives and careers is very different. This causes them to attend differently to each of the elements in a given situation. Finally,

- What determines the specific way individuals decide to perform their jobs and how they interpret each situation?

From *The Invisible War: Pursuing Self-Interest at Work* by Samuel A. Culbert and John J. McDonough, 1980. pp. 60–71, 219–222. New York: John Wiley & Sons, Inc. © 1980. This material is used by permission of John Wiley & Sons, Inc.

Easy again, it's what we've termed alignment. People proceed with a job orientation that spontaneously spins out interpretations and meanings that serve the unique way they need reality constructed in order to be a "success." How individuals do a job and what they see are influenced by what they find personally interesting, by the concepts they can master and the skills they can perform with excellence, by the self-ideals and values they seek to attain, by their unique ideas of what constitutes career advancement, by what they believe will score on the checklist that others will use in evaluating their performance, and by what they genuinely believe the organization needs from someone in their role.

Few people are all that aware of their alignment. Even fewer are conscious of the fact that systematic biases permeate their view of the organizational world. And, almost no one understands that such biases play a major role in making organizations effective. All this is because most people work their alignment out implicitly and take its presence for granted until a change in the external scene, in other people's views of their effectiveness, or in their own sense of satisfaction show it to be obsolete. Then they can appreciate what they lost and strive for a new alignment that will again allow them to satisfy self-interests and personal pride while getting acclaim for doing a good job. For example, consider what happened to a middle manager named Pete who had a marvelous alignment until he got promoted and suddenly found himself faced with a serious gap between his own and the organization's definition of success.

Pete was one of twenty in his corporation who, some five years ago, agreed to take on a newly created mission, that of improving communications and managerial competence within his company. This function seemed right up Pete's alley. He'd attended sensitivity training sessions, had a reputation of being genuinely concerned with people,

and was respected up and down the ranks for his leadership ability even though he had not burned up the track with his progress.

Pete saw the new assignment as a chance to bolster a lagging career. He had never been overly concerned with rising in the hierarchy, but his failure to take a fast track to the top was presenting him with daily redundancies that left him feeling somewhat stale. At forty-five he needed another challenge and this assignment held the potential to revitalize his career. Eagerly he accepted.

Pete threw himself into the new position. He enrolled in outside courses and hired skilled consultants to design training programs for the corporation's managers. Whenever possible he assisted the consultants and within a short time he understood their technology and was able to play a role in tailoring their inputs to the specific needs of his corporation. His learning continued and soon he was running programs on his own, involving personnel from each divisional level. Almost immediately his reputation as a man who genuinely cared was enhanced by widespread recognition of his competence in the management development technologies. And he was no soft touch either. He aggressively challenged managers on their "self-sealing" logics and constructed boat-rocking experiments to confront higher-ups with the demotivating and profit-eroding consequences of their autocratic styles.

Pete's involvements took an exciting turn with the advent of minority and women's consciousness. If the corporation's managers weren't racist, their de facto hiring and promotion policies were. This meant a greater volume of work and warranted an increase in the size of his staff. From a resource base that started with himself and a secretary, his department increased to two professionals, an administrative assistant, and two secretaries. Their operation hummed. They did career development counseling with secretaries. They got involved with the corporation's recruiters, both to encourage the hiring of blacks and females and to create programs that would support the new employees' progress in an essentially all white male management structure. They hired racial-awareness consultants to get managers in touch with their prejudices and help them work these out. And with this heightened workload, Pete even found time to continue his efforts in getting managers to identify areas in which their style intruded on the effectiveness of others.

Pete also had marvelous latitude in job definition which he exploited to match his interests and values. He enrolled in personal growth courses, attended conventions, joined professional associations, and on occasion even used the company plane. Because Pete identified both with the welfare of people and the productivity of the corporation and was concerned that his work produce tangible outcomes, his indulgences were hardly noticed—rather they were seen as part of his power. The people on his staff looked up to him and nondefensively brought him their toughest problems for coaching and support. His credibility with people lower in the hierarchy provided him a position of influence with those at the highest corporate levels. And, delightfully for Pete, his reputation among blacks and women was impeccable.

Within a couple of years Pete had worked out an ideal *alignment*. He had a way of engaging each constituency that allowed them to see how his actions related to results they valued. There seemed to be a 99 percent overlap between his personal definition of success and the missions and responsibilities assigned to him, and no one in the company could perform them better.

The other nineteen managers receiving the same charter as Pete, but working elsewhere in the corporation, didn't fare nearly as well. Perhaps lack of know-how, perhaps enculturation in the corporation's way of doing things, or perhaps a different tolerance for conflict had made them reluctant to aggressively challenge higher-ups. With time, to a greater or lesser degree, their roles degenerated to those of commiserator and management "go-for." They always seemed to be on the defensive, trying to prove themselves rather than challenging others to be more excellent. Their weakness and low-keyed tactics made Pete's strength and accomplishments look all the more potent.

Eventually those sitting in upper corporate echelons took notice of the overall situation and decided that Pete was the role model of what they were trying to achieve. They approached Pete with an offer of a promotion if he would agree to supervise and train the other nineteen managers. Pete's first reaction was to accept, but something held him back. At the time, he didn't understand his hesitancy, so he merely used it to negotiate a sweeter deal. He would not take responsibility for the others, there were too many bad habits to overcome. But he would step up a level in his current territory and accept overall responsibility for recruitment, career planning, minority advancement, and improved managerial functioning.

Pete's promotion put him on the same level with other line managers. He became a regular member of the management team and now directly supervised three managers who were responsible for about forty professional employees and oversaw the hiring of outside consultants.

Unfortunately, at this point, his alignment fell apart and his work life became filled with aggravation. *First*, his former associates began treating him like their boss, which he was, and this severely undermined his ability to coach and openly suggest. Now his suggestions were heard as orders and his inadvertent questions were received as well-thought-out criticisms.

Next, his relationships with blacks and women went to pot. His elevation in the hierarchy caused him to be seen as manager rather than human rights worker and he was treated to rounds of Mau-Mauing and confrontations, as what formerly had been received as his in-group remarks were interpreted as racial and sexist slurs.

Next, Pete found that the added amount of time his new job required for supervision, staff meetings, and report writing reduced the time available for the internal consulting role he prized.

On top of everything else, a "screw-up" in another division involving a racial-awareness consultant set off a reactionary wave up to an executive vice-president who responded by ordering sharp cutbacks in the use of outside consultants. For Pete, this had the personal effect of cutting off sources of his support and learning and the task effect of withdrawing the quality resources needed to keep his operation competently stationed and challenging to the status quo.

To top these disappointments, after about three months in the new job, Pete's boss called him in for a coaching session where he received word that his new peers were concerned that he was hurting his career by appearing to be such a deviant and advocate for minorities. Pete returned to his office screaming, "What the hell is going on here, these are the same jokers who wanted me promoted because I *was* such a deviant?!"

This was the last straw. Not only were his former constituents treating him like one of the "other guys" but the "other guys" were claiming that he was too much of a deviant for them.

From our perspective Pete was caught without either a personally effective or an organizationally successful alignment. His personal viewpoint wasn't registering anywhere. Nowhere was he actively shaping reality. His alignment had become obsolete. He was in the same position his nineteen former counterparts had found themselves in when they were charged with a mission to which they could not personally relate and thus could not confidently assert an articulate point of view.

Incidentally, and no pun intended, this is not a case of the "Peter Principle." We know Pete and he's anything but a person who had been promoted above his level of competence. We believe it is just a matter of time before Pete constructs a new alignment, one that allows him to use his new job for personal expression and to further the missions he values. But until he gets realigned, the self-deliberations entailed in trying to match self-interests with what seems to be required by his job will provide him with many lonely hours of unhappiness and frustration.

Pete's story was chosen because it illustrates the active dimension of the orienting process we call alignment. It shows the importance of an individual's commitment to inner values. That Pete could succeed, both inwardly and outwardly, where nineteen others could not is a tribute to his success in finding a good match between his personal needs and interests and what he saw as needed by the job. He had an effective alignment. The nineteen others lacked an effective alignment and most of them became either *cynics or careerists*. The cynics converged on alignments that subordinated the organization's needs to their own interests and values. They saw management's view as constraints to be navigated around, not perspectives to be joined and possibly learned from. Conversely, the careerists adopted alignments that subordinated their personal interests and values to what they thought would score on the organization checklist. They ground out workshop after workshop, training event after training event, but without the conversations and conflicts that could budge the status quo.

The concept of alignment, and Pete's story, provides support for most people's contention that repackaging themselves to fit a particular job or role does not constitute a sell-out to the job, although to an outsider their compromises frequently appear fatal. As Pete's situation illustrates, people need to shift alignments when they change jobs or experience a new set of external demands, even though their interests, skills and values remain the same. While self-interests remain relatively constant, the form in which they are pursued and expressed must shift. How often we've seen people criticize the way their boss operates only to themselves embody much of the same behavior as they shift alignments upon moving up to the boss's level in the organization.

In summary, we see the concept of alignment as a key addition to how people should be thinking about organizations. There's a level of organization residing within each individual that explains how that person does his or her job and views external organization events. If there's an external organization that determines how groups of people relate in doing work together then there's an *internal organization*, far more encompassing than an individual's personality, that determines how individuals within groups transact their business and work for the greater institutional good. Moreover, despite their lack of prominence in how people present themselves, self-interests are a dominant factor in determining what gets produced in the name of organizationally required product and how what is produced is received. And you don't need the skills of a psychoanalyst to understand these self-interests. You merely need to comprehend what an individual is trying to express personally and achieve in his or her career, and what he or she perceives as making a valuable contribution to the job. At every point personal needs and organization goals impact on one another, and it's always up in the air whether the needs of the job or the interests of the individual will swamp the other or whether a synergy of interests will evolve.

Thus *alignment* is our term for the highly personal orientation one takes to the job that must be known before we can comprehend the meaning and intent of someone's actions. Sometimes people do different things for the same reason. Sometimes people do the same things for different reasons. Without knowing people's alignment, taking their actions on face value—even those with a direct connection to bottom-line product—leads to erroneous conclusions. The only way to comprehend what people are about is to know what they are trying to express and achieve personally and what assumptions they are making about the organizational avenues for doing so.

At this point we provide a guide to comprehending the personal side of an individual's orientation to the job. It's a set of questions which, when thoughtfully answered, provide a new perspective on why an individual does his or her job the way he or she does it, and why that person views organization events in a particular way. Add in the task requisites of the job, as the individual sees them, and you've got that person's alignment. Incidentally, we've had marvelous results using an abbreviated list of these questions as preparation for team-building meetings at which a boss and his or her subordinates get together for a long session to discuss opportunities for improving their work-group's effectiveness. Twenty to forty minutes each, around the group, and the edge comes off many premeeting criticisms. Instead of being programmed to fault one another for inadequacy, the discussion takes a constructive turn as participants contrast the fit between an individual's needs and talents with what participants see as the task requisites of that person's job.

The questions we use in seeking to understand the self-interest side of an individual's alignment fall into three categories: personal, career, and organizational. Specifically we ask questions drawn from, but not limited to, the following list.

Self-Interest Questions

Personal

What are you trying to prove to yourself and, very importantly, why?

What are you trying to prove to others? Give an instance that illustrates why and how.

What style of life are you trying to maintain or achieve? (Does this entail a change in income? geography? family size? etc.)

Name the people who have played significant roles in your life and say what those roles were.

What dimensions would you like to add to your personal life and why?

What motto would you like to have carved on your tombstone and how do you want to be remembered by the people who are close to you?

Career

What profession do you want to wind up in? (If you are an engineer and you say "management," tell why. If you are not in that profession, say how you plan to get into it.)

How did you, or will you, develop competency in that profession?

What do you want to accomplish in that profession?

What honor or monument would you like to have symbolize your success in that profession? Say why it would constitute a personal hallmark.

Organizational

What has been your image in your organization and what would you like it to be?

Describe a bum-rap or overly simplistic category others have used in describing you and tell either why you are different now or why their statement was simplistic or too categorical.

What is the next lesson you need to learn and what are your plans for doing so?

What would you like to be doing two to five years out?[1]

What would you like to be doing ten years out?

While we encourage people to share perspectives generated by these questions with work associates whom they trust, we do not recommend that they reveal specific instances in which self-interests played a role in determining one of their organizational actions. We don't because we fear that others, however well-intentioned, will inadvertently misuse such candor later on. What we advocate is that each individual simply provide associates a more valid context for viewing his or her goals and accomplishments. . . .

Conclusion

It's appropriate that we've saved our favorite story for the end. It's a story about a manager who embodies the best of both the subjective and the rational approaches to leadership and for us is a symbol that it can be done. This manager is able to go toe to toe with hard-boiled characters like Charlie and at the same time remain sensitive to the contributions made by leaders like Fred.[2] He's a manager who searches for ways of relating to the uniqueness of those reporting to him while he shuns calling "objective" that which he sees as arbitrary and a matter of personal convenience.

The manager we have in mind demonstrated the effectiveness of much that we

---

[1]Think of "doing" in terms of a specific assignment (job, position, status) and specify it in terms of a specific role (player, coach, expert) and how you would like to be performing it.

[2]Charlie and Fred are characters introduced earlier in the book from which this except is taken—*Ed. note.*

are advocating in three distinct settings: industry, education, and public service. First, he fought his way through the highly competitive world of consumer products where he became chairman of the board of one of the nation's largest and most successful conglomerates. Next, in the educational field, he became the dean of a large and prestigious professional school, instituting changes that brought national recognition to that institution. And most recently he was the President's choice to head a world-renowned agency and this appointment brought instant acclamation from the Senate Hearings Committee. All this took place before his forty-seventh birthday!

In our view the key to this manager's success lies in his ability to see the connection between personal effectiveness and organizational efficiency. To him, these are highly related issues. He believes that organizations exist to serve people, not the other way around, and he constantly searches to understand what people are trying to achieve in the way of personal meaning and career success. Nevertheless, his style is one which frequently gets misinterpreted as soft and permissive leadership and does not produce an easy route to universal love and appreciation. His understanding of personal projects allows him to penetrate many of the facades people construct, and this makes him the target of behind-the-scenes ambivalence and face-to-face suspicion. Let's examine his impact more closely.

In the first place, he resists spending the bulk of his energies responding to problems defined by others as "crises." This orientation allows him to take tough stands with respect to the succession of "crises" any top administrator faces, and which, if passed down through the organization, can make it impossible for anyone to align self-interests with the task requirements of their job in a way that's constructive for the institution. In the short run his "nonresponsiveness" makes him vulnerable to the charge that he is not on top of a situation. In the long run, however, he frees himself and the people in his organization from the oppressive burden of always responding to someone else's fire drill.

We certainly don't want to mislead you into thinking that our hero, or any other leader, could emerge from each of these settings totally unscarred. To the contrary, on his way to the board chairmanship he spent more than three years going eyeball to eyeball with a manager whose style was the antithesis of his own and whose subordinates consider him to be "the biggest prick you're ever going to find in a chief executive's office." When our leader realized that he was going to be locked in mortal combat for as long as he stayed with the conglomerate, he began to look around. That's when he got into education. Some say things got too hot for him to handle. In our minds his decision revealed that he saw more to life than surviving corporate death struggles.

It's interesting to contrast the subordinates who value his leadership style with those who don't. Those who see flexibility in the construction of their own alignments generally appreciate his style. But he causes fits among those with careerist and martyr mentalities. These people are confused by his respect for the personal side of their alignments. They mistake his sensitivity to what is personally meaningful to them as agreement with their self-beneficial formulations of what the organization needs to do. Consequently they experience small betrayals when learning of a decision he takes after surveying their perspective. What they don't understand is that our hero seriously considers competing perspectives prior to making a decision and that his integration is almost always original, with even the people who influenced him the most finding themselves unable to identify their input in what he prints out. But for those with open ended questions, his print-outs are almost always educational. By factoring out what he added, they deduce what this leader sees as the limitations in their formulations.

For almost everyone, his style is disarming. His searching respect for the subjective side of an individual's participation is responded to as a warm and irresistible invitation to tell all. This makes it quite difficult to fragment. Knowing that he knows their subjective interests causes most people to tell their whole story—either out of a fear of looking stupid or one of getting caught telling a half-truth. In subtle ways this leader conveys the message that he's not there simply to serve the self-indulgent needs of individuals but to provide another perspective on what the organization needs and to challenge people to find a more synergistic means of relating their needs to organization product. And he's been able to do this and still score on the traditional checklist.

In many ways this leader is bigger than life; certainly his accomplishments surpass what most of us are externally striving to achieve. Today's society seems to worship external success, yet each of us knows that we're up to so much more. Our hero often strikes us as a very lonely man and we can't help but think that a major part of what appears to be a self-imposed solitude derives from an understanding that, in today's world, his accomplishments are valued for reasons which bear little resemblance to what he sets out to do. But help should be on the way. We believe the evaluation categories which convey illusions of objectivity and overemphasize externals will gradually change. And as more people demonstrate an enhanced appreciation for the subjective involvements that everyone brings to organization life, this leader, together with the rest of us, will have an easier time being himself and gaining recognition for just that.

III-3: Behind Open Doors
Colin Powell's Seven Laws of Power

Oren Harari

He has commanded armies and headed government agencies—and now as U.S. Secretary of State, Colin Powell is in every sense a world leader. Through the years, in each position of growing authority, he has followed a code of leadership that inspires confidence, trust, and admiration.

Powell and I became friends after we both spoke at an IBM-sponsored conference in 1996. Over time and from our many discussions, I formulated a point-by-point guide to Powell's style, a kind of Leadership 101.

Surprisingly, for a lifelong Army man, many of his strategies seem to fly in the face of traditional military thinking. As I began developing these principles into a book about Powell's innate management skills, I at first viewed the project as primarily for business leaders. But in the days following the September attacks in New York and Washington—as Powell displayed his assured, dignified, and well-prepared style—it became clear to me that everyone has a vital interest in having a clear understanding of the Powell Way. What's more, I firmly believe that Powell's insights are of immense practical value for anyone faced with important decisions, whether business or personal. Here are seven of his key principles.

The day soldiers stop bringing you their problems is the day you have stopped leading them.

1. DARE TO BE THE SKUNK

"Every organization," says Powell, "should tolerate rebels who tell the emperor he has no clothes and this particular emperor expects to be told when he is naked." As a young officer out of the ROTC program at New York's City College, Powell headed a platoon in Vietnam—where he learned something about how not to lead others. "We accepted that we had been sent to pursue a policy that had become bankrupt," he wrote in his best-selling autobiography. "The top leadership never went to the Secretary of Defense or the President and said, 'This war is unwinnable the way we are fighting it.' They bowed to group-think pressures and kept up pretenses."

Powell and many other junior officers vowed that someday, when they were in charge, they would not make the same mistake. Years later, during Desert Storm, he would put that principle into practice. Almost immediately after becoming Chairman of the Joint Chiefs of Staff in 1989, Powell huddled with President George Bush's senior staff, debating how best to respond to the invasion of Kuwait by Iraq. The group agreed that the United States should continue to defend Saudi Arabia

from invasion. But what about pushing the Iraqis out of Kuwait? Only Powell was willing to bring up that potentially devastating question. "I guess some people suggested that that was not the correct thing for me to ask," he says. "But I asked it."

He went even further, suggesting that the President draw his famous rhetorical "line in the sand." And, he recalls, "That was not a well-received statement." In fact, then Secretary of Defense Dick Cheney bluntly criticized Powell.

"Perhaps I was the ghost of Vietnam," he says. "There had been cases in our past when senior leaders, military leaders, did not force civilians to make those kinds of clear choices, and if it caused me to be the skunk at the picnic, take a deep breath."

Of course, Powell is a gentleman. He's not rude or mean. As a good leader, he patiently builds a consensus, prodding people while simultaneously listening, learning, and involving them. But in the final analysis, he says, "Being responsible sometimes means pissing people off."

2. TO GET THE REAL DIRT, HEAD FOR THE TRENCHES

"The people in the field are closest to the problem," Powell says. "Therefore, that is where the real wisdom is." On the eve of the Desert Storm campaign, Powell solicited enlisted men and women for advice on winning the war.

"When a captain came to see me," he recalls, "I would tell him to sit down. I'd say, 'Talk to me, son. What have you got?' And then I'd let him argue with me, as if he were arguing with an equal. After all, he knew more about the subject than I did.

"I also knew he'd tell his friends that he had argued with the Chairman of the Joint Chiefs of Staff. Word would spread, and people would understand that when they came into my office I really wanted to hear what they thought." And that he trusted their opinions.

Leaders who ask for straight talk from the trenches must graciously accept information and diverse opinions—even ideas they don't want to hear. "The day soldiers stop bringing you their problems is the day you have stopped leading them," says Powell. Such encouragement can be non-verbal. The first time I walked into his office, Powell came around his vast desk and warmly ushered me into an alcove, where we sat, almost touching, at a far smaller, round table. He explained that the table sends a message of intimacy and trust. He wants visitors to know that he genuinely wants to hear what they have to say.

3. SHARE THE POWER

"Plans don't accomplish work," says Powell. "It is people who get things done." He adheres to two basic leadership premises: 1) People are competent and 2) Every job is important.

"Everybody has a vital role to play," he told his State Department staff when he took over as Secretary. "And it is my job to convey down through every layer to the last person in the organization the valuable role they perform."

The flip side to that leadership style is more responsibility on the part of those being led. The day he was promoted to lieutenant general and placed in command of V Corps in Germany, Powell received this letter from the Chief of Staff of the Army: "If in two years you have not heard from me offering you a second position or promoting you to four stars, I expect you to have your resignation on my desk." Two years later, four-star General Powell was in the White House as National Security Adviser.

"He expected me to retire if he couldn't use me anymore," Powell explains simply.

4. KNOW WHEN TO IGNORE YOUR ADVISERS

Experts, advisers, and consultants will only get you so far. Eventually a leader must make the final decisions. In Vietnam, Powell recalls asking a Vietnamese army officer why an outpost had been put in such a vulnerable spot. The officer explained that some military experts wanted it there to supply a nearby airfield. So then, asked Powell, why was the airfield there? The officer replied, "To resupply the outpost."

"Experts often possess more data than judgment," says Powell. "Elites can become so inbred that they produce hemophiliacs who bleed to death as soon as they are nicked by the real world." The best leaders, he believes, should never ignore their own hard-won experience.

5. DEVELOP SELECTIVE AMNESIA

Too many leaders get so trapped in fixed ways of seeing things that they can't cope when the world changes. In the spring of 1988, Powell flew to Moscow to prepare for a presidential summit. Sitting across the table, Soviet Premier Mikhail Gorbachev delivered momentous news, saying, in effect: "I'm ending the Cold War, and you're going to have to find a new enemy."

As Powell recalls it, his initial mental reaction was, "But I don't want to!" After investing 28 years in seeing the Soviet Union as an enemy, he realized that "everything I had worked against no longer mattered." But he regained his footing, adjusted to the new world order, and helped guide modern U.S. foreign policy.

While we all have preconceived notions, Powell says, "Never let ego get so close to your position that when your position goes, your ego goes with it."

6. COME UP FOR AIR

Powell demands excellence from his staff, but he also insists they have lives outside the office. Again, he leads by example: He has always devoted as much time as possible to Alma, his wife of 39 years, and their children, Mike, Linda, and Annemarie. "I don't have to prove to anybody that I can work sixteen hours a day if I can get it done in eight," he told his State Department staff. "If I'm looking for you at 7:30 at night and you are not in your office, I'll consider you a wise person. Anybody who is logging hours to impress me, you are wasting time."

7. DECLARE VICTORY AND QUIT

"Command is lonely," says Powell. And so is the decision to withdraw from the position of authority—a choice he says not every leader makes soon enough. His own retirement from the military was, in his word, "traumatic."

"One of the saddest figures in all of Christendom," he says, "is the Chairman of the Joint Chiefs of Staff, once removed, driving around with a baseball cap pulled over his eyes, making his strategic choice as to whether it's going to be McDonald's or Taco Bell."

Powell didn't stay retired in 1993. Now in civilian clothes, he helps lead not only the military but the nation itself. He is equal to the task in no small measure because of the lessons he has learned and the principles he lives by.

"Leadership," he says, "is not rank, privilege, titles, or money. It's responsibility."

III-4: Courage

Richard L. Daft and Robert H. Lengel

A farmer one spring enjoyed watching two eagles flying near a distant bluff. After failing to see the eagles for a couple of days, he went to investigate. He found an abandoned nest that held an egg, which he took back to the farm. With the faint hope that it might hatch, and a baby eagle grow up and fly, he placed the egg in a nest in the henhouse.

Two weeks later, the egg hatched, and the strange-looking baby eagle joined the chicks in the yard of the henhouse. As the first days passed, the eaglet learned the habits of the chickens, feeding on the corn provided by the farmer. Noticing birds flying overhead one beautiful morning, the eaglet remarked, "Wouldn't it be wonderful to fly like that! I wish I could fly." But you know how chickens are. They quickly admonished this foolish thinking. "You are a chicken," they said. "You are not meant to fly." The fearful mother hen said, "If you try to fly, you will surely get caught in the chicken wire and break your neck." The strutting rooster father added logically, "Even

(continued)

Reprinted with permission of the publisher. From *Fusion Leadership*, copyright © 1998 by Daft/Lengel, Berrett-Koehler Publishers, Inc., San Francisco, CA. All rights reserved. www.bkconnection.com

(*continued*)

if you flew over the fence, it would be hard to find food and you would probably starve." All the chickens agreed the baby eagle should not try to fly.

"It sure would be wonderful to fly and soar like that," the eaglet repeated to himself. "I wish I could do it." But he did not try. He believed the chickens. As the days and weeks passed, the eaglet said little about flying. He spent more time alone, often in the henhouse.

Then one day, the farmer noticed that the eaglet was no longer in the chicken yard. He hoped the eaglet had grown big enough to fly away, but went to investigate. The henhouse was dark, and when he turned on the light, he noticed a clump of dark feathers in the corner. He picked it up, saw that it was the young eagle. The eaglet was dead.

This story is sad because the eaglet saw his inner dream in the birds flying overhead, and if only he had tried, he too could have flown. Instead, he listened to the chickens and died without ever fulfilling his true identity.

The eaglet story is applicable to people, especially managers, who have identified their dream but have not acted on it. Dreams are not achieved automatically. You have to make dreams happen in the face of resistance from the "chickens."

Companies that rely exclusively on strong forces appeal not to courage but to fear. Fear appeals to the conditioned ego, not to the deeper, essential self. When fear prevails, the deeper sources of courage within managers and employees go untapped, and remain so until people begin to wonder why risk taking and courage are so rare. Courage, like mindfulness and vision, can be remembered and unlocked.

A dream comes from the heart. Acting on the dream takes courage. Courage enables you to fly. Courage carries you through deprivation, ridicule, rejection, and potential failure to achieve something you love. Corporate America was misled by years of stability, abundance, and the assumption that courage wasn't needed. Managers learned: "Keep your nose clean. Don't fail. Let somebody else go first. Don't have a mark on your record. Be careful. If you are cautious and gather enough data, you won't make a mistake."

This approach is so safe, and so ridiculous. Life in an out-of-kilter world is as safe as a roll of the dice. Things constantly change, one thing depends on everything else, and nothing significant can be controlled. Leaders thrive by solving problems through trial and error, which means many errors. In a turbulent world, caution is no match for reality. Action is demanded. Acting precedes planning, not vice versa. Leaders create the future by moving forward in the face of uncertainty, by taking chances, by behaving with courage. Yet many aspiring leaders seem blocked from risk taking and initiating real change. Their fears overwhelm them. In this chapter, we will help leaders understand and break through such fears.

WHAT IS LEADERSHIP COURAGE?

In images from folklore, courage is seen as doing battle with intrusive elements from the external world. It is the virtue of the archetypal warrior who takes the offensive, loves action, and abhors inaction. Similarly, the inner warrior has a strong spirit, engages life, seizes opportunities, and enjoys an outpouring of life energy toward a valued goal, a higher mission or cause. A courageous leader is an adventurer, an explorer.

Courage is the stuff that underlies a leader's choice to put in long hours, endure pain, and overcome obstacles, lack of sleep, and repeated rejection.

In *Iron John*, Robert Bly asks the reader to consider whether he is made of copper or iron. Copper is a conductor. A manager made of copper lives as an unhealthy bridge for others. The demands of the organization, the expectations of others, the boss's whims, all run through a copper person without resistance. The copper manager suppresses his real opinions and beliefs, carries out orders, tries to gain acceptance by being a nice person, and may become an apologist for actions that violate his own true values. Managers made of copper accept change initiated by others so that they will obtain corporate approval.

Iron represents strength, armor, and protection. Iron means healthy resistance. Arrows bounce from an iron shield. The leader made of iron sets limits, knows when to say "Enough," and will sacrifice charm, niceness, and the approval of others in the risky cause of the dream. Leaders made of iron have opinions. They disagree with the boss. They express subtle forces, and protect others' right to do so. They promote new ideas in the pursuit of a higher purpose. The leader made of iron has an internal shield to protect himself and his boundaries.

Courage and risk taking seem nonexistent in some of today's large, bureaucratic organizations. We visited a large agency of the federal government and were amazed at the obsessive avoidance of risk taking in that corporate culture. The slightest mistake created a whirlwind of blaming, finger pointing, and extra effort to avoid responsibility. Culpability was passed down the chain of command: one lower-level employee suffered the penalty for a superior's error because he had no power to avoid it. The absence of courage froze the agency. People were almost afraid to do normal tasks. Innovation was impossible.

Yet there are also examples of great courage in organizations. A study sponsored by Korn-Ferry International found many leaders unafraid to take risks. "They spoke out, they changed jobs, they argued with bosses, they tackled assignments with uncertain prospects for success. They consistently voiced a strong point of view, and pushed for what they believed." Courage is the CEO who was proud to admit, "We make mistakes on an hourly basis." That attitude was the basis of his company's success. Courage is Hewlett-Packard's medal of defiance given to people who disobey the system and succeed anyway. Courage is the executive who gave the highest performance evaluations to people who made mistakes while stretching beyond their traditional responsibilities.

COURAGE IS NONCONFORMITY

Not too many years ago, large companies would hire business graduates by the truckload. The students who went to work in staff jobs at IBM would soon start to look and think alike in important ways. The same is true of those hired to work at the headquarters of General Motors or Ford. And the Ford people would be different from the IBM people. An important reason for homogenization is that the business graduates want to succeed. They want approval. The organization has enormous power over those who will do whatever it takes to succeed. Business graduates use their talent to tune into politics and protocol and give the company what it wants, hoping someday to "succeed" with a big salary and high position. But this success-oriented behavior is conformity, not leadership.

Leadership in a destabilized world means nonconformity. It means breaking tradition, boundaries, and norms. One obvious trait that distinguishes a leader from a manager is a willingness to take risks, to deviate from the system, to change the system. Leaders do not play it safe, and they encourage others to take chances. Managers are fine for stability, leaders are needed to initiate change. It takes courage to jump into a new way of doing things when you don't know for sure whether there is water in the pool. Leaders extend themselves, they try new things. Rather than avoid surprises, courageous leaders welcome surprises because this is where progress is made.

At its easiest, courageous leadership means championing change in the form of a new idea, product, procedure, or improvement. At its hardest, courageous leadership means being a maverick, pursuing guerrilla warfare, dismantling the system, perhaps creating a new culture or a new paradigm. The courageous leader does whatever is needed to help the organization and its people grow, improve, and adapt.

Understood in this way, leadership is difficult. Leadership is a struggle. Leaders who pursue a dream to improve the organization will find cooperation, but they will also meet resistance. Just as the Red Sea parted for Moses, the organization may yield to a leader's dream and passion, but leakages will slosh back on the leader. Well-intended people will resist, disagree, or drag their feet. When nudging subordinates into new territory, you will encounter opposition, uncertainty, and doubt. You will make mistakes, be outvoted, and fail. Other managers will challenge you, and you will feel hurt and rejected. Leadership is a struggle, both within yourself and within the organization. That's why warrior courage is so critical. *If what you are doing comes easily, it is probably not leadership*.

It is important to note that nonconformity must be verbal if it is to influence others. Consider the Texas farm family and guests who decided to drive forty miles to town for dinner on a hot day when their car's air conditioner wasn't working. They were miserable. Talking about it afterward, each person admitted that he or she hadn't wanted to go, but went along to please the others. The father said he had suggested going to town only as a way to make conversation and find out what the others wanted to do. No one in the family wanted to go to town on that hot day, yet no one honored their mindful inner voice and said no.

Jerry Harvey calls this The Abilene Paradox. He found that people often don't voice their independent thoughts because they want to please others. The need to please blocks the truth. Often, in company teams, no one says how he really feels or what she really thinks. The reason is partly our cultural predisposition to conform. People want approval and hence fail to listen to or act spontaneously on the subtle voice within.

COURAGE IS NAMING THE TRUTH

The old Newtonian wisdom for a stable world was to fake it, to maintain an appearance of strength, to keep your nose clean, to go along with the company crowd. Steering a course through the chaos of the modern workplace requires that the hard problems that at first glance seem insurmountable must be faced honestly. Giant bureaucracies like IBM, GM, or Sears Roebuck were impossible to streamline as long as leaders failed to acknowledge the reality of their own and the companies' weaknesses.

Like the medicine man in a tribal culture, the courageous leader today recognizes and names the "undiscussable" demons that plague his organization. To face the faults within himself, his coworkers, and his organization is to acquire the demon's power.

> Consider Pat Riley's naming of the demon in the New York Knicks after he took over as coach. The players couldn't see how their cliques and dislike for each other fed negative attitudes and a losing mindset. He had the players report to a room one hour before practice.

They all sat together while Riley named the members of each clique and described their characteristics. Then he had each clique sit together in separate corners. The chair-shifting exercise made visible a new reality for the team. Riley held up a mirror to their separateness and hostility. The players fumed, but they got the message, along with an hourlong discussion about tolerance, openness, and team spirit. Riley's mindful naming of the demon started the team on a cooperative path that led to the playoffs. He helped the players remember the truth of why they were there.

A fusion leader seeks truth as the ultimate foundation for effective communication and trust. Denying the truth strains everyone as people tiptoe around obvious issues.

Expressing vulnerability takes courage, and leaders are admired when they acknowledge their responsibility for a blunder. President Kennedy earned great political capital from publicly admitting his responsibility for the Bay of Pigs fiasco. His honesty attracted people to him. Some think that Richard Nixon's refusal to admit mistakes about Watergate caused the threat of impeachment and his ultimate resignation. It is fear that prevents people from admitting failure.

A delightful example of vulnerability was Captain Asoh, a pilot for Japan Air Lines, who landed his DC-8 two miles short of the San Francisco runway—in the bay. When asked how he did what he did, Captain Asoh replied, "As you Americans say, Asoh f. . . up." Asoh knew that admitting the mistake was the best strategy for himself and J.A.L. He continued to fly for Japan Air Lines until his retirement, and having made the big mistake, he was a better pilot than ever.

As illustrated in the Greek myth of Orestes, even the gods admire people who openly take responsibility for their mistakes:

Orestes' grandfather was punished by the gods, who put a curse on his descendants. The curse upon Orestes was realized when his mother murdered his father. A son was obliged under the Greek code of honor to slay his father's murderer, yet the greatest sin a Greek could commit was to kill his mother. After agonizing over the decision, Orestes decided to kill his mother. The gods punished him by assigning three Furies to torment him day and night.

After many years of trying to atone for his crime and be relieved of the Furies, Orestes asked the gods to reconsider. A trial was held. Apollo spoke in Orestes' defense, claiming that he arranged the situation in which Orestes chose to kill his mother. Orestes jumped up and contradicted Apollo. "It was I, not Apollo, who murdered my mother!" He took personal responsibility. The gods were surprised because people always blamed the gods for what went wrong. Never before had the gods seen someone take total responsibility for his behavior. They decided the trial in Orestes' favor. They removed the Furies and assigned instead loving spirits to ensure Orestes' good fortune.

The moral of this story is clear: taking responsibility for your actions and mistakes brings acceptance and respect from others, and even good fortune. Denial of your mistakes and responsibilities brings pain and punishment.

COURAGE IS FIGHTING FOR WHAT YOU BELIEVE

In today's corporate world, where people seem so focused on their own careers, the idea gets lost that warriors use courage in the pursuit of the larger purpose, dream, or social outcome. Warriors venture beyond traditional boundaries, and risks are taken for an important purpose. The warrior fights for what he or she really believes in. A true warrior is not just out for number one, but fights for valued outcomes that benefit the community. Commitment to higher values is the foundation for risk taking.

Leadership courage does not mean using warrior energy to violate or hurt others. Courage is not conquest. Warriors do not venture beyond boundaries to triumph over the weak and powerless or to destroy things valued by others. True strength is gentle. The desire for conquest or destruction arises from fear, not courage. When the courageous leader becomes a destroyer, it is to destroy senseless procedures, thoughtless actions, corruption, pettiness, abuse, stifling bureaucracy, or unfair corporate demands. The warrior battles against obstacles that stand in the way of employee growth, the overall vision, and higher values.

COURAGE IS SETTING BOUNDARIES

Although warriors venture beyond traditional boundaries, courage also protects boundaries. Risks are taken and battles fought to protect the warrior's family, community, department, or organization. The warrior battles evil and injustice that threaten his or her community. The highest use of courage is to protect others, to be assertive for human values. Marshal Matt Dillon in *Gunsmoke* stood for justice by drawing a line in the dust against a mob that wanted to lynch a prisoner. The "Magnificent Seven" used their courage to defend a helpless Mexican community against ransacking bandits. Courageous leaders protect associates who take worthwhile risks and fail.

Courage also means protecting one's personal boundaries. Courage is the ability to say no. A strong individual will not give his or her entire life to the company, working endless hours in the hope of gaining approval. Saying no to unreasonable demands from bosses or subordinates protects your personal boundaries. The courage to say no in the interests of self-protection is as important as saying no to protect your family, department, or community.

Managers with courage are able to claim their rightful power as human beings, as leaders, as employees. Such managers ask for what they want, for what their department or project needs. They pursue the department's vision, they facilitate change, they improve things, they say no.

FEAR AND FAILURE STRENGTHEN COURAGE

Courage is the ability to step forward through fear. Courage is the will to overcome fear. Courage means acting when you are afraid to act, whether giving a speech when you feel desperately shy or approving a multimillion-dollar contract that could sink your career.

People experience all kinds of fears, including fear of death, mistakes, failure, change, loss of control, loneliness, intimacy, pain, uncertainty, engulfment, abuse, embarrassment, rejection, success, and public speaking. Fear may reveal itself as a tightening in the stomach or as avoidance and procrastination. Recognizing the symptoms of fear is the first step in overcoming it. Avoidance is unproductive. Many fears can be conquered when you can admit to them.

Fears have a physical or psychological base. Physical fear has its roots in mortality. In our work with managers, fully 95 percent of the fears that influence their leadership behaviors are psychological. Psychological fear has roots in childhood, when we depend on acceptance and approval. The fear that the love of a parent might be lost persists into adulthood as an unconscious fear of any rejection or failure.

Everyone is vulnerable to fear when going beyond his or her comfort zone. In social or risk-taking situations, we may walk into an invisible wall—we would like to move forward, but can't. Single people may feel this wall of fear when asking someone for a date. Or it may loom up when a person is about to confront the boss, break off a relationship, launch an expensive new project, double the size of a building, or change careers. The wall is within us. It is our own fear projected onto the situation.

FEAR IMAGINES TERRIBLE CONSEQUENCES

What we've learned time and again is that fear of failure is worse than the failure itself. The imagined loss of reputation, dollars, love, respect, or whatever, is typically far worse than the real loss that occurs when a risk does not pay off. We can handle failure. We dust ourselves off and move on. Actual failure is not so bad. It's fear that stops us.

At a critical point in his life, Bob Lengel found himself confronting the irrational fear of consequences:

> My disenchantment with Wall Street became a watershed for courage in my life. The pull of financial success versus fulfillment kept me from peaceful sleep. As my discomfort mounted, my wife and I decided to join friends on a trip to Bermuda. I love the sea and looked forward to some time for

serious thought. On the second morning, as the group walked through the lobby of the Southampton Princess, I spotted a ticker-tape machine on the wall. Four men sat in front of it staring at the stream of symbols and numbers that passed before them. I told my friends I would join them at the beach after I learned how the market was doing. As I focused on the stream of stock quotes, I felt sorry for those men spending this beautiful morning worrying about their money and ignoring the beauty and spiritual joys only steps away. Then I realized I was one of them.

> During the downhill stroll to the beach, my mind was on fire. My impulse was to call in my resignation, but anxiety stopped me. What would I do to make a living? Would others think I quit because I couldn't cut it in the world of investments? The stream of terrible consequences that would surely occur if I acted from my heart blinded me. I walked along the water's edge by myself, absorbed in the sights, sounds, and smells that brought back memories of my childhood summers on the beaches of New Jersey. I remembered what it felt like to be fully engaged in a moment. Every sand crab, every seagull, lives at the edge of life and death. The lives of people like myself were insulated from living and dying by artificial walls of certainty and security. Maybe to be alive is to be at risk.

> A source of courage began to flow from within me. Within minutes, there was no doubt—there was a choice between preparing to live and continuing to die. As I rejoined my friends, the song

I Want to Live, by John Denver, was playing on the radio, and the lyrics about growing and giving and being will forever mean courage to me. Within two months, I was back in school studying to become a teacher.

Bob faced the invisible wall of fear that in the moment seemed to be made of concrete. He was scared and asked, "How can I do it?" But when he stepped forward, the wall disappeared. Suddenly the question changed to "Why did I wait so long?" Looking back, the decision was obviously correct, no matter how it turned out. He had to try. By stepping through fear, new opportunities sprang up.

Risk takers discover parts of themselves waiting to blossom. They grow strong. And they often experience unimagined success. The majority of risks work out. Either the risk succeeds as planned or the so-called failure produces growth that exceeds the originally desired outcomes.

Whenever leaders defer to fear, they lose their voice, the opportunity to express themselves. This is powerlessness, and it is self-imposed. It comes from not asking for what you want, not stepping into your fears, and not speaking your truth. People never really know themselves until they step through the wall of fear and gain the enormous benefits of either "success" or "failure."

FAILURE IS THE FIRST STEP TOWARD SUCCESS

An ice-skating instructor who had trained several "star" pupils was asked if she could tell which students would become champions. She answered that future champions were the ones willing to make fools of themselves. Nonconformity involves risk and the possibility of failure. And the failures are more important than the successes. Without failure, we don't learn. Many people mistakenly believe that failure leads to failure and must be avoided at all costs. This is absolutely untrue. Over time, success breeds failure, and failure breeds success. Everyone can recall an embarrassing failure that was the trigger for growth and learning and new success. Success and failure are phases in the normal cycle of leadership growth.

Sam Walton understood that his role was to take risks and change things. As David Glass, Wal-Mart's CEO said:

> Two things about Sam Walton distinguish him from almost everyone else I know. First, he gets up every day bound and determined to improve something. Second, he is less afraid of being wrong than anyone I've ever known. And once he sees he's wrong, he just shakes it off and heads in another direction.

If you don't have failures to look back on, something is wrong. You aren't acting like a leader. You've been playing it safe. One of our friends was proud of having skied all day without falling, and she said so. Another friend replied, "If you're not falling, you're not skiing." His point was that when a skier stretches to improve, she will naturally fall. In a short time, this woman became an outstanding skier.

A Zen teacher said, "Having many difficulties perfects the will; having no difficulties ruins the being." Thus gain is the edge of loss, loss is the heart of gain.

The poet Kahlil Gibran wrote that we must know fear and failure to enjoy success: "Your pain is the breaking of the shell that encloses your understanding. Even as the stone of the fruit must break, that its heart may stand in the sun, so must you know pain."

The strength gained from risk taking grows from a transformation similar to rebirth. The image of death followed by new life is symbolic of courageous leadership.

The writings of Joseph Campbell emphasize that failure and destruction are the beginning of new life. Death, decay, and pain are the creative forces producing new possibilities. Leaders affirm the life-giving opportunities in failure. The old life, the familiar organizational routine, has been outgrown. Leaders see that the time has arrived for the organization to cross a threshold into the new.

The leader may symbolically go inward, to be born again. Jonah went into the whale and survived. The Greek hero Herakles threw himself into the throat of a sea monster, then cut his way out through the belly, killing the beast. Each move forward is associated with loss, with the pain of giving up something. No leader or company can transform itself without ceasing to exist in some sense, leaving the old behind, leaping into the maw of the monster. The courageous hero, intent on protecting others, risks his or her own death in the effort to slay the monster. But having passed through fear, the hero comes away from the act a new person, stronger than ever.

This process of death and rebirth was experienced at Video Star, a company that provided temporary satellite networks to corporate clients. Executives took no chances in bidding for an all-important order from Digital Equipment, a prized special-event customer. All sixty employees geared up to win the order, which they expected to receive.

The order went to a competitor. Stunned and bewildered, Video Star undertook an agonizing postmortem. Its harsh self-analysis revealed much about how the company positioned itself in relation to prospective clients, and these findings led Video Star to redefine what it was and what it wanted to be. The company underwent a transformation that produced astonishing dividends in future bidding competitions. Without the failure, the rebirth and subsequent growth would not have happened.

SOURCES OF LEADER COURAGE

To be a fusion leader in a destabilized world is to frequently live outside your comfort zone. What can you do to push through your fear? How can you be forcefully assertive in the face of risk, let your warrior energy flow outward, and serenely accept losses and failures? Perhaps the best way to find courage is to connect risk taking to other subtle forces—emotions, a higher vision, and an attitude that welcomes failure.

EMOTION IS A SOURCE OF COURAGE

Emotion is the foundation of courage, the source of forward energy. Anger and love are two powerful emotions. Harnessing anger occasionally allows people to blast through fear. When someone has to be fired, it is often put off until an incident makes you angry enough to carry it out. In moderate amounts, anger is a healthy emotion that provides forward energy.

Perhaps less obvious, but even more important, is love. Positive emotions such as love, passion, and bliss pull us toward the objects that inspire them. When we are engaged with our hearts, our head is less likely to overanalyze possible short-comings (a symptom of fear), and we have greater confidence to push ahead. It's like being in love with an opportunity, however risky. As Barker described in *Future Edge*, rational judgment does not empower us to move into a paradigm shift. The courage to move forward is a leap of faith based on attraction, belief, and trust, rather than logic. When rational evidence is the only basis for risk taking, the path chosen is likely to be the safe one.

Emotion also means being connected to other people, which increases courage. Clarissa Pinkola Estes tells a story that describes the way of old African kings:

An old man is dying, and calls his people to his side. He gives a short, sturdy stick to each of his many offspring, wives, and relatives. "Break the stick," he instructs them. With some effort, they all snap their sticks in half.

"This is how it is when a soul is alone without anyone. They can be easily broken."

The old man next gives each of his kin another stick, and says, "This is how I would like you to live after I pass. Put your sticks together in bundles of twos and threes. Now, break these bundles in half."

No one can break the sticks when there are two or more in a bundle. The old man smiles. "We are strong when we stand with another soul. When we are with another, we cannot be broken."

Having support from others is a potent source of courage in an out-of-kilter world. Although rugged individualists in corporate America prefer to stand alone, being part of a team that is supportive and caring, or having a loving family at home, reduces the fear of failure. When a person is all alone, the consequences of failure seem enormous.

In *Band of Brothers*, Stephen Ambrose describes the astonishing fusion among members of E Company, 101st Airborne, in Europe during World War II. Having bonded together under seemingly impossible conditions during eighteen months of training and six months of fighting, these men cared about each other more deeply than brothers, more deeply even than lovers. In the harsh cold of a German winter, they gave up blankets to one another. When surrounded at Bastogne in Belgium, running low on supplies, they gave up food to one another and accepted scouting assignments to protect one another. If wounded, a soldier would use every device to get back to the front and rejoin the company. E Company was assigned the most difficult engagements, suffering 150 percent casualties (some soldiers were wounded multiple times). On learning that they were surrounded by Germans at Bastogne, one of the soldiers was heard to say, "They've got us surrounded, the poor bastards." A short time later, the company broke out and overran the German positions. Loving one another was their source of extreme courage.

COURAGE RESPONDS TO A HIGHER PURPOSE

The archetypal warrior has courage because he fights for what he believes. He is committed to something larger than himself, whether a community, a people, a task, a nation, a cause, or a god. Higher values and service to a larger vision are the great enablers of our inner warriors. Courage is easy when we fight for something that really matters.

Gandhi endured many deprivations in pursuit of the higher goal of expelling the British from India. Martin Luther King, Jr., received death threats against himself and his family almost every day during the civil rights movement. The moral rightness of his cause enabled King to move forward. What is the higher cause, the larger meaning, in your work and in the work of your division or department? Finding a meaning as simple as serving others can release the courage to innovate and even shift the paradigm. Immature leaders often pursue goals just for themselves. To them, failure means the loss of everything, rather than a minor setback on the road to a larger vision.

Bob Lengel witnessed a striking demonstration of the motivating power of higher purpose in a class he taught:

In a policy course, I had a student group that produced a creative paper about the downsizing of middle management. The group made the unusual argument that a company has a responsibility, beyond producing goods and services, to create jobs for people. I talked to a couple of the students in the group after their paper was graded, and they explained that they saw the paper as a big risk, but they took the risk so that Betty could receive an A. Betty was the first in her family to go to college, and now she wanted to go to medical school. The group decided to pull out all the stops for an A, which would increase the chances of her realizing that dream. These students had a higher mission, and they cared about each other. Their passionate priorities gave them the courage to make a daring leap. And they did earn their A.

Courage can increase simply as a result of your clarifying what you want to achieve. Risk taking then is only a matter of trying to reach your goal. Trial and error produces plenty of errors, but it also creates ultimate success.

WELCOME FAILURE AS A NATURAL PART OF THINGS

Joseph Campbell, in the study of myths and dreams, pondered why images of failure seem fewer in the twentieth century. He commented on an early saying by Heraclitus: "The upward way and the downward way are one and the same." The point is that our life journey can be seen as a harmonious relationship between upward and downward movement. It is a life-death-life cycle. Success and failure form a unity; these opposites are two sides of a coin. But modern man wants to have success without failure, believing that everything should be good and perfect, and that success arrives without difficulty.

Acceptance of failure fosters courage. Japanese samurai warriors learned to face the biggest possible failure—death. *The Book of Five Rings*, written centuries ago, prescribes the samurai practice of visualizing death in battle before the actual encounter. In a meditative state, a warrior could vividly see his own death and accept it. This allayed his fear, and he could go on and fight with abandon. Accepting failure and the worst possible outcome makes it easier to move the mission forward.

Leaders know that failure ultimately leads to success, that pain of learning strengthens the person and the organization. A courageous leader understands that the biggest risk of all is not taking risks, not experimenting, not taking action. Both the leader and the organization become healthier, trimmer, and more capable through trial and error. They know that danger comes from change that is too slow. A frog that jumps into a pan of boiling water will immediately jump out again. A frog that sits in a pan of cold water that gradually comes to a boil will perish.

Authentic courage is a human attractor. People want to follow someone with courage, especially the courage to be a nonconformist, pursue a higher purpose, serve others, admit failure, and be willing to act on faith and trust.

These ideas about courage are summarized in Exhibit 3-1.

Courageous risk taking is the price of fusion leadership. The eagle cannot soar if it listens to the chickens and remains afraid to fly. Courage is the foundation for personal action and achievement. Courage mentors others by its example. By developing their warrior potential, fusion leaders become strong and inspire others to be risk takers.

EXHIBIT 3-1 Courage	
Conventional Strong-Force View	*Fusion Leader Subtle View*
• Assert conformity	• Assert nonconformity
• Follow self-interest	• Follow higher purpose
• Seek to conquer	• Seek to serve
• Act as copper	• Act as iron
• Deny fear and failure	• Feel fear, admit failure
• Support success, avoid failure	• Support failure as way to grow and learn
• Avoid demons	• Name demons, speak truth
• Go along	• Disagree, say no
• Seek rational evidence	• Act on faith and trust
• Be self-sufficient	• Accept support from others

They energize both themselves and the organization.

● ● ● ● ● ● ● ● ● ●
PERSONAL REMEMBERING

- What are your three worst failures? What did you learn from those experiences? Are you taking enough risks? If not, why?

- What is the one thing you most want to do in your organization but have not? What fear is holding you back?

- What sources of courage can you call on to take a risk or step through fear?

- Reach out to someone in your work or social life who puts you off. Build a bridge to that person. What did this experience teach you?

III-5: Epic of Survival
Shackleton

Caroline Alexander and Frank Hurley

IT IS ONE of the very greatest survival stories in the annals of exploration. Sir Ernest Shackleton, his ship *Endurance* crushed by ice in Antarctica's Weddell Sea, led his men to safety through a series of impossible journeys over land and sea that, more than 80 years later, still leaves one gasping. When I was reading *South*, Shackleton's account of his adventure, I stood one evening in New York City, at a 79th Street bus stop, with the

book tucked under my arm. Feeling an insistent tug on my sleeve, I turned to meet the gaze of a man who was staring at me with the burning eyes of a zealot.

"Shackleton," he said, in half-whispered complicity, knowing that if I had read even part of the book, I would be a convert.

The Imperial Trans-Antarctic Expedition left Plymouth, England, on August 8, 1914, just at the outbreak of the First World War. Shackleton's ship was a three-masted wooden sailing vessel—a barkentine—specially designed to withstand ice. Called *Polaris*, the ship had been built by Norway's

"Epic of Survival: Shackleton" by Caroline Alexander from *National Geographic*, Nov. 1998, Vol. 194, Issue 5. Reprinted with permission.

most renowned shipyard out of oak, Norwegian fir, and greenheart, a wood so dense that it has to be worked with special tools. Shackleton renamed her the *Endurance*, after his family motto, "Fortitudine vincimus—By endurance we conquer."

Heading south, the expedition's last port of call was the island of South Georgia, a wild sub-antarctic outpost of the British Empire inhabited by a small community of Norwegian whalers. From here the *Endurance* set sail for the Weddell Sea, the dangerous ice-infested ocean abutting the Antarctic continent. Battling her way through one thousand miles of pack ice over a six-week period, the *Endurance* was about a hundred miles from her destination—one day's sail away—when on January 18, 1915, the ice closed in around her. A drastic drop in temperature caused the seawater to freeze, effectively cementing the compressed ice. The *Endurance* was trapped, "frozen," as the ship's storekeeper wrote, "like an almond in a piece of toffee."

Shackleton was by this time already a famous polar explorer. He had first been south with Capt. Robert Falcon Scott in 1901, drawn to Antarctica by the ideal of heroic quest. But the expedition ended in failure for Shackleton when he was invalided home with scurvy after the first winter. Five years later, at the head of his own expedition, he won renown for marching to within one hundred miles of the South Pole, the farthest south anyone had been. In December 1911 Roald Amundsen claimed the South Pole for Norway, leaving only one prize remaining in polar exploration— the crossing on foot of the Antarctic continent. It was on this Shackleton had set his sights.

Now, with the entrapment in the ice, his most daring venture was thwarted. More important, he was responsible for the care of 27 men—as well as 60 sledging dogs, two pigs, and the ship's cat, Mrs. Chippy. For the next ten months the *Endurance* zigzagged more than a thousand miles with the northwest drift of the pack. As each day passed Shackleton and his crew knew that the Antarctic continent was falling farther and farther away.

Some of the men were professional sailors from the Royal Navy; some were rough trawler hands who had worked in the brutal cold of the North Atlantic; some were recent graduates of Cambridge University who had come along as scientists. One, the youngest man on board, Perce Blackborow, had stowed away in Buenos Aires. All had come with different hopes, which had now evaporated.

For Shackleton, the disappointment was particularly bitter. He was 40 years old, and the expedition had taken considerable energy to prepare. Europe was consumed by war, and he was unlikely to have this opportunity again. Nonetheless, he knew that his men would look to "the Boss" as they called him, for direction and morale, Disguising his emotions, Shackleton gave the appearance of being confident and relaxed, and the long months on the *Endurance* passed almost enjoyably.

All hands on board knew that one of two things would eventually happen: Come spring, the pack would thaw and disperse, freeing them. Or, the pressure exerted by the grinding floes would take hold of the little ship and crush her like an eggshell. In October 1915 the signs were ominous.

In his diary, now in the State Library of New South Wales, Australia, Frank Hurley, expedition photographer, wrote on October 26: "At 6 p.m., the pressure develops an irresistible energy. The ship groans and quivers, windows splinter, whilst the deck timbers gape and twist. Amid these profound and overwhelming forces, we are the absolute embodiment of helpless futility. This frightful strain is observed to bend the entire hull some 10 inches along its length."

On the following day, Shackleton gave the order to abandon ship. The men spent their first night on the ice in linen tents so thin the moon shone through them. The temperature was minus 16 degrees Fahrenheit.

"A terrible night," wrote expedition physicist Reginald James in his diary, "with the ship sullen dark against the sky & the noise of the pressure against her seeming like the cries of a living creature."

Most of the expedition's food supplies were still trapped in the *Endurance*. Their warmest clothes were their long woolen underwear and Burberry windbreakers, about the weight of umbrella fabric. They had no radio communication, and no one in the world knew where they were. To get to safety once the ice broke up, they had only three salvaged lifeboats—and Shackleton to lead them.

"I can't remember the matter being discussed or argued in any way," James would recall. "We were in a mess, and the Boss was the man who could get us out."

In London's Royal Geographical Society, a venerable institution that has sponsored innumerable expeditions of discovery, the archivist brought me a Bible. I turned to the 38th chapter of the Book of Job—or, more accurately, to where the 38th chapter of Job once was. The page, as I already knew, was missing.

The day after the abandonment of the *Endurance*, Shackleton gathered his men and quietly told them they were going to try to march over the ice to Paulet Island, nearly 400 miles to the northwest. Only the barest essentials could be carried, and personal gear had to be sacrificed. By way of example, Shackleton took the ship's Bible and, ripping out a page from Job, deposited the book on the ice. The verses he saved read:

Out of whose womb came the ice?
And the hoary frost of Heaven,
who hath gendered it?
The waters are hid as with a stone,
And the face of the deep is frozen.

It was a dramatic gesture. What Shackleton never learned was that one of the sailors, a superstitious old salt named Tom McLeod, secretly carried the Bible away, believing that leaving it would invite bad luck.

The march to land was reluctantly abandoned: Dragging the loaded boats, each of which weighed at least a ton, over the colossal fragments of pressure ice and through deep snow proved impossible. The expedition now regrouped, and Shackleton determined there was nothing to do but pitch camp on the drifting ice and see where the current and winds would take them before conditions permitted the use of the boats.

Ocean Camp—the first of two camps pitched on the ice—was their new home. An eccentric supply of food was salvaged from the half-sunk *Endurance*; the crates that first floated to the surface—soda carbonate, walnuts, onions—were not necessarily what the men would have chosen for starvation rations. Sledging rations originally intended for the transcontinental trek were put aside for use in the boats.

It was now summer in the Southern Hemisphere, and temperatures crept as high as 33 Fahrenheit. The soft slush of snow made walking difficult, and the men's clothing was always wet; then the temperatures dropped each night, freezing the sodden tents and clothes. The principal diet was penguin and seal, and seal blubber provided the only fuel.

The men spent most of their time analyzing the direction of the ice drift. Their greatest hope was that the drift would continue north by northwest, carrying them within striking distance of Paulet Island, off the tip of the Antarctic Peninsula, where there was a hut with supplies from an earlier Swedish expedition. Shackleton's prime concern was not food or shelter but morale, and he feared the advent of depression as much as scurvy, the traditional bane of polar expeditions. The latter could be prevented by eating the organs of freshly killed animals, but the former required more complex management.

"Optimism is true moral courage" Shackleton often said. His particular concern was for the sailors, who more than the other men had been devastated by the loss of the *Endurance*. As Shackleton acknowledged, "To a sailor his ship is more than a floating home." From his earliest days as an explorer Shackleton had mixed easily with both the lower deck and the officers, and this now paid off. He was also well tuned to the temperaments of his men and catered to each. Hurley was somewhat vain, and Shackleton flattered him by making a pretense of consulting him privately on all matters of importance. A man found complaining that "he wished he were dead" was curtly assigned galley duties to distract him. Two of the more solitary and vulnerable men of the company were taken into Shackleton's own tent.

Other tactics were more controversial. The scientists and other educated personnel believed that the gravest danger facing the party was lack of food, and they wanted to kill and stockpile any wildlife that came their way. For the sailors who had been quartered in the fo'c'sle, on the other hand, the greatest imaginable hardship was remaining long months on the ice before being able to take to the boats. When Lionel Greenstreet, the first officer, urged Shackleton to put by more meat, Shackleton's response was instructive.

"Oh," he said. "You're a bloody pessimist. That would put the wind up the fo'c'sle crowd, they'd think we were never going to get out."

In mid-January four teams of sledging dogs were shot; the ice had become too treacherous for them to be safely used, and meat for their food was in increasingly short supply.

"This duty fell upon me & was the worst job I ever had in my life," reported Shackleton's loyal second-in-command, Frank Wild, in his memoir, also in the State Library of New South Wales. "I have known many men I would rather shoot than the worst of the dogs."

By March the northerly drift of the pack had carried them abreast of Paulet Island—but far to the east of it.

"One might as well try to cross from Ostend to Dover on water lily leaves as get over the pack from where we are now;" wrote Thomas Orde Lees, the expedition's storekeeper. "What is going to happen remains to be seen."

March was bleak. The last of the dogs were shot—and this time eaten. The men lay in the tents, huddled in their bags that had frozen as stiff as sheet iron, too cold to read or play cards.

In April the ice cracked through their camp, and Shackleton knew that the long-awaited breakup was at hand. On April 9 he gave the order to launch the three boats, the *James Caird*, the *Dudley Docker*, and—barely seaworthy—the *Stancomb Wills*, all named after sponsors of the expedition. Twenty-eight men crammed aboard them with their basic camping gear and rations. The temperature dropped to minus 10 Fahrenheit, and high seas poured over the open boats and men, who had no waterproof clothing.

Day and night, through the minefield of grinding ice, then through the crashing waves of the open sea, the helmsman of each boat tried to hold his course, while his shipmates bailed. The boats were too small to maneuver in gale force winds, and after several changes of direction, Shackleton gave the order to run due north, with the wind behind them, for a splinter of land called Elephant Island.

This boat journey was made most vivid to me by a trip I took on a fine, calm winter day—not to the Antarctic but to East Anglia, England. The son of Huberht Hudson, navigator of the *Endurance*, had agreed to let me see the sextant his father had once steered by. Serene in its packing case, its brass somewhat faded, it was an evocative relic—but not as evocative as the single image Dr. Hudson recalled of his father.

"My father's fingers were bent, you see," he said quietly, contorting his own hands. "From the frostbite."

For seven sleepless, nightmarish days and terrifying black nights, the men endured cold that froze their clothing into solid plates of icy armor. Out of the night-dark sea, with explosive, rhythmic exhalations, white-throated killer whales rose beside the boats, taking the measure of the men with their small, knowing eyes. Ernest Holness, who had braved the North Atlantic on trawlers, covered his face with his hands and wept. Blackborow, the popular young stowaway whom Shackleton had made ship's steward, quietly mentioned that his "feet felt funny." And Hudson, bent over the tiller with ungloved hands, finally collapsed. Shackleton's exhaustion was extreme.

"Practically ever since we had first started Sir Ernest had been standing erect day and night on the stern counter of the *Caird*," wrote Orde Lees. Shackleton knew it was important to his men that they see him in charge.

At last, on April 15, the boats hove under the forbidding cliffs of Elephant Island, and a landing was made.

"Many were suffering from temporary aberation," was Hurley's description of his shipmates' mental state. Many lay on the ground burying their faces in the stones or reeled down the small beach, laughing uproariously. It had been 497 days since they had last set foot on land, but, as they soon discovered, a more godforsaken, blizzard-raked part of the Earth could scarcely exist. Howling 80-mile-an-hour winds off the glacial peaks shredded their tents and swept away precious remaining possessions— blankets, ground sheets, cooking utensils. The

sailors crawled into the boats to take cover; others lay with the cold wet tent canvas collapsed about them, draped over their faces.

Shackleton knew that the outside world would never come to Elephant Island. There was only one remotely feasible course of action, and it was terrifying. He would take the largest lifeboat, the *James Caird*, and with a small crew sail 800 miles across some of the most dangerous water on the planet, the South Atlantic, in winter, to the whaling stations of South Georgia. They could expect to encounter waves as high as 50 feet from tip to trough, the notorious Cape Horn rollers. They would navigate by sextant and a chronometer whose accuracy was unknown, depending on sightings of the sun—but they knew that in these latitudes weeks of overcast weather could prevent a single sighting.

It is possible to make a pilgrimage to the boat itself, now retired in Shackleton's old school, Dulwich College, and one day I went there on a day trip from London. To conjure the scale of the seas that this unremarkable-looking wooden craft had survived was beyond both my experience and imagination, and standing beside the *Caird*, I was struck by a more banal consideration—that six men had found room in so small a craft. Overcome by unexpected emotion, I wept.

The *James Caird* was a 22 1/2-foot-long wooden lifeboat, whose gunwales had been raised by the skill of Henry "Chippy" McNish, Shackleton's gifted Scottish carpenter. Working outside with frost-nipped hands as the blizzards raged on Elephant Island, McNish salvaged what timber he could from packing cases and old sledge runners. The "decking" was made of canvas, painfully thawed over a blubber flame and stitched with brittle needles. The nails were secondhand, extracted from packing cases.

In lieu of hemp and tar for caulking, Chippy used lamp wicks, seal blood, and the oil paints of the ship's artist. The ballast was two tons of rough Elephant Island beach stone.

Shackleton chose five men whose seamanship and fortitude he felt he could trust; two of the men—McNish and John Vincent, a bullying sailor who had worked on trawlers—were also known to be "difficult" characters, and he wanted them on board under his watchful eye. His navigator would be Frank Worsley, a high-spirited, somewhat rambunctious New Zealander, whose talent for navigation under impossible conditions had already helped bring them safely to Elephant Island. Tim McCarthy was a cheerful young Irish sailor, well liked by the whole company. The sixth man, Tom Crean, was a powerful, apparently indestructible Irishman who had sailed on both of Scott's expeditions; on the last he had been awarded the Albert Medal for bravery when he trekked 35 miles alone through snow, supplied only with three biscuits and two pieces of chocolate, to bring help to a stricken companion.

The *Caird* set out on April 24, 1916, on a rare afternoon of relative calm. "Bravo! Brave leader" Orde Lees exclaimed in his diary, now in the National Library of New Zealand, as they left. The men Shackleton left behind faced their own trials, surviving on penguins and seals and living in a makeshift shelter under the two remaining overturned boats. Frank Wild, Shackleton's lieutenant, was in charge of the demoralized and shaken men, some of whom—Blackborow, Hudson, and Rickinson, the engineer, who had suffered a heart attack—were in grave need of medical attention.

The Day After departure the *Caird's* ordeal began in earnest. Of seventeen days sailing, there would be ten days of gales. Icy waves soused the men. Beneath the canvas decking, the off-duty watch lay for four hours on stone ballast in wet and putrefying reindeer-skin sleeping bags; the dark space beneath the thwarts was so narrow that it gave the men the sensation of being buried alive. One night they awoke to find the boat staggering in the water. Ice as much as 15 inches thick encased every sodden inch of wood and sail. Despite the dangerous pitching and rolling of the boat, the men had to crawl onto the glassy decking and hack the ice away.

If Shackleton noticed that any one of the men seemed to be suffering more than usual, he ordered hot drinks prepared for all hands on their little Primus stove.

"He never let the man know that it was on his account," Worsley recorded, "lest he become nervous about himself." Despite Shackleton's care, Vincent collapsed after the first few days, and McNish was in a bad way, although still soldiering on. All six found that their feet, which were constantly wet, were white and swollen and had lost all surface feeling, while their bodies were cruelly chafed by their salt-ridden, icy clothes. Yet grimly, mechanically, through all the upheaval of wind and surf, they kept their watches, prepared their meals, took their turns at the makeshift pump, worked the sails, and held their course.

McCarthy shamed them all.

"[He] is the most irrepressible optimist I've ever met" Worsley scrawled in his navigating book. "When I relieve him at the helm, boat iced & seas pourg: down yr neck, he informs me with a happy grin 'It's a grand day, sir.'"

As feared, Worsley was able to take few sightings with the sextant he had borrowed from Hudson. Drawing on experience and an uncanny instinct for assessing wind and tide, Worsley navigated mostly by dead reckoning, the sailor's calculation of courses and distance. Their proposed landfall, South Georgia, represented a mere speck in thousands of miles of ocean. Reluctantly the men decided to aim for the island's uninhabited southwest coast; if they overshot this landfall, prevailing winds would blow them east to other land. If they aimed for the inhabited northeast coast and missed—they would be blown into oblivion,

Near dusk on May 7, the 14th day, a piece of kelp floated by. With mounting excitement they sailed east-northeast through the night, and at dawn on the 15th day spotted seaweed. Land birds appeared in the thick fog, and when the fog cleared just after noon, McCarthy cried out that he saw land.

"There, right ahead, through a rift in the flying scud, our glad but salt-blurred eyes saw a towering black crag, with a lacework of snow around its flank," wrote Worsley. "One glimpse, and it was hidden again. We looked at each other with cheerful, foolish grins. The thoughts uppermost were: 'We've done it.'"

It was a triumph of navigation as much as seamanship and endurance; even the five sightings Worsley had been able to make had involved a degree of guesswork, as the boat had pitched too wildly for him to gain secure fixes of the sun. As if out of spite, a full-blown hurricane roared up to thwart any attempt at landing that day. On top of all else, the men had discovered that their remaining water supply was brackish, and they were tormented with thirst. But on the evening of May 10, with Shackleton and his men at their very limits, the *Caird* ground onto a gravelly beach on South Georgia.

The nearest whaling stations lay about 150 miles distant by sea, too far for the battered boat and debilitated crew. Instead, Shackleton determined that he and two companions—Worsley and Crean—would cross overland to the stations at Stromness Bay. The distance was only 22 miles as the crow flies, but over a confusion of jagged rocky upthrusts and treacherous crevasses. While the coasts of the island had been charted, the interior had never been crossed, and their map depicted it as a blank.

Shackleton's main concern was the weather, as a blizzard in the mountains could finish them. But at 3 A.M. on May 19 the conditions were right, and by a gift of providence there was a full, guiding moon.

The highest mountains on the island were less than 10,000 feet, and by strict mountaineering standards the journey was not technically difficult. A modern professionally guided traverse requires that each climber take the following equipment: Sleeping bag (rated to +10 Fahrenheit), closed-cell foam sleeping pad, climbing boots (preferably double), waterproof gaiters, one set pile jacket and pants, one extra pile jacket, one waterproof jacket, one waterproof pants, two sets of mitts (one waterproof), spare gloves, lightweight balaclava, face mask, camp booties, vapor-barrier socks, long underwear, one large pack, crampons, one ice ax, two ice screws, sunglasses, goggles, water bottle, Swiss army knife, sunscreen, skis with climbing skins, ski poles, waterproof bags. Guides provide tents, stoves, radio, first aid kits, climbing ropes, snow shovel, food and fuel, and crevasse rescue equipment.

"We decided to make the journey in very light marching order," wrote Shackleton. "We would take three days' provisions for each man in the form of sledging ration and biscuit. The food was to be packed in three socks, so that each member of the party could carry his own supply." They also carried matches, a cooking pot, two compasses, a pair of binoculars, 50 feet of rope, a Primus stove filled with enough fuel for six hot meals, and McNish's adze in lieu of an ice ax. They were dressed in threadbare long woolen underwear worn under ordinary clothing that had not been changed for seven months. For traction on the ice McNish had also put screws from the *James Caird* in their boot soles. Their frostbitten feet had not regained feeling in the nine days since their landing.

With moonlight glinting off the glaciers, Shackleton, Worsley, and Crean left their companions and set out from the head of King Haakon Bay into the mountains. Guided only by common sense, they made three failed attempts to pass through the rocky crags that lay athwart their path. The fourth pass took them over just as daylight was failing. After an initial precipitous drop, the land on the other side merged into a long, declining snow slope, the bottom of which lay hidden in mist.

"I don't like our position at all," Worsley quotes Shackleton as saying. With night coming, they were in danger of freezing at that elevation. Shackleton remained silent for some minutes. "We'll slide," he said at last. Coiling the length of rope beneath them, the three men sat down, one behind the other, each locking his arms around the man in front. With Shackleton in the lead and Crean bringing up the rear, they pushed off toward the pool of darkness below.

"We seemed to shoot into space," wrote Worsley. "For a moment my hair fairly stood on end. Then quite suddenly I felt a glow, and knew that I was grinning! I was actually enjoying it. I yelled with excitement, and found that Shackleton and Crean were yelling too."

Their speed slackened, and they came to a gentle halt in a snowbank. Rising to their feet, they solemnly shook hands all round. In only minutes they had descended 1,500 feet.

They tramped on through the night, half asleep. More blunders were made as they became too tired to calculate the lay of the land. But as dawn was breaking, they passed over a ridge and saw below the distinctive, twisted rock formation that identified Stromness Bay. They stood in silence, then for the second time turned and shook each other's hands.

At 6:30 A.M. Shackleton thought he heard the sound of a steam whistle. He knew that about this time the men at the whaling stations would be roused from bed: If he had heard correctly, another whistle should sound at seven o'clock, summoning the men to work. With intense excitement, Shackleton, Worsley, and Crean waited, watching as the hands moved round Worsley's chronometer. At seven o'clock to

the minute, they heard the whistle again. Now they knew they had succeeded.

At three o'clock on the afternoon of May 20, after 36 hours without rest, they walked into the outskirts of Stromness station. Filthy, their faces black with blubber smoke, their matted, salt-clogged hair hanging almost to their shoulders, they presented a fearsome sight, and two small children—their first human contact—ran from them in fright.

Eventually they came upon the station foreman, and Shackleton asked to be taken to the manager. Tactfully unquestioning, the foreman led the trio to the home of Thoralf Sorile, whom they had met when the *Endurance* came to South Georgia, nearly two years before.

"Mr. Sorlle came out to the door and said, 'Well?'" Shackleton recorded.

"'Don't you know me?' I said.

'I know your voice' he replied doubtfully. 'You're the mate of the *Daisy*.'

'My name is Shackleton,' I said."

Aghast at their story, the Norwegian whalers received the castaways with admiration and open hearts. A ship was sent to collect the other three members of the *James Caird* crew—and the *James Caird* itself, which was carried into the station on the shoulders of the whalers like a sacred relic.

Dawn came clear and cold on Elephant Island. It was August 30, 1916, nearly five months since the *Caird* had departed, and Frank Wild had privately begun preparations to mount his own rescue.

Food reserves had become alarmingly low. Perce Blackborow's badly frostbitten foot had been operated on by the expedition's two surgeons, but bone infection had set in, and his condition was grave. Since their arrival on the island, he had lain without complaint in his sodden sleeping bag.

At one in the afternoon, Wild was just serving a "hoosh," a stew of limpets scavenged from tidal pools, when George Marston, the expedition's artist, excitedly poked his head inside the shelter they had made under the two remaining boats.

"Wild, there's a ship," he said. "Shall we light a fire?"

"Before there was time for a reply there was a rush of members tumbling over one another," Orde Lees reported, "all mixed up with mugs of seal hoosh making a simultaneous dive for the door-hole which was immediately torn to shreds."

Outside, the mystery ship drew closer, and the men were puzzled to see it raise the Chilean ensign. Within 500 feet from shore the ship lowered a boat, and as she did so, the men recognized the sturdy, square-set figure of Shackleton, and then of Tom Crean.

"Then there was some real live cheers given," recalled William Bakewell, one of the sailors. This was Shackleton's fourth attempt to reach Elephant Island; pack ice around the island had thwarted three earlier efforts.

For the fourth journey the Chilean government had given Shackleton the use of the *Yelcho,* a small steelhulled tug that had last served as a lighthouse tender, and her crew. In this eminently unsuitable vessel, he, Worsley, and Crean had set forth.

In one hour, the entire company of Elephant Island and their few possessions were aboard the *Yelcho,* Hurley bringing along his canisters of photographic plates and film that he had cached in the snow.

"2.10 All Well!" Worsley recorded in his log. He had been watching from the bridge. "At last! 2.15 full speed ahead."

Through all the long months of their terrible ordeal, Shackleton had lost—not a man.

"Tell me, when was the war over?" Shackleton had asked Sorlle, on arriving at Stromness station after crossing South Georgia.

"The war is not over" Sorlle replied. "Millions are being killed. Europe is mad. The world is mad."

Shackleton and his men returned to a different world than they had left. Everything had changed, including ideals of heroism. With millions of Europe's young men dead, England was not much interested in survival stories. Captain Scott, the Royal Navy officer who had brought honor to his country by dying in the Great White South, better fit the mourning nation's idea of heroism than did an entrepreneurial survivor like Shackleton.

Hard-pressed for money, at a loose end, his greatest dreams already thwarted, in 1921 Shackleton headed south again. An old school chum from Dulwich sympathetically financed this expedition in a somewhat shaky ship called the *Quest.* It was unclear exactly what the purpose of the expedition was; plans ranged from circumnavigating Antarctica to looking for Captain Kidd's treasure. It didn't matter. All that counted was to go south again.

On January 4, 1922, after a stormy passage, the *Quest* arrived at South Georgia, where Shackleton was warmly greeted by the Norwegian whalers. After an idyllic day ashore, he returned to his ship for dinner, bade his friends good night, retired to his cabin—and died. The cause was a massive heart attack; he was 47.

"Shackleton's popularity among those he led was due to the fact that he was not the sort of man who could do only big and spectacular things," Worsley wrote. "When occasion demanded, he would attend personally to the smallest details, and he had unending patience and persistence, which he would apply to all matters concerning the well-fare of his men." Shackleton believed that quite ordinary men were capable of heroic feats if the circumstances required; for him, the weak and the strong must survive together.

On hearing of her husband's death, Shackleton's wife, Emily, requested that he be buried on South Georgia. His body still rests in the island's small cemetery, lying among the sea-hardened whalers who perhaps best appreciated his achievements. Mountain and sea surround him, and the wild beauty of the harsh landscape that forged his greatness.

Shackleton's photographer, Frank Hurley, kept his taste for adventure, shooting in Papua, New Guinea and other exotic locales. He died in 1962.

III-6: Creating Courageous Organizations

Monica C. Worline

The world's largest energy trading organizations, suddenly bankrupt. The largest bankruptcy in the history of the United States left stockholders holding worthless shares and employees without jobs or pension plans. Later headlines revealed that senior executives encouraged employees to buy stock at the same time that they knew the company was headed for disaster. Employees who spoke out against questionable practices were ignored or ostracized, while the senior management continued to make decisions that put money into their own pockets without regard to legal or ethical practices. The organization deliberately contributed to an energy crisis in California, depriving citizens of electric power in order to bolster profits. In the wake of the scandal, one senior manager committed suicide before testifying, while others claimed their constitutional rights against self-incrimination in front of television cameras and American Congressional investigation committees. And it wasn't only Enron, of course, touched by the growing scandal. Independent auditors, whose job was to ensure that accounting practices were honest and fair, were implicated in the collapse of the organization. Wall Street traders were indicted for collusion. The first major American scandal of the twenty-first century turned out to be a deeply organizational scandal.[1]

We have a tendency to individualize courage and talk about it as if it resides within people, yet a deeply organizational scandal calls for a deeply organizational notion of courage as well. When we see someone disavow responsibility from the top of a corrupt organization, we cannot simply comment on his cowardice without regard to the fact that environments can heighten or lower people's ideals. Creating courageous organizations is important because organizations strengthen, or silence, people's courage. In the wake of large-scale disillusionment and organizational failure, we need courageous organizations.

A courageous organization is one that is designed, structured, and managed to call forth the best in people. Portraits of Enron whistle-blowers show that employees who spoke up about wrongdoing or asked questions about business practices were either ignored or shunted aside. Courageous organizations foster active voice and multiple opinions from their members, using information from all levels to refine the organization's goals, practices, products, and

[1]For summaries of the Enron and Arthur Andersen cases, see summaries such as "Out of Control at Andersen" in *Business Week*, April 8, 2002, or "Wall Street's Den of Thieves" in *Fast Company Magazine*, May 2002.

strategies.[2] Portraits of people working at Enron also reveal that many of them were emotionally connected to the organization's mission but were discouraged from understanding the details of the organization's work. Courageous organizations create missions that seem both sensible and worthy to their members. Insider views of the work environment at Enron reveal fierce and consuming internal competition that encouraged employees to ignore external implications and logistics. Courageous organizations build a sense of shared humanity among members that reinforces the shared values of the organization and guides people toward making moral and ethical decisions. Finally, some analysts have noted in the wake of the Enron scandal that the economy rests on a moral contract between organizations and their stakeholders—whether they be shareholders, customers, or employees. Courageous organizations employ and promote many quiet leaders who are able to sense and respond to the needs of the organizations as they embody this moral contract.

WHAT IS COURAGE?

Some writers have claimed that courage is an ethically neutral idea—in this view, regardless of the end, courageousness is simply the ability to overcome fear in order to engage in dangerous or risky behavior. The flaw inherent in such a definition becomes obvious when we see that it might lead us to an analysis of the courage of the senior management of Enron and Arthur Andersen, because they were certainly operating in a climate of great risk with seeming fearlessness. To understand courageous organizations, we need an idea of courage that goes beyond overcoming fear or engaging in danger. Many of our typical notions of courage involve cultivating an attitude of confrontation and opposition, untempered by a notion of humanity or compassion. Yet if organizations simply cultivate an oppositional, confrontational attitude that is not tempered with other values such as honesty or humanity, this definition of courage can lead to more harm than good.

In everyday life, courage is not an ethically neutral concept. For Thomas Aquinas, who spent his life exploring the idea of courage, it became critical to distinguish between false courage, which involves showmanship and recklessness, and true courage, which consists of reasoned pursuit of what is good, regardless of fear yet heedful of risk. This link among ethics, morality, and courage is alive today in the actions of everyday people working in organizations who must choose what is "right" over the exigencies of what is simply acceptable or efficient. Nancy, an employee in a financial services firm, notes that "the many pressures of the marketplace can compromise an individual's values in favor of what is expedient.[3] Courage in organizations involves a sense of action that is deliberately directed toward what is right rather than what is expedient.

Aristotle asserted that courage is the "golden mean" between reason and action. William James thought that courage energized the will to do what is right. In organizations people need a notion of courage related to these capacities to be thoughtful and reasonable as well as active and vigorous. The contemporary philosopher Walton calls courage an "excellence of practical action." This definition of courage, which includes a balance of reason and action, will and excellence, makes courage into an eminently organizational idea.

---

[2]For portraits of former Enron employees, see "Bad Business: What If You'd Worked at Enron?" In *Fast Company Magazine,* May 2002.

[3]See the website www.winningyourway.com for quotes related to courage at work from people in a variety of industries.

- -

COURAGEOUS VOICES: WHAT ARE YOU WILLING TO GET FIRED FOR?

One of the most important ingredients for creating a courageous organization is the wisdom that is carried in the voices of its members. This is exemplified by Jeff, a senior manager at a high-tech software company, who commented that his job is all about giving voice to courage. "Every meeting," he says, "before you walk in the door, you have to know what you're willing to get fired for."[4] Courageous organizations attend to the moral and ethical decisions that employees and managers such as Jeff make every day. For Jeff, acting with courage becomes a regular practice. For the people who work with him, and the customers and shareholders who benefit from his choices, Jeff is an organizational hero.

We don't often talk about our work in such grand terms, though. The collapse of Enron is a wake-up call for our thinking about courage in organizations. It shows us why we need to cultivate managers like Jeff, who understand the daily practice of courage in organizational life. Precisely because of the possibilities for exploitation and damage that arise with complex, global organizations, we need to build an accompanying emphasis on important human values in organizations and management. Without such an emphasis, organizational worlds become chaotic, destructive, or simply unlivable.

CULTIVATING DISSENT

Calls for change in the wake of the Enron scandals include the idea that CEO's and managers must encourage dissent in the organization, from front-line employees all the way up to the board of directors.[5] Andy Grove, former CEO of Intel, asserted that management teams must have a healthy paranoia about what they know and what they don't know because in many situations, top management will be the last to know about important developments in an organization or changes among its technologies and customers.[6] These calls for organizations' ability to cultivate dissent are related to the idea that courageous organizations rest on courageous voices.

In a world in which management assumes that it cannot have all the important information it might need, attention to employee input becomes critical. This input can appear in the form of dissent, as in this story told by Janine, an employee in a small start-up firm:

> A colleague of mine, a software developer with less than two years of experience, questioned the complete product line and direction of the product just a month before our firm was going to have its initial stock offering. He told our manager and the Chief Technology Officer directly that the technology was wrongly focused. He was well prepared, with data, articles, reviews, and market research to back up his claim. I had some doubts about the products and technology, but I never openly questioned them. When I saw this colleague vocalize his doubts, I felt inspired and motivated to stand up with my own thoughts and doubts.
>
> In addition, my thinking about "upper management knows everything" changed. I learned to ask

---

[4]This example and others that discuss courage in high-technology companies are adapted from the author's dissertation work that examines the role of courage in organizations. All names have been changed.

[5]See "How to Fix Corporate Governance" in *Business Week*, May 6, 2002.
[6]Andy Grove, *Only the Paranoid Survive*, Bantam Books, 1999.

good questions and prepare supporting data. In my workplace, management acknowledged that the technology and product lines needed revisiting, and a number of reviews and follow-up alignments of product line and technology followed.

Janine notes that daring voices open space in the organization for further daring. When the "management knows everything" ethos begins to dissipate in an organization, many more people can imagine themselves holding critical roles in the company.

Cultivating dissent isn't always easy, however. Sanjay, a worker from a firm that makes computer hardware, says, "The closest I get to courage is that from time to time I interrupt my superiors or managers when they are talking too much bullshit." Sanjay's sentiments encapsulate the fact that many people in organizations recognize times when poor decisions are being made or when things are not being done correctly, yet fail to raise their voices because the organization silences dissent. Because people rely on the structure of the organization for such material and psychological resources, work organizations have amazing power to shape what people are willing to do. Cultivating dissent and raising courageous voices involves designing organizations that recognize and reward employees who know what they are willing to be fired for.

COURAGEOUS WORK: A MISSION WORTH ACCOMPLISHING

We haven't often described working as courageous. When we have, our typical images come in the form of firefighters or explorers, rather than knowledge workers in their cubicles or sales forces making calls in the field. It makes sense that people who face danger in their daily work must have reserves of courage. What we often fail to recognize is that these employees' courage is born not from facing danger but rather from being passionately engaged in a mission that is worthwhile. Regardless of types of work, when people believe in the worth of a mission, they are often able to access their courage in unimaginable ways.

When the explorer Shackleton was stranded in the polar ice, left with nothing to do but abandon his ship, he was forced to announce to his crew that they must abandon their home and attempt to survive without reliable food or shelter for hundreds of miles across the barren Antarctic. Shackleton needed his crew to do courageous work.[7] On the morning that Shackleton and crew abandoned the *Endurance*, he took the captain aside and said: "I am going to hoist the King's Flag to-morrow. I think it will be a fine thing to have the flag flying here, especially as the King himself presented it to us. It'll buck the men up." The captain wrote in his log the next day: "It seemed a splendid gesture of defiance to the ice to see the flag flying proudly, even though it were only over a floating, freezing wilderness."[8] Shackleton's use of the flag as a rallying point for his crew communicated that the mission of the expedition had not changed. The crew had a duty, commanded by the King, to go on with their appointed tasks. No matter that they had lost their ship, they were still in Antarctica to expand humankind's knowledge of the globe. Being a brilliant and attentive leader, Shackleton understood that the crew's courage could be sustained by reminding them that they had undertaken a mission worth accomplishing.

[7]Read more about Shackleton's Antarctic voyage in a companion article in this section.
[8]Worsley, Frank, *Endurance: An Epic of Polar Adventure*, New York: Jonathan Cape and Harrison Smith Inc., 1931, p. 25.

Doing courageous work, as Shackleton implicitly understood, is not simply about a momentary rally in the face of danger. Courageous organizations engage the entire system in a purpose that is worthy of courage. The fact is that people who act with courage rarely think of themselves as doing so. In fact, most people who act courageously will say to those who marvel at their bravery: "I was just doing what needed to be done." When reporters wanted to interview New York City firefighters after their efforts to rescue people from the World Trade Center towers, most firefighters refused the interviews. They consistently told reporters, "I was just doing my job."[9] The fact that people who act with courage do not think of themselves as courageous is more than simple modesty. It reveals an important fact about courage in organizations—that in order to sustain courage, people need a sense of purpose and usefulness that can absorb their attention and make them feel that their effort is worthwhile. The more solid and valuable the mission becomes in the minds of those who work toward it, the more they are able to sustain their belief and direct their energy toward it.

Leaders can have a tremendous impact in creating courageous organizations through developing and communicating a sense of mission that directs people's action. In 1994, Bonnie Reitz took over as Vice President of Sales and Distribution at Continental Airlines, a declining airline that had alienated most of its travel agents, was notorious for a poor on-time flight record, and was rapidly losing its lucrative business travel customers.[10] Reitz felt convinced that it was possible to turn the organization around,

and she acted fast to spark the same determination in her staff. She created a new sales force dedicated to corporate customers and spearheaded a new advertising campaign to draw business travelers. She worked hard, along with the management team and others in the organization, to boost on-time performance and let people know about it. Her main message to her employees was to listen to customers. She told her staff that listening to customers was the only way to know whether what they were doing was right. Her dedication and determination were inspiring to her staff, but with over 26,000 employees who needed to regain faith in the organization's mission, getting the customer-focused message out was difficult. Reitz organized a party for 100 elite-level Continental customers at the home of the CEO. When word of the party and the fact that the CEO was inviting customers to his home, and apologizing to them in person for the decline of the airline, spread around the company, employees were shocked. It was a jolt to the organization, just as Shackleton's British flag had been, reinforcing that the staff had a mission worth accomplishing. The story of the customer-focused parties ignited the passion of employees, who became dedicated to serving customers better. By 2001, Continental was one of the only two large airlines in the U.S. that was profitable, and the courageous work of Reitz and her employees was a stunning success.

Continental Airlines was severely impacted by the tragedy of September 11, which threatened to kill their turnaround success just as it was coming to fruition. Reitz and her staff used their passion for the mission to sustain courage at Continental headquarters even in the midst of crisis. On September 11, the staff immediately began to telephone corporate clients, figuring out which of their employees were stranded and offering them office space and hotel rooms. On the same day that the planes hit the

---

[9]For interviews with firefighters who did talk about their efforts on September 11, see "The Firefighters: Their Own Stories" in *Men's Journal*, November 2001, pp. 56–93.
[10]This story is excerpted from Keith H. Hammonds, "Continental's Turnaround Pilot," *Fast Company Magazine*, December 2001, pp. 96–101.

World Trade Center and Pentagon, Reitz worked with the electronic marketing team to remove all sales pitches from the Continental website and transform it into an online center for emergency information. Use of the site soared 80%. She and her team wrote and faxed letters to business travelers around the world, explaining new security procedures and addressing their concerns. Even when Continental had to furlough one-fifth of their workforce, Reitz made sure to address those who were leaving personally. She told them that they were great, and that the company would fight to win their jobs back. She told them that their dedication and courage were a tribute to the company. Reitz says, "My people know that no matter what they do, I will be right there next to them. Stand up. Have strength of character in good times and in bad. If you do those things—and people know that's how you operate—that's how they start to lead."[11]

COURAGEOUS HUMANITY: INSPIRATION THROUGH CONNECTION WITH OTHERS

Though people seldom see themselves as courageous, they are quick to recognize courage in others. Most people, when asked, can tell a story about courage at work, and most people who have witnessed courage at work feel that they themselves are more able to act with boldness or heightened honesty and candor because of the example of others. Courage at work is related to humanity because courage changes the connections between people,

heightening respect and trust among coworkers. Maria, a manager in a software firm, remarked that "each time someone steps up to the plate and takes responsibility, I see that as courage. I think it creates confidence, both in yourself to take on bigger challenges, and in your peers—they will trust you more."

Because courage is so deeply connected to the quality of relationships, it is no surprise that in a 2001 national poll conducted in the United States, one third of Americans who talked about having a hero referred to a close relative.[12] Most others who named heroes mentioned people such as Martin Luther King, Jr., Jesus Christ, or Mother Theresa—people who combined a message of courageous action with a notion of shared humanity. This is an important point for those who want to create courageous organizations, because it emphasizes the importance of connections between people in fostering inspiration. When people witness courage, they implicitly sense the humanity of others. Cultivating a sense of shared humanity among people in organizations is one of the most powerful forces that sustains courageous action.

A classic example of the power of shared humanity to foster courage comes from soldiers in World War II. Soldiers who were members of small, close-knit groups were less traumatized by the war, more able to cope with difficulties, and more likely to return from their missions safe and successful. Soldiers who were isolated or who faced missions alone had the highest rates of mental distress and were less likely to return safely from battle. The small group structures that emphasized the soldiers' shared humanity were the one thing that sustained soldiers in their darkest hours. For those who aim to build courageous organizations, everyday examples of

---

[11]Hammonds, "Continental's Turnaround Pilot," *Fast Company Magazine*, December 2001, pp. 96–101, p. 100.

[12]See "Heroes," A special issue of *US News and World Report*, August 20–27, 2001. pp. 25–29.

moments in which human connection seems courageous abound in the workplace. Jacques, a contract employee in a design firm, tells a story about a moment of courageous connection:

> A high level manager dropped by my office one day when I was a contractor. He asked in a nutshell if I was bored. I was so shocked that I retreated and gave the safe answer, "no." The fact of the matter was that I was extremely bored and considering leaving. So, I summoned my courage and approached him with the truth. He was amazed and said "how refreshing."
>
> It took courage to tell someone I had not been truthful. But more to the point, it took courage for him to ask me that question, because it reflected poorly on his organization. I was truly energized by his humanity and enjoy the relationship that I have with this manager now.

Jacques recognized a courageous question from a manager as a moment of shared humanity that allowed him to radically change his engagement with his work. After that moment, he says, "I am no longer afraid to tell the hard truths when necessary. They can in fact be triggers to new and great things."

● ● ● ● ● ● ● ● ● ● ● ● ●
COURAGEOUS LEADERSHIP: STEERING TOWARD WHAT IS RIGHT

Talk of creating courageous organizations contains a risk that leaders may come to see everything in heroic terms. When we think of examples such as firefighters saving lives, soldiers from World War II battling for free-

dom, or leaders such as Churchill delivering speeches to keep the citizenry of London strong, we might fail to see or appreciate the small daily actions that pepper the places where we study or work or worship. Badaracco[13] writes about "quiet leaders," who understand their organizations and their coworkers well enough to do courageous things without making them seem grand. These are people who work within the rules and routines of the organization to accomplish what is right. These "quiet heroes" struggle with where to draw the line, as in Jeff's worry about what he is willing to get fired for, or Sanjay's wrestling with speaking up to senior managers. These people aren't heroes in the grand and tragic sense of firefighters or soldiers. Neither are they crusaders, willing to throw away their hard-won careers at the drop of a hat. Rather, they work with an excellence of practical action that brings out the best in those around them. Courageous leaders draw upon a sense of their own and others' humanity, acknowledging fear and weakness but not deterred from doing what is right.

As an example of a "quiet hero," Badaracco describes a new bank manager who is charged with improving performance in his branch. The manager knows that his promotion comes with a silent expectation that he will fire several long-time employees who are underperforming in their jobs. Instead of directly firing these long-term employees, however, the bank manager uses his knowledge of the organization to stall for time and find more creative solutions, such as early retirement and revised performance incentives. This might not be what we typically think of as courageous behavior—but it is courageous humanity that quietly steered the organization toward what was right. Most organizational courage isn't of the tragic hero vari-

---

[13]See "We Don't Need Another Hero," Joseph L. Badaracco, *Harvard Business Review*, September 2001.

ety, but rather is based in concern about organizational performance coupled with concern for people.

There are moments, however, when leaders can be the force that galvanizes a group into a courageous system. Like Shackleton flying the king's flag, in moments of crisis leaders become living embodiments of collective values. Lincoln transformed America with the Gettysburg Address. Churchill is credited with his tireless rousing speeches that sustained the courage of the British people while they were under attack in World War II. On September 11, 2001, in the wake of the fall of the World Trade Center, Rudy Giuliani galvanized New York with his combination of determination and humanness, symbolized in his vow that: "The people of New York City will be whole again." In the days following the tragedies of September 11, Rudy Giuliani inspired people to be at their best. He organized memorial and prayer services that spanned denominations; he directed the efforts of volunteers and personally visited families in hospitals and emergency centers, giving them a sense of hope; he cut red tape as much as possible for the families of victims, and he consistently used all of his channels of communication to convey a sense of calm and competence, even as he displayed powerful emotions.[14]

Courageous leaders who steer people toward what is right are inspiring to those around them. Giuliani, steering a city through grief, was inspiring to an entire nation. Psychologists who study feelings of inspiration have discovered that when people feel inspired, they are often moved to try to serve others or become better people. Courageous leaders do not need to think of themselves as heroes to sustain courage in their organizations, because they inspire others with their competence and humanity regardless of how they see themselves. Rebecca describes a quiet, inspiring leader who changed her view of herself and her work in a software company:

> I knew a leader who was stripped of his authority by a new executive. The new executive assumed the leader would be indignant and quit. He did not. Instead, he held his head up with dignity, grace and courage, and without criticism continued to lead his people, in his revised capacity, forward until he was ready to leave.

This leader, someone who fits the definition of "quiet hero," inspired Rebecca because he consistently lived out the values he had always advocated, fostering his own and others' maturity and humanity. "After he left," Rebecca says, "I felt a responsibility to embrace and carry on his concern for people. He reminded me to never compromise my values or integrity and to do my best each day."

Michael Useem, a professor of management and scholar of leadership, writes about effective leaders as those who are led by the needs of those around them. Documenting leadership lessons that students have gleaned by trekking the Himalayas to put their study of leadership into action. Useem echoes Rebecca when he writes that: "Leaders should be led by the group's need."[15] Far from an isolated heroic vision, Useem characterizes the key abilities of leaders who sustain courage as deeply social and connected to others. Leaders who sustain courage tend to work hard to sense the needs of the group and to respond with humble service. This notion of leadership is a staple of Buddhist thought. A Buddhist monk teaching Useem and his students in the Himalayas encapsulates the quality of

---

[14]For a description of the Giuliani administration in the days following September 11, see "The Mayor of America" in *Talk Magazine*, November 2001.

[15]Michael Useem, "The Leadership Lessons of Mount Everest," *Harvard Business Review*, October, 2001.

leaders who steer toward what is right: "When leaders truly serve and subordinate their private welfare to that of others, their authority often becomes unquestionable." As leaders begin to listen to the courageous voices of others in the organization, foster a mission worth accomplishing, recognize and value the humanity of others around them, and engage in service to the needs of the group, they inspire others to similar courage, humanity, and service.

III-7: The Creation

Anonymous

In the beginning was the plan
and then came the assumptions
and the assumptions were without form
and the plan was completely without
   substance
and darkness was upon the faces of the
   workers.
And they spake unto their group heads,
   saying:
"It is a crock of shit, and it stinketh."
And the group heads went unto their
   section heads, and sayeth:
"It is a pail of dung, and none may
   abide the odour thereof."
And the section heads went unto their
   managers, and sayeth unto them:
"It is a container of excrement, and it is
   very strong,
such that none here may abide by it."
And the managers went unto their
   Director, and sayeth unto him:

"It is a vessel of fertilizer, and none
   may abide its strength."
And the Directors went unto their
   Director-General, and sayeth:
"It contains that which aids plant
   growth, and it is very strong."
And the Director-General went unto
   the assistant Deputy Minister, and
   sayeth unto him:
"It promoteth growth, and it is very
   powerful."
And the ADM went unto the Deputy
   Minister, and sayeth unto him:
"This powerful new plan will actively
   promote the growth and
efficiency of the department, and this
   area in particular."
and the Deputy Minister looked upon
   the plan,
and saw that it was good,
and the plan became policy.

III-8: How Management Teams Can Have a Good Fight

Kathleen M. Eisenhardt, Jean L. Kahwajy, and L. J. Bourgeois III

The absence of conflict is not harmony, it's apathy.

Top managers are often stymied by the difficulties of managing conflict. They know that conflict over issues is natural and even necessary. Reasonable people, making decisions under conditions of uncertainty, are likely to have honest disagreements over the best path for their company's future. Management teams whose members challenge one another's thinking develop a more complete understanding of the choices, create a richer range of options, and ultimately make the kinds of effective decisions necessary in today's competitive environments.

But, unfortunately, healthy conflict can quickly turn unproductive. A comment meant as a substantive remark can be interpreted as a personal attack. Anxiety and frustration over difficult choices can evolve into anger directed at colleagues. Personalities frequently become intertwined with issues. Because most executives pride themselves on being rational decision makers, they find it difficult even to acknowledge—let alone manage—this emotional, irrational dimension of their behavior.

The challenge—familiar to anyone who has ever been part of a management team—is to keep constructive conflict over issues from degenerating into dysfunctional interpersonal conflict, to encourage managers to argue without destroying their ability to work as a team.

We have been researching the interplay of conflict, politics, and speed in strategic decision making by top-management teams for the past ten years. In one study, we had the opportunity to observe closely the work of a dozen top-management teams in technology-based companies. All the companies competed in fast changing, competitive global markets. Thus all the teams had to make high-stakes decisions in the face of considerable uncertainty and under pressure to move quickly. Each team consisted of between five and nine executives; we were allowed to question them individually and also to observe their interactions firsthand as we tracked specific strategic decisions in the making. The study's design gives us a window on conflict as top-management teams actually experience it and highlights the role of emotion in business decision making.

The challenge is to encourage members of management teams to argue without destroying their ability to work together.

In 4 of the 12 companies, there was little or no substantive disagreement over major issues and therefore little conflict to observe. But the other 8 companies experienced considerable conflict. In 4 of them, the top-management teams handled conflict in a way that avoided interpersonal hostility or discord. We've called those companies Bravo Microsystems, Premier Technologies, Star Electronics, and Triumph Computers. Executives in those companies referred to their colleagues as "smart," "team player," and "best in the business." They described the way they work as a team as "open," "fun," and "productive." The executives vigorously debated the issues, but they wasted little time on politicking and posturing. As one put it, "I really don't have time." Another said, "We don't gloss over the issues; we hit them straight on. But we're not political." Still another observed of her company's management team, "We scream a lot, then laugh, and then resolve the issue."

The other four companies in which issues were contested were less successful at avoiding interpersonal conflict. We've called those companies Andromeda Processing, Mega Software, Mercury Microdevices, and Solo Systems. Their top teams were plagued by intense animosity. Executives often failed to cooperate, rarely talking with one another, tending to fragment into cliques, and openly displaying their frustration and anger. When executives described their colleagues to us, they used words such as "manipulative," "secretive," "burned out," and "political."

The teams with minimal interpersonal conflict were able to separate substantive issues from those based on personalities. They managed to disagree over questions of strategic significance and still get along with one another. How did they do that? After analyzing our observations of the teams' behavior, we found that their companies used the same six tactics for managing interpersonal conflict. Team members

- worked with more, rather than less, information and debated on the basis of facts;
- developed multiple alternatives to enrich the level of debate;
- shared commonly agreed-upon goals;
- injected humor into the decision process;
- maintained a balanced power structure;
- resolved issues without forcing consensus.

Those tactics were usually more implicit than explicit in the decision-making work of the management teams, and if the tactics were given names, the names varied from one organization to the next. Nonetheless, the consistency with which all four companies employed all six tactics is testimony to their effectiveness. Perhaps most surprising was the fact that the tactics did not delay — and often accelerated — the pace at which the teams were able to make decisions.

FOCUS ON THE FACTS

Some managers believe that working with too much data will increase interpersonal conflict by expanding the range of issues for debate. We found that more information is better — if the data are objective and up-to-date — because it encourages people to focus on issues, not personalities. At Star Electronics, for example, the members of the top-management team typically examined a wide variety of operating measures on a monthly, weekly, and even daily basis. They claimed to "measure everything." In particular, every week they fixed their attention on indicators such as bookings, backlogs, margins, engineering milestones, cash, scrap, and work-in-process. Every month, they reviewed an even more comprehensive set of measures that gave them extensive knowledge of what was actually happening in the corporation. As one executive noted, "We have very strong controls."

Star's team also relied on facts about the external environment. One senior executive was charged with tracking such moves by competitors as product introductions, price changes, and ad campaigns. A second followed the latest technical developments through his network of contacts in universities and other companies. "We over-M.B.A. it," said the CEO, characterizing Star's zealous pursuit of data. Armed with the facts, Star's executives had an extraordinary grasp of the details of their business, allowing them to focus debate on critical issues and avoid useless arguments rooted in ignorance.

At Triumph Computer, we found a similar dedication to current facts. The first person the new CEO hired was an individual to track the progress of engineering-development projects, the new-product lifeblood of the company. Such knowledge allowed the top-management team to work from a common base of facts.

In the absence of good data, executives waste time in pointless debate over opinions. Some resort to self-aggrandizement and ill-formed guesses about how the world might be. People — and not issues — become the focus of disagreement. The result is interpersonal conflict. In such companies, top managers are often poorly informed both about internal operations, such as bookings and engineering milestones, and about external issues, such as competing products. They collect data narrowly and infrequently. In these companies, the vice presidents of finance, who oversee internal data collection, are usually weak. They were often described by people in the companies we studied as "inexperienced" or "detached." In contrast, the vice president of finance at Premier Technologies, a company with little interpersonal conflict, was described as being central to taking "the constant pulse of how the firm is doing."

Management teams troubled by interpersonal conflict rely more on hunches and guesses than on current data. When they consider facts, they are more likely to examine a past measure, such as profitability, which is both historical and highly refined. These teams favor planning based on extrapolation and intuitive attempts to predict the future, neither of which yields current or factual results. Their conversations are more subjective. The CEO of one of the four high-conflict teams told us his interest in operating numbers was "minimal," and he described his goals as "subjective." At another such company, senior managers saw the CEO as "visionary" and "a little detached from the day-to-day operations." Compare those executives with the CEO of Bravo Microsystems, who had a reputation for being a "pragmatic numbers guy."

There is a direct link between reliance on facts and low levels of interpersonal conflict. Facts let people move quickly to the central issues surrounding a strategic choice. Decision makers don't become bogged down in arguments over what the facts *might* be. More important, reliance on current data grounds strategic discussions in reality. Facts (such as current sales, market share, R&D expenses, competitors' behavior, and manufacturing yields) depersonalize the discussion because they are not someone's fantasies, guesses, or self-serving desires. In the absence of facts, individuals' motives are likely to become suspect.

Building decisions on facts creates a culture that emphasizes issues instead of personalities.

MULTIPLY THE ALTERNATIVES

Some managers believe that they can reduce conflict by focusing on only one or two alternatives, thus minimizing the dimensions over which people can disagree. But, in fact, teams with low incidences of interpersonal conflict do just the opposite. They deliberately develop multiple alternatives, often considering four or five options at once. To promote debate, managers will even introduce options they do not support.

For example, Triumph's new CEO was determined to improve the company's lackluster performance. When he arrived, new products were stuck in development, and investors were getting anxious. He launched a fact-gathering exercise and asked senior executives to develop alternatives. In less than two months, they developed four. The first was to sell some of the company's technology. The second was to undertake a major strategic redirection, using the base technology to enter a new market. The third was to redeploy engineering resources and adjust the marketing approach. The final option was to sell the company.

Working together to shape those options enhanced the group's sense of teamwork while promoting a more creative view of Triumph's competitive situation and its technical competencies. As a result, the team ended up combining elements of several options in a way that was more robust than any of the options were individually.

The other teams we observed with low levels of interpersonal conflict also tended to develop multiple options to make major decisions. Star, for example, faced a cash flow crisis caused by explosive growth. Its executives considered, among other choices, arranging for lines of credit from banks, selling additional stock, and forming strategic alliances with several partners. At Bravo, managers explicitly relied on three kinds of alternatives: sincere proposals that the proponent actually backed, support for someone else's proposal, even if only for the sake of argument; and insincere alternatives proposed just to expand the number of options.

There are several reasons why considering multiple alternatives may lower interpersonal conflict. For one, it diffuses conflict: choices become less black and white, and individuals gain more room to vary the degree of their support over a range of choices. Managers can more easily shift positions without losing face.

Generating options is also a way to bring managers together in a common and inherently stimulating task. It concentrates their energy on solving problems, and it increases the likelihood of obtaining integrative solutions—alternatives that incorporate the views of a greater number of the decision makers. In generating multiple alternatives, managers do not stop at obvious solutions; rather, they continue generating further—usually more original—options. The process in itself is creative and fun, setting a positive tone for substantive, instead of interpersonal, conflict.

By contrast, in teams that vigorously debate just one or two options, conflict often does turn personal. At Solo Systems, for instance, the top-management team considered entering a new business area as a way to boost the company's performance. They debated this alternative versus the status quo but failed to consider other options. Individual executives became increasingly entrenched on one side of the debate or the other. As positions hardened, the conflict became more pointed and personal. The animosity grew so great that a major proponent of change quit the company in disgust

while the rest of the team either disengaged or slipped into intense and dysfunctional politicking.

CREATE COMMON GOALS

A third tactic for minimizing destructive conflict involves framing strategic choices as collaborative, rather than competitive, exercises. Elements of collaboration and competition coexist within any management team: executives share a stake in the company's performance, yet their personal ambitions may make them rivals for power. The successful groups we studied consistently framed their decisions as collaborations in which it was in everyone's interest to achieve the best possible solution for the collective.

They did so by creating a common goal around which the team could rally. Such goals do not imply homogeneous thinking, but they do require everyone to share a vision. As Steve Jobs, who is associated with three high-profile Silicon Valley companies—Apple, NeXT, and Pixar—has advised, "It's okay to spend a lot of time arguing about which route to take to San Francisco when everyone wants to end up there, but a lot of time gets wasted in such arguments if one person wants to go to San Francisco and another secretly wants to go to San Diego."

More information is better. There is a direct link between reliance on facts and low levels of interpersonal conflict.

Teams hobbled by conflict lack common goals. Team members perceive themselves to be in competition with one another and, surprisingly, tend to frame decisions negatively, as reactions to threats. At Andromeda Processing, for instance, the team focused on responding to a particular instance of poor performance, and team members tried to pin the blame on one another. That negative framing contrasts with the positive approach taken by Star Electronics executives, who, sharing a common goal, viewed a cash crisis not as a threat but as an opportunity to "build the biggest war chest" for an impending competitive battle. At a broad level, Star's executives shared the goal of creating "*the* computer firm of the decade." As one Star executive told us, "We take a corporate, not a functional, viewpoint most of the time."

In teams that vigorously debate just one or two options, conflict often turns personal, as positions harden.

Likewise, all the management team members we interviewed at Premier Technologies agreed that their common goal—their rallying cry—was to build "the best damn machine on the market." Thus in their debates they could disagree about critical technical alternatives—in-house versus offshore manufacturing options, for example, or alternative distribution channels—without letting the conflict turn personal.

Many studies of group decision making and intergroup conflict demonstrate that common goals build team cohesion by stressing the shared interest of all team members in the outcome of the debate. When team members are working toward a common goal, they are less likely to see themselves as individual winners and losers and are far more likely to perceive the opinions of others correctly and to learn from them. We observed that when executives lacked common goals, they tended to be closed-minded and more likely to misinterpret and blame one another.

● ● ● ● ● ● ● ● ● ● ● ●
USE HUMOR

Teams that handle conflict well make explicit—and often even contrived—attempts to relieve tension and at the same time promote a collaborative esprit by making their business fun. They emphasize the excitement of fast-paced competition, not the stress of competing in brutally tough and uncertain markets.

All the teams with low interpersonal conflict described ways in which they used humor on the job. Executives at Bravo Microsystems enjoyed playing gags around the office. For example, pink plastic flamingos—souvenirs from a customer—graced Bravo's otherwise impeccably decorated headquarters. Similarly, Triumph Computers' top managers held a monthly "dessert pig-out," followed by group weight watching. Those seemingly trivial activities were part of the CEO's deliberate plan to make work more fun, despite the pressures of the industry. At Star Electronics, making the company "a fun place" was an explicit goal for the top-management team. Laughter was common during management meetings. Practical jokes were popular at Star, where executives—along with other employees—always celebrated Halloween and April Fools' Day.

At each of these companies, executives acknowledged that at least some of the attempts at humor were contrived—even forced. Even so, they helped to release tension and promote collaboration.

Humor was strikingly absent in the teams marked by high interpersonal conflict. Although pairs of individuals were sometimes friends, team members shared no group social activities beyond a standard holiday party or two, and there were no conscious attempts to create humor. Indeed, the climate in which decisions were made was often just the opposite—hostile and stressful.

Humor works as a defense mechanism to protect people from the stressful and threatening situations that commonly arise in the course of making strategic decisions. It helps people distance themselves psychologically by putting those situations into a

TABLE 3-1 How Teams Argue but Still Get Along	
Tactic ────────────────────────→	*Strategy*
Base discussion on current, factual information. Develop multiple alternatives to enrich the debate.	} Focus on issues, not personalities.
Rally around goals. Inject humor into the decision-making process.	} Frame decisions as collaborations aimed at achieving the best possible solution for the company.
Maintain a balanced power structure. Resolve issues without forcing consensus.	} Establish a sense of fairness and equity in the process.

broader life context, often through the use of irony. Humor—with its ambiguity—can also blunt the threatening edge of negative information. Speakers can say in jest things that might otherwise give offense because the message is simultaneously serious and not serious. The recipient is allowed to save face by receiving the serious message while appearing not to do so. The result is communication of difficult information in a more tactful and less personally threatening way.

Humor can also move decision making into a collaborative rather than competitive frame through its powerful effect on mood. According to a large body of research, people in a positive mood tend to be not only more optimistic but also more forgiving of others and creative in seeking solutions. A positive mood triggers a more accurate perception of others' arguments because people in a good mood tend to relax their defensive barriers and so can listen more effectively.

BALANCE THE POWER STRUCTURE

We found that managers who believe that their team's decision-making process is fair are more likely to accept decisions without resentment, even when they do not agree with them. But when they believe the process is unfair, ill will easily grows into interpersonal conflict. A fifth tactic for taming interpersonal conflict, then, is to create a

sense of fairness by balancing power within the management team.

Our research suggests that autocratic leaders who manage through highly centralized power structures often generate high levels of interpersonal friction. At the other extreme, weak leaders also engender interpersonal conflict because the power vacuum at the top encourages managers to jockey for position. Interpersonal conflict is lowest in what we call *balanced power structures*, those in which the CEO is more powerful than the other members of the top-management team, but the members do wield substantial power, especially in their own well-defined areas of responsibility. In balanced power structures, all executives participate in strategic decisions.

> *Autocratic leaders often tend to generate high levels of interpersonal friction.*

At Premier Technologies, for example, the CEO—described by others as a "team player"—was definitely the most powerful figure. But each executive was the most powerful decision maker in some clearly defined area. In addition, the entire team participated in all significant decisions. The CEO, one executive observed, "depends on picking good people and letting them operate."

The CEO of Bravo Microsystems, another company with a balanced power structure, summarized his philosophy as "making quick decisions involving as many people as possible." We watched the Bravo team over several months as it grappled with a major strategic redirection. After many group discussions, the final decision was made at a multiday retreat involving the whole team.

In contrast, the leaders of the teams marked by extensive interpersonal conflict were either highly autocratic or weak. The CEO at Mercury Microdevices, for example, was the principal decision maker. There was a substantial gap in power between him and the rest of the team. In the decision we tracked, the CEO dominated the process from start to finish, identifying the problem, defining the analysis, and making the choice. Team members described the CEO as "strong" and "dogmatic." As one of them put it, "When Bruce makes a decision, it's like God!"

At Andromeda, the CEO exercised only modest power, and areas of responsibility were blurred within the top-management team, where power was diffuse and ambiguous. Senior executives had to politick amongst themselves to get anything accomplished, and they reported intense frustration with the confusion that existed at the top.

Most executives expected to control some significant aspect of their business but not the entirety. When they lacked power—because of either an autocrat or a power vacuum—they became frustrated by their inability to make significant decisions. Instead of team members, they became politicians. As one executive explained, "We're all jockeying for our spot in the pecking order." Another described "maneuvering for the CEO's ear."

The situations we observed are consistent with classic social-psychology studies of leadership. For example, in a study from the 1960s, Ralph White and Ronald Lippitt examined the effects of different leadership styles on boys in social clubs. They found

that boys with democratic leaders—the situation closest to our balanced power structure—showed spontaneous interest in their activities. The boys were highly satisfied, and within their groups there were many friendly remarks, much praise, and significant collaboration. Under weak leaders, the boys were disorganized, inefficient, and dissatisfied. But the worst case was autocratic rule, under which the boys were hostile and aggressive, occasionally directing physical violence against innocent scapegoats. In imbalanced power situations, we observed adult displays of verbal aggression that colleagues described as violent. One executive talked about being "caught in the cross fire." Another described a colleague as "a gun about to go off." A third spoke about "being beat up" by the CEO.

● ● ● ● ● ● ● ● ● ● ● ● ● ● ● ●
SEEK CONSENSUS WITH QUALIFICATION

Balancing power is one tactic for building a sense of fairness. Finding an appropriate way to resolve conflict over issues is another—and, perhaps, the more crucial. In our research, the teams that managed conflict effectively all used the same approach to resolving substantive conflict. It is a two-step process that some executives call *consensus with qualification*. It works like this: executives talk over an issue and try to reach consensus. If they can, the decision is made. If they can't, the most relevant senior manager makes the decision, guided by input from the rest of the group.

When a competitor launched a new product attacking Premier Technologies in its biggest market, for example, there was sharp disagreement about how to respond. Some executives wanted to shift R&D resources to counter this competitive move, even at the risk of diverting engineering talent from a more innovative product then in design. Others argued that Premier should simply repackage an existing product, adding a few novel features. A third group felt that the threat was not serious enough to warrant a major response.

> *Executives may believe that consensus is always possible, but insisting on agreement can lead to endless haggling.*

After a series of meetings over several weeks, the group failed to reach consensus. So the CEO and his marketing vice president made the decision. As the CEO explained, "The functional heads do the talking. I pull the trigger." Premier's executives were comfortable with this arrangement—even those who did not agree with the outcome—because everyone had had a voice in the process.

People usually associate consensus with harmony, but we found the opposite: teams that insisted on resolving substantive conflict by forcing consensus tended to display the most interpersonal conflict. Executives sometimes have the unrealistic view that consensus is always possible, but such a naïve insistence on consensus can lead to endless haggling. As the vice president of engineering at Mega Software put it, "Consensus means that everyone has veto power. Our products were too late, and they were too expensive." At Andromeda, the CEO wanted his executives to reach consensus, but persistent differences of opinion remained. The debate dragged on for months, and the frustration mounted until some top managers simply gave up. They just wanted a decision, any decision. One was finally made when several executives who favored one point of view left the company. The price of consensus was a decimated team.

In a team that insists on consensus, deadlines can cause executives to sacrifice

---

Building a Fighting Team

How can managers encourage the kind of substantive debate over issues that leads to better decision making? We found five approaches that help generate constructive disagreement with a team:

1. **Assemble a heterogeneous team, including diverse ages, genders, functional backgrounds, and industry experience.** If everyone in the executive meeting looks alike and sounds alike, then the chances are excellent that they probably think alike too.

2. **Meet together as a team regularly and often.** Team members that don't know one another well don't know one another's positions on issues, impairing their ability in argue effectively. Frequent interaction builds the mutual confidence and familiarity team members require to express dissent.

3. **Encourage team members to assume role beyond their obvious product, geographic, or functional responsibilities.** Devil's advocates, sky gazing visionaries, and action oriented executives can work together to ensure that all sides of an issue are considered.

4. **Apply multiple mind sets to any issue.** Try role playing, putting yourself in your competitors shoes, or conducting war games. Such techniques create fresh perspectives engage team members spurring interest in problem solving.

5. **Actively manage conflict.** Don't let the team, acquiesce too soon or too easily. Identify and treat apathy early, and don't confuse a look of conflict with agreement. Often, what passes for consensus is really disengagement.

fairness and thus weaken the team's support for the final decision. At Andromeda, executives spent months analyzing their industry and developing a shared perspective on important trends for the future, but they could never focus on making the decision. The decision-making process dragged on. Finally, as the deadline of a board meeting drew imminent, the CEO formulated and announced a choice—one that had never even been mentioned in the earlier discussions. Not surprisingly, his team was angry and upset. Had he been less insistent on reaching a consensus, the CEO would not have felt forced by the deadline to act so arbitrarily.

How does consensus with qualification create a sense of fairness? A body of research on procedural justice shows that process fairness, which involves significant participation and influence by all concerned, is enormously important to most people. Individuals are willing to accept outcomes they dislike if they believe that the process by which those results came about was fair. Most people want their opinions to be considered seriously but are willing to accept that those opinions cannot always prevail. That is precisely what occurs in consensus with qualification. As one executive at Star said, "I'm happy just to bring up my opinions."

Apart from fairness, there are several other reasons why consensus with qualification is an important deterrent to interpersonal conflict. It assumes that conflict is natural and not a sign of interpersonal dysfunction. It gives managers added influence when the decision affects their part of the organization in particular, thus balancing managers' desires to be heard with the need to make a choice. It is an equitable and egalitarian process of decision making that encourages everyone to bring ideas to the table but clearly delineates how the decision will be made.

Finally, consensus with qualification is fast. Processes that require consensus tend to drag on endlessly, frustrating managers with what they see as time-consuming and useless debate. It's not surprising that the managers end up blaming their frustration on the shortcomings of their colleagues and not on the poor conflict-resolution process.

LINKING CONFLICT, SPEED, AND PERFORMANCE

A considerable body of academic research has demonstrated that conflict over issues is not only likely within top-management teams but also valuable. Such conflict provides executives with a more inclusive range of information, a deeper understanding of the issues, and a richer set of possible solutions. That was certainly the case in the companies we studied. The evidence also overwhelmingly indicates that where there is little conflict over issues, there is also likely to be poor decision making. "Groupthink" has been a primary cause of major corporate- and public-policy debacles. And although it may seem counterintuitive, we found that the teams that engaged in healthy conflict over issues not only made better decisions but moved more quickly as well.

Without conflict, groups lose their effectiveness. Managers often become withdrawn and only superficially harmonious. Indeed, we found that the alternative to conflict is usually not agreement but apathy and disengagement. Teams unable to foster substantive conflict ultimately achieve, on average, lower performance. Among the companies that we observed, low-conflict teams tended to forget to consider key issues or were simply unaware of important aspects of their strategic situation. They missed opportunities to question falsely limiting assumptions or to generate significantly different alternatives. Not surprisingly, their actions were often easy for competitors to anticipate.

In fast-paced markets, successful strategic decisions are most likely to be made by teams that promote active and broad conflict over issues without sacrificing speed. The key to doing so is to mitigate interpersonal conflict.

Kathleen M. Eisenhardt is professor of strategy and organization at Stanford University in Stanford, California, where her consulting and research focus on strategy in fast-paced industries. Jean L. Kahwajy is a management consultant with Strategic Decision Group in Menlo Park, California, and is pursuing research at Stanford University on organizational influences on decision making. L. J. Bourgeois III is professor of business administration at the University of Virginia's Darden Graduate School of Business in Charlottesville.

III-9: Offbeat Majors Help CEOs Think Outside the Box

Del Jones

Abstract

Just one-third of CEOs running the USA's largest 1,000 companies have a master's of business administration degree, according to executive search firm Spencer Stuart. Cisco's John Chambers added an MBA to his law degree, and Enron Chairman Kenneth Lay added a Ph.D. in economics to his MBA. But for every CEO who takes a businesslike approach, there are those who follow pure interests and trample practicality on the way to the top.

No one disputes that there is a place for the traditional MBA. Miramar Systems just hired a Harvard MBA for business development. But CEO Neal Rabin, who majored in creative writing (UCLA '80), says chief executives who learn at the knee of Harvard case studies know too many ways that companies fail. They find themselves paralyzed by fear, he says.

Unlike President [George W. Bush] (MBA Harvard '75; B.A. history Yale '68), 87% of Fortune 300 CEOs did not attend an Ivy League school, according to Spencer Stuart's Route to the Top survey last year. Corning's [John Loose] got his degree from Earlham College, a 1, 200-student school founded by Quakers in Richmond, Ind. Denison University, attended by both [Michael Eisner] and history major Terry Jones ('70), CEO of Travelocity.com, is a 2,100-student college in Granville, Ohio.

• • • • • • • • • •
FULL TEXT

George W. Bush may be the first president with an MBA degree, but U.S. business is run by CEOs with a hodgepodge of degrees in everything from atmospheric physics to French literature.

Hewlett-Packard CEO Carly Fiorina, a medieval history and philosophy major (Stanford '76), says her curiosity about the transformation from the Middle Ages to the Renaissance folds neatly into the digital awakening she now must address.

"A century of sustained and enduring human achievement" long ago leaves her confident that "we have, in fact, seen nothing yet," Fiorina says.

Walt Disney CEO Michael Eisner never took a single business course, getting a double major in English and theater (Denison '64), and he has nudged his three sons into liberal arts. He was reminded of a favorite English professor, Dominic Consolo, when reading the script for *Dead Poets Society*, a movie about a passionate poetry teacher starring Robin Williams. Eisner considers it to be one of the best movies Disney has made.

"Literature is unbelievably helpful, because no matter what business you are in, you are dealing with interpersonal relationships," Eisner says. "It gives you an appreciation of what makes people tick."

Ambitious college grads peddling offbeat degrees in a job market gone sour can take heart that such success stories are far from rare.

Just one-third of CEOs running the USA's largest 1,000 companies have a master's of business administration degree, according to executive search firm Spencer Stuart. Cisco's John Chambers added an MBA to his law degree, and Enron Chairman Kenneth Lay added a Ph.D. in economics to his MBA.

But for every CEO who takes a businesslike approach, there are those who follow pure interests and trample practicality on the way to the top.

No one disputes that there is a place for the traditional MBA. Miramar Systems just hired a Harvard MBA for business development. But CEO Neal Rabin, who majored in creative writing (UCLA '80), says chief executives who learn at the knee of Harvard case studies know too many ways that companies fail. They find themselves paralyzed by fear, he says.

Michael Dell, founder and CEO of Dell Computer, was a pre-med biology major at the University of Texas before dropping out after his freshman year.

"I took one course that was remotely related to business: macroeconomics," Dell says. "One of the things that really helped me is not approaching the world in a conventional sense. There are plenty of conventional thinkers out there."

Microsoft Chairman Bill Gates also left college without earning a degree— Harvard's most famous dropout had been studying computer science. More typical, however, are executives who completed school but whose course of study now seems irrelevant.

These CEOs say their offbeat majors have been anything but irrelevant. Some say they still apply the knowledge learned in pursuing those degrees in making day-to-day business decisions. Others say the degrees helped launch their careers where economics, finance or business may have not.

STUDYING HISTORY AND CULTURE

Any good education would have been enough to get a foot in Corning's door 37 years ago, CEO John Loose says. But it's unlikely he would have been chosen for his first big international assignment without a degree in East Asian history (Earlham '64).

"To have an understanding of the history and culture of Koreans, Japanese, Indians and Chinese was invaluable," Loose says. Even today, Corning continues to court Asia as a rare bright spot in the depressed fiber-optic market.

Likewise Sue Kronick, now group president of Federated Department Stores, was an Asian studies major (Connecticut College '73). Her rise from a Bloomingdale's buyer was helped by understanding India's economic system so well that she found ways to slash the cost of imports.

"My background served me well," Kronick says. "You tend to get a more narrow in point of view as time marches on. Liberal arts is about approaching problems from a different point of view."

Michaela Rodeno, CEO of the French-owned St. Supery winery in California, had no idea how to put her French literature degree (University of California at Davis '68) to use until she moved with her husband to Napa Valley, where he set up a law practice.

French wineries happened to be venturing into the valley for the first time. Rodeno's fluency in the language would have been enough to land a job, but knowledge of "France's institutions, arts and letters" stunned French executives and put her on the fast track.

SMALL-COLLEGE EDUCATION

Unlike President Bush (MBA Harvard '75; B.A. history Yale '68), 87% of Fortune 300 CEOs did not attend an Ivy League school, according to Spencer Stuart's Route to the Top survey last year. Cornings Loose got his degree from Earlham College, a 1,200-student school founded by Quakers in Richmond, Ind. Denison University, attended by both Eisner and history major Terry Jones ('70), CEO of Travelocity.com, is a 2,100-student college in Granville, Ohio.

Eisner says he knew nothing of Denison. But he had gone to all-boys schools since kindergarten and was won over to co-ed Denison by a friend's brochure.

Offbeat routes to the top are not restricted to CEOs with liberal arts degrees. After earning a master's ('71) and Ph.D. ('73) in chemical engineering from Drexel University, Ramani Ayer accepted an entry-level job with Hartford Financial Services Group.

"My professors thought I was nuts," Ayer says. Today, he is Hartford's CEO.

"The mathematical ways of looking at the world are very transferable from engineering to insurance," Ayer says. Those who rise to the top know why things happen the way they do, he says. "Engineering is very good training for knowing why."

An industrial engineering degree (North Carolina State '71) eventually landed Gordon Harton, president of jean company Lee, in fashion. "I wouldn't be the person you'd want to select the hottest colors for next spring," he says. "And I can't remember using calculus in any marketing decisions."

Harton worked 15 years in operations, doing plant layout, scheduling and capacity planning, but he discovered he was more interested in marketing and fashion. Engineering teaches that the best solution is the most simple—a principle Lee applied when its marketers were quick to spot the trend for baggy fitting jeans simply by talking to boys who rode skateboards.

Upoc CEO Gordon Gould says his environmental studies degree (Pitzer College '92) has transferred easily to computer systems and helped him understand how a computer virus might spread. Upoc is a service that lets teens and young adults get tailored information and exchange messages on mobile phones and pagers.

Frank Moss, chairman of e-business company Bowstreet, was working with the Apollo space team still earning a master's degree in astronautics (Princeton '71). He was getting his Ph.D. in aeronautics (MIT '76) when he became a pioneer in what is now known as the Internet.

"In the space program, you learned how to get things done quickly as a team," Moss says. "We solved things in 24 hours, sometimes in 24 minutes. There was a sense of urgency I brought to computers and software, where it's highly competitive."

The marriage of computers with biology is the next frontier, and business needs more bright leaders with backgrounds in history, philosophy and the like to sort out ethical questions about such issues as genetic patents and the cloning of a human being, Moss says.

"We need not just scientists who say what we can do, but people with broad intellectual and liberal arts backgrounds who say what we shouldn't do," Moss says.

LEARNING HOW TO THINK

Blue Shield of California CEO Bruce Bodaken has a bachelor's (Colorado State '72) and a master's (Colorado '75) degree in philosophy and once taught an introduction to ethics course.

"Philosophy teaches you to ask deeper questions, how to think through a tough problem," Bodaken says.

High-tech companies are increasingly bringing on CEOs who know relatively little about technology. There are several reasons Uniscape CEO Steve Adams, who has a Ph.D. in 20th-century British literature (Florida State '82), quit a college teaching job at the University of Louisiana at Monroe. One was a 50% pay raise to become an entry-level technical writer.

Not long ago, "I thought a chip was something you had with dip," says Adams, who runs a company that helps global companies with Web sites that must reach out to a variety of languages and cultures.

Adams says he brings something fresh to the table, often quoting poetry to computer scientists and electrical engineers. One of his favorites comes from Ralph Waldo Emerson: "A foolish consistency is the hobgoblin of little minds."

Where CEOs of some of the biggest companies got their sheepskins			
Company	*Executive*	*Degree*	*University*
ExxonMobil	Lee Raymond	B.A. and Ph.D. in chemical engineering	University of Minnesota
Wal-Mart	H. Lee Scott Jr.	B.S. in business	Pittsburg State U. (Pittsburg, Kan.)
General Motors	G. Richard Wagoner Jr.	B.A. in economics M.A. in business administration	Duke University Harvard University
Ford	Jacques Nasser	Business studies	Royal Melbourne Institute of Technology
General Electric	Jeffrey Immelt[a]	B.S. in applied mathematics MBA	Dartmouth College Harvard University
General Electric	Jack Welch Jr.[a]	B.S., M.S. and Ph.D. in chemical engineering	University of Massachusetts and University of Illinois
Citigroup	Sanford Weill	B.A. in government	Cornell University
Enron	Jeffrey Skilling	B.S. in applied science MBA	Southern Methodist University Harvard Business School
IBM	Louis Gerstner Jr.	B.A. in engineering MBA	Dartmouth College Harvard University
AT&T	C. Michael Armstrong	B.S. in business and economics	Miami University (Ohio)
Verizon[b]	Charles Lee	B.A. in metallurgical engineering MBA	Cornell University Harvard University

(continued)

Company	Executive	Degree	University
Verizon[b]	Ivan Seidenberg	B.A. in mathematics MBA	City University of New York Pace University
Philip Morris	Geoffrey Bible		Attended the Institute of Chartered Accountants in Australia and the Chartered Institute of Management Accountants in the United Kingdom
J.P. Morgan Chase	William Harrison Jr.	B.A. in economics	University of North Carolina
Bank of America	Kenneth Lewis	B.A. in finance	Georgia State University
SBC Communications	Edward Whitacre Jr.	B.S. in industrial engineering	Texas Tech University
Boeing	Philip Condit	B.A. in mechanical engineering	University of California at Berkeley
		M.S. in aeronautical engineering	Princeton University
		MBA	Massachusetts Institute of Technology
		Ph.D. in engineering	University of Tokyo
Texaco	Glenn Tilton	B.A. in international relations	University of South Carolina
Duke Energy	Richard Priory	B.S. in civil engineering	West Virginia Institute of Technology
		M.S. in engineering	Princeton University
Kroger	Joseph Pichler	B.A. in marketing	University of Notre Dame
		MBA and Ph.D. in business	University of Chicago
Hewlett-Packard	Carly Fiorina	B.A. in medieval history and philosophy	Stanford University
		MBA (marketing and business administration)	University of Maryland
		M.S. in business administration	Massachusetts Institute of Technology
Chevron	David O'Reilly	B.A. in chemical	University College (Dublin)

[a]Jeffrey Immelt replaces Jack Welch Jr. as chairman and CEO effective Sept. 7.
[b]Verizon has co-CEOs.

III-10: The Leader of the Future

William C. Taylor

Harvard's Ronald Heifetz offers a short course on the future of leadership.

It's hard to imagine discussing "the leader of the future" without having a discussion with Ronald Heifetz—one of the world's leading authorities on leadership. Heifetz, 48, director of the Leadership Education Project at Harvard University's John F. Kennedy School of Government, is a scholar, a teacher, and a consultant. His course at Harvard, "Exercising Leadership," is legendary for its popularity with students and for its impact on them. His students (many of them in mid-career) include leaders from all walks of life: business executives, generals, priests and rabbis, politicians. His clients have included senior executives at Bell-South, who brought him on to conduct a two-year program on leadership in a fast-changing world, and the president of Ecuador, who is struggling to lead that nation through tough economic times.

What makes Heifetz's approach to leadership so compelling is that he is so honest about what real leadership demands. The book that rocketed him to prominence was called *Leadership Without Easy Answers* (Belknap/Harvard University Press, 1994). The role of the leader is

changing, Heifetz argues. The new role is "to help people face reality and to mobilize them to make change." And making change is painful: "Many people have a 'smiley face' view of what it means to lead. They get a rude awakening when they find themselves with a leadership opportunity. Exercising leadership generates resistance—and pain. People are afraid that they will lose something that's worthwhile. They're afraid that they're going to have to give up something that they're comfortable with."

So why bother to lead? "There are lots of things in life that are worth the pain," he says. "Being a leader is one of them." In a series of conversations with Fast Company, Heifetz offered ideas, advice, and techniques for the leaders of the future.

● ● ● ● ● ● ● ● ● ● ● ● ● ● ● ●
HOW LEADERS SEE

There is so much hunger for leadership in business today. Everyone wants better leaders. What do great leaders do?

The real heroism of leadership involves having the courage to face reality—and helping the people around you to face reality. It's no accident that the word "vision" refers to our capacity to see. Of course, in business, vision has come to mean something abstract or even inspirational. But the quality of any vision depends on its accuracy, not just on its appeal or on how imaginative it is.

Mustering the courage to interrogate reality is a central function of a leader. And that requires the courage to face three realities at once. First, what values do we stand for—and are there gaps between those values and how we actually behave? Second, what are the skills and talents of our company—and are there gaps between those resources and what the market demands? Third, what opportunities does the future hold—and are there gaps between those opportunities and our ability to capitalize on them?

Now, don't get the wrong idea. Leaders don't answer those questions themselves. That's the old definition of leadership: The leader has the answers—the vision—and everything else is a sales job to persuade people to sign up for it. Leaders certainly provide direction. But that often means posing well-structured questions, rather than offering definitive answers. Imagine the differences in behavior between leaders who operate with the idea that "leadership means influencing the organization to follow the leader's vision" and those who operate with the idea that "leadership means influencing the organization to face its problems and to live into its opportunities." That second idea—mobilizing people to tackle tough challenges—is what defines the new job of the leader.

Most companies have a remarkable tendency to underestimate their external threats and to overestimate their own power. Why is it so hard for leaders to convince people to face reality?

Companies tend to be allergic to conflict—particularly companies that have been in operation for a long time. Being averse

to conflict is understandable. Conflict is dangerous: It can damage relationships. It can threaten friendships. But conflict is the primary engine of creativity and innovation. People don't learn by staring into a mirror; people learn by encountering difference. So hand in hand with the courage to face reality comes the courage to surface and orchestrate conflicts.

Leaders of the future need to have the stomach for conflict and uncertainty—among their people and within themselves. That's why leaders of the future need to have an experimental mind-set. Some decisions will work, some won't. Some projects will pay off, some won't. But every decision and every project will teach you and your organization something about how the world is changing—and about how your company compares with its competition.

In other words, facing reality means facing up to mistakes and failures—especially your own failures. In the mid-1990s, Bill Gates made a big decision about the Internet. He decided that the Net wasn't going to be all that important. Then he changed his decision, because the people whom he was listening to contradicted his earlier decision. In the mid-1980s, Ken Olsen, the cofounder of Digital Equipment Corp., decided that personal computers weren't going to be all that important. He didn't change his decision very quickly, and Digital suffered as a result. These days, leaving any big decision in one person's hands is like playing Russian roulette. It's much safer to run multiple experiments. You never know which ideas are going to flourish and which ones are going to die.

If everything is subject to change, how can leaders help people keep their bearings?

Not everything is subject to change. If the role of the leader is first to help people face reality and then to mobilize them to make change, then one of the questions that defines both of those tasks is this: What's precious, and what's expendable? Which values and operations are so central to our core that if we lose them, we lose ourselves? And which assumptions, investments, and businesses are subject to radical change? At the highest level, the work of a leader is to lead conversations about what's essential and what's not.

Examples from politics abound. The civil-rights movement posed several questions: What's most precious about America? What values do we stand for? Do we stand for freedom and equal opportunity? Or do we stand for how we are living today? By posing those questions in such terms, Martin Luther King Jr. and the movement's other strategists generated conflict within the hearts and minds of many people around the country. People faced an internal contradiction between the values they espoused and the way they lived. Millions of people had to decide for themselves what was precious about their country and what was expendable about the supremacist lessons that they had learned.

Now, that is a very difficult inner conversation for anyone to have. Imagine how hard it was for Lew Platt, CEO of Hewlett-Packard, to lead conversations about breaking up that company—and about leaving the HP name with the computer business rather than with the test-and-measurement business, which is where William Hewlett and David Packard got their start. I wasn't privy to those conversations, but my guess is that they were quite emotional. You can understand the business logic: HP's technology is so established in the test-and-measurement world that the company can survive a name change in that business without losing market share. The HP name isn't what's precious. Even so, if you grew up in that business, immersed in the legend of Hewlett and Packard's innovation in a garage, it might seem awfully precious.

HOW LEADERS LISTEN

With leaders, the sense of sight—vision—is closely linked to the sense of hearing. People who love their boss often say, "She's a great listener." What does it mean to be a "great listener"?

Most leaders die with their mouths open. Leaders must know how to listen—and the art of listening is more subtle than most people think it is. But first, and just as important, leaders must want to listen. Good listening is fueled by curiosity and empathy: What's really happening here? Can I put myself in someone else's shoes? It's hard to be a great listener if you're not interested in other people.

Think about some of the best-known leaders in the airline business: Jan Carlzon at SAS (Scandinavian Airlines System) in the early 1980s, Colin Marshall at British Airways in the early 1990s, Herb Kelleher at Southwest Airlines today. These executives are always flying on their own airlines' planes. They're always talking with customers. They're always encouraging ticket agents and baggage handlers to be creative about helping customers to solve problems. They're in "dynamic listening" mode, asking questions all the time—and not getting seduced into trying to provide all of the answers. If you're the boss, the people around you will invariably sit back and wait for you to speak. They will create a vacuum of silence, and you will feel a compelling need to fill it. You need to have a special discipline not to fill that vacuum.

What else does it take to be a great listener?

Great listeners know how to listen musically as well as analytically. As president, Jimmy Carter relied on "rational discourse" to weigh the pros and cons of various initiatives. He would have people prepare papers, and then he would sift their views in private. Doing it that way enabled him to listen to their arguments analytically but not musically. What do I mean by that? Jimmy Carter did not enjoy being in meetings with people who were posturing, arguing, haggling. But there's an enormous amount of information in the haggling, and that information tells us quite a lot about the values, the history, and the personal stakes that people bring to an argument. It's difficult for someone who's lost the last six arguments to say in a policy paper, "I've lost the last six arguments. If I don't win the next one, what am I going to tell my people?"

But in a conversation, the tone of voice and the intensity of the argument give clues to that subtext. Listening musically enables leaders to get underneath and behind the surface to ask, "What's the real argument that we're having?" And that's a critical question to answer—because, in the absence of an answer to that question, you get superficial buy-in. People go along in a pseudo-consensus, or in a deferential way, but without commitment.

If curiosity is a prerequisite for listening, what's the enemy?

Grandiosity. Leaders need to check their sense of self-importance. But you shouldn't think that grandiosity arises from bad intentions. It usually grows out of the normal human need to feel important. I don't know any human being who doesn't want to feel important, who doesn't want to matter to other people. And those of us who have a strong need to be needed—I happen to have that need, so I know a lot about it—spend our lives solving other people's problems. It makes us feel needed: "Surely you have a problem that I can solve." But that orientation creates its own kind of problem. The more we demonstrate our capacity to take problems off other people's shoulders, the more authority we gain in their eyes—until, finally, we become a senior executive or a CEO. And, by then, the tracks have been laid so deeply inside our brain that it becomes hard to stand back, hard to listen, hard to learn from others. Our normal need

to feel important—"Let me help you"—has been transformed into grandiosity: "I have all the answers."

HOW LEADERS FAIL

Why do so many people dislike their bosses? Why do so many of us not respect our leaders?

For decades, I've been interested in that question—because it sounds like a paradox: "Our leadership isn't exercising any leadership." Why do so many people feel that way about those who lead their companies or their communities? One reason is that people in positions of authority are frequently asked not to exercise their leadership. Instead of mobilizing their constituents to face tough, frustrating challenges, they are asked to protect those constituents from having to make adjustments. It's very hard for a congressman to go to his district and say, "Good news: The Cold War is over. Time for 10,000 of you to lose your jobs." He has been elected to his post to protect people from challenges that will require adjustments to their way of life.

That's why leadership is dangerous. Sure, you have to protect people from change. But you also have to "unprotect" them. It's dangerous to challenge people in a way that will require changes in their priorities, their values, their habits. It's dangerous to try to persuade people to take more responsibility than they feel comfortable with. And that's why so many leaders get marginalized, diverted, attacked, seduced. You want to be able to stir the pot without letting it boil over. You want to regulate disequilibrium, to keep people in a productive discomfort zone.

How do you keep people in a "productive discomfort zone"?

Attention is the currency of leadership. To a leader with formal authority, attention comes naturally. Fidel Castro can give a two-hour speech, and people will pay attention. So can Nelson Mandela. The president of the United States can give a State of the Union address that lasts an hour and 15 minutes. The big questions for that kind of leader are "How do I use that attention? What do I focus it on? When does a broad agenda become too broad? How do I push the organization without alienating my core constituency?" You have to remember: Drawing attention to tough challenges generates discomfort. So you want to pace the rate at which you frustrate or attempt to change expectations.

That means distinguishing between "ripe" and "unripe" issues. A ripe issue is one in which there is a general urgency for action. An unripe issue is one in which there is local urgency—a readiness to change within just one faction. The work that it takes to ripen an unripe issue is enormous—and quite dangerous. It needs to be done, but it's different from working a ripe issue.

Lyndon Johnson exercised wonderful leadership in helping to ripen civil rights as an issue. Six weeks after Kennedy's assassination, he called Roy Wilkins, executive secretary of the NAACP, and said, "When are you going to get down here and start civil rights?" Then he gave Wilkins counsel on how to lobby Everett Dirksen, the senate minority leader. Johnson was ripening an unripe issue: He couldn't get out front on the Civil Rights Act of 1964, but as an authority figure, he could provide counsel and cover for leaders without authority—leaders who could then disseminate a sense of urgency. He did the same thing with King. Basically, he said, "If you open the door, if you create the political will, I'll drive through that opening." Johnson was asking King to ripen the issue for him. He was expected to be president for all the people. So, unless King and other civil-rights leaders generated the necessary political will, he couldn't move on that issue. He was pre-vented from exercising leadership by virtue of his authority.

What about grassroots leaders—people without formal authority?

Again, it starts with attention. People who lead without authority, who lead from below, must draw attention to the issues that they raise without drawing too much attention to themselves. Grassroots leaders often generate "sticky" attention—attention that sticks to them personally, rather than to their agenda. To use a different metaphor, it's never comfortable to be a lightning rod. The easiest way for an organization to neutralize the disturbance that you represent is to neutralize you.

There's a second big difference between people who lead with authority and people who lead without authority. If you're leading without authority, other people's attention spans are going to be short whenever you try to communicate with them. Forget two-hour speeches—most people aren't willing to give you more than 30 seconds! So you have to use their attention wisely. You have to make your interventions short, simple, intelligible, and relevant.

I've met many in-the-trenches leaders who blame the people above them when they fail to make progress on their agenda: "I know where we have to go, but my boss doesn't get it. He's standing in the way." That's usually a complete misdiagnosis of the situation. Don't attack your boss. Look at the situation from his or her point of view. You should treat his or her attitude as a barometer of stress in the organization.

Let's say there's a well-meaning person—we'll call him Max—who has an imaginative idea, an idea with plenty of merit. Max speaks up in the middle of a meeting, off the agenda, and offers his inspired intuition. What the boss notices is how Max's colleagues fidget, roll their eyes, demonstrate their impatience. That's because they're all saying to themselves, "I've got an agenda item that I need to get covered, because my troops are expecting me to bring home the bacon. And there goes Max with his enthusiasms again." The boss immediately picks up on that attitude and takes Max down.

Now, the boss isn't the problem. Max is the problem. Max has to find a smarter way to intervene in behalf of his agenda. He has to understand the dilemma that he's creating for the boss, and he has to figure out how to help the boss resolve that dilemma. Remember: Most bosses are already operating near the limit of how much distress they can tolerate—of how much disequilibrium, confusion, and chaos they can stomach. Naturally, they're inclined to suppress additional disturbances. So Max needs to understand the pains of change that he represents and to choose his tactics accordingly.

HOW LEADERS STAY ALIVE

Leadership is hard—on the people who work with leaders as well as on leaders themselves. How do leaders maintain the stamina, the energy, and the passion that they need to keep pushing ahead?

I'm working on this question with a Kennedy School colleague, Martin Linsky. We're writing a book for leaders that will be called *Staying Alive*. To sustain yourself over the long term, you must learn how to distinguish role from self. Or, to put it more simply: You can't take things personally. Leaders often take personally what is not personal and then misdiagnose the resistance that's out there.

Remember: It's not you they're after. It may look like a personal attack, it may sound like a personal attack—but it's the issues that you represent that they're after. Distinguishing role from self helps you maintain a diagnostic mind-set during trying times.

There's a second point: Because we get so swept up in our professional roles, it's hard to distinguish role from self on our own. That's why we need partners who can help us stay analytical. And we need two different kinds of partners. We need allies inside the organization—people who share our agenda. And we need confidants inside or outside the organization—people who can keep us from getting lost in our role.

Leaders also need a sanctuary, a place where they can go to get back in touch with the worth of their life and the worth of their work. I'm not necessarily talking about a physical place or an extended sabbatical. I'm talking about practical sanctuaries—daily moments that function as sanctuaries. One sanctuary that I recently developed for myself involves getting an email that's sent out by a rabbinic friend, who's a mystic and a biblical scholar. Every day, he sends out an interpretation of one word from the Bible. It's just a few screens long, but as I'm going through my email every day, I take a few minutes to read this thing, and it roots me in a different reality, a different source of meaning.

I'm not peddling any particular kind of sanctuary; we all have to find our own structures. Unfortunately, though, people who get swept up in fast-moving companies often treat their partners and their sanctuaries as expendable luxuries rather than as necessities: "I don't have time to have lunch with my friend"; "I don't have time to go to the gym in the morning, or to pray or meditate." I live in Boston. No one would live in Boston without owning a winter coat. But countless people think that they can exercise leadership without partners or without a sanctuary. To stay alive as leaders—to tend the wounds that we inevitably receive when we raise tough questions—requires maintaining these structures in our lives.

You make leadership sound so hard, so demanding. Do you worry that more people are going to start opting out?

Recognizing the challenges of leadership, along with the pains of change, shouldn't diminish anyone's eagerness to reap the rewards of creating value and meaning in other people's lives. There's a thrill that comes with the creation of value—and of course there's money and status — and those rewards are surely worth the pain that comes with the territory. There are lots of things in life that are worth the pain. Leadership is one of them.

William C. Taylor (wtaylor@fastcompany.com) is a founding editor of Fast Company.

III-11: Sharpening Saws

Robert Quinn

A hermit, who lived far out in a forest, would cut enough wood each summer to heat his cabin through the winter. One fall day, he heard on his shortwave radio that an early winter storm was heading for his area. Because he had not yet cut enough wood, he rushed to his wood pile.

Examining his dull and rusty saw, he realized that it needed sharpening. He paused for a moment, looked at his watch, looked at the height of his uncut wood pile, and shook his head. Instead of sharpening his saw, he began to cut. As he worked, he noted that the saw was getting increasingly dull and that he was working harder and harder. He told himself repeatedly that he needed to stop and sharpen the saw, but he continued to cut anyway. At the end of the day, as the snow began to fall, he sat exhausted next to a sizable pile of uncut wood.

"Sharpening Saws" from *Deep Change* by Robert E. Quinn. Jossey-Bass Publisher, 1996, p. 59. This material is used by permission of John Wiley & Sons, Inc.

III-12: Questions That Matter
Stories of Courage and Grace

Wayne Muller

As a therapist and minister, I've spent more than twenty years in the company of people who suffer. As I listen more deeply in each encounter, I notice something happens in a moment of suffering, something that can be quite precious—a moment that simultaneously breaks us down and also breaks us open.

(continued)

(*continued*)

At such times, we can respond to suffering by bringing everything we have—body, heart, spirit—as a sacramental offering into the company of others, be they friend, child, parent, lover, family, or community.

If we allow ourselves to be awake, an almost inevitable fountain of grace begins to open. Certain questions begin to arise in our hearts and our minds. One of the first questions, of course, is Why did this happen to me? But beyond that other deeper questions arise: What does this all mean about the nature of life? What do I hold to be sacred? What can I touch, that when I hold it in my hand will make me feel safe?

Over the years, I and others have wrestled with some deep questions—questions that don't have pat answers, and whose answers change from year to year, often from hour to hour. The questions are like mantras, they're like koans, they're something to hold in our hearts as we make our way through life.

WHO AM I?

Most spiritual traditions begin the process of pilgrimage with this question—whether a vision quest, a naming ceremony, or some other way of beginning to listen to the names we call ourselves. This is because our identities color everything we do. Who I believe myself to be will influence the paths I choose to walk, the friends I take as mine, and the enemies I choose.

For example, if I wake up in the morning and call myself a Christian, then I will look with Christian eyes at a world that seems to be moving from sin to salvation, and perhaps I will remember the teachings of Jesus about the lilies of the field. "They neither toil nor spin and yet I tell you that Solomon in all his glory was not arrayed as one of these . . . and therefore I tell you do not worry about tomorrow." And maybe I heed his prescriptions to feed the hungry, clothe the naked, and visit the sick and those in prison.

If I wake up in the morning and I think of myself as a Jew, then perhaps I feel my life as part and parcel of an enormous sweep of history from slavery to liberation, and I recite the covenants that God has made with my people. I vow to do those things that are necessary to walk humbly and do justice.

If I wake in the morning and see the world through Buddhist eyes, then perhaps I'll be thinking about the Four Noble Truths, the nature of suffering, the origin of suffering, alleviation of suffering, and escape from the wheel of birth-death-rebirth. Perhaps I take the vow as a Boddhisatva to alleviate the suffering of all beings.

And so it is with every name that we take—Democrat or Republican, mother or father, employer or employee—every name we use as our identity colors and shapes the way we walk and the way we feel about ourselves and the people we meet.

I've noticed a distressing trend in this regard during the last twenty years or so, where people have named themselves using psychological terminology—diagnostic names like "adult child of alcoholic" or "manic-depressive" or "multiple personality" or "incest survivor." While these terms may apply to some aspects of our lives, they're not names that are large enough to hold the true nature of who we are.

Jesus said, "You are the light of the world." The Buddha said, "You are saturated with Buddha nature." Jesus did not say "You are the light of the world as long as your parents were really nice and you lived in a nice neighborhood and you got a red wagon every year for Christmas, and you go to church every Sunday." He simply said "You are the light of the world."

This means that regardless of what sorrow or suffering or ache or loss or fear that travels through your body, there is this light of the world, this Buddha nature, this still small voice, this kingdom of God, that will not leave you uncomforted.

Where I live in New Mexico, Native Americans often take their names from nature, perhaps from the color of the sky, or the way an eagle seems to defy gravity and makes its way into the air, or the way an animal exhibits its power as it walks across the face of the Earth. And so, when they speak their name, they remember their strength or courage or wisdom—even when frightened, lost, or confused. Their name calls forth what doesn't break; it keeps them company. However, if I take as my name Adult Child of Alcoholic, for example, while that may be true of my experience, it doesn't touch that place that can't be named.

Telling stories about how people treated us may be useful up to a point, but there is another way of looking at this. A wonderful parable by the Buddha expresses it so well: Imagine coming to the edge of a river, and you need to get to the other side. You take grasses, sticks, and branches, lash them together to make a raft, and paddle across the river. When you get to the other side, you're so grateful to the raft that you carry it with you for the rest of your life. This would be rather silly, wouldn't it? Of course, what you would do with such a raft is tie it on the bank, and let someone else use it, or just let it float down the river. So it is with the story of our life, and even with the Buddha's teachings—certain things have usefulness to a point, but to carry them on our back for the rest of our life is just silly.

As circumstances change, what we need and what is useful in life also changes. Curiously enough, our names actually change as we grow because we ourselves become deeper and more spacious—our names get larger. Another wonderful Buddhist parable captures this: Imagine taking a hefty spoonful of salt and stirring it into a cup of water. It would be very unpleasant to drink. But if you took that same hefty spoonful of salt and stirred it into an enormous, clear blue mountain lake, and drank a mouthful, it would be so sweet. The problem is not the salt, it's the size of the container.

And so as you take your name, when you say who you are, I invite you to begin to investigate what kind of name can be large enough to hold the truth of who you are.

WHAT DO I LOVE?

The Chinese say that when a teapot has been in use in a family for over a hundred years, after a while you only need pour hot water into the pot, and the pot itself will make you tea. Because if we do something day after day, year after year, generation after generation, our lives will come to hold the fragrance of that thing. If we hold something in our hands, day after day, year after year, our hands will come to hold the shape of that thing.

And so it is that if we do what we love, day after day, year after year, generation after generation, then we become what we love. This is not magic, of course; this is simple "spiritual physics." So, like our names, it is important to know what we love. What do you love? If God is love, as most of the spiritual traditions seem to suggest in one form or another, then if we follow what we love we will be led inevitably up the steps and onto the doorstep of the divine.

Many of us have spent perhaps quite a bit of time getting rid of the things we don't love—part of our histories, our stories about the aches and struggles we've carried. This is useful work. Yet at a certain point it will bring us back up only to zero. All of the poets and mystics and saints of the world have indicated that a human life can go higher than zero. And what star we choose to follow is the star of what we love.

What opens our hearts? What excites our spirit? What galvanizes our passion and our curiosity? "Curiosity," of course, shares the same root as "cure," so in a way what we love and what captures our curiosity draws us forward into some place of great destiny.

Another reason to pay attention to what we love is that it will live in our eyes: What we love will actually change what we see. I'll give an example. A couple of years ago, in the Santo Domingo Pueblo, I joined a family of close friends on an Easter-egg hunt in the hills. Now, when you picture Easter-egg hunting in northern New Mexico, it's not at all like on the White House lawn. There's wind and dust blowing into your eyes and teeth, and you're also competing with cactus, gophers, and rattlesnakes. It's a different sort of Easter experience.

I was with my son Maxwell, who was about three, and we had found a few eggs. Timothy, the son of our host family, had quite a few more—obviously having much greater success. We asked him where he found the eggs, and whether there were any left. All of sudden, Tim looked down, and said, pointing to some yellow sand on the ground, "You know, I need that yellow sand for my pots." Tim's a potter, from generations of potters, and loves making pots. His family, of course, doesn't go to "Clays-R-Us" they get their clay from the earth. Tim's eyes know to look for those colors that he loves, and because he loves that particular color yellow he stopped in the middle of a conversation about the egg hunt and said, "I need to go get a plastic bag and the pickup, and bring some yellow clay back for my glazes."

Because Tim loves pots, he could see that yellow in a way that I, standing right next to him, could never have seen: What we love lives in our eyes. What we love actually changes what we see.

It is important, therefore, to be mindful of what we love. Do you love dance? Do you love God? Do you love color? Do you love beauty? Do you love justice? Do you love children? Those things that you love will guide your steps, and they will also live in your eyes.

HOW SHALL I LIVE, KNOWING I WILL DIE?

What kind of people shall we be, knowing that we have only a short period left here on this Earth? Shall we be courageous? Shall we be playful? Shall we be loving? Shall we be quiet people? How shall we live, knowing that we will die?

A friend of mine had a son, Forrest, four years old, who used to keep a journal. He didn't actually keep the journal, of course. His mother would sit down on his bedside every evening and ask him, "Forrest, do you have anything you would like to say about how it was for you today?" And she would write down what he said, so as he got older he could have this journal as a memory of his childhood. She read me some of Forrest's entries when he was four:

> Thursday, May 5: "I love dinosaurs, I love 'em, love 'em, love 'em. I love sharks. T. Rex is the most fierce hunter. It's Thursday today. My days are getting different now because we're doing different stuff. I don't know why my pterodactyl's sick for three days. I love my dinosaurs."
>
> Sunday, June 12: "I'm happy today. I wish we'd go out on a hike. I wish there were butterflies in rainforests. Is there a rainforest in Micronesia? I played on my tricycle. I slipped and almost fell, but I didn't. I ran over Sissy's tail and hand. Sissy growled, I said I'm

sorry. I want to go to the rainforest sometime."

On June 24, Forrest was killed in a car accident. His mother was driving. Forrest and his brother Bryce, who was one, were in the back seat, and both were killed—her only two children, along with her father, who was in the front passenger's seat. She somehow miraculously survived.

I was blessed to be in the company of Forrest's parents for quite a period after that, trying to listen along with them for what doesn't break, for what still lives, in the midst of such unspeakable grief.

Knowing what we know, now, about Forrest's life and death, pay attention again for a moment to some of the things he had to say:"I love dinosaurs, I love'em, love 'em, love 'em. I want to go to the rainforest sometime."

We listen to Forrest's words differently when we feel his life framed by his death. I would like to suggest that the difference between Forrest and ourselves is really quite small, that our lives, like Forrest's, are also brief and also framed by death. There's a kind of poignancy that we ascribe to Forrest's life because it seems somehow unnaturally short. And yes, our lives as well are simply naturally short.

When I'm in the company of people dying of cancer or AIDS or other terminal illnesses, one of the things that happens, not always but often, is that people begin to feel the preciousness of what it means to breathe and to be able to love one another, to be able to put one day at the service of someone who is in need, or to be able to be in the company of other beings in love or kindness. Every touch of the hand becomes a miracle, every word of kindness shared is a symphony, every day that the sun rises miraculously and bathes the Earth in sunlight is an epiphany, because this could be the last time I see this unspeakably magnificent event.

Those of us who believe we will live for a very long time tend to get sloppy, and we live by accident. Yet every breath we take, every prayer we speak, every conversation we have, can be a moment of great healing, or grace, or creation, or birth. Can we be that awake? How do we live, knowing that we will die?

One of the things that happens, paradoxically, to people who are close to their death is they become grateful, which makes no sense from the outside. Yet from the inside there is sometimes this deep pool of gratefulness. Thank you for coming to see me. Thank you for this cookie that you baked for me with your loving kindness. Thank you for sitting with me on this bed.

I remember sitting with a man close to death who said, "You know, I've done an awful lot of spiritual practice, I've prayed, I've meditated, I've taken vows, I've taken initiations, and I think I'm ready to die. But to be perfectly honest, I wish I had just ten years of cancer-free life, just ten years." So I said, "If I could grant you that boon, if I could give you those ten years, what would you do with them?" And without skipping a beat he said, "I would be kind. I would teach children everything I've ever learned about how things work, and how to be strong, and how to be courageous, and how to be loving."

WHAT IS MY GIFT TO THE FAMILY OF THE EARTH?

All of the practices we do—every prayer we speak, every meditation, every invocation, every vow, every ordination—is not for our own healing alone. We do this work for the healing of all beings.

One of the most painful things for me as a minister, as a therapist, working with people who have been given some suffering or some illness, some poverty, some injustice, or some violation, is that they feel so hurt or broken down or ripped open or defective because of the depth of the

What Do You Love?

I met Max Cordova through our work with Bread for the Journey—an organization I started in New Mexico to assist people committed to enhancing the quality of life in their community. Max often calls me with ideas about what can be done to help people of Truchas in the northern part of the state. Max is warm and kind, and his heart is given to helping others.

This time Max wanted to talk about water. Truchas—like all of northern New Mexico—was settled by the Spanish in the sixteenth and seventeenth centuries. The Spanish irrigated these lands by climbing high into the mountains to dig a wide irrigation ditch that would bring water to the fields and villages. What the Spanish learned about irrigation from the Incas in South America they brought to the mountains of the Southwest.

Max took me up to the mouth of the ditch, a two-hour drive in his pickup. The *acequia madre*, or mother ditch, feeds a smaller ditch which runs for twelve miles into town. Three hundred years ago, the families that settled Truchas worked for years to dig this ditch by hand. Like their Inca counterparts, they had only donkeys and shovels. When they found their way blocked by a large boulder, they would dig a small pit under a portion of the rock and light a fire underneath the stone. When the rock was heated they poured cold water on it to crack it open. Then they could continue digging. Some boulders were so large it took a month of heating and cracking simply to get through them.

Max and I walked alongside the ditch. The water flowed so quietly, cradled in the earth beneath a canopy of ponderosa and aspen. Every year, in spring, the people of Truchas climb this mountain to clean the ditch, as they have for the last three hundred years. As water poured forth from the mountain, so had the life of these people been poured into this Acequia. This was sacred ground.

"The Army Corps of Engineers wants to tear this all out," Max finally told me. "They want to replace it with plastic pipe. They got some money from the government, and they decided to use it to fill in this ditch. They say that plastic pipe will be more efficient, that we will not lose any water and that we can direct it anywhere we want." Max paused. He was clearly upset. "They say it will be better for us, and we should be happy we will not have to clean the ditch."

"But we don't think this is a good idea," Max went on, slowly, quietly. "We love this ditch, When we all climb Truchas peak in the spring and clean the ditch, it holds us together. The ditch is our life. It feeds us: it is like glue that holds the soul of Truchas together. How can they take it away from us?"

I did not know what to say. It was inconceivable anyone would want to destroy this place. I marveled again at the frequency with which people in small villages, people of color, people with little financial or political influence, must relentlessly confront powers that regularly impose their will from the outside, so often bringing unnecessary suffering and grief.

Max continued, "It is true, we have many problems. We have a lot of poverty here. We have drinking, alcoholism; sometimes there is violence. There is hardly anything for our young people. But the ditch, it is a beautiful thing. These things, they can unite us, give us hope. This ditch holds us together. Without the ditch, I am afraid we will come apart."

For the next three months Bread for the Journey worked with Max, finding lawyers fluent in the language of environmental and historical preservation. The Corps was forced to hold public hearings, open their documents to the public, and allow the people of Truchas to have a voice in the future of the ditch. There were emotional meetings, passionate encounters where people spoke of their parents and grandparents and great-grandparents and of cleaning the ditch, drawing the water for their fields, tasting the sweetness of the mountain's gift to them. How could they let this die?

Finally the lawyers and representatives of the community presented the Army Corps of Engineers with a petition to keep the ditch. Of the

(continued)

ache they carry in their body. They believe they have no gift at all to bring to the family of the Earth. And this, to me, is perhaps greater suffering even than the original abuse or illness.

What is your gift to the family of the Earth? One of the first things that happens to us when we think about our gift is we think that it must be something large and magnificent. "If we're going to be truly spiritual saviors of the planet, we must have something terribly impressive and dramatic to offer to the world." But our gifts need not be dramatic or magnificent. In point of fact, they can be quite small and unobtrusive.

Sometimes we wait until we're quite certain that our gifts will be useful. And this of course is a trap, because we never really know whether our gifts will be useful. We cannot wait until we know the results of our gifts before we offer them. The Buddha in the Eight-fold Path speaks quite passionately about right understanding and right mindfulness and right effort and right action, but the Buddha never speaks of right result. We do not know what will happen to what we bring, and we can't hold the world hostage waiting for the promise that what we bring will do some good. As a matter of fact, sometimes our gifts will at first blush seem as if they do nothing at all.

A good friend of mine, Sharon Salzberg, wrote a book about eight or nine years ago. She was studying with a particular Buddhist teacher, and she and some friends decided to collect his meditations and teachings into a book. Wisdom Publications published it, and it sold a couple of thousand copies.

Many years later, Sharon was reading about Aung San Suu Kyi, who was imprisoned in Burma for her work trying to lead her people to freedom and democracy. She was placed under house arrest for many years. She was alone and frightened and mishandled. When she was eventually released some people asked her, "What sustained you during that time?" And she said, "Well, I learned how to meditate." They asked her how she learned. She said, "I had this little book, and it taught me everything I needed to know in order to survive my imprisonment." And, of course, it was Sharon's book.

We don't know where our gift will bear fruit, but we do know that our gift is required. All it requires is for you to listen to the impulse that arises, as it does in each and every one of us—not because it's dramatic, not because it's particularly spiritual, but just because it's yours.

You are the light of the world. What permission are you waiting for before you feel as if you could offer your gift with ease and playfulness and grace? What is your gift to the family of the Earth?

Source: Adapted from a talk at IONS conference "Questing Spirit," Palm Springs, July 1997.

Wayne Muller is a therapist, public speaker, minister, and author of *Legacy of the Heart*, the best-selling book that explores the resilience of the spirit in the face of human sorrow. His second book, *How Then Shall We Live?*, examines four simple questions that reval our natural, inner abundance and liberate our ability to be joyfully kind and helpful in our families and communities. His third book, *Sabbath: Restoring the Sacred Rhythm of Rest*, explores how, in the relentless busyness of modern life, we have lost of the essential rhythm between work and rest. *Sabbath* provides simple, traditional practices that renew and refresh our lives with a healing rhythm of rest and delight. His latest book is called *Learning to Pray: How We Find Heaven on Earth*, a guide for finding peace in ourselves and in the world in the midst of troubled times.

Wayne is the founder of Bread for the Journey, a nonprofit organization that supports the natural generosity of ordinary people as they learn to become neighborhood philanthropists. He is also the founder of the Institute for Engaged Spirituality, a consultant with the Fetzer Institute, and a fellow with The Institute of Noetic Sciences (IONS). IONS members and local groups who are interested in starting a local chapter of Bread for the Journey can contact Marianna Cacciatore at Bread for the Journey, 267 Miller Ave, Mill Valley, CA 94941, (415) 383-6600, mariannac@pacbell.net.

III-13: The Learning Executive

Jim Collins

● ● ● ● ● ● ● ● ● ● ● ● ● ●

THE LONG VIEW

Asking why you need to put learning objectives before performance objectives is like asking for a financial justification for breathing.

How would your day be different if you organized your time, energy, and resources primarily around the objective of learning, instead of around performance? For many people, their daily activities—what they do and how they go about doing it—would be dramatically changed. Indeed, despite all the buzz around the concept of the "learning organization," I'm struck by how few people seem to have embraced the idea of being a true learning person.

This came home to me during an interview with a television producer developing a documentary on Sam Walton. After about

45 minutes, she asked if I had anything else to add, indicating the end of the interview. "No," I said, "but I'd like to ask you some questions." She paused, obviously not prepared for my request, and then gave an uncertain, "OK." For the next 15 minutes, I had the great pleasure of asking her questions about what she had learned in her research. The producer had no background in business—having done most of her documentaries on historical figures like Stalin and Mozart—so I thought she might have a fresh and illuminating perspective. She did, and I learned some new information and gained new insights about one of my favorite subjects.

"That's the first time that's ever happened to me," she said. "I interview professors and experts all the time, but I've never had one turn the tables and begin asking me questions. At first I was taken aback—surprised, really—but it's refreshing to see that experts can still learn."

Stop and think about that for a minute. Here's a bright television producer who

Source: Inc Magazine, August 1, 1997.

spends her life delving into specific subjects — a walking treasure trove of knowledge — and people whose profession is to continually learn don't pause to take the opportunity to expand their expertise by talking with her. They act as knowers rather than learners, which, incidentally, is just the opposite of what Sam Walton did.

Walton viewed himself not as a definitive expert on retailing but as a lifelong student of his craft, always asking questions and talking every opportunity to learn. A Brazilian businessman once told me that of 10 U.S. retailing CEOs he wrote to asking for an appointment after he'd purchased a discount retailing chain in South America, only Walton said yes. "We didn't know much about retailing, so we wanted to talk to executives who knew the business," he explained. "Most didn't bother to reply. Sam said, 'Sure, come on up.' Only later did I realize he was as interested in learning from us as we were in learning from him; he pummeled us with questions about Brazil. Later we launched a joint venture with Wal-Mart in South America."

Becoming a learning person certainly involves responding to every situation with learning in mind, a Walton did. But it involves more than that; it requires setting explicit learning objectives. Look at your personal list of long-term objectives and midterm objectives, and your current to-do list. How many items fall into the performance genre and how many fall into the learning genre? How many begin with the structure "My objective is to learn x" rather than "My objective is to accomplish y"? Most people operate off of to-do lists. They're a useful mechanism for getting things done. A true learning person also has a "to-learn" list, and the items on that list carry at least as much weight in how one organizes his or her time as the to-do list does.

Granite Rock, in Watsonville, Calif., one of the few authentic learning organizations,

has institutionalized this idea by replacing performance goals for individuals with learning goals. The stone, concrete, and asphalt supplier makes the shift explicit by asking each employee to set his or her annual objectives in the format "Learn _____ so that I can _____."

Learning people also develop explicit learning mechanisms, such as "learning logs" or formal "autopsies" — time explicitly set aside to discuss or reflect on events and extract the maximum knowledge and understanding from them. Such people plant seeds of learning that will flower later. One prominent thinker I spent a day with ended our discussion with the statement, "I have a small consulting fee: you must keep me informed as to your learning and progress." Every six months or so I send him a letter, and I imagine he gets dozens of such learning letters a year. I've also found the mechanism of a learning notebook to be useful; in it I keep track of my learning and observations about life, work, myself, or whatever seems interesting, much the same way a scientist keeps a lab book on any subject of inquiry. It's a powerful mechanism for identifying not only learning but also the activities in which I'm not learning (which I then unplug or redesign).

I'm not yet as much of a learning person as I'd like to be. Like most Americans, I'm driven largely by an urge to perform, accomplish, achieve, and get things done. Yet as I begin to consciously shift to filtering everything through a learning lens, I find both dramatic and subtle differences in the way I do things and how I spend my time. With a "get things done" lens, I'll leave a voice-mail message; with a learning lens, I'll seek a real-time phone call during which I can ask questions and learn from conversation. With a performance lens, I'll try to impress the interviewer with my knowledge; with a learning lens, I'll ask her questions. Even mundane activities like washing dishes, shaving, and walking through airports can be transformed by carrying a portable tape player and listening to unabridged books on tape.

John W. Gardner, author of the classic book *Self-Renewal: The Individual and Innovative Society* (and a man who keeps an active learning and teaching schedule well into his eighties), captured the spirit of the learning person with his admonition "Don't set out in life to be an interesting person; set out to be an interested person." Learning people, of which Gardner is a prime example, learn till the day they die, not because learning will "get them somewhere" but because they see learning as part of the reason for living. When asked for an economic justification for learning, they find the question as odd as being asked for a financial justification for breathing. The link between learning and performance is self-evident, but for a true learning person (or organization, for that matter), performance is not the ultimate why of learning. Learning is the why of learning. And until we grasp that fact and organize accordingly, we will not—indeed cannot—build the elusive learning organization.

Jim Collins is the coauthor of *Built to Last: Successful Habits of Visionary Companies* (Harper Business, 1994) and operates a management laboratory in Boulder, Colorado.

III-14: Cat's in the Cradle

Harry Chapin

My child arrived just the other day;
he came to the world in the usual way.
But there were planes to catch and bills
  to pay;
he learned to walk while I was away.
And he was talkin' 'fore I knew it,
and as he grew he'd say,
"I'm gonna be like you, Dad,
you know I'm gonna be like you."

And the cat's in the cradle and the silver spoon,
little boy blue and the man in the
  moon.
"When you comin' home Dad?"
"I don't know when, but we'll get
  together then,
you know we'll have a good time then."

My son turned ten just the other day;
he said, "Thanks for the ball, Dad,
come on let's play.
Can you teach me to throw?"

I said, "Not today, I got a lot to do."
He said, "That's okay."
But his smile never dimmed, it said,
"I'm gonna be like him, yeah,
you know I'm gonna be like him."

Chorus

Well he came from college just the
  other day;
so much like a man I just had to say,
"Son, I'm proud of you, can you sit for
  a while?"
He shook his head and he said with a
  smile,
"What I'd really like, Dad,
is to borrow the car keys;
see you later, can I have them please?"

Chorus

I've long since retired,
my son's moved away;
I called him up just the other day.
I said, "I'd like to see you if you don't
  mind."

He said, "I'd love to Dad, if I could find
  the time.
You see, my new job's a hassle and the
  kids have the flu,
but it's sure nice talking to you, Dad,
  it's been sure nice talkin' to you."

As I hung up the phone,
it occurred to me,
he'd grown up just like me;
my boy was just like me.

Chorus

III-15: If I Had My Life to Live Over

Nadine Stair

I'd dare to make more mistakes next
  time. I'd relax. I would limber up. I
  would be sillier than I have been this
  trip. I would take fewer things seriously. I would take more chances. I
  would take more trips. I would climb
  more mountains and swim more
  rivers. I would eat more ice cream and
  less beans. I would perhaps have
  more actual troubles, but I'd have
  fewer imaginary ones.

You see, I'm one of those people who
  live sensibly and sanely hour after
  hour, day after day. Oh, I've had my

moments and if I had it to do over
  again, I'd have more of them. In fact,
  I'd try to have nothing else. Just
  moments, one after another, instead
  of living so many years ahead of
  each day. I've been one of those persons who never goes anywhere without a thermometer, a hot water bottle, a raincoat, and a parachute. If I
  had to do it again, I would travel
  lighter than I have.

If I had my life to live over, I would
  start barefoot earlier in the Spring
  and stay that way later in the Fall. I
  would go to more dances. I would
  ride more merry-go-rounds. I would
  pick more daisies.

A Free verse poem frequently attributed to Nadine
Stair, based on a text by Don Herold, copyright
Readers Digest.

III-16: Leading from Any Chair

Rosamund Stone Zander and Benjamin Zander

BEN: A conductor can be easily seduced
by the public's extraordinary attention to his
unique offering and come to believe that he is

personally superior. The near-mythical maestro Herbert von Karajan was reputed to have
jumped into a taxi outside the opera house
and shouted to the driver, "Hurry, hurry!"
"Very good, sir," said the driver. "Where to?"
"It doesn't matter," said von Karajan impa-
tiently. "They need me everywhere!"

Orchestral players will forgive a great conductor—one who has a far-reaching artistic vision—many personal transgressions in facilitation of the all-important performance, much the way a family will administer to the extraordinary needs of a woman giving birth. Yet in the music business, as in all walks of life, a leader who feels he is superior is likely to suppress the voices of the very people on whom he must rely to deliver his vision alive and kicking.

The conductor, a magical figure for the audience, enjoys a leadership mystique of significant magnitude. It may seem strange to the orchestral musician that the corporate world would be interested in hearing a conductor's views on leadership or that the metaphor of the orchestra is so frequently used in the literature of leadership because, in fact, the profession of conductor is one of the last bastions of totalitarianism in the civilized world!

There is a famous tale of Toscanini, the great Italian maestro, whose temper and blatantly autocratic ways—as much as his transcendent musicianship—were the stuff of legend. It is said that once in the middle of a rehearsal, in a fit of anger, he fired a long-standing member of the double bass section, who now had to return home to tell his wife that he was out of a job. As the bass player packed up his instrument, he mentioned a few things that he had hitherto kept to himself, and, as he left the hall for the final time, shouted at Toscanini, "You are a no-good son-of-a-bitch!" So oblivious was Toscanini to the notion that a player would dare to challenge his authority, that he roared back: "It is too late to apologize!"

This kind of domination of the orchestra by the conductor—widespread, if not the norm, fifty years ago—is less common today. But vanity and tyranny are prevalent in the music world even in these enlightened times, and the picture of orchestral musicians as infantile and submissive, caught

between willful conductors, insensitive management, and hypervigilant unions, is not as rare as one would hope. Perhaps that is part of the reason why a recent study of various professions revealed that orchestral players, while not the *most* disaffected in the survey, experience a job satisfaction level just below that of prison guards.[1]

I had been conducting for nearly twenty years when it suddenly dawned on me that the conductor of an orchestra does not make a sound. His picture may appear on the cover of the CD in various dramatic poses, but his true power derives from his ability to make other people powerful. I began to ask myself questions like "What makes a group lively and engaged?" instead of "How good am I?" So palpable was the difference in my approach to conducting as a result of this "silent conductor" insight, that players in the orchestra started asking me, "What happened to you?" Before that, my main concerns had been whether my interpretation was being appreciated by the audience and, if the truth be known, whether the critics liked it because if they did it might lead to other opportunities and greater success. In order to realize my interpretation of the work in question, it seemed all I had to do was to gain sway over the players, teach them my interpretation, and make them fulfill my musical will. Now, in the light of my "discovery," I began to shift my attention to how effective I was at enabling the musicians to play each phrase as beautifully as they were capable. This concern had rarely surfaced when my position appeared to give me absolute power and I had cast the players as mere instruments of my will.

But how, actually, could I know what the players were feeling about my effectiveness

---

[1] Paul R. Judy, "Life and Work in Symphony Orchestras: An Interview with J. Richard Hackman," *Harmony: Forum of the Symphony Orchestra Institute,* vol. 2 (Aril 1996), 4

in releasing their power? Certainly I could tell a lot by looking into their eyes—the eyes never lie, after all—and at their posture, their whole demeanor, and I could ask myself, "Are they engaged?" But at some point, I found I wanted more information, and more relationship. Our eyes meeting across a crowded room was simply not enough; I wanted to hear what they had to say. It was completely impractical to attempt to be on speaking terms with a hundred players at every rehearsal, however, and anyway, there was no precedent for it. Traditionally, all verbal communication in an orchestral rehearsal is directed from the podium to the players and almost never the other way around. Any communication back to the conductor is through a few leading players, especially the concertmaster, and then almost invariably in the form of a question, usually preceded by a semi-diffident, often secretly mocking, "Maestro. . . ."

"Virtually every communication from the musicians to a conductor in a rehearsal is phrased as a question, even when it is really a statement of fact or belief," wrote Seymour and Robert Levine in an article in *Harmony* magazine.

> One of [us] once heard the principal clarinetist of a major American orchestra ask the conductor whether he wanted the notes with dots over them ". . . short, or like the brass were playing them?" [A dot over a note indicates that it is to be played short.] This rather complex statement, masquerading as a question, conveyed both the musician's lack of respect for the brass players in question, and scorn for the conductor's failure to notice the problem. But to fit the myth of the omniscient conductor, the comment had to be phrased as a question, for how could a musician possibly inform an omniscient being?

The myth dictates that a musician can only tap into that well of knowledge, not add to it.[2]

One time, as we were rehearsing Mahler's Sixth Symphony, I made a seemingly routine apology to the players of the Philharmonia Orchestra of London. You see, I had shouted out after one passage, "Cowbells, you didn't come in!" A few minutes later I realized that the cowbells weren't supposed to play at that moment, so I called out to the percussion section, "I'm so sorry, I was wrong about that entrance. I see you don't play there." After the rehearsal, I was amazed that no less than three musicians came to me separately and in private to say that they couldn't remember the last time they had heard a conductor admit his own mistake. One player commented on how dispiriting it is for players when a conductor, as often happens, gets angry and blames the orchestra when he himself made the mistake, in the vain hope that nobody will have noticed. Many corporate heads and managers I have spoken to have since let me know that the orchestra is not the *only* hierarchical setting where this dynamic occurs.

With the intention of providing a conduit for orchestra members to be heard, I initiated a practice of putting a blank sheet of paper on every stand in each rehearsal. The players are invited to write down any observation or coaching for me that might enable me to empower them to play the music more beautifully. At first I braced myself for criticism, but surprisingly the responses on the "white sheets," as they have come to be called, rarely assume that form.

Initially, out of habit, players confined their remarks to practical issues, such as the agreement between the parts and the score. Gradually, when they trusted that I was genuinely interested in what they had to say,

---

[2]Seymour Levine and Robert Levine, "Why They Are Not Smiling," *Harmony* vol. 2 (April 1996): 18.

they began to support me, not by bolstering my authority, nor my ego, but by giving recognition to my role as an essential conduit for the full realization of the possibility of the music. Now that the "white sheet" practice is familiar and accepted by all the orchestras that I regularly conduct; the comments, which are usually signed to facilitate further discussion, are most often practical ones about my conducting or about the interpretation of the music. Musicians do not hesitate to ask me, for instance, to conduct a certain passage in two rather than in four, so they can better fulfill the sense of the musical line.

Frequently I receive comments that are deeply insightful about the interpretation, comments that I almost always take on board and that affect the performance. An orchestra of a hundred musicians will invariably contain great artists, some with an intimate or specialized knowledge of the work being performed, others with insight about the tempo or structure or relationships within the piece, a subject about which no one has ever asked them to communicate.

Whenever I take on an idea from a member of the orchestra, I try to make some eye contact with them at the moment the passage is played, sometimes several times during the rehearsals and even at the concert. Magically, that moment becomes *their* moment. "*You did my crescendo!*" said a cellist with a mixture of disbelief, pride, and delight after the concert; she had written on her white sheet only that morning at the dress rehearsal that we weren't doing justice to one of Bruckner's majestic climaxes.

One of the most supremely gifted and accomplished artists I have known sat for decades as a modest member of the viola section of one of America's leading orchestras. Eugene Lehner had been the violist of the legendary Kolisch Quartet, and had coached the distinguished Julliard String Quartet as well as innumerable other famous ensembles. Many of Boston's finest musicians considered Lehner to be a semi-

nal, formative influence on their musical lives. How often I have consulted him on thorny points of interpretation—to have the scales removed from my eyes by his incandescent insight into the music!

Yet, had any conductor visiting the Boston Symphony ever consulted him or called on his profound knowledge and understanding of the particular piece they were performing together? Indeed, I believe such a notion is almost unthinkable. One Friday, when he was a guest coach at my Interpretation class, I raised this issue; for the benefit of the class I asked him, "How can you bear to play day after day in an orchestra led by conductors, many of whom must know so much less than you?" In his habitual humility, he sidestepped the compliment and then indicated that he did indeed have something to say on the subject:

> One day, during my very first year playing with the orchestra, I remember an occasion when Koussevitsky was conducting a Bach piece and he seemed to be having some difficulty getting the results he wanted—it simply wasn't going right. Fortunately, his friend, the great French pedagogue and conductor Nadia Boulanger, happened to be in town and sitting in on the rehearsal, so Koussevitsky took the opportunity to extricate himself from an awkward and embarrassing situation by calling out to her, "Nadia, please, will you come up here and conduct? I want to go to the back of the hall to see how it sounds." Mademoiselle Boulanger stepped up, made a few comments to the musicians, and conducted the orchestra through the passage without a hitch. Ever since that time, in every rehearsal, I have been waiting for the conductor to say, "Lehner, you come up

here and conduct, I want to go to the back of the hall to hear how it sounds." It is now forty-three years since this happened, and it is less and less likely that I will be asked. However, in the meantime, I haven't had a single dull moment in a rehearsal, as I sit wondering what I would say to the orchestra should I suddenly be called upon to lead.

During a recent stint guest-conducting the orchestra at the Royal College of Music in London, I told, as I often do, the story of Lehner, as a way of encouraging the greatest possible attentiveness and participation of all the players. Then, in the middle of the rehearsal, I suddenly turned to one of the violinists sitting in the fourth stand of the second violins, whose passion had been evident to me from the very first rehearsal, and said, "John, you come up here and conduct. I want to go to the back to hear how it sounds." That day on his white sheet he wrote that I had enabled him to realize a lifelong dream. Suddenly, the full extent of the resources of the orchestra presented itself to my view, and I leapt to offer some of the other musicians the same gift. One wrote, "*I have been so critical of conductors, and now I see that what you have to do is as demanding as playing an instrument.*" Others commented that this exercise shifted the whole experience of playing in an orchestra from a passive one to one in which, like Lehner, they became active participants.

HOW MUCH GREATNESS ARE WE WILLING TO GRANT?

The conductor decides who is playing in his orchestra. Even when he comes in fresh to guest-conduct players who are already in

their seats, he determines who is there. When he sees instrumentalists who look listless, he can decide that they are bored and resigned, or he can greet in them the original spark that enticed them into music, now dimmed to a flicker. He can say, "Of course! They have had to go against their passionate natures and interrupt the long line of their commitment on account of the many competing demands of the music profession. They want to be recognized as the true artists they really are." He can see, sitting before him, the jaded and the disaffected—or the tender and glorious lover of music.

A monumental question for leaders in any organization to consider is: How much greatness are we willing to grant people? Because it makes all the difference at every level who it is we decide we are leading. The activity of leadership is not limited to conductors, presidents, and CEOs, of course—the player who energizes the orchestra by communicating his newfound appreciation for the tasks of the conductor, or a parent who fashions in her own mind that her children desire to contribute, is exercising leadership of the most profound kind.

Listening for passion and commitment is the practice of *the silent conductor* whether the players are sitting in the orchestra, on the management team, or on the nursery floor. How can this leader know how well he is fulfilling his intention? He can look in the eyes of the players and prepare to ask himself, "Who am I being that they are not shining?" He can invite information and expression. He can speak to their passion. He can look for an opportunity to hand them the baton.

Today was exceptional in that I learned leadership is not a responsibility—nobody has to lead. It's a gift, shining silver, that reminds people huddled nearby why each shimmering moment matters. It's in the eyes, the voice, this swelling song that warms up from the toes and tingles with endless possibilities. Things change when you care enough to grab whatever you love, and give it everything.

—Amanda Burr, student at the Walnut Hill School

LEADERS EVERYWHERE

BEN: On our 1999 tour to Cuba with the Youth Philharmonic Orchestra, we decided to begin a concert in Havana with two pieces to be performed in combination with the National Youth Orchestra of Cuba, a Cuban and an American sitting at each stand. The first piece to be played was written by the outstanding conductor of the Cuban orchestra. It was colorful and brilliant, and contained many complicated Cuban rhythms. I had decided not to prepare our orchestra in advance because I thought it was a rare opportunity to start work on a piece under the direction of the composer himself.

Maestro Guido Lopez Gavillan began rehearsing his work, but it soon seemed evident that the complex Cuban rhythms were so unfamiliar to the American kids that the piece was beyond them. They simply couldn't play it. The maestro became concerned, frustrated, and then resigned himself to failure. He declared from the podium, "I'm afraid this is not going to work. We have to cancel the performance."

This outcome was completely unacceptable to me. It was one of the cornerstones of this trip that our young musicians be able to perform with their counterparts. Without thinking, I leapt to the stage and said to the young Cuban players through an interpreter, "Your job is to teach these rhythms to your stand partner." And to the American players I said, "Just give yourselves over to the leaders sitting next to you. You will get the support you need." I asked the maestro to try again.

What happened next startled us all. The focus shifted away from the maestro, toward the stand partners. Already more expressive than most young players I had seen, the Cubans became fantastically energized, exuberantly conducting with their instruments, each leading along his American stand partner enthusiastically. The American kids, basking in the lavish attention, gave themselves over to the process and began to play the rhythms the way they were intended to be played. Maestro Gavillan, who appeared as surprised and as pleased as I was, nodded to me that everything would be fine.

Then it was my turn, and I rose to conduct the other piece that was to open the program: Bernstein's fiendishly difficult little masterpiece, his overture to *Candide*. This piece was so tricky to play that we had sent the parts down to Havana three months earlier to make sure that the Cuban orchestra would have the opportunity to prepare. As we were getting ready to rehearse, I asked their leader in passing whether they had enjoyed working on the overture. "But we've never seen it," he said, obviously perplexed. It turned out that the music had been languishing in the Cuban post office for all that time.

I could feel the blood drain from my face. I felt panic overcoming me, realizing the impossibility of performing *this* piece under *these* conditions. Our youth orchestra had taken months to master the overture! Then, I looked at the players and saw many of them smiling. Of course! We had only to reverse the process that had been so successful earlier in the rehearsal! The American kids now sprang to life, energetically leading their stand partners through the bar lines—and it went off perfectly.

Again, the attention shifted away from the conductor on the podium to the partnership in the pit. The energy level of each local "conductor" rose dramatically. No less remarkable was the willingness of the young Cuban players to be supported and led by their close companions—and how much more effectively than by the distant figure on the podium.

Like Lehner's tale, the story of these young people highlights another meaning of the phrase *silent conductor*. A leader does not need a podium; she can be sitting quietly on the edge of any chair, listening passionately and with commitment, fully prepared to take up the baton. In fact, to make reference to the Rabbi's gift at the end of chapter 3, the leader may be any one of us.

Mr. Zander,

This is my first white sheet. Sitting at the back of the cello section, when I have always sat at the front, was the hardest thing I've done in a long while. But over the nine days of our work together I began to discover what playing in an orchestra was really about. Your shine has inspired me to believe that I have the force of personality to power the section from wherever I sit and I believe that I led that concert from the 11th chair. Thank you for helping me know that. From this day I will be leading every section in which I sit—whichever seat.

—Georgina, cellist in the
New Zealand National Youth
Orchestra

Here is a final story of a committed and passionate man, a colleague of Eugene Lehner's, who led as a peer from the edge of his chair with so little fanfare that no one actually noticed him. They just heard the remarkable result.

The legendary Kolisch Quartet had the singular distinction of playing its entire repertoire from memory, including the impossibly complex modern works of Schoenberg, Webern, Bartok, and Berg. Eugene Lehner was the violist for the quartet in the 1930s. Lehner's stories about their remarkable performances often included a hair-raising moment when one player or another had a memory slip. Although he relished the rapport that developed between them without the encumbrance of a music stand, he admits there was hardly a concert in which some mistake did not mar the performance. The alertness, presence, and attention required of the players in every performance is hard to fathom, but in one concert an event occurred that surpassed their ordinary brinkmanship.

In the middle of the slow movement of Beethoven's String Quartet op. 95, just before his big solo, Lehner suddenly had an inexplicable memory lapse, in a place where his memory had never failed him before. He literally blacked out. But the audience heard Opus 95 as it was meant to be played, the viola solo sounding in all its richness. Even the first violinist, Rudolph Kolisch, and cellist, Bennar Heifetz, both with their eyes closed and deeply absorbed in the music, were unaware that Lehner had dropped out. The second violinist, Felix Khuner, was playing Lehner's melody, coming in without missing a beat at the viola's designated entrance, the notes perfectly in tune and voiced like a viola on an instrument tuned a fifth higher. Lehner was stunned, and offstage after the performance asked Khuner how he could have possibly known to play. Khuner answered with a shrug: "I could see that your third finger was poised over the wrong string, so I knew you must have forgotten what came next."

III-17: The Invisible Leader

Phil Jackson

John Paxson once came across a Chinese fable in the *Harvard Business Review* that he said reminded him of my leadership style.

The story was about Emperor Liu Bang, who, in the third century B.C., became the first ruler to consolidate China into a unified empire. To celebrate his victory, Liu Bang held a great banquet in the palace, inviting many important government officials, military leaders, poets, and teachers, including Chen Cen, a master who had given him guidance during the campaign. Chen Cen's disciples, who accompanied him to the banquet, were impressed by the proceedings but were baffled by an enigma at the heart of the celebration.

Seated at the central table with Liu Bang was his illustrious high command. First there was Xiao He, an eminent general whose knowledge of military logistics was second to none. Next to him was Han Xin, a legendary tactician who'd won every battle he'd ever fought. Last was Chang Yang, a shrewd diplomat who was gifted at convincing heads of state to form alliances and surrender without fighting. These men the disciples could understand. What puzzled them was how Liu Bang, who didn't have a noble birth or knowledge comparable to that of his chief advisers, fit into the picture. "Why is he the emperor?" they asked.

Chen Cen smiled and asked them what determines the strength of a wheel. "Is it not the sturdiness of the spokes?" one responded. "Then why is it that two wheels made of identical spokes differ in strength?" asked Chen Cen. After a moment, he continued, "See beyond what is seen. Never forget that a wheel is made not only of spokes but also of the space between the spokes. Sturdy spokes poorly placed make a weak wheel. Whether their full potential is realized depends on the harmony between. The essence of wheelmaking lies in the craftman's ability to conceive and create the space that holds and balances the spokes within the wheel. Think now, who is the craftsman here?"

The disciples were silent until one of them said, "But master, how does a craftsman secure the harmony between the spokes?" Chen Cen asked them to think of sunlight. "The sun nurtures and vitalizes the trees and flowers," he said. "It does so by giving away its light. But in the end, in which direction do they grow? So it is with a master craftsman like Liu Bang. After placing individuals in positions that fully realize their potential, he secures harmony among them by giving them all credit for their distinctive achievements. And in the end, as the trees and flowers grow toward the giver, the sun, individuals grow toward Liu Bang with devotion."

● ● ● ● ● ● ● ● ● ● ● ● ● ●
THE MIDDLE WAY

Many coaches are control-oholics. They keep a tight rein on everyone from the players to the equipment manager, and set strict guidelines for how each person should perform. Everything flows from the top, and the players dare not think for themselves. That approach may work in isolated cases, but it usually only creates resentment, particularly with the NBA's young breed of players, who are more independent than their predecessors. Witness what happened to Don Nelson when he was head coach/general manager of the Golden State Warriors. He got into a battle of wills with a sensitive star, Chris Webber, that destroyed the team and ultimately forced Nelson to resign.

Other coaches are far more *laissez-faire*. Feeling helpless about controlling their players, who generally make much more money than they do, they give them total freedom, hoping that somehow they'll figure out a way to win on their own. It's a difficult situation: even when coaches want to exercise more control, the league doesn't give them much ammunition with which to discipline players. Fines of $250 a day, the maximum that coaches can mete out, are meaningless to the new generation of multimillionaires. When Butch Beard took over as head coach of the New Jersey Nets in 1994, he instituted a simple dress code for road trips. Free spirit Derrick Coleman objected to the policy and, rather than cooperate, paid fines the whole season. Given this climate, some coaches believe the only sensible solution is to pander to their players' absurd demands. They coddle the top two or three stars, try to keep the next five or six players as happy as possible, and hope that the rest don't start a rebellion. Unless they're incredibly gifted psychologists, these coaches inevitably end up feeling as if they're being held hostage by the players they're supposed to be leading.

Our approach is to follow a middle path. Rather than coddling players or making their lives miserable, we try to create a supportive environment that structures the way they relate to each other and gives them the freedom to realize their potential.

I also try to cultivate everybody's leadership abilities, to make the players and coaches feel that they've all got a seat at the table. No leader can create a successful team alone, no matter how gifted he is.

What I've learned as a coach, and parent, is that when people are not awed or overwhelmed by authority, true authority is attained, to paraphrase the *Tao Te Ching*. Every leader has weaknessness and screws up some of the time; an effective leader learns to admit that. In coaching the Bulls I try to stay in touch with the same "beginner's mind" I learned to cultivate in Zen practice. As long as I know I *don't* know, chances are I won't do too much harm.

My shortcomings are painfully obvious to me. I have high expectations and don't hand out praise easily. That places an unrealistic burden on some of the players, particularly the younger ones, making them feel that whatever they do will never be enough. Though most players find me compassionate, I'm not a touchy-feely kind of guy who'll slap a fellow on the back and console him when he doesn't perform. I also can be stubborn and intractable, and sometimes I get caught in conflicts with players that rumble on in the background for months before they get resolved.

THE LESSONS OF COMPASSION

The prevailing myth in sports, and the business world, is that managing from the top down and keeping your charges constantly guessing about their status within the organization is an effective way to stimulate creativity. A friend of mine who works for a large corporation told me about a meeting he attended that showed how pervasive this style of management is. His company had been losing some of its best performers to the competition, and top management was perplexed about how to keep the remaining workers happy. A young female executive who had recently been promoted to a senior-level position suggested being more nurturing and compassionate to the worker bees, to encourage them to be more productive. She was roundly attacked by almost everyone at the table. The solution, as top management saw it, was to hire a bunch of "superstars" from outside and give everybody else the message that if they didn't improve dramatically, they would soon be history. Shortly after the meeting, the boss instituted that policy, and, not surprisingly, productivity declined even further.

In his book, *Leading Change*, management consultant James O'Toole talks about a different style of leadership, known as "value-based" management, that closely resembles my approach. "Value-based" leaders, O'Toole says, enlist the hearts and minds of their followers through inclusion and participation. They listen carefully to their followers out of a deep respect for them as individuals and develop a vision that they will embrace because it is based on their highest aspirations. "To be effective," writes O'Toole, "leaders must begin by setting aside that culturally conditioned 'natural' instinct to lead by push, particularly when times are tough. Leaders must instead adopt the unnatural behavior of *always* leading by the pull of inspiring values."

What O'Toole is talking about essentially is compassionate leadership. In the Buddhist tradition, compassion flows from an understanding that everything derives its essential nature, or Buddha nature, from its dependence on everything else. As Pema Chodron, an American Buddhist nun, puts it in her insightful book, *Start Where You Are*: "By being kind to others—if it's done properly, with proper understanding—we benefit as well. So the first point is that we are completely interrelated. What you do to others, you do to yourself. What you do to yourself, you do to others."

In terms of leadership, this means treating everyone with the same care and respect you give yourself—and trying to understand their reality without judgment. When we can do that, we begin to see that we all share basic human struggles, desires, and dreams. With awareness, the barriers between people gently give way, and we begin to understand, directly, remarkably, that we're part of something larger than ourselves.

Horace Grant taught me this lesson. When I became head coach, Horace was still making a lot of mistakes, and I decided to do something drastic to shake him up. I asked him if he minded being criticized in front of the group, and he said no. So I rode him hard in practice—thinking that my words would not only motivate Horace, but also galvanize the other players. If I was particularly harsh in my criticism, the rest of the team would rally around to give him support.

As Horace matured, he asked me to stop treating him that way, and I respected his wish. Then in 1994 a conflict erupted between us when he decided to play out the option on his contract. Early on, Horace had asked my advice on whether he should declare himself a free agent. I told him that if he could live with the risks, he would probably do extremely well financially. But if he went ahead with it, I would expect him to play just as hard in his option year as John Paxson had done a few years earlier. Once the 1993–94 season began, however, I could sense that Horace was pulling away from the team.

During the All-Star Game, he had a flare-up of tendinitis and asked to sit out the next several games. At the time, we were also missing Kukoc, Paxson, and Cartwright, and our lock on first place was in jeopardy. After a few games I told Horace we needed to reactivate him, but he balked, saying, "Coach, I've got to think about next year."

That was the wrong answer. As far as I was concerned, he was getting paid to play *this* year, not next year. The fact that he was going to be a free agent was no excuse. Many of his teammates were in the same situation, but they hadn't retreated from the team.

My anger made me shut down and freeze Horace out of the group. I told him in front of the team that he wasn't living up to the code the Bulls had always honored: play hard, play fair, play *now*. And when he walked out in the middle of practice complaining of tendinitis, I started yelling at him in the trainers' room: "Go home. I don't want to see you around here until you get it together." There were a few expletives mixed in there, as well.

This confrontation troubled me. Why had I been so hard-hearted with Horace? Why did I take his rebellion as a personal affront? Talking it over with my wife, I realized that my own agenda for Horace was getting in the way of seeing the situation clearly. When I stepped back, I saw how much I blamed Horace for trying to sabotage the season when all he was doing was looking out for his future. What I needed to do was open my heart and try to understand the situation from his point of view. I needed to practice the same selflessness and compassion with Horace that I expected from him on court. When I was able to relax the steel grip on my heart and finally see him through a less self-centered lens, our relationship was repaired.

● ● ● ● ● ● ● ● ● ● ● ● ● ● ●

THE DARK SIDE OF SUCCESS

One thing I needed to be particularly mindful of was the effect success was having on the players. Success tends to distort reality and make everybody, coaches as well as players, forget their shortcomings and exaggerate their contributions. Soon they begin to lose sight of what made them successful in the first place: their connection with each other as a team. As Michael Jordan puts it, "Success turns we's back into me's."

I had seen that happen with the New York Knicks after the 1970 championship, and I desperately wanted to protect the Bulls from the same fate. It wasn't easy. After we won our first championship, success nearly tore the team apart. Everybody wanted to take credit for the victory, and several players began clamoring for a bigger role. Scott Williams wanted to shoot more; B. J. Armstrong wanted to be a starter; Horace Grant wanted to be more than just a "blue-collar worker." All of a sudden, I had to spend a lot of time babysitting fragile egos.

I also had to fend off the media invasion. After we won the championship in 1991, the media presence grew and started feeding off the team. Players who didn't have Jordan's gift for handling reporters were given a national soapbox, and the results were sometimes unfortunate. The first incident occurred before the next season even started. We were invited to a postchampionship celebration at the White House in October. Jordan decided not to attend because he had met President Bush before and felt that, if he went, he would be the center of attention. Horace thought it was unfair that Michael was the only player allowed to skip the event and told reporters so. Jordan, he added, "is going to be the death of this team."

Michael wasn't pleased with these remarks, particularly since he had been spending more time with Horace, trying to strengthen their relationship. My guess was that Horace had been manipulated by reporters into speaking out against Jordan. Horace considered it a badge of honor to be honest and forthright, and sometimes he got lured into making pronouncements that sounded a lot more inflammatory than he intended. Jordan seemed to understand this about Horace and didn't take him to task for his remarks.

I could empathize with Horace and other players who got caught in that trap because it had happened to me when I was with the Knicks. Reporters are seductive—that's their job—and if you're inexperienced, they can often trick you into saying something provocative that you'll regret the next day. As a player, I had made some off-the-wall comments to get a laugh or, on occasion, to make a reporter I didn't particularly like stop pestering me. Sometimes I went too far. In 1977 All-Star forward George McGinnis and I got into a tussle, and he leveled what could have been a knockout punch at me from behind. Luckily, I stepped out of the way and the blow merely grazed the side of my head, but I was furious at the refs for not throwing him out of the game. A month or so later when Kermit Washington hit Rudy Tomjanovich in the face and put him out of action for the rest of the season, I was still angry, and made a flip remark to reporters about how it took a black player to hit a white *star* for the league to do something about the violence issue. Out of context, my remarks sounded racist, and insensitive to Tomjanovich, who had sustained massive head injuries. From that point on, I was more circumspect about what I said to the press.

Some coaches try to force players to be close-mouthed by humiliating them in front of their teammates. Former Knicks coach Hubie Brown used to read newspaper stories to his team, sometimes extending practice by a half an hour or more to get through his pile of clips. When Bill Fitch was coaching the Houston Rockets, he used to have the *players* give the readings. Once he had 7'4″ center Ralph Sampson, who had made some divisive remarks, stand on a stool in practice and read his quotes aloud to the team.

In my view, that approach only increases the media's power in the players' minds. Instead I try to play the stories down. Once the season starts, I don't pay much attention to the news unless a problem crops up that I have to address. Whenever a "big" story develops, I try to laugh it off in front of the players to show them that I don't consider what appears in the papers to be very important.

When you're young and in the public eye, it's easy to get caught up in fame's seductive web. But the truth is the players aren't fighting for the media or the public, they're fighting for the inner circle of the team. Anyone outside that circle who can destroy the team harmony has to be handled with care.

I'm not always perfectly detached. Sometimes I'll step in if I think a player is trying to manipulate the media for selfish reasons. At one point, Will Perdue, whose wry wit has made him a media darling, started making noise in the papers about getting more playing time. When I asked him why he had gone public, he said he thought he'd try it because it had worked for Stacey King. I reminded him that Stacey's experiment backfired in the end, costing him a lot of money *and* playing time.

The players have learned a lot about fame watching how Michael Jordan is treated by the press. Writers usually portray him as a larger-than-life superhero or a tarnished celebrity with dark hidden flaws—neither of which is true. That helps the players see through the media's game and become less vulnerable to criticism. Talking about the Bulls' championship run, B.J. Armstrong recalls, "We didn't care about anything they said in the press. That's what kept us together. If a guy said something bad to the press, we didn't care because he was one of our group. That's what enabled us to win three championships in a row."

Over the years the Bulls have been caught up in a number of controversies, such as the White House flap, Pippen and Grant's contract disputes and Jordan's gambling adventures. But none of those well-publicized problems shook the unity of the group. Even when credible rumors that Scottie was going to be traded hovered over the team for the first half of the 1994–95 season, the effect on team play was minimal. Once the game starts, the players know how to tune out those distractions because of the trust they have in each other. The untold story of the Bulls, says B.J. Armstrong, is "the respect each individual has for everybody else."

ALCHEMY

When everything is running smoothly, I, like Lao-tzu's craftsman, try to leave few traces. In the first half of the 1991–92 season, the Bulls were in such perfect harmony they rarely lost. During that period, according to B.J., it felt as if the team was "in tune with nature" and that everything fell into place "like fall and winter and spring and summer."

The team went 36–3 during that stretch. At one point Jerry Reinsdorf asked me if I was driving the team toward the record, and I said no. In truth, it was out of my hands. The Bulls were too good that year to try to slow them down. The only thing that threw them off track briefly was when Michael was ejected from a game, then suspended from another for protesting the call and bumping the ref. We lost both games, and racked up our longest losing streak of the season: two.

This is what I'd been striving for ever since I had started coaching: to become an "invisible" leader. University of Indiana coach Bobby Knight once said that he could never work in the NBA because the coaches don't have any control over the players. My question is: How much control do you need? It's true that NBA coaches don't have the autocratic power of someone like Knight, but we have far more power than it appears. The players are used to having an authority figure telling them what to do, and

the only reason they've made it as far as they have is that at some point they listened to what some coach somewhere had to say. The way to tap into that energy is not by being autocratic, but by working *with* the players and giving them increasing responsibility to shape their roles.

SPOKES IN A WHEEL

That's why I like to have strong people around me. When I took over as head coach, I named Tex Winter offensive coordinator and Johnny Bach defensive coordinator. In truth, those distinctions were somewhat artificial; the lines of authority on basketball teams are never that clear cut. But I wanted to make it clear to the players that Tex and Johnny's views should be taken seriously. Tex, Johnny, and I didn't always see things the same way, but the interplay of ideas stimulated everybody's creativity.

The players have also taken on key leadership roles. Scottie Pippen is a good floor leader, energizing the team and inspiring the players to stay focused. B.J. Armstrong provided behind-the-scenes support for the young players; John Paxson was a much-needed voice of reason in the locker room; and Cliff Levingston had an uncanny knack for smoothing over conflicts.

During the championship years, the most important leaders were Bill Cartwright and Michael Jordan. I relied on them to solve minor problems and give me an accurate reading of what was going on with the team. Once during the 1992–93 season, the team went into a slump, losing four out of five games, our worst slide in two years. The next game was against the Utah Jazz, always a tough opponent. On the plane to Salt Lake City, I asked Bill and Michael what they thought we could do to revive the team. They said that some of the players had split themselves off from the group, and I should do something to bring them back together. Bill and Michael were especially concerned about Scottie and Horace, who had recently cooled toward one another after being close friends for so many years.

It was Super Bowl Sunday. When we arrived at the hotel, I told the players to get some pizzas and beers after practice and watch the Super Bowl in their hotel rooms. "You guys need to get together and remember what you're doing this for," I said. "You're *not* doing it for money. It may seem that way, but that's just an external reward. You're doing it for the internal rewards. You're doing it for each other and the love of the game." Michael had a lively Super Bowl party in his room that afternoon, and the players reconnected. The next day they came alive, erasing a 17-point deficit in the fourth quarter to beat Utah 96–92. After that, they settled down and cruised through the rest of the season.

SKILLFUL MEANS

In Buddhist teachings the term *skillful means* is used to describe an approach to making decisions and dealing with problems in a way that is appropriate to the situation and causes no harm. Skillful means always arise out of compassion, and when a problem emerges, the idea is to address the offense without denying the humanity of the offender. A parent who packs a kid off to bed for spilling milk instead of handing the child a sponge is not practicing skillful means.

Like large families, basketball teams are highly charged, competitive groups. Because you win or lose as a *team*, individual recognition sometimes gets lost in the larger effort. The result is heightened sensitivity. Everybody is competing with everybody else all the time, and alliances are sometimes tentative and uneasy—a fact of pro sports life that works against deepening intimacy. Players are always complaining about

not getting their fair share of playing time or having their role on the team diminished.

Though some coaches try to settle differences in team meetings, I prefer to deal with them on an individual basis. This helps strengthen my one-on-one connection with the players, who sometimes get neglected because we spend so much of our time together *en masse*. Meeting with players privately helps me stay in touch with who they are out of uniform. During the 1995 playoffs, for instance, Toni Kukoc was troubled by reports that Split, Croatia, where his parents live, had been hit by a barrage of artillery fire. It took several days for him to get through on the phone and learn that his family was all right. The war in his homeland is a painful reality of Toni's life. If I ignored that, I probably wouldn't be able to relate to him on any but the most superficial level.

Athletes are not the most verbal breed. That's why bare attention and listening without judgment are so important. When you're a leader, you have to be able to read accurately the subtle messages players send out. To do that means being fully present with beginner's mind. Over the years I've learned to listen closely to players—not just to what they say, but also to their body language and the silence between the words.

I find it amusing when people ask me where I get my ideas for motivating players. The answer is: *in the moment*. My approach to problem-solving is the same as my approach to the game. When a problem arises, I try to read the situation as accurately as possible and respond spontaneously to whatever's happening. I rarely try to apply someone else's ideas to the problem—something I've read in a book, for instance—because that would keep me from tuning in and discovering a fresh, original solution, the most skillful means.

During the 1991 playoffs, Philadelphia's Armon Gilliam was doing a dance on our front line. Scottie was too small to guard him, and Horace had trouble containing him. So, in an inspired moment, I decided to throw Scott Williams, then an untested rookie, at Gilliam, and it worked. To keep Scott from losing his composure in the closing minutes of the game, I told Jordan to keep his eye on him. From then on, Scott, who like Michael is a North Carolina alum, became Jordan's personal project. All because I refused to play the game by the book.

Ultimately, leadership takes a lot of what St. Paul called faith: "the substance of things hoped for, the evidence of things not seen" (Hebrews 11:1). You have to trust your inner knowing. If you have a clear mind and an open heart, you won't have to search for direction. Direction will come to you.

FIVE FINGERS ON A HAND

The Bulls certainly had faith in themselves in 1991–92. At one point, Johnny Bach proclaimed, "Only the Bulls can beat the Bulls," and he was right. Except for a few minor flareups, everything flowed smoothly. There were no serious injuries and only one change in the roster: backup shooting guard Dennis Hopson was replaced by Bobby Hansen. After the All-Star break, the team lost only six games, and we finished with the best record in the league: 67–15.

The playoffs were a different story. After breezing past Miami, we ran into our toughest opponent to date: the New York media. Former Knicks coach Pat Riley had a gift for waging psychological warfare in the papers, and I could see early on when he started complaining to reporters that Jordan was getting breaks from the refs, that this was going to be an explosive series. Riley's strategy worked in the beginning. The combination of the Knicks' brutal style of play, questionable officiating, and negative reporting in the press distracted the players

enough to disrupt their game. I decided I had to take a more aggressive stance.

The showdown came in Game 4 in New York. We were ahead in the series, 2–1, and the Knicks needed a win desperately. They started shoving with both hands and tackling dribblers without getting called. Horace compared the game to a World Wrestling Federation match, and Michael told me he thought the officiating was so bad it would be impossible to win. I began making a lot of noise on the sidelines and got thrown out of the game in the second half.

There was something about Riley's manner that brought out my irreverent side. The more self-righteous he got, the more flippant I became. At the press conference after the game, which we lost, 93–86, I said, "I think they're probably licking their chops on Fifth Avenue where the NBA offices are. I think they kind of like that it's a 2–2 series. I don't like 'orchestration' . . . it sounds a little too fishy . . . but they control who they send as referees and if it goes to seven, everybody will be really happy. Everybody will get the TV revenues and ratings they want."

Actually it was Riley who was licking his chops. My remarks, for which I was fined $2,500, gave him the perfect opportunity to work the media. "What [Jackson] is doing is insulting us basically," he said the next day. "I was part of six championship teams. I've been to the finals thirteen times. I know what championship demeanor is all about. The fact that he's whining and whimpering about officiating is an insult to how hard our guys are playing and how much our guys want to win. That's what championship teams are about. They've got to take on all comers. They can't whine about it."

The reporters loved that story line: former New York Knick leaves town and turns into kvetch. I hit back with a few zingers, but I realized Riley had staked out the higher ground and anything I said would only fuel the story. This was an important lesson for me. Though I didn't agree with Riley's characterization of me or the team, there was a grain of truth in what he said. We were the champions, and that meant we had to prove ourselves on every level. The best rejoinder to his remark would be to keep quiet and win the series.

That's what we did. Inspired by Jordan in Game 7, the team finally stopped playing New York's slow, rough-and-tumble game and speeded up the action. In the first quarter, Michael set the tone when he chased down Xavier McDaniel, who had been beating up on Scottie Pippen throughout the series, and blocked one of his shots from behind. The message: you're going to have to go through me to win this one. In the second half, our defense rose to another level, and the Knicks became disheartened. The final score was 110–81. Riley was gracious in defeat. He told reporters he felt we had rediscovered our identity in the final game. "They played like they are," he said.

The rest of the playoffs weren't any easier. The Cleveland Cavaliers, another tough team, took the next series to six games, and the Portland Trail Blazers gave us a scare in the finals when they won Game 2 in Chicago. But we were able to take two out of three in Portland and finished them off in Game 6. Our bench, which had been struggling earlier in the playoffs, came through in that game. The starters had run out of energy, and we had fallen behind by 17 points. But in the fourth quarter a reserve unit, led by Bobby Hansen, who scored a key three-pointer, turned the game around and erased the deficit. For me, this was the sweetest victory because *everybody* on the team made a significant contribution.

The celebration lasted all night. This was the first, and only, time we won a championship in Chicago, and the fans didn't want to leave. After the ceremonies in the locker room, the players returned to the court with the trophy and showed it off to the crowd, dancing in a makeshift chorus line on top of the scorers' table. Later that night, June and I watched our kids play a raucous game of pickup in the backyard. We fell asleep to the sound of basketballs bouncing on the blacktop.

The next season I loosened up. Cartwright had sore knees and a bad back, and we were worried he wouldn't make it to the playoffs. Paxson also had knee problems, and Jordan and Pippen had been worn down by playing in the Olympics. I excused them all from part of training camp, and we started off the season at a much slower pace. Our playbook usually contains a page of specific goals for the season. This time I left that page out. Everyone knew what the goal was: to become the first team since the 1960s to win three championships in a row. In large type on the cover of the playbook, I put the word I felt best described the upcoming season: Triumphant.

We staggered through the season, finishing behind New York in the conference with a 57–25 record. But losing the home-court advantage seemed to energize the players. After winning a brutal six-game series against the Knicks, we faced Charles Barkley and the Phoenix Suns in the finals. They pulled out every trick; we even had to contend with Robin Ficker, a guerrilla fan who sat behind our bench and read excerpts from *The Jordan Rules*.

The crucial turn in the series came in the final seconds of Game 6. The Suns were ahead by 4 with less than a minute to go. But Jordan picked off a rebound and drove down court to bring us within 2. Then with 3.9 seconds left, John Paxson put in a 3-pointer that won the game. I'll never forget what he said afterwards: "You know, it's just like when you're a kid. You go out to your driveway and start counting down. 'Three, two, one . . .' I don't know how many shots like that I've taken in my lifetime, but this was the one that really counted."

In my mind, what was impressive about that shot was the pass from Horace Grant that set it up. Horace got the ball from

Pippen near the basket and could have tried to muscle his way in for a dunk. But instead he read the court and found Paxson wide open on the periphery. It was a completely unselfish act. This was the player who, four years earlier, Michael Jordan thought would never be able to learn the triangle offense.

But when the game was on the line, he did the right thing. Without hesitating he made a selfless play instead of trying to be a hero.

In that split-second all the pieces came together and my role as leader was just as it should be: invisible.

III-18: Narcissistic Leaders
The Incredible Pros, the Inevitable Cons

Michael Maccoby

THERE'S SOMETHING NEW AND DARING about the CEOs who are transforming today's industries. Just compare them with the executives who ran large companies in the 1950s through the 1980s. Those executives shunned the press and had their comments carefully crafted by corporate PR departments. But today's CEOs—superstars such as Bill Gates, Andy Grove, Steve Jobs, Jeff Bezos, and Jack Welch—hire their own publicists, write books, grant spontaneous interviews, and actively promote their personal philosophies. Their faces adorn the covers of magazines like *Business Week, Time*, and the *Economist*. What's more, the world's business personalities are increasingly seen as the makers and shapers of our public and personal agendas. They advise schools on what kids should learn and lawmakers on how to invest the public's money. We look to them for thoughts on everything from the future of e-commerce to hot places to vacation.

There are many reasons today's business leaders have higher profiles than ever before. One is that business plays a much bigger role in our lives than it used to, and its leaders are more often in the limelight. Another is that the business world is experiencing enormous changes that call for visionary and charismatic leadership. But my 25 years of consulting both as a psychoanalyst in private practice and as an adviser to top managers suggest a third reason—namely, a pronounced change in the personality of the strategic leaders at the top. As an anthropologist, I try to understand people in the context in which they operate, and as a psychoanalyst, I tend to see them through a distinctly Freudian lens. Given what I know, I believe that the larger-than-life leaders we are seeing today closely resemble the personality type that Sigmund Freud dubbed narcissistic. "People of this type impress others as being 'personalities,'" he wrote, describing one of the psychological types that clearly fall within the range of normality. "They are especially suited to act as a support for others, to take on the role of leaders, and to give a fresh stimulus to cultural development or damage the established state of affairs."

Productive narcissists have the audacity to push through the massive transformations that society periodically undertakes.

Throughout history, narcissists have always emerged to inspire people and to shape the future. When military, religious, and political arenas dominated society, it was figures such as Napoléon Bonaparte, Mahatma Ghandi, and Franklin Delano Roosevelt who determined the social agenda. But from time to time, when business became the engine of social change, it, too, generated its share of narcissistic leaders. That was true at the beginning of this century, when men like Andrew Carnegie, John D. Rockefeller, Thomas Edison, and Henry Ford exploited new technologies and restructured American industry. And I think it is true again today.

But Freud recognized that there is a dark side to narcissism. Narcissists, he pointed out, are emotionally isolated and highly distrustful. Perceived threats can trigger rage. Achievements can feed feelings of grandiosity. That's why Freud thought narcissists were the hardest personality types to analyze. Consider how an executive at Oracle describes his narcissistic CEO Larry Ellison: "The difference between God and Larry is that God does not believe he is Larry." That observation is amusing, but it is also troubling. Not surprisingly, most people think of narcissists in a primarily negative way. After all, Freud named the type after the mythical figure Narcissus, who died because of his pathological preoccupation with himself.

Yet narcissism can be extraordinarily useful—even necessary. Freud shifted his views about narcissism over time and recognized that we are all somewhat narcissistic. More recently, psychoanalyst Heinz Kohut built on Freud's theories and developed methods of treating narcissists. Of course, only professional clinicians are trained to tell if narcissism is normal or pathological. In this article, I discuss the differences between productive and unproductive narcissism but do not explore the extreme pathology of borderline conditions and psychosis.

Leaders such as Jack Welch and George Soros are examples of productive narcissists. They are gifted and creative strategists who see the big picture and find meaning in the risky challenge of changing the world and leaving behind a legacy. Indeed, one reason we look to productive narcissists in times of great transition is that they have the audacity to push through the massive transformations that society periodically undertakes. Productive narcissists are not only risk takers willing to get the job done but also charmers who can convert the masses with their rhetoric. The danger is that narcissism can turn unproductive when, lacking self-knowledge and restraining anchors, narcissists become unrealistic dreamers. They nurture grand schemes and harbor the illusion that only circumstances or enemies block their success. This tendency toward grandiosity and distrust is the Achilles' heel of narcissists. Because of it, even brilliant narcissists can come under suspicion for self-involvement, unpredictability, and—in extreme cases—paranoia.

It's easy to see why narcissistic leadership doesn't always mean successful leadership. Consider the case of Volvo's Pehr Gyllenhammar. He had a dream that appealed to a broad international audience—a plan to revolutionize the industrial work-place by replacing the dehumanizing assembly line caricatured in Charlie Chaplin's *Modern Times*. His wildly popular vision called for team-based craftsmanship. Model factories were built and publicized to international acclaim. But his success in pushing through these dramatic changes also sowed the seeds for his downfall. Gyllenhammar started to feel that he could ignore the concerns of his operational managers. He pursued chancy and expensive business deals, which he publicized on television and in the press. On one level, you can ascribe Gyllenhammar's falling out of touch with his workforce simply to faulty strategy. But it is also possible to attribute it to his narcissistic personality. His overestimation of himself led him to believe that others would want him to be the czar of a multinational enterprise. In turn, these fantasies led him to pursue a merger with Renault, which was tremendously unpopular with Swedish employees. Because Gyllenhammar was deaf to complaints about Renault, Swedish managers were forced to take their case public. In the end, share-holders aggressively rejected Gyllenhammar's plan, leaving him with no option but to resign.

Given the large number of narcissists at the helm of corporations today, the challenge facing organizations is to ensure that such leaders do not self-destruct or lead the company to disaster. That can take some doing because it is very hard for narcissists to work through their issues—and virtually impossible for them to do it alone. Narcissists need colleagues and even therapists if they hope to break free from their limitations. But because of their extreme independence and self-protectiveness, it is very difficult to get near them. Kohut maintained that a therapist would have to demonstrate an extraordinarily profound empathic understanding and sympathy for the narcissist's feelings in order to gain his trust. On top of that, narcissists must recognize that they can benefit from such help. For their part, employees must learn how to recognize—and work around—narcissistic bosses. To help them in this endeavor, let's first take a closer look at Freud's theory of personality types.

● ● ● ● ● ● ● ● ● ● ● ●
THREE MAIN PERSONALITY TYPES

While Freud recognized that there are an almost infinite variety of personalities, he identified three main types: erotic, obsessive, and narcissistic. Most of us have elements of all three. We are all, for example, somewhat narcissistic. If that were not so, we would not be able to survive or assert our needs. The point is, one of the dynamic tendencies usually dominates the others, making each of us react differently to success and failure.

Freud's definitions of personality types differed over time. When talking about the erotic personality type, however, Freud generally did not mean a sexual personality but rather one for whom loving and above all being loved is most important. This type of individual is dependent on those people they fear will stop loving them. Many erotics are teachers, nurses, and social workers. At their most productive, they are developers of the young as well as enablers and helpers at work. As managers, they are caring and supportive, but they avoid conflict and make people dependent on them. They are, according to Freud, outer-directed people.

Obsessives, in contrast, are inner-directed. They are self-reliant and conscientious. They create and maintain order and make the most effective operational managers. They look constantly for ways to help people listen better, resolve conflict, and find win-win opportunities. They buy self-improvement books such as Stephen Covey's *The 7 Habits of Highly Effective People*. Obsessives are also ruled by a strict conscience—they like to focus on continuous improvement at work because it fits in with their sense of moral improvement. As entrepreneurs, obsessives start businesses that express their values, but they lack the vision, daring, and charisma it takes to turn a good idea into a great one. The best obsessives set high standards and communicate very effectively. They make sure that instructions are followed and costs are kept within budget. The most productive are great mentors and team players. The unproductive and the uncooperative become narrow experts and rule-bound bureaucrats.

Narcissists, the third type, are independent and not easily impressed. They are innovators, driven in business to gain power and glory. Productive narcissists are experts in their industries, but they go beyond it.

They also pose the critical questions. They want to learn everything about everything that affects the company and its products. Unlike erotics, they want to be admired, not loved. And unlike obsessives, they are not troubled by a punishing superego, so they are able to aggressively pursue their goals. Of all the personality types, narcissists run the greatest risk of isolating themselves at the moment of success. And because of their independence and aggressiveness, they are constantly looking out for enemies, sometimes degenerating into paranoia when they are under extreme stress. (For more on personality types, see the sidebar "Fromm's Fourth Personality Type" on page 285.)

STRENGTHS OF THE NARCISSISTIC LEADER

When it comes to leadership, personality type can be instructive. Erotic personalities generally make poor managers—they need too much approval. Obsessives make better leaders—they are your operational managers: critical and cautious. But it is narcissists who come closest to our collective image of great leaders. There are two reasons for this: they have compelling, even gripping, visions for companies, and they have an ability to attract followers.

GREAT VISION

I once asked a group of managers to define a leader. "A person with vision" was a typical response. Productive narcissists understand the vision thing particularly well, because they are by nature people who see the big picture. They are not analyzers who can break up big questions into manageable problems, they aren't number crunchers either (these are usually the obsessives). Nor do they try to extrapolate to understand the future—they attempt to create it. To paraphrase George Bernard Shaw, some

people see things as they are and ask why, narcissists see things that never were and ask why not.

Consider the difference between Bob Allen, a productive obsessive, and Mike Armstrong, a productive narcissist. In 1997, Allen tried to expand AT&T to reestablish the end-to-end service of the Bell System by reselling local service from the regional Bell operating companies (RBOCs). Although this was a worthwhile endeavor for shareholders and customers, it was hardly earth-shattering. By contrast, through a strategy of combining voice, telecommunications, and Internet access by high-speed broad-band telecommunication over cable, Mike Armstrong has "created a new space with his name on it," as one of his colleagues puts it. Armstrong is betting that his costly strategy will beat out the RBOC's less expensive solution of digital subscriber lines over copper wire. This example illustrates the different approaches of obsessives and narcissists. The risk Armstrong took is one that few obsessives would feel comfortable taking. His vision is galvanizing AT&T. Who but a narcissistic leader could achieve such a thing? As Napoléon—a classic narcissist—once remarked, "Revolutions are ideal times for soldiers with a lot of wit—and the courage to act."

As in the days of the French Revolution, the world is now changing in astounding ways; narcissists have opportunities they would never have in ordinary times. In short, today's narcissistic leaders have the chance to change the very rules of the game. Consider Robert B. Shapiro, CEO of Monsanto. Shapiro described his vision of genetically modifying crops as "the single most successful introduction of technology in the history of agriculture, including the plow" (*New York Times*, August 5, 1999). This is certainly a huge claim—there are still many questions about the safety and public acceptance of genetically engineered fruits and vegetables. But industries like agricul-

---

Fromm's Fourth Personality Type

Not long after Freud described his three personality types in 1931, psychoanalyst Erich Fromm proposed a fourth personality type, which has become particularly prevalent in today's service economy. Fromm called this type the "marketing personality," and it is exemplified by the lead character in Woody Allen's movie *Zelig*, a man so governed by his need to be valued that he becomes exactly like the people he happens to be around.

Marketing personalities are more detached than erotics and so are less likely to cement close ties. They are also less driven by conscience than obsessives. Instead, they are motivated by a radarlike anxiety that permeates everything they do. Because they are so eager to please and to alleviate this anxiety, marketing personalities excel at selling themselves to others.

Unproductive marketing types lack direction and the ability to commit themselves to people or projects. But when productive, marketing types are good at facilitating teams and keeping the focus on adding value as defined by customers and colleagues. Like obsessives, marketing personalities are avid consumers of self-help books. Like narcissists, they are not wedded to the past. But marketing types generally make poor leaders in times of crisis. They lack the daring needed to innovate and are too responsive to current, rather than future, customer demands.

---

ture are desperate for radical change. If Shapiro's gamble is successful, the industry will be transformed in the image of Monsanto. That's why he can get away with painting a picture of Monsanto as a highly profitable "life sciences" company—despite the fact that Monsanto's stock has fallen 12% from 1998 to the end of the third quarter of 1999. (During the same period, the S&P was up 41%.) Unlike Armstrong and Shapiro, it was enough for Bob Allen to win against his competitors in a game measured primarily by the stock market. But narcissistic leaders are after something more. They want—and need—to leave behind a legacy.

SCORES OF FOLLOWERS

Narcissists have vision—but that's not enough. People in mental hospitals also have visions. The simplest definition of a leader is someone whom other people follow. Indeed, narcissists are especially gifted in attracting followers, and more often than not, they do so through language. Narcissists believe that words can move mountains and that inspiring speeches can change people. Narcissistic leaders are often skillful orators, and this is one of the talents that makes them so charismatic. Indeed, anyone who has seen narcissists perform can attest to their personal magnetism and their ability to stir enthusiasm among audiences.

Yet this charismatic gift is more of a two-way affair than most people think. Although it is not always obvious, narcissistic leaders are quite dependent on their followers—they need affirmation, and preferably adulation. Think of Winston Churchill's wartime broadcasts or J.F.K.'s "Ask not what your country can do for you" inaugural address. The adulation that follows from such speeches bolsters the self-confidence and conviction of the speakers. But if no one responds, the narcissist usually becomes insecure, overly shrill, and insistent—just as Ross Perot did.

One of his greatest problems is that the narcissist's faults tend to become even more pronounced as he becomes more successful.

Even when people respond positively to a narcissist, there are dangers. That's because charisma is a double-edged sword — it fosters both closeness and isolation. As he becomes increasingly self-assured, the narcissist becomes more spontaneous. He feels free of constraints. Ideas flow. He thinks he's invincible. This energy and confidence further inspire his followers. But the very adulation that the narcissist demands can have a corrosive effect. As he expands, he listens even less to words of caution and advice. After all, he has been right before, when others had their doubts. Rather than try to persuade those who disagree with him, he feels justified in ignoring them — creating further isolation. The result is sometimes flagrant risk taking that can lead to catastrophe. In the political realm, there is no clearer example of this than Bill Clinton.

WEAKNESSES OF THE NARCISSISTIC LEADER

Despite the warm feelings their charisma can evoke, narcissists are typically not comfortable with their own emotions. They listen only for the kind of information they seek. They don't learn easily from others. They don't like to teach but prefer to indoctrinate and make speeches. They dominate meetings with subordinates. The result for the organization is greater internal competitiveness at a time when everyone is already under as much pressure as they can possibly stand. Perhaps the main problem is that the narcissist's faults tend to become even more pronounced as he becomes more successful.

SENSITIVE TO CRITICISM

Because they are extraordinarily sensitive, narcissistic leaders shun emotions as a whole. Indeed, perhaps one of the greatest paradoxes in this age of teamwork and part-nering is that the best corporate leader in the contemporary world is the type of person who is emotionally isolated. Narcissistic leaders typically keep others at arm's length. They can put up a wall of defense as thick as the Pentagon. And given their difficulty with knowing or acknowledging their own feelings, they are uncomfortable with other people expressing theirs — especially their negative feelings.

Indeed, even productive narcissists are extremely sensitive to criticism or slights, which feel to them like knives threatening their self-image and their confidence in their visions. Narcissists are almost unimaginably thin-skinned. Like the fairy-tale princess who slept on many mattresses and yet knew she was sleeping on a pea, narcissists — even powerful CEOs — bruise easily. This is one explanation why narcissistic leaders do not want to know what people think of them unless it is causing them a real problem. They cannot tolerate dissent. In fact, they can be extremely abrasive with employees who doubt them or with subordinates who are tough enough to fight back. Steve Jobs, for example, publicly humiliates subordinates. Thus, although narcissistic leaders often say that they want teamwork, what that means in practice is that they want a group of yes-men. As the more independent-minded players leave or are pushed out, succession becomes a particular problem.

POOR LISTENERS

One serious consequence of this oversensitivity to criticism is that narcissistic leaders often do not listen when they feel threatened or attacked. Consider the response of one narcissistic CEO I had worked with for three years who asked me to interview his immediate team and report back to him on what they were thinking. He invited me to his summer home to discuss what I had found. "So what do they think of me?" he asked with seeming nonchalance. "They think you are very creative and courageous," I told him, "but they also feel that you don't listen." "Excuse me, what did you say?" he shot back at once, pretending not to hear. His response was humorous, but it was also tragic. In a very real way, this CEO could not hear my criticism because it was too painful to tolerate. Some narcissists are so defensive that they go so far as to make a virtue of the fact that they don't listen. As another CEO bluntly put it, "I didn't get here by listening to people!" Indeed, on one occasion when this CEO proposed a daring strategy, none of his subordinates believed it would work. His subsequent success strengthened his conviction that he had nothing to learn about strategy from his lieutenants. But success is no excuse for narcissistic leaders not to listen.

LACK OF EMPATHY

Best-selling business writers today have taken up the slogan of "emotional competencies"—the belief that successful leadership requires a strongly developed sense of empathy. But although they crave empathy from others, productive narcissists are not noted for being particularly empathetic themselves. Indeed, lack of empathy is a characteristic shortcoming of some of the most charismatic and successful narcissists, including Bill Gates and Andy Grove. Of course, leaders do need to communicate persuasively. But a lack of empathy did not prevent some of history's greatest narcissistic leaders from knowing how to communicate—and inspire. Neither Churchill, de Gaulle, Stalin, nor Mao Tse-tung were empathetic. And yet they inspired people because of their passion and their conviction at a time when people longed for certainty. In fact, in times of radical change, lack of empathy can actually be a strength. A narcissist finds it easier than other personality types to buy and sell companies, to close and move facilities, and to lay off employees— decisions that inevitably make many people

angry and sad. But narcissistic leaders typically have few regrets. As one CEO says, "If I listened to my employees' needs and demands, they would eat me alive."

There is a kind of emotional intelligence associated with narcissists, but it's more street smarts than empathy.

Given this lack of empathy, it's hardly surprising that narcissistic leaders don't score particularly well on evaluations of their interpersonal style. What's more, neither 360-degree evaluations of their management style nor workshops in listening will make them more empathic. Narcissists don't want to change—and as long as they are successful, they don't think they have to. They may see the need for operational managers to get touchy-feely training, but that's not for them.

There is a kind of emotional intelligence associated with narcissists, but it's more street smarts than empathy. Narcissistic leaders are acutely aware of whether or not people are with them wholeheartedly. They know whom they can use. They can be brutally exploitative. That's why, even though narcissists undoubtedly have "star quality," they are often unlikable. They easily stir up people against them, and it is only in tumultuous times, when their gifts are desperately needed, that people are willing to tolerate narcissists as leaders.

DISTASTE FOR MENTORING

Lack of empathy and extreme independence make it difficult for narcissists to mentor and be mentored. Generally speaking, narcissistic leaders set very little store by mentoring. They seldom mentor others, and when they do they typically want their protégés to be pale reflections of themselves. Even those narcissists like Jack Welch who are held up as strong mentors are usually more interested in instructing than in coaching.

Narcissists certainly don't credit mentoring or educational programs for their own development as leaders. A few narcissistic leaders such as Bill Gates may find a friend or consultant—for instance, Warren Buffet, a superproductive obsessive—whom they can trust to be their guide and confidant. But most narcissists prefer "mentors" they can control. A 32-year-old marketing vice president, a narcissist with CEO potential, told me that she had rejected her boss as a mentor. As she put it, "First of all, I want to keep the relationship at a distance. I don't want to be influenced by emotions. Second, there are things I don't want him to know. I'd rather hire an outside consultant to be my coach." Although narcissistic leaders appear to be at ease with others, they find intimacy—which is a prerequisite for mentoring—to be difficult. Younger narcissists will establish peer relations with authority rather than seek a parentlike mentoring relationship. They want results and are willing to take chances arguing with authority.

AN INTENSE DESIRE TO COMPETE

Narcissistic leaders are relentless and ruthless in their pursuit of victory. Games are not games but tests of their survival skills. Of course, all successful managers want to win, but narcissists are not restrained by conscience. Organizations led by narcissists are generally characterized by intense internal competition. Their passion to win is marked by both the promise of glory and the primitive danger of extinction. It is a potent brew that energizes companies, creating a sense of urgency, but it can also be dangerous. These leaders see everything as a threat. As Andy Grove puts it, brilliantly articulating the narcissist's fear, distrust, and aggression, "Only the paranoid survive." The concern, of course, is that the narcissist finds enemies that aren't there—even among his colleagues.

AVOIDING THE TRAPS

There is very little business literature that tells narcissistic leaders how to avoid the pitfalls. There are two reasons for this. First, relatively few narcissistic leaders are interested in looking inward. And second, psychoanalysts don't usually get close enough to them, especially in the workplace, to write about them. (The noted psychoanalyst Harry Levinson is an exception.) As a result, advice on leadership focuses on obsessives, which explains why so much of it is about creating teamwork and being more receptive to subordinates. But as we've already seen, this literature is of little interest to narcissists, nor is it likely to help subordinates understand their narcissistic leaders. The absence of managerial literature on narcissistic leaders doesn't mean that it is impossible to devise strategies for dealing with narcissism. In the course of a long career counseling CEOs, I have identified three basic ways in which productive narcissists can avoid the traps of their own personality.

FIND A TRUSTED SIDEKICK

Many narcissists can develop a close relationship with one person, a sidekick who acts as an anchor, keeping the narcissistic partner grounded. However, given that narcissistic leaders trust only their own insights and view of reality, the sidekick has to understand the narcissistic leader and what he is trying to achieve. The narcissist must feel that this person, or in some cases persons, is practically an extension of himself. The sidekick must also be sensitive enough to manage the relationship. Don Quixote is a classic example of a narcissist who was out of touch with reality but who was constantly saved from disaster by his squire Sancho Panza. Not surprisingly, many narcissistic leaders rely heavily on their spouses, the people they are closest to. But dependence on spouses can be risky, because they may further isolate the narcissistic leader from his company by supporting his grandiosity and feeding his paranoia. I once knew a CEO in this kind of relationship with his spouse. He took to accusing loyal subordinates of plotting against him just because they ventured a few criticisms of his ideas.

It is much better for a narcissistic leader to choose a colleague as his sidekick. Good sidekicks are able to point out the operational requirements of the narcissistic leader's vision and keep him rooted in reality. The best sidekicks are usually productive obsessives. Gyllenhammar, for instance, was most effective at Volvo when he had an obsessive COO, Hakan Frisinger, to focus on improving quality and cost, as well as an obsessive HR director, Berth Jönsson, to implement his vision. Similarly, Bill Gates can think about the future from the stratosphere because Steve Ballmer, a tough obsessive president, keeps the show on the road. At Oracle, CEO Larry Ellison can afford to miss key meetings and spend time on his boat contemplating a future without PCs because he has a productive obsessive COO in Ray Lane to run the company for him. But the job of sidekick entails more than just executing the leader's ideas. The sidekick also has to get his leader to accept new ideas. To do this, he must be able to show the leader how the new ideas fit with his views and serve his interests. (For more on dealing with narcissistic bosses, see the sidebar "Working for a Narcissist" on page 291.)

INDOCTRINATE THE ORGANIZATION

The narcissistic CEO wants all his subordinates to think the way he does about the business. Productive narcissists—people who often have a dash of the obsessive

The Rise and Fall of a Narcissist

The story of Jan Carlzon, the former CEO of the Scandinavian airline SAS, is an almost textbook example of how a narcissist's weaknesses can cut short a brilliant career. In the 1980s, Carlzon's vision of SAS as the businessperson's airline was widely acclaimed in the business press, management guru Tom Peters described him as a model leader. In 1989, when I first met Carlzon and his management team, he compared the ideal organization to the Brazilian soccer team—in principle, there would be no fixed roles, only innovative plays. I asked the members of the management team if they agreed with this vision of an empowered front line. One vice president, a former pilot, answered no. "I still believe that the best organization is the military," he said. I then asked Carlzon for his reaction to that remark. "Well," he replied, "that may be true, if your goal is to shoot your customers."

That rejoinder was both witty and dismissive, clearly, Carlzon was not engaging in a serious dialogue with his subordinates. Nor was he listening to other advisers. Carlzon ignored the issue of high costs, even when many observers pointed out that SAS could not compete without improving productivity. He threw money at expensive acquisitions of hotels and made an unnecessary investment in Continental Airlines just months before it declared bankruptcy.

Carlzon's story perfectly corroborates the often-recorded tendency of narcissists to become overly expansive—and hence isolated—at the very pinnacle of their success. Seduced by the flattery he received in the international press, Carlzon's self-image became so enormously inflated that his feet left the ground. And given his vulnerability to grandiosity, he was propelled by a need to expand his organization rather than develop it. In due course, as Carlzon led the company deeper and deeper into losses, he was fired. Now he is a venture capitalist helping budding companies. And SAS has lost its glitter.

personality—are good at converting people to their point of view. One of the most successful at this is GE's Jack Welch. Welch uses toughness to build a corporate culture and to implement a daring business strategy, including the buying and selling of scores of companies. Unlike other narcissistic leaders such as Gates, Grove, and Ellison, who have transformed industries with new products, Welch was able to transform his industry by focusing on execution and pushing companies to the limits of quality and efficiency, bumping up revenues and wringing out costs. In order to do so, Welch hammers out a huge corporate culture in his own image—a culture that provides impressive rewards for senior managers and shareholders.

Welch's approach to culture building is widely misunderstood. Many observers, notably Noel Tichy in *The Leadership Engine*, argue that Welch forms his company's leadership culture through teaching. But Welch's "teaching" involves a personal ideology that he indoctrinates into GE managers through speeches, memos, and confrontations. Rather than create a dialogue, Welch makes pronouncements (either be the number one or two company in your market or get out), and he institutes programs (such as Six Sigma quality) that become the GE party line. Welch's strategy has been extremely effective. GE managers must either internalize his vision, or they must leave. Clearly, this is incentive learning with a vengeance. I would even go so far as to call Welch's teaching brain washing. But Welch does have the rare insight and know-how to achieve what all narcissistic business leaders are trying to do—namely, get the organization to identify with them, to think the way they do, and to become the living embodiment of their companies.

GET INTO ANALYSIS

Narcissists are often more interested in controlling others than in knowing and disci-

plining themselves. That's why, with very few exceptions, even productive narcissists do not want to explore their personalities with the help of insight therapies such as psychoanalysis. Yet since Heinz Kohut, there has been a radical shift in psychoanalytic thinking about what can be done to help narcissists work through their rage, alienation, and grandiosity. Indeed, if they can be persuaded to undergo therapy, narcissistic leaders can use tools such as psychoanalysis to overcome vital character flaws.

Consider the case of one exceptional narcissistic CEO who asked me to help him understand why he so often lost his temper with subordinates. He lived far from my home city, and so the therapy was sporadic and very unorthodox. Yet he kept a journal of his dreams, which we interpreted together either by phone or when we met. Our analysis uncovered painful feelings of being unappreciated that went back to his inability to impress a cold father. He came to realize that he demanded an unreasonable amount of praise and that when he felt unappreciated by his subordinates, he became furious. Once he understood that, he was able to recognize his narcissism and even laugh about it. In the middle of our work, he even announced to his top team that I was psychoanalyzing him and asked them what they thought of that. After a pregnant pause, one executive vice president piped up, "Whatever you're doing, you should keep doing it, because you don't get so angry anymore." Instead of being trapped by narcissistic rage, this CEO was learning how to express his concerns constructively.

Leaders who can work on themselves in that way tend to be the most productive narcissists. In addition to being self-reflective, they are also likely to be open, likable, and good-humored. Productive narcissists have perspective; they are able to detach themselves and laugh at their irrational needs. Although serious about achieving their goals, they are also playful.

Working for a Narcissist

Dealing with a narcissistic boss isn't easy. You have to be prepared to look for another job if your boss becomes too narcissistic to let you disagree with him. But remember that the company is typically betting on *his* vision of the future — not yours. Here are a few tips on how to survive in the short term:

- Always empathize with your boss's feelings, but don't expect any empathy back. Look elsewhere for your own self-esteem. Understand that behind his display of infallibility, there hides a deep vulnerability. Praise his achievements and reinforce his best impulses, but don't be shamelessly sycophantic. An intelligent narcissist can see through flatterers and prefers independent people who truly appreciate him. Show that you will protect his image, inside and outside the company. But be careful if he asks for an honest evaluation. What he wants is information that will help him solve a problem about his image. He will

resent any honesty that threatens his inflated self-image and will likely retaliate.

- Give your boss ideas, but always let him take the credit for them. Find out what he thinks before presenting your views. If you believe he is wrong, show how a different approach would be in his best interest. Take his paranoid views seriously, don't brush them aside — they often reveal sharp intuitions. Disagree only when you can demonstrate how he will benefit from a different point of view.

- Hone your time-management skills. Narcissistic leaders often give subordinates many more orders than they can possibly execute. Ignore the requests he makes that don't make sense. Forget about them. He will. But be careful: carve out free time for yourself only when you know there's a lull in the boss's schedule. Narcissistic leaders feel free to call you at any hour of the day or night. Make yourself available, or be prepared to get out.

As leaders, they are aware of being performers. A sense of humor helps them maintain enough perspective and humility to keep on learning.

THE BEST AND WORST OF TIMES

As I have pointed out, narcissists thrive in chaotic times. In more tranquil times and places, however, even the most brilliant narcissist will seem out of place. In his short story *The Curfew Tolls*, Stephen Vincent Benét speculates on what would have happened to Napoléon if he had been born some 30 years earlier. Retired in prerevolutionary France, Napoléon is depicted as a lonely artillery major boasting to a vacationing British general about how he could have

beaten the English in India. The point, of course, is that a visionary born in the wrong time can seem like a pompous buffoon.

Historically, narcissists in large corporations have been confined to sales positions, where they use their persuasiveness and imagination to best effect. In settled times, the problematic side of the narcissistic personality usually conspires to keep narcissists in their place, and they can typically rise to top management positions only by starting their own companies or by leaving to lead upstarts. Consider Joe Nacchio, formerly in charge of both the business and consumer divisions of AT&T. Nacchio was a supersalesman and a popular leader in the mid-1990s. But his desire to create a new network for business customers was thwarted by colleagues who found him abrasive, self-promoting, and ruthlessly ambitious.

Two years ago, Nacchio left AT&T to become CEO of Qwest, a company that is creating a long-distance fiber-optic cable network. Nacchio had the credibility—and charisma—to sell Qwest's initial public offering to financial markets and gain a high valuation. Within a short space of time, he turned Qwest into an attractive target for the RBOCs, which were looking to move into long-distance telephony and Internet services. Such a sale would have given Qwest's owners a handsome profit on their investment. But Nacchio wanted more. He wanted to expand—to compete with AT&T—and for that he needed local service. Rather than sell Qwest, he chose to make a bid himself for local telephone operator U.S. West, using Qwest's highly valued stock to finance the deal. The market voted on this display of expansiveness with its feet—Qwest's stock price fell 40% between last June, when he made the deal, and the end of the third quarter of 1999. (The S&P index dropped 5.7% during the same period.)

> *More and more corporations are finding there is no substitute for narcissistic leaders in this age of innovation.*

Like other narcissists, Nacchio likes risk—and sometimes ignores the costs. But with the dramatic discontinuities going on in the world today, more and more large corporations are getting into bed with narcissists. They are finding that there is no substitute for narcissistic leaders in an age of innovation. Companies need leaders who do not try to anticipate the future so much as create it. But narcissistic leaders—even the most productive of them—can self-destruct and lead their organizations terribly astray. For companies whose narcissistic leaders recognize their limitations, these will be the best of times. For other companies, these could turn out to be the worst.

Michael Maccoby is an anthropologist and a psychoanalyst. He is also the founder and president of the Maccoby Group, a management consultancy in Washington, DC. The former director of the Program on Technology, Public Policy, and Human Development at Harvard University's Kennedy School of Government in Cambridge, Massachusetts, Maccoby is the author of *The Leader: A New Face for American Management* (Simon & Schuster, 1981), *The Gamesmen: The New Corporate Leaders* (Simon & Schuster, 1977), and *Why Work? Motivating the New Workforce* (Second Edition, Miles River Press, 1995).

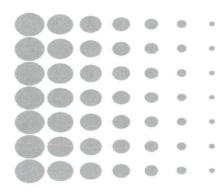

SECTION IV

ISSUES OF SUSTAINED ORGANIZING

The term *organization* implies that, once assembled, establishments persist in a static state. In fact, sustaining a successful, purposeful entity is an ongoing accomplishment requiring that structures, practices, and individual actions adapt to ever-changing internal and external circumstances. The term *organizing* more aptly conveys the continuing nature of organizational effort than *organization*, an important distinction in comprehending organizational reality. Only in a dynamic view are the topics in this section apparent—pain and trauma experienced as a consequence of organizing, enduring struggles of control and resistance, implications for action derived from failure, realignments to increase resilience, puzzles of coping with moral ambiguity in oganizations, and tensions from globalization.

DEALING WITH PAIN AND TRAUMA

Management rhetoric often favors the positive—the exhilaration of successful accomplishment—but at times organizational members experience something different—the sting and anguish of organizationally generated pain and trauma. The articles in this section address these negative consequences of organizing and how to deal with them.

The first of the readings "Toxic Shock," deals with the toxicity of adverse events and the toll they take on individuals and organizations. Additional readings detail some of the organizational sources of toxicity.

"Two Generations of Wage Slaves" by Jolene Sundlie describes the life of a waitress. The toxicity here stems as least in part from the difficulty of making ends meet despite the hard work.

Pace and change are two sources of difficulty. In an excerpt from *White Collar Sweatshop*, Jill Fraser concentrates on links between the "seismic" increase in the demands of managerial work in the last several decades, even while the rewards were diminishing, and personal problems of employees. With stress from difficult and insecure working conditions as a constant, heart-pounding companion, social costs of white-collar sweatshops may be as high as $200 billion a year.

Corporate downsizing common during this period has been another source of emotional turmoil for employees. Clive Gilson describes his own discomfort and inability to maintain eye contact as he had to let go an employee from whom he had learned the ropes and who now couldn't comprehend the termination decision. Although communicating such decisions will never be easy, from his experiences as an outplacement consultant, Bob Evans recommends the golden rule: "Do unto others as you would have others do unto you."

Job and organizational design are at issue in the final selection The "Early PT Cruiser" illustrates how awareness of the human factor can facilitate organizational adjustments.

Originally, workers could build only one car per day rather than one every 2 minutes as targeted because of difficulties fitting the engine within narrow tolerances. Instead of declaring a "no build," a Chrysler manager asked workers to practice and, after much effort and frustration, they eventually exceeded the targeted production time while maintaining quality.

UNDERSTANDING CONTROL AND RESISTANCE

Organizations face a difficult dilemma. The primary concern of individuals might be to satisfy their own self-interests, but the concern of organizations is to induce individuals to work toward collective ends. To resolve this dilemma, organizations go to great lengths to control what individuals do. In response, individuals try to avoid such constraints. In short, controlling and resisting are two processes that permeate organizational life.

At the turn of the twentieth century, Frederick Taylor tried to convince all who would listen that workers and managers had compatible interests. Since that time, many organizational writers have echoed this theme. That so much has been written about the possibility of organizational harmony suggests another fact—commonality of interests is not all that obvious to many. We, too, believe a considerable amount of organizational conflict could be avoided, but we also see substantial evidence of inherent conflict. Potential divergence of individual and organizational ends is not limited to lower organizational levels, it extends to the highest level of the organization.

Moreover, efforts of organizational members to assert their own interests can be perceived and labeled in different ways. An employee's refusal to follow a supervisor's directive to use a more economical production method could be viewed as insubordination, resistance, or evidence that the employee has an authority problem. Alternatively, the same act could be construed as principled commitment to quality work, to professional norms, or to personal ethics.

Labels themselves are part of the process through which individuals pursue their own purposes—by seeking to control others and resisting the efforts of others to control them. Efforts to win and to resist control are some of the most interesting facets of organizational reality. The selections in this section approach these struggles from a variety of perspectives.

O'Day focuses on the successively more onerous sanctions, the "intimidation rituals" that those with formal authority employ to persuade would-be organizational reformers to abandon their efforts. "The Catbird Seat," James Thurber's well-known short story, describes a sophisticated scheme devised to fight back against a controlling manager. In reading this story, it is useful to follow how the resister defines situations and finds sources of power in these definitions. Debra Meyerson then explores how tempered radicals become "everyday leaders" by using "the power of difference" to work toward organizational change.

Conflicts posed by the organization of work are the subject of the final selection. As "More Plants Go 24/7" discusses, workers face a difficult juggling act trying to maintain personal values, including commitments to family and to faith, while meeting the demands of new work schedules.

We do not want to suggest that members of organizations are always at cross-purposes. However, as this section makes clear, organizations cannot be understood without considering the formal and informal means that that those at all levels use to try to assert their own interests.

LEARNING FROM FAILURE

Although we often wish to disassociate ourselves with failure, it can be an important, if uncomfortable, source of organizational learning. This section draws lessons from three organizational disasters: the loss of the space shuttle *Challenger*, the fiery crash of two departing aircraft on the island of Tenerife, and the loss of smoke jumpers fighting the Mann Gulch fire in Montana. In each of these cases, calamity resulted not from a single malfunction but from breakdowns in several interrelated areas. Together these three analyses highlight the crucial part that organizational interdependence plays in many disasters.

From her reanalysis of primary documents related to the *Challenger* disaster, Diane Vaughn contests simplistic explanations derived from prior summaries. The fatal decision to launch *Challenger* in cold weather wasn't really an anomaly. It was the outcome of decision processes that had evolved as layers of bureaucratic and political cultures were added to and complicated NASA's original technical culture. Vaughn suggests that organizations interested in reducing odds of catastrophic events should target three areas for concern: complex cultures, missed signals, and the trickle-down effects of actions by organizational elites.

Karl Weick finds somewhat different factors operating in the takeoff crash on Tenerife and the loss of smoke jumpers at Mann Gulch. Because of bomb threats, two large aircraft were diverted to Tenerife, a cloud-shrouded airport not equipped for such planes. Under stress, a breakdown in coordinated action, regression to habituated ways of acting, and difficulties in speech exchange contributed to the fiery crash as one plane clipped the other on takeoff. The 1949, Mann Gulch fire was the first time smoke jumpers were lost fighting a fire. Expecting a relatively standard "10 o'clock fire," smoke jumpers lost the capacity for sense making and thus for effective group action when the fire blew up. From this tragedy, in which only 3 of 12 firefighters survived, Weick emphasizes approaching new situations with an "attitude of wisdom," being able to improvise, and respectful interaction among group members.

Vaughn and Weick both argue that their analyses have relevance for other organizations. One way to test their contention is to see if the issues highlighted for one disaster might have relevance for understanding the other two. For example, Vaughn delineates cultures, signals, and elites as salient to the decision to launch *Challenger*. Although Weick does not focus directly on these factors, would they be helpful in understanding the details Weick presents about Tenerife or Mann Gulch? Similarly, could elements Weick finds significant at Tenerife or Mann Gulch facilitate making sense of the fatal *Challenger* decision? For us, these writings do generalize—aspects Vaughn and Weick have identified prove useful in generating a rich understanding of other difficult situations.

INCREASING RESILIENCE IN ORGANIZATIONS

The prior section on learning from failure reveals the importance of organizational resilience in responding to difficulty, unanticipated events, or a changing environment. Rather than being unusual, such circumstances are common, and organizations need to be prepared for the unexpected. Thus, increasing resilience is a priority for many organizations.

In the leadoff reading in this section, Peter Frost and his colleagues emphasize the importance of compassion, which can easily be overlooked as leaders try to be "in charge." Leaders who demonstrate their own compassion in times of difficulty help ease collective anguish by permitting others to show their feelings and support one another in making sense of events, often to the benefit of the organization as well as individuals.

Details from organizations that evidence resilience are the focus of the remaining selections. "Amid Crippled Rivals, Southwest Again Tries to Spread Its Wings" describes how Southwest Airlines responded to difficulties in the airline and travel industries in the weeks and months following the tragedy of September 11, 2001. Consistent with its own unique culture of commitment to employees and concern for customers, Southwest maintained service rather than cutting back as its major competitors did. "Improvisations in Green" shows how the Green Berets in effect followed Weick's (see Learning from Failure) prescription for adaptive response when sent on a mission to help stabilize Haiti.

Finally, in coaching the Chicago Bulls to six NBA championships, Phil Jackson went against the grain in basketball. At a time of star players and big egos, he instilled "selflessness in action" or "substituting the we for the me" among his players, including the legendary Michael Jordan. Using similar tactics, he has now coached the Los Angeles Lakers to several consecutive NBA championships (three as of 2002). Many of the elements Weick and Vaughn consider important are evidenced in his own account of his early success with the Chicago Bulls.

COPING WITH MORAL MAZES

Details emerging from the bankruptcy of Enron in 2001, followed by similar revelations of difficulties at other prominent organizations, involved accounting irregularities, executive greed, and corporate governance failures. Renewed calls for morality or ethics in management came in response to repeated tales of executives who "earned" millions for managing their organizations into shambles, often leaving investors with little and lower-level employees with no jobs and retirement accounts worth only pennies on the dollar. Executive and legislative branches of the government considered a variety of regulatory approaches that might enhance corporate responsibility.

All individuals experience pressures to behave ethically—that is, to do what is right and not what is wrong. These pressures come from external and internal sources. One's actions are evaluated by others, who will reward or punish the individual according to how they judge the actions vis-à-vis their criteria for right and wrong. Individuals also have their own internal standards of ethical behavior. These standards are developed through life experiences, including efforts by parents, schools, and other institutions to inculcate ethical standards and the accumulated encounters with judgments of others.

Although there is broad agreement that individuals should behave ethically, universal agreement has not been reached on the content of ethical standards. Substantial differences exist between and within cultures. Of particular relevance to American business is the tension between the pursuit of self-interests and the achievement of social good. Our long-standing acceptance of the invisible hand, which operates through free markets to channel individual self-interests into actions promoting the common good, is a major ethical force underlying the free-enterprise system. At the extreme, the invisible hand has been used to justify the view that greed is enough and additional ethical principles for managers are unnecessary. On the other hand, many argue that self-interest requires further restraint for anything approaching ethical management to emerge. This debate, seldom far from the surface in discussion of business ethics in the United States, is central to the renewed interest in moral or ethical management and to the articles in this section.

When organizations are superimposed on human relationships, new dimensions are added to knowing what is right and wrong and doing what is appropriate. In light of Enron's bankruptcy, CEO Ken Lay's forward to the Enron Code of Ethics is an important reminder that having a policy isn't sufficient to generate ethical action, even on the part of the CEO who promulgated the policy. The selection from Robert Jackall's oft-cited *Moral Mazes* explores why actions on the part of organizational members might deviate from ethical precepts. Ethical issues are often clearer in retrospect than when originally faced in organizations. The ambiguous nature of organizational life makes organizational climate and top management example particularly powerful when it comes to ethical action. Faced with uncertainty, individuals search for clues in organizational practice and are extremely susceptible to social influence, especially from above.

According to John Bryne's article, "After Enron: The Ideal Corporation," companies would return to the values articulated in many selections in this book. Trust, integrity, and fairness, he argues, do matter to the bottom line. Transparency in operations, giving employees an ownership stake, and correcting the excesses in top management pay would help establish organizations that are more likely to maintain ethical standards.

• • • • • • • • • • • • • • •

GOING GLOBAL

The increasing significance of globalization to business success has become obvious. Operating in a global environment, however, is far from easy. The United States, regretfully, is distinctly insular and not particularly knowledgeable about other cultures. Americans often fail to study local culture, observe the necessary courtesies, and otherwise adapt their behavior to local situations. The selections in this section elaborate on this theme. The initial selection focuses on experiences of a specific U.S.-based organization, Wal-Mart. Two additional articles provide more general food for thought on the complexities of globalization.

The *Economist's* "Wal Around the World" notes the importance to going global to Wal-Mart's future and traces the difficulties they have encountered while trying to extend U.S.-style retail operations to other countries. Despite their remarkable success in the United States adaptations are needed to achieve similar results elsewhere.

"Dangerous Liaisons" was included in the previous edition of *Managerial Reality,* and we asked the authors, Marta Calas and Linda Smircich, to revisit it for this edition, combining readings from prior editions of *Organizational Reality* and *Managerial Reality* with new material. The original article, written in 1992, expressed concern that an American perspective on globalization was being uncritically celebrated by many management writers. Their reconsideration in this edition explores similar themes.

Finally, labor leader (AFL-CIO Secretary-Treasure) Richard Trumka takes a nuanced perspective on issues of globalization. Rather than opposing internationalization per se, he argues that specifics matter a great deal—some alternatives are preferable to others.

We, too, wish to take a nuanced view of globalization. It brings problems and opportunities. Only with thought and care can problems be addressed while opportunities are pursued.

IV-1: Toxic Shock

Peter Frost

Pain is a fact of organizational life. Companies will merge; bosses will make unrealistic demands; people will lose their jobs. The emotions that accompany events such as these aren't in themselves toxic; rather, it's how that pain is handled throughout the organization that determines whether its long-term effects are positive or negative. What turns emotional pain into toxicity, especially in organized settings, is when others respond to that pain in an insensitive and harmful, rather than healing, way.

The consequences of such harmful responses are far from benign. Toxicity, the outcome of emotionally insensitive attitudes and actions of managers and of the practices of their companies, doesn't simply ruffle a few feathers. Instead, it acts as a noxious substance, draining vitality from individuals and the entire organization, potentially causing everything from missed deadlines to a mass exodus of key staff—and the effects of toxicity don't stop at these sorts of outcomes, which disrupt the workflow.

Left unchecked, toxicity will seep into an organization's performance and right down to the bottom line.

However, despite the pervasiveness of emotional toxins in organizations and their negative effects on people and on profit, no one raises the subject because such discussions tend to be seen as "weak" or "soft." Those who do see it—and help to resolve it—are left with their mouths shut and their heads down.

Toxicity is produced when an individual's attitudes or an organization's policies, or both, fail to take into account the emotional attachment people have to their work contributions. They discount the human qualities of people at the receiving end of an initiative, intervention or retort. Unfortu-nately, this lack of sensitivity to others (conscious or otherwise) is an all-too-common trait among people who hold high levels of power and influence, where the name of the game is surviving, prospering, and acquiring control. In themselves, these goals aren't inherently toxic, but they tend to become so when the players ignore how their actions affect others.

One veteran senior manager from a major U.S. corporation put it this way: "The toxic producers, disconnected from their humanity, deliver practices that create damage to others, who are hurt in the process."

A senior human resources executive in the retail industry had this to say about the pain-inducing practices of top management: "Fish stinks from the head! The higher up the toxic person is, the more widely spread is the pain, the more people there are who behave in the same way as that person. All the lieutenants begin to talk and act the same way as the toxic boss. If you have a CEO who delivers public lashings—when he, in effect, does his performance appraisals in public—then you will find that the lieutenants begin to join in."

The point is that top managers influence the attitudes and actions of a wide circle of subordinates. When a leader's behavior is dictatorial, dismissive of the feelings and value of other people in their organization, that style becomes a model in the culture.

Although the behaviors and attitudes of managers often are a major source of pain in organizations today, other sources can be traced to a company's policies and practices; sometimes there's a direct connection between how individuals create toxicity and the way the corporation conducts its business. Some degree of toxicity at work, however, is simply inevitable, arising from the changes, traumas, and crises that people and companies experience from time to time.

The work of the company frequently gets done because of the often unrecognized work of "toxin handlers." These are individuals, managers, or staff members who step into toxic situations and work to identify, contain, neutralize, or disperse emotional poison so that those in pain can begin to heal and refocus their efforts on effectively getting the job done. Such handlers may be HR specialists, but often they are line managers, project managers, or team members who know the value of a healthy workplace and act constructively when they see toxic situations.

They are not only caregivers who help heal people who hurt; they are also leaders who work with pain in ways that are designed to sustain or enhance performance in the workplace. Handlers focus on the emotional needs of individuals and on the emotional linkages and relationships within organizations.

Toxin handlers respond to pain in many ways, small and large, but their work tends to reflect five major themes:

- Listening: They listen with attention and compassion to someone else's pain.
- Holding space for healing: They recognize that someone is in pain, then find ways to create and hold a space that will give the person "breathing room." It might be to provide a private office or time off or a reduced workload.
- Buffering pain: Handlers will take the pain in a harsh message from the top or from other managers and hold it so none of the toxins get through. A message that the employees are incompetent and lazy ("those idiots") can be rephrased to appeal to their pride in getting the planned work done.
- Extricating others from painful situations: Handlers may use their political skills to get a promising employee transferred to a more receptive department.

- Transforming pain: Many potentially toxic situations in organizations cannot be changed in the short run and therefore require the constructive "translation" that toxin handlers can offer. For example, difficult chief executive officers or senior managers will rarely change their styles even if they understand that they're hurting people. Much of the toxin handler's work to transform situations, then, occurs through changing the view of painful experiences.

When done successfully, the toxin handler can feel extreme joy and satisfaction in the work as he or she observes the people who have been helped to begin to heal, but there can also be considerable costs and risks in store for people who do the difficult work of toxin handling. One of the biggest dangers is of becoming toxic themselves. Too often, handlers become so immersed in the work of healing others that they are unable or unwilling to recognize the toll being taken on their own mental and physical health.

The result? Toxin handlers, over time, experience a number of negative effects that, if untreated, begin to dull their sensitivities as handlers, the effectiveness of their work, and the health and quality of their own lives. They become overwhelmed by all the pain they are trying to cope with and to heal; it numbs them to their own and other people's feelings. And because handlers usually work alone, keeping to themselves the pain they're managing, they become isolated and trapped in the role. The confidential, behind-the-scenes work they do rarely allows them opportunities to unburden themselves to others or to otherwise dissipate the toxicity.

As well, working to alleviate the pain of others in organizations is rarely rewarded, encouraged, or supported.

However, there are ways that formal leaders and their organizations can step up to the plate and respond to the need for more widespread handling of organizational toxins.

Leaders can consciously assume the work of the toxin handler. The load thereby shifts from the few to the many, and this work is no longer relegated to a back burner. Distributing the work of managing toxicity among multiple leaders accomplishes at least three things.

First, it lifts some of the relentless burden of dealing with organizational toxins from those who have stepped in simply because no one else would do so. Second, it puts the responsibility for managing the toxins with those who have power, resources, visibility, and connections—enabling real and effective interventions when necessary and rooting out toxicity where it has taken hold. Third, an organization that expects and reinforces toxin handling in its leaders creates a force for positive experiences. It naturally engenders a more healthy work environment than one that ignores or blocks this competency. A crucial contribution to developing support and understanding for the toxin-handling activities of leaders is that they be seen and supported as part of normal work—not as an "extra" or an activity that is "bootlegged" into the daily agenda.

Skills that should become part of the repertoire of the compassionate leader include:

- Pay attention: Be alert to the presence and signals of others around you and be open-minded, rather than prejudicial or defensive, to emotional "data" they experience. Being open-minded enables you to discover workable responses to a situation. Being open-hearted encourages compassionate and caring behavior. There is always grief somewhere in the room.
- Put people first: Recognize that employees are assets, not expenses. Leadership includes making tough

decisions that sometimes set very tight performance deadlines, pushing people beyond their comfort zones, or involve letting staff go. However, by thinking first about the person and his or her feelings and then assessing that person's performance, you can create a culture in which compassionate responses to pain become a natural part of doing business. Handling toxins becomes more naturally one of the things that leaders, formal and informal, do for one another.

- Practise professional intimacy: When leaders step in to defuse toxic emotions, they must strike a tricky balance between detachment from the pain of those they're helping and an excessive emotional involvement with the situation. They are most effective when they use their emotions as a guide to responding to what has transpired and its effect on others, but managers are most helpful when they can do this with "professional intimacy"—without clouding their judgment by over-identifying with the sufferer.
- Plant seeds: Get the organization to invest in processes that prepare people to respond to each other and to difficult situations in caring, attentive, and respectful ways.
- Push back: Occasionally, leaders must take bold steps to eradicate emotional pain in their workplaces. They need to push back on the sources of the pain to eliminate their effects. The Benjamin Group, a Silicon Valley–based public relations firm, demonstrates its values by taking a stand on how employees are treated, not only by their colleagues and managers, but also by their customers, suppliers, and other business partners. These values are represented in a code of principles that includes the statement: "We're all in this together." One message implicit in this code of

principles is that the company is prepared to cancel an account (and has done so) if a client develops a track record of being abusive to its staff.

Organizations can face the challenge of managing toxicity in the workplace with three strategies:

- Prevention: Choose employees for attitude and competence, develop people and help them shine, build fair-minded workplaces, and create a healthy atmosphere by allowing spaces for healing.
- Intervention: Deal with downturns by building bridges for people to leave with hope and opportunity, and deal with people's personal pain by creating policies that are compassionate and systematic.
- Restoration and recovery: Show patience and trust in the belief that time heals, help people see positive options, provide focus so that active routines are restored and foster rituals and symbols for "letting go."

Work is the place where many of us live much of our lives. Much of what we hold dear and a great deal of what happens in our lives takes place at work, or spills into or out of our time there. Having this reality acknowledged, respected, and compassionately "handled" makes this intense and essential part of our lives immensely richer and more productive. When toxin-handling work is done in an environment that acknowledges and supports them, the types of positive outcomes multiply for everyone involved, including loyalty, commitment, and effort toward bottom-line results.

Peter Frost is the author of *Toxic Emotions at Work,* published by Harvard Business School Press, and the Edgar F. Kaiser professor in organizational behavior in the Faculty of Commerce at the University of British Columbia in Vancouver.

IV-2: Two Generations of Wage Slaves
A Family of Waitresses

Jolene Sundlie

Barbara Ehrenreich's book *Nickel and Dimed: On (Not) Getting by in America* gives the reader an abridged version of life as a blue-collar, manual laborer in modern-day America. Ehrenreich works as a maid in both homes and hotels, a nursing home attendant, a Wal-Mart employee, and a waitress. The *Nickel and Dimed* research was not intended to be an in-depth analysis of each job worked. Ehrenreich more or less admits that she barely scratches the surface of real life as a minimum wage employee in America. In spite of that, the book caused enough of a stir to prompt cable's A&E network to do an *Investigative Report based on Nickel and Dimed* titled, "Wage Slaves: Not Getting by in America."

Even though Ehrenreich only worked each job for a short time and offers just a glimpse of what each job is really like, I found the portrayal of her job as a waitress to be strikingly accurate. I feel I am qualified to make such a determination, having been raised in a serving family and working as a waitress myself for the past nine years. While looking for more literature about experiences as a waitress/server, I found *Waiting: True Confessions of a Waitress* by Debra Ginsberg which offers a more detailed and personal look at a woman's perspective of her job as a server for several years. Using these manuscripts and the television documentary as a guide, I will offer additional insight into the world of the working waitress and wage slaves as I have known them.

Waitressing tends to be one of those professions that is often passed down through the generations. My mother has worked as a waitress most of her adult life. While my siblings and I were young, our dad worked days as a sheet metal worker while our mother was a homemaker who would occasionally work nights at a local fraternal organization. My mom started her current day job working at the local elementary school the same day I started kindergarten. The eighties were not kind to our family. My mom's day job was extra income to our family and offered excellent and stable benefits, which were important because my dad's job was often affected by the economy and layoffs were common. I do not think my mother ever intended to continue serving once she started her "career" at the school, but the incomes from her two jobs helped us move out of our mobile home and into a four bedroom house with a big yard.

If things would have been different, my father (who was one of the better workers in his blue-collar field) would have eventually made enough money for my mother to quit serving. Like many of the women that were alluded to in the literature, my mother became a victim of circumstance. My father was diagnosed with a genetic lung disorder that forced him to quit working when he was only forty-four years old. He received social security benefits which equaled or exceeded my mother's income. Although there were potentially other jobs my mother could have taken that would have earned her more money, our family could not afford to have her quit her paraprofessional job at the school. Her job was the only way our family would have medical and dental insurance. My father's illness made insurance not

a luxury, but a necessity. My mom's job at the school, while providing important benefits, paid little more than minimum wage. A second job was our only option; without it we surely would have been on welfare.

Mom continued to work at the fraternal club until the day it closed its doors; not out of boredom or a reason to get out of the house, but because we could not have made it without her tips. Once her longtime waitressing job was gone, so was the extra income. Summers were especially hard because once school ended for the summer, so did my mom's paychecks. She has worked the oddest jobs just to make ends meet. The ultimate was when she sold apples out of a semi trailer parked on the side of a road near our hometown. Eventually, she started bartending at the local bar. When my dad died four years ago, my mom had to work even more hours at the bar in order to pay for the mortgage on the house. My mom is fifty-eight years old and has worked two jobs for over twenty-three years.

My mother is a "wage slave." As I read *Nickel and Dimed,* I saw my mother as one of the women Ehrenreich worked with. As I watched the A&E special, I thought about my mom. "Wage Slaves" mentioned that many workers in low-wage jobs are "two paychecks away from homelessness." When my mother owned our home, she certainly fit this description. She recently sold our home and bought a mobile home. The documentary also pointed out that 24% of Americans make less than $16,000 per year and must "piece jobs together" and "juggle bills." Although finances are not typically discussed in my family, I have seen my mother's tax forms and I know that she is one of those 24%. My mother is not stupid; she is not an alcoholic or drug addict, yet she is still poor. It is hard to reason why a hard working person cannot make a living in the richest country in the world.

One issue that Ehrenreich briefly touches on is the dehumanizing affect of working a low-wage job. My mother is a resilient woman, but she is still human. It is tremendously humiliating to have to sell apples on the side of the road in order to pay your bills, especially in a small town. To have to depend on your friends and neighbors for tips puts one at an awkward social position. How can you ever really disagree or argue with someone when you must rely on them for your rent? I have seen the toll these jobs have had on my mother. There is a defeated attitude about her. She does not argue with anyone, partly because she does not want to offend anyone who she might need to wait on, but also because she is just too damn tired.

Both Ehrenreich and Ginsberg point out that waitressing is exhausting, physically and mentally. Physically the body is always at risk of injury both chronic or temporary. From my own experiences, a typical day begins as I have to take down the chairs from the night before. Depending on the restaurant or bar that could be up to seventy chairs, which are generally sturdy (heavy) enough to sustain any size customer. Ice bins must be filled using five gallon buckets of ice which probably weigh around twenty pounds each. It can take up to six buckets to fill all the ice bins. Beer coolers in the bar must be restocked from the cooler in the back of the kitchen. Most beer coolers I have been in have their beer stocked vertically and in no particular order, which means I have to move case after case to get to what I need. Sometimes I have to climb on top of kegs and cases of beer to reach a case of beer, which I then must somehow carry down with me while standing on top of the keg. There are also kegs to be changed which weigh about twenty pounds each when empty.

While there are plenty of heavy things that need to be lifted and swung and stocked daily in a bar, that is not the end of the bodily harm you put yourself through on a daily basis. There are burns from hot water, steam, and hot plates. When a server tells a customer "Watch out for this plate (or soup), it is very hot," they generally know from experience.

Cuts are another daily occurrence. They can be small, such as poking your finger while you cut fruit for garnishes, but there are also the meat slicer cuts, the broken glass slashes, and the worst one I have seen yet: a forearm lacerated to the bone by a knife used to cut through rib bones. While a cut may result in a scar, the scariest result could be hepatitis.

I never really thought about contacting a disease at work, but when you work in a bar and restaurant you are constantly in contact with human fluids. Daily I touch glasses people drink from, plates and silverware they have eaten from, and on rarer occasions have had to plunge public toilets and clean up blood and vomit. I am not a well-paid health care professional with benefits and a 401(k), I make $3.50 per hour and am not compensated for these additional tasks. Generally if someone leaves a place vomiting or bleeding, they are not going to leave you a big tip.

Interestingly, the most common injuries a waitress' body sustains are the result of day-to-day wear and tear. It manifests itself in the calloused feet of repeated eight hour shifts; the carpal tunnel syndrome in the wrists and arms from lifting trays day in and day out; the varicose veins that appear behind the knees (I got mine at age twenty-two); the scaly hands, cracked nails, and hangnails from constantly washing dishes, hands, and tables with nuclear strength sanitizer; and the allergies, sinus infections, and sore throats that come from breathing in toxic levels of second-hand smoke.

Another health related issue that plagues a full-time waitress/server is insurance. Many younger servers are still in school and covered by their parents' insurance and some servers may be married and covered by their spouses. Generally, restaurants do not offer insurance to their part-time employees, which most employees are.[1]

I know for a fact that my allergies are worse when I work a long weekend in a smoke-filled bar. Unfortunately, I do not have insurance and cannot afford my pre-scription allergy medicine. My allergies stick around longer because of the smoke and the lack of drugs. Although allergies and sinus infections are common, they are minute worries compared to the possibility that something will happen to me at work. I have been "lucky" so far that none of my inci-dents at work have been permanently dis-abling. I know of one person who broke his neck in the kitchen of a corporate restau-rant where he worked. The company took the employee to court to avoid paying his medical bills, claiming his injury took place after hours. Another person I know was injured in a fight bouncing a drunk out of the bar. He was instructed to pay for his hos-pital bill out of his own pocket for which he would be reimbursed. The owner did not want to file workman's comp, because that would increase his insurance. The employee has only been reimbursed for half of his medical bills and none of his lost wages.

While injuries incurred on the job should be covered by the business' insur-ance or workman's compensation, I am just as worried about the long term effects serv-ing has had on my body that will not be revealed until I have quit my job and have no recourse. I am afraid that I will develop carpal tunnel disease and be unable to play softball ever again. I am afraid that my father's genetic lung disease coupled with my constant exposure to second-hand smoke will produce cancer in my lungs. These constant fears of physical injury are one of the causes of the second kind of damage incurred by a full-time waitress; mental or emotional despair.

Mental or emotional despair sounds dramatic. Not every waitress or bartender or server is depressed or defeated. The younger servers generally enjoy their part-time job as they work their way through col-lege. I know I did. Yet, when serving is your only job, it affects you. Initially, you come to resent your customers, because as Ginsberg points out,

> On a small scale, customers liter-ally hold the server's fate in his pockets. This imbues the customer with a certain amount of power as soon as he sits down at the table. And power, as the saying goes, cor-rupts. In a way, the server is imme-diately placed on the defensive. Her livelihood is not determined so much by whether or not she takes an order correctly, brings the food on time, or smiles often. Rather, she must gauge a customer's mood, pick up cues as to his background, and based on all of this anticipate his needs and wants. The server is, effectively, the customer's private dancer for the two hours he sits at her table.

Ginsberg's account is sad and true. When you go to work, you have to be able to put your problems and worries aside and worry about your customers' needs and wants. You are in limbo; every decision you make and every action you take seemingly decides your fate at each table. I used to be able to handle this. It was nerve-wracking but excit-ing in the same way gambling can be. Things change.

I am, like my mother and sister, a good server. I have been recruited to work at sev-eral places and praised for jobs well done. Sometimes, I go to work and I look forward to the adrenaline rush I get during a busy

---

[1]Restaurants are careful to keep employees under a 40 hour week to keep them from earning overtime ($5.25 for a server) and making them ineligible for benefits. This is why many servers work more than one job; there are usually not enough hours available at one job.

spurt. Lately, it is not the job itself that I find difficult. It is the internal struggle that I see my mother and my sister deal with every day.

Waitressing can be terribly degrading. It is humiliating to have to wait on certain people. I am more educated than most of the people I wait on, yet I am relying on them for a living. Smart capable women go to work to earn a paycheck and are talked down to, condescended to, and treated more like servants or prostitutes than hard working blue-collar people. I have often been embarrassed to admit that I am (still) a waitress, I usually tell people that my mom works in an elementary school, not in a bar, and I usually mention what my brother-in-law does without offering that my sister is still working in a restaurant. People have preconceived notions about waitresses. Ginsberg gives an example, "A general societal attitude toward waiting on tables was outlined for me a few years ago on the game show *Family Feud*. The question was "What job would you least like your wife to have?" The number one answer. . . was "waitress." Not stripper, mind you, or prostitute. Waitress" (Ginsberg, 2000:112). I had a similar experience when I dated a guy a few years ago. He told me that he really liked me, but did not like that I was a waitress because "waitresses are slutty and flirt with guys all day to make their tips." Never mind that I met him at work. I have also been called a "stupid waitress" and "just a waitress."

The feeling like a prostitute comes from the practice that sometimes you do flirt a little with your customers to up your tip. It is practically expected from a cocktail waitress. There are the male customers who take it too far. They tell sexist jokes; they drop things for you to pick up; they ask inappropriate, personal questions and expect answers. If you do not play along with their drunken idiot games, you are "no fun," "a prude," "stuck up," and your tip goes down dramatically.

Surprisingly, I find it easier to wait on the creeps than to wait on demeaning, condescending people. With a pervert, there is probably some room for retorts such as, "Would you talk to your daughter this way?" or the threat of telling the manager, bartender, or bouncer and having them thrown out. You can then go on with your night thinking he was just a drunk jerk. With the other group, the haughty, arrogant blue bloods (and those that think they are), there is no way to win with them without bowing to their every wanton need.

These are the customers that make you feel like there is something wrong with YOU. Customers like this make people cry, get people fired, and they get in your head. Their remarks hurt and scar; they make you doubt your abilities, intelligence, and self worth. It is impossible to describe the shame that you can feel just for doing your job. I have walked away from tables with my ears burning, my chest tight, and my head swimming for an explanation as to what I did to be treated so poorly.

If you have to put up with people that make you doubt yourself year after year, eventually you just believe that you are not worth a crap and give up. Like I mentioned before, my mom has been defeated by her job. My sister works at a country club where arrogance reigns supreme. It is apparent to me that my creative, talented sister has let the job depress her. My sister is much more feisty than my mother and I hope she gets out of the business before it overwhelms her too. I feel my sister will probably go out in a server's blaze of glory; one of those episodes that many servers dream about, complete with telling off the customer, spilling food and drinks, and insulting everyone else in earshot.

My mother has told me that she wished neither my sister nor I had ever gotten into the serving business. She did not try to stop either one of us, not that she could have. I think she wanted us to see for ourselves how hard waitressing can be. While I think that Ehrenreich's research was impressive and her findings shocking, I think some people will read Ehrenreich and think they understand the perils of waitressing or cleaning toilets or working at Wal-Mart, but being an underpaid, overworked American is something that is hard to describe. One has to experience the back-breaking work, the stress of not having enough money for bills, and the humiliation of being poor to truly understand what it means to be a "wage slave."

Works Cited

Ehrenreich, Barbara. 2001. *Nickel and Dimed: On (Not) Getting By in America.* Henry Holt and Company: New York.

Ginsberg, Debra. 2000. *Waiting: The True Confessions of a Waitress.* HarperCollins Publishers, Inc.: New York.

Investigative Reports. August 2002. *Wage Slaves: Not Getting by in America.*

IV-3: "The Pace Was Insane"
Less Time, More Stress

Jill Andresky Fraser

"The whole theme of your book is my life," one IBM veteran in her early forties told me during the first of a series of conversations we shared.

Catherine described to me her steady progression from a junior position at "Big Blue" back in the early 1980s through a fairly continual string of promotions into the ranks of management during the next decade. Early on, she had been identified as a strong performer and, as she put it, "placed on the management fast track." While still in her twenties, she worked twenty-hour days. "It was pretty unbelievable" is the way she recalls it now.

One two-year assignment kept her on the road, visiting IBM's customers, five days a week. "I'd only go home on the weekends. That was just accepted. It was part of the culture. You just did it—kept working and traveling at that kind of pace." Since her husband also worked for the company, he didn't complain; fortunately, his travel schedule was lighter than hers, which allowed them to maintain a semblance of a home life.

Then she was promoted into a line-management position. The good news was, she was on her way up and no longer needed to maintain that relentless travel schedule. The bad news was, her responsibilities included a regular rotation during which she was placed "on call" twenty-four hours a day, on a shift that lasted a week at a time.

To an outsider looking in, what was perhaps most remarkable about Catherine's work and home life was just how unremarkable it all seemed to her and her colleagues. "A customer could get in touch with me anytime. If you were on call, that meant you were their first point of contact." She paused, then added, "At two o'clock in the morning, you would get calls from a customer. But you were still expected to be in the office by 8 A.M. I did it for two years. I'd come home at eight or nine at night. In the midst of that, I had my first back operation. The pace was insane. When you'd get home, you'd go for the wine. And then, pretty much crash and go to sleep."

Although the working conditions were brutal, Catherine never contemplated complaining or switching to another employer.

From *White Collar Sweatshop: The Deterioration of Work and Its Rewards in Corporate America* by Jill Andresky Fraser. Copyright © 2001 by Jill Andresky Fraser. Used by permission of W.W. Norton & Company, Inc.

"This was known as a job you had to do to 'get your ticket punched,'" she explained. Little wonder she wanted it punched: this was still the 1980s, when a management job at IBM was the pot of gold at the end of many a white-collar rainbow, thanks to the company's longtime domination of the mainframe computer business, unflaggingly powerful stock performance, and well-earned reputation as a blue-chip provider of employee benefits and incentives.

Then the competitive arena shifted, and IBM's market preeminence (as well as the dominance of mainframes) was challenged by the growing popularity of personal computers. Its stock price began a long downhill slide, various corporate reorganizations were announced, and finally, in 1993, Louis Gerstner, a veteran of the RJR Nabisco restructuring, took the helm with a mandate for change.

For Catherine and her colleagues, the demands of their already difficult jobs were notched up several levels as the company gradually entered a crisis management mode. As they worked harder and harder, many of the benefits they had prized most dearly during their days at Big Blue started slipping away. For one thing, "we used to get one hundred percent medical coverage," she recalled. "Then they switched married couples to coordinated benefits, then they switched us to an HMO. It was just, holy s—!" Worst of all was the damage done by the company's falling stock price, which went from a high around 170 to a low in the 40s; that downward trajectory drastically reduced, among other things, the value of many employees' retirement savings, traditionally one of the biggest benefits of life as one of IBM's "blue suits."

Workloads kept increasing, as the company announced numerous early-retirement initiatives and then layoffs, driving its workforce down from a high of over four hundred thousand to the low two hundred thousands. "It began to trickle down that you had this pace of work and meetings during the day. You couldn't get to your e-mails during the day, so you'd do them at night." Catherine's laugh was bitter. "It was like you didn't have a home life. IBM gave you a computer at home. That made it easy to work." Again the laugh. "I used to pride myself on thinking, I'm not going to complain. I can take it all on. I can do anything."

In the hours Catherine spent describing her grueling working conditions to me — as I came to understand the ways that work had enveloped just about every aspect of her personal life since she first entered the corporate arena back in her early twenties — I kept asking her, and myself, why she had stayed on at IBM, especially as the company began shedding its paternalistic practices and cutting back on the once-traditional rewards for all that hard labor.

Our conversations illuminated several points. She accepted her workload in large part because it was the norm within the corporation: as it increased for her, it increased for her colleagues, too, which meant that it still seemed within the bounds of the acceptable. Also, Catherine was emotionally attached to her employer, identifying with both its successes and failures, in a way that encouraged her to hang on, despite the difficulties of her position. Finally, although certainly not of least importance, she was a success at IBM and had been for some years now. As she continued to rise within the corporate hierarchy, to build her own network of mentors, colleagues, and friends within the organization — to spend most of her waking hours thinking about IBM, working for IBM, *being* at IBM — it was tough to imagine turning her back on so many years of accumulated experiences and ties.

The demands of her job still took their toll. There were two more back operations for Catherine, and more and more problems with her husband, during those few hours they managed to spend together away from the office. By this time, the couple had been trying unsuccessfully to get pregnant for years. Catherine blamed their failure on her chronic exhaustion and job-related stress: the cause also, she was convinced, of her incessant back ailment.

Bt this time, she was working sixteen-hour days *at* the office, then going home to check—among other tasks—her e-mails and voice-mail messages. Her travel pace had picked up again as well. "My husband was traveling then, too. We'd do what we called 'calendar coordination' every two weeks," she told me. "We'd sit down at dinner and plan for every single day. Where would he be and where would I be?" Worn out by a pace of work that she had been maintaining for more than a decade, she decided a few years ago to join a health club, naturally choosing one that was open twenty-four hours a day. "I'd try to go at ten o'clock at night, after I left the office."

LONGER WORKDAYS

Experiences like Catherine's reflect seismic changes that have taken place within corporate America during the past two decades, most especially during the 1990s, in respect to the rules, the rewards, and the demands of work. This shift is equivalent to an industrial revolution for white-collar workers who, by necessity, have learned to adjust to (and often successfully function within) whatever versions of the white-collar "sweatshop" have evolved within their own companies and industries.

People are working longer and harder, the kind of hours one once might have expected to see logged in only by chief executives or would-be CEOs (or sweatshop workers!). There may be no greater testament to this reality than the best-selling success of Juliet Schor's *The Overworked American,* which argued, "If present trends continue, by the end of the century Americans will be spending as much time at their jobs as they did back in the nineteen twenties."

Currently, over 25 million Americans work more than forty-nine hours each week, some a good bit more. Here's how those numbers break down: Nearly 12 percent of the workforce, about 15 million people, report spending forty-nine to fifty-nine hours weekly at the office; another 11 million, or 8.5 percent, say they spend sixty hours or more there. Most of these people are white-collar professionals: among them, corporate managers, marketing staffers, investment bankers, office administrators, software designers, lawyers, editors, engineers, accountants, business consultants, and the secretaries, word processors, computer programmers, and back-office clerks who support their activities.

Most people, of course, don't spend sixteen or so hours a day at their offices, at least not on a regular basis, year after year. They might not be able to relate to all the career successes Catherine has had along the way. Odds are pretty strong as well that they haven't lived through the painful medical procedures she has; indeed, it might not be so simple to draw a straight line between their work-related stresses and whatever problems have emerged within their personal lives.

But Catherine is far from unique when it comes to the back-breaking pace of her work life. "Men and women come in all the time, begging for help, more and more stressed out," Zoe confided. A mid-level manager at Levi Strauss, she had worked her way through layoffs and cutbacks during the 1990s. She told me, as she laughed, that she had been with the company so long that she remembered a time when it was still thought of as a good place to work. But no longer, she emphasized, adding, "I'd say the average person is now doing the job of two and a half people."

At workplaces across the nation, most people working more than forty hours each week are between twenty-five and forty-four years old. A good many of them are likely to be juggling the intense demands of these job schedules with the also intense demands of a family, which may include responsibilities for aging parents, as well as spouses and children.

Manny is a good example. He was a technical writer at Intel and, also, the single father of two elementary-school-age girls. "Nominally, Intel has work hours, usually eight to five," he told me. But "life at Intel is intense . . . incredibly hard work." So he evolved his own strategy to cope: "I'd get the kids up, give them breakfast, then I'd take off. Get there about seven in the morning. Usually I'd leave right at five." He'd come home to prepare dinner and eat it with his daughters. "Then I'd put them to bed at eight," leaving them at home alone, he explained, "and come back to the office until about 1 A.M."

In some industries, among them the technology and financial services sectors, the norms—everyday expectations about just how much time people should spend at the office each day—have become so extreme that a twelve-hour workday can seem positively lightweight. As the culture of overwork spread across the United States, inflexibly high demands like these began to seem like a badge of honor, at least from the business world's perspective. Lexus, the car manufacturer, ran advertisements that boasted, "Sure, We Take Vacations. They're Called Lunch Breaks," and "We Don't Have a Company Softball Team. It Would Lower Productivity by .56%."

Newcomers who try to leave such workplaces early, maybe to get home in time to have dinner with their families, must either adapt to the rigors of the daily routine or risk the loss of their jobs. "I see a lot of people who have a hard time understanding families and family pressures," one public relations executive in his mid-thirties confided to me. With a career that has already encompassed three different mergers at three financial corporations and one merger-related layoff,

Marc has drawn a drastic, if perhaps understandable, conclusion from his workplace observations: "I personally feel that having a family is not necessarily a good thing."

In industries like his, where white-collar workers can typically spend seventy, eighty, ninety hours a week, or even more, in their offices, machismo attitudes surface—especially in group situations—when people describe just how long and how hard they work. (Remember Catherine's sense of pride about "never complaining"?) When Harvard Business School professor Rosabeth Moss Kanter ran focus groups with about three hundred professionals working in the software industry, she was told about an "ethic that is far and above 8-to-5." Black humor abounded: "Only a half-day?" "That's 8 P.M. to 5 P.M." "This is like a poker game. I'll see you your hours and raise you." Another person explained, "The long hours aren't because we want to outshine everybody; we want to keep up with everybody."

This pace of work is physically and emotionally draining, however, whether or not people choose to complain about it to their friends, relatives, or colleagues. Robert, a thirty-two-year-old financial executive at American Express, described his working conditions to me this way: "I don't get home until nine-thirty some nights. I'm dead tired ninety percent of the time. I think it's slowly sinking in with my wife about the idea that we're going to have to do something with Robert's life."

Two paychecks means twice as much potential for overwork and exhaustion, with just that much less time left over for child-rearing and other priorities. One recent study of multidecade work patterns among two-career couples concluded, in the words of Marin Clarkberg, a Cornell University sociologist, "People are working longer hours, and it's not because they want to." Among the study's findings: 43 percent of husbands and 34 percent of wives reported working more hours than they would like.

What keeps people in their offices all these hours? One would assume—especially in a tight labor market—that the big difference between today's educated and empowered white-collar workers and the sweatshop seamstress would be the former's freedom to "just say no": to refuse to punch these round-the-clock time cards and instead insist upon a humane pace of work.

The explanation is as complex as the corporate world. Some people don't have the clout or the outside options to permit them to strive for more balanced schedules and workloads. Some industries effectively squash resistance early on by expecting their managers to train early recruits to accept (and even expect) excessive demands upon their time. On Wall Street, for example, it is common for a supervisor to instruct new hires to keep a spare set of clothes and toothbrush in the office for all those late night work episodes when it just won't make sense to head home for a quick snooze. Managers like these quickly impose their company's demanding work schedules upon their staffers' psyches and work habits, since they themselves put in extra long hours and can easily identify "slackers."

There are other ways, of course, to make certain that white-collar men and women meet their employers' tough standards. Legal, consulting, and accounting firms track numbers of billable hours, which has always made it simple for them to identify those professionals who fail to work long enough and bring in whatever levels of revenue currently seem adequate. With the development of new software products, other companies have the option—whether they choose to take advantage of it or not—of using personal computers to track the in-office productivity of all kinds of staffers.

As many people rise within their organizations, there's no need for the corporation to *impose* work-hour guidelines or track time spent at their desks. Their workloads are so heavy that they have no choice but to spend long hours there. If they want to hold on to their paychecks and benefit packages, if they want to keep rising within the corporate hierarchy, if they still care about their careers, they will put in whatever hours are necessary to handle their workloads. And they require neither timekeepers nor shop-floor supervisors to crack the whip, since they will *self-impose* whatever work schedule—nine-to-nine, six-to-eight (meaning A.M. to P.M., of course), or well into the morning hours—is necessary to get the job done.

JOB SPILL

One of the most insidious features of today's white-collar "sweatshop" is the way that increased work time and job demands get disguised, since many work-related activities take place in the ever more blurry terrain between life inside and outside the office.

Remember lunch hours? The very term has become an anachronism for many inhabitants of the corporate world. Thirty-nine percent of workers surveyed by the National Restaurant Association report that they are too busy to take a lunch break . . . they just work through it. Another 45 percent complain that they have less time for lunch than they used to have. While it's tough to tell exactly *how much less*—two recent surveys concluded that the sixty-minute lunch break has shrunk to either thirty-six or twenty-nine minutes—one conclusion is clear: we're gulping down our sandwiches quicker so that we can speed our way back to work.

In Manhattan, for example, where "power lunches" have traditionally been a way of life (and integral to the publishing, entertainment, fashion, legal, and other industries), tony restaurants such as Le Bernardin now offer thirty-minute quickies for working men and women who are too pressed for time to ingest their gourmet meals at a leisurely pace. The latest trend among rising professionals? They schedule two or more mini-meals, with one set of business guests arriving at the table as another departs: "There's no foreplay to lunch anymore," one confided.

The daily commute has also changed. For many men and women, the hours they spend in their cars or on trains getting to and from their offices used to include precious and uninterrupted moments of quiet which they now use, not for personal relaxation, but to return work-related phone calls they were too busy to respond to during the workday. When they get a free moment, or maybe get stalled in traffic, they check voice mail back at the office for new messages. Odds are, they don't even think of this activity as work; for many, it's just catch-up time. They might even blame themselves for being too disorganized or inefficient at the office to get done everything they need to do.

All those people in all those cars, however, with one hand on the steering wheel and the other on the cell phone, are part of a larger trend that has little to do with their personal efficiency. In most cases, after all, they'll have just as many phone calls to return during tomorrow's commute as they do today, even if they manage to catch up on all of them now. For lack of a better term, think of the cause as job "spill," like an oil spill. Then imagine job tasks seeping from the office to the home in much the same way as oil can invade a body of water and a beach. The seepage is just as difficult to block. And it's the dirty secret behind many a corporation's thriving bottom line.

Job spill encroaches upon far more than commuting time. Like Catherine, many of the people who write memos during their train rides home or return phone calls from the highway are the same ones who then proceed to check their e-mails and voice-mail messages after dinner: sometimes several times after dinner and sometimes for quite a long time after dinner. Their nighttime reading material might well be a proj-

ect update or a stack of memos from colleagues, or a book they're editing, or an investment prospectus they're writing. As with commuting, they usually don't tote this up as additional time spent after an already long workday, although of course it is.

People try to minimize the disruption of their home life by playing their own equivalent of the commuter "catch-up" game: they tell themselves that by working at home during the evening, they're making their lives "easier" at the office tomorrow. Of course, they need to tell themselves the same thing when faced with tomorrow's job spill. Or, they can try not to think too much about it; after all, that's just "the way things are."

Job spill also seeps into the weekend. Although there always were some people—mainly go-getters on the rise and plain old workaholics—who brought office work home with them to do on Saturday and Sunday, the weekend has typically been an inviolate private space, a chance to unwind and get together with relatives or friends or simply relax. As Witold Rybczynski put it in *Waiting for the Weekend,* "It's a time apart from the world of mundane problems and mundane concerns, from the world of making a living. On weekends time stands still, and not only because we take off our watches."

No longer. For many men and women, the pace of work is so intense and unrelenting that they simply cannot squirrel away the time to take off their watches and forget about their offices all weekend long. "I had no hobbies, no outside interests," recalled Patricia, one of a small group of female engineers at one of the nation's most prestigious (and demanding) high-tech giants. "I believe that the divorce rate at these very aggressive companies must be higher than the norm. If you make the choice to have a home life, your career will suffer. You've got to be willing to work the endless hours, come in on weekends, travel to the ends of the earth."

Weekend work is now just unavoidable for a good number of white-collar staffers.

Electronic mail has fueled the trend in making it both easier for people to contact their colleagues and more difficult for colleagues to fail to respond (and respond quickly). People are fortunate who can squeeze their weekend work in along with other activities, confine it to *only* Saturday or Sunday, or limit it to a couple of weekends each month.

There are countless subtle, but significant, signs of the invasion of the office into the once-inviolate weekend. FedEx, for example, launched a Sunday delivery service to a series of select U.S. zip code destinations in order to serve a customer base in which "more and more businesses were operating on Sunday. . . [or] were faced with either the occasional situation or the demanding customer who needed things on what was once an impossible deadline."

Bill, a longtime public relations executive, pointed out to me that more and more press conferences and news releases are being scheduled for Sunday. "It's a subtle breakdown of the old rules," he commented. "Maybe next we'll see these announcements coming out on Christmas. Hell, that's only another Wednesday or Thursday or whatever!"

Weekend work can take many different forms, running the gamut from a briefcase full of papers that will demand hours of reading and response time at one's home "office," to cell phone calls that interrupt a Sunday jitney ride back from the Hamptons, to beeper alerts that summon a mother or father away from a child's baseball game. The low point, at least with regard to weekend work, came for Marc one Saturday morning when he was wheeling his toddler daughter in a stroller to a local delicatessen for a breakfast alone.

"There we were in the mall and my beeper goes off." He paused in anger, as if he were still hearing it ring. "Here I am. My daughter deserves my attention, *but* all of a sudden Marc is a husband, a father, and a manager, all at the same time." He paused again, then added, "But that's not right,

because when I'm at the office, they don't want to hear that I'm also Marc a father and Marc a husband."

Whether weekend work takes place at a shopping mall (or some other extension of one's home turf) or at the office generally depends upon the norms for each person's industry and particular company. Parking lots may be as much as half full at a high-tech company like Microsoft on a Saturday or Sunday, and it's easy to tell what that signifies: more people working more hours. (Manny reported to me that he used to "sneak [his] daughters in below the security cameras," when he worked weekends at Intel, because he was so desperate to spend time with them, even if only at the office.)

On the other hand, the cubicles and hallways may be empty at a publishing company like HarperCollins during the weekend. But that doesn't mean its editors aren't blue-lining manuscripts from their desks or dining room tables at home, or performing other tasks they are simply too busy to handle during their workweek.

● ● ● ● ● ● ● ● ● ●
LESS TIME TO UNWIND

"You *are* being asked to work weekends," complained Robert, the financial executive from American Express. "You *have* to travel. People don't consider it an acceptable excuse to say, 'I'm burned out and I need to spend time with my family.' People *do* keep mental notes. You see it in their faces."

Few people possess the valuable ability to shut work out of their personal lives, at least for a long enough period to unwind from the intense job schedules they must cope with seven days a week. Since weekends scarcely provide relief for many overloaded men and women, vacations and holidays loom ever more important as an opportunity to restore balance. Yet these too are under siege in the white-collar "sweatshop," both from cost-cutting corporations and from the ever-present job spill.

In *The Overworked American,* Juliet Schor concluded that during the 1980s "U.S. workers have gotten *less* time off—on the order of three and a half fewer days each year of vacation time, holidays, sick pay, and other paid absences." She added, "This decline is even more striking in that it reverses thirty years of progress in terms of paid time off." Symptomatic of the corporate trend was DuPont's decision to reduce the highest-paid vacation level for employees from seven to four weeks, while also eliminating three company-wide holidays from its annual calendar.

With less time off (and jobs whose demands may be such that getting-away-from-it-all for two weeks is virtually impossible), quickie vacations have become increasingly popular. According to the Travel Industry Association of America, weekend vacations now represent more than half of all U.S. travel.

Even a weekend off is more time than some people can now steal away from their workplaces. So a new trend has evolved: twenty-four-hour vacations, which may take the form of overnights at a nearby hotel or spa. (Others manage to cram in round-trip airline flights, boat cruises, or some other type of long-distance conveyance that provides at least the illusion of a full-scale respite from work.) The *Wall Street Journal* termed such vacationers "deadline tourists," suggesting a heart-pounding compression of time that merely mirrors the intensity of their work and home lives.

Most people still cling to the more traditional forms of vacation (including enough time to work on a suntan or overcome jetlag). But a fair number bring along with them their laptops, portable fax machines, or electronic organizers, no matter how far from the office they go. They're the ones we all see who are speaking to their offices or their clients from cellular phones on the beach or the fishing boat. Intrusions like these from the workplace can even seem funny, so long as they're not happening to you or me. That was the way I felt when one thirty-something Wall Streeter described the time her cellular phone rang during a crowded train ride to her rented beach house in the Hamptons. Everyone within her sight range on the train checked his or her own phone; all were carrying them, in briefcases or handbags, as a matter of course.

Like all those men and women who squeeze work time into their commutes or evenings with the family, working vacationers may tell themselves that a little (or a lot) of work isn't really too bad, so long as it can be done *during* a stay at the beach or a trendy resort. How painful can it be to check one's voice mail, after all, if one can do it while watching the kids play beach volleyball or perfecting a suntan?

People who pacify themselves this way fail to appreciate that any work at all defeats the goal of a vacation, which is to restore one's sense of personal balance, enjoyment in life, and independence from the office. They cannot unwind, not really. The sad thing is, many people have basically accepted that this, too, is "the way things are."

TOO MUCH STRESS

Corporate America has always been a demanding place. For large numbers of men and women, however, the traditional demand-and-reward equation that has governed work life within the nation's largest companies no longer adds up. And that's true whether they're earning $30,000 a year or multiples more.

What's tipped the balance for many corporate staffers is the way that increased work time and job spill (with reduced opportunities to relax and recover) has contributed to stress loads so overwhelming that "job stress" and "personal stress" seem inextricably connected and inescapable. The personal toll can be overwhelming. Manny, the single father from Intel, confided to me, "Sometimes I would crash. A crash would mean I'd sit there and stare at the computer—couldn't move, couldn't hear anything. One time, I got a warning from my supervisor."

Many people find themselves pushed close to their own versions of Manny's "crash." International Survey Research Corporation, a Chicago-based opinion research firm, found that 44 percent of employees surveyed from a variety of corporations believe that their workloads are "excessive." (That percentage rose in six of the seven years surveyed, from a low of 37 percent in 1988.) Nearly as many people report that they are often bothered by excessive job pressures.

Just think about it for a moment. People are working ten or twelve or more hours a day. They're working through their lunch hours, during their commutes to and from the office, in squeezed-in spare moments during their evening hours, and whenever else they absolutely need to on weekends and holidays. And many of them still feel that they cannot keep up, that their workloads are excessive.

When the American Management Association conducted an overnight fax survey of its members to explore what it called "the emotionally charged workplace," its results were disturbing. Fifty-one percent of those surveyed cited "frustration" and 49.4 percent "stress" in response to a question about which emotions best described their feelings throughout the workday. The problem of "having more to do than time to do it" ranked highest on a five-point scale that measured respondents' intensity of feelings.

The National Center for Health Statistics, a division of the U.S. Department of Health and Human Services, tracked forty thousand workers to learn that more than

half reported feeling either a lot or a moderate amount of stress during the two weeks prior to the survey. In the majority of instances, that stress was work-related. Clearly, the problem abounds. More than 40 percent of professional and clerical workers surveyed by Gallup complained about stress on a daily or almost daily level. Business and sales staffers reported comparable loads.

Unlike hours spent in the office or productivity demands, stress is difficult to quantify. But a person knows it when he or she feels it—and, as I came to discover during my research, one also knows it when one hears it. I heard it in Jerome's voice when he and I met for a rushed lunch on Wall Street to discuss his career.

During more than twenty years in the marketing departments of major banks, including Citibank and Marine Midland, Jerome had worked his way through numerous corporate reorganizations and mergers, surviving some and losing his job after another. In his current position, he was earning less than he had earned five years earlier but was working harder, without any promotion opportunities in sight.

Jerome was plagued by the memory of the time, a few years ago, when he had failed to follow up on a headhunter's telephone call: after all, that job *might* have taken him to a better place and position than the spot where he has ended up. With a son graduating from high school that coming June, he confessed that worries about college tuition were never far from his mind. It would be difficult enough to handle those bills at his current salary, but what if he somehow lost his job again? He had learned the hard way that you couldn't count on anything in the corporate world.

All this added up to stress: stress that was apparent in the angry, clipped tones he used during our conversation and the way that his fingers kept banging the table to punctuate his points. "How long can they tighten the screws on people?" he asked me. Then he answered his own question. "As long as people take it. But they take it. They take it. They accept that this is what's happening to them. And it happened to their friends." He paused, then added in a tone laced with sarcasm. "They can commiserate with each other. If every company's doing it, the norm has just changed forever."

It has. These days stress is a way of life for many white-collar workers, regardless of their particular employer, age, or position on the corporate ladder. Today's pumped-up, high-pressure corporations thrive on stress, which helps motivate people to meet inflated and sometimes unrealistic short-term goals, regardless of the long-term toll it takes on their employees. Within the white-collar "sweatshop," there is little effort to disguise stressing techniques: in fact, the practice has been elevated to the level of business "philosophy." As one management consultant expressed his version, "The workplace is never free of fear—and it shouldn't be. Indeed, fear can be a powerful management tool."

Fear, insecurity, and exhaustion all contribute to rising stress levels in today's large corporations. And these pressures reinforce each other as overworked, stressed-out colleagues take their anxieties and resentments out on their fellow workers. "You should check out workplace bullying," Maureen, a thirty-year-old marketing representative at Simon and Schuster, advised me.

The problem, in Maureen's assessment, was not so much outright confrontation between professional colleagues: it was a "subtle" hostility between them that often manifested itself in rude behavior, angry or dismissive conversational tones, or short fuses. In her own office, she complained, people were quick to blame others for anything that ever went wrong. "The underlying thing is the sense of fear. They're feeling very insecure about their jobs," she commented.

A tour through the vast body of work-related websites on the Internet reveals "The Work Doctor," a site started up in 1998 by two self-described employee advocates and psychologists by training, who promise to "listen unconditionally . . . support the hurting." Calling itself the "U.S. Campaign Against Workplace Bullying Headquarters," the site attracts an average of nearly thirty-five thousand visitors per month, ranging in age from seventeen to fifty-eight—a strong indicator that others agree with Maureen's assessment of the significance of this problem. (The site's demographic surveys suggest that about 30 percent of this visitors are "professionals" and another 40 percent work in some type of management position. The majority of these have been female so far.)

According to the "Work Doctors," "the American workplace's 'dirty little habit' is that harassment, abuse, cheating, power plays, denial of simple rights, and other forms of mistreatment occur regularly. Rarely is the wrongdoing illegal. It is bullying." Among the classic workplace types they describe is the "opportunistic bully" who has "learned well the lessons of contemporary workplace dealings. He is only copying what he sees the parent [corporation] do," which includes "seizing the opportunity" to compete with and "obliterate" coworkers.

"The backbiting and politicking that you see at big companies these days is unbelievable," noted Zoe, the veteran of Levi Strauss's downsizing campaigns. "People become territorial because they're so scared. They're vying for power. If you know that cutbacks are coming, you'll do anything to position yourself so that you'll survive, even if nobody else does. There's lots of nastiness. All kinds of false accusations."

Along with verbal abuse and bullying, physical violence can surface in today's stressed-out offices. The phrase "going postal" has entered the lexicon of today's high-pressure, lean-and-mean workplaces:

shorthand for people who crack under the strain of working conditions too tough for them to handle. But although few of us even give a thought to the risk of office violence, some studies suggest that it may be more common than many people imagine. According to a survey conducted by the Society for Human Resource Management, nearly 10 percent of employers can expect some type of violent altercation to break out in their offices each year.

Direct links clearly exist between corporate developments and the personal problems facing many workers. In Maureen's office, relationships between coworkers deteriorated during the period when Simon and Schuster's corporate parent, Viacom, began to publicize its intention to sell part or all of the publishing company as soon as an acceptable bid came along.

I spoke to her during that period of complete instability (while she and her colleagues were, as she reported, plagued by anxieties about whether they could expect good severance packages if and when they got laid off, if and when the company got sold). "The fear level *is* pretty high," she concluded, then added that for a lot of people, including herself, these kinds of stress "also delay what seems like the passage to adulthood. Things like buying a house. Because people feel like even if they're employed, they don't know if they can hold on to their jobs long enough to live with a mortgage."

White-collar men and women also move in the opposite direction—fueling credit card binges and other forms of risky overextension that thrived during the 1990s—as they seek to alleviate their anxieties about the future of their careers or their feelings of personal inadequacy (because they haven't managed to get their hands on stock options or some of the other corporate goodies they keep reading about in the newspapers).

To make matters worse, with cost control a major priority at most large corporations, workplace conditions have deteriorated in ways that may even seem, at first glance, to be too petty to notice. But they quickly add up for stressed-out workers whose tempers are frayed and whose patience is short. "Did you hear about the water yet?" is a question I was asked by three different white-collar employees whose company, NYNEX, had merged with Bell Atlantic in the course of the many months I spoke with each of them.

They were different types of people, and each one had his or her own perspective on what had gone wrong with the company during many years of employment. But all three were preoccupied with water— or, to be more specific, with the *lack* of drinkable water at the company's office on Manhattan's Avenue of the Americas.

"The quality of water in our building is rather poor," one told me, his voice positively dripping with understatement. He explained that NYNEX had made it a practice to provide employees at this facility with bottled water: scarcely the most decadent of perquisites (especially when one considers the time it took people to ride the elevator downstairs and walk to a nearby grocery or coffee shop, inevitably crowded, instead). But after the merger, "in the interests of cost reduction," this manager said, drawing out every word, "they eliminated the bottled water."

He wanted to make certain I understood just how discomforting this decision had proven to be. (In fact, all three NYNEX veterans spent considerable time describing the water situation.) "No water means no coffee either." From her vantage point at Simon and Schuster, Maureen would not have been surprised to learn that heated confrontations soon broke out between departments that decided to ante up for their own water so as to be able to make their own coffee in the office, and those coworkers from other departments who occasionally crept in during a busy morning or afternoon to sneak a spare cup to which they were not entitled.

Annoyances of all scales abound. For all the jokes Scott Adams pokes at cubicles in his Dilbert cartoons, life in a cubicle is far from funny for most of the estimated 35 million white-collar workers who reside in one during eight-, ten-, twelve-, or longer-hour work-days. For one thing, cubicles keep getting smaller: Facility Performance Group Inc., an Ann Arbor, Michigan-based organization that tracks office trends at seventy large corporations, has reported that work spaces have shrunk by 25 to 50 percent over the past ten years for most workers.

Far from creating the collaborative, open environments that many top executives boast of when describing their "bullpen" designs (often from their own, multi-windowed and lushly furnished offices), cubicles foster all kinds of negative feelings. As one workplace observer aptly described, cubicles (whether of the relatively larger or relatively smaller variety) remain "mechanisms of constant surveillance." Their ticky-tacky, one-size-fits-all, institutional-gray designs demean white-collar professionals just as surely as do the lack of a door and any illusion of privacy. Meanwhile, their very air of impermanence—since most can be set up, moved, or reconfigured at will—is a not-so-subtle daily reminder of the lack of stability and security in the corporate workplace. If there is any lesson that the 1980s and 1990s have taught white-collar workers, it is that they can be replaced easily.

Other new arrangements convey similar, unspoken messages. With the virtual office or "hoteling" trend, employees are stripped of anything resembling a workspace and become "floaters" who may claim a desk or an office only on an as-needed basis. Despite the impact on people's day-to-day work lives, the strategy has its appeal for companies looking for ways to cut real estate and operating costs.

Cubicles, "hoteling" offices, and other arrangements like these help ratchet up job pressures by creating corporate atmospheres that are anything but comfortable, secure, and permanent. Most people understand the subtext. For cubicle dwellers: Work harder, because we can all see, smell, and hear what you're doing . . . or not doing. For hotelers: Be productive, or your "stay" at this company will soon be over.

● ● ● ● ● ● ● ● ● ●
THE TOLL

Unpleasant working conditions, difficult job demands, and rising career insecurities have combined to make stress the constant companion of many of today's white-collar men and women. It is a complaint so common as to seem banal, boring, perhaps the most hackneyed cliché of our age. But the reality of it is the very opposite: a heart-pounding, anxiety-ridden emotional state that regularly plagues men and women at work and outside of work, leading to migraines, ulcers, pinched nerves, insomnia, clammy palms, skipped heartbeats, and any number of other symptoms of our stressed-out age.

One estimate pegged the annual cost to the U.S. economy of such work-related stress at $200 billion. Talk to enough corporate staffers these days and that seems quite believable. "I've started getting heart palpitations. I just went through stress tests. I'm trying now to detach myself, to focus on my own health," Donald told me.

Just forty years old, he was a marketing staffer who had spent more than a decade at NYNEX, where he managed to hold on to his post through a number of layoffs and, eventually, the company's merger with Bell Atlantic. But between the years of cutbacks, the career uncertainty, the increasing workload, he was bitter. "I don't have any pride in this company. I don't feel any attachment. I don't feel any loyalty. It's only money. That's all I care about—the money." His father had been a blue-collar worker, employed by a municipal agency. Donald recalled, "He hated his job. He was powerless. He pushed me to become a professional. But even though I'm a professional, it doesn't mean anything. We're all just trying to survive."

The long-term toll of job-related stress appears to include all kinds of health risks. One ten-year study, which tracked about one thousand Swedes and was conducted by UCLA and the Karolinska Institute in Stockholm, found that serious work-related problems made a person "five times more likely to develop colorectal cancer." Meanwhile, "unemployment of more than six months doubled the cancer risk."

A University of California at Davis research team that tracked female lawyers found that those who worked long hours were "five times as likely to experience great stress at work and three times as likely to suffer miscarriages as [were] female lawyers who work fewer than 35 hours a week." A University of Michigan study of nearly fifteen hundred nurses found that women who worked more than forty hours during the week or experienced high job stress were 70 to 80 percent more likely to deliver premature, underweight babies.

I discussed job stress with Ida, a sociologist by training, whose career path had taken her through a series of human resources jobs at large corporations. "What helps people who are living through life at a lot of these companies is that there's the mortgage to pay and all those bills. Their outlet is sports, the Internet," she told me, adding, "The fact is that for many people, they have no choice."

Ida started working in corporate America during the 1960s, when she believed that the nation's prosperity would help make people's work lives more challenging, secure, *and* rewarding. But she lost those illusions after participating in a huge round of cutbacks at a big-name manufacturing firm. "People were literally dying. There were heart attacks, all kinds of medical responses." Now, she believes something very different: that job stress is responsible for "the decline of the civil society, the increase in traffic, in rage."

Damaging as they may be, however, recent increases in stress and workloads are only part of the problem for the inhabitants of today's white-collar "sweatshops." Despite nearly two decades of economic prosperity, many people have found themselves working harder within a business world whose reward structure has deteriorated in a variety of important ways.

IV-4: The Termination of Eric Clark

Clive Gilson

Yes, I had several summer jobs during my time as a student, but the real world always seemed to be somewhere over the horizon. My world was one which flowed between papers, exams and results. And back again. In fact the completion of my Ph.D signalled almost ten years in higher education. It was

The Termination of Eric Clark by Clive Gilson, St. Francis Xavier University, Antigonish, Nova Scotia, Canada. Reprinted with permission.

now September of 1979 and I was about to begin another year at University, this time as an educator.

While sitting in my office preparing for the coming semester, I pondered the reality of my position. A simple problem. It did not seem real at all. Taking stock I decided with uncharacteristic clarity that I should leave at once—escape if you will, perhaps I might even learn how to be human. So I left. Within 48 hours and with Ph.D in hand, I took a job as a medium haul truck driver at a large local bakery, which employed close to 1,000 workers.

I will never forget my first morning. It started at 4:00 A.M. My lasting memory will always be the smell of sweet fresh cream amid the acrid aroma of diesel fuel and exhaust fumes. The assault upon my senses also included the earthy didactic commentary of a grizzled supervisor named Johnny Poole, who frequently called into question the status of my parentage and also implied for good measure that relations between myself and my mother were at best unconventional. No place for dignity here. I was shocked. However, I was lucky enough to be sent out on the road with driver Eric Clark who was to show me the ropes and without conscious knowledge, transmit to me some of the values and behaviors of those who "really" worked for a living. Eric was the educator; I had come to school.

I could barely keep up, Eric was 55 years old yet seemed able to cope with the constant grinding strain of the road and the loading and unloading of bakery goods (which incidentally are much heavier than you could ever imagine). Several times I would verbalize my admiration, commenting that his fortitude in the face of hard work, low pay and a perniciously cruel supervisor, was hard to understand. His response was always the same — "Press on regardless." Much later I was to learn that such phrases were important mechanisms which enabled workers at the bakery to find solace and meaning in their labours. Like his co-workers Eric rarely, if ever, questioned his subjugation to managerial authority and only occasionally, its terms. Anyway, that's pretty much how Eric coped, actually more than coped. He retained a wonderfully optimistic approach towards all people. His infectious zest for life even under what I considered to be considerable adversity, was remarkable. He was an honest man whose essential nature was to do a good day's work. And taking his example, I tried to do the same. Finally, I was actually *working* for a living.

My three weeks spent with Eric Clark made a brutalizing experience manageable. Not only was I able to master the art of handling a 40-ton trailer, more importantly, I had obtained a valuable lesson in how workers see the world — and the distance between them and those who controlled our destiny. I had no idea that 5 years later our paths would cross again and I would learn another lesson which would alter my world forever.

Christmas of 1979 brought unbelievable exhaustion. I had not realised that eating was a seasonal habit. Our work load doubled and then tripled. Days seemed to merge together. In the week before Christmas "piggy-back" shifts started at 3:00 A.M. and finished at 9:00 P.M. For once my pay-check appeared reasonable, although my initial pleasure was fettered somewhat by the knowledge that January would almost certainly bring at best short-time working and at worst, extended lay-off until the Spring months. Through all this I had grown very cynical towards the management. I was astonished at their ineptitude and apparent distance from the workers. This compelled me to join the local union and seek representative office as Shop Steward. In the Summer of the following year I was elected to the position of plant Convener in charge of negotiations for just under 1,000 workers. I was both proud and filled with trepidation. My fellow workers expected and demanded miracles. From management I got hostility.

For the next two years I struggled mightily to improve the working conditions which my fellow workers endured. Many times I would come off the road from an eight-hour shift and have to represent one of my members who, unable to deal with the daily pressures, had engaged in verbal acts of insubordination — and sometimes worse behaviour still. This was not the rational world which I had frankly expected. My emotional and physical investment also conspired to rob me of many of the critical and analytical faculties which I had nurtured during my "academic" years. Reading and cultural activities were reduced to tabloid newspapers and watching sitcom re-runs. Bed at 8:30 P.M. or 9:00 P.M.

In the Autumn of 1981 I was called into the office of the owner and Managing Director and given an ultimatum. Join management or face dismissal. My role as an articulate workers' advocate apparently caused considerable disquiet among some managers, who felt threatened by my persistent questioning of their decisions—they simply wanted me out. The Managing Director saw the situation differently and reasoned that in the right place I could be an asset rather than an irritant. Driven by naivety and selective optimism I assumed the role of Transport and Distribution Manager. In the first few months of the job, my new power enabled me to introduce many of the changes which I had long sought as a union official. The workers greatly appreciated my progressive style. So did the owner of the company. Within six months I had been promoted to the position of Assistant Director in charge of all company operations.

For the next two years I was immersed in the world of executive decision making. Work began at 7:30 A.M. or 8:00 A.M. (although I still woke up at 3:45–4 A.M.—a legacy which continues to this day) and was full of creativity and responsibility. Power and influence became seductive aphrodisiacs. I had finally found the real world.

Unfortunately, the real world also included the storm clouds of economic recession. By late 1983 it seemed as if people had stopped eating. The company had a very poor Christmas period and the Winter months looked bleak. For the first time I instituted strict performance and appraisal programs with the intention of reducing our labour costs. I had no choice, the books spoke the unequivocal truth. In

February of 1984 my General Manager made a sombre yet excellent presentation which concluded that the appraisals had revealed that we should release 150 workers—permanently. Each decision was based on a combination of seniority and performance. Since I was the one who carried the responsibility for this critical initiative, I announced that I would personally inform each worker that he was going to be released. I asked the general manager to prepare the list and to leave it on my desk so I could begin this unenviable task the following morning.

After sleeping well I arrived at work a little earlier than usual and sat down at my desk. I opened the envelope and found six pages of names—those who were to be terminated. At the top of the list was Eric Clark. I was stunned. In haste I retrieved his personal file. It made devastating reading. Twelve months earlier his wife, June (whom I had also met) had died of cancer of the brain—I knew that Eric worshipped her. I had not known that his work had deteriorated since then. Apparently, he had slowed down considerably, become forgetful and incurred a number of minor traffic violations. I had not known of June's death either.

Eric was summoned to see me early in the afternoon. By now the word had spread and Eric knew what our meeting was about. He entered my office walking tall with his shoulders square. He shook my hand and said, "Good afternoon, Sir." Despite the difficult circumstances, Eric's dignity enabled him to maintain his natural deference to authority. I asked him to be seated and began my long explanation concerning the rationale behind his release. After I had finished there was a long and uneasy silence. At this point I remember that I found it difficult to look Eric in the face.

Eventually, in a quiet voice Eric started to speak. I cannot remember his precise words so I will try to summarise them for you. He told me that in the Second World War he was a marine commando and was part of the allied forces which liberated Italy. He had fought for his own and future generations and he could not understand that within his own lifetime, he was being discarded. Why? More directly he expressed his disbelief that he was being rejected by the very generation which he had fought for. Eric, of course, was the same age as my own parents, which made my task doubly awkward. Indeed, not a few years earlier, I had heard similar incantations from my father whenever I had acted selfishly or had been disrespectful to my elders. I had also heard many stories about the bravery and heroism of the marine commandos—at school we were taught that they were the ones who won the war. Eric also told me that his last operation was on the beaches at Anzio, where he was seriously wounded. I also remember my father telling me that the carnage at Anzio was so appalling that those who fought, lived and died on those beaches were legends who were accorded a special status. They stood next to God.

Eric had never mentioned or talked about his life to me in those few weeks we had spent together in the fall of 1979. In fact I suspect that he had never related his story to anyone. I do not think for one moment that he deliberately tried to make me feel uncomfortable (although this was clearly the result). I sensed that he truly could not comprehend the world, its values and its short memory.

IV-5: In Downsizing, Do Unto Others . . .

Bob Evans

First we read of Wilfred Popoffs bewilderment and sense of betrayal over his firing by the Saskatoon Star-Phoenix (One Day You're Family; The Next Day You're Fired—March 14) and in particular of his distress over the churlish and insensitive way in which it was done.

Five days later, Cheryl Tibbetts responded with a well-crafted distillation of the finest in 19th-century management philosophy (A Sheep In Capitalist's Clothing—March, 19), unimproved by the slightest understanding of the psychological and social realities of work, or the longer-term deleterious effects upon the whole economy that proceed from actions that rupture the already tattered employer-employee relationship.

I have been involved in the curious business called outplacement for over 20 years. It might be a conceit to say that I have seen it all but I do not think that I have missed too much. An outplacement consultant's job is to advise organizations on how to plan and execute a downsizing or an individual dismissal in a way that minimizes the social, psychological and economic damage that attends these almost always unpleasant activities. As well, it is my job to counsel, train and support the dismissed employees so as to expedite their efforts to find new employment.

Mr. Popoff's reactions to his firing was about as normal as you are likely to find. As he pointed out, he went in a moment from trusted employee to convicted felon, from respected senior member of a team of men and women putting out a newspaper to one more body on the discard pile. He was hurt, he was deeply offended, he was bewildered by the turn of events and as a result he was questioning everything in an effort to make sense of his situation.

"In Downsizing, Do Unto Others . . ." by Bob Evans, *The Globe and Mail*.

Did he turn his back on capitalism? It is more likely that he never turned toward it with anything approaching Ms. Tibbetts's ideological zeal. Capitalism for him and for most of us is an abstraction accepted with long personal lists of exceptions — a wishy-washy liberalism that, far from being a weakness, is the strength that defines this country and makes us the envy of the world.

I doubt that capitalism is the sort of "ism" that informed and guided his life. Certainly, it did not rank with civility in his hierarchy of values, nor with his good sense of community and fair play.

Mr. Popoff was fired and he reacted as you and I would have — as an ordinary human being who collided with an ugly reality.

I have a problem with Ms. Tibbetts's nasty and narrow little take on that reality. To begin with, her assumption (or presumption) that business is purely an economic game flies in the face of our collective experience. It may be an economic game for the capitalists (in her definition). For the rest of us, businesses are where we earn our daily bread. Work is also where we find community — that sense of belonging and contributing and being somebody that our great-grandparents had and enjoyed and that has been lost as our society has changed; become urban, dispersed, mechanistic and individualistic.

Society changed, but our need for community did not. We want our business organizations to be our communities. In good times, they have done so — more or less. In bad times, they have let us down.

Ms. Tibbetts believes that this is irrelevant and that "our ideologies are a function of our current circumstances," as she put it. Ideologies are what we fall back upon when things become incomprehensible, and in that sense she is right. But ideologies are subordinate to basic human values. Ideologies change or die, values proceed. Ask Wilfred Popoff.

In 20 years of advising on the process of prying people loose from their work, com-munity and self-definition, I have observed many things. Here are a few insights born of the experience of my "vocationally challenged" clients and the organizations that did the challenging.

Most employees do not buy in to the "corporate vision." They do not get excited about selling more Dino Puffs or capturing another 3 percent market share. The rhetoric that amuses the financial analysts does not always amuse the troops. What employees do buy into is honesty and consistency, even if the message is uniformly bleak. They often enjoy the work that they do and most of them do it well. And they treasure most the companionship, community and sense of belonging that their work provides.

Most downsizings do not achieve their started purposes; in fact, they often produce results quite different from the ones intended. Terminations that are perceived by others in the work force as ill-conceived or unfair or that are conducted harshly and disrespectfully can destroy morale and commitment, cause the best and brightest to put their resumes on the street, turn the lot of middle management into a living hell and hamstring the organization's ability to recruit good people. In time, that ill will can show up on the bottom line — in red.

The most important single task in a termination or downsizing is the protection and preservation of the dignity of the persons being fired. I realize that Ms. Tibbetts cannot factor this into her economic equation and I am sorry to hear that the outplacement types who orchestrated Mr. Popoff's departure seem to have the same problem. The problem is one of attitude. Let me explain it this way, using Mr. Popoff as an example. For 30 years he worked willingly and well for his company. We can safely assume that he was and is an honest, responsible, ethical and non-violent man. By what stretch of lunatic logic does senior management and the outplacement firm determine that at the moment of his firing and thereafter he is likely to take leave of the values and beliefs that have informed and guided his behavior for 54 years and become malevolent, dishonest and untrustworthy? Why would anyone assume that he cannot be permitted into his office for fear he might trash the computer or pee in the potted plants?

Firing does not turn people into ogres. In my experience, it usually has the opposite effect, causing them to fall back on their core values and stand tall on the moral high ground. In all of my years as an outplacement consultant, the worst behavior I witnessed during a firing took the form of a loud and colorful cascade of obscenities.

If you assume that people are going to behave badly at the time of dismissal and thereafter, you are then inclined to take "protective measures" such as delivering the news off-site, having gaggles of security guards and outplacement consultants doing crowd control, shaking people down for their passcards and keys, denying unsupervised access to the workplace, escorting people to the parking lot and so on.

A number of years ago, a smart psychologist named McGregor managed to sum up a good part of his life's work in one brilliant aphorism. He said, speaking to managers and executives, that "people will behave about the way you expect them to."

To Cheryl Tibbetts and her ilk, to the consultants who managed the downsizing at the StarPhoenix, to the senior managers there and to anyone now planning a termination or downsizing: Please check your assumptions and manage your expectations accordingly. It is the least we can do in the interest of maintaining the civility and mutual respect that have been our hallmarks as Canadians.

IV-6: Early PT Cruiser Took a Bruisin'
But Resolute Workers Triumphed over Obstacle to Quick Assembly

Elliot Blair Smith

TOLUCA, Mexico—DaimlerChrysler almost didn't build PT Cruiser, its runaway hit and the 2001 North American Car of the Year, because of a last-minute manufacturing glitch.

When Gary Henson, the automaker's global manufacturing chief, arrived here in late 1999, he thought the brash new PT Cruiser would be a snap to build.

Instead, he found a problem so basic— putting the engine in each Cruiser stopped the assembly line dead—that "we didn't think we could do it. We had what we thought was a 'no build.'"

At that point, it took the workers a day to build each Cruiser. They needed to make each one in less than 2 minutes.

That the automaker and its workers saved the car is a triumph of ingenuity and persistence over manufacturing limitations. Now they are gearing up to make more of the wildly popular cars at an even brisker pace.

A PT Cruiser wipeout would have been costly for both Chrysler and Mexico.

The financially ailing automaker had spent $600 million to develop PT Cruiser, which has become a profit machine. Cruiser contributed pre-tax profits of about $494 million to DaimlerChrysler last year, a badly needed infusion almost equal to the $501 million operating profit posted by the troubled Chrysler Group.

And Mexico's automotive industry avoided what would have been a black eye. Seven global automakers built 1.9 million vehicles in the country last year, 76% for export, most to the USA.

The Cruiser didn't wipe out, and now DaimlerChrysler is investing $300 million to expand the Toluca plant, an hour outside Mexico City, so it can build 260,000 next year, a 44% increase. That's because demand vastly outstrips supply. The only other place Cruisers will be built is at a factory in Austria, now ramping up to produce the car for the European market.

Once work is complete on the Toluca expansion, a PT Cruiser will roll off the line every 56 seconds.

That's a far cry from January 2000, when the factory, one of the company's most mod-ern, efficient plants, could build just one a day.

The problem: Once the assembly line accelerated to production speed, factory workers found they didn't have time to wedge the PT Cruiser's 24-liter engine into the vehicle's narrow snout.

DaimlerChrysler production engineers had devised two moving production lines—one for the motor, one for the chassis—which converged at the point where the motor was to be inserted from below. But designers working on simulators at the company's Auburn Hills, Mich., headquarters, had left the assemblers a tiny 0.6-inch clear-ance in which to work, more than a third smaller than the tightest engine tolerance on any previous Chrysler vehicle.

"You've got a moving vehicle, you've got a moving engine. You're moving them horizontally—parallel to one another—and all of a sudden, you start moving the engine up vertically," says Henson. "It's kind of like try-ing to put your shoe on while you're running."

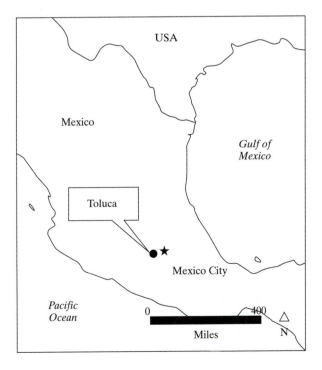

Only by stopping the production line and working from a standstill could workers fit the motor into the chassis. At that pace, the PT Cruiser never would be profitable.

Henson had dealt with unforeseen manufacturing problems before. One year earlier, Chrysler had introduced the LHS luxury sedan with front-door bolts inaccessible to factory tooling. "We couldn't get the frigging door on," Henson recalls. Daimler-Chrysler temporarily solved that problem by hand-bolting the doors and adjusted the tooling later.

But never before the PT Cruiser had Henson experienced a potentially fatal flaw so late in a new model's development. "You either put the engine in, or you don't run," Henson says.

Daimler Chrysler's manufacturing chief looked at the Mexican factory workers' stricken faces, weighed the financial consequences and decided he had to solve the problem right there, not back in Michigan, the land of sophisticated design computers.

"Before we declare we can't build this," Henson says he told the workers, "here's what I want to do: Until I come back in 2 weeks, I want you to just practice." Mexican factory officials, led by plant manager Luis Rivas, cleared a corner of the 1.4 million-square-foot factory to repeatedly practice inserting the motor.

● ● ● ● ● ● ● ● ● ● ● ● ●
STEP BY STEP

Rivas, 48, broke the task into small steps, each timed to the second. And he painted sections of the factory floor in colors—green, yellow, red—corresponding to the steps. If the workers—teams of five—were unable to complete their assigned tasks before the vehicle moved to the next color grid, they were instructed to pull an emergency alarm to stop production and begin again.

It was a skirmish of man vs. machine that could be measured in fractions of an inch. Time and again, frustrated workers pulled the alarm, stopped the assembly line and started over.

When Henson returned 2 weeks later, the factory had improved its performance to one vehicle—motor inserted properly— every 10 minutes. That was a long way from the target production speed, but better than a "no build."

> *"Once they saw this huge obstacle they had, and solved it, everything else looked pretty minuscule."*
> —GARY HENSON,
> DaimlerChrysler global
> manufacturing chief

"It was a turning point in the launch. Once they saw this huge obstacle they had, and solved it, everything else looked pretty minuscule," Henson recalls. "I said, 'Good, I'm coming back again in another 2 weeks.'"

Two weeks later, PT Cruisers rolled off the line at a rate of one every 4 minutes.

Practice. More practice. And more practice, eventually resulting in the factory producing one PT Cruiser every 1 minute, 20 seconds.

Next year's goal is to reduce the production time by 25%. The Mexican workers' footwork and faded paint marks on the factory floor reveal they are well on their way. Back at Chrysler headquarters, Henson says, engineers also improved their factory-simulation skills.

● ● ● ● ● ● ● ● ● ● ● ● ●
MAINTAINING QUALITY

Despite the incredible decrease in production time, the Toluca workers didn't make the improvement at the cost of quality. J.D. Power & Associates, in a private study of a half-dozen Mexican automotive plants, rates the plant as No. 1 in quality, above GM's car factory in Guanajuaco, Nissan's plant in Aguascalientes, another DaimlerChrysler plant in Saltillo, the VW plant in Puebla, and a Ford plant in Hermosillo.

Moreover, J.D. Power rates the Toluca plant as the second-best manufacturing operation worldwide for DaimlerChrysler, which has established its reputation on the basis of the excellence of its Mercedes-Benz automobiles. And J.D. Power rates the PT Cruiser among the top five highest quality premium compact cars.

FIGURE 4-1   DaimlerChrysler Tops in Mexican Exports

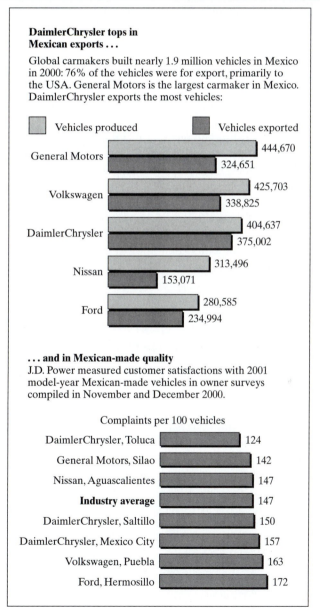

DaimlerChrysler tops in Mexican exports . . .

Global carmakers built nearly 1.9 million vehicles in Mexico in 2000: 76% of the vehicles were for export, primarily to the USA. General Motors is the largest carmaker in Mexico. DaimlerChrysler exports the most vehicles:

☐ Vehicles produced   ☐ Vehicles exported

General Motors — 444,670 / 324,651
Volkswagen — 425,703 / 338,825
DaimlerChrysler — 404,637 / 375,002
Nissan — 313,496 / 153,071
Ford — 280,585 / 234,994

. . . and in Mexican-made quality
J.D. Power measured customer satisfactions with 2001 model-year Mexican-made vehicles in owner surveys compiled in November and December 2000.

Complaints per 100 vehicles

DaimlerChrysler, Toluca — 124
General Motors, Silao — 142
Nissan, Aguascalientes — 147
Industry average — 147
DaimlerChrysler, Saltillo — 150
DaimlerChrysler, Mexico City — 157
Volkswagen, Puebla — 163
Ford, Hermosillo — 172

Source: J.D. Power and Associates

That's unusual for a new model. "Typically with new-model launches, we see quality problems as the vehicle is coming off the line, and the plant is working to deal with any problems," says Rich Bongiorno, manager of product research for J.D. Power. PT Cruiser "did launch quite respectably."

The PT Cruiser also has been a saving grace for the Chrysler Group, acquired by Daimler in 1998 and an earnings albatross almost ever since. Last year. Chrysler Group unit sales dipped 6% in an expanding U.S. auto market. In December, Wall Street's two major credit-rating agencies, Standard & Poor's and Moody's, downgraded the company's debt.

But the $22,000 Cruiser has become one of Chrysler's most profitable vehicles, because the company needs to spend almost no money on advertising or financial incentives to sell it.

Although some automotive analysts view the Cruiser as a fad with limited staying power, sales were 72,295 for the first 6 months of the year, roughly what Chrysler planners thought a full year's sales would be. That generated revenue of about $1.5 billion, about 10% of Chrysler Group's revenue for the first half.

The success of PT Cruiser is helping the Mexican factory and its workers as well.

At a time when Chrysler is laying off 26,000 employees, the Toluca plant plans to increase its 3,200-person workforce by one-third, all devoted to Cruiser.

And the factory is beginning to fashion bold variations of the basic Cruiser model that likely will incorporate new colors, flame-decal sides, wood paneling, convertible tops and turbo engines—moves designed to maintain the vehicle's sales momentum.

"We're very proud that the PT Cruiser is made in Mexico," says Rivas, the plant manager.

With an engineer's nonchalance, he shrugs off the difficulty posed by the now-solved engine-placement problem. Says Rivas: "Mexico is entering the big leagues of global manufacturing."

IV-7: Intimidation Rituals
Reactions to Reform

Rory O'Day

The reaction of authority in social systems to the reform initiatives of a subordinate is viewed as a series of intimidation rituals. These rituals divide into two major phases, each involving two distinct steps. The first phase, *Indirect Intimidation,* includes the rituals of *nullification and isolation;* the second, *Direct Intimidation,* the rituals of defamation and expulsion. Why these rituals for protest-suppression in organizations are powerful tools in the hands of the middle manager is discussed. Attention is also given to various images projected by the organizational reformer and reasons for resistance to reform from within an organization.

This paper characterizes the reactions of superiors in social systems to a reform-minded subordinate as a series of intimidation rituals. Each successive "ritual of control" represents an escalation in the efforts of authority to discourage an individual

Rory O'Day, *Journal of Applied Behavioral Science,* copyright 1974 by Sage Publishing. Reprinted by Permissions of Sage Publications, Inc.

(and those who may support him or her) from continuing to seek reform.

MIDDLE MANAGEMENT'S MECHANISM OF CONTROL

The rituals of intimidation satisfy the two primary concerns of authorities confronted by a subordinate who appears not only able to articulate the grievances of a significant number of other system members but also capable of proposing solutions to them. Their first concern is, of course, to control the reformer so that he does not succeed in recruiting support. Their other concern is to exercise this control in ways that absolve them of any wrongdoing in the matter. The individual in question must be controlled in such a way that he neither continues to be an effective spokesman nor becomes a martyr. When superiors are confronted with a reform-minded subordinate, they want his silence or his absence, whichever is easier to achieve. The "authorities" must also preserve their carefully managed image of reasonableness, and would prefer that the reformer leave voluntarily rather than be removed officially.

For purposes of illustration, this presentation will describe intimidation rituals used by various organizations in the service of protest-suppression, for organizational authorities prefer to *intimidate* a reform-minded individual rather than commit organizational energy to the structural and personnel changes required to transform a "non-conforming enclave" into a legitimate subunit.[1] It is further suggested that an organization undergoes major changes that incorporate and accommodate a group of dissidents only when the intimidation rituals do not succeed in silencing the individuals who constitute the "leading edges" of the reform movement.

In the discussion that follows, I will be concerned primarily with the reformer who emerges from the lower hierarchy in an organization and challenges the *middle hierarchy*. A reformer threatens middle management in three distinctly different ways. The first threat is a function of the validity of his accusations about the inadequacy of specific actions of middle-level members and his suggestions for correcting them. If the reformer is correct, those in the middle will fear that those at the top will punish them when they discover the truth. The second threat comes from the moral challenge presented by such a reformer, for his demand for action will reveal the strength or weakness of middle management's commitment to the organization. And thirdly, the reformer's challenge may indicate to people at the top that middle management is unable to maintain order in its own jurisdiction. To protect their interests, middle-level bureaucrats therefore feel their only defense against reform-minded subordinates is intimidation.[2]

The rituals of intimidation involve two phases: *Indirect Intimidation,* which has two steps, *nullification* and *isolation;* and *Direct Intimidation,* which also comprises two steps, *defamation* and *expulsion.*

PHASE I: INDIRECT INTIMIDATION

STEP 1: NULLIFICATION

When a reformer first approaches his immediate superiors, they will assure him that his accusations or suggestions are invalid—the result of misunderstandings and misperceptions on his part. His superiors, in this phase, hope that the reformer will be so awed by authority that he will simply take their word that his initiative is based on error. If, however, the reformer insists, his superiors will often agree to conduct an "investigation."

The results of such an investigation will convince the reformer that his accusations are groundless and that his suggestions for enhancing organizational effectiveness or revising organizational goals have been duly noted by the appropriate authorities.

Bureaucratic justification for this response usually rests on the argument that this method copes with the system's "crackpots" and "hot-heads," discouraging them from disturbing the smooth, routine functioning of the organization with their crazy ideas and their personal feuds. But middle management also uses these rituals of nullification to handle a potentially explosive (for them and others in the organization) situation quickly and quietly, in order to prevent unfavorable publicity, maintain the organization's state of pluralistic ignorance, and prevent the development of a sympathetic and concerned audience for the reformer's ideas. The explicit message is: "You don't know what you're talking about, but thank you anyway for telling us. We'll certainly look into the matter for you." Members of the middle hierarchy then proceed to cover up whatever embarrassing (for them) truth exists in the reformer's arguments.

The protest-absorption power of the ritual of nullification derives from an element inherent in bureaucracies: the always-attractive opportunity to avoid personal responsibility for one's actions. Thus, if people attempt reform at all, they generally do not proceed beyond the first ritual, which is a process designed to quash the reformer and allow his superiors to reaffirm the collective wisdom of the organization, while clearing their consciences of wrongdoing. Nullification even gets the would-be reformer off the book—and he may remain grateful to the organization for this added convenience. This shedding of personal responsibility allows the reformer and the authorities alike to compromise in the belief that although it might not be a perfect organizational world, it is nevertheless a self-correcting one.

Repeated exposure to the nullification ritual (the "beating your head against the wall" phenomenon) is expected to convince any sane organizational member that a reformist voice or presence is unwelcome. He is expected to take the hint and stop pestering his superiors with his misguided opinions. Gestures of generosity on the part of the middle hierarchy are not unusual if he decides to leave the organization—and such concern is usually expressed by offering to help the individual find employment opportunities elsewhere.

STEP 2: ISOLATION

If the reformer persists in his efforts, middle management will separate him from his peers, subordinates, and superiors, thereby softening his impact on the organization and making it extremely difficult for him to mobilize any support for his position.

Middle managers argue that these procedures represent the exercise of their rights of office in the service of protecting the organization. But these attempts to isolate the reformer can also be seen as a show of force, as a way of reassuring their own superiors (if they are paying attention), their subordinates, and perhaps themselves that they can maintain order in their own jurisdiction.

Attempts at isolating the reformer include closing his communication links, restricting his freedom of movement, and reducing his allocation of organization resources. If these do not neutralize the reformer, he will be transferred to a less visible position in the organization. In these rituals, the bureaucratic message is: "If you insist on talking about things which you do not understand, then we will have to prevent you from bothering other people with your nonsense."

Systematic unresponsiveness to a reformer's criticism and suggestions is a particularly interesting form of isolation. This lack of response is meant to convince the reformer of the invalidity of his position; but if he presses his right to be heard, it may be used to create a feeling of such impotence that the reformer overreacts in order to elicit a response from his superiors. This overreaction may then be used to demonstrate the reformer's psychological imperfections.

When subjected to organizational isolation, most people come to see the error of their ways or the handwriting on the wall. When an individual learns that there is still time to mend his ways, he usually steps back in line and becomes a silent participant in the organization. When he realizes his career in the organization is at a standstill, he may decide to leave as gracefully as possible while he can still leave under his own steam. Middle managers closest to him then often offer him assistance in finding a new job, with the assurance that *"we* only want what is best for *you."*

Most forms of isolation are designed to persuade the reformer of the futility of trying to initiate change until such time as he is instructed by his superiors to concern himself with change. The reformer practically guarantees his defeat if he reacts to systematic organizational unresponsiveness by confronting his superiors in ways that violate policy or law. The temptation to confront administrative unresponsiveness in dramatic and often self-defeating ways stems in large part from the intense frustration induced by the reformer's belief that systematic unresponsiveness violates his basic rights of freedom of expression and carries with it the implication that he is personally ineffectual (Turner, 1973). Administrative unresponsiveness to what the reformer believes are crucial issues both for himself and for the organization may be sufficiently frustrating to compel him to act, however rashly, in order to clarify the situation. From the administration's point of view, this can be seen as "flushing the rebels out into the open," "giving them

enough rope to hang themselves," or, more formally, deviance-heresy conversion (Harshbarger, 1973).

● ● ● ● ● ● ● ● ● ● ● ● ● ● ●
PHASE II: DIRECT INTIMIDATION

Step 3: Defamation

Should the reformer refuse to remain silent, and instead mobilizes support for his position, middle management will begin to impugn his character and his motives. "When legitimate techniques fail—the middle hierarchy might resort to illegitimate or non-legitimate ones" (Leeds, 1964, p. 126). Middle managers will often distort events or even fabricate instances of misconduct in order to intimidate not only the reformer but also those who would listen to or believe him.

Defamation attempts to cut the reformer off from a potentially sympathetic following by attributing his attempts at reform to questionable motives, underlying psychopathology, or gross incompetence. This three-pronged attack is meant to blackmail the reformer into submission and to transform a sympathetic following into a mistrustful crowd of onlookers or an angry mob that feels resentful at having been deceived by the reformer.

From the vantage point of the reformer, the Kafkaesque or Alice-in-Wonderland quality of the rituals of intimidation becomes particularly evident at this time. The reformer finds himself faced with charges which only he and his accusers know are either false or irrelevant in relation to the value of his reform initiatives. The reformer is in a double bind. His superiors will use their offices and positions of trust and responsibility to create the impression in the minds of others in the organization that their accusations of incompetence, self-interest, or psychopathology are true. If the reformer continues in the face of these accusations, he risks being viewed as power-hungry or irrational. If he allows himself to be intimidated by the threat of lies, he allows his superiors to win by default.

One tactic of the superior is to accuse the reformer of acting out his Oedipal conflicts. Such a personalization of a subordinate's reform efforts (especially a younger subordinate) permits his superior to present himself as a harassed "father" faced with a troubled "son," and blocks any examination of his conduct that might reveal provocation on his part. In this way the bureaucrat hopes to persuade others in the organization to respond to the reformer as a sick person in need of therapy or as a child in need of nurturing—a stance that allows him to take on the role of "good father" in relation to other subordinates and to the reformer, if and when the latter capitulates and admits his need for help and guidance.

Rituals of defamation are undertaken by superiors in order to focus attention away from themselves and onto the reformer. The superiors hope that by casting enough doubt on the motives, intentions, and personality of the reformer, enough people in the organization will think that "where there is smoke, there must be fire." The message of this ritual is: "Don't listen to him (his message) because you can't trust a person like him."

Like the rituals of nullification and isolation, the ritual of defamation is both an end in itself and a preliminary to the final ritual of expulsion. The superiors hope by threatening to destroy the reformer's reputation and his character, he will retreat into silence and passivity or leave the organization for greener pastures; if, however, the reformer continues his efforts, his superiors have laid the groundwork for his expulsion.

If the ritual of defamation is undertaken, its target is usually indeed a reformer and not simply a nonconformist or a deviant. His superiors would not need to engage in public tactics of intimidation if there were no substance to his challenge. It is precisely the validity of his reform initiatives that leads his superiors to attempt to destroy his credibility. If this destruction of the reformer's credibility with his peers, subordinates, and top management is effectively conducted, others in the organization will desert his cause and he can be dismissed easily as an undesirable member of the intact organizational team.

STEP 4: EXPULSION

When neither nullification, isolation, nor defamation can silence the reformer or force his "voluntary withdrawal" from the organization, the middle hierarchy seeks an official decision for his dismissal.

If successful, at least three aims may be achieved thereby. Obviously, by expelling the reformer, his superiors will cut him off from any actual or potential following and weaken any opposition to their authority. An official dismissal also serves as a warning to other budding reformers that middle management has the necessary power and authority to expel troublemakers. Finally, the act of expulsion—a verdict of unfitness—supports the contention that the reformer is an immoral or irrational person.

Of course, the middle hierarchy would prefer the reformer to withdraw voluntarily. Managers want to avoid the public and formal proceedings that often accompany an official request for dismissal of an employee, for the accuser (superior) can often then be scrutinized as carefully as the accused, if the accused person wishes to avail himself of the opportunity. The expulsion ritual involves the formal submission of evidence, the keeping of records, the establishment of independent investigative bodies, and the right of cross-examination, which all function to threaten the image of managers as reasonable, honest, and hardworking servants of the organization. Formal dismissal proceedings are also avoided by middle management because in some fundamental sense they imply that the organization has failed and that they, in particular, have shown themselves unable to maintain order.

THE RITUAL CYCLE ABSORBS AND DESTROYS

Indirect Intimidation attempts to absorb the accusations and suggestions of the reformer, first by depriving him of effectiveness or validity, then by treating him as if he were an "invisible person." The object here is to define the reformer as "harmless." It also attempts to absorb protest by psychologically and physically exhausting the reformer so that he comes to doubt his own experience of reality, his abilities to accomplish the task he sets for himself, and its significance. The authorities hope that the reformer will come to believe the task he has set for himself is humanly impossible and that his fatigue and confusion are the result of his inability to accept human nature for what it is. Short of this, they hope that the reformer will come to feel so inadequate that he will be grateful for continued employment by the organization, in any capacity. ("You're welcome to stay aboard as long as you don't rock the boat.")

Direct Intimidation attempts to destroy protest through destruction of the *character* of the reformer (defamation) or, if necessary, of his *position* in the organization (expulsion). Direct Intimidation represents middle management's active attempt to destroy the reformer as a source of legitimate grievances and suggestions and to terrorize, if necessary, other organizational members. Successful rituals of defamation create a "bad" person, enabling the "good" organization to close ranks once again and benefit from the curative properties of solidarity when he is cast out of the system. In this sense, the ritual destruction of the person (Garfinkel, 1956) necessarily precedes the destruction of his place in the organization.

In sum, Figure 1 portrays the specific cycles of intimidation rituals. Cycle 1 is most preferred by all organizations, while Cycle 4 is the least preferred. Cycle 2 is preferred to Cycle 3.

THE REFORMER IMAGE

Throughout this discussion, the individual subjected to the rituals of intimidation has been referred to as the *reformer,* a generic term for any organizational member who resorts to voice rather than to avoidance when faced with what *he* regards as a situation or organizational deterioration or imperfection. Voice is defined as

> . . . any attempt at all to change, rather than escape from, an objectionable state of affairs, whether through individual or collective petition to the management directly in charge, through appeal to a higher authority with the intention of forcing a change in management, or through various types of actions and protests, including those that are meant to mobilize public opinion (Hirschman, 1970, p. 30).

Therefore, in the sense in which it is being used here, "reformer" includes the various meanings contained in such labels as "internal muckraker" or "pure whistle-blower" (Peters & Branch, 1972), "innovator in innovation-resisting organizations" (Shepard, 1969), "crusader for corporate responsibility" (Heilbroner, 1972), "nonconforming individual" (Etzioni, 1961; Leeds, 1964), and "heretic" (Harshbarger, 1973); but it is not intended to include the various meanings inherent in the term "organizational change agent."[3] Thus *"reformer"* refers to any member who acts, in any way and for any reason, to alter the structure

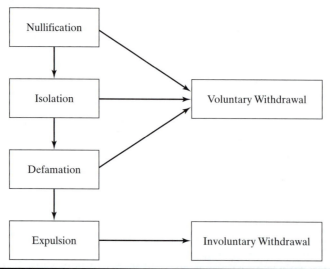

FIGURE 4-2   Cycles of Intimidation Rituals

and functioning of the organization, when he has *not* been formally delegated authority to institute change.

WHY INTIMIDATION WORKS

From this definition we can see that it is the organization which has the power to define the "reformer" as such, and attaches the stigma to many a well-meaning individual who does not see himself in a protest role. It is often the case that a potential reformer initially thinks of himself or herself only as a hard-working and loyal member of the organization who is simply trying to make things "better" and wishes to be "understood" by busy but well-meaning superiors. However, by the time authorities begin the rituals of defamation, the most naive individual usually realizes that, at least in the eyes of his superiors, he poses a threat to the established order (Herbert, 1972).

The inside reformer is vulnerable to all the intimidation rituals that his particular organization has at its disposal. The reformer outside an organization is usually vulnerable only to the rituals of nullification, isolation (in the form of systematic unresponsiveness), and defamation, unless the organization he is challenging is able to pressure the parent organization into doing the intimidating for it (McCarry, 1972).

Authorities in formal organizations are rarely directly challenged by subordinates. As in the Hans Christian Andersen tale, most individuals do not presume to stand in public judgment of their organizational superiors. Belief in the wisdom and power of the people at the top serves to keep most individuals silent about their grievances concerning the status quo and their ideas (if they have any) for enhancing organizational effectiveness or revising organizational goals. Subordinates do not generally demand, as part of their organizational contractual arrangements, the power to hold their superiors accountable for actions in direct and continuing ways. So intimidation rituals are held to be a last resort—reserved for organizational members who resist, for whatever reason, the usual mechanisms of social control (Millham, Bullock, & Cherrett, 1972).

In their discussion of the obstacles to whistle-blowing, Peters and Branch (1972) include the "loyal-member-of-the-team" trap, the feeling that "going public" is unseemly and embarrassing, and the fear of current and future job vulnerability. Thompson (1968) and Peters and Branch (1972) also refer to the subconscious accommodative device of the "effectiveness trap," an organizational argument that permits its members to avoid conflict on an immediate issue in order to ensure "effectiveness" on some more important issue, at some future time. The curator mentality and emotional detachment generated by the bureaucratic role; the tendency to resort to wishful thinking that organizational deterioration and the consequences of bad policy must soon stop simply because they cannot go on; and the fear that one disagrees with a particular exercise of power only because one is too weak to handle it further contribute to inaction on the part of most "loyal" organizational members (Thompson, 1968).

REFORMER AS BAD GUY

In point of fact, the protest-absorbing and protest-destroying power of intimidation rituals derives, in large measure, from their infrequent use by organizations. Conversely, if more members were willing to turn their various dissatisfactions into reformist activities, intimidation rituals would lose much of their power.

To understand the effectiveness of organizational intimidation one must examine the reasons why peers and subordinates usually fail to support the reformer withdraw support, or even actively resist his efforts. Their passive or active resistional members who continue to harbor some doubt about the reformer's guilt, the fear of retaliation against "sympathizers" usually dampens their enthusiasm for the reformer's cause and suppresses all but ritualistic expressions of concern for his plight.

SEIZE THE DAY

It is not possible here to do more than raise the issue of whether one should attempt to change organizations from within or whether one should create alternative organizations. Large formal organizations are going to be with us for a long time to come (Heilbroner, 1972), and their members are going to have to devise ways to make them more democratic, because there really is no place to run to anymore.

The serious reformer should be prepared to take advantage of organizational crises. He must learn how to recognize, expose, and make concrete those administratively designed arrangements that do not satisfactorily resolve critical problems. For it is in a time of crisis that an organization is open to solutions to the basic problem of survival. Organizational members will be eager to adopt new structures that promise to relieve the uncertainty and anxiety generated by a crisis (Shepard, 1969). If the organization has become weak internally, if it contains corruption and indolence at various levels, if the organization is beset by energy-consuming external pressures, and if the organizational elite lack the resources or the will to initiate changes essential for organizational survival, then the organization might well be ready for successful reform from within (Leeds, 1964). Such an organization might not be capable of successfully administering the intimidation rituals.

Internal organization reform is a difficult process. The cause of reform as well as constructive revolution cannot be served by deluding ourselves as to the ease of restructuring human society (Heilbroner, 1972; Schon, 1973). The reformer's life is not an easy one. But neither need he feel doomed from the start by the inevitability of the success of intimidation rituals mobilized against him.

Notes

1. "Nonconforming enclave" refers to the existence of a number of organizational members who, through collective effort, ". . . could potentially divert organization resources from their current commitments, undermine organizational effectiveness, or form a front capable of capturing control of the organization" (Leeds, 1964, p. 155).
2. In a related context, Etzioni (1961, p. 241) asserts, "Once deviant charisma has manifested itself, despite . . . elaborate preventive mechanisms, counter-processes are set into motion. These are of two kinds: those which attempt to eliminate the deviant charisma; and those which seek to limit its effect."
3. It is possible, however, that an organizational change agent might find himself undergoing the rituals of intimidation if he insists that effective action be taken on his proposals for change, particularly if such action would threaten certain organizational power arrangements.

References

Bion, W. R. *Experiences in Groups.* New York: Basic Books, 1959.

Etzioni, A. *A Comparative Analysis of Complex Organizations.* New York: The Free Press, 1961.

Garfinkel, H. "Conditions of Successful Degradation Ceremonies," *American Journal of Sociology,* 1956, *61,* 420–424.

Harshbarger, D. "The Individual and the Social Order: Notes on the Management of Heresy and Deviance in Complex Organizations," *Human Relations,* 1973, *26,* 251–269.

Hartz, L., *The Liberal Tradition in America.* New York: Harcourt, Brace and World, 1955.

Heilbroner, R. L. *In the Name of Profit.* New York: Doubleday, 1972.

Herbert, A. *Soldier.* New York: Holt, Rinehart and Winston, 1972.

Hirschman, A. O. *Exit, Voice, and Loyalty.* Cambridge, Mass.: Harvard University Press, 1970.

Leeds, R. "The Absorption of Protest: A Working Paper," in W. W. Cooper, H. J. Leavitt, and M. W. Shelly, II (eds.), *New Perspectives in Organization Research.* New York: Wiley, 1964.

McCarry, C. *Citizen Nader.* New York: Saturday Review Press, 1972.

Millham, S., Bullock, R., and Cherrett, P. "Social Control in Organizations," *The British Journal of Sociology,* 1972, *23,* 406–421.

Peters, C., and Branch, T. *Blowing the Whistle: Dissent in the Public Interest.* New York: Praeger, 1972.

Schon, D. S. *Beyond the Stable State.* New York: Norton, 1973.

Shepard, H. A. "Innovation-resisting and Innovation-producing Organizations," in W. G. Bennis, K. D. Benne, and R. Chin (Eds.), *The Planning of Change,* Rev. ed. New York: Holt, Rinehart and Winston, 1969, pp. 519–525.

Slater, P. E. "On Social Regression," *American Sociological Review,* 1963, *29,* 339–364.

Slater, P. E. *The Pursuit of Loneliness.* Boston: Beacon Press, 1970.

Thompson, J. C. "How Could Vietnam Happen? An Autopsy," *Atlantic Monthly,* April 1968, *221* (4), 47–53.

Turner, R. H. "Unresponsiveness as a Social Sanction," *Sociometry,* 1973, *36,* 1–19.

Walzer, M. "Corporate Responsibility and Civil Disobedience," *Dissent,* Sept.–Oct., 1969, pp. 395–406.

Wilcox, H. G. "The Cultural Trait of Hierarchy in Middle Class Children," *Public Administration Review,* 1968, *28,* 222–235.

IV-8: The Catbird Seat

James Thurber

Mr. Martin bought the pack of Camels on Monday night in the most crowded cigar store on Broadway. It was theater time and seven or eight men were buying cigarettes. The clerk didn't even glance at Mr. Martin, who put the pack in his overcoat pocket and went out. If any of the staff at F & S had seen him buy the cigarettes, they would have been astonished, for it was generally known that Mr. Martin did not smoke, and never had. No one saw him.

It was just a week to the day since Mr. Martin had decided to rub out Mrs. Ulgine Barrows. The term "rub out" pleased him because it suggested nothing more than the correction of an error—in this case an error of Mr. Fitweiler. Mr. Martin had spent each night of the past week working out his plan and examining it. As he walked home now he went over it again. For the hundredth time he resented the element of imprecision, the margin of guesswork that entered into the business. The project as he had worked it out was casual and bold, the risks were considerable. Something might go wrong anywhere along the line. And therein lay the cunning of his scheme. No one would ever see in it the cautious, painstaking hand of Erwin Martin, head of the filing department of F & S, of whom Mr. Fitweiler had once said, "Man is fallible but Martin isn't." No one would see his hand, that is, unless it were caught in the act.

Sitting in his apartment, drinking a glass of milk, Mr. Martin reviewed his case against Mrs. Ulgine Barrows, as he had every night for seven nights. He began at the beginning. Her quacking voice and braying laugh had first profaned the halls of F & S on March 7, 1941 (Mr. Martin had a head for dates). Old Roberts, the personnel chief, had introduced her as the newly appointed special adviser to the president of the firm, Mr. Fitweiler. The woman had appalled Mr. Martin instantly, but he hadn't shown it. He had given her his dry hand, a look of studious concentration, and a faint smile. "Well," she had said, looking at the papers on his desk, "are you lifting the oxcart out of the ditch?" As Mr. Martin recalled that moment, over his milk, he squirmed slightly. He must keep his mind on her crimes as a special adviser, not on her peccadillos as a personality. This he found difficult to do, in spite of entering an objection and sustaining it. The faults of the woman as a woman kept chattering on in his mind like an unruly witness. She had, for almost two years now, baited him. In the halls, in the elevator, even in his own office, into which she romped now and then like a circus horse, she was constantly shouting these silly questions at him. "Are you lifting the oxcart out of that ditch? Are you tearing up the pea patch? Are you hollering down the rain barrel? Are you scraping around the bottom of the pickle barrel? Are you sitting in the catbird seat?"

It was Joey Hart, one of Mr. Martin's two assistants, who had explained what the gibberish meant. "She must be a Dodger fan," he had said. "Red Barber announces the Dodger games over the radio and he uses those expressions—picked 'em up down South." Joey had gone on to explain one or two. "Tearing up the pea patch" meant going on a rampage; "sitting in the catbird seat" meant sitting pretty, like a batter with three balls and no strikes on him.

Mr. Martin dismissed all this with an effort. It had been annoying, it had driven him near to distraction, but he was too solid a man to be moved to murder by anything so childish. It was fortunate, he reflected as he passed on to the important charges against Mrs. Barrows, that he had stood up under it so well. He had maintained always an outward appearance of polite tolerance. "Why, I even believe you like the woman," Miss Paird, his other assistant, had once said to him. He had simply smiled.

A gavel rapped in Mr. Martin's mind and the case proper was resumed. Mrs. Ulgine Barrows stood charged with willful, blatant, and persistent attempts to destroy the efficiency and system of F & S. It was competent, material, and relevant to review her advent and rise to power. Mr. Martin had got the story from Miss Paird, who seemed always able to find things out. According to her, Mrs. Barrows had met Mr. Fitweiler at a party, where she had rescued him from the embraces of a powerfully built drunken man who had mistaken the president of F & S for a famous retired Middle Western football coach. She had led him to a sofa and somehow worked upon him a monstrous magic. The aging gentleman had jumped to the conclusion there and then that this was a woman of singular attainments, equipped to bring out the best in him and in the firm. A week later he had introduced her into F & S as his special adviser. On that day confusion got its foot in the door. After Miss Tyson, Mr. Brundage, and Mr. Bartlett had been fired and Mr. Munson had taken his hat and stalked out, mailing in his resignation later, old Roberts had been emboldened to speak to Mr. Fitweiler. He mentioned that Mr. Munson's department had been a "little disrupted" and hadn't they perhaps better resume the old system there? Mr. Fitweiler had said certainly not. He had the greatest faith in Mrs. Barrows' ideas. "They require a little seasoning, a little seasoning, is all," he had added.

Mr. Roberts had given it up. Mr. Martin reviewed in detail all the changes wrought by Mrs. Barrows. She had begun chipping at the cornices of the firm's edifice and now she was swinging at the foundation stones with a pickaxe.

Mr. Martin came now, in his summing up, to the afternoon of Monday, November 2, 1942—just one week ago. On that day, at 3 P.M., Mrs. Barrows had bounced into his office. "Boo!" she had yelled. "Are you scraping around the bottom of the pickle barrel?" Mr. Martin had looked at her from under his green eyeshade, saying nothing. She had begun to wander about the office, taking it in with her great, popping eyes. "Do you really need *all* these filing cabinets?" she had demanded suddenly. Mr. Martin's heart had jumped. "Each of these files," he had said, keeping his voice even, "plays an indispensable part in the system of F & S." She had brayed at him, "Well, don't tear up the pea patch!" and gone to the door. From there she had bawled, "But you sure have got a lot of fine scrap here!" Mr. Martin could no longer doubt that the finger was on his beloved department. Her pickaxe was on the upswing, poised for the first blow. It had not come yet; he had received no blue memo from the enchanted Mr. Fitweiler bearing nonsensical instructions deriving from the obscene woman. But there was no doubt in Mr. Martin's mind that one would be forthcoming. He must act quickly. Already a precious week had gone by. Mr. Martin stood up in his living room, still holding his milk glass. "Gentlemen of the jury," he said to himself, "I demand the death penalty for this horrible person."

The next day Mr. Martin followed his routine, as usual. He polished his glasses more often and once sharpened an already sharp pencil, but not even Miss Paird noticed. Only once did he catch sight of his victim; she swept past him in the hall with a patronizing "Hi!" At five-thirty he walked home, as usual, and had a glass of milk, as usual. He had never drunk anything stronger in his life—unless you could count ginger ale. The late Sam Schlosser, the S of F & S, had praised Mr. Martin at a staff meeting several years before for his temperate habits. "Our most efficient worker neither drinks nor smokes," he had said. "The results speak for themselves." Mr. Fitweiler had sat by, nodding approval.

Mr. Martin was still thinking about that red-letter day as he walked over to the Schrafft's on Fifth Avenue near Forty-sixth Street. He got there, as he always did, at eight o'clock. He finished his dinner and the financial page of the *Sun* at a quarter to nine, as he always did. It was his custom after dinner to take a walk. This time he walked down Fifth Avenue at a casual pace. His gloved hands felt moist and warm, his forehead cold. He transferred the Camels from his overcoat to a jacket pocket. He wondered, as he did so, if they did not represent an unnecessary note of strain. Mrs. Barrows smoked only Luckies. It was his idea to puff a few puffs on a Camel (after the rubbing-out), stub it out in the ashtray holding her lipstick-stained Luckies, and thus drag a small red herring across the trail. Perhaps it was not a good idea. It would take time. He might even choke, too loudly.

Mr. Martin had never seen the house on West Twelfth Street where Mrs. Barrows lived, but he had a clear enough picture of it. Fortunately, she had bragged to everybody about her ducky first-floor apartment in the perfectly darling three-story red-brick. There would be no doorman or other attendants; just the tenants of the second and third floors. As he walked along, Mr. Martin realized that he would get there before nine-thirty. He had considered walking north on Fifth Avenue from Schrafft's to a point from which it would take him until ten o'clock to reach the house. At that hour people were less likely to be coming in or going out. But the procedure would have made an awkward loop in the straight thread of his casu-

alness, and he had abandoned it. It was impossible to figure when people would be entering or leaving the house, anyway. There was a great risk at any hour. If he ran into anybody, he would simply have to place the rubbing-out of Ulgine Barrows in the inactive file forever. The same thing would hold true if there were someone in her apartment. In that case he would just say that he had been passing by, recognized her charming house and thought to drop in.

It was eighteen minutes after nine when Mr. Martin turned into Twelfth Street. A man passed him, and a man and a woman talking. There was no one within fifty paces when he came to the house, halfway down the block. He was up the steps and in the small vestibule in no time, pressing the bell under the card that said "Mrs. Ulgine Barrows." When the clicking in the lock started, he jumped forward against the door. He got inside fast, closing the door behind him. A bulb in a lantern hung from the hall ceiling on a chain seemed to give a monstrously bright light. There was nobody on the stair, which went up ahead of him along the left wall. A door opened down the hall in the wall on the right. He went toward it swiftly, on tiptoe.

"Well, for God's sake, look who's here!" bawled Mrs. Barrows, and her braying laugh rang out like the report of a shotgun. He rushed past her like a football tackle, bumping her. "Hey, quit shoving!" she said, closing the door behind them. They were in her living room, which seemed to Mr. Martin to be lighted by a hundred lamps. "What's after you?" she said. "You're as jumpy as a goat." He found he was unable to speak. His heart was wheezing in his throat. "I—yes," he finally brought out. She was jabbering and laughing as she started to help him off with his coat. "No, no," he said. "I'll put it here." He took it off and put it on a chair near the door. "Your hat and gloves, too," she said. "You're in a lady's house." He put his hat on top of the coat. Mrs. Barrows seemed larger than he had thought. He kept his gloves on. "I was passing by," he said. "I recognized—is there anyone here?" She laughed louder than ever. "No," she said, "we're all alone. You're as white as a sheet, you funny man. Whatever *has* come over you? I'll mix you a toddy." She started toward a door across the room. "Scotch-and-soda be all right? But say, you don't drink, do you?" She turned and gave him her amused look. Mr. Martin pulled himself together. "Scotch-and-soda will be all right," he heard himself say. He could hear her laughing in the kitchen.

Mr. Martin looked quickly around the living room for the weapon. He had counted on finding one there. There were andirons and a poker and something in a corner that looked like an Indian club. None of them would do. It couldn't be that way. He began to pace around. He came to a desk. On it lay a metal paper knife with an ornate handle. Would it be sharp enough? He reached for it and knocked over a small brass jar. Stamps spilled out of it and it fell to the floor with a clatter. "Hey," Mrs. Barrows yelled from the kitchen, "are you tearing up the pea patch?" Mr. Martin gave a strange laugh. Picking up the knife, he tried its point against his left wrist. It was blunt. It wouldn't do.

When Mrs. Barrows reappeared, carrying two highballs, Mr. Martin, standing there with his gloves on, became acutely conscious of the fantasy he had wrought. Cigarettes in his pocket, a drink prepared for him—it was all too grossly improbable. It was more than that; it was impossible. Somewhere in the back of his mind a vague idea stirred, sprouted. "For heaven's sake, take off those gloves," said Mrs. Barrows. "I always wear them in the house," said Mr. Martin. The idea began to bloom, strange and wonderful. She put the glasses on a coffee table in front of a sofa and sat on the sofa. "Come over here, you odd little man," she said. Mr. Martin went over and sat beside her. It was difficult getting a cigarette out of the pack of Camels, but he managed it. She held a match for him, laughing. "Well," she said, handing him his drink, "this is perfectly marvelous. You with a drink and a cigarette."

Mr. Martin puffed, not too awkwardly, and took a gulp of the highball, "I drink and smoke all the time," he said. He clinked his glass against hers. "Here's nuts to that old windbag, Fitweiler," he said, and gulped again. The stuff tasted awful, but he made no grimace. "Really, Mr. Martin," she said, her voice and posture changing, "you are insulting our employer." Mrs. Barrows was now all special adviser to the president. "I am preparing a bomb," said Mr. Martin, "which will blow the old goat higher than hell." He had only had a little of the drink, which was not strong. It couldn't be that. "Do you take dope or something?" Mrs. Barrows asked coldly. "Heroin," said Mr. Martin. "I'll be coked to the gills when I bump that old buzzard off." "Mr. Martin!" she shouted, getting to her feet. "That will be all of that. You must go at once." Mr. Martin took another swallow of his drink. He tapped his cigarette out in the ashtray and put the pack of Camels on the coffee table. Then he got up. She stood glaring at him. He walked over and put on his hat and coat. "Not a word about this," he said, and laid an index finger against his lips. All Mrs. Barrows could bring out was "Really!" Mr. Martin put his hand on the doorknob. "I'm sitting in the catbird seat," he said. He stuck his tongue out at her and left. Nobody saw him go.

Mr. Martin got to his apartment, walking, well before eleven. No one saw him go in. He had two glasses of milk after brushing his teeth, and he felt elated. It wasn't tipsiness, because he hadn't been tipsy. Anyway, the walk had worn off all effects of the whisky. He got in bed and read a magazine for a while. He was asleep before midnight.

Mr. Martin got to the office at eight-thirty the next morning, as usual. At a quarter to nine, Ulgine Barrows, who had never before arrived at work before ten, swept into his office. "I'm reporting to Mr. Fitweiler now!" she shouted. "If he turns you over to the police, it's no more than you deserve!" Mr. Martin gave her a look of shocked surprise. "I beg your pardon?" he said. Mrs. Barrows snorted and bounced out of the room, leaving Miss Paird and Joey Hart staring after her. "What's the matter with that old devil now?" asked Miss Paird. "I have no idea," said Mr. Martin, resuming his work. The other two looked at him and then at each other. Miss Paird got up and went out. She walked slowly past the closed door of Mr. Fitweiler's office. Mrs. Barrows was yelling inside, but she was not braying. Miss Paird could not hear what the woman was saying. She went back to her desk.

Forty-five minutes later, Mrs. Barrows left the president's office and went into her own, shutting the door. It wasn't until half an hour later that Mr. Fitweiler sent for Mr. Martin. The head of the filing department, neat, quiet, attentive, stood in front of the old man's desk. Mr. Fitweiler was pale and nervous. He took his glasses off and twiddled them. He made a small, bruffing sound in his throat. "Martin," he said, "you have been with us more than twenty years." "Twenty-two, sir," said Mr. Martin. "In that time," pursued the president, "your work and your—uh—manner have been exemplary." "I trust so, sir," said Mr. Martin. "I have understood, Martin," said Mr. Fitweiler, "that you have never taken a drink or smoked." "That is correct, sir," said Mr. Martin. "Ah, yes." Mr. Fitweiler polished his glasses. "You may describe what you did after leaving the office yesterday, Martin," he said. Mr. Martin allowed less than a second for his bewildered pause. "Certainly sir," he said. "I walked home. Then I went to Schrafft's for dinner. Afterward I walked home again. I went to bed early, sir, and read a magazine for a while. I was asleep before eleven." "Ah, yes," said Mr. Fitweiler again. He was silent for a moment, searching for the proper words to say to the head of the

filing department. "Mrs. Barrows," he said finally, "Mrs. Barrows has worked hard, Martin, very hard. It grieves me to report that she has suffered a severe breakdown. It has taken the form of a persecution complex accompanied by distressing hallucinations." "I am very sorry, sir," said Mr. Martin. "Mrs. Barrows is under the delusion," continued Mr. Fitweiler, "that you visited her last evening and behaved yourself in an—uh—unseemly manner." He raised his hand to silence Mr. Martin's little pained outcry. "It is the nature of these psychological diseases," Mr. Fitweiler said, "to fix upon the least likely and most innocent party as the—uh—source of persecution. These matters are not for the lay mind to grasp, Martin. I've just had my psychiatrist, Dr. Fitch, on the phone. He would not, of course, commit himself, but he made enough generalizations to substantiate my suspicions. I suggested to Mrs. Barrows when she had completed her—uh—story to me this morning, that she visit Dr. Fitch, for I suspected a condition at once. She flew, I regret to say, into a rage, and demanded—uh—requested that I call you on the carpet. You may not know, Martin, but Mrs. Barrows had planned a reorganization of your department—subject to my approval, of course, subject to my approval. This brought you, rather than anyone else, to her mind—but again that is a phenomenon for Dr. Fitch and not for us. So, Martin, I am afraid Mrs. Barrows' usefulness here is at an end." "I am dreadfully sorry, sir," said Mr. Martin.

It was at this point that the door to the office blew open with the suddenness of a gas-main explosion and Mrs. Barrows catapulted through it. "Is the little rat denying it?" she screamed. "He can't get away with that!" Mr. Martin got up and moved discreetly to a point beside Mr. Fitweiler's chair. "You drank and smoked at my apartment," she bawled at Mr. Martin, "and you know it! You called Mr. Fitweiler an old windbag and said you were going to blow him up when you got coked to the gills on your heroin!" She stopped yelling to catch her breath and a new glint came into her popping eyes. "If you weren't such a drab, ordinary little man," she said, "I'd think you'd planned it all. Sticking your tongue out, saying you were sitting in the catbird seat, because you thought no one would believe me when I told it! My God, it's really too perfect!" She brayed loudly and hysterically, and the fury was on her again. She glared at Mr. Fitweiler. "Can't you see how he has tricked us, you old fool? Can't you see his little game?" But Mr. Fitweiler had been surreptitiously pressing all the buttons under the top of his desk and employees of F & S began pouring into the room. "Stockton," said Mr. Fitweiler, "you and Fishbein will take Mrs. Barrows to her home. Mrs. Powell, you will go with them." Stockton, who had played a little football in high school, blocked Mrs. Barrows as she made for Mr. Martin. It took him and Fishbein together to force her out of the door into the hall, crowded with stenographers and office boys. She was still screaming imprecations at Mr. Martin, tangled and contradictory imprecations. The hubbub finally died out down the corridor.

"I regret that this has happened," said Mr. Fitweiler. "I shall ask you to dismiss it from your mind, Martin." "Yes, sir," said Mr. Martin, anticipating his chief's "That will be all" by moving to the door. "I will dismiss it." He went out and shut the door, and his step was light and quick in the hall. When he entered his department he had slowed down to his customary gait, and he walked quietly across the room to the W20 file, wearing a look of studious concentration.

IV-9: Tempered Radicals
How People Use Difference to Inspire Change at Work

Debra E. Meyerson

WHO TEMPERED RADICALS ARE AND WHAT THEY DO

tempered\tem-perd\adj l a: having the elements mixed in satisfying proportions: TEMPERATE b: qualified, lessened, or diluted by the mixture or influence of an additional ingredient: MODERATED

radical\ra-di-kel\adj 1: of, relating to, or proceeding from a root. . . 2: of or relating to the origin: FUNDAMENTAL 3 a: marked by a considerable departure from the usual or traditional: EXTREME 4 b: lending or disposed to make extreme changes in existing views, habits, conditions, or institutions[1]

Martha Wiley sits in her tenth-floor office in a prestigious high-rise building in downtown Seattle. Decorated with earth-tone sofa and chair, overgrown ivies, and floor-to-ceiling ficus tree, her office looks as if she has inhabited it for years. Traditional management books line her bookshelves, interrupted only by a few recognizable volumes on women and management, a stone abstract carving of a woman and child, and a half-dozen silver-framed pictures of her two children and husband. Neatly stacked piles of paper cover her desk, suggesting that an orderly and busy executive sits behind it. Only running shoes and sweats in the corner disrupt the traditional mood of this office.

At 44, Martha has spent the past ten years working her way up to her current position as senior vice president and highest-ranking woman in the real estate division of Western Financial. She shows no sign of slowing down. From the time Martha walked into her office at 7:00 A.M. until this last meeting of the day at 5:30 P.M. she has sprinted from one meeting to the next, stopping only for a one-hour midday workout. This last meeting, before she rushes home to relieve her nanny, was requested by one of her most valued employees to talk about "the future." Her employee nervously explains that since returning from maternity leave with her second child, she has found it increasingly difficult to be in the office five long days each week. She needs to find an alternative way to continue performing her job.

After thirty minutes, the two women agree to a plan: the employee will work two days from home and three days in the office, and every other week she will take one day off. Martha's only request is that the employee remain flexible and be willing to come into the office when it is absolutely necessary for her work.

Martha is pleased that she can meet this employee's needs. In fact, she has actively looked for opportunities to initiate changes that accommodate working parents and that make her department more hospitable to women and people of color. A full 30 percent of her staff now have some sort of flexible work arrangement, despite a lack of formal policy to guide these initiatives. Martha has little doubt that her experiments in work arrangements, even though she has kept them quiet, have been slowly paving the way for broader changes at Western. She had heard that word of her successes was spreading, and that it was only a matter of time before the institution caught up to her lead. (Eventually, the organization did initiate some policies that have given employees more flexibility in arranging their work schedules.)

This example is typical of Martha's approach to change at Western. Though her agenda for change is bold—she wants nothing less than to make the workplace more just and humane—her method of change is modest and incremental. Martha constantly negotiates the path between her desire to succeed within the system and her commitment to challenge and change it; she navigates the tension between her desire to fit in and her commitment to act on personal values that often set her apart. As a result, she continues to find ways to rock the boat, but not so hard that she falls out of it.

All types of organizations—from global corporations to small neighborhood schools—have Marthas. They occupy all sorts of jobs and stand up for a variety of ideals. They engage in small local battles rather than wage dramatic wars, at times operating so quietly that they may not surface on the cultural radar as rebels or change agents. But these men and women of all colors and creeds are slowly and steadily pushing back on conventions, creating opportunities for learning, and inspiring change within their organizations.

Sometimes these individuals pave alternative roads just by quietly speaking up for their personal truths or by refusing to silence aspects of themselves that make them different from the majority. Other times they act more deliberately to change the way the organization does things. They are not heroic leaders of revolutionary change; rather, they are cautious and committed catalysts who keep going and who slowly make a difference. They are "tempered radicals."[2]

COMPETING PULLS

Tempered radicals are people who operate on a fault line. They are organizational insiders who contribute and succeed in their jobs. At the same time, they are treated as outsiders because they represent ideals or agendas that are somehow at odds with the dominant culture.[3]

People operate as tempered radicals for all sorts of reasons. To varying extents, they feel misaligned with the dominant culture because their social identities—race, gender, sexual orientation, age, for example—or their values and beliefs mark them as different from the organizational majority. A tempered radical may, for example, be an African American woman trying to make her company more hospitable to others like herself. Or he may be a white man who holds beliefs about the importance of humane and family-friendly working conditions—or someone concerned for social justice, human creativity, environmental sustainability, or fair global trade practices that differ from the dominant culture's values and interests.

In all cases they struggle between their desire to act on their "different" selves and the need to fit into the dominant culture. Tempered radicals at once uphold their aspiration to be accepted insiders and their commitment to change the very system that often casts them as outsiders. As Sharon Sutton, an African American architect, has explained "We use our right hand to pry open the box so that more of us can get into it while using our left hand to be rid of the very box we are trying to get into."[4]

Tempered radicals are therefore constantly pulled in opposing directions: toward conformity and toward rebellion. And this tension almost always makes them feel ambivalent toward their organizations.* This ambivalence is not uncommon. Psychologists have found that people regularly feel ambivalent about their social relations, particularly toward institutions and people who constrain their freedom. Children, for example, regularly hold strong opposing feelings, such as love and hate, towards their parents.[5] Sociologists have observed a comparable response in employees toward their organizations. They frequently counter organizational attempts to induce conformity and define their identities with efforts to express their individuality.[6] People who differ from the majority are the most likely targets of organizational pressures toward conformity, and at the same time they have the greatest reason to resist them.

A RANGE OF RESPONSES

If ambivalence is the psychological reaction to being pulled in opposing directions, how does it lead people to behave? Some people make a clear choice, relieving their ambivalence by moving clearly in one direction or the other.[7] Others become paralyzed and ultimately so frustrated that escaping the situation is their only relief. Some people flame out in anger. They grow to feel unjustly marginalized and focus on how to avenge perceived wrongs. They feel victimized by their situation and ultimately come to be at the mercy of their own rage. While the pain and anger are often justified, they can become debilitating.

Tempered radicals set themselves apart by successfully navigating a middle ground.

---

*Though this is a pervasive state, it is nonetheless a simplification that people are pulled only in two directions. The nature of the "self" is complex and people are pulled in multiple directions. Here, I emphasize this general stance that results from two types of pulls that are at odds with each other. Later, we discuss the specific content of the pulls toward difference and ways people respond to them.

They recognize modest and doable choices in between, such as choosing their battles, creating pockets of learning, and making way for small wins.

Tempered radicals also become angry, but they mitigate their anger and use it to fuel their actions. In the world of physics, when something is "tempered" it is toughened by alternately heating and cooling. Tempered steel, for example, becomes stronger and more useful through such a process. In a similar way, successfully navigating the seemingly incongruous extremes of challenging and upholding the status quo can help build the strength and organizational significance of tempered radicals.[8]

Note, though, that *tempered* radicals are not radicals. The distinction is important. The word *radical* has several meanings: "of, relating to, or proceeding from a root," or fundamental, as well as "marked by a considerable departure from the usual or traditional," or extreme.[9] Tempered radicals may believe in questioning fundamental principles (e.g., how to allocate resources) or root assumptions, but they do not advocate extreme measures. They work *within* systems, not against them.

Martha, for example, could stridently protest her firm's employment policies or could take a job within an activist organization and advocate for legalistic remedies to the inequities she perceives. But she has chosen the tempered path, in part because she believes that she can personally make more of a difference by working within the system. Her success has created a platform from which to make changes—often seemingly small and almost invisible—which over time have the potential to affect many people.

Martha also has chosen her course because she likes it. She is quick to admit that she loves her job, takes pride and pleasure in moving up the corporate ladder, and enjoys the status and spoils of her success.

She likes living in a comfortable home and taking summer vacations in Europe. While Martha clearly enjoys the privileges that come with success, she believes that the criteria by which the system distributes these privileges need to be changed. Does this belief make her a hypocrite? Or does it simply speak to a duality she and other tempered radicals constantly straddle?

A SPECTRUM OF STRATEGIES

Martha makes choices every day, some conscious, some not, in order to strike a balance. She is committed to chipping away at her "radical" agenda, but not so boldly as to threaten her own legitimacy and organizational success. What is the right balance to strike? More generally, how do tempered radicals navigate the often murky organizational waters to pursue their ideals while fitting in enough to succeed? How do they successfully rock the organizational boat without falling out?

These questions drove my research and form the heart of this book. Not surprisingly, there is no single formula for finding a successful course. Rather, tempered radicals draw on a wide variety of strategies to put their ideals into practice, some more forceful and open, others subtler and less threatening. By choosing among these strategies, each tempered radical creates the balance that is appropriate for him or her in a given situation.

Figure 4-3 presents a spectrum of strategies. It is anchored on the left side by a collection of strategies I have labeled "resisting quietly and staying true to one's 'self,'"[9] which includes acts that quietly express people's "different" selves and acts that are so subtle that they are often not visible to those they would threaten. The other end of the spectrum, "organizing collective action," reflects actions people take to get others involved in deliberate efforts to advance

Resisting quietly and staying true to one's "self"	Turning personal threats into opportunities	Broadening the impact through negotiation	Leveraging small wins	Organizing collective action

FIGURE 4-3   **How Tempered Radicals Make a Difference**

change. Martha's initiatives around flexible work arrangements and similar strategies fall in the category of "leveraging small wins," between the two endpoints.[10]

The spectrum varies along two primary dimensions. First, it speaks to the immediate scope of impact of a tempered radical's actions. At the far left, only the individual actor and a few people in his or her immediate presence are likely to be directly affected by the action. At the opposite end of the spectrum, tempered radicals' actions are meant to provoke broader learning and change. At the far left, the action is invisible or nearly so and therefore provokes little opposition; at the far right, the action is very public and is more likely to encounter resistance.

The second overlapping dimension is the intent underlying a person's actions. At the left, people primarily strive to preserve their "different" selves. Many of these people who operate quietly are not trying to drive broad-based change; they simply want to be themselves and act on their values within an environment where that may feel difficult. Others who resist quietly do intend to provoke some change, but they do it from so far behind the scenes that the actions are not visible. At the right end of the spectrum, people are motivated by their desire to advance broader organizational learning and change. In reality, of course, no one person sits on a specific point on the spectrum, and the strategies themselves blur and overlap. I've distinguished them for the purpose of contrast, rather than to suggest that they

reflect distinct responses. A few examples may help bring this spectrum to life.

Sheila Johnson is a black woman from a working-class family. She has worked her way up to senior vice president in the private equity division at Western Financial. Even though she is one of only a handful of black women in Western's professional ranks, she thought that she would have a reasonable chance of succeeding here because of Western's stated commitment to "diversity." Sheila has tried over the years to keep a low profile, but when she has a chance to help other minorities, or when she feels she must speak up, she usually does so.

Sheila recalls a period when her division's human resource manager complained about the inability to find and hire "qualified minorities" at every level. She knew that standard recruiting procedures at elite college and graduate schools did not constitute the kind of pipeline that would bring in enough diverse candidates to change the face of Western. So she took it upon herself to post descriptions of entry-level jobs throughout minority communities. She did not call attention to her intervention—she didn't ask for permission or insist that the practice become recruiting policy. But through her quiet efforts, she helped create a more diverse pool of candidates, many of whom were hired into entry-level jobs.

Sheila could have broadened the impact of her actions by talking openly about them to enable others to recognize why their standard recruiting practices had failed to fill the bill. Had she made this link clear, she would have pushed others to learn from her actions, which might have led to additional adaptations. Although taking these additional steps could have broadened the impact of her actions, Sheila probably would have had to overcome opposition and assume a potentially greater risk. Because she undertook her actions so quietly, and outside the scope of the organization, I see her behind-the-scenes efforts as an example of "quiet resistance."

John Ziwak is a tempered radical of a different sort. On the surface, he seems to have little in common with Sheila. John has enjoyed all the privileges of growing up in a white middle-class family. He attended an elite university, went to business school at a branch of the University of California, and landed a plum job at a local high-technology company. Six years later, now married with two children, John accepted his current post as manager of business development at Atlas Tech. Although he wants to continue to rise within Atlas, he has no intention of shirking his duties as parent and partner. He can't. His wife also works in a demanding career, and they have always shared responsibilities—and plan to continue.

But it isn't that easy. John, like his wife, faces ongoing pressure from his organization to choose between his commitment to his work and his commitment to his family. John doesn't think that this choice is reasonable; he doesn't believe that he should have to give up his duties at home to prove his commitment and to succeed at Atlas. So in both big and small ways he resists pressure to make such choices and, when appropriate, he challenges prevailing expectations.

One morning John's boss told him that he needed to get on that night's red-eye flight to New York to meet with an important candidate for acquisition. His wife was already out of town and he did not want to ask the babysitter to stay overnight, so he told his boss that he couldn't go: "I told him

that I was sorry I would miss this meeting because I would have brought a lot to the discussion." At the same time, John made sure to point out that he usually can travel, but that he needs some advance notice owing to his wife's travel schedule. John hoped that his boss would understand the broader implications of his resistance—that only a subset of employees can be available on such short notice and that the boss's expectations penalize those who can't pick up and go at the last minute. Whether the boss understood the bigger issue or not, he did begin to give John advance notice about travel whenever possible.

John's act was not dramatic or proactive. A normal reaction in a normal encounter between himself and his boss, it illustrates the strategy I have called "turning threats into opportunities." In this instance, John turned an immediate threat to his personal values and priorities—a request to meet organizational expectations that clash with personal values—into an opportunity for learning. Though John cannot tell how much his boss actually learned, he thinks he made at least a start.

The actions taken by John, Sheila, and Martha fall at different points on the spectrum shown in Figure 4-3. On another day, any one of them might take another action that might fall elsewhere on the spectrum, depending on the opportunity, the situation, the importance of the issue to them, and—as Sheila admitted—"how much sleep [I] had on a given day." Though the actions of some tempered radicals tend toward one end of the spectrum versus the other, most take different actions at different times. It is important to understand that *the spectrum represents different strategies for acting, not different types of people.*

The spectrum does not imply that the quiet responses on the left are in any way less important than those on the right. As we will see, a lifetime of quiet resistance can require enormous patience, conviction, and fortitude. And sometimes persistent behind-the-scenes actions cumulate over time for lasting change or set the context for more public and revolutionary acts.

GUIDING MODELS

Tempered radicals face two primary sets of challenges: those related to the preservation of their "selves" and those that involve advancing an agenda for change from within. Given the centrality of these themes, I want to make explicit my assumptions about how organizations change, the nature of the "self," and how the two are connected through action. These ideas are supported by my own research and guided by the research of others.

HOW ORGANIZATIONS CHANGE

My "theory" of change begins with the notion that organizations are always changing, continually adapting in response to an ongoing flow of inputs and activities.[11] Since most changes are small, incremental adaptations scattered throughout organizations, it may be difficult to recognize this movement as *change,* except retrospectively when small effects have had time to accumulate. In addition, because this process is diffuse, specific *causes* of change are often difficult to pinpoint. Indeed, the change process looks more like random events and chaos than it does rational cause-effect sequences.

Here's an example of the difficulty of pointing to the source of change: Four years after my first interview at Western, a senior human resources officer explained that during the previous five years, the culture had shifted dramatically to be more hospitable to working parents. Whereas once a 5:30 P.M. staff meeting would have been the norm, now it would be seen as completely inappropriate to schedule meetings that late. She was at a loss to point to the specific cause of this shift. The change evolved, she concluded, because many employees, over a period of years, pushed back on the old expectations and set examples for new ones.

This image of change as a continuous and fragmented process bears little resemblance to portraits of episodic and revolutionary change processes you read in many best-selling management texts. These more dramatic pictures of transformation see organizational change occurring not continuously, but periodically as a result of specific trigger events, such as crises, technological innovations, top-down strategic mandates, or bottom-up revolutions. These moments of large-scale transformation are the "figure" against the "ground" of periods of stability.[12] While I do not deny the significance of the occasional crisis, technological innovation, or dramatic intervention, there is significant evidence that such events do not drive much of the adaptation that occurs in organizations.[13]

Many mundane processes that play a part in incremental adaptation disappear as organizational noise if we think of organizational change strictly as episodic and revolutionary. If, however, we look at change as emergent and ongoing, little prods like Sheila's recruiting efforts, which redirect organizational momentum slightly, suddenly appear as significant catalysts of adaptation. So too are small, local accommodations that accumulate into something bigger, such as Martha's flexible work initiative. Interpretation and learning are also pivotal components of this adaptive change process. As people understand things differently, they act differently, and different actions inspire more change.

This view of organizational and social change makes room for lots of normal people to effect change in the course of their everyday actions and interactions. It is an inclusive model that sees people on the margin as well as at the center making a difference in a wide variety of ways. Change agents are not just those characterized by bold visions and strategic savvy, but also those characterized by patience, persistence, and resourcefulness. In this model, change agents are sensitive improvisers who are able to recognize and act on opportunities as they arise.

This view of change and change agents is less dramatic, less inspiring, and less breathless than portraits of grand transformation and revolutionary leaders. It is also more inclusive, more realistic, and more hopeful for most people who care to make a difference in their worlds. I believe it is also more reflective of how most real and lasting change occurs.

THE "SELF"

My assumptions about the "self" also follow from theories that emphasize fluidity. I begin with the notion that who we are—our "selves"—is at the same time stable and mutable.[14] Some aspects of our core identities remain relatively stable, and other, more mercurial aspects are highly sensitive to social cues.[15] For example, some people may want to downplay a part of their identities, but if colleagues see and reinforce those aspects of their identities, they will be compelled to acknowledge these aspects of themselves more explicitly.[16] High-level women who want to ignore their gender identity, for example, are often forced by others who interact with them *as women* to acknowledge and address this aspect of themselves. The reverse is also true. Say an individual defines his religion as a core part of his identity. If, however, others challenge or criticize him when he acts on his faith by, say, reading the Bible in public or praying in a group setting or even talking about being a regular churchgoer, he may be less inclined to express that part of his "self" explicitly in the future. In this context, he may completely suppress it.

Thus the "self" is not immune to external cues; it is built and sustained in relationships with others. Accordingly, both sides of a tempered radical's competing "selves" develop in interactions with others. Since work life tends to be full of relationships that enforce the part of the "self" that identi-

fies with the majority culture, the social cues that lure the "self" toward conformity are strong. It is crucial, then, for people to interact with people inside and outside their organizations who affirm the nonconforming parts of their "selves." These relationships help keep their threatened identities alive.

ACTION, THE "SELF," AND CHANGE

So what is the connection between people's "selves" and the outcomes of organizational learning and change? One piece, as I mentioned earlier, is that asserting the nonconforming aspects of oneself can pave the way for learning and change by questioning current practice and expectations and providing an alternative.

This dynamic can also be self-reinforcing. When people act in ways that outwardly express a valued part of their selves, they make that part of their selves "real." The act of putting this part of themselves out in the world for affirmation and challenge often reminds them, and others, that they will not silence these valued parts of their selves and that they will not allow the dominant culture to define who they are. Not only is action driven by people's valued selves, but it helps construct and fortify those selves.

Actions produce other consequences as well. When people act on their different selves, they make it possible for others who share their social identities and values to find each other. When environmentalists do something *as environmentalists,* for instance, they become visible to other environmentalists. Gay people report that once they come out of the closet, they suddenly discover dozens of other coworkers who are gay. In this way, people's actions have the unintended effect of creating relationships with similar others, thus making the context more friendly.

Actions can also bolster people's sense of efficacy, proving to themselves and to others that they can make a difference, even if the direct consequences of their actions are small.[17] When people believe they can make a difference, they are more likely to search for opportunities to act, which makes it more likely that they will locate opportunities. When people recognize opportunities for action, their environment will seem less threatening and more amenable to action.[18]

This self-fulfilling cycle suggests the crucial importance of *action* as a starting point and trigger for a wide range of outcomes. Actions help develop sustaining relationships with similar others, affirm threatened "selves," generate organizational learning and change, fuel a sense of efficacy, and heighten attention to opportunities. The first and last of these create a context more amenable to action.[19] (See Figure 4-4.) While most people talk about action being driven by people who see themselves as change agents, I've observed how the reverse is true—and very powerful; actions transform people from the stance of passive bystander or victim to that of constructive agent.

WHY PEOPLE ACT AS TEMPERED RADICALS

Why do people bother to navigate such a difficult maze of conformity and rebellion? Why might you want to do so? Given the multitude of organizational processes that steer people toward conformity, wouldn't it be easier to go along, at least until you have "enough" power to make "real" change without jeopardizing your job? Challenging the status quo can be very risky, which puts an extra burden on tempered radicals to perform well in their jobs. Wouldn't it be simpler to find an organization where all parts of your core "self" are valued, where you don't face extra pressures? It certainly is not easy to act in ways that keep these competing selves alive, nor is it comfortable psychologically to remain in an ongoing state of ambivalence. So why do people take this path?

The most straightforward answer is that they don't like the alternatives. While the lures toward conformity can be overwhelming in some contexts, for some people this route is unacceptably demoralizing and draining. If they conform completely, they essentially silence a core part of their selves. Some people feel that they are "selling out" on their values and turning their backs on their communities. This route can also enervate people, as they come to see themselves as victims of their situations. For many of the tempered radicals I interviewed, complete conformity was not an option.

A person could also stay consistently true to his or her self, and simply start fresh when the friction gets too great to bear or

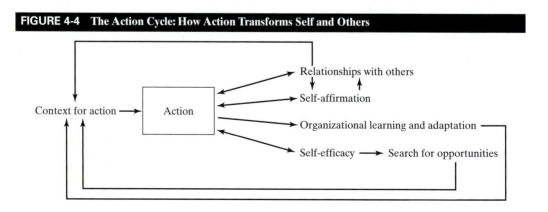

FIGURE 4-4 The Action Cycle: How Action Transforms Self and Others

Context for action → Action
- Relationships with others
- Self-affirmation
- Organizational learning and adaptation
- Self-efficacy → Search for opportunities

when he or she is forced from the organization. But most people have neither the desire nor the luxury to risk the alienation (and displacement) that would likely result. Those who end in this direction don't survive in conventional organizations; they are often the ones better suited to the role of pure radical, advocating from outside the organization, from a position closer to their ideals.

With these alternatives, we might ask the opposite question: Why aren't more people tempered radicals? The obvious answer, as I mentioned earlier, is that it creates a difficult ambivalence to tolerate and manage. And for many, the rewards of conformity—combined with the risk of exclusion—are too great to pass up. While this simple answer is undoubtedly true, I suggest that in fact *many people are tempered radicals and just don't realize it.* They struggle silently with their ambivalence, reluctant to acknowledge it and uncertain how they might make it work better for themselves and constructively for their organizations.

Fortunately, when people do act on their convictions, they set in motion a powerful cycle (see Figure 4-4) and make a start at managing the ambiguity of their situations. Even small acts can have far-reaching effects, affirming an actor's sense of self, fueling their sense of efficacy, and making a difference for others.

TEMPERED RADICALS AS EVERYDAY LEADERS

Few of the tempered radicals mentioned in these pages see themselves as heroes or champions of organizational revolutions. They often are not the CEOs, presidents, or senior professionals in their organizations, and yet they sometimes play a role in organizational adaptation as crucial as that of their colleagues with more authority. They have become the "everyday leaders" in their organizations, often unrecognized but nevertheless essential agents of organizational learning and change.

When these individuals push back on conventional expectations, challenge assumptions about what is "normal," and revise work practices to meet unaddressed needs, they push others to learn and force systems to adapt to impending challenges. Martha's initiatives, for example, have responded to the needs of certain employees who cannot continue to work effectively in traditional, full-time work arrangements. As word of her successes has spread, the organization has been challenged to confront this issue in a more systemic way. John's push back on his boss' expectations about travel brought into focus entrenched practices and assumptions that inadvertently penalized certain groups of employees and made them less effective at work. Sheila's efforts to hire from the community addressed an immediate recruiting challenge her group was facing. Had she intervened more visibly, she could have pointed to the limitations of the organizationally endorsed approach to recruiting. To different extents, each of these relatively small actions took steps toward surfacing and addressing an important adaptive challenge facing the system.[20]

Tempered radicals also provoke learning and adaptation through the perspective they bring as people who are not fully assimilated into the system. Tempered radicals are more likely to think "out of the box" because they are not fully in the box. As "outsiders within," they have both a critical and a creative edge.[21] They speak new "truths."

For example, someone concerned about environmental sustainability probably has a different view of time than others, seeing the longterm effects of current actions. That person thus brings an entirely new set of perspectives, asks different questions, and might pose different solutions to problems such as urban growth and development. In the film industry, we have the example of Robert Redford, who is both an insider and yet a self-appointed outsider, an atypical member of the film community. His innovations in independent filmmaking, born as an alternative to Hollywood, have been an influential force for creativity *inside* Hollywood. His stance as an "outsider within" gives him a critical edge that both questions "normal" ways of doing things in his profession and offers new possibilities. Redford is, in many ways, a quintessential tempered radical, and whether he intends to be or not, a leader within his industry.

Conclusion

Tempered-radical-as-leader is a more inclusive, realistic, and inspiring way to think about leadership—and life—than are images of leadership found in fairy tales and the popular business press. To gauge the efficacy of one's efforts against portraits of leaders as lone crusaders at the helm of dramatic transformation is to resign oneself to falling short, to feeling that one's efforts have not made *a real* difference. The depiction of tempered-radical-as-leader provides more compelling metrics and ideals. It allows that through a wide range of ways people make a difference for others, create new truths, and live lives of integrity, meaning, and purpose.

Tempered radicals exist at all levels in all kinds of organizations. Not only do they exist, but they persist and, to varying extents, succeed. Even if they don't feel "radical" or have an explicit agenda for change, countless people act as tempered radicals, at least over some portions of their careers and under certain circumstances. They know that the challenges they pose may bring some risk to their careers, yet many feel that going along in silence can bring even greater costs to their souls.

Notes

1. *Merriam-Webster's Collegiate Dictionary,* 10th ed. (Springfield, MA: Merriam-Webster, 1998).

2. Debra Meyerson and Maureen Scully, "Tempered Radicalism and the Politics of Ambivalence and Change," *Organizational Science* 6, no. 5 (1995): 585–601.

3. In her autobiographical account, *Trespassing: My Sojourn in the Halls of Privilege* (New York: Houghton Mifflin, 1997), Gwendolyn Parker describes the feeling of being an outsider even as she climbed up the ladder of success at American Express Company.

4. Sharon Sutton, *Finding Our Voice in a Dominant Key* (unpublished manuscript, University of Michigan, 1991).

5. See Sigmund Freud, *Civilization and its Discontents* (New York: Norton, 1961).

6. On ambivalence see Gideon Kunda's *Engineering Culture* (Philadelphia: Temple University Press, 1991). Kunda describes the way people construct their selves in relation to a culture that attempts to be all-consuming. See also Ken Smith and David Berg. *Paradoxes of Group Life* (San Francisco: Jossey-Bass, 1987) and Blake Ashforth and Fred Mael. "The Power of Resistance: Sustaining Valued Identities," in *Power and Influence in Organizations.* ed. Roderick Kramer and Margaret Neale (Thousand Oaks, CA: Sage, 1998), 89–102. Both these works speak to the opposing inclinations of self in relation to conformity-inducing social institutions. See also Neil Smelsner's 1998 Presidential Address to the American Sociological Association: Neil J. Smelsner, "The Rational and the Ambivalent in the Social Sciences," *American Sociological Review* 63 (1998): 1–15 for a discussion of the ubiquity of ambivalence in social life and the conditions that foster it.

7. These two strategies are comparable to the strategies of "exit" and "loyalty" described by Albert Hirschman, *Exit, Voice and Loyalty* (Cambridge, MA: Harvard University Press, 1970), in this classic treatment of people's ambivalence toward the state and constraining social institutions.

8. Meyerson and Scully, "Tempered Radicalism."

9. *Merriam-Webster's New Collegiate Dictionary,* 10th ed. (Springfield, MA: Merriam-Webster, 1998).

10. Karl E. Weick, "Small Wins," *American Psychologist* 39, no. 1 (1984): 40–49.

11. Karl E. Weick and Robert E. Quinn, "Organizational Change and Development," *Annual Review of Psychology* 50 (1999): 361–386; Karl E. Weick, "Emergent Change as a Universal in Organizations," in *Breaking the Code of Change,* ed. Michael Beer and Nitin Noria (Boston: Harvard Business School Press, 2000), 223–241.

12. Michael Tushman and Elaine Romanelli, "Organizational Determinants of Technological Change: Toward a Sociology of Technological Evolution," in *Research in Organizational Behavior* 14, ed. Barry Staw and Larry Cummings (Greenwich, CT: JAI, 1992), 311–347.

13. Weick and Quinn, "Organizational Change and Development."

14. One's identity—and therefore one's deviance based on identity—is defined in part by one's cultural and historical situation. What being an Indian woman means is different in the United States than it is in India. After an Indian woman spends time in the United States, it means something different to be a woman when she returns her home country. The point is, it is hard to answer the question "who am I?" in a vacuum. People's identities change over time and place, and they change as their place in a web of relations changes. This notion is relatively alien to Western notions of the "self" as autonomous and stable, but it is familiar within Eastern conceptions of self as defined relationally. See Dorinne Kondo, *Crafting Selves: Power, Gender, and Discourses of Identity in a Japanese Workplace* (Chicago: University of Chicago Press, 1990) and Hazel Marcus and Shinobu Kitayama, "Culture and the Self: Implications for Cognition, Emotion, and Motivation," *Psychological Review* 98, no. 2 (1991): 224–253. What this means for tempered radicals is that the tensions they experience and their feelings of deviance are specific to time and context. And, although I view ambivalence as a starting point, how people experience ambivalence, the extent to which their selves are at odds, and what they do

with these felt tensions can vary enormously over time and situation.

15. It has also been found that people's conception of the "self" is culturally specific, e.g., Marcus and Kitayama, "Culture and the Self."

16. William B. Swann, Jr., "Identity Negotiation: Where Two Roads Meet." *Journal of Personality and Social Psychology* 53, no. 6 (1987): 1038–1051; Viktor Gecas, "The Self-concept," *Annual Review of Sociology* 8 (1982): 1–33. See also Erving Goffman, *The Presentation of Self in Everyday Life* (New York: Doubleday, 1959).

17. Karl E. Weick, "Small Wins."

18. Jane E. Dutton, "The Making of Organizational Opportunities: An Interpretive Pathway to Organizational Change," in *Research in Organizational Behavior* 15, ed. Barry Staw and Larry Cummings (Greenwich, CT: JAI, 1992). 195–226. Dutton describes the psychological mechanisms by which "opportunity framing" motivates action. The first of these is the suppression of perceived threat, which lowers anxiety and allows for greater search for response options. The second is a "positive gloss" effect, which heightens one's sense of mastery and efficacy, which in turn provides motivation for action.

19. Ibid.

20. Ronald Heifetz, *Leadership Without Easy Answers* (Cambridge, MA: Harvard University Press, 1994). Heifetz, who teaches a popular leadership course at Harvard's Kennedy School of Government, argues that enabling a system to meet its adaptive challenges is the most crucial component of leadership.

21. Patricia Hill Collins, "Learning from the Outsider Within," *Journal of Social Problems* 33, no. 6 (1986): 53. Sociologists have made similar observations about the creativity and insight black women bring to the field of sociology as a result in part of their "outsider within" status in the field. Outsiders within occupy a special place— they become different people, and their difference sensitizes them to patterns that may be more difficult for established sociological insiders to see.

IV-10: More Plants Go 24/7, and Workers Are Left at Sixes and Sevens
Long Shifts, Odd Schedules Disrupt Life Off the Job; Safety, Health Are Issues

Timothy Aeppel

Sunday is rough for a pastor.

DANVILLE. Va.—Herman Lea recalls the chilly January day in 1996 when he accepted "the calling" from God to become a preacher. Little did he know that this would put him on a collision course with a different sort of higher power: Goodyear Tire & Rubber Co.

The world's biggest tire maker soon announced that its sprawling Danville plant, where Mr. Lea works, would join most other Goodyear factories around the world in producing tires around the clock, seven days a week, including Sunday. The whole tire industry has gone this way, the company said, and Danville had to adapt or die.

Mr. Lea now works at least two Sundays each month, which means there is no way he could become a pastor. He receives invitations to fill in for those on vacation or ill, but that's tough, too. "I've had to give up a lot of engagements" to preach because of conflicts with work, he says.

Mr. Lea and his co-workers have discovered the unspoken reality of manufacturing: Increasingly it is structured around the machines, rather than the people who run them. The reason is economics. Every hour a costly plant sits idle is a drain on a company's bottom line, something no one can afford in the face of today's sharply slowing economy.

Compounding the new schedule is Goodyear's move to 12-hour shifts, which is common when companies go nonstop. Mr. Lea gets more days off with the longer shifts, but the longer workday is far more grueling for the 50-year-old. Moreover, his days off vary each week, complicating his life. He had a stroke in February, which he blames partly on the stress of juggling his schedule.

Running factories nonstop can take a heavy toll on workers, disrupting homes and relationships. Single parents, Little League coaches, students as well as preachers must contort their lives to meet their schedules, or give up things they love to do. The pressures affect not only workers' quality of life, but also their health and safety. Critics say workers often don't get enough rest to do their jobs safety.

• • • • • • • • • •
A MASSIVE CONVERSION

No one tracks how many factories have gone this way, but economists and consultants say it has become more common. Bill Sirois, vice president of Circadian Technologies Inc., a consulting firm that assists companies shifting to nonstop operations, says industries such as steel and chemicals always ran plants continuously, because it was costly and hazardous to stop and restart them. But "in the last decade or so, you've seen a massive conversion to running 24/7," Mr. Sirois says, and the practice has spread to the manufacture of things such as plastics and toothpaste.

Joseph Martha, a consultant with Mercer Management Consulting, says he sees more companies shutting plants as part of restructuring, but managing to maintain overall capacity by running their remaining factories continuously. "I've seen it accelerate in the first half of this year and the last quarter of last year," as the economy slowed, he says.

Unilever PLC, the Anglo-Dutch consumer-products company, said last year it would shed 100 factories world-wide and consolidate in its remaining 150 locations. "It's not that we're going to start working all our factories 24 hours a day," says Stephen Milton, a company spokesman, although many locations will do just that, including a toothpaste factory in Jefferson City, Mo., that plans to go nonstop in September. Some Unilever plants, such as ice cream factories, will work continuously only when demand calls for it.

DESIGNED TO RUN NONSTOP

As plants become more automated, they are often designed to run nonstop. Inside Delphi Automotive Systems Corp.'s new plant in Cortland, Ohio, the air temperature and humidity level are closely monitored and held constant—at the level the company has found allows the banks of plastic injection-molding machines to work more smoothly and therefore produce better parts and go longer between repairs.

Those who move to continuous operation often find it tough to implement and tough to maintain. Last year, at the peak of the economic boom, the GNB industrial-power division of Exide Technologies pushed to get the four of its five factories in the U.S. and Canada that weren't on continuous operations to make the change. The maker of industrial batteries had a huge backlog of orders and needed to increase capacity.

Two plants made the switch, but the union at another plant voted against it, and negotiations at the fourth factory continue. In the meantime, the economy slumped and slowing demand forced one plant that had switched to reverse course.

The company says it still prefers running plants continuously if it can, because it saves money and allows GNB to boost production faster in response to increases in demand. And "once an operation goes 7/24, you don't want to mess with the schedule," says Tim Robertson, a spokesman, since getting people to accept it is so difficult in the first place.

Which points up one of the biggest sticking points: Many workers don't like continuous operations. Some unions have gone on strike over it. In Danville, the union initially fought Goodyear's plan, but eventually relented. It didn't hurt that the plant needed to hire about 500 more people in order to fill the extended shifts. That fattened the union's roster and gave the faded textile town some badly needed jobs.

Mr. Sirois, the consultant, says how people react to continuous operations hinges on where they are in life. "If you're a single parent, you now have weekend child-care requirements," he says. "If you're a student, now you find it hard to make it to courses."

Mr. Sirois estimates that 90% of companies that adopt nonstop schedules move to 12-hour shifts. The longer workdays mean not just more days off but more weekends off each month. Companies consider that crucial in enticing workers to accept continuous schedules. Some also pay premiums to make up for the overtime pay which is lost when Saturdays and Sundays become just another set of workdays.

The increasingly prevalent longer shifts have fueled the debate over whether they undermine safety and quality. Mr. Sirois says such shifts don't necessarily cause such problems, noting that a worker with more days off each month overall is less likely to build up sleep deprivation over time.

Research by safety experts, labor unions and physicians has found a link between worker fatigue and accidents. "Fatigue undermines every aspect of human capability — from decision-making abilities to alertness," says Mark Rosekind, president of Alertness Solutions, a consulting firm in Cupertino, Calif., and former director of the Fatigue Countermeasures Program at NASA's Ames Research Center. He says the most dangerous period is 3 A.M. to 5 A.M. — when the body's internal clock is at its lowest ebb. Dr. Rosekind estimates 15% to 20% of all accidents in transportation operations, for example, are related to fatigue.

But the debate is rife with conflicting evidence. A 1998 study in Germany determined that the risk of accidents starts to rise rapidly after nine hours on a job. Circadian Technologies, the consulting firm, has found workers themselves rate the physical demands of eight-hour and 12-hour shifts about the same. Part of this may be a form of worker denial. Fatigue is often difficult for workers or others to recognize in themselves. Many feel it a point of pride to work through their tiredness.

There are no statistics that compare injury rates at plants that run continuously with rates at other factories. Evaluating the potential health and safety impact of 24/7 operations is also complicated by a number of factors. How shifts are structured can vary greatly from one plant to another. For instance, plants that shift workers from days

to nights are more likely to cause sleep disruptions than plants that assign workers to fixed shifts. And workers themselves can respond differently to the same demands, depending on their age and general health.

● ● ● ● ● ● ● ● ● ● ●
SHIFT INTO DEPRESSION

For Michael Tucker, the demands of around-the-clock operations eventually plunged him into depression. The 51-year-old works at Corning Inc.'s factory in Blacksburg, Va., making ceramic cores for catalytic converters used on automobiles. The plant has always operated continuously with 12-hour shifts. But Mr. Tucker, who has worked there 12 1/2 years, says he never got used to it, particularly steadily switching from days to nights. Corning doesn't believe it is fair to give half the work force plum day shifts, so workers have to alternate.

"You're tired all the time, and it keeps you feeling down," Mr. Tucker says. He often got home too tired to do things around the house, instead focusing on resting for his next stint at the factory. He found himself spending less time with his wife and five children.

About four years ago, he sought counseling provided through Corning. He was put on antidepressants, which helped. But the turning point came in January — when he won a coveted specialized position that allows him to work only day shifts for the next 18 months. He still puts in 12-hour days. "But at least now I'm getting quality rest," he says. "When you're constantly switching from days to nights, you feel trapped." He has stopped taking the medication. His main concern now, he says, is what will happen when he goes back to alternating shifts.

Mr. Tucker's counselor, James Walsh, works with factory workers from a variety of companies in the region, most of them on some form of continuous operations. He says workers never come to him "saying, 'My problem is shift work,' but there's no question that it's a factor." Disruptive work schedules don't cause depression, but if they interfere with sleep patterns and other normal routines, they can add to the stress and demands that do, he says.

Such schedules also are hard on relationships. "If you're off on a Wednesday, Thursday and a Friday—and the rest of the world is working—you find other avenues to fill your time, other people to spend your time with," Mr. Walsh says.

A DIFFERENT LIFESTYLE

Advocates of continuous operations say most people do adapt. And for its part, Goodyear says there are advantages that make up for the disruptions. "It's a different lifestyle," says Darrell Finney, the Danville plant manager, especially for workers who have never had days off in the middle of the week. "But under this schedule, they get a three-day weekend every other weekend. So people with small children love it: they get more time with their children."

Danny Travis is a believer. When Danville made the switch in 1998, he had worked nights for 23 years, starting at 11 P.M., finishing at 7 A.M. Under the new schedule, workers had to be divided into four new groups, two of which were assigned to days. With his seniority, Mr. Travis was able to land a day shift.

He also likes the chunks of time off that the new schedule affords. During a recent week, for instance, he was off on Monday and Tuesday, worked Wednesday and Thursday, and then had a three-day weekend. But even he admits such a pattern can disrupt things. When he worked his old night shift, he would usually sleep until early afternoon—leaving him plenty of daylight hours every day of the week to do chores.

Workers at the plant juggle their lives with mixed results. Mr. Travis coaches his daughter's fast-pitch softball team, and the league has accommodated him by scheduling his games in the evenings.

But Mike Bakers, a maintenance worker at the plant who used to be very active in his church, often had trouble making board meetings. So he stopped serving. This year he also stopped working as an umpire for high-school baseball games. This is the first year I haven't umpired in I don't know how long," he says. "It's hard to give it up."

The Danville plant, which opened in 1966, has 49 acres under its low-slung roofs. In the past, Goodyear would spend heavily to build worker amenities at such plants, something few companies would consider today. The plant has a golf course, a shooting range, baseball diamonds and a stocked fishing pond. But many workers say the new schedule has left them with little energy to make much use of them. Part of this is certainly due to broader changes in society. With more two-income families, there is more pressure on working people to cover a variety of family responsibilities, such as attending children's soccer matches or shopping for groceries.

But one of the Danville plant's most striking features—though relatively common in the Bible Belt—is the number of preachers who work there. Among its 2,500 workers there are about 20 employees who are ministers. Most are like Mr. Lea, doing it part time.

Julius B. Baldridge, who goes by "J.B.," is one of the few who serve as full-time pastors. He has a flock of about 35 at the Bethlehem Baptist Church in the nearby town of Brosville, Va. His night shift sometimes forces him to shoehorn in his pulpit work. On weekends when he works, he leaves the plant at 7 A.M. Sunday, preaches his morning sermon, takes a nap, then gets up and preaches again at 5:30 in the afternoon.

Then, he's off to work for the start of his shift again at 7 P.M. He also has other duties, like visiting people in the hospital.

Even so, Mr. Baldridge says he's never too tired to preach. "Preaching give me life," he says. Then pointing around him dourly at the plant, he adds: "I get tired *here.*"

Still, his schedule has taken a toll on his marriage, he says. His wife works as an insurance clerk in a doctor's office and they're now raising two of their grandchildren on top of everything else. "Right now," he says, "we're going through a stage when I walk through the door, she's saying goodbye" on the way out to work.

● ●

A DREAM POSTPONED

Mr. Lea has adapted to the new schedule as best he can. He helped set up a "praise service," held each Sunday inside the plant at 6 A.M. He also has gone ahead with his seminary studies through a night course. He has one semester left. And every Friday, he goes to the county jail to minister to prisoners.

Strolling between the empty pews at the River Zion Missionary Baptist Church, Mr. Lea says his dream of being a pastor is postponed, not forgotten. The church, set on a country lane in Blaneh, N.C., is the one he grew up with; his father helped build it, and several of the stained-glass windows carry the names of family members who donated money to pay for them. It was here that he gave his first sermon, in May of 1996. He doesn't covet the job of the current pastor, figuring that he'll have his own church one day.

He worries about his age. People want young pastors these days, he says, but he want to keep his factory job at least until his daughter, Cherie, is through college in two years. Goodyear pays him well: more than $19 an hour.

The solution, he says, is to retire and devote himself to finding a flock. "I pray I will soon," says Mr. Lea.

IV-11: The Trickle-Down Effect
Policy Decisions, Risky Work, and The *Challenger* Tragedy

Diane Vaughan

The *Challenger* launch decision often is used in business schools and management training seminars as a classic exemplar of how-not-to-do-it. Depending on how the cause of the decision failure is portrayed, however, the lessons for administrators change. In the months following the *Challenger* disaster, the official investigations and media accounts led many citizens to believe that managerial wrongdoing was behind the launch decision. Locating the cause in managers and their potential for unethical conduct, the preventive strategy seemed clear: strengthen individual ethics. As scholars began to analyze the event, however, many located the cause in the dynamics of the teleconference itself. Although this research is diverse and eludes easy classification into tidy categories, three general themes appeared: poor engineering analysis, communication failure, and (perhaps most prominently) Groupthink. Again, strategies to prevent similar decision failures in other workplaces flowed logically from the causes identified: improving training for engineers, sharpening communication and decision-making skills, or altering group dynamics.

Another body of scholarship looked beyond the teleconference, locating the cause of the disaster in NASA's political, economic, and institutional environment. This research indicated that historic policy decisions made by top agency administrators, responding to environmental threats to the agency and their own power base, changed the culture of the space agency so that production pressures dominated the workplace. The thesis—sometimes explicitly stated, sometimes implied—was that decisions by lower participants, in particular, NASA middle managers, were influenced by an organization culture in which production concerns took priority over safety. These scholars directed attention to environmental contingencies that affected the NASA organization. Locating the cause of the flawed decision in NASA's own distinctive history created the impression that the tragedy was an anomaly—a mistake peculiar to NASA. Also, this research left an empirical gap: it did not show *how* those historic policy decisions and the culture that resulted affected engineering decisions about the Solid Rocket Boosters, the technical cause of the disaster. Not only were specific lessons for managers making daily decisions difficult to identify, but the idea that the organization was uniquely flawed led many to conclude that "it couldn't happen here."

What happened at NASA was no anomaly, but something that could happen in any organization. Drawing on archival data and interviews unused by other analysts, this research revises conventional wisdom about the *Challenger* launch decision in several ways. First, it affirms that prior policy decisions played a pivotal role in the *Challenger* tragedy. Thus, this analysis shifts attention

from the launch decision to NASA's larger system of organizational relations and to the past. Second, it reveals how the decisions of top space agency administrators trickled down through the organization, altering both the structure and culture of the organization, affecting official engineering risk assessments made at the bottom of the hierarchy. Third, it affirms that production concerns permeated the culture of the workplace, but challenges conventional understandings by revealing that the culture was governed by three cultural imperatives: production concerns, bureaucratic accountability, and the original technical culture. Fourth, it shows how this complex culture affected all people doing the risky work, managers and engineers alike.

The connection between policy decisions and mistakes in the workplace is an issue relevant to all organizations, but of particular concern where loss of life and/or extensive social harm is a possible outcome. Many organizations that do risky work are devoting resources to identifying the causes of errors and eliminating them: for example, hospitals are concerned with errors in surgery, anesthesiology, medication, and diagnosis: U.S. Forest Service Wildland Firefighters explore decision making by firefighters in a crisis; social work agencies try to eliminate errors in placement and monitoring that result in abuse and death of children; naval aircraft carriers aim to avoid disasters at sea; the U.S. Air Force seeks to eliminate deaths in military training exercises and errors in judgment during combat; the FAA targets decision errors in flawed aircraft production and maintenance, airline cockpit crews, and air traffic control. What all these examples of risky work have in common is that decisions are being made under conditions of uncertainty in complex organizations, where history and political contingency are facts of life. Yet inmost of these organizations, error-reducing activities have concentrated upon the decision-making situation and the individuals who participated in it. Much less attention—if any—is paid to the organizational system and its environment, as they contribute to decision errors.

To be effective, strategies for control should target the causes of a problem. The purpose of this discussion is to examine the *Challenger* launch decision in order to draw attention to factors that systematically produce errors in organizations but routinely receive little attention in error-reduction efforts. First, I contrast the conventional wisdom about events at NASA with contradictory information found in primary data sources in order to challenge commonly-held views about the launch decision and prepare readers for the analysis that follows. Second, I analyze the history of decision making at NASA, 1977–1985, and the eve of the *Challenger* launch teleconference. An overview, I lay out the structure of the argument only, omitting details that support my inferences and claims. This discussion will be suggestive, rather than definitive, isolating a few key factors for attention. Interested readers should see the original.[1] Third, I present new information describing the social impact of the *Challenger* disaster on the space agency. These sections lay the groundwork for a discussion of three targets for administrators interested in reducing the possibility of mishap, mistake, and disaster: policy decisions, organization culture, and signals of danger.

REVISING THE CONVENTIONAL WISDOM

The Presidential Commission investigating the *Challenger* disaster revealed that the O-ring failure on the Solid Rocket Boosters was preceded by questionable middle management actions and decisions. First, the Commission learned of a midnight hour teleconference on the eve of the *Challenger* launch, in which contractor engineers located at Morton Thiokol in Wasatch, Utah, protested launching *Challenger* in the unprecedented cold temperatures predicted for launch time the next morning. Following a heated discussion, NASA middle managers at Marshall Space Flight Center proceeded with the launch, apparently violating safety rules about passing information up the hierarchy in the process. Second, the Commission discovered that in the years preceding the January 28, 1986 tragedy, NASA repeatedly proceeded with shuttle launches in spite of recurring damage on the O-rings. They were flying with known flaws, accepting more risk each time.

The Commission concluded that the disaster was not simply a technical failure, but an organizational failure of tragic proportion. Based primarily on the Presidential Commission's findings about economic strain, production pressures at the space agency, and repeated safety rule violations by Marshall managers responsible for the Solid Rocket Booster Project, the conventional wisdom conveyed by the media was this: NASA managers at Marshall Space Flight Center, warned that the launch was risky, succumbed to production pressures and violated safety rules in order to stick to the schedule.

The televised hearings of the Presidential Commission and Volume I of the Commission's report were the basis of the media-generated conventional wisdom as well as subsequent research by scholars. However, primary data sources stored at the National Archives showed that many taken-for-granted aspects of the tragedy were more complex than they appeared and, in many cases, completely mistaken. The archival record contained many surprises about the technology. The shuttle had not "exploded," as most media accounts reported. According to engineers, there was a fireball and a structural breakup, but no explosion. More surprising, the technical cause of the failure was not as the conventional wisdom portrayed. The primary O-ring in the aft joint of the right Solid Rocket Booster was badly charred, but the charred material itself helped to seal the joint. Then, 50 seconds into the launch, an unprecedented, unpredicted wind shear violently shook the vehicle, jarring loose the charred material and allowing the hot propulsion gases to penetrate the booster joint. Had it not been for the wind shear, the joint would have remained sealed through the two-minute burn of the boosters, and *Challenger*—barring other technical failures—would have returned.

Equally startling were original documents and archival data, unexamined by other researchers, that revealed that much of the conventional wisdom about NASA decision making also was wrong. Some examples:

• In the years preceding the *Challenger* teleconference, NASA repeatedly launched with known flaws in the Solid Rocket Boosters. Memos, written by worried engineers during this period, created the public impression that NASA managers had a history of ignoring engineering concerns. But Morton Thiokol engineers, not NASA managers, initiated official risk assessments and launch recommendations about the Solid Rocket Boosters. All official launch decisions originated with contractor engineers at the bottom of the launch decision chain. For each of the controversial decisions prior to 1986, Thiokol engineers—the very engineers who authored the memos and protested the *Challenger* launch—had repeatedly recommended that NASA managers accept risk and fly.

• On the eve of the launch, the dichotomous view of "good" engineers versus "bad" managers was not borne out. Not all working engineers were opposed to the launch: only the ones who were opposed were called to testify before the Presidential Commission. Moreover, eleven of the fourteen engineers present that night stated that Thiokol's engineering analysis was flawed and unlikely to convince managers.

• Rumor had it that NASA managers needed to launch because of a planned hook-up between the *Challenger* crew and President Reagan, who was making his State of the Union address the evening of the launch. But NASA rules prohibited outside communication with the crew during the first 48 hours in orbit because the crew were too busy, and those rules had never been violated. Moreover, every launch has two launch windows, morning and afternoon. If NASA managers truly believed they were making an unsafe decision but felt an urgent pressure to get the launch off, they could have launched *Challenger* in the afternoon when the temperature was predicted to reach between 40 and 50 degrees, with no political repercussions for the program.

• The image of rule-violating middle managers was unfounded. In the history of decision making on the Solid Rocket Boosters, 1977–1985, and on the eve of the launch, Marshall middle managers abided by every NASA launch decision rule.

Primary data sources indicated that key aspects of conventional post-tragedy wisdom—and thus many of the facts on which other research was based—were wrong. With all the public scrutiny this event received, how could this be? First, post-tragedy analysts, viewing what happened at NASA retrospectively, saw key incidents and events very differently that the managers and engineers responsible for risk assessments as the problem unfolded. In large part, this was due to retrospection. Starbuck and Milliken point out that when observers who know the results of organizational actions try to make sense of them, they tend to see two kinds of analytic sequences.[2] Seeking to explain the bad result, observers readily identify the incorrect actions, the flawed analyses, that led inexorably to it. In contrast, when the outcome is good, observers invariably identify the wise choices and persistence that were responsible. Second, it was clear that post-tragedy analysts had not grasped key aspects of NASA culture: the rules, procedures, and bureaucratic and technical language that were essential to understanding how engineering decisions were made in the space agency. Culture was even an obstacle to the understanding of the Presidential Commission, which spent three months and enormous resources to investigate the incident. Third, many post-tragedy investigators based their analysis on secondary sources. Most relied extensively on Volume 1 of the Presidential Commission's report, published in June 1986, which was an extensive summary, but a summary nonetheless, of a 5-volume report. Omitted from scrutiny were the other four volumes, the report of the House Committee on Science and Technology, published later, and over 200,000 pages of original materials available at the National Archives.[3]

Using the full documentary record, I reconstructed a chronology of engineering decisions at NASA that explores the meaning of actions to insiders as the Solid Rocket Booster problems unfolded. Despite the acknowledged importance of culture in organizations, ethnographies of decision-making processes as they unfold in natural settings are rare. Occasionally, however, the outcome of a decision is such a public calamity that information becomes available allowing us to reconstruct what happened.[4] As a profession, engineers are particularly attentive to maintaining written records. Perhaps most important in this research were National Archives documents containing engineering post-flight analyses, risk assessments, NASA procedures, and 160 lengthy interview transcripts collected by government investigators working for

the Commission. The latter represent a rich untapped resource, as only 40 percent of those interviewed were called before the Commission. These archival data, plus personal interviews, were the basis of an ethnographic account that shows how top policy decisions altered both culture and structure, undermining safety at NASA.

AN INCREMENTAL DESCENT INTO POOR JUDGMENT

In *Man-Made Disasters,* Turner found disasters usually were preceded by "failures of foresight": long incubation periods typified by signals of potential danger that were either ignored or misinterpreted.[5] The infamous teleconference can only be understood as one decision in a long line of decisions that show an incremental descent into poor judgment. From 1977 through 1985, the decision-making history was studded with early warning signs. Anomalies—deviations from design expectations—were found on many missions prior to *Challenger*. But in post-flight analysis, Marshall and Thiokol working engineers responsible for initiating risk assessments of the boosters continually normalized the technical deviation that they found. By "normalized," I mean the remarkable fact that, individual perceptions and concerns notwithstanding, *in all official engineering analyses and launch recommendations prior to the eve of the* Challenger *launch,* Morton Thiokol and NASA engineers analyzed evidence that the design was not performing as predicted and reinterpreted it as acceptable and non-deviant. Based on engineering calculations, tests, and analysis showing that if the primary O-ring failed, a second O-ring would back it up, Marshall and Thiokol working engineers continued to recommend to their superiors that it was safe to fly. Circumstances changed on the eve of the *Challenger* launch. But in the years preceding it, engineering analyses demonstrated that the O-rings operated as a redundant system; therefore, they were an "acceptable risk."

Perhaps most salient and puzzling about the normalization of deviance in official risk assessments was that as missions continued, Marshall and Thiokol working engineers gradually expanded the boundaries of acceptable risk. History and precedent were influential. The critical decision was the first one, when, expecting no damage to the O-rings, in-flight damage occurred and they found it acceptable. This precedent, created early, started the work group on a slippery slope. The engineering analysis and testing that supported this decision were foundational: they resulted in a set of engineering decision rules about how the O-rings operated. Over the years, that first set of decision rules was reinforced by increasingly sophisticated tests and analyses that supported the redundancy of the O-rings. Gradually, in their formal engineering risk assessments, the work group accepted more and more risk. Each of these decisions, taken singly, seemed correct, routine, and, indeed, insignificant and unremarkable, but they had a cumulative directionality, stunning in retrospect.[6]

Presidential Commission member Richard Feynman observed that it was as if they were "playing Russian roulette."[7] Starbuck and Milliken called it an example of "fine-tuning the odds until something breaks."[8] Why, if working engineers were concerned and writing memos, as the historic record indicates they did, did these same engineers repeatedly recommend launching in the years prior to the *Challenger* teleconference?

SIGNALS OF POTENTIAL DANGER: INFORMATION AND ITS CONTEXT

Sensemaking is context-dependent.[9] At NASA, having problems was not itself a signal of potential danger. Because of the inno-

vative, uncertain character of the technology, they were working in an organization culture where having problems was expected and taken-for-granted. The shuttle was composed of many component parts, made by different manufacturers, that had to be put together by NASA. Since many parts were purchased "off-the-shelf" and not designed specifically to fit with others, there were bound to be problems in assembly. Also, because the shuttle design was unprecedented, the working engineers had no rules to guide them about how it would operate.[10] Despite engineering lab tests, field tests, and calculations, they could never predict and prepare for all the forces of the environment that the shuttle would experience once it left the launch pad. The sky was the laboratory. They were learning by doing, and post-flight analysis taught them the most important lessons about how the vehicle behaved. Finally, the shuttle was designed to be reusable. They knew that the shuttle would experience in-flight damage that required new analysis and correction before it could be launched again.

Taking this uncertainty and risk into account before missions began, in 1981 NASA created a document titled "The Acceptable Risk Process," in which the agency acknowledged that after they had done everything that could be done, the shuttle would still contain residual risks.[11] The residual risk of each component part had to be analyzed to determine whether or not that part was an acceptable risk prior to each flight. The document articulated, in broad strokes, the directions that the Acceptable Risk Process must take prior to each flight. These decision-making guidelines were reflected in the language appearing in engineering hazard analyses: "acceptable risk;" "acceptable erosion;" "anomalies;" "discrepancies." To outsiders after the disaster, this language looked like rationality gone wild. To insiders, it was normal, everyday talk. Record keeping and computerized problem-tracking systems made "blizzards of paperwork" a part of the information context that concealed more than it revealed.[12]

This cultural context contributed to the normalization of deviance because having problems was unremarkable and routine. In addition, when the Solid Rocket Boosters began behaving in unexpected ways, the interpretive work of engineers was influenced by the pattern of information as problems began to occur.[13] What, in retrospect, appeared to be clear signals of potential danger that should have halted shuttle flights were interpreted differently at the time by the engineers responsible for risk assessments. As the problems unfolded, signals were mixed, weak, or routine.

MIXED SIGNALS

A mixed signal was one where a signal of potential danger was followed by signals that all was well, convincing engineers that the problem had been successfully diagnosed, corrected, and thus, that the component was an acceptable risk. When returning flights showed anomalies on the booster joints—a signal of potential danger—engineers analyzed and corrected the problem (a piece of lint on an O-ring was enough to cause damage to an O-ring). Subsequently, a number of flights would return showing no problems—a signal that all was well.

WEAK SIGNALS

A weak signal was one that was unclear, or one that, after analysis, seemed such an improbable event that working engineers believed there was little probability of it recurring. To illustrate: A launch in January 1985—a year before *Challenger*—showed the worst O-ring damage prior to that date.[14] Cold temperature was thought to be a factor, because the vehicle was on the launch pad through three consecutive days of 19–20 degree overnight Florida temperatures. Knowing that *Challenger* was affected by the cold, we saw this as a strong signal. In

fact, Thiokol engineer Roger Boisjoly, who was present at Kennedy Space Center for post-flight disassembly, observed the damage and was alarmed.[15] However, according to Boisjoly, they had no quantitative data proving that temperature was responsible for the damage they found—many factors had been causing problems—and they believed such a long run of record cold temperatures was unlikely to happen again.[16] Thiokol began some temperature testing but, in the words of Boisjoly, there was "no scramble to get temperature data" because no one expected a recurrence.[17] The vehicle was tested and designed to withstand extremes of heat, not cold. Cold temperature was, to them after analysis, a weak signal—until the eve of the *Challenger* launch.

ROUTINE SIGNALS

Routine signals are those that occur frequently. The frequent event, even when acknowledged to be inherently serious, loses some of its seriousness as similar events occur in sequence and methods of assessing and responding to them stabilize.[18] In mid-1985, O-ring erosion began occurring on every flight. Post-disaster analysts were incredulous that flights continued. However, these anomalies also were determined to be acceptable risks in official engineering risk assessments. For Marshall and Thiokol working engineers assigned to the Solid Rocket Booster Project, multiple instances of erosion indicated not danger, but assurance that they correctly understood the problem. Marshall and Thiokol engineers had instituted a new procedure that guaranteed that the O-rings would be properly positioned. This procedure increased the probability of erosion, but erosion was not viewed as a problem. Better they assure redundancy by getting the rings in proper position than worry about erosion, which was, in fact, occurring exactly as they predicted. What we saw, in retrospect, as signals of potential danger were to them, routine signals showing the joint was operating exactly as they expected.[19]

THE TRICKLE-DOWN EFFECT POLICY DECISIONS AND RISK ASSESSMENTS AT NASA

After the disaster, the Presidential Commission and other post-tragedy analysts unanimously concluded that policy decisions had been a contributing cause of the tragedy. Political bargains and goal-setting by agency elites had altered the organization culture so that production concerns dominated the space agency, contributing to NASA's incremental descent into poor judgment. These post-disaster analysts were correct. NASA's relationships with its connected communities—Congress, the White House, contractors—altered the organization culture. Political accountability and thus, production pressures were introduced into the agency. However, these policy decisions resulted in a three-faceted culture comprised of the space agency's original technical culture, bureaucratic accountability, and political accountability. All three contributed to the Solid Rocket Booster work group's repeated decisions to accept risk and fly in launch recommendations prior to the *Challenger* teleconference.

THE ORIGINAL TECHNICAL CULTURE

The standards of engineering excellence that were behind the splendid successes of the Apollo era made up NASA's original technical culture.[20] Integral to that culture was the reliance on and deference to in-house professional technical expertise and experiential knowledge of the technology, known as the "dirty hands" approach.[21] Also, the original technical culture insisted upon scientific positivism.[22] It required that risk assessments be guided by extensive testing, engineering principles,

and rigorous quantitative analysis. Hunches, intuition, and observation, so essential to engineering, had a definite place in lab work. But when it came to decisions about whether to proceed with a mission or not, the subjective and intuitive were not allowed: flawless, precise, engineering analysis, based on quantitative methods, grounded in solid engineering data, was required for launch decisions.

This original technical culture still existed at NASA during the shuttle program. It was perhaps most visible in NASA's formal pre-launch decision structure known as Flight Readiness Review, where contractor engineers brought forward their engineering analyses and recommendations about risk acceptability. These contractor launch recommendations and the engineering analysis that supported them were challenged in four hierarchical Flight Readiness Review levels in harshly adversarial, public confrontations designed to test engineering risk assessments.[23] But these mandates for excellence integral to the original Apollo technical culture were struggling to survive amidst two other cultural mandates that resulted from policy decisions early in the Space Shuttle Program: political accountability and bureaucratic accountability.[24]

POLITICAL ACCOUNTABILITY

During the Apollo era, Congress gave NASA a blank check. As the Apollo program neared completion, changes in U.S. domestic and international affairs eroded the consensus for space exploration that had produced both autonomy and money for NASA. NASA barely managed to get the shuttle program endorsed. Top administrators did so by selling the shuttle to Congress as a project that would, to great extent, pay its own way. The space shuttle, they argued, would be like a bus, routinely ferrying people and objects back and forth in space. It could carry commercial satellites, and at the projected launch rate, could produce enough income a year to support the program. Thus, the shuttle would survive as a business, and concerns about cost effectiveness and production pressures were born.[25]

Impression management was the name of the game: after the fourth shuttle flight in 1982, top NASA officials (aided by a ceremonial declaration by President Reagan) declared the program "operational," meaning the developmental or test period was over and henceforth space flight would be "routine and economical." Top administrators continued to establish program goals consistent with the public imagery of an "operational program," even though advised by safety regulators that the shuttle was a developmental, not operational, system. Among those were efforts to accelerate the turnaround time between launches in order to increase the launch rate, and later, taking non-astronauts on missions for political purposes. Meeting the schedule became the key to continued funding from Congress. Consequently, for middle managers and engineers assigned to the hardware, performance pressures and political accountability invaded the original technical culture of the workplace.[26]

BUREAUCRATIC ACCOUNTABILITY

The agency became bureaupathological. During Apollo, the "dirty hands" approach was maintained, although occasionally contractors were used. After Apollo, as a consequence of international space competition, the multi-component shuttle design, and its complex mission, top agency administrators institutionalized the practice of "contracting out."[27] The expanded NASA/contractor structure required ever more rules to coordinate vehicle assembly, launch and mission. Attention to rules and burgeoning paperwork became integral to organization culture. In addition, the Reagan Administration required greater accountability of all government agencies.

Both these developments affected working engineers in the shuttle program. The entire launch decision process always had been guided by rigid rules for procedural accountability. Policy decisions now joined these rules with rules that governed nearly every aspect of the work process. The "dirty hands" approach was undercut by contracting out: instead of getting their hands dirty, many NASA engineers were assigned responsibility for contractor oversight. They spent much more time doing desk work, filling out forms. For each launch, 60 million components and thousands of count-down activities had to be processed. With the accelerated launch schedule, managers and engineers were working evenings and weekends just to turn around all the paperwork necessary to qualify the vehicle for launch.

THE TRICKLE-DOWN EFFECT

Between 1977–1985, the original technical culture, bureaucratic accountability, and political accountability contributed to the normalization of deviance in official launch recommendations as follows:

The original technical culture required that rigorous, scientific, quantitative engineering arguments back up all engineering recommendations. As long as the managers and engineers in the Solid Rocket Booster work group had convincing quantitative data affirming risk acceptability (which they did), they could not interrupt the schedule to do tests necessary to understand *why* it was operating as it was. Policy decisions and impression management at the top eroded the ability of engineers to live up to some of the precepts of the original technical culture. Once the shuttle was declared operational, engineers could not request money for additional developmental testing unless analysis showed a component was an unacceptable risk.

It is important to point out that even though the agency was experiencing economic strain, the schedule was the problem, not money for hardware redesign. The budget was based on an over-optimistic launch rate. Budgeted to launch twelve in 1985, they actually launched nine. The inflated mission model gave them plenty of money for new hardware.[28] But unless data indicated a component was a threat to flight safety, delay was out of the question. Many launches were delayed during this period when data indicated a particular component was not an acceptable risk for an upcoming launch. Marshall and Thiokol engineers in the Solid Rocket Booster work group even delayed launches, one requiring a two-month postponement for a different booster problem. But within the culture, quantitative data were necessary: engineering concerns and intuitions were insufficient reason to interrupt the schedule.

Bureaucratic accountability contributed to the normalization of deviance in official launch recommendations in an ironic way. The sensemaking of managers and working engineers was affected by the fact that they followed all the rules. Interviews showed that the working engineers and managers assigned to shuttle hardware had not lost sight of the inherent riskiness and developmental nature of the technology. Indicating a healthy respect for their innovative design and the mysterious forces of nature it would encounter on a mission, many reported praying before every launch. Many experienced a "gut check," or a nauseatingly tight stomach every time countdown proceeded to its final stages. Macho risk taking was not in the cultural script of these managers and engineers, and in proof of it are the many times they canceled launches prior to *Challenger*.[29] In spite of their concerns about escalating O-ring problems, they reported a belief in their official launch recommendations to accept risk and fly that was based in bureaucratic accountability: if they followed all the rules, all the procedures, then they had done everything they could to reduce residual risk and to assure safety.

THE ANATOMY OF A MISTAKE

Together, information and its context, a three-faceted organization culture composed of the original technical culture, political accountability, and bureaucratic accountability, and the NASA/contractor organization structure shaped the sensemaking of individual participants, and thus the *Challenger* teleconference outcome. Historic policy decisions changing culture and structure had dramatic impact. Two things are striking: the subtlety of their effect upon the proceedings; and that they affected managers and engineers alike. A few examples, condensed from a lengthy reconstruction, show how all factors combined to create a disaster.[30]

The launch decision was the outcome of a two-hour teleconference between 34 people gathered around tables in three locations: Morton Thiokol in Utah, Kennedy Space Center in Florida, and Marshall Space Flight Center in Alabama. Bear in mind that the participants came to the teleconference with a historic understanding of how the joints worked that was based on a cumulatively developed, science-based, paradigmatic engineering analysis that supported redundancy. The engineering analysis supporting risk acceptability in the past was a critical context for the discussion. Bear in mind also that this decision scenario was unprecedented in three ways:

- the predicted cold temperature was below that of any previous launch;
- although teleconferences were routine at NASA, launch decisions based on formal contractor engineering analysis and presentation always were discussed face-to-face in Flight Readiness Review, held two weeks before a launch;[31]
- Thiokol engineers had never before come forward with a no-launch recommendation.

Concern about the cold temperature arose earlier in the day. The influence of political accountability appeared immediately. When a Marshall manager telephoned contractor engineers at Morton Thiokol in Utah to see if they had any concerns about the predicted cold temperature, Thiokol engineers chose a time for the teleconference to begin. The engineers were used to working in a deadline-oriented culture deeply concerned about costs. If they could make a decision before 12:30 A.M. EST, when the ground crew at Kennedy Space Center in Florida would begin putting fuel into the External Tank, they could avoid the costly de-tanking if the decision was "No-Go." NASA always de-tanked in the event a launch was canceled, but de-tanking was an expensive, time-consuming operation. So Thiokol engineers established an 8:15 P.M. EST starting time. As a consequence, the engineers had to hurry to put together the engineering charts containing their risk assessments. They divided up the work, taking responsibility for creating different charts according to specialization. Some people were putting together the final recommendation chart without seeing the data analysis charts the other engineers were creating. Unprepared at 8:15 P.M., they took the extra time necessary to finish the charts, but the full group did not examine and discuss all the charts prior to faxing them to people in the other two locations. Political accountability took its toll.

As it turned out, the engineering charts contained inconsistencies that did not live up to the standards of NASA's original technical culture.[32] The original technical culture required quantitative, scientific data for every engineering launch recommendation. However, patterns of information undermined the credibility of their engineering position. The charts contained mixed, weak, and routine signals. Thiokol's launch recommendation chart stated "Do not launch unless the temperature is equal to or greater than 53 degrees." They chose the 53 degree limit because that was the temperature of the coldest launch, which had suffered the most O-ring damage. However, data on some of the Thiokol charts contradicted the 53 degree limit they proposed.

One chart indicated that the O-rings would be redundant at 30 degrees; another indicated the second worst damage occurred at 75 degrees—the warmest launch. Thus, Thiokol's charts contained mixed signals that undermined the correlation between cold temperature and damage. Also, Thiokol engineers, hurrying to meet the teleconference deadline, had included some charts used in previous engineering presentations, *where the same data had been used to recommend launches.* To people in other locations, those charts were routine signals, because they had been seen before. Finally, the 53 degree limit was not based on quantitative data, but qualitative data: observations made in post-flight analysis of that particular mission. Within the positivistic norms of the original technical culture, the engineering analysis overall was a weak signal, insufficient to overturn the pre-existing, science-based engineering analysis that had supported redundancy and launch recommendations in all the previous years.

We see political accountability operating again, in the angry voices of Marshall managers who challenged Thiokol's data analysis and conclusions, intimidating the engineers. Infamously, Marshall's Larry Mulloy said hotly, "when do you want me to launch, Thiokol, next April?" Marshall managers would be the ones who would have to carry forward the launch recommendation and defend the engineering analysis behind it to top administrators in a system where schedule was important. Marshall managers frequently had delayed launches for safety reasons, but this time it appeared they would be in the position of arguing for delay with an engineering analysis that was, within the original technical culture, not only flawed, but based on observational data that were unacceptable for launch decisions. Moreover, political accountability was at work in another way: a 53 degree launch limit, if imposed for this launch, would stand as a new decision criterion for all launches—an awesome complication in a system required to meet a tight schedule. Under these circumstances, a tight engineering argument seemed particularly essential.

The effects of hierarchy and organization structure on the discussion were equally devastating. In three locations, people could not see each other, so words and inflections were all important. Midway in the teleconference, the people assembled at Morton Thiokol in Utah held an off-line caucus. In it, a senior Thiokol administrator who knew little about the technology took charge, repeating the challenges of the Marshall managers. Without any new data to support their arguments, the engineers could not build a stronger data analysis. Four administrators in Utah reversed the original engineering recommendation, going back on-line and announcing that Thiokol had reexamined their data, reversed the decision, and recommended launch. When Marshall managers asked, "Does anybody have anything more to say?" no one spoke up. Ironically—and fatally—people at Marshall and Kennedy did not know that the Thiokol engineers still objected. Moreover, Thiokol engineers did not know that during the caucus, people at the other two locations believed the launch was going to be canceled. They also were unaware that the top Marshall administrator, participating in Alabama, was making a list of people to call in order to stop the launch.

Bureaucratic accountability also played a critical role in the outcome. In an unprecedented situation, all participants invoked the usual rules about how decisions are made. These rules were designed to assure safety. They included adversarial challenges to engineering analyses and charts to assure no flaws, insistence on scientific, quantitative evidence, hierarchical procedures, and norms about the roles of managers and engineers in engineering disagreements. In conditions of uncertainty, people revert to habits and routines. Weick, in research on firefighting fatalities, observed that those who died failed to drop their heavy tools at critical moments when doing so might have allowed them to escape an out-of-control wildland fire.[33] He pointed out that dropping tools is difficult because not only are firefighters trained that always having them in hand enhances safety, but also the tools are part of a firefighter's identity.

The rules and procedures of formal launch decision making and the original technical culture were the tools that assured managers and engineers in the Solid Rocket Booster work group that they had done everything possible to assure mission safety. In a decision-making crisis unprecedented in three ways, no one thought to do it a different way. This was a "no-launch" recommendation. Yet managers and engineers alike abided by all the usual rules and norms in an unprecedented situation where (hindsight shows) the usual rules were inappropriate. Adversarial challenges to engineering risk assessments were normative in Flight Readiness Review as a strategy to assure the rigor of engineering analyses. However, in a situation of uncertainty, perhaps a cooperative, democratic, sleeves-rolled-up, "what can we make of all this" decision-making session would have produced a different outcome than the adversarial legalism usually employed. Further, people in other locations had potentially useful information and opinions that they did not enter into the conversation because they were subordinates: rules and norms about who was empowered to speak inhibited them from talking on the teleconference.

Conformity to all three cultural imperatives permeated the teleconference proceedings. As Starbuck and Milliken put it,

"People acting on the basis of habits and obedience are not reflecting on the assumptions underlying their actions."[34] If anyone could be argued to be deviant that night, it was the two Thiokol engineers, Arnie Thompson and Roger Boisjoly, who continued to argue vigorously for safety based on observational data—a position that they were aware violated the mandates of the original technical culture, political accountability, and bureaucratic accountability. Although a quantitative argument always was required for a "go" launch decision, engineering concern and hunches should have been enough to stop a launch. But retrospection also shows a great irony: had they dropped their tools and done it differently, they might have discovered that they did have the data to put together an engineering analysis that was a sufficiently strong signal to delay the launch.[35]

· · · · · · · · · · · · · · · · · · ·
IMPACT: THE POST-DISASTER PERIOD

Whenever organizations have tragedies that cost lives, post-disaster activities seem to follow patterns that have near ritualistic qualities: a public investigation; flaws and errors leading to the tragedy are identified; a set of recommendations to prevent similar incidents is made, followed by a period of implementation, change, and high-attention to problems. The public is quieted and business-as-usual resumes. NASA followed this pattern.

Initially, there was shock and grief. Grieving personnel automatically began to act in their organization roles, trying to figure out what had happened: saving and backing up console data; examining telemetry data; beginning a fault tree analysis to find the cause of the technical failure. At the same time, the agency was bombarded by questions from devastated astronaut families, Congress, the White House, the press, and an angry public seeking an explanation. Significantly, top NASA officials had not created a plan about how to handle the social consequences if mission and crew were lost, and chaos reigned. The Presidential Commission was formed and an official investigation was conducted. The Commission's investigation created a huge extra workload, as relevant personnel were interviewed, documents pre-dating the disaster were retrieved, photocopied, listed, and turned over, and NASA's own internal accident investigation got underway.

Typical of other cases when organizational failures cost lives, the work-load dramatically increased at a time when people needed to grieve. NASA and Thiokol were torn by internal conflict, finger-pointing, and official and unofficial attempts to save face. Teleconference participants blamed each other, lodging responsibility for the disaster in the failure of other individuals on that fateful night. They grappled with the loss of their astronaut colleagues and their own possible contribution to their demise. Not knowing the answer themselves, they struggled to answer the questions of family and friends about why the astronauts had died. Most difficult were those of other astronauts and their own children, who had been watching the "Teacher in Space" mission in classrooms. In retrospect, the official investigators, the public, and NASA personnel saw clearly the signals of danger that had looked so different to insiders as the problem unfolded. Teleconference participants focused on the past, identifying turning points where they should have acted differently, passionately wishing they had said or done other than they had. They feared for themselves, their jobs, the agency, and the future. While they had understood all along that failure was always possible, the awareness that they had followed all the usual rules and procedures and still lost *Challenger* generated deep doubts about the organization, its mission and capabilities, and their own competencies. People dealt with their grief in different ways. Some have never resolved it. Unable to move forward, they still focus on the past, working it through again and again.

Then the post-disaster ritual entered a different phase: the report of the official investigation and a series of recommendations that targeted the causes the Commission identified. In common with most post-disaster rituals, the investigation following *Challenger* focused attention on the physical cause of the accident and the individuals responsible for the flawed decision: middle-level managers at Marshall Space Flight Center. Having identified the causes of the disaster, the strategy for control was fairly simple: fix the technology, replace the responsible individuals, and tighten up decision rules. In terms of individual accountability, middle managers were, of course, responsible. But their isolation in the spotlight deflected attention from the responsibility of top decision makers who made political bargains, established goals, allocated resources, and made other key decisions that altered both the structure and culture of the agency, converting it from an R&D organization to a business complete with allegiance to hierarchical relations, production cycles, and schedule pressures. It was top NASA administrators who elected to take civilians on shuttle missions, not the technical people who attended the teleconference. The emphasis on individual middle managers also obscured from the public the truly experimental nature of the technology, its unpredictability under even the best of circumstances, and the logical possibility

of another failure. The final phase of the post-disaster ritual was completed when the Commission's recommendations were implemented, convincing the public that the disaster was an anomaly that would not recur. Spaceflight resumed.

THE CONNECTION BETWEEN CAUSE AND CONTROL

The *Challenger* disaster cannot be accounted for by reductionist explanations that direct attention only toward individual actors, nor theories that focus solely on communication failure or the social psychological dynamics of the teleconference itself. Several scholarly accounts published in the years since the disaster have concluded that Janis's theory of Groupthink—perhaps the leading theory of group dynamics and decision making—was responsible for the launch decision.[36] But many of the elements of Groupthink were missing, and those that were present have explanations that go beyond the assembled group to cultural and structural sources.[37] It was, as sociologist Robert K. Merton has so famously written, "the unanticipated consequences of purposive social action."[38] To a great extent, group dynamics during the teleconference—and the outcome—were shaped by decision makers not present at the teleconference who made historic political bargains that caused political accountability and bureaucratic accountability to become institutionalized and taken for granted in the workplace, having a profound impact on the proceedings.

Mistakes are indigenous, systematic, normal by-products of the work process,[39] and thus could happen in any organization, large or small, even one pursuing its tasks and goals under optimal conditions. The possibility of error and mistake are exacerbated by the complexity of risky work: the more complex the technology, the more complex the organization, the greater the possibility of the kind of "failures of foresight" that Turner identified.[40] When environmental contingency, politics, and structures of power are added to this formula, risky work becomes even more risky. We can never eliminate the possibility of error and mistake in organizations. For this reason, some kinds of risky work are too costly to society to undertake.[41] For others, however, learning from failures as well as successes can reduce the possibility that failures will occur.[42] Errors and failures come in many varieties, so the lessons will vary from one to another. Keep in mind that the *Challenger* disaster was an organizational-technical system error, the former feeding into the latter, so there are many lessons.[43] Here we focus only on three strategic targets that flow from this discussion: policy decisions, organization culture, and the sending and receiving of signals.

TARGET ELITE DECISIONS

Safety goals routinely get subverted as administrators respond to environmental forces, both to further the survival of the organization and their own interests. *Top administrators must take responsibility for mistake, failure, and safety by remaining alert to how their decisions in response to environmental contingencies affect people at the bottom of the hierarchy who do risky work.* The obstacles to achieving this goal are great, making it perhaps the most difficult strategy to employ.[44] First, accidents and errors in risky work tend to get blamed on the proximate cause—human error by operators (nurses, firefighters, case workers, technicians, anesthesiologists, assemblyline workers)—rather than the administrators who determine the conditions in which they work. Second,

policy decisions have deferred results, so that by the time a failure occurs, responsible administrators have left the organization or are in other positions in it, so are not publicly associated with the harmful outcome. Third, the "politics of blame" protects the powerful when organizations have bad outcomes.[45] The *Challenger* case explicitly shows the relationship between goal-setting, negotiations, and bargains with external competitors, suppliers, regulators, and customers. One obvious lesson is the importance of policy that brings goals and the resources necessary to meet them into alignment. When this is not the case, the organization is in a condition of strain, with the people responsible for the hands-on work caught in the squeeze, increasing risk and the possibility of mishap, mistake, and disaster.

Decisions to change organization structure should not be undertaken without research evaluating the effect on safety. Changes that make the system more complex—as many do—also create new ways an organization can fail.[46] Efforts to downsize, which in theory should enhance safety by reducing system complexity, may enhance safety in the long run. But in the short run, the organization may encounter "liabilities of newness"[47] that create new possibilities for error. Altering the structure of an organization can also alter the culture, in both visible and imperceptible ways. When structure is in transition, risk of error and mistake increases as cultures combine and clash, old ways of doing things conflict with new, the institutional memory is lost as files are thrown out and people are discharged or moved, technological changes are introduced. Observers trained in field methods—organization theorists, anthropologists, sociologists—could act as consultants both in planning and implementing change.

Top administrators must remain in touch with the hazards of their own workplace. Administrators in offices removed from the hands-on risky work are easily beguiled by the myth of infallibility. After the *Challenger* disaster, media reports charged that a "can-do" attitude at NASA contributed to the technical failure. That "can-do" attitude was not equally distributed throughout the organization, however. Working engineers at NASA remained keenly aware of risks and the developmental, experimental character of shuttle technology, but three policy decisions, in particular, indicated that NASA top administrators had lost touch with, minimized, or ignored the failure possibilities of the shuttle: extensive cuts to NASA's internal safety regulatory system after the shuttle was declared operational;[48] taking civilians on missions, as part of their attempt to convince Congress and commercial satellite customers that shuttle flight was routine and safe; and the absence of a plan about what to do in the event of a disaster.

Plan for the worst-case scenario. Because a failure has not happened does not mean that one cannot happen. If a post-disaster plan is not in place, top administrators should develop one and set aside resources for enacting a strategy to effectively counteract the social harm of a technical failure. Lee Clarke's research on the Exxon *Valdez* oil spill and other failures shows that most disaster plans are not based in reality, but "fantasy documents," underestimating harm and backed by insufficient resources to control a disaster situation.[49] A plan should encompass both the physical consequences of error and human recovery of affected people. Administrators should also consider how employees can best be helped to move on. One possibility would be to make counseling available to help co-workers deal with the deep emotions experienced when organizations are responsible for social harm. Not only is it humane to do so, but in the long run properly coming to grips with individual feelings may help assure future safety. Implementing the plan deserves equal attention. Even the best of plans can

fail because organizations seldom devote the same attention to developing an implementation strategy.[50]

TARGET CULTURE

Don't make assumptions about organization culture. Although aspects of culture—certain norms, values, and beliefs in an organization that are shared—may be obvious, typically cultures have great variation and diversity.[51] In the *Challenger* incident, the organization culture was much more complicated and its effects on decision making more subtle and hard to detect that even insiders realized. As members of an organization, we are sensitive to certain aspects of the culture, resisting it, but others become taken-for-granted, so that we unquestioningly follow its dictates without realizing exactly what the culture is, how it is operating on us, or how we both use and contribute to it. Research could provide some insights into culture that might prevent future "failures of foresight."

Rules—and whether to obey them or not—are part of an organization's culture. Organizations create rules to assure safety. But in practice, the rules themselves may create additional risks. *In order to assure effective systems of rules, research should examine both rule-following and rule-violating behavior in normal work situations.* Organizations would benefit from learning how extensive rule violations are, which ones are violated, and why. People violate rules for numerous reasons.[52] A rule may be complex, so [it] is violated out of lack of understanding; a rule may be recent, so people are unaware of it; a rule may be vague or unclear, so [it] is violated because people don't see that it applies to the situation they face; a rule may be perceived as irrelevant to the task at hand, or in fact an obstacle to accomplishing it, so the rule is ignored; a rule may conflict with norms about how best to get the work done. A particularly challenging administrative problem that we can extract from the *Challenger* tragedy is how to instill a rule-following mentality that will assure coordination and control in a crisis, and at the same time teach people to "drop their tools": to recognize the situation for which no rules exist and for which the existing rules do not apply.

Cultural assumptions about diversity exist in the workplace. Workgroups, teams, and organizations can be a diverse social composite: sex, race, ethnicity, social class. Also important, members often differ in experience. Kanter identified problems that result from skewed distributions in organizations.[53] *To mitigate risk, research could also explore the effects of diversity on safety.* For example, how do contingent workers and core workers relate to one another, and what can be done to develop reliable working relationships? What are the effects of age, race, gender, or experience differences on decision making? Does diversity affect deployment of personnel and job assignments, so that some are underutilized as resources? Do all employees get the same quality feedback on their performance?

TARGET SIGNALS

Weick stresses the importance of sensemaking in organizations, pointing out that information and how it is interpreted is critical to safety.[54] The social organization of information and its context affected the interpretation of both written and oral exchange about risk at NASA. In organizations where most people are buried in paperwork, signals conveyed in written form can easily be lost, ignored, or misinterpreted. Technical language creates standard ways of communicating that neutralize language as a means of communicating risk and danger. *In decision making, all participants should be alert to the categories of mixed, weak, routine, and strong signals and how they influence others'* *interpretation of a situation, and therefore, how those others respond.* A challenge for organizations is to design systems that maximize clarity of signals and to train individuals to do the same in written and oral communication about risky work.

Minimizing missing signals is another challenge. In face-to-face discussions, not only words and actions, but inflection, gestures, and body language affect how others make sense of what is happening. Face-to-face communication in an important decision-making situation has obvious advantages over written communication, e-mail, or teleconferences, but still is no guarantee. Professional or organizational status can silence subordinates. *Extra effort must go into assuring that all relevant information gets entered into the conversation.* Significant in the eve-of-launch decision were the many missing signals: Thiokol engineers did not know support existed for their view in other locations; information important to the engineering discussion did not get brought up, and so forth. There is nothing so deadly in a crisis as the sound of silence. It is prosaic but worth repeating to acknowledge that subordinates, newcomers, and others who feel marginal or powerless in an organization often have useful information or opinions that they don't express. Democratic practices and respectful practices empower people to speak. However, some kinds of information will still be hard to pass on in settings where people are trained that suppressing individuality to the collective well-being and following the commands of a leader are central to safety. More difficult still is passing on information contradicting what appears to be the leader's strategy or the group consensus. This is the equivalent of two engineers continuing to argue "don't launch" when all around them appear to want to go.

Beware the slippery slope. From 1977–1985. Thiokol and NASA working engineers gradually expanded the bounds of risk acceptability in official risk assessments. Although some engineers expressed concern informally, in official decision-making venues they recommended that the boosters were an acceptable flight risk. The long incubation period that Turner identified as typical in man-made disasters existed at NASA. Hypothetically, a long incubation period would provide more opportunities to intervene. The normalization of deviance in official launch decisions during the years prior to the *Challenger* launch raises an important issue. Sensitivity to risk is essential in organizations that deal with hazards. Yet collective blindness is also possible in an organization where change is introduced gradually, routinization is necessary to accomplish tasks, problems are numerous, and systems are complex. Patterns of information and the wider problem context may obscure gradual change, indicated by signals of potential danger that emerge incrementally. The challenge for administrators is how to develop the kind of common frame of reference necessary for a "collective mind" and "heedful interrelating" in risky decision settings,[55] and still encourage the fresh perspective, the deviant view, the "stranger's eyes" that will be sensitive to gradually developing patterns that normalize signals of potential danger, leading to failures of foresight, mistake, and disaster.

Notes

1. D. Vaughan, *The Challenger Launch Decision: Risky Technology, Culture, and Deviance at NASA* (Chicago, IL: University of Chicago Press, 1996).
2. W. H. Starbuck and F. J. Milliken, "Executives' Perceptual Filters: What They Notice and How They Make Sense," in D. C. Hambrick, ed., *The Executive Effect* (Greenwich, CT: JAI, 1988).
3. Presidential Commission on the Space Shuttle Challenger Accident, *Report to the President by the Presidential Commission on the Space Shuttle Challenger Accident,* 5 vols.

(Washington, D.C.: Government Printing Office, 1986); U.S. Congress, House, *Investigation of the Challenger Accident: Report; Hearings,* 3 vols. (Washington, D.C.: U.S. Government Printing Office, 1986).
4. See, e.g., G. Allison, *The Essence of Decision: Explaining the Cuban Missile Crisis* (Boston, MA: Little, Brown, 1971).
5. B. Turner, *Man-Made Disasters* (London: Wykeham, 1978).
6. Vaughan, op. cit., pp. 77–195.
7. Presidential Commission, *Report,* op. cit, vol. 1, p. 148. See also R.P. Feynman, "Personal Observations on Reliability of Shuttle," In Presidential Commission, *Report,* op. cit., vol. 2, Appendix F.
8. W. H. Starbuck and F. J. Milliken, "*Challenger:* Fine-Tuning the Odds until Something Breaks," *Journal of Management Studies,* 25 (1988): 319–340.
9. K. E. Weick, *Sensemaking in Organizations* (Thousand Oaks, CA: Sage, 1995).
10. B. Wynne, "Unruly Technology: Practical Rules, Impractical Discourses, and Public Understanding." *Social Studies of Science,* 18 (1988): 147–167.
11. J. B. Hammack and M. L. Raines. *Space Shuttle Safety Assessment Report,* Johnson Space Center, Safety Division, March 5, 1981, National Archives, Washington, D.C.
12. For illuminating general discussions, see M. S. Feldman, *Order Without Design: Information Production and Policy Making* (Stanford, CA: Stanford University Press, 1989); and A. L. Stinchcombe, *Information and Organizations* (Berkeley, CA: University of California Press, 1990).
13. Vaughan, op. cit., pp. 243–264.
14. Ibid., pp. 154–163.
15. Presidential Commission, *Report,* op. cit., vol. 1, p. 135.
16. Although after the disaster Boisjoly strongly objected to NASA middle managers' failure to pass information about problems on this mission up the hierarchy, contradictory to the conventional wisdom, Boisjoly's own Project Manager A. McDonald participated in this decision, and both McDonald and Boisjoly agreed that the temperature data were inconclusive, which was the reason Marshall and Thiokol Project Managers

did not carry it forward. Vaughan, op. cit., pp. 157–161.

17. Roger M. Boisjoly, personal interview by author, February 8, 1990.

18. Emerson, op. cit., p. 433.

19. Vaughan, op. cit., pp. 246–247.

20. H. E. McCurdy, *Inside NASA: High Technology and Organizational Change in the U.S. Space Program* (Baltimore, MD: Johns Hopkins University Press, 1993); P. Tompkins, *Organizational Communication Imperatives: Lessons of the Space Program* (Los Angeles, CA: Roxbury, 1993); W. A. McDougall, *And the Heavens and the Earth; A Political History of the Space Age* (New York, NY: Basic Books, 1985).

21. M. Wright, Office of Space History, Marshall Space Flight Center, Huntsville, Alabama, personal interview by author, June 2, 1992; Tompkins, op. cit.

22. Vaughan, op. cit., pp. 89, 91, 202, 208, 221.

23. Vaughan, op. cit., pp. 82–84, 90–95.

24. McCurdy, op. cit.; H. E. McCurdy. "The Decay of NASA's Technical Culture," *Space Policy* (November 1989), pp. 301–310; B. S. Romzek and Melvin J. Dubnick, "Accountability in the Public Sector: Lessons from the *Challenger* Tragedy," *Public Administration Review,* 47 (1987): 227–238; Vaughan, op. cit., pp. 209–227.

25. A. Roland, "The Shuttle: Triumph or Turkey?" *Discover* (November 1985), pp. 29–49; Vaughan, op. cit., pp. 17–28, 209–227.

26. Romzek and Dubnick, op. cit.

27. Romzek and Dubnick, op. cit.; Tompkins, op. cit.

28. Vaughan, op. cit., p. 235.

29. P. Humphlett, "Shuttle Launch Delays," Science Policy Research Division, Congressional Research Service, Library of Congress, Washington, D.C., February 25, 1986, reproduced in Vaughan, op. cit., pp. 51–52.

30. Vaughan, op. cit., pp. 278–386.

31. Two weeks earlier, at the Flight Readiness Review for *Challenger,* the Thiokol engineers had presented a risk assessment that recommended the boosters were safe to fly.

32. The thirteen Thiokol charts are reproduced in D. Vaughan, op. cit., pp. 293–299.

33. K. E. Weick, "The Collapse of Sensemaking in Organizations: The Mann Gulch Disaster," *Administrative Science Quarterly,* 38 (1993): 628–652.

34. Starbuck and Milliken, "*Challenger:* Fine-Tuning the Odds," op. cit., p. 324.

35. Vaughan, op. cit., pp. 382–383.

36. I. L. Janis, *Groupthink* (Boston, MA: Houghton Mifflin, 1982). See, for example, J. K. Esser and J. S. Lindoerfer, "Groupthink and the Space Shuttle Challenger Accident: Toward a Quantitative Case Analysis," *Journal of Behavioral Decision Making,* 2 (1989): 167–177; A. W. Kruglanski, "Freeze-think and the Challenger," *Psychology Today* (August 1986), pp. 48–49.

37. For example, the antecedent conditions that Janis posits were not present. In fact, the constraints on collective thinking that Janis suggests should be present, were present, scripted in the proceedings by organizational rules and norms. Teleconference participants were not an "inner circle" consisting of a cohesive small group of decision makers who liked each other and valued membership in the group. Instead, 34 people were present; not all knew each other; and several had not even participated in launch decisions before. Physically, the group was insulated from others in the organization, but NASA's matrix system functioned to bring in experts not normally assigned to the Solid Rocket Booster Project, specifically to interject alternative views and information. The discussion did not lack norms requiring methodical procedures for decision making. It was guided by norms and rules of the organization about how technical discussions must be conducted. Readers interested in pursuing this issue should see D. Vaughan, op. cit., Chapters 8 and 9, and the detailed discussion of groupthink at p. 525, n41.

38. R. K. Merton, "The Unanticipated Consequences of Purposive Social Action," *American Sociological Review,* 1 (1936): 894–904.

39. E. C. Hughes, "Mistakes at Work," *Canadian Journal of Economics and Political Science,* 17 (1951): 320–327; M. A. Paget, *The Unity of Mistakes: A Phenomenological Interpretation of Medical Work* (Philadelphia, PA: Temple University Press, 1995); C. Bosk, *Forgive and Remember: Managing Medical Failure* (Chicago, IL: University of Chicago Press, 1979).

40. C. B. Perrow, *Normal Accidents: Living with High Risk Technologies* (New York, NY: Basic Books, 1984); S. D. Sagan, *The Limits of Safety* (Princeton, NJ: Princeton University Press, 1993); B. Turner, "The Organizational and Interorganizational Development of Disasters." *Administrative Science Quarterly,* 21 (1976): 378–397.

41. Perrow, op. cit.

42. Perrow, op. cit.; M. E. Pate-Cornell, "Risk Analysis and Risk Management for Offshore Platforms: Lessons from the Piper Alpha Accident," *Journal of Offshore Mechanics and Arctic Engineering,* 115 (August 1993): 179–190; K.H. Roberts, "Managing High Reliability Organizations," *California Management Review,* 32/4 (Summer 1990): 101–113; T. R. LaPorte, "A Strawman Speaks Up: Comments on The Limits of Safety," *Journal of Contingencies and Crisis Management,* 2 (December 1994): 207–212; G. I. Rochlin, T. R. LaPorte, and K. H. Roberts, "The Self-Designing High-Reliability Organization: Aircraft Carrier Flight Operations at Seas," *Naval War College Review,* 40 (1987): 76–90; S. D. Sagan, "Toward a Political Theory of Organizational Reliability." *Journal of Contingencies and Crisis Management,* 2 (December 1994): 228–240.

43. D. Vaughan, op. cit., pp. 387–422.

44. For detailed discussion, see Sagan, op. cit.; C. B. Perrow, "The Limits of Safety: The Enhancement of a Theory of Accidents," *Journal of Contingencies and Crisis Management,* 2 (December 1994): 212–220.

45. S.D. Sagan, *The Limits of Safety.*

46. Perrow, op. cit.; Sagan, op. cit.; Vaughan, op. cit.

47. A. L. Stinchcombe, "Social Structure and Organizations," in J. G. March, ed., *Handbook of Organizations* (Chicago, IL: Rand McNally, 1965).

48. D. Vaughan, "Autonomy, Interdependence, and Social Control: NASA and the Space Shuttle Challenger," *Administrative Science Quarterly,* 35 (1990): 225–258.

49. L. Clarke, *Fantasy Documents* (Chicago, IL: University of Chicago Press, forthcoming).

50. J. Pressman and A. Wildavsky, *Implementation: How Great Expectations in Washington are Dashed in Oakland; or, Why It's Amazing That Federal Programs Work at All* (Berkeley, CA: University of California Press, 1974).

51. For helpful reading on this topic, see M. Douglas and A. Wildavsky, *Risk and Culture* (Berkeley, CA: University of California Press, 1982); A. Swidler, "Culture in Action," *American Sociological Review,* 51 (1986): 273–286; K. E. Weick, "Organizational Culture as a Source of High Reliability," *California Management Review,* 29/2 (Winter 1987): 116–136; J. Martin, *Cultures in Organizations* (New York, NY: Oxford University Press, 1992); P. J. Frost et al., eds., *Organizational Culture* (Beverly Hills, CA: Sage, 1985): L. Smircich, "Concepts of Culture and Organizational Analysis," Administrative Science Quarterly, 28 (1983): 339–358; S E. H. Schein, *Organizational Culture and Leadership* (San Francisco, CA: Jossey-Bass, 1992); H. M. Trice and J. M. Beyer, *The Cultures of Work Organizations* (Upper Saddle River, NJ: Prentice Hall, 1993).

52. D. Vaughan, *Controlling Unlawful Organizational Behavior* (Chicago, IL: University of Chicago Press, 1983), pp. 107–108.

53. R. M. Kanter, *Men and Women of the Corporation* (New York, NY: Basic Books, 1977).

54. K. E. Weick (1995), op. cit.

55. K. E. Weick and K. H. Roberts, "Collective Mind in Organizations: Heedful Interrelating on Flight Decks," *Administrative Science Quarterly,* 38 (1993): 357–381.

IV-12: The Vulnerable System*
An Analysis of the Tenerife Air Disaster

Karl E. Weick

The Tenerife air disaster, in which a KLM 747 and a Pan Am 747 collided with a loss of 583 lives, is examined as a prototype of system vulnerability to crisis. It is concluded that the combination of interruption of important routines among interdependent systems, interdependencies that become tighter, a loss of cognitive efficiency due to autonomic arousal, and a loss of communication accuracy due to increased hierarchical distortion, created a configuration that encouraged the occurrence and rapid diffusion of multiple small errors. Implications of this prototype for future research and practice are explored.

There is a growing appreciation that large-scale disasters such as Bhopal (Shrivastava, 1987) and Three Mile Island (Perrow, 1981) are the result of separate small events that become linked and amplified in ways that are incomprehensible and unpredictable. This scenario of linkage and amplification is especially likely when systems become more tightly coupled and less linear (Perrow, 1984).

"The Valuable System: An Analysis of the Tenerife Air Disaster," by Karl E. Weick from *Journal of Management*, 1990, Vol. 16, No. 3, 571–593. Reprinted with permission.
*Early abbreviated versions of this article were presented at the dedication of the Stanford Center for Organizational Research, at the School of Library and Information Management at Emporia State University, and at the Strategic Management Research Center at the University of Minnesota. Animated discussions with people at all three locations contributed immeasurably to the final product, and I deeply appreciate the interest and help of those people.
Address all correspondence to Karl E. Weick, School of Business Administration. The University of Michigan, Ann Arbor, MI 48109-1234.

What is missing from these analyses, however, is any discussion of the processes by which crises are set in motion. Specifically, we lack an understanding of ways in which separate small failures become linked. We know that single cause incidents are rare, but we don't know how small events can become chained together so that they result in a disastrous outcome. In the absence of this understanding, people must wait until some crisis actually occurs before they can diagnose a problem, rather than be in a position to detect a potential problem before it emerges. To anticipate and forestall disasters is to understand regularities in the ways small events can combine to have disproportionately large effects.

The purpose of the following analysis is to suggest several processes that amplify the effects of multiple small events into potentially disastrous outcomes. These processes were induced from an analysis of the Tenerife air disaster in which 583 people were killed. The processes include, the interruption of important routines, regression to more habituated ways of responding, the breakdown of coordinated action, and misunderstandings in speech-exchange systems. When these four processes occur in the context of a system that is becoming more tightly coupled and less linear, they produce more errors, reduce the means to detect those errors, create dependencies among the errors, and amplify the effects of these errors.

These processes are sufficiently basic and widespread that they suggest an inherent vulnerability in human systems that, up until now, has been overlooked. The processes suggest both a research agenda for the 90s as well as a managerial agenda.

● ● ● ● ● ● ● ● ● ● ● ● ● ● ●

DESCRIPTION OF TENERIFE DISASTER

On March 27, 1977, KLM flight 4805, a 747 bound from Amsterdam to the Canary Islands, and Pan Am flight 1736, another 747 bound from Los Angeles and New York to the Canary Islands, were both diverted to Los Rodeos airport at Tenerife because the Las Palmas airport, their original destination, was closed because of a bomb explosion. KLM landed first at 1:38 P.M., followed by Pan Am which landed at 2:15 P.M. Because Tenerife is not a major airport, its taxi space was limited. This meant that the Pan Am plane had to park behind the KLM flight in such a way that it could not depart until the KLM plane left. When the Las Palmas airport reopened at 2:30, the Pan Am flight was ready to depart because its passengers had remained on board. KLM's passengers, however, had left the plane so there was a delay while they reboarded and while the plane was refueled to shorten its turnaround time at Las Palmas. KLM began its taxi for takeoff at 4:56 P.M. and was initially directed to proceed down a runway parallel to the takeoff runway. This directive was amended shortly thereafter and KLM was requested to taxi down the takeoff runway and at the end, to make a 180 degree turn and await further instruction.

Pan Am was requested to follow KLM down the takeoff runway and to leave the takeoff runway at taxiway C3, use the parallel runway for the remainder of the taxi, and then pull in behind the KLM flight. Pan Am's request to hold short of the takeoff runway and stay off it until KLM had departed, was denied. After the KLM plane made the 180 degree turn at the end of the takeoff runway, rather than hold as instructed, it started moving and reported,

"we are now at takeoff." Neither the air traffic controllers nor the Pan Am crew were certain what this ambiguous phrase meant, but Pan Am restated to controllers that it would report when it was clear of the takeoff runway, a communique heard inside the KLM cockpit. When the pilot of the KLM flight was asked by the engineer, "Is he not clear then, that Pan Am?" the pilot replied "yes" and there was no further conversation. The collision occurred 13 seconds later at 5:06 P.M. None of the 234 passengers and 14 crew on the KLM flight survived. Of the 380 passengers and 16 crew on the Pan Am plane, 70 survived, although 9 died later, making a total loss of 583 lives.

A brief excerpt from the Spanish Ministry of Transport and Communication's investigation of the crash, describes interactions among the KLM crew members immediately before the crash. These interactions, reconstructed from the KLM cockpit voice recorder (CVR), are the focus of the remainder of our analysis.

As the time for the takeoff approached, the KLM captain "seemed a little absent" from all that was heard in the cockpit. He inquired several times, and after the copilot confirmed the order to backtrack, he asked the tower if he should leave the runway by C-1, and subsequently asked his copilot if he should do so by C-4. On arriving at the end of the runway, and making a 180 degree turn in order to place himself in takeoff position, he was advised by the copilot that he should wait because they still did not have an ATC clearance. The captain asked him to request it, and he did, but while the copilot was still repeating the clearance, the captain opened the throttle and started to take off. Then the copilot, instead of requesting takeoff clearance or advising that they did not yet have it, added to his read-back, "We are now at takeoff."

The tower, which was not expecting the aircraft to take off because it had not been given clearance, interpreted the sentence as,

Tenerife Air Disaster

Tenerife Airport Diagram	T_1 = 1659:10 (GMT)	T_3 = 1705:53 (GMT)
accident between	Pan Am on range	Pan Am passing C3
	KLM enters runway	KLM receiving ATC
KLM 4805 and PAA 1736		clearance
March 27, 1977	T_2 = 1702:08 (GMT)	
Elevation: 2073 feet	Pan Am enters runway	T_4 = 1706:49 (GMT)
runway: 3400 x 45 meters	KLM at C3	Impact point near C4

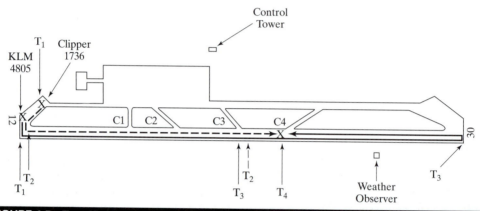

FIGURE 4-5   Tenerife Airport Diagram

"We are now at takeoff position." (When the Spanish, American and Dutch investigating teams heard the tower recording together and for the first time, no one, or hardly anyone, understood that this transmission meant that they were taking off.) The controller replied: "O.K.,... stand by for takeoff... I will call you." Nor did the Pan Am, on hearing the "We are now at takeoff," interpret it as an unequivocal indication of takeoff. However, in order to make their own position clear, they said, "We are still taxiing down the runway." This transmission coincided with the "Stand by for takeoff... I will call you," causing a whistling sound in the tower transmission and making its reception in the KLM cockpit not as clear as it should have been, even though it did not thereby become unintelligible.

The communication from the tower to the PAA requested the latter to report when it left the runway clear. In the cockpit of the KLM, nobody at first confirmed receiving these communications until the Pan Am responded to the tower's request that it should report leaving the runway with an "O.K., we'll report when we're clear." On hearing this, the KLM flight engineer asked, "Is he not clear then?" The captain did not understand him and he repeated, "Is he not clear that Pan American?" The Captain replied with an emphatic "Yes." Perhaps influenced by his great prestige, making it difficult to imagine an error of this magnitude on the part of such an expert pilot, both the copilot and flight engineer made no further objections. The impact took place about 13 seconds later (*Aviation Week*, 1978b: 71).

TENERIFE AS
A STRESSFUL
ENVIRONMENT

Stress is often defined as a relation between the person and the environment, as in Holyroyd's and Lazarus's (1982) statement that "psychological stress requires a judgment that environmental and/or internal demands tax or exceed the individual's resources for managing them" (22). Their use of the word *judgment* emphasizes that stress results from an appraisal that imposes meaning on environmental demands. Typically, stress results from the appraisal that something important is at stake and in jeopardy (McGrath, 1976).

There were several events impinging on people at Tenerife that are likely to have taxed their resources and been labeled as threatening. These events, once appraised as threatening, had a cumulative, negative effect on performance (George, 1986). After we review some of the more prominent of these events, we look more closely at which concepts used in the stress literature help us most to make sense of the Tenerife disaster. It is these concepts that deserve closer attention in subsequent research on how crises are mobilized. The concepts to be discussed include size of discrepancy between demands and abilities, regression to first learned responses, and interruption as the occasion for stress. First, however, we review the demands at Tenerife.

ENVIRONMENTAL DEMANDS
AT TENERIFE

The KLM crew felt growing pressure from at least three sources: Dutch law, difficult maneuvers, and unpredictable weather. Because the accident took place near the end of March, members of the KLM crew were very near the limits of time they were allowed to fly in one month. This was more serious than a mere inconvenience because in 1976 the Dutch enacted a tough law on "Work and Rest Regulations for Flight Crews" (Roitsch, Babcock, & Edmunds, 1979: 14) that put strict limits on flight and duty time. The computation of these limits was complex and could no longer be done by the captain nor did the captain have any discretion to extend duty time. Therefore, the KLM crew faced the possibility of fines, imprisonment, and loss of pilot license if further delays materialized. The crew was informed that if they could leave Las Palmas by 7 P.M. their headquarters thought they could make it back to Amsterdam legally, but headquarters would let them know in Las Palmas.

Further pressure was added because the maneuver of turning a 747 around (backtracking) at the end of a runway is difficult, especially when that runway is narrow. It takes a minimum width of 142 feet to make a 180 degree turn in a 747 (Roitsch et al., 1979:19) and the Tenerife runway was 150 feet wide.

Finally, the weather was unpredictable, and at Tenerife that creates some unique problems. Tenerife is 2073 feet above sea level and the sea coast is just a few miles away. This means that clouds rather than fog float into the airport. When KLM's crew backtracked, they saw a cloud 3000 feet down the runway moving toward them at 12 knots (Roitsch et al., 1979: 12), concealing the Pan Am plane on the other side. Pan Am was taxiing inside this cloud and passed its assigned runway exit because it could not see it. KLM entered that same cloud 1300 feet into its takeoff roll and that is where the collision occurred. The tower did not see the collision or the resulting fire because of the cloud, nor could the firefighters find the fire at first when they were summoned. The density of the cloud is further shown by the fact that when the firefighters started to put out the fire on one plane, the KLM plane, they didn't realize that a second plane was on fire nearby because they couldn't see it (*Aviation Week,* 1978a: 117-119).

The KLM crew was not the only group that was under pressure. Las Palmas airport had reopened for traffic at 2:30, barely 15 minutes after Pan Am had landed at Tenerife. Pan Am was ready to leave Tenerife immediately except that they were blocked by KLM 4805 and continued to be blocked for another 2-1/2 hours. Reactions of the Pan Am crew to the lengthening delays undoubtedly were intensified by the fact that they had originally asked to circle over Las Palmas because they had sufficient fuel to do so, a request that was denied by Spanish controllers. The Pan Am crew also saw the weather deteriorating as they waited for KLM to leave. They had been on duty 11 hours, although they were not close to the limits of their duty time.

Controllers at Tenerife were also under pressure because they were short-handed, they did not often handle 747s, they had no ground radar, the centerline lights on the runway were not operating, they were working in English (a less familiar second language), and their normal routines for routing planes on a takeoff and landing were disrupted because they had planes parked in areas they would normally use to execute these routines.

RESEARCH LEADS TO BE PURSUED

The events at Tenerife provide a pretext to think more carefully about discrepancy size, regression, and interruption as components of stressful environments. These three concepts figure prominently in the events we have just reviewed, and by implication, they may also be a source of system vulnerability in other environments.

McGrath (1976) has shown that the traditional formulation of stress as a discrepancy between demands and ability operates differently from what most people thought. The highest arousal occurs when abilities are only slightly less than what is demanded and there is a chance that the person can cope. Small discrepancies create the most intense stress.

Despite all of the pressures operating at Tenerife, and despite all of the ways in which demands were mounting, the people involved were nearly able to cope successfully. Abilities almost matched demands. When the KLM captain saw the Pan Am plane in front of him on the runway, he pulled back fully on the control column in an attempt to fly over it. The tail of his plane scraped the runway and left a 66 foot long streak of metal embedded in the runway. It was only the KLM's wheels that hit the right wing and rear cabin of the Pan Am plane (which the Pan Am pilot had almost been able to steer off the takeoff runway) (Roitsch et al., 1979: 13), and when the KLM settled back on the runway after the collision, it was intact. Ignition of the extra fuel taken on to speed up departure from Las Palmas caused the KLM fatalities.

Tenerife is important, not just because it illustrates that small discrepancies can have large effects, but even more important because it seems to be an usually clear example of the much discussed, but seldom pursued idea that stress can produce regression to first learned responses (Allnutt, 1982: 11; Barthol & Ku, 1959). If there is a key to understanding the Tenerife disaster, it may lie in this principle.

The pilot of KLM 4805 was Head of the Flight Training Department of KLM. He was a training captain: the flights he was most familiar with were those which followed a script, had fewer problems, and were shorter in duration. Furthermore, he had not flown on regular routes for 12 weeks. The importance of this background becomes evident in the context of a footnote in the Spanish Ministry's report:

> Although the captain [KLM captain] had flown for many years on European and intercontinental

routes, he had been an instructor for more than 10 years, which relatively diminished his familiarity with route flying. Moreover, on simulated flights, which are so customary in flying instruction, the training pilot normally assumes the role of controller: that is, he issues takeoff clearances. In many cases no communications whatsoever are used in simulated flights, and for this reason takeoff takes place without clearance. (*Aviation Week,* 1978a: 121)

Pressure leads people to fall back on what they learned first and most fully. In the case of the KLM pilot, this was giving himself clearance to takeoff. Giving clearance is what he had done most often for the last 10 years when sitting at the head of a runway and it is the response he may have reverted to as pressures mounted at Tenerife.

Both the Pan Am crew and the air traffic controllers seem also to show evidence of regression. The Pan Am captain wanted to hold short of the active runway, but he was asked to proceed down the active runway by a ground controller who spoke with a heavy accent and who did not seem to comprehend fully what Pan Am was requesting. Rather than attempt a potentially more complex negotiation to get permission to hold short, the Pan Am captain chose the more overlearned option of compliance with the controller's directive. Controller communiques also became more cryptic and harder to understand as controllers tried to cope with too many aircraft that were too big. These pressures may have made their use of English, a language which they used less frequently, more tenuous and increased the likelihood that more familiar Spanish language constructions would be substituted.

The more general implication of the disruptive effects of regression is that more recently learned complex rationales and complex collective responses are all more vulnerable to disruption than are older, simpler, more overlearned, cultural and individual responses. Requisite variety (Zeleny, 1986) is much harder to achieve than it looks. When people acquire more complex responses so that they can sense and manage more complex environments, they do not become more complex all at once. Instead, they develop their complexity serially. Under pressure, those responses acquired more recently and practiced less often, should unravel sooner than those acquired earlier, which have become more habitual. Thus, requisite variety may disappear right when it is most needed. Hypothetically, the KLM pilot had high requisite variety because he was both a training pilot and a line pilot. In reality, however, his more recent habits of line flying disappeared under pressure and were replaced by his older habits of flying under training conditions.

Among the many theories of stress that could be applied to the incidents at Tenerife, one of the most fitting is Mandler's (1982) because it encompasses so many properties of Tenerife, including interruption, limited information processing, cognitive narrowing, interpretation, plans, and autonomic arousal.

The centerpiece of Mandler's theory is the idea that interruptions trigger activity in the autonomic nervous system. This autonomic activity absorbs information processing capacity, which then decreases the efficiency of complex thought processes. By way of background, the autonomic nervous system is the branch of the peripheral nervous system that regulates the body's internal environment and maintains homeostasis. The sympathetic branch of the ANS, through the secretion of adrenaline and noradrenaline; mobilizes the common symptoms of stress such as accelerated heart rate, increased blood pressure, and increased glucose secretion (Frankenhauser, 1986).

In Mandler's theory, autonomic activity is triggered by interruption, which he defines as "Any event, external or internal to the individual, that prevents completion of some action, thought sequences, plan, or processing structure" (92). Both action structures and intrapsychic cognitive structures can be interrupted, either when an expected event fails to occur or an unexpected event occurs.

The degree of autonomic activity that occurs following an interruption depends on two factors: first, the degree of organization of the action or thought process that is interrupted (invariant, habituated actions with high degree of expectancy among parts create a sharp increase in autonomic activity when interrupted); and second, the severity of interruption (high external demand to complete an action, coupled with repeated attempts to restart the action and repeated interruptions combine to facilitate arousal).

The autonomic activity triggered by an interruption focuses attention on two things, both of which consume considerable information processing capacity. Attention is focused on the interrupting event, and if it is not altered, on the internal autonomic activation itself. When autonomic arousal consumes scarce information processing capacity, this reduces the number of cues that can be processed from the activity that was underway at the time of the interruption.

In Mandler's model, stress is an interruption that signals an emergency and draws attention to events in the environment. In the short run, this signalling is adaptive and improves coping. Autonomic activity alerts people to the existence of threatening events, but if the threat is not dealt with and the arousal continues, then it registers in consciousness and interferes with ongoing cognitive activity. Thus, consciousness becomes the arena for troubleshooting, but unless the diagnosis and coping is swift, and the response being interrupted is weak in its organization, the troubleshooting consumes information processing capacity and this leads to the omission of important cues for task performance and an increase in cognitive inefficiency.

If we apply Mandler's concepts to the situation of the KLM pilot, we pay closer attention to such aspects as the following. The diversion to Los Rodeos was an interruption of the plan to get back to Amsterdam legally. And the cloud moving down the runway toward the KLM plane represents a potential interruption of a lower order plan to leave Las Palmas. Because neither interruption can be removed directly, autonomic arousal increases, displaces more information processing capacity, and decreases attention to peripheral cues such as radio transmissions. The severity of the interruption should be substantial because a well-organized takeoff routine is interrupted, but most of all because there is a continuing, intense demand to complete the interrupted action (there is no realistic substitute activity that will get the passengers to Las Palmas unless they leave Los Rodeos on KLM 4805).

The pilot's potential focus on the interruption created by the diversion to Los Rodeos and on the consequent lengthening of duty time, coupled with potential awareness of his own internal agitation (which would be hard to label as "pleasure" but easy to label as "frustration" or "fear"), all use up information processing capacity. This leaves little remaining capacity for the immediate task of taxiing the plane to a difficult takeoff position and then flying it safely off the runway. Furthermore, there would appear to be little remaining capacity available to process cryptic, non-standard, sometimes noisy transmissions from the tower and other aircraft.

Thus, to use Mandler's phrase, consciousness became "the arena for troubleshooting," but the troubleshooting was devoted to the question of a legal return to Amsterdam, a higher order plan, rather than to the immediate plan of leaving Los Rodeos. Attention devoted to interruption of the higher order plan used up the major share of attention that could have been allotted to the lower order, more immediate plan.

The point I want to demonstrate is that crises in general typically involve the interruption of plans or cognitive structures or actions that are underway. Because interruption is a generic accompaniment of crisis, a theory of stress and emotion that uses interruption as the point of departure is ideally suited for further investigation and application to settings involving crisis. Furthermore, susceptibility to interruption is an important predictor of system vulnerability.

THE BREAKDOWN OF COORDINATION UNDER STRESS

The phrase "operator error" is misleading in many ways, but among the most subtle problems is the fact that the term is singular (Hayashi, 1985). An operator error is usually a collective error (e.g., Gardenier, 1981), but it is only recently that efforts have been made to understand the ways in which team interaction generates emergent potentialities for and remedies of local failures (e.g, Hirokawa, Govran, & Martz, 1988). The crew in the KLM cockpit provides a unique glimpse of some ways in which crises become mobilized when crew interaction breaks down.

INDIVIDUALISM IN THE COCKPIT

The setting in the KLM cockpit was unusual, not only because the captain was the head of flight training and a member of the top management team, but also because this captain had given the copilot (first officer) his qualification check in a 747 just 2 months earlier. This recently certified first officer made only

two comments to try to influence the captain's decision during the crucial events at the head of the runway. The ALPA report of the crash describes those comments this way:

> The KLM first officer was relatively young and new in his position and appeared to be mainly concerned with completing his tasks so as not to delay the captain's timing of the takeoff. He only made two comments in order to try to influence the captain's takeoff decision. When the captain first began pushing up the thrust levers, he said, "Wait a minute, we do not have an ATC clearance." The captain, rather than admitting to an oversight, closed the thrust levers and responded by saying, "No, I know that, go ahead ask." The second occurrence was at the end of the ATC clearance readback. The KLM first officer observed that the captain had commenced the takeoff and finished the ATC clearance readback by stating, "We are, uh, taking off" or "We are at takeoff" over the radio. After many hours of replaying the tapes, it is difficult to be sure what statement the first officer made. For this reason, we assume that neither the approach controller nor the Pan Am crew were positive about what was said. The Study Group believes that this ambiguous statement by the first officer was an indication that he was surprised by the KLM captain's actions in commencing the takeoff. We believe the first officer thought something was wrong with the takeoff decision by the captain, and tried to alert everyone on frequency that they were commencing takeoff. The

KLM captain did not comment on his first officer's radio transmission but rather became immediately involved in setting takeoff power and tracking the runway centerline. (Roitsch et al., 1979: 18)

The first officer is not the only person acting in a manner that is more individual than collective (Wagner & Moch, 1986). The same was true for the engineer. The flight engineer was the first and current president of the European Flight Engineers Organization. There is an odd statement about him in the ALPA documents. It says that he was not in favor of integrating the functions of the engineering position with those of the pilot crewmembers, such as communication, navigation, and general monitoring of the operation of the flight. "He is said to have felt that flight engineering should consist of specialized emphasis on power-plant and systems analysis and maintenance consideration" (Roitsch et al., 1979: 5). Recall that the engineer was the last point where this accident could have been prevented when he asked, "Is he not clear then, that Pan Am?" Recordings suggest that he made this statement in a "tentative manner" (Roisch et al., 1979: 22) just as the plane entered the thick cloud and the pilots had their hands full keeping the plane on the runway.

RESEARCH LEADS TO BE PURSUED

These several observations suggest that the KLM crew acted less like a team (Hackman, 1987) than like three individuals acting in parallel. That difference becomes important in the context of an important generalization suggested by Hage (1980): "Microsociological hypotheses usually require limits. The human scale is much smaller than the organizational one—at least as far as hypotheses are concerned. Beyond this the 'world' of the individual appears to be domi-

nated by normal curves where too much of a good thing is as bad as too little. In contrast, linearity appears to be a good first approximation in the organizational 'world'" (202).

We should expect that most microhypotheses are curvilinear and most macrohypotheses are linear. McGuire's (1968) model of individual persuasion, for example, is curvilinear and predicts that people with moderately high intelligence are more persuasible than are those who are higher or lower in intelligence. Dailey (1971) argues that individual perceptual accuracy is curvilinear and reflects a tradeoff between increasing confidence in one's own judgment and decreasing openness to new information.

When we move from individual to group, we move from micro in the direction of macro and should expect to find fewer curvilinear relationships and more linear relationships. For example, the recurrent finding that the relationship between stress and performance is curvilinear, holds for individuals, but when it is examined as a group phenomenon, the relationship is found to be more linear (Lowe & McGrath, 1971). Thus, as we move from individual to group, increase in stress should lead to increases in performance, not decreases. However, this shift is dependent on whether individuals coalesce into a team that is a distinctive entity exhibiting distinctive functional relationships or whether they merely act in the presence of another and respond and fall apart, more like individuals than like groups.

A KLM crew that is not a team is subject to curvilinear relationships, whereas a crew that is a team is more subject to linear relations. It is conceivable that more stress improves team performance but degrades individual performance, because teamwork lowers task complexity. A well-functioning team may face a simpler task than does a poorly functioning team. And research on the Yerkes-Dodson (e.g., Bregman & McAllister, 1982) law shows that performance of simple tasks is less susceptible to the disruptive effects of arousal than is performance of complex tasks.

What Hage describes resembles what Hackman (1987) seems to have in mind when he describes group synergy: synergy "refers to group-level phenomena that (1) emerge from the interaction of group members, and (2) affect how well a group is able to deal with the demands and opportunities in its performance situation" (324). Group synergy creates outcomes that "may be quite different from those that would be obtained by simply adding up the contributions of individual members" (321–322). Synergy can be either positive or, as appears to be the case with the KLM crew, negative: negative synergy is described as "a failure of coordination within the group so severe that *nobody* knows what he or she is supposed to be doing" (322). Although it is true that the plane was accelerating in a mechanically correct manner and the crew had in hand a clearance routing them to Las Palmas, lingering uneasiness about pilot judgments was neither voiced nor resolved until it was too late. What is unclear is whether the KLM crew represents a case of negative synergy with a defective group interaction process, or a case of three individuals who never became a group in the first place, or a case where a group became transformed into a collection of separate individuals when stress led the three people to fall back on dissimilar idiosyncratic ways of responding (Lazarus & Folkman, 1984; 104).

Hackman's model seems to suggest that the KLM crew in the Tenerife disaster is an example of a group where there was a slight deficiency of knowledge and skill (pilot unfamiliar with route flying, first officer recently certified on 747) but mainly a deficiency in the performance strategies (328–331) they adopted to review their design and their process and to alter it to fit the abnormal demands created by the diversion.

Helmreich's continuing research on flightcrew behavior has direct relevance to

our understanding of the Tenerife disaster. As part of this program, Helmreich has assessed the managerial aspect of flight operations using a 25-item "Cockpit management attitudes survey" (Helmreich, 1984). The instrument, administered to more than 5000 pilots, has been validated on pilots classified as high and low in resource management (Helmreich, Foushee, Benson, & Russini, 1985) and covers such topics as personal reactions to stress (e.g., "pilots should feel obligated to mention their own psychological stress or physical problems to other flight-crew personnel before or during a flight"), interpersonal communication (e.g., "the pilot flying the aircraft should verbalize his plans for maneuvers and should be sure that the information is understood and acknowledged by the other pilot"), and crew roles (e.g., "There are no circumstances [except total incapacitation] where the first officer should assume command of the ship").

The items in the survey are of special interest in the context of Tenerife. It was found (Helmreich, 1984: 586) that captains and first officers differed significantly in their answers to item 5, which read, "First officers should not question the decision or actions of the captain except when they threaten the safety of the flight." The first officers agreed with the contention significantly more often than did the captains. However, on item 6, which read "Captains should encourage their first officers to question procedures during normal flight operations and in emergencies," captains were significantly less enthusiastic about encouraging input than were first officers. Thus, the idea of coordinated activity and coordinated decision making in the cockpit is a source of ambivalence and a potential source of errors that could enlarge.

These two items remained diagnostic in the validation study, because they were 2 of the 6 items that discriminated most sharply between 114 pilots rated below average or outstanding by evaluators, who actually rode with these pilots and evaluated their flight crew performance. Pilots evaluated as outstanding felt more strongly that first officers should be encouraged to question their decisions and that the first officers should question decisions other than those that threaten the safety of the flight. Pilots with below average performance held the opposite attitudes. Parenthetically, it should be noted that the item that discriminated most sharply between the outstanding and the below average was the item that read, "My decision-making ability is as good in emergencies as in routine flying situations." Below average pilots agree with this item; outstanding pilots disagree with it. Thus, not only do the outstanding pilots realize that their ability to make decisions can change under stress, but in realizing this, they may become more receptive to inputs from others that will help the crew cope.

SPEECH-EXCHANGE SYSTEMS AS ORGANIZATIONAL BUILDING BLOCKS

KLM as an airline is in large part constituted by its speech exchanges. When people employed by KLM talk among themselves and with outsiders, not only do they communicate within an organization, they also construct the organization itself through the process and substance of what they say. As their talk varies, the solidity and predictability of the organization itself varies. Conversations with headquarters about duty time, conversations with the KLM agent at Las Palmas about ways to hasten the departure, conversations (or the lack of them) among crew members that construct the hypothesis that the runway is empty, all are the building blocks of the order and disorder that is the hallmark of organized activity.

The unfolding of the Tenerife disaster reminds us that macroprocesses such as centralization are made up of repetitious microevents that occur frequently and in diverse locations. Organizations are built, maintained, and activated through the medium of communication. If that communication is misunderstood, the existence of the organization itself becomes more tenuous.

The Tenerife disaster was built out of a series of small, semi-standardized, misunderstandings, among which were the following:

1. KLM requested 2 clearances in one transmission (we are now ready for takeoff and are waiting for ATC clearance). Any reply could be seen as a comment on both requests.

2. The controller, in giving a clearance, used the words "after takeoff" ("maintain flight level niner zero right after takeoff proceed with heading zero four zero until intercepting the three two five radial from Las Palmas"), which could have been heard by the KLM crew as permission to leave. The ATC Manual (7110.650, October 25, 1984) clearly states, under the heading "Departure Terminology" that controllers should, "Avoid using the term 'takeoff' except to actually clear an aircraft for takeoff or to cancel a takeoff clearance. Use such terms as 'depart,' 'departure,' or 'fly' in clearances when necessary" (heading 4-20: 4-5). Thus, the Tenerife controller could have said "right turn after departure" or "right turn fly heading zero four."

3. As we have seen, the phrase "We are now taking off" is non-standard and produced confusion as to what it meant.

4. When the controller said to KLM, "Okay . . . stand by for takeoff . . . I will call you," a squeal for the last portion of this message changed the timbre of the controller's voice. This may have led the KLM crew to assume that a different station was transmitting and that the message was not intended for them.

5. The controller did not wait to receive an acknowledgement (e.g., "Roger") from KLM after he had ordered them to "standby for takeoff." Had he done so, he might have discovered a misunderstanding (Hurst, 1982: 176).

6. Shortly before the collision, for the first and only time that day, the controller changed from calling the Pan Am plane "Clipper 1736" to the designation "Pappa Alpha 1736." This could sound like the controller is referring to a different plane (Roitsch et al., 1979: 22).

The point to be emphasized is that speech exhange and social interaction is an important means by which organization is built or dismantled. This is not to say that social interaction is a local, self-contained production that is unaffected by anything else in the setting. There clearly are "non-interpretational foundations of interpretation in social interaction" (Munch & Smelser, 1987: 367). The interpretation process itself is shaped by shared language, authority relationships that assign rights of interpretation, norms of communication, and communication. The meanings that actors co-construct are not self-created. So microanalysis cannot go it alone without macroinput. As Mead put it, people carry a slice of society around in their heads (Alexander & Giesen, 1987: 9). But to acknowledge that slice, is also to acknowledge the carrier and the fact that the slice is realized, made visible, and given shape, in discourse.

RESEARCH LEADS TO BE PURSUED

We have already discussed several issues regarding communication and here will merely supplement those by suggesting that (a) communication is necessary to detect false hypotheses and (b) crises tend to create vertical communication structures when, in fact, lateral structures are often more appropriate for detection and diagnosis of the crisis.

In any crisis situation, there is a high probability that false hypotheses will develop and persist. It is largely through open exchange of messages, independent verification, and redundancy, that the existence of false hypotheses can be detected. There are at least four kinds of situations in which false hypotheses are likely to occur and in which, therefore, there is a premium on accuracy in interpersonal communication (O'Reilly, 1978). These four, identified by Davis (1958), are the following:

1. Expectancy is very high. If a pilot hears a distorted message and knows the tower would not say something meaningless, then the pilot tries to fill in the gaps, and hears the message he or she "should" have heard. This tendency increases the likelihood that a dubious hypothesis will be preserved. Applied to Tenerife, because the crew was expecting takeoff clearance and because they wanted to hear takeoff clearance, it is probable that when the tower said, "Okay, stand by for takeoff, I will call you," and when a squeal accompanied the middle portion of that message, they could have heard "OK, takeoff," which is what they expected to hear.

2. The hypothesis serves as a defense. People interpret communiques in ways that minimize anxiety. In nuclear power plant control rooms, for example, "it is easy for each operator to assume the other knows best, and, in being a good fellow, to reinforce the other's misperceptions. Thus error probabilities for people working together may be better or worse than error probabilities for individuals working independently and not communicating" (Sheridan, 1981: 23). Occasionally, a pilot's seniority and status "may be an even greater bar to admitting his mistakes—and he will only publicly

reject his false hypothesis when it is too late" (Allnutt, 1982: 9). Applied to Tenerife, the hypothesis that there is no one on the runway, given the limited amount of current information present in the radio traffic that had been processed, could easily be bolstered if the pilot and the first officer both assumed that, if there were someone on the runway, surely the head of Flight Training would know it.

3.   Attention is elsewhere. We have already encountered this explanation in the context of Mandler's theory. Allnutt (1982: 9) supplements the earlier discussion when he notes that, "if a pilot has a number of immediate tasks, and if one of those requires special attention, he is likely to be less critical in accepting hypotheses about other components of the work load." Thus a person may ignore information that conflicts with the prevailing hypothesis when it comes from instruments that are on the periphery of attention. Applied to Tenerife, the pilot was undoubtedly more focussed on the takeoff including the approaching cloud, the difficult backtrack maneuver, and tracking the centerline on the runway without the help of lights than he was on the radio communiques that were being handled by the first officer.

4.   It is after a period of high concentration. There is often a let-up near the end of a journey, when the most difficult part of the procedure has been completed. False hypotheses can persist in the face of this decreased attentiveness. Applied to Tenerife, the Spanish Ministry report of the accident actually raised this possibility: "Relaxation—after having executed the difficult 180-degree turn, which must have coincided with a momentary improvement in the visibility (as proved by the CVR, because shortly before arriving at the runway approach they turned off the widescreen wipers), the crew must have felt a sudden feeling of relief which increased their desire to finally overcome the ground problems: the desire to be airborne" (*Aviation Week,* 1978a: 121). The false hypothesis that the runway was clear was something the crew expected to be true, something they wanted to be true, something they dimly felt might not be true, but in the context of hierarchical communications was something they jointly treated as if it were true.

The likelihood that crises impose hierarchical constraints (Stohl & Redding, 1987) on speech-exchange systems is a straightforward extrapolation from the finding that stress leads to centralization (see Staw, Sandelands, & Dutton, 1981). This finding traditionally has been interpreted in a way that masks a potentially key cognitive step that allows us to understand Tenerife more fully. Before stress creates centralization, it must first increase the salience of hierarchies and formal authority, if it is to lead to centralization. It is the increased salience of formal structure that transforms open communication among equals into stylized communications between unequals. Communication dominated by hierarchy activates a different mindset regarding what is and is not communicated and different dynamics regarding who initiates on whom. In the cockpit, where there is a clear hierarchy, especially when the captain who outranks you is also the instructor who trained you, it is likely that attempts to create interaction among equals is more complex, less well-learned, and dropped more quickly in favor of hierarchical communication, when stress increases.

What is especially striking in studies of communication distortion within hierarchical relationships (Fulk & Mani, 1985), is that the "types of subordinate message distortion [to please the receiver] are quite similar to the strategies used to address message overload. They include gatekeeping, summarization, changing emphasis within a message, withholding, and changing the nature of the information" (Stohl & Redding, 1987: 481).

The similar effects of hierarchy and overload on communication suggests that one set of distortions can solve two different problems. A mere change in emphasis in a communication upward can both reduce message overload and please the recipient. These mutually reinforcing solutions to two distinct problems of crises—overload and centralization—should exert continuing pressure on communication in the direction of distortion and away from accuracy.

INTERACTIVE COMPLEXITY AS INDIGENOUS TO HUMAN SYSTEMS

As the day unfolded at Tenerife after 1:30 in the afternoon, there was a gradual movement from loosely coupled events to tightly coupled events, and from a linear transformation process to a complex transformation process with unintended and unnoticed contingencies. Human systems are not necessarily protected from disasters by loose coupling and linear transformation systems, because these qualities can change when people are subjected to stress, ignore data, regress, centralize, and become more self-centered.

Thus it would be a mistake to conclude from Perrow's (1984) work that organizations are either chronically vulnerable to normal accidents or chronically immune from them. Perrow's (1984:63) structural bias kept him from seeing clearly that, when you take people and their limitations into account, susceptibility to normal accidents can change within a relatively short time.

Several events at Tenerife show the system growing tighter and more complex:

1. Controllers develop ad hoc routing of 2 jumbo jets on an active runway because they have no other place to put them (Roisch et al., 1979:8).

2. Controllers have to work with more planes than they have before, without the aid of ground radar, without a tower operator, and with no centerline lights to help in guiding planes.

3. Controllers keep instructing pilots to use taxiway "Third Left" to exit the active runway, but this taxiway is impossible for a 747 to negotiate. It requires a 148 degree left turn followed by an immediate 148 degree right turn onto a taxiway that is 74 feet wide (Roisch et al., 1979: 19). Thus, neither the KLM pilot nor the Pan Am pilot are able to do what the controller tells them to do, so both pilots assume that the controller really means for them to use some other taxiway. Nevertheless, the KLM pilot may have assumed that the Pan Am pilot had exited by taxiway third left (Roisch et al., 1979: 24).

4. The longer the delay at Tenerife, the higher the probability that all hotel rooms in Las Palmas would be filled, the higher the probability that the air corridor back to Amsterdam would be filled with evening flights, occasioning other air traffic delays, and the greater the chance for backups at Las Palmas itself, all of which increased the chances that duty time would expire while the KLM crew was in transit.

5. Throughout the afternoon there was the continuing possibility that the terrorist activities that had closed Las Palmas could spread to Tenerife. In fact, when the tower personnel heard the KLM explosion, they first thought that fuel tanks next to the tower had been blown up by terrorists (Roisch et al., 1979: 8).

RESEARCH LEADS TO BE PURSUED

Stress paves the way for its own intensification and diffusion because it can tighten couplings and raise complexity. Each of the several effects of stress that we have reviewed up to this point either increases dependencies among elements within the system or increases the number of events that are unnoticed, uncontrolled, and unpredictable. For example, the same stress that produces an error due to regression paves the way for that error to have a much larger effect by increasing the complexity of the context in which the error first occurred. As stress increases, perception narrows, more contextual information is lost, and parameters deteriorate to more extreme levels before they are noticed, all of which leads to more puzzlement, less meaning, and more perceived complexity. Not only does stress increase the complexity, it also tightens couplings. Threat leads to centralization, which tightens couplings between formal authority and solutions that will be influential, even though the better solutions may be in the hands of those with less authority. Notice how the same process that produces the error in the first place, also shapes the context so that the error will fan out with unpredictable consequences.

Normally, individual failures stay separate and unlinked if they occur in a linear transformation system where they affect only an adjacent step and if they occur in a loosely coupled system where that effect may be indeterminate (Perrow, 1984: 97, characterizes "airways" as linear, modestly coupled systems). If the couplings become tighter (e.g., slack such as excess duty time is depleted) and if the linear transformation process becomes more complex through the development of a greater number of parallel events having unknown but multiple logical entailments (Douglas, 1985: 173), then more failures can occur and they can affect a greater number of additional events.

Cost cutting at the Bhopal plant prior to the disastrous gas leak illustrates the subtle way in which minor changes can tighten couplings and increase complexity:

> When cost cutting is focused on
> less important units [in Union
> Carbide], it is not just decreased

maintenance which raises susceptibility to crisis. Instead, it is all of the indirect effects on workers of the perception that their unit doesn't matter. This perception results in increased inattention, indifference, turnover, low cost improvisation, and working-to-rule, all of which remove slack, lower the threshold at which a crisis will escalate, and increase the number of separate places at which a crisis could start. As slack decreases, the technology becomes more interactively complex, which means there are more places where a minor lapse can escalate just when there are more minor lapses occurring. (Weick, 1988: 313)

The point of these details is that "normal accidents" may not be confined to obvious sites of technical complexity such as nuclear power plants. Instead, they may occur in any system that is capable of changing from loose to tight and from linear to complex. As we have suggested, any system, no matter how loose and linear it may seem, can become tighter and more complex when it is subjected to overload, misperception, regression, and individualized response.

● ● ● ● ● ● ● ● ● ● ● ● ● ● ● ● ● ●
IMPLICATIONS AND CONCLUSIONS

Although we have examined closely only a single incident, we have done so in the belief that Tenerife is a prototype of system vulnerability in general. Among the generic properties of Tenerife that are likely to be found in other systems, we would include the interruption of important routines among and within interdependent systems, interdependencies that become tighter, a loss of cognitive efficiency due to autonomic arousal, and a loss of communication accuracy due to increased hierarchical distortion. This configuration of events seems to encourage the occurrence and rapid diffusion of multiple errors by creating a feedback loop which magnifies these minor errors into major problems.

Implications for both research and practice of the processes observed in this prototype have been scattered throughout the preceding account and I conclude by reviewing some of those which seem especially important. The concepts that I found most helpful were concepts that have been around for some time. The good news is that much of the old news about crises and behavior remains viable news. What I have basically done is gather these bits and pieces of understanding in one place, sort through them for their relevance to a single dramatic event, and then propose that the resulting assemblage represents a plausible configuration that explains the genesis of a large crisis from small beginnings. The account I have assembled is as much a reminder of tools already in hand as it is a set of speculations about new variables.

Nevertheless, in assembling, editing, and reformulating existing ideas, several themes for future research were identified and I review seven of them below.

First, the concept of temporary systems (e.g., Bryman, Bresnen, Beardsworth, Ford, & Keil, 1987; Goodman & Goodman, 1976; Miles, 1964) has been around for some time, but seems worth resuscitating because air crews, task forces and project teams are both plentiful and doing increasingly consequential work. It is not just air crews with their constantly changing personnel that form an odd mix of the mechanistic and the organic. Any group with a transient population is subjected to some of the same dynamics (e.g., see Gaba, Maxwell, & DeAnda, 1987 on mishaps during anesthesia administration). Thus, it would be instructive to learn to what extent parallels of Tenerife occur in the larger category of organizational forms called temporary systems.

Second, it goes without saying that we must continue to refine and make more precise the concept of stress. The concept plays an important role. It blends together emotion, anxiety, strain, pressure, and arousal. This blending can be troublesome because of the resulting ambiguity, but the global concept of stress nevertheless serves the important function of reminding investigators that affect is a vital part of experience and the human condition (Kemper, 1987). That reminder is worth whatever terminological distress it may occasion.

Third, there appears to be an important but little understood tradeoff between cohesion and accuracy in groups (e.g., Weick, 1983). Janis's (1982) important research on groupthink demonstrates the many insidious ways that sensing and criticism can be sacrificed in the service of group maintenance. Tenerife reminds us again of how delicate this balance can be and of the necessity to see the conditions under which the dilemma can be accommodated.

Fourth, in a related vein, we may need to restudy the possibility that pluralistic ignorance (Miller & McFarland, 1987) is a potential contributor to early stages of crisis. Pluralistic ignorance applied to an incipient crisis means I am puzzled by what is going on, but I assume that no one else is, especially because they have more experience, more seniority, higher rank. That was the error with the Enterprise at Bishop Rock (Robert, in press) (i.e., "surely the captain knows that is a rock just ahead") as well as with the KLM takeoff (i.e., "surely the captain knows that the runway may not be clear").

The first officer, who is reluctant to take off for Las Palmas but assumes no one else is, may not be all that different from the person who is reluctant to ride to Abilene (Harvey, 1974) on a sticky Sunday afternoon, but assumes no one else is. The conditions under which that paradox gets resolved before damage is done remain important to articulate.

Fifth, if the elements that form the pre-crisis context become tightly coupled and more complex, then failures occur more often because of complexity and spread farther and more quickly because of tighter couplings. That is important, but fairly obvious. What is less obvious, and what the analysis of Tenerife suggests, is that persistent failures (those that remain unresolved and lead to a buildup of autonomic arousal) can also tighten couplings and increase complexity. Failures use up information processing capacity. With less information processing capacity, people ignore more central cues, invoke simpler mental models that leave out key indicators, and become more tolerant of unexplained and unpredicted entailments. Failures make authority structures, divisions of labor, and assigned responsibilities more salient. This can tighten the coupling between assigned roles and role behavior in the crises, even though such in-role behavior may be dysfunctional. Notice that this tightening between assigned pre-crisis roles and action during crisis is especially likely if those pre-crisis roles are overlearned. Even though improvisation might reduce the impact of a crisis, it is difficult when arousal is high and when, as Helmreich (1984) demonstrated, captains are wary of the idea that there are times when first officers should override their judgment. This wariness surely does not get lost on ambitious first officers.

Special attention should be directed at systems that are either loose/linear, loose/complex, or tight/linear, because they all are potentially vulnerable to small failures that are difficult to contain. The fact that so many systems are included within these three categories is the basic point being emphasized.

If tightening and complication of systems can be blocked, slowed, or dampened, or if people can be trained and rewarded to redesign the performance strategies when both their context and their structure become tighter and more complex, then failures should stay small and local.

Sixth, we need to see whether, as group interaction improves, task complexity (Wood, 1986) decreases? If so, we then need to see if this is a plausible means by which cohesive groups are less susceptible to disruption from stress than are un-cohesive groups? This may be one means by which cohesive groups continue to function productively even though they are subjected to very high levels of stress.

And seventh, we need to see whether an increment in stress increases the salience of formal structure and authority relations. If so, this may be a considerable deterrent to expertise rather than position controlling the content of an early diagnosis. Given the tendency for communication among equals to turn hierarchical under stress, it would appear necessary that those at the top of the hierarchy explicitly legitimate and model equal participation, if they are to override that salience of hierarchy.

IMPLICATIONS FOR PRACTICE

Again, the implications for practice that emerge from an analysis of Tenerife are not unusual, but they bear repeating because we are likely to see many more situations in the future that assume the outlines of Tenerife.

First, part of any job requirement must be the necessity for talk. Strong, silent types housed in systems with norms favoring taciturnity can stimulate unreliable performance because misunderstandings are not detected. Of the four implications for managerial practice derived by Sutton and Kahn (1987) in their influential stress review, three concern talk: be generous with information, acknowledge the information functions of the informal organizations, do not hold back bad news too long. LaPorte, Rochlin, and Roberts (e.g., LaPorte & Consolini, 1989) find that reliable performance and amount of talk exchanged co-vary.

What our analysis of Tenerife has uncovered is the possibility that with communication a complex system becomes more understandable (you learn some missing pieces that make sense of your experience) and more linear, predictable, and controllable.

The recommendation that people should keep talking is not as simple as it appears, because one of the problems at Three Mile Island was too many people in the control room talking at one time with different hunches as to what was going on. The din created by tense voices plus multiple alarms, however, would make it all but impossible to single out talk as uniquely responsible for confusion, misdiagnosis, and delayed responding. The crucial talk at TMI should have occurred in hours before the control room got cluttered, not after.

If things do not make sense, speak up. This is the norm that needs to be created. Only by doing so can you break pluralistic ignorance (i.e., "you too, I thought I was the only one who didn't know what was going on").

Second, cultivate interpersonal skills, select people on the basis of their interpersonal skills, and devote training time to the development of interpersonal skills (Helmreich, 1983). As technologies become more complex than any one person can comprehend, groups of people will be needed to register and form collective mental models of these technologies. Requisite variety is no longer an individual construct; it must be viewed as a collective accomplishment (Orton, 1988). But to create collective requisite variety, leaders must create a climate in which trust, doubt, openness, candor, and pride can co-exist and be rewarded.

Third, remember that stress is additive, and that off the job stressors cumulate with those that arise on the job. Encourage norms that people under stress should alert others who are dependent on them that their performance may be sub-par. That norm is hard to implant in a macho culture where coping is perceived as grounds for promotion and an admission of problems is seen as grounds for being plateaued.

Fourth, treat chaos as a resource and reframe crises into opportunities to demonstrate and reaffirm competence as well as to enlarge response repertoires. One of the most important contributions of chaos theory (e.g., Gleick, 1987) as well as the counsel to "thrive on chaos" (Peters, 1987) is that they suggest that disorder contains some order; therefore, prediction, if not control, is possible. If chaos theory is not convincing on those instrumental grounds, then at least it suggests that chaos is indigenous, patterned, normal, and to be expected. Appreciation of those aspects of chaos may cushion the arousal that occurs when it becomes the source of interruption. Any response is seen as susceptible to interruption: one never becomes wedded to a single strategy but instead, repeatedly cultivates options and alternative routes by which projects can be completed.

Fifth, controllability makes a difference (Karasek, 1979; Sutton & Kahn 1987), which means discretion must be generously distributed throughout the system. The removal of the KLM pilot's discretion to extend duty hours increased the severity of the interruption occasioned by the diversion to Tenerife and may have produced more cognitive narrowing than would have occurred had the effects of that interruption been bypassed by an extension of duty time.

Sixth, if a strong case can be made that new complex skills should be learned to replace old skills that are no longer appropriate, then the new skills should be overlearned, but with a clear understanding of the tradeoffs involved. It is important to overlearn new skills to offset the tendency for that skill to unravel in favor of earlier learning under pressure of stress. But, overlearning is a mixed blessing. It reduces the likelihood of regression, but in doing so it heightens the disruptive effects of an interruption because overlearning makes the sequence of the response more invariant. The remedy would seem to be to give people more substitute routes by which an interrupted response can be carried to completion and inoculate people against the disruptive qualities of interruption. Help them expect interruption and give them a mindset and actions to cope with interruption.

And seventh, forewarn people about the four conditions under which they are especially vulnerable to false hypotheses. Remind people to be mindful when they are most tempted to act in a mindless fashion (i.e., when they expect something, when they want something, when they are preoccupied with something, and when they finish something).

In conclusion, small details can enlarge and, in the context of other enlargements, create a problem that exceeds the grasp of individuals or groups. Interactive complexity is likely to become more common, not less so in the 90s. It is not a fixed commodity, nor is it a peculiar pathology confined to nuclear reactors and chemical plants. It may be the most volatile linkage point between micro and macro processes we are likely to find in the next few years.

References

Alexander, J. C. & Giesen, B. 1987. From reduction to linkage: The long view of the micro-macro debate. In J. C. Alexander, B. Giesen, R. Munch, & N. J. Smelser (Eds.), *The macro-micro link:* 1–42. Berkeley. University of California.

Allruitt, M. 1982. Human factors: Basis principles. In R. Hurst & L. R. Hurst (Eds.), *Pilot error* (2nd ed.): 1–22. New York: Jason Aronson.

Aviation Week and Space Technology. 1978a. Spaniards analyze Tenerife accident. November 20: 113–121.

Aviation Week and Space Technology. 1978b. Clearances cited in Tenerife collision. November 27: 69–74.

Barthol, R. P., & Ku, N. D. 1959. Regression under stress to first learned behavior. *Journal of Abnormal and Social Psychology,* 59: 134–136.

Bregman, N. J. & McAllister, H. A. 1982. Motivation and skin temperature biofeedback: Yerkes-Dodson revisited. *Psychophysiology,* 19: 282–285.

Bryman, A., Bresnen, M., Beardsworth, A. D., & Ford, J. & Keil, E. T. 1987. The concept of the temporary system: The case of the construction project. *Research in the Sociology of Organizations,* 5: 253–283.

Dailey, C. A. 1971. *Assessment of lives.* San Francisco: Jossey-Bass.

Davis, R. D. 1958. Human engineering in transportation accidents. *Ergonomics,* 2: 24–33.

Douglas, M. 1985. Loose ends and complex arguments. *Contemporary Sociology,* 14 (2): 171–173.

Frankenhaeuser, M. (1986). A psychological framework for research on human stress and coping. In M. H. Appley & R. Trumbull (Eds.), *Dynamics of stress:* 101–116. New York: Plenum.

Fulk, J., & Mani, S. 1985. Distortion of communication in hierarchical relationships. In M. McLaugulin (Ed.), *Communication yearbook 9:* 483–510. Newbury Park, CA: Sage.

Gaba, D. M., Maxwell, M. & DcAnda, A. 1987. Anesthetic mishaps: Breaking the chain of accident evolution. *Anesthesiology,* 66: 670–676.

Gardenier, J. S. 1981. Ship navigational failure detection and diagnosis. In J. Rasmussen & W. B. Rouse (Eds.), *Human detection and diagnosis of system failures:* 49–74. New York: Plenum.

George, A. L. 1986. The impact of crisis-induced stress on decision making. In F. Solomon & R. Q. Marston (Eds.), *The medical implications of nuclear war:* 529–552. Washington, DC: National Academy of Science Press.

Gleick, J. 1987. *Chaos: Making a new science,* New York: Viking.

Goodman, R. A., & Goodman, L. P. 1976. Some management issues in temporary systems: A study of professional development and manpower—the theater case. *Administrative Science Quarterly,* 21:494–501.

Hackman, J. R. 1987. The design of work teams. In J. W. Lorsch (Ed.), *Handbook of organizational behavior:* 315–342. Upper Saddle River, NJ: Prentice Hall.

Hage, J. 1980. *Theories of organizations.* New York: Wiley.

Harvey, J. B. 1974. The Abilene paradox. *Organizational Dynamics,* 3 (1): 63–80.

Hayashi, K. 1985. Hazard analysis in chemical complexes in Japan—especially those caused by human errors. *Ergonomics,* 28: 835–841.

Helmreich, R. L. 1983. *What changes and what endures: The capabilities and limitations of training and selection.* Paper presented at the Irish Air Line Pilots/Air Lingers Flight Operations Seminar, Dublin.

Helmreich, R. L., 1984. Cockpit management attitudes. *Human Factors,* 26: 583–589.

Helmreich, R. L., Foushee, H. C., Benson, R., & Russini, W. 1985. *Cockpit resource management: Exploring the attitude—performance linkage.* Paper presented at Third Aviation Psychology Symposium, Ohio State University, Columbus.

Hirokawa, R. Y. Gouran, D. S., & Martz, A. E. 1988. Understanding the sources of faulty group decision making: A lesson from the Challenger disaster. *Small Group Behavior* 19: 411–433.

Holroyd, K. A. & Lazarus, R. S. 1982. Stress, coping, and somatic adaptation. In L. Goldberger & S. Breznitz (Eds.), *Handbook of stress:* 21–35. New York: Free Press.

Hurst, R. 1982. Portents and challenges. In R. Hurst & L. R. Hurst (Eds.), *Pilot error* (2nd ed.): 164–177. New York: Jason Aronson.

Janis, I. R. (1982). *Victims of groupthink* (2nd ed.). Boston: Houghton-Mifflin.

Karasek, R. A. 1979. Job demands, job decision latitude and mental strain: Implications for job redesign. *Administrative Science Quarterly,* 24: 285–308.

Kemper, T. D. 1987. How many emotions are there? Wedding the social and the autonomic

components. *American Journal of Sociology,* 93: 263–289.

LaPorte, T., & Consolini, P. M. 1989. *Working in practice but not in theory: Theoretical challenges of high reliability organizations.* Unpublished manuscript, Department of Political Science, University of California at Berkeley.

Lazarus, R. S., & Folkman, S. 1984. *Stress, appraisal, and coping.* New York: Springer.

Lowe, R., & McGrath, J. E. 1971. *Stress, arousal, and performance: Some findings calling for a new theory.* Project report, AF1161–67, APOSR, University of Illinois.

Mandler, G. 1982. Stress and thought processes. In L. Goldberger & S. Breznitz (Eds.), *Handbook of stress:* 88–104. New York: Free Press.

McGrath, J. E. 1976, Stress and behavior in organizations. In M. D. Dunnette (Ed.), *Handbook in industrial and organizational psychology:* 1351–1395. Chicago: Rand-McNally.

McGuire, W. J. 1968. Personality and susceptibility to social influence. In E. F. Borgatta & W. W. Lambert (Eds.), *Handbook of personality theory and research:* 1130–1187. Chicago: Rand-McNally.

Miles, M. B. 1964. On temporary systems. In M. B. Miles (Ed.), *Innovation in education:* 437–490. New York: Teachers College Bureau of Publications.

Miller, D. T. & McParland, C. 1987. Pluralistic ignorance: When similarity is interpreted as dissimilarity. *Journal of Personality and Social Psychology,* 53: 298–305.

Munch, R., & Smelser, N. J. 1987. Relating the micro and macro. In J. C. Alexander, B. Giesen, R. Munch, & N. J. Smelser (Eds.), *The macro-micro link:* 356–387. Berkeley: University of California.

O'Reilly, C. A. 1978. The intentional distortion of information in organizational communication: A laboratory and field approach. *Human Relations,* 31: 173–193.

Orton, J. D. 1988. *Group design implications of requisite variety.* Unpublished manuscript, School of Business Administration, University of Michigan.

Perrow, C. 1981. Normal accident at Three Mile Island. *Society,* 18(5): 17–26.

Perrow, C. 1984. *Normal accidents.* New York: Basic.

Peters, T. J. 1987. *Thriving on chaos.* New York: Knopf.

Roberts, K. H. in press. Bishop Rock dead ahead: The grounding of U.S.S. Enterprise, *Naval Institute Proceedings.*

Roitsch, P. A., Babcock, G. L. & Edmunds, W. W. 1979. *Human factors report on the Tenerife accident.* Washington, D.C.: Airline Pilots Association.

Sheridan, T. B. 1981. Understanding human error and aiding human diagnostic behavior in nuclear power plants. In J. Rasmussen & W. B. Rouse (Eds.), *Human detection and diagnosis of system failures:* 19–35. New York: Plenum.

Shrivastava, P. 1987. *Bhopal: Anatomy of a crisis.* Cambridge. MA: Ballinger.

Staw, B. M., Sandelands, L. E., & Dutton, J. E. 1981. Threat-rigidity effects in organizational behavior: a multilevel analysis. *Administrative Science Quarterly,* 26: 501–524.

Stohl, C. & Redding, W. C. 1987. Messages and message exchange processes. In F. M. Jahlin,

L. L. Putnam, K. H. Roberts, & L. W. Porter (Eds.). *Handbook of organizational communication:* 451–502. Newbury Park, CA: Sage.

Sutton, R. I. & Kahn, R. L. 1987. Prediction, understanding, and control as antidotes to organizational stress. In J. W. Lorsch (Ed.), *Handbook of organizational behavior:* 272–285. Upper Saddle River NJ: Prentice-Hall.

Wagner, J. A. & Moch, M. K. 1986, Individualism collectivism: Concept and measure. *Group and Organization Studies,* 11: 280–304.

Weick, K. E. 1983. Contradictions in a community of scholars: the cohesion-accuracy trade-off. *The Review of Higher Education,* 6(4): 253–267.

Weick, K. E. 1988. Enacted sensemaking in crisis situations. *Journal of Management Studies,* 25: 305–317.

Wood, R. E. 1986. Task complexity: definition of the construct. *Organizational Behavior and Human Performance,* 37: 60–82.

Zeleny, M. 1986. The law of requisite variety: is it applicable to human systems? *Human Systems Management,* 6: 269–271.

IV-13: The Collapse of Sensemaking in Organizations
The Mann Gulch Disaster

Karl E. Weick

The death of 13 men in the Mann Gulch fire disaster, made famous in Norman Maclean's *Young Men and Fire,* is analyzed as the interactive disintegration of role structure and

"The Collapse of Sensemaking in Organizations: The Mann Gulch Disaster" by Karl E. Weick, University of Michigan © 1993 Cornell University (from ASO December 1993). Reprinted with permission.

sensemaking in a minimal organization. Four potential sources of resilience that make groups less vulnerable to disruptions of sensemaking are proposed to forestall disintegration, including improvisation, virtual role systems, the attitude of wisdom, and norms of respectful interaction. The analysis is then embedded in the organizational literature to show that we need to reexamine our thinking about temporary systems, structuration, nondisclosive intimacy, intergroup dynamics, and team building.

The purpose of this article is to reanalyze the Mann Gulch fire disaster in Montana described in Norman Maclean's (1992) award-winning book *Young Men and Fire* to illustrate a gap in our current understanding of organizations. I want to focus on two questions: Why do organizations unravel? And how can organizations be made more resilient? Before doing so, however, I want to strip Maclean's elegant prose away from the events in Mann Gulch and simply review them to provide a context for the analysis.

THE INCIDENT

As Maclean puts it, at its heart, the Mann Gulch disaster is a story of a race (p. 224). The smokejumpers in the race (excluding foreman "Wag" Wagner Dodge and ranger Jim Harrison) were ages 17–28, unmarried, seven of them were forestry students (p. 27), and 12 of them had seen military service (p. 220). They were a highly select group (p. 27) and often described themselves as professional adventurers (p. 26).

A lighting storm passed over the Mann Gulch area at 4 P.M. on August 4, 1949 and is believed to have set a small fire in a dead tree. The next day, August 5, 1949, the temperature was 97 degrees and the fire danger rating was 74 out of a possible 100 (p. 42), which means "explosive potential" (p. 79). When the fire was spotted by a forest ranger, the smokejumpers were dispatched to fight it. Sixteen of them flew out of Missoula, Montana at 2:30 P.M. in a C-47 transport. Wind conditions that day were turbulent, and one smokejumper got sick on the airplane, didn't jump, returned to the base with the plane, and resigned from the smokejumpers as soon as he landed ("his repres-

sions had caught up with him, " p. 51). The smokejumpers and their cargo were dropped on the the south side of Mann Gulch at 4:10 P.M. from 2000 feet rather than the normal 1200 feet, due to the turbulence (p. 48). The parachute that was connected to their radio failed to open, and the radio was pulverized when it hit the ground. The crew met ranger Jim Harrison who had been fighting the fire alone for four hours (p. 62), collected their supplies, and ate supper. About 5:10 (p. 57) they started to move along the south side of the gulch to surround the fire (p. 62). Dodge and Harrison, however, having scouted ahead, were worried that the thick forest near which they had landed might be a "death trap" (p. 64). They told the second in command, William Hellman, to take the crew across to the north side of the gulch and march them toward the river along the side of the hill. While Hellman did this, Dodge and Harrison ate a quick meal. Dodge rejoined the crew at 5:40 P.M. and took his position at the head of the line moving toward the river. He could see flames flapping back and forth on the south slope as he looked to his left (p. 69).

At this point the reader hits the most chilling sentence in the entire book: "Then Dodge saw it!" (p.70). What he saw was that the fire had crossed the gulch just 200 yards ahead and was moving toward them (p. 70). Dodge turned the crew around and had them angle up the 76-percent hill toward the ridge at the top (p. 175). They were soon moving through bunch grass that was two and a half feet tall and were quickly losing ground to the 30-foot-high flames that were soon moving toward them at 610 feet per minute (p. 274). Dodge yelled at the crew to drop their tools, and then, to everyone's astonishment, he lit a fire in front of them and ordered them to lie down in the area it had burned. No one did, and they all ran for the ridge. Two people, Sallee and Rumsey, made it through a crevice in the ridge unburned, Hellman made it over the ridge burned horribly and died at noon the next day, Dodge lived by lying down in the ashes of his escape fire, and one other person, Joseph Sylvia, lived for a short while and then died. The hands on Harrison's watch melted at 5:56 (p. 90), which has been treated officially as the time the 13 people died.

After the fire passed, Dodge found Sallee and Rumsey, and Rumsey stayed to care for Hellman while Sallee and Dodge hiked out for help. They walked into the Meriwether ranger station at 8:50 P.M. (p. 113), and rescue parties immediately set out to recover the dead and dying. All the dead were found in an area of 100 yards by 300 yards (p. 111). It took 450 men, five more days to get the 4,500-acre Mann Gulch fire under control (pp. 24, 33). At the time the crew jumped on the fire, it was classified as a Class C fire, meaning its scope was between 10 and 99 acres.

The Forest Service inquiry held after the fire, judged by many to be inadequate, concluded that "there is no evidence of disregard by those responsible for the jumper crew of the elements of risk which they are expected to take into account in placing jumper crews on fires." The board also felt that the men would have been saved had they "heeded Dodge's efforts to get them to go into the escape fire area with him" (quoted in Maclean, p. 151). Several parents brought suit against the Forest Service, claiming that people should not have been jumped in the first place (p. 149), but these claims were dismissed by the Ninth Circuit U.S. Court of Appeals, where Warren E. Burger argued the Forest Service's case (p. 151).

Since Mann Gulch, there have been no deaths by burning among Forest Service firefighters, and people are now equipped with backup radios (p. 219), better physical conditioning, the tactic of building an escape fire, knowledge that fires in timber west of the Continental Divide burn differently than do fires in grass east of the Divide, and the insistence that crew safety take precedence over fire suppression. . . .

· · · · · · · · · · ·

COSMOLOGY EPISODES IN MANN GULCH

Early in the book (p. 65), Maclean asks the question on which I want to focus: "what the structure of a small outfit should be when its business is to meet sudden danger and prevent disaster." This question is timely because the work of organizations is increasingly done in small temporary outfits in which the stakes are high and where foul-ups can have serious consequences (Heydebrand, 1989; Ancona and Caldwell, 1992). Thus, if we understand what happened at Mann Gulch, we may be able to learn some valuable lessons in how to conceptualize and cope with contemporary organizations.

Let me first be clear about why I think the crew of smokejumpers at Mann Gulch was an organization. First, they have a series of interlocking routines, which is crucial in Westley's (1990: 339) definition of an organization as "a series of interlocking routines, habituated action patterns that bring the same people together around the same activities in the same time and places." The crew at Mann Gulch have routine, habituated action patterns, they come together from a common pool of people, and while this set of individual smokejumpers had not come together at the same places or times, they did come together around the same episodes of fire. Westley's definition suggests it doesn't take much to qualify as an organization. The other side is, it also may not take much to stop being one.

Second, the Mann Gulch crew fits the five criteria for a simple organizational structure proposed by Mintzberg (1983: 158). These five include coordination by direct supervision, strategy planned at the top, little formalized behavior, organic structure, and the person in charge tending to formulate plans intuitively, meaning that the plans are generally a direct "extension of his own personality." Structures like this are found most often in entrepreneurial firms.

And third, the Mann Gulch crew has "generic subjectivity" (Wiley, 1988), meaning that roles and rules exist that enable individuals to be interchanged with little disruption to the ongoing pattern of interaction. In the crew at Mann Gulch there were at least three roles: leader, second in command, and crewmember. The person in the lead sizes up the situation, makes decisions, yells orders, picks trails, sets the pace, and identifies escape routes (pp. 65–66). The second in command brings up the rear of the crew as it hikes, repeats orders, sees that the orders are understood, helps the individuals coordinate their actions, and tends to be closer to the crew and more of a buddy with them than does the leader. And finally, the crew clears a fire line around the fire, cleans up after the fire, and maintains trails. Thus, the crew at Mann Gulch is an organization by virtue of a role structure of interlocking routines.

I want to argue that the tragedy at Mann Gulch alerts us to an unsuspected source of vulnerability in organizations. Minimal organizations, such as we find in the crew at Mann Gulch, are susceptible to sudden losses of meaning, which have been variously described as fundamental surprises (Reason, 1990) or events that are inconceivable (Lanir, 1989), hidden (Westrum, 1982), or incomprehensible (Perrow, 1984). Each of these labels points to the low probability that the event could occur, which is why it is meaningless. But these explanations say less about the astonishment of the perceiver, and even less about the perceiver's inability to rebuild some sense of what is happening.

To shift the analytic focus in implausible events from probabilities to feelings and social construction. I have borrowed the term "cosmology" from philosophy and stretched it. Cosmology refers to a branch of philosophy often subsumed under metaphysics that combines rational speculation and scientific evidence to understand the universe as a totality of phenomena. Cosmology is the ultimate macro perspective, directed at issues of time, space, change, and contingency as they relate to the origin and structure of the universe. Integrations of these issues, however, are not just the handiwork of philosophers. Others also make their peace with these issues, as reflected in what they take for granted. People, including those who are smokejumpers, act as if events cohere in time and space and that change unfolds in an orderly manner. These everyday cosmologies are subject to disruption. And when they are severely disrupted, I call this a cosmology episode (Weick, 1985: 51–52). A cosmology episode occurs when people suddenly and deeply feel that the universe is no longer a rational, orderly system. What makes such an episode so shattering is that both the sense of what is occuring and the means to rebuild that sense collapse together.

Stated more informally, a cosmology episode feels like vu jàdé—the opposite of déjà vu: I've never been here before, I have no idea where I am, and I have no idea who can help me. This is what the smokejumpers may have felt increasingly as the afternoon wore on and they lost what little organization structure they had to start with. As they lost structure they became more anxious and found it harder to make sense of what was happening, until they finally were unable to make any sense whatsoever of the one thing that would have saved their lives, and escape fire. The disaster at Mann Gulch was produced by the interrelated collapse of sensemaking and structure. If we can understand this collapse, we may be able to forestall similar disasters in other organizations.

SENSEMAKING IN MANN GULCH

Although most organizational analyses begin and end with decision making, there is growing dissatisfaction with this orthodoxy.

Reed (1991) showed how far the concept of decision making has been stretched, singling out the patching that James G. March has done in recent discussions of decision making. March(1989:14) wrote that "decision making is a highly contextual, sacred activity, surrounded by myth and ritual, and as much concerned with the interpretive order as with the specifics of particular choices." Reed (1991: 561) summarized March this way: "decision making preferences are often inconsistent, unstable, and externally driven; the linkages between decisions and actions are loosely-coupled and interactive rather than linear; the past is notoriously unreliable as a guide to the present or the future; and . . . political and symbolic considerations play a central, perhaps overriding, role in decision making." Reed wondered aloud whether, if March is right in these descriptions, decision making should continue to set the agenda for organizational studies. At some point a retreat from classic principles becomes a rout.

There have been at least three distinct responses to these problems. First, there has been a shift, reminiscent of Neisser and Winograd's (1988) work on memory, toward examining naturalistic decision making (Orasanu and Connolly,1993) with more attention to situational assessment and sensemaking (Klein, 1993). Second, people have replaced an interest in decision making with an interest in power, noting, for example, that "power is most strategically deployed in the design and implementation of paradigmatic frameworks within which the very meaning of such actions as 'making decisions' is defined" (Brown, 1978: 376). And third, people are replacing the less appropriate normative models of rationality (e.g., Hirsch, Michaels, and Friedman, 1987) based on asocial "economic man"(Beach and Lipshitz) with more appropriate models of rationality that are more sophisticated

about social relations, such as the model of contextual rationality (White, 1988).

Reed (1991) described contextual rationality as action motivated to create and maintain institutions and traditions that express some conception of right behavior and a good life with others. Contextual rationality is sensitive to the fact that social actors need to create and maintain intersubjectively binding normative structures that sustain and enrich their relationships. Thus, organizations become important because they can provide meaning and order in the face of environments that impose ill-defined, contradictory demands.

One way to shift the focus from decision making to meaning is to look more closely at sensemaking in organizations. The basic idea of sensemaking is that reality is an ongoing accomplishment that emerges from efforts to create order and make retrospective sense of what occurs. Recognition-primed decision making, a model based in part on command decisions made by fire-fighters, has features of sensemaking in its reliance on past experience, although it remains grounded in decision making (Klein, 1993). Sensemaking emphasizes that people try to make things rationally accountable to themselves and others. Thus, in the words of Morgan, Frost, and Pondy (1983: 24), "individuals are not seen as living in, and acting out their lives in relation to, a wider reality, so much as creating and sustaining images of a wider reality, in part to rationalize what they are doing. They realize their reality, by reading into their situation patterns of significant meaning."

When the smokejumpers landed at Mann Gulch, they expected to find what they had come to call a 10:00 fire. A 10:00 fire is one that can be surrounded completely and isolated by 10:00 the next morning. The spotters on the aircraft that carried the smokejumpers "figured the crew would have it under control by 10:00 the next morning" (Maclean, p. 43). People rationalized this image until it was too late. And because they did, less and less of what they saw made sense:

1. The crew expects a 10:00 fire but grows uneasy when this fire does not act like one.

2. Crewmembers wonder how this fire can be all that serious if Dodge and Harrison eat supper while they hike toward the river.

3. People are often unclear who is in charge of the crew (p. 65).

4. The flames on the south side of the gulch look intense, yet one of the smokejumpers, David Navon is taking pictures, so people conclude the fire can't be that serious, even though their senses tell them otherwise.

5. Crewmembers know they are moving toward the river where they will be safe from the fire, only to see Dodge inexplicably turn them around, away from the river, and start angling upslope, but not running straight for the top. Why? (Dodge is the only one who sees the fire jump the gulch ahead of them.)

6. As the fire gains on them, Dodge says, "Drop your tools," but if the people in the crew do that, then who are they? Firefighters? With no tools?

7. The foreman lights a fire that seems to be right in the middle of the only escape route people can see.

8. The foreman points to the fire he has started and yells, "Join me," whatever that means. But his second in command sounds like he's saying, "To hell with that, I'm getting out of here" (p. 95).

9. Each individual faces the dilemma, I must be my own boss yet follow orders unhesitatingly, but I can't comprehend what the orders mean, and I'm losing my race with the advancing fire (pp. 219–220).

As Mann Gulch loses its resemblance to a 10:00 fire, it does so in ways that make it increasingly hard to socially construct reality. When the noise created by wind, flames, and exploding trees is deafening; when people are strung out in a line and relative strangers to begin with; when they are people who, in Maclean's words, "love the universe but are not intimidated by it" (p. 28); and when the temperature is approaching a lethal 140 degrees (p. 220), people can neither validate their impressions with a trusted neighbor nor pay close attention to a boss who is also unknown and whose commands make no sense whatsoever. As if these were not obstacles enough, it is hard to make common sense when each person sees something different or nothing at all because of the smoke.

The crew's stubborn belief that it faced a 10:00 fire is a powerful reminder that positive illusions (Taylor, 1989) can kill people. But the more general point is that organizations can be good at decision making and still falter. They falter because of deficient sensemaking. The world of decision making is about strategic rationality. It is built from clear questions and clear answers that attempt to remove ignorance (Daft and Macintosh, 1981). The world of sensemaking is different. Sensemaking is about contextual rationality. It is built out of vague questions, muddy answers, and negotiated agreements that attempt to reduce confusion. People in Mann Gulch did not face questions like where should we go, when do we take a stand, or what should our strategy be? Instead, they faced the more basic, the more frightening feeling that their old labels were no longer working. They were outstripping their past experience and were not sure either what was up or who they were. Until they develop some sense of issues like this, there is nothing to decide.

ROLE STRUCTURE IN MANN GULCH

Sensemaking was not the only problem in Mann Gulch. There were also problems of structure. It seems plausible to argue that a major contributor to this disaster was the loss of the only structure that kept these people organized, their role system. There were two key events that destroyed the organization that tied these people together. First, when Dodge told Hellman to take the crew to the north side of the gulch and have it follow a contour down toward the river, the crew got confused, the spaces between members widened appreciably, and Navon—the person taking pictures (p. 71)—made a bid to take over the leadership of the group (p. 65). Notice what this does to the role system. There is now no one at the end of the line repeating orders as a check on the accuracy with which they are understood. Furthermore, the person who is leading them, Hellman, is more familiar with implementing orders than with constructing them or plotting possible escape routes. So the crew is left for a crucial period of time with ill-structured, unacknowledged orders shouted by someone who is unaccustomed to being firm or noticing escape routes. Both routines and interlocking are beginning to come apart.

The second, and in some way more unsetting threat to the role system occured when Dodge told the retreating crew "throw away your tools!"(p. 226). A fire crew that retreats from a fire should find its identity and morale strained. If the retreating people are then also told to discard the very things that are their reason for being there in the first place, then the moment quickly turns existential. If I am no longer a firefighter, then who am I? With the fire bearing down,

the only possible answer becomes, An endangered person in a world where it is every man for himself. Thus, people who, in Maclean's words, had perpetually been almost their own boss (p. 218) suddenly became completely their own boss at the worst possible moment. As the entity of a crew dissolved, it is not surprising that the final command from the "crew" leader to jump into an escape fire was heard not as a legitimate order but as the ravings of someone who had "gone nuts" (p. 75). Dodge's command lost its basis of legitimacy when the smoke jumpers threw away their organization along with their tools.

PANIC IN MANN GULCH

With these observations as background, we can now look more closely at the process of the cosmology episode, an interlude in which the orderliness of the universe is called into question because both understanding and procedures for sensemaking collapse together. People stop thinking and panic. What is interesting about this collapse is that it was discussed by Freud (1959: 28) in the context of panic in military groups: "A panic arises if a group of that kind [military group] becomes disintegrated. Its characteristics are that none of the orders given by superiors are any longer listened to, and that each individual is only solicitous on his own account, and without any consideration for the rest. The mutual ties have ceased to exist, and a gigantic and senseless fear is set free." Unlike earlier formulations, such as McDougall's (1920), which had argued that panic leads to group disintegration, Freud, reversing this causality, argued that group disintegration precipitates panic. By group disintegration, Freud meant "the cessation of all the feelings of consideration which the members of the group otherwise show one another"(p. 29). He described the mechanism involved this way: "If an individual in panic fear begins to be solicitous only on his own account, he bears witness in so doing to the fact that the emotional ties, which have hitherto made the danger seem small to him, have ceased to exist. Now that he is by himself in facing the danger, he may surely think it greater."

It is certainly true in Mann Gulch that there is a real, palpable danger that can be seen, felt, heard, and smelled by the smoke-jumpers. But this is not the first time they have confronted danger. It may, however, be the first time they have confronted danger as a member of a disintegrating organization. As the crew moved toward the river and became more spread out, individuals were isolated and left without explanations or emotional support for their reactions. As the ties weakened, the sense of danger increased, and the means to cope became more primitive. The world rapidly shifted from a cosmos to chaos as it became emptied of order and rationality.

It is intriguing that the three people who survived the disaster did so in ways that seem to forestall group disintegration. Sallee and Rumsey stuck together, their small group of two people did not disintegrate, which helped them keep their fear under control. As a result, they escaped through a crack in the ridge that the others either didn't see or thought was too small to squeeze through. Wag Dodge, as the formal leader of a group he presumed still existed, ordered his followers to join him in the escape fire, Dodge continued to see a group and to think about its well-being, which helped keep his own fear under control. The rest of the people, however, took less notice of one another. Consequently, the group, as they knew it, disintegrated. As their group disintegrated, the smokejumpers became more frightened, stopped thinking sooner, pulled apart even more, and in doing so, lost a leader-follower relationship as well as access to the novel ideas of other people who are a lot like them. As these relationships disappeared, individuals reverted to primitive tendencies of flight. Unfortunately, this response was too simple to match the complexity of the Mann Gulch fire.

What holds organization in place may be more tenuous than we realize. The recipe for disorganization in Mann Gulch is not all that rare in everyday life. The recipe reads, Thrust people into unfamiliar roles, leave some key roles unfilled, make the task more ambiguous, discredit the role system, and make all of these changes in a context in which small events can combine into something monstrous. Faced with similar conditions, organizations that seem much sturdier may also come crashing down (Miller, 1990; Miles and Snow, 1992), much like Icarus who overreached his competence as he flew toward the sun and also perished because of fire.

FROM VULNERABILITY TO RESILIENCE

The steady erosion of sense and structure reached its climax in the refusal of the crew to escape one fire by walking into another one that was intentionally set. A closer look at that escape fire allows us to move from a discussion of what went wrong at Mann Gulch, to a discussion of what makes organizations more resilient. I want to discuss four sources of resilience: (1) improvisation and bricolage, (2) virtual role systems, (3) the attitude of wisdom, and (4) respectful interaction.

IMPROVISATION AND BRICOLAGE

The escape fire is a good place to start in the search for sources of resilience simply because it is clear evidence that, minimal though the organization of the crew might have been, there still was a solution to the crisis inside the group. The problem was, no one but Dodge recognized this. The question then becomes, How could more people either see this escape fire as a solution or develop their own solution? This is not an easy question to answer because, from everything we know, Dodge's invention of burning a hole in a fire should not have happened. It should not have happened because there is good evidence that when people are put under pressure, they regress to their most habituated ways of responding (e.g., Barthol and Ku, 1959). This is what we see in the 15 people who reject Dodge's order to join him and who resort instead to flight, a more overlearned tendency. What we do not expect under life-threatening pressure is creativity.

The tactic of lighting a fire to create an area where people can escape a major prairie fire is mentioned in James Fenimore Cooper's 1827 novel *The Prairie,* but there is no evidence Dodge knew this source (Maclean, p. 104). Furthermore, most of Dodge's experience had been in timbered country where such a tactic wouldn't work. In timber, an escape fire is too slow and consumes too much oxygen (p. 105). And the fire that Dodge built did not burn long enough to clear an area in which people could move around and dodge the fire as they did in the prairie fire. There was just room enough to lie down in the ashes where the heat was less intense (p. 104).

While no one can say how or why the escape fire was created, there is a line of argument that is consistent with what we know. Bruner (1983: 183) described creativity as "figuring out how to use what you already know in order to go beyond what you currently think." With this as background, it now becomes relevant that Dodge was an experienced woodsman, with lots of hands-on experience. He was what we now would call a bricoleur, someone able to create order out of whatever materials were at hand (e.g., Levi-Strauss, 1966: Harper, 1987). Dodge would have known at least two things about fires. He would have

known the famous fire triangle—you must have oxygen, flammable material, and temperature above the point of ignition to create a fire (Maclean, p. 35). A shortage of any one of these would prevent a fire. In his case, the escape fire removed flammable material. And since Dodge had been with the Forest Service longer than anyone else on the crew, he would also have known more fully their four guidelines at that time for dealing with fire emergencies (p. 100). These included (1) start a backfire if you can, (2) get to the top of a ridge where the fuel is thinner, (3) turn into the fire and try to work through it, and (4) don't allow the fire to pick the spot where it hits you. Dodge's invention, if we stretch a bit, fits all four. It is a backfire, though not in the conventional sense of a fire built to stop a fire. The escape fire is lit near the top of a ridge. Dodge turns into the main fire and works through it by burning a hole in it, and he chooses where the fire hits him. The 15 who tried to outrun the fire moved toward the ridge but by not facing the fire, they allowed it to pick the spot where it hit them.

The collapse of role systems need not result in disaster if people develop skills in improvisation and bricolage (see Janowitz, 1959: 481). Bricoleurs remain creative under pressure, precisely because they routinely act in chaotic conditions and pull order out of them. Thus, when situations unravel, this is simply normal natural trouble for bricoleurs, and they proceed with whatever materials are at hand. Knowing these materials intimately, they then are able, usually in the company of other similarly skilled people, to form the materials or insights into novel combinations.

While improvised fire fighting may sound improbable, in fact, Park Service firefighters like those stationed at the Grand Canyon approximate just such a style. Stephen Pyne (1989), a Park Service firefighter, observed that people like him typically have discretion to dispatch themselves, which is unfathomable to the Forest Service crews that rely on dispatchers, specialization, regimentation, rules, and a conscious preference for the strength of the whole rather than the versatility and resourcefulness of the parts. Forest Service people marvel at the freedom of movement among the Park people. Park Service people marvel at how much power the Forest Service is able to mobilize on a fire. Pyne (1989: 122) described the Park Service fire operations as a nonstandard "eclectic assembly of compromises" built of discretion and mobility. In contrast to the Forest Service,where people do everything by the book, "The Park Service has no books; it puts a premium on the individual. Its collective behavior is tribal, and it protects its permanent ranks." If improvisation were given more attention in the job description of a crew person, that person's receptiveness to and generation of role improvisations might be enhanced. As a result, when one organizational order collapses, a substitute might be invented immediately. Swift replacement of a traditional order with an improvised order would forestall the parelysis that can follow a command to "drop your tools."

VIRTUAL ROLE SYSTEMS

Social construction of reality is next to impossible amidst the chaos of a fire, unless social construction takes place inside one person's head, where the role system is reconstituted and run. Even though the role system at Mann Gulch collapsed, this kind of collapse need not result in disaster if the system remains intact in the individual's mind. If each individual in the crew mentally takes all roles and therefore can then register escape routes and acknowledge commands and facilitate coordination, then each person literally becomes a group (Schutz, 1961). And, in the manner of a holograph, each person can reconstitute the group and assume whatever role is vacated,

pick up the activities, and run a credible version of the role. Futhermore, people can run the group in their head and use it for continued guidance of their own individual action. It makes just as much sense to talk about a virtual role system as it does to talk about a virtual anything else (e.g., Bruner,1986: 36–37). An organization can continue to function in the imagination long after it has ceased to function in tangible distributed activities. For the Mann Gulch fire, this issue has bearing on the question of escape routes. In our research on accidents in flight operations off nuclear carriers (Weick and Roberts, 1993), Karlene Roberts and I found that people who avoid accidents live by the credo, "never get into anything without making sure you have a way out." At the very last moment in the Mann Gulch tragedy. Dodge discovered a way out. The point is that if other people had been able to simulate Dodge and/or his role in their imagination, they too might have been less puzzled by his solution or better able to invent a different sensible solution for themselves.

THE ATTITUDE OF WISDOM

To understand the role of wisdom (Bigelow, 1992) as a source of resilience, we need to return to the crew's belief that all fires are 10:00 fires. This belief was consistent with members' experience. As Maclean put it, if the major purpose of your group is to "put out fires so fast they don't have time to become big ones" (p. 31), then you won't learn much about fighting big fires. Nor will you learn what Maclean calls the first principle of reality: "little things suddenly and literally can become big as hell, the ordinary can suddenly become monstrous, and the upgulch breezes can suddenly turn to murder" (p. 217). To state the point more generally, what most organizations miss, and what explains why most organizations fail to learn (Scott, 1987: 282), is that "Reality backs up while it is approached by the subject who tries to understand it. Ignorance and knowledge grow together" (Meacham, 1983: 130). To put it a different way, "Each new domain of knowledge appears simple from the distance of ignorance. The more we learn about a particualr domain, the greater the number of uncertainties, doubts, questions and complexities. Each bit of knowledge serves as the thesis from which additional questions or antithesis arise" (Meacham, 1983: 120).

The role system best able to accept the reality that ignorance and knowledge grow together may be one in which the organizational culture values wisdom. Meacham (1983: 187) argued that wisdom is an attitude rather than a skill or a body of information:

> To be wise is not to know particular facts but to know without excessive confidence or excessive cautiousness. Wisdom is thus not a belief, a value, a set of facts, a corpus of knowledge or information in some specialized area, or a set of special abilities or skills. Wisdom is an attitude taken by persons toward the beliefs, values, knowledge, information, abilities, and skills that are held, a tendency to doubt that these are necessarily true or valid and to doubt that they are an exhaustive set of those things that could be known.

In a fluid world, wise people know that they don't fully understand what is happening right now, because they have never seen precisely this event before. Extreme confidence and extreme caution both can destroy what organizations most need in changing times, namely, curiosity, openness, and complex sensing. The overconfident shun curiosity because they feel they know most of what there is to know. The overcautious shun curiosity for fear it will only deepen their uncertainties. Both the cautious and the confident are closed-minded, which means neither makes good judgments. It is this sense in which wisdom, which avoids estremes, improves adaptability.

A good example of wisdom in groups is the Naskapi Indians' use of caribou shoulder bones to locate game (Weick, 1979). They hold bones over a fire until they crack and then hunt in the directions to which the cracks point. This ritual is effective because the decision is not influenced by the outcomes of past hunts, which means the stock of animals is not depleted. More important, the final decision is not influenced by the inevitable patterning in human choice, which enables hunted animals to become sensitized to humans and take evasive action. The wisdom inherent in this practice derives from its ambivalence toward the past. Any attempt to hunt for caribou is both a new experience and an old experience. It is new in the sense that time has elapsed, the composition of the hunter band has changed, the caribou have learned new things, and so forth. But the hunt is also old in the sense that if you've seen one hunt, you've seen them all: There are always hunters, weapons, stealth, decoys, tracks, odors, and winds. The practice of divination incorporates the attitude of wisdom because past experience is discounted when a new set of cracks forms a crude map for the hunt. But past experience is also given some weight, because a seasoned hunter "reads" the cracks and injects some of his own past experience into an interpretation of what the cracks mean. The reader is crucial. If the reader's hunches dominate, randomization is lost. If the cracks dominate, then the experience base is discarded. The cracks are a lot like the four guidelines for fire emergencies that Dodge may have relied on when he invented the escape fire. They embody experience, but they invite doubt, reassembly, and shaping to fit novelties in the present.

RESPECTFUL INTERACTION

The final suggestion about how to counteract vulnerability makes explicit the preceding focus on the individual and social interaction. Respectful interaction depends on intersubjectivity (Wiley, 1988: 258), which has two defining characteristics: (1) Intersubjectivity emerges from the interchange and synthesis of meanings among two or more communicating selves, and (2) the self or subject gets transformed during interaction such that a joint or merged subjectivity develops. It is possible that many role systems do not change fast enough to keep up with a rapidly changing environment. The only form that can keep up is one based on face-to-face interaction. And it is here, rather than in routines, that we are best able to see the core of organizing. This may be why interaction in airline cockpit crews, such as discussed by Foushee (1984), strikes us so often as a plausible microcosm of what happens in much larger systems. In a cockpit under crisis, the only unit that makes sense (pun intended) is face-to-face synthesis of meaning.

Intersubjectivity was lost on everyone at Mann Gulch, everyone, that is, but Sallee and Rumsey. They stuck together and lived. Dodge went his own individual way with a burst of improvisation, and he too lived. Perhaps it's more important that you have a partner than an organization when you fight fires. A partner makes social construction easier. A partner is a second source of ideas. A partner strengthens independent judgment in the face of a majority. And a partner enlarges the pool of data that are considered. Partnerships that endure are likely to be those that adhere to Campbell's three

imperatives for social life, based on a reanalysis of Asch's (1952) conformity experiment: (1) Respect the reports of others and be willing to base beliefs and actions on them (trust); (2) Report honestly so that others may use your observations in coming to valid beliefs (honestly); and, (3) Respect your own perceptions and beliefs and seek to integrate them with the reports of others without deprecating them or yourselves (self-respect) (adapted from Campbell, 1990: 45–46)

Earlier I noted a growing interest in contextual rationality, understood as actions that create and maintain institutions and traditions that express some conception of right behavior and a good life with others (Reed, 1991). Campbell's maxims operationalize this good life with others as trust, honesty, and self-respect in moment-to-moment interaction. This triangle of trust, honesty, and self-respect is conspicuously missing (e.g., King, 1989: 46–48) in several well-documented disasters in which faulty interaction processes led to increased fear, diminished communication and death. For example, in the Tenerife air disaster (Weick, 1990), the copilot of the KLM aircraft had a strong hunch that another 747 airplane was on the takeoff runway directly in front of them when his own captain began takeoff without clearance. But the copilot said nothing about either the suspicions or the illegal departure. Transient cockpit crews, tied together by narrow definitions of formal responsibilities, and headed by captains who mistakenly assume that their decision-making ability is unaffected by increases in stress (Helmreich et al., 1985), have few protections against a sudden loss of meaning such as the preposterous possibility that a captain is taking off without clearance, directly into the path of another 747.

Even when people try to act with honesty, trust, and self-respect, if they do so with little social support, their efforts are compromised. For example, linguists who analyzed the conversations at Tenerife and in the crash of Air Florida flight 90 in Washington concluded that the copilots in both cases used "devices of mitigation" to soften the effects of their requests and suggestions:

> A mitigated instruction might be phrased as a question or hedged with qualifications such as "would" or "could.". . . (I)t was found that the speech of subordinate crew members was much more likely to be mitigated than the speech of captains. It was also found that topics introduced in mitigated speech were less likely to be followed-up by other crew members and less likely to be ratified by the captain. Both of these effects relate directly to the situation in which a subordinate crew member makes a correct solution that is ignored. . . The value of training in unmitigated speech is strongly suggested by these results. (O'Hare and Roscoe, 1990: 219)

If a role system collapses among people for whom trust, honesty, and self-respect are underdeveloped, then they are on their own. And fear often swamps their resourcefulness. If, however, a role system collapses among people where trust, honesty, and self-respect are more fully developed, then new options, such as mutual adaptation, blind imitation of creative solutions, and trusting compliance, are created. When a formal structure collapses, there is no leader, no roles, no routines, no sense. That is what we may be seeing in Mann Gulch. Dodge can't lead because the role system in which he is a leader disappears. But what is worse, Dodge can't rely on his crewmembers to trust him, question him, or pay attention to him, because they don't know him and there is

no time to change this. The key question is, When formal structure collapses, what, if anything, is left? The answer to that question may well be one of life or death.

STRUCTURES FOR RESILIENCE

. . . If there is a structure that enables people to meet sudden danger, who builds and maintains it? A partial answer is Ken Smith's intergroup analysis, suggesting that the needed structure consists of many structures, built and maintained by a shifting configuration of the same people. As I said, this perspective makes sense when time is extended, demands change, and there is no formal leader at the beginning of the episode. But there is a leader in Mann Gulch, the foreman. There is also a second in command and the remaining crew, which means there is a top (foreman), middle (second in command), and bottom (remaining crew). If we take this a priore structure seriously, then the Mann Gulch disaster can be understood as a dramatic failure of leadership, reminiscent of those lapses in leadership increasingly well documented by people who study cockpit/crew resource management in aircraft accidents (e.g., Wiener, Kanki, and Helmreich, 1993).

The captain of an aircrew, who is analogous to a player-coach on a basketball team (Hackman, 1993: 55), can often have his or her greatest impact on team functioning *before* people get into a tight, time-critical situation. Ginnett (1993) has shown that aircraft captains identified by check airmen as excellent team leaders spent more time team building when the team first formed than did leaders judged as less expert. Leaders of highly effective teams briefed their crewmembers on four issues: the task, crew boundaries, standards and expected behaviors (norms), and authority dynamics.

Captains spent most time on those of the four that were not predefined by the organizational context within which the crew worked. Typically, this meant that excellent captains did *not* spend much time on routinized tasks, but less-excellent captains did. Crew boundaries were enlarged and made more permeable by excellent captains when, for example, they regarded the flight attendants, gate personnel, and air traffic controllers as members of the total flight crew. This contrasts with less-excellent captains, who drew a boundary around the people in the cockpit and separated them from everyone else.

Excellent captains modeled norms that made it clear that safety, effective communication, and cooperation were expected from everyone. Of special interest, because so little communication occurred at Mann Gulch, is how the norm, "communication is important," was expressed. Excellent crews expect one another to enact any of these four exchanges: "(1) I need to talk to you; (2) I listen to you; (3) I need you to talk to me; or even (4) I expect you to talk to me" (Ginnett, 1993: 88). These four complement and operationalize the spirit of Campbell's social imperatives of trust, honesty, and self-respect. But they also show the importance of inquiry, advocacy, and assertion when people do not understand the reasons why other people are doing something or ignoring something (Helmreich and Foushee, 1993: 21).

Issues of authority are handled differently by excellent captains. They shift their behaviors between complete democracy and complete autocracy during the briefing and thereafter, which makes it clear that they are capable of a range of styles. They *establish competence* and their capability to assume legitimate authority by doing the briefing in a rational manner, comfortably, with appropriate technical language, all of which suggests that they have given some thought to the upcoming flight and have constructed a framework within which the crew will work.

Less autocratic than this enactment of their legitimate authority is their willingness to *disavow perfection*. A good example of a statement that tells crewmembers they too must take responsibility for one another is this: "I just want you guys to understand that they assign the seats in this airplane based on seniority, not on the basis of competence. So anything you can see or do that will help out, I'd sure appreciate hearing about it" (Ginnett, 1993: 90). Notice that the captain is not saying, I am not competent to be the captain. Instead, the captain is saying, we're all fallible. We all make mistakes. Let's keep an eye on one another and speak up when we think a mistake is being made.

Most democratic and participative is the captain's behavior to *engage the crew*. Briefings held by excellent captains last no longer than do those of the less-excellent captains, but excellent captains talk less, listen more, and resort less to "canned presentations."

Taken together, all of these team-building activities increase the probability that constructive, informed interactions can still occur among relative strangers even when they get in a jam. If we compare the leadership of aircraft captains to leadership in Mann Gulch, it is clear that Wag Dodge did not build his team of smokejumpers in advance. Furthermore, members of the smokejumpers crew did not keep each other informed of what they were doing or the reasons for their actions or the situational model they were using to generate these reasons. These multiple failures of leadership may be the result of inadequate training, inadequate understanding of leadership processes in the late '40s, or may be attributable to a culture emphasizing individual work rather than group work. Or these failures of leadership may reflect the fact that even the best leaders and the most team-conscious members can still suffer when structures begin to pull apart, leaving in their wake senselessness, panic, and cosmological questions. If people are lucky, and interpersonally adept, their exposure to questions of cosmology *is* confined to an episode. If they are not, that exposure stretches much further. Which is just about where Maclean would want us to end.

References

Ancona, Deborah G., and David F. Caldwell (1992) "Bridging the boundary: External activity and performance in organizational teams."*Administrative Science Quarterly*, 37: 634–665.

Asch, Soloman (1952) *Social Psychology*. Englewood Cliffs, NJ: Prentice Hall.

Barley, Stephen R. (1988) "Technology as an occasion for structuring: Evidence from observations of CT scanners and the social order of radiology departments." *Administrative Science Quarterly*, 31: 78–108.

Barthol, R. P., and N. D. Ku (1959) "Regression under stress to first learned behavior." *Journal of Abnormal and Social Psychology*, 59: 134–136.

Bass, Barnard M. (1960) *Leadership, Psychology, and Organizational Behavior*. New York: Harper. (1990) *Bass and Stogdill's Handbook of Leadership*. New York: Free Press.

Beach, Lee R., and Raanan Lipshitz (1993) "Why classical decision theory is an inappropriate standard for evaluation and aiding most human decision making." In Gary A. Klein, Judith Orasanu, Roberta Calderwood, and Caroline E. Zsambok (eds.), *Decision Making in Action: Models and Methods*: 21–35. Norwood, NJ: Abtex.

Bigelow, John (1992) "Developing managerial wisdom."*Journal of Management Inquiry*, 1: 143–153.

Brown, Richard Harvey (1978) "Bureaucracy as praxis: Toward a political phenomenology of formal organizations." *Administrative Science Quarterly*, 23: 365–382.

Bruner, Jerome (1983) *In Search of Mind*. New York: Harper. (1986) *Actual Minds, Possible Worlds*. Cambridge, MA: Harvard University Press.

Campbell, Donald T. (1990) "Asch's moral epistemology for socially shared knowledge." In Irwin Rock (ed.), *The Legacy of Solomon Asch: Essays in Cognition and Social Psychology*: 39–52. Hillsdale, NJ: Erlbaum.

Daft, Richard L., and Norman B. Macintosh (1981) "A tentative exploration into the amount and equivocality of information processing in organizational work units." *Administrative Science Quarterly*, 26: 207–224.

DiMaggio, Paul (1991) "The micro-macro dilemma in organizational research: Implications of role-system theory." In Joan Huber (ed.), *Micro-macro Changes in Sociology*: 76–98. Newbury Park, CA: Sage.

Elsenbarg, Eric M. (1990) "Jamming: Transcendence through organizing." *Communication Research*, 17: 139–164.

Eisenhardt, Kathleen M. (1993) "High reliability organizations meet high velocity environments: Common dilemmas in nuclear power plants, aircraft carriers, and microcomputer firms." In Karlene H. Roberts (ed.), *New Challenges to Understanding Organizations*: 117–135. New York: Macmillan.

Foushee, H. Clayton (1984) "Dyads and triads at 35,000 feet." *American Psychologist*, 39: 885–893.

Freud, Sigmund (1959) *Group Psychology and the Analysis of the Ego*. (First published in 1922.) New York: Norton.

Giddens, Anthony (1984) *The Constitution of Society*. Berkeley: University of California Press.

Ginnett, Robert C. (1983) "Crews as groups: Their formation and their leadership." In Earl L. Wiener, Barbara G. Kanki, and Robert L. Helmreich (eds.), *Cockpit Resource Management*: 71–98. San Diego: Academic Press.

Hackman, J. Richard (1993) "Teams, leaders, and organizations: New directions for crew-oriented flight training." In Earl L.Wienar, Barbara G. Kanki, and Robert L. Helmreich (eds.), *Cockpit Resource Management*: 47–69. San Diego: Academic Press.

Harper, Douglas (1987) *Working Knowledge: Skill and Community in a Small Shop.* Chicago: University of Chicago Press.

Helmrich, Robert L., and Clayton Foushee (1993) "Why crew resource management? Empirical and theoretical bases of human factors training in aviation." In Earl L. Wiener, Barbara G. Kanki, and Robert L. Helmreich (eds.), *Cockpit Resource Management*: 3–45. San Diego: Academic Press.

Helmreich, Robert L., Clayton H. Foushee, R. Benson, and W. Russini (1985) "Cockpit resource management: Exploring the attitude-performance linkage." Paper presented at Third Aviation Psychology Symposium, Ohio State University.

Heydebrand, Wolf V. (1989) "New organizational forms." *Work and Occupations*, 16: 323–357.

Hirsch, Paul, Stuart Michaels, and Ray Friedman (1987) "'Dirty hands' vs. 'clean models': Is sociology in danger of being seduced by economica?" *Theory and Society*, 16: 317–336.

Janowitz, Morris (1959) "Changing patterns of organizational authority: The military establishment." *Administrative Science Quarterly*, 3: 473–493.

King, Jonathan B. (1989) "Confronting chaos." *Journal of Business Ethics*, 8: 39–50.

Klein, Gary A. (1993) "A recognition-primed decision (RPD) model of rapid decision making." In Gary A. Klein, Judith Orasanu, Roberta Calderwood, and Caroline E. Zsambok (eds.), *Decision Making in Action: Models and Methods*: 138–147, Norwood, NJ: Ablex.

Lanir, Zvl (1989) "The reasonable chice of disaster: The shooting down of the Libyan airliner on 21 February 1973." *Journal of Strategic Studies*, 12: 479–493.

Levi-Strauss, Claude (1968) *The Savage Mind.* Chicago: University of Chicago Press.

Maclean, Norman (1992) *Young Men and Fire.* Chicago: University of Chicago Press.

March, James G. (1989) *Decisions and Organizations.* Oxford: Blackwell.

Maruyama, Magorah (1963) "The second cybernetics: Deviation-amplifying mutual causal process." *American Scientist*, 61: 164–179.

McDougall, William (1920) *The Group Mind.* New York: Putnam.

Meacham, John A. (1983) "Wisdom and the context of knowledge." In D. Kuhn and J.A. Meacham (eds.), *Contributions in Human Development*, 8: 111–134. Basel: Karger.

Miles, Ray E., and Charles C. Snow (1992) "Causes of failure in network organizations." *California Management Review*, 34(4): 53–72.

Miller, Danny (1990) *The Icarus Paradox.* New York: Harper.

Mintzberg, Henry (1983) *Structure in Fives: Designing Effective Organizations.* Englewood Cliffs, NJ: Prentice Hall.

Morgan, Gareth, Peter J. Frost, and Louis R. Pondy (1983) "Organizational symbolism," in L. R. Pondy, P. J. Frost, G. Morgan, and T. C. Dandridge (eds.), *Organizational Symbolism*: 3–35. Greenwich, CT: JAI Press.

Neisser, Ulric, and Eugene Winograd (1988) *Remembering Reconsidered: Ecological and Traditional Approaches to the Study of Memory.* New York: Cambridge University Press.

O'Hare, David, and Stanley Roscoe (1990) *Flightdeck Performance: The Human Factor.* Ames, IA: Iowa State University Press.

Orasanu, Judith, and Terry Connolly (1993) "The reinvention of decision making," In Gary A. Klein, Judith Orasanu, Roberts Calderwood, and Caroline E. Zsambok (eds.), *Decision Making in Action: Models and Methods*: 3–20. Norwood, NJ: Ablex.

Perrow, Charles (1984) *Normal Accidents.* New York: Basic Books. (1986) *Complex Organizations*, 3rd ed. New York: Random House.

Poole, M. Scott, David R. Selbold, and Robert D. McPhee (1985) "Group decision-making as a structurational process." *Quarterly Journal of Speech*, 71: 74–102.

Pyne, Stephen (1989) *Fire on the Rim.* New York: Weidenfeld & Nicolson.

Random House (1987) *Dictionary of the English Language*, 2d ed.: Unabridged. New York: Random House.

Ranson, Stewart, Bob Hinings, and Royston T. Greenwood (1980) "The structuring of organizational structures." *Administrative Science Quarterly*, 25: 1–17.

Read, P. P. (1974) *Alive*. London: Pan Books.

Reason, James (1990) *Human Error*. New York: Cambridge University Press.

Reed, M. (1991) "Organizations and rationality: The odd couple." *Journal of Management Studies*, 28: 559–567.

Riley, Patricia (1983) "A structurationalist account of political culture." *Administrative Science Quarterly*, 28: 414–437.

Runkel, Phillip J., and Joseph E. McGrath (1972) *Research on Human Behavior*. New York: Holt, Rinehart, and Winston.

Schutz, William C. (1981) "The ego, FIRO theory and the leader as completer." In Louis Petrulla and Bernard M. Bass (eds.), *Leadership and Interpersonal Behavior*: 48–65. New York: Holt, Rinehart, and Winston.

Scott, W. Richard (1987) *Organizations: Rational Natural, and Open Systems*, Englewood Cliffs, NJ: Prentice Hall.

Smith, Ken K. (1983) "An Intergroup perspective on individual behavior." In J. Richard Heckman, Edward E. Lawler, and Lyman M. Porter (eds.), *Perspectives on Behavior in Organizations*: 397–408. New York: McGraw-Hill.

Taylor, Shelby E. (1989) *Positive Illusions*. New York: Basic Books.

Weick, Kari E. (1979) *The Social Psychology of Organizing*, 2d ed. Reading, MA: Addison-Wesley. (1985) "Cosmos vs. chaos: Sense and nonsense in electronic contexts." *Organizational Dynamics*, 14(Autumn): 50–84. (1990) "The vulnerable system: Analysis of the Tenerife air disaster." *Journal of Management*, 16: 571–593.

Weick, Kari E., and Kariene H. Roberts. (1993) "Collective mind in organizations: Heedful interrelating on flight decks." *Administrative Science Quarterly*, 38: 357–381.

Westley, Frances R. (1990) "Middle managers and strategy: Microdynamics of inclusion." *Strategic Management Journal*, 11: 337–351.

Westrum, Ron (1982) "Social intelligence about hidden events." *Knowledge*, 3: 381–400.

White, S. K. (1988) *The Recent Work of Jurgen Habermas: Reason, Justice, and Modernity*. Cambridge: Cambridge University Press.

Wiener, Earl L., Barbara G. Kanki, and Robert L. Helmreich (1993) *Cockpit Resource Management*, San Diego: Academic Press.

Wiley, Norbert (1988) "The micro-macro problem in social theory." *Sociological Theory*, 6: 254–261.

IV-14: Narratives of Compassion in Organizations

Peter J. Frost, Jane E. Dutton, Monica C. Worline, and Annette Wilson

As my illness progressed I was trying to keep on teaching, was trying to keep doing everything and I was keeping on, keeping on. I was on medications and increasingly ill and finally I called a friend and senior colleague on a Sunday and I said: 'You have to help me figure out how to quit doing what I am doing. I can't do another day.' And she came over and spent the afternoon with me on a Sunday, reassigning my students, figuring out all

"Naratives of Compassion in Organizations" by Peter J. Frost, Jane E. Dutton, Monica C. Worline, and Annette Wilson. Sage Publications, 2000. Reprinted with permission.

the paperwork that needed to be done and doing all of those things. (Colleen, Professor)

Organizations are sites of everyday healing and pain. Colleen's story is a story of organizational compassion, organizational response to pain. As one of our participants reminded us: "I see lots of pain which people bring to their workplaces simply because they are human beings. . . most people actually walk in through the doors as wounded people"

What do others do in the face of this wounding? While not often talked about, and easily missed if one is not looking for them, compassionate acts are part of the weave that keeps work communities on the mend. The giving and receiving of compassion restores a sense of humanity and connection to the experiences that people have at work (Frost, 1999). Compassion is an essential part of care-giving that is "part of, rather than separate from, work interaction" (Kahn, 1998: 43). Pain and compassion are not separate from "being a professional" and the "doing of work" in organizations. They are a natural and living representation of people's humanity in the workplace.

This chapter explores some foundational assumptions in our conceptualization of compassion and its link to emotion in organizations. These foundations provide the canvas for a painting of compassion stories that reveal two important insights about compassion and organization. One insight is that people often act compassionately in the face of pain without knowing what is appropriate or how compassion should be conveyed.

Compassion involves people allowing feeling to guide action, rather than the reverse. A second insight is that organizations create an emotional ecology where care and human connection are enabled or disabled. We use these two insights to pose an invitation to further study of compassion

in organizations. We close with a found poem that weaves together our study participants' words, representing what we learned in a very different way. We hope that the text and the poem together awaken recognition and interest in compassion as concept and compassion as human expression.

FOUNDATIONS

We were guided in collecting these narratives of compassion by four assumptions. We assume that organizations are social systems and that people's interactions with others in the organization will comprise much of their experience of their work. The embeddedness of people's work experiences in interpersonal interactions and relationships means that the emotional tone and impact of these interactions is vital to an understanding of people's work experience (Berschied, 1994; Brass, 1985; Dutton et al., 1999; Gersick et al., 2000; Ibarra, 1992; Ibarra and Smith-Lovin, 1997; Uzzi, 1996). Because work organizations are such important centres of people's time and energy, we assume that people in organizations seek a feeling of connection with one another, a feeling of belonging, and a feeling of being cared for and respected. Such feelings are provided in part by daily interactions that are caring (Baumeister and Leary, 1995; Kahn, 1993; Meyerson, 1998; Miller and Stiver,1997). At the centre of our notion of compassion is the assumption that the absence or presence of caring interactions at work dramatically impact people's experience of organizations.

Our second assumption is that people are inherently emotional beings and that people experience connection and belonging through feeling (Baumeister and Leary, 1995; Miller and Stiver, 1997). As other scholars have noted, dominant discourse separates emotion from rationality and divides people in organizations from their emotional responses (Meyerson, 1998;

Mumby and Putnam, 1992). Rather than separate emotion from work, we assumed that people bring emotions into their work and that emotions infiltrate the doing of work (Kahn, 1998). Sharing these emotions and responding to emotions of others is at the heart of experiences of pain and compassion in organizations.

We further assumed that people's actions and feelings are not completely determined by the organization. We attempt to understand the ways in which organizational practices bound, limit, enable and encourage the expression of pain and compassion (Shotter, 1995). We assume a world in which organizational practices provide a framework within which people experience their work (Bell and Staw, 1989).

Finally, traditional discourse in organizations often seeks to divide public from private, home from office, personal from professional (Bardbury and Lichtenstein, 1999; Meyerson, 1998; Mumby and Putnam, 1992). We assume that these divisions are largely impossible. When we ask about acts of compassion in the workplace, we receive information about both personal and professional lives. Participants in this research described tensions that are inherent in living both a personal and an organizational life. Such tensions often limit the expression of pain in organizations. In the end, however, we cannot divide ourselves or separate pain from work (Kahn, 1998; Meyerson, 1998). Compassion is directed toward those who are suffering, regardless of whether that suffering is the result of a personal or a professional wound.

WHAT IS COMPASSION?

We focus on a definition of compassion that centres on the connection between people. Some define compassionate acts as forms of empathy or personal support that are offered from one person to another. Psychologists who study the motivation for

helping each other when in need see compassion as one of the emotions associated with empathetic concern (for example, Batson, 1991). Like empathy, compassion involves on "other-oriented feelings that are most often congruent with the perceived welfare of the other person" (Batson, 1994; 606). We assume, however, that compassion goes beyond an individual feeling of empathy and is expressed through action of some sort. In organizations, this form of caregiving often involves conveying "an emotional presence by displaying warmth, affection and kindness" (Kahn, 1993: 546). In this sense, compassionate acts often display a form of emotional intelligence (Goleman, 1995, 1998) and are guided by a mutual concern that allows action in connection with others (Miller and Stiver, 1997).

One can also think about compassion as "the heart's response to the sorrow" (Kornfield, 1993: 326). In compassion, a person surrenders him or herself to the pain of another by being with that person, at least for a moment. Compassion is associated with feelings that are fundamentally "other regarding rather than self-regarding" (Solomon, 1998: 528). The Dalai Lama discusses "genuine compassion [as] based on a clear acceptance or recognition that others, like oneself, want happiness and have the right to overcome suffering. On that basis one develops some kind of concern about the welfare of others, irrespective of one's attitude to oneself" (1981: 63). This focus outside of oneself facilitates another's feeling of being cared for, joined, seen, felt, known, and not alone (Kahn, 193; Noddings, 1984).

WHY NARRATIVES OF COMPASSION?

This chapter is built on stories that people shared about how others responded to their pain and the pain of others in their work organizations. Our empirical context involves people in university settings.[1] Thus the narratives of compassion have double meaning. As a methodology and phenomena, narratives are windows into life in organizations (Boje, 1991; Barry and Elmes, 1997; Czarniawska, 1998; Martin et al., 1983; O'Connor, 1996; Weick and Browning, 1986). As a research setting, these narratives provide openings into the organizational worlds in which we live. Through collecting stories of how people in universities experience compassion, we have become much more attuned to universities as sites of human pain and healing. While we will use primarily the voice of "researchers", behind this stance is an unwritten text of how all four of us as university participants—two PhD students and two faculty members—have been affected deeply by the dialogues that shaped these research observations.

For organizational researchers interested in emotion at work, compassion narratives are carriers of both the feelings of being in pain and the feelings of responding to pain as they play out during the conduct of people's work. They highlight features of emotions at work that have received scant attention. First, stories of compassion at work breathe life into deadened accounts of work feeling. As Sandelands (1998:17) describes, "Society [and as applied here, organization] is dissected as a cadaver, a logical structure of inert elements", extinguishing the life in the social connection that exists between people. Fineman makes a similar graphic assertion when he argues that our field is "emotionally anorexic" (Fineman, 1993: 9). Reliance on stories as data helps to hold onto a fuller and more living account to people's feelings at work.

Organizational studies has focused on display rules and how these shape the forms of expressed feelings in organizational settings (for example, Hochschild, 1983; Rafaeli and Sutton, 1987, 1989). Compassion narratives, while evidencing some effects of these constraints, also convey feelings of care that emerge spontaneously in response to observed or known suffering. Expressed pain is often a violation of basic display rules that divide emotion from work. When these basic display rules are transgressed others often act within the space that is opened. While it does not deny the existence of toxic organizational contexts, acts of compassion are more than normative compliance to well-grooved display rules. While compassionate expression is subject to culturally bounded display rules, we found that people experienced authentic connection with each other in the context of work when pain was expressed and response was necessary.

STORIES

THE IMPORTANCE OF PAIN

Understanding compassion in organizations means recognizing the ubiquity of pain in the workplace. Our participants helped us to see that pain in work organizations lives in many forms and emerges from many places. Their accounts of pain were vivid, honest and sometimes horrifying.

Some people described the pain of acute losses—deaths and suicides of family members and friends. For others, the losses were of connections and relationships with others as marked by divorces, separations, and ruined friendships or working relationships. Still others described the pain of career losses inflicted by demotions, rejections and tenure denials. Not all pain was brought on by significant losses. Participants also described the pain of small slights, disrespect and uncivil acts (Pearson and Porath, 1999) and being treated as invisible or unimportant. Experienced pain is part of the daily rhythm of organizational participation.

For example, faculty described working with the pain of students who had suffered traumatic events such as rape, suicide, sexual harassment, and abuse. They described acknowledging and working with this pain as a necessary part of the teaching experience. Similarly, staff members described working with the pain of students, other staff and faculty who they knew to be suffering. Students described other student's suffering in enduring the painful setbacks and degradations of being a student. Many people described the pain of being overloaded, experiencing crushing workloads, making it difficult to spend meaningful time with themselves, with partners and with families. The pain was often accentuated because people in universities described feeling so alone in much of their work.

COMPASSION IN THE FACE OF PAIN-THREE INSTANCES

Three examples of compassion in the face of pain introduce a discussion of what we discovered about compassion through the stories we collected. Ken told us about responding compassionately to a colleague's illness over several years.

> He was a colleague in my department, in my field. We were on committees together. Then one [day] he showed up at my house distraught and at loose ends . . . He was sobbing and incoherent, so I stayed with him. And eventually I took him to the hospital for a kind of urgent clinical care. For three years or so he was not so good . . . But for some reason he glommed on to me. And every once in a while, once a month or so, I'd get a call and I would have to go wherever he was and be with him.

Lynn told of a small gesture from a student when she was overwhelmed by an illness in her family and the demands from her doctoral studies. As she described it:

> I was working on this project and trying to do my own stuff and I felt like I was going to go crazy. And

there was a baby shower that was coming up . . . I didn't know how I was going to be able to do everything I had to do and get to the store to get a present . . . One of my colleagues' students called me and said she was going to the store to get a present and said, 'Can I pick up one for you?' I know that it sounds crazy but it was such a gift. It was such a small little thing, she bought a present for me. It was just wonderful. She had thought about me and done that.

Finally, acts of compassion often involved someone offering comfort in the face of the painful loss of someone loved. Ralph, a professor and former dean told the following story:

> My wife and I lost three close relatives in one year, my mother and father, and her brother died of a heart attack at 37 years of age. A lot of people came to our door and chatted about relatives that had died, and so on, but one couple came to our door and wept. And I said 'Well, come on in.' So, they came in. They didn't say anything . . . And it's interesting, because at the end of the day, my wife and I would go over the day's grieving. And the couple that really served us and cared for us and showed compassion was the couple that had said nothing, but had listened and hugged and wept with us.

VISIONS OF COMPASSION

Compassion is one way in which people reach out to others when they are hurting. The picture of compassion seen through the stories we collected reveals a rich range of possible ways that people express and receive compassion at work—from small gestures such as buying a gift to much larger and more extensive acts such as going to a colleague's aid over a period of years.

Sometime the acts of compassion were planned and deliberate, as when someone learned about another's loss or difficulty and consciously made the effort to connect. We see this in Ralph's story of how others responded to the deaths his family suffered. We heard inspiring accounts of how people altered the rhythms of their own lives to accommodate and respond to the suffering of others. Consider the case of Abe, a graduate school dean who deliberately stepped in to help a faculty member in pain. A witness to the act told us the story:

> Jerry was a very bright academic who had a history of emotional pain that included a very unhappy and unloving childhood. He was in a faculty where he felt under-appreciated and he was regarded by most of his colleagues as a jerk. He was also a poor teacher. He would act up with the dean of the department. If the dean wanted him to write a paper or do something he was often so angry that he would put the request in his drawer and refuse to do it. One day this dean came over to him and said, 'Let's go for lunch. I want to take you out.' And he took him for lunch and he said: 'What's going on, tell me about this, what's happening?' And Jerry told him he was having all these problems, and he was just starting to work [them] out. And the dean said, 'Oh I see. Why don't you come to my place every Tuesday and Thursday evening and we will work together.' And they worked on his papers and the dean was an incredible mentor to him.

Many of the compassionate tales were of spontaneous and unplanned giving in the face of someone else's suffering. Sometimes these were the hugs, e-mails, cards or other gestures of care that people extended immediately upon learning of a colleague's suffering. On other occasions whole groups of people dropped what they were doing and responded as a collective. Angela told a heartbreaking story of her husband's death from an inheritable disease and the yearly terror of having to test her children to see if there were signs that they also harboured the disease. She described getting the dreaded phone call that indicated her son had been diagnosed as positive with the disease and having to go immediately to run a staff meeting:

> I sort of ran the meeting and they said "we're planning for next year." And somebody said, "Oh Angela, you know you look a little burned out, maybe we shouldn't be talking about planning right now." And then I said, "Oh, it's not my job. It's not because of that," and then I started weeping, and saying what it was, and all of a sudden, everybody in that room was offering help.

Compassionate acts can be solo or collective. In Ken's story, one colleague provides comfort and assistance to another. In Angela's story it is a group of people gathered for a meeting who spontaneously offer help. We also heard about organized efforts from groups that provided comfort in the face of experienced pain. Clare, a graduate student undergoing chemotheraphy treatments for cancer, described how fellow graduate students organized a meal-cooking intervention for her and her husband. In her words:

> When I was going through treatment, shortly after I had been diagnosed with cancer, some of my fellow doctoral students volunteered to cook for my husband and me. So

they would come over every two weeks with a big cooler full of prepared meals at their own expense. We decided to start paying them for the food because the gesture was just too large for us to accept. So they would just bring us ten prepared meals every couple of weeks and we would stock up our freezers and our bellies would be full.

Compassion was expressed directly and indirectly. Direct forms of compassion involved fact-to-face verbal interactions or physical expressions of touch that communicated a presence and care for another. Indirect expressions of compassion were different. Sometimes people acted as buffers in attempts to alleviate the pain of another. Nathan described a boss who tried to prepare others to help a co-worker if needed:

When Alan was breaking up with Mary he was late to work, he was making mistakes, and the boss was understanding about it. He allowed him to make more mistakes than he usually would have. He sort of let the rest of us know that we needed to keep an eye out to help him or whatever. He talked to everybody about it.

Compassion also comes in its own time. Compassionate acts were sometimes as short as the time it took to write a card or give a hug. Alternatively, expressions of compassion sometimes spanned the space of years as a person responded to repeated episodes of the same kind of pain, as in Ken's story above. Compassion often means giving time to another. As one interviewee expressed: "To me, a compassionate work would be to make yourself available when you don't have time." Compassionate responding involves recognizing when there is a limited opening through which people can connect. As Ken put it, "You know these opportunities come and they slip by and you let them go and you get on with your life." They are not moments that can be easily recovered. When someone shares that they have lost a parent or that their job is being restructured, in the words of one of our participants: "You just have that interstitial space, that moment between the two of you where you can make a difference"

● ● ● ● ● ● ● ● ● ● ●
KNOWLEDGE

One of our faculty participants, after feeling the difference others' responses made to the healing from his father's death, provided this advice:

If you don't know what to say, say anything. If you don't know what to say, at least say something to acknowledge it happened . . . I think even if you don't know the person well enough to do it, acknowledging it in some way is infinitely better than to not say anything. (Greg, professor)

ACTING IN THE FACE OF NOT-KNOWING

At the core of compassion is the idea that in some way one is moved by someone else's pain and acts to connect with the person to signal that one cares. As Josh described: compassion involves "giving them the space to express their pain, whatever that pain might be about and to listen in a way that, you know, that is both just listening but also being active. . . in how you respond back, that is sensitive to the person. And it is more than just a passing acknowledgement that this person is in pain." Miller and Stiver (1997) have described the kind of connection that Josh articulates as mutual empathy. They describe ways in which people connect with others and use feelings of connection to guide responses.

Often we assume that people must know before they act. However, Josh shows us that compassion is action in the face of not-knowing. The emotional connection with another provides a direction for action. Shotter (1995) describes this as "feeling one's way forward" (p. 127) in organizations. Connection with another often demands immediate action and interplay. People rarely know when or under what circumstances compassion will be required. They do not know the facts of their co-workers' lives. Instead, people must allow room for a connection to be established and they must follow the feelings in the connection to respond in the best way they know how.

This kind of connecting seems to entail an ability to attune to the needs of the other. Being able to see or imagine another's pain implies a form of empathy or connected knowing (Belenky et al., 1986). Patricia Benner and her colleagues (196) describe a skill of emotional attunement in highly proficient nurses that illustrates this quality. Attuned nurses have a capacity to read a situation in a patient and to grasp its emotional tone: to know when something is "off" when it looks "ok" on the surface, or to sense that its actually 'ok' despite appearances to the contrary. Compassionate action involves moving from not-knowing and using attunement to guide action.

We speculate that people who are skilled in compassionate responding are able to attune themselves quickly to what others are feeling, and are also able to act out of that attunement. One participant describes the feeling of attunement when his co-worker reaches out to him: "like the times when Jenny asks me if I'm okay, I know that somebody cares about me . . . There's no rhyme or reason for when she asks me, but when she asks me I need to be asked. She knows that somehow . . . We feel the life of each other . . . And it means so much to me and I know she knows that." In this sense, compassion involves the align-ment of action with attunement. Miller and Stiver (1997) suggest that people develop larger repertoires of responses as they engage in this type of mutuality and resonance with another's feelings. Few of our participants felt that they knew how to express compassion or that they knew how to engage in compassionate action before they were called to do so. Compassion involves reaching toward another in ways that allow feeling to guide action.

WHEN COMPASSION FAILS

People's suffering is not always met with compassionate responses when it is shared in organizations. Just as there are barriers to the sharing of pain, such as fear of being seen as weak or fear of burdening others, there are also barriers to the expression of compassion in organizations. Time and timing are important barriers. When people are overloaded or overwhelmed they often feel incapable of responding compassionately. When organizations emotionally exhaust their members, people disconnect from their work and their co-workers (Kahn, 1993).

In addition to time pressure, acts of compassion are blocked when people feel unsure about what kind of expression of compassion is appropriate. Sometimes a lack of knowledge about a person or their situation creates barriers to compassionate action. As our participants told us, when people encounter pain from others whom they don't know too well, they wait for a sign that someone wants help. They worry about "crossing a line" and getting too personal when someone may wish to keep their pain private. As Vicki explained, "Unless they've conveyed to me that it's a problem, I don't go prying because I'm concerned they may not want to talk about it."

People struggle with the lack of knowledge about what to do in the face of tremendous loss. Cindy asks the questions all of us face when confronting the ultimate pain of death:"So how do we relate? How do we give them space? What do you do with the person who you are sitting across from, who knows they have only got maybe next week or maybe the next day. What do you do to relate to them?" Though we can provide no simple answers to these poignant questions, they are the questions with which all organizational members grapple. Because these questions can seem overwhelming, organizational members may be daunted by tremendous loss and compassionate responses may be hindered or lost.

Finally, not everyone is prepared to receive compassion from others, as it implies vulnerability and closeness. Some of our participants expressed not wanting compassionate-attention from their colleagues. One academic gave explicit instructions that no condolences be sent on the loss of a partner. Another, whose parent had passed away, explained: "It wasn't something I wanted to hide, but I didn't want to be getting e-mails from people I'd never known." Sometimes too there was a sense that talking to others doesn't help, that "There's nothing that someone can say to you to make [the pain] go away; it's just there."

Issues of power imbalance and hierarchy may play an important role in people's reluctance to reveal their pain. Fear of unwanted repercussions on the job prevents some from opening up. An untenured professor worried about how a senior colleague would see her professionally: "I was afraid she'd think less of me if I let her into some of the personal problems I was going through." Internalized voices, such as "You imagine you're handicapped in some way" or "I don't feel as smart as I used to . . . I feel damaged and less capable . . . reinforced the sense that revelation could hurt a career. One participant explained that it is: "The pain of uncertainty, the pain of wondering if they're going to be used in some way, or manipulated in some way, or even, the pain of thinking the worst about yourself and your prospects within the company."

Fear of jeopardizing one's employment future also affected those responding compassionately. When Fred took time to be with his child he would think: "what am I doing here? It's 3 in the afternoon and I'm supposed to work on trying to get promoted, and I'm at the park for four hours on a Thursday afternoon." Another expressed his concern: "If I show solidarity or compassion . . . to a co-worker that is in disfavour with the . . . supervisor, then I could be looked at in a very different light professionally." John, a supervisor, speculates that sometimes people may feel coerced to open up when they'd rather not. "If your boss asks you a personal question . . . you may not feel like you know that person well enough to talk to them . . . It's hard, you don't want to tell the boss that it's none of her business, or that you don't feel like talking about it." He worries about the double bind: that he now may be seen as uninterested or uncompassionate.

These fears were realized for some who experienced uncompassionate responses to their pain. One woman, who experienced severe financial hardship following a disability, states: "I have been treated with extreme levels of condescension, contempt, and exclusion because of it." A professor whose father had passed away recalls a colleague's impatient response to his pain: "He said to me, 'So how long do you think it will take you to get over this [death of his father]? Three weeks, maybe?'. . . and I almost said 'f— — —you', you know. And I just looked at him and said, 'No I think it's going to take a lot longer than that.'"

ORGANIZATIONS

Ralph, a former dean of a religious college, noted:

> I think a compassionate organization deals with the pain [of the organization]. There will always be

failure and mistakes and one of the things we look for in an organization is how it treats people when they make mistakes. We just made a huge mistake with our catalogue. One faculty member's picture and name was left out, a senior member of the faculty. Now that's a huge mistake when you have 5000 copies of the catalogue actually printed, sitting in a carton. It was a senior but new administrator who made the mistake. The president exercised very important leadership in saying that we will pay the price as a community to do the right thing in this and do it in such a way that there is no dishonor brought to anyone.

Expressed pain is an invitation to connect. Expressed compassion is a response that affirms the human connection. While these expressions are often exchanged between two or a few people, they are facilitated or hindered by the organizations where people study and work.

AN ECOLOGY OF COMPASSION

Organizations as behavioural settings can ease or make more difficult people's compassion giving. Universities as organizations create cultures, develop rules and procedures, promote leaders, and structure people's time in ways that affect compassionate responding. At a basic level, organizations are distinguished by shared values, beliefs and norms that place different levels of emphasis on being caring towards others. Kahn (1998) demonstrates patterns of orgnizational care that flow throughout organizational systems. Behaviour within these systems serves either to replenish or deplete people's emotional and caring resources (Kahn, 1993). Different cultures give rise to different value for compassion-

ate expressions as normal or not, valued or not, deviant or not. Cialdini (1999), writing about dishonest practices in organizations, finds that organizational practices spread like tumours and beget similar practices across the organization. An organizational system that responds with compassion time and again thus fosters compassionate seeing and acting in its members.

Several participants had worked in different university settings and noted the difference in compassionate responses. For example, faculty members talked about differences in responses to tenure decisions and the departure of organizational members at different universities. Jacques (1993) describes an organizational culture of connection that facilitates informational exchanges and creates a value of caring. Clearly universities as organizations establish an emotional ecology within which their members interact. That emotional ecology can facilitate or retard compassionate action.

One important aspect of an emotional ecology is a working envirnoment in which people are given permission and space to attend to their pain. Kahn (1998) describes the importance of emotional attachments that create whole social systems, with compassionate and caring relationships being developed by the collective. Meyerson (1998) describes organizations that normalize and make room for caring for people who are overloaded and experience burnout. Universities varied considerably in the degree to which they exhibited responses to their members' suffering. For example, one participant described an institution that made an apartment near a hospital available to a staff member to allow her to be near a family member in a coma. We heard stories of administrators arranging workloads and providing help for those experiencing difficulties. We heard of the importance of organizational routines such as sending flowers, notes of condolence, and other actions that represent a form of regularized caring.

Actions like these help to establish a framework for compassionate action by organizational members and create a pattern of organizational care that comes out of such an emotional ecology (Kahn, 1993). The absence of these behaviours also creates patterns of organizational response that are perceived as cold or uncaring (Cialdini, 1999).

Organizational leaders and prominent organizational citizens can exemplify compassionate or uncompassionate reactions to the suffering of organizational members, and by doing so, reinforce or diminish a sense that compassionate responding is valued (Bass, 1990; Kahn, 1993). We heard several other stories of how deans' and administrators' actions were actively interpreted as signals of what the organizations cared about, and therefore the kinds of actions that would be valued (Pfeffer, 1981).

CHARACTERISTICS OF AN ECOLOGY OF COMPASSION

Compassion can help make others in an organization feel cared for, seen, felt, known and not alone (Kahn, 1993; Noddings, 1984). In this way, compassion can be healing, even if the healing is not directed toward the initial source of pain. Because feeling and mutual empathy guides compassionate action, healing is a transformation of the connection and emotion in both the compassion giver and the recipient. Through our collection of compassion narratives we identified five characteristics of interactions within an ecology of compassion.

Compassionate responses affirm a person's existence by making the other person "present" (Buber, 1974). Compassion requires authentic human presence with another. In "The human moment at work," psychiatrist Edward Hallowell (1999) talks about people's need to experience moments of authentic psychological connection. He describes the human moment as having two prerequisites:

"people's physical presence and their emotional and intellectual attention" (p. 59). For the human moment to work: "You have to set aside what you are doing, put down the memo you were reading, disengage from your laptop, abandon your day dream and focus on the person you are with" (p. 60). This skill of recognizing the need in another person is an integral part of the process of giving compassion. One of our participants explained: "Compassion is the willingness to drop what you are engaged in, in order to attend to a person's real feelings, longings, aspirations, pain . . . to leave a task unfinished and to attune to a person is a real act of love in the organizational context." In a similar vein, another participant told us: "Compassion demands our patience, sensitivity, a giving over of ourselves. When people act compassionatey, their world shifts to being present with another." Conveying felt presence is a powerful message in an organizational setting, where invisibility and production are often the essence of daily experience. As Sarah Lawrence-Lightfoot (1999) claims: "As we hurtle through our lives, such moments are altogether too rare, and the relationships in which they occur provide a reminder of what nourishes us most profoundly, perhaps even an echo or reminder of our earliest relationships. In such moments, we feel present and acknowledged" (p. 197).

Compassion giving and receiving sometimes altered the felt connection between people. In the terms of network theorists, a compassionate response in the face of pain often changes a weak tie into a strong tie (Granovetter, 1973), with a change in attendant levels of felt trust and reliance. Compassionate acts can change attachments from weak to strong, where a relationship gains greater emotional weight in someone's life (Kahn, 1998). The compassion receiver often recognized that the quality of connection between two people had been transofrmed. As Greg told us, "After someone has been compassionate, they loom as an important person in my life."

Sometimes the transformation in connection was profound. Margaret described a colleague who comforted her during a painful divorce. In this case, a compassionate response dulled the pain in the short term, and created a lasting friendship in the long term. In her words, "Wow, how did that make me feel? It made me laugh; it stopped the pain for a moment and made me laugh. It was an amazing friendship that formed through that. And again, she is not only a great friend, but a great colleague, also in academia struggling her own struggles."

There were cases where witnessing the compassionate actions modelled a form of contact that changed the quality of connection between the whole. Anne, a faculty member in the arts, told of a student's struggle with representing her partner's suicide in a class assignment. When the student shared her creation with other class members, the professor responded in a way that affected everyone who saw it. As she described: "We have all been touched by death, if not suicide, in some way . . . So I just talked about that . . . None of us could understand the pain she had experienced . . . And that it was incredibly valuable for all of us to have her share it with us, what it meant, and how her life would be forever affected. And that art allows us to do this." The student's courage and openness moved the other students deeply, enabling them to share. "They were so supportive of her and thanked her and talked about it. Some of them opened up and said things about deaths that had affected them."

Organizational environments can be transformed by compassion. Similarly, a professor describes how a senior colleague has "set up an environment of cooperation and collaboration of mutual support," by taking compassionate action to help others: "She is very conscious of graduate students and adjuncts, women who are struggling, who are alone . . . argu[ing] long and hard with the dean, fearlessly, on their behalf to keep them in their classes." As a result, the participant felt that corner of her workplace was transformed from a competitive "snake pit" to a place she felt "comfortable and so at home." A number of participants mentioned that they felt their units were unusually supportive: oases within a larger, hostile institution. One supervisor felt that some of his staff had transferred into his unit because of the compassionate climate, suggesting that the compassionate workplace may be a factor in both attracting and retaining staff.

AN INVITATION TO STUDY COMPASSION IN ORGANIZATIONS

An inquiry into compassion narratives offered our participants the possibility of sharing stories in which they were caregivers to others at work. The fact is everyone we asked had stories to tell. The roles that employees took in these stories—whether staff, faculty or students—were as validators and responders to others' suffering. The compassion stories revealed the myriad of ways that compassion is "done" as a form of competent relational practice (Fletcher, 1999). At the same time, the stories were occasions in which people saw themselves as deeply human, emotional beings—affected by and troubled by the witnessing of another person's pain. While most people expressed doubt and discomfort about whether they were responding the "right way," all of the storytellers expressed a form of engagement and empathy for the other (Frank, 1992).

Thus, we see in these stories the possibility of rewriting caregiving in organizational life as a daily, everyday activity in which all people participate (Kahn 1993, 1998; Meyerson, 1998). In the same way that Kolb (1992) finds that people utilize informal channels of dispute resolution in organizations, we find that compassion is practised by all organizational members. Compassion giving is not something done only by designated professionals (such as social workers, human resource practitioners or crisis counsellors), but is done by most organizational members in the everyday doing of work in organizational communities. Like Kahn (1993) we find that caregiving and compassionate action are woven into the daily interactions in organizations.

DANGER AND BLINDSPOTS IN A COMPASSION FRAME

It is also important to name some of the silences and blindspots in our study account. Of course, any attempt to do so is always incomplete. First, we chose a wide brush to paint the look of compassion through the words of 22 people living in academic settings. Differences and variations are brushed over in this type of account. It was often the variation or the anomalies that were most moving or informative, and yet we have focused on patterned similarities, pushing differences into the background. This makes the compassion portrait look neater, tidier and more coherent than in fact it is. No doubt compassion varies across cultures, organizations and industries. We hope that other researchers will repaint differences that exist between individuals engaging in compassionate action in different national and organizational contexts.

Second, we have not fully explored the dynamics of power and status. Our account does not address how superior power enables people to express pain differently and, similarly, how inferior status may coerce revelation or silence, and enable or disable expression. For example, greater power in organizations is typically associated with freedom, flexibility and resources that equip people to respond compassionately. We have also not addressed the gendering of compassion giving as a partial

explanation for why it is so invisible in organizations (for example, Fletcher, 1999; Jacques, 1992). There are similar silences about race, social class and other differences that could shape how compassion looks and how it feels in organizational settings.

Third, we have portrayed compassion giving implicitly as positive action. However, it is also an action that can injure the people who do it. Some of our participants noted the emotional exhaustion that can come from giving compassion without recourse to some "protection" from the wash of pain one is dealing with. Although she loves helping, one participant reflects, "sometimes I feel I'm not respected very much for being interested . . . They sort of think of me as something to . . . empty their wastes into . . . Or they don't think about me and my feelings very much." As Frost and Robinson note: "Managing organizational pain that is too intense and/or too protracted can inflict great cost on the health of those who step in and try to be compassionate. The most common roll of toxic handling . . . is burnout, both psychological and professional" (1999: 100; see also Meyerson, this volume). Beyond exhaustion and burnout, the positive valuing of compassionate action offered by "good people" masks the ambivalence and conflict that some people felt when faced with other people's pain. The possibility of acting compassionately or not calls forth the very human dilemma of whether one wants to care for another at a particular time, in a particular place, or at a particular level of connection.

• • • • • • • • • •
EPILOGUE

We have devoted this chapter to an exploration of the nature of compassion and the complex and nuanced issues that surround giving and receiving compassion in the workplace. We have discussed the notion of an ecology of compassion as a way to create the beginnings of a framework for viewing organizations in terms of how effectively they enhance or diminish the emotional and caring resources of the people who work in them. We have identified some of the limitations in our study of compassion in organizations.

We close with what we call a "found poem," created from the words of our interview participants by Monica Worline. She writes: "In the words of Annie Dillard, whose work inspired the idea to create a found poem, poems 'seldom require explanation, but this one does . . . I did not write a word of it. Other hands composed the poem's lines-the poem's sentences . . . I lifted them. Sometimes I dropped extra words; I never added a word.'" This poem weaves the words of our participants into an original order, but captures for us the extraordinary depth and eloquence of the stories we have collected, a part of which are evidenced in this chapter.

BECAUSE YOU DARE TO NAME IT

Commiseration, support, problem
    solving, advocacy, a feeling of
    togetherness.
I think we get worn down. Like your
    edges are worn.
You just don't stand out like you used
    to.
So, it's leaning in. It's not just a job, it's
    caring for people.
You can see a tension in the person's
    face, for one thing:

    Sometimes, you see it in their eyes
    Sometimes, in their body movements
    Sometimes, even in what they are
        saying.

Everybody was praying, sending condolences, sending cards, expressions,
    support;
real caring, listening, little gifts; people
    picking up pieces, you know, to help
    practically.

Is fear a form of pain?
Because you have to hide your true self
    and your true feelings;
it looks like people feeling like second
    class citizens;
there was a real norm in our department of modesty and always presenting a good face.
    Keep your skeletons at home.
    You're not supposed to have a personal life.
    You're supposed to take care of
        business.

The pain of uncertainty, the pain of
    wondering
if they're going to be used in some way,
    or manipulated in some way, or even
the pain of thinking the worst about
    yourself and your prospects within
    the company.
Mostly what people do is avoid you.
I understand it. Boy, I did it.
I have to catch myself from doing it
    again.
And so I have this memory of people
    who just backed away and didn't say
    anything,
thinking it was the best thing.

But I was so moved that she wanted to
    do that:
to go into the ugly personal slop of
    my life.

I think, no, I want to change this
    language.
I want there to be a language for saying
    that I have pain with dignity.

For someone on behalf of an aggrieved
or someone who is representative of
    the organizaion
to be able to say, "I forgive you";
or "We forgive you and we do not hold
    this against you:"

It changed things tremendously.

I was throwing up all over the house
    and she hung on to my rear end,
    and I said, "Oh my god, this is so
    humiliating."
And she said, "Oh, fuck it, this is the
    bonding moment."
That's her. Wow, how did that make
    me feel?
It made me laugh. It stopped the pain
    for a moment and made me laugh.

Well, for me, the great threshold is to
    do something.

And, you know, everybody put their
    arms around me and said,
"We want things to work out"
and everybody was offering help; it's
    incredible. People offering their ser-
    vices,
whether it's watch your house, take
    your dog, can I go to the store
    for you?
Bring you meals, cover your desk.
And you don't forget that. You do not
    forget that.

To actually feel what other people felt
and the ability to insist that the feeling
    be addressed.

She is very conscious of graduate stu-
    dents and adjuncts who are women
    and who are struggling;
who are alone;
who are barely making it financially;
and she argues long and hard with the
    dean fearlessly on their behalf to
    keep them in their classes.

Compassion is not in that sense a qual-
    ity or a thing, it's a capacity.
I mean, we say the right things; we say
    that people are important,
our most important resource,
but then look at—what do people
    really need?

I think most people really need to feel
    that somewhere along the line
    they're doing something valuable,
or right, or meaningful, or it's
    appreciated;
People work more hours than is
    humanly possible
and they get criticized for their
    mistakes
more than thanked for what they
    do well.

I mean, I just honestly believe that you
    have the moment;
An opportunity right then for some-
    thing that may never come up again.
It's hard to live in the truth of that.

The story of my life is not dealing with
    pain;
dealing with pain is what I have to do
    to have my life.

So I think it's where the humanity of
    one person meets the humanity of
    another person.
This is a really significant thing:
If an organization can be listening and
    caring and compassionate.
That was what the whole miracle was.
    We did get to do that.
Because there is so much;
People suffer so alone and there is
    so much.

ACKNOWLEDGMENTS

An earlier version of this chapter was presented at the Academy of Management
National Meetings, Chicago, 8–11 August
1999. We wish to thank the colleagues
whom we interviewed for the generous contributions of time and insight. Thanks to
Martha Feldman, Stephen Fineman, Linda
Groat, Jane Hassinger, Deb Meyerson,
Beth Reed, Denise Rousseau and Amy

Wrezesniewski for comments on earlier drafts. We also wish to thank the William Russell Kelly professorship for its support of this project.

Note

1. We interviewed 22 people from three university settings, including faculty, staff and students. They told us stories of their own pain, of the pain they have seen in others, and of the ways in which they have been the givers, the receivers, and the observers of compassionate acts in organizations. We have given fictional names to our informants to provide them with anonymity and to protect their confidences. The people we interviewed were all people we knew and people with whom we had some connection. The connection to our interviewees was consequential in how the interviews unfolded and the kinds of stories shared. Our interviews were often conversations—sharing what we had learned from our own life experiences about what compassion is and how it works(or does not work)in the organizations that we inhabit as places of employment and as places of study.

References

Barry, D. and Elmes, M. (1997) "Strategy retold: toward a narrative view of strategy discourse," *Academy of Management Review,* 22 (2): 428–52.

Bass, B. M. (1990) *Bass and Stodgill's Handbook of Leadership.* New York: Free Press.

Batson, C. D. (1991) *The Altruism Question: Toward a Social-Psychological Answer.* Hillsdale, NJ: Erlbaum.

Batson, C. D. (1994) "Why act for the public good: 4 answers," *Personality and Social Psychological Bulletin,* 20 (5): 603–10.

Baumcister, R. and Leary, M. (1995) "The need to belong: desire for interpersonal attachments as a fundamental human motivation," *Psychological Bulletin,* 117 (3): 497–529.

Belenky, M. F., Clinchy, B. M., Goldberger, N. R. and Tarule, M. (1986) *Women's Ways of Knowing.* New York: Basic Books.

Bell, N. and Staw, B. M. (1989) "People as sculptors vs. sculpture: The roles of personality and personal control in organizations," in M. B. Archur, D. T. Hall and B. S. Lawrence (eds.), *The Handbook of Career Theory.* Cambridge: Cambridge University Press.

Benner, P., Tanner, C. and Chesla, C. (1996) *Expertise in Nursing Practice: Caring, Clinical Judgement and Ethics.* New York: Springer Publishing Company.

Berscheid, E. (1994) "Interpersonal relationships," *Annual Review of Psychology,* 45: 79–129.

Boje, D. (1991) "The storytelling organization: A study of story performance in an office-supply firm," *Administrative Science Quarterly,* 36(1): 106–26.

Bradbury, H. and Lishtenstein, B. (1999) "Relationality in organizational research: exploring the space between." Working paper.

Brass, D. J. (1985) "Men's and women's networks: A study of interaction patterns and influences on organizations," *Acadamy of Management Journal,* 28: 327–43.

Buber, M. (1974) *I and Thou.* New York: Macmillian Publishing.

Cialdini, R. (1999) "Of tricks and tumors: Some little-recognized costs of dishonest use of effective social influence," *Psychology and Marketing,*18 (2): 91–8.

Czarniawska, B. (1998) *A Narrative Approach in Organization Studies.* Thousand Oaks, CA: Sage.

Dalai Lama (1981) *The Power of Compassion.* London: Thorsons.

Dillard, A. (1995) *Mornings Like This: Found Poems.* New York: HarperCollins Publishers.

Dutton, J., Dehebe, G. and Wrzesniewski, A. (1999) "Being valued and devalued at work: A social valuing perspective" Working paper, University of Michigan, Ann Arbor.

Fineman, S. (1993) *Emotions in Organizations.* London: Sage.

Fletcher, J. (1999) *Disappearing Acts: Gender, Power and Relational Practice at Work.* Cambridge, MA: MIT Press.

Frank, A. W. (1992) "The pedagogy of suffering: Moral dimensions of psychological therapy and research," *Theory and Psychology,* 2: 467–85.

Frost, P. F. (1999) "Why compassion counts," *Journal of Management Inquiry*, 8 (2): 127–33.

Frost, P. and Robinson, S. (1999) "The toxic handler: Organizational hero and casualty," *Harvard Business Review*, July–August, 96–106.

Gersick, C., Bartunek, J. M. and Dutton, J. E. (2000) "Learning from academia: The importance of relationships in professional life," *Academy of Management Journal*, forthcoming.

Goleman, D. (1995) *Emotional Intelligence*. New York: Bantam Books.

Goleman, D. (1998) *Working with Emotional Intelligence*. New York: Bantam Books.

Granovetter, M. S. (1973) "The strength of weak ties,"*American Journal of Sociology*, 78 (6): 1360–80.

Hallowell, E. M.(1999) "The human moment at work," *Harvard Business Review*, Jan.–Feb., 58–66.

Hochschild, A. R. (1983) *The Managed Heart: Commercialization of Human Feeling*. Berkeley: University of California Press.

Ibarra, H. (1992) "Homophily and differential returns: Sex differences in network structure and access in an advertising firm," *Administrative Science Quarterly*, 37: 422–47.

Ibarra, H. and Smith-Lovin, L. (1997) "New directions in social network research on gender and organizational careers," in C. L. Cooper and S. Jackson (eds.), *Creating Tomorrow's Organization: A Handbook for Future Research in Organizational Behaviors*. Sussex: John Wiley & Sons.

Jacques, R. (1992) "Critique and theory building: producing knowledge from the kitchen," *Academy of Management Review*, 17(3): 582–606.

Jacques, R. (1993) "Untheorized dimensions of caring work: Caring as structural practice and caring as a way of seeing," *Nursing Administration Quarterly*, 17 (2):1–10.

Kahn, W. A. (1993) "Caring for the caregivers: Patterns of organizational caregiving," *Administrative Science Quarterly*, 38 (4): 539–63.

Kahn, W. A.(1998) "Relational systems at work," in B. M. Staw and L. L. Cummings (eds.), *Research in Organizational Behavior*, vol. 20. Greenwich, CT: JAI Press, pp. 39–76.

Kolb, D. (1992) "Women's work: Peacemaking in organizations,"in D. Kolb and J. Bartunek (eds.), *Hidden Conflict in Organizations*. Newbury Park, CA: Sage.

Kornfield, J. (1993) *A Path with Heart*. New York: Bantam Books.

Lawrence-Lightfoot, S. (1999) *Respect*. Reading, MA: Perseus Books.

Martin, J., Feldman, M. S., Hatch, M. J. and Sitkin, S. B. (1983) "The uniqueness paradox in organizational stories,"*Administrative Science Quarterly*, 28: 438–53.

Meyerson, D. E. (1998) "Feeling stressed and burned out: A feminist reading and re-visioning of stress-based emotions within medicine and organizational science," *Organizational Science*, 8(1):103–18.

Miller, J. B. and Stiver, I. (1997) *The Healing Connection*. Boston, MA: Beacon Press.

Mumby, D. K. and Putnam, L. L. (1992) "The politics of emotion: A feminist reading of bounded emotionality," *Academy of Management Review*, 17: 465–86.

Noddings, N. (1984) *Caring: A Feminine Approach to Ethics and Moral Education*. Berkeley, CA: University of California Press.

O'Connor, E. S. (1996) "Telling decisions: The role of narrative in organizational decision making," in Z. Shapira (ed.), *Organizational Decision Making*, New York: Cambridge University Press, pp. 304–23.

Pearson, C. and Porath, C. (1999) "Workplace incivility: The target's eye view," Paper presented at the National Academy of Management Meetings, Chicago.

Pfeffer, J. (1981) "Management as symbolic action: The creation and maintenance of organizational paradigms," in L. L. Cummings and Barry M. Staw (eds.), *Research in Organizational Behavior*, vol. 3. Greenwich, CT: JAI Press.

Rafaeli, A. and Sutton, R. (1987) "The expression of emotions as part of the work role," *Academy of Management Review*, 12:23–37.

Rafaeli, A. and Sutton, R. (1989) "The expression of emotion in organizational life," in L.

Cummings and B. Staw (eds), *Research in Organizational Behavior*, vol. 11. Greenwich, CT: JAI Press, pp.1–42.

Sandelands, L. E. (1998) *Feeling and Form in Social Life.* Lanbam, MD: Rowman & Littlefield.

Shotter, J. (1995) "The manager as practical author: A rhetorical-responsive, social constructionist approach to social organizational problems," in D. Hosking, H. Dachler and K. Gergen (eds.), *Management and Organizations: Relationship Alternatives to Individualism.* Aldershot: Avebury.

Solomon, R. C. (1998) "The moral psychology of business: Care and compassion in the corporation," *Business Ethics Quarterly,* 8 (3): 515–33.

Uzzi, B. (1996) "The sources and consequences of embeddedness for the economic performance of organizations: The network effect," *American Sociological Review,* 61: 674–98.

Weick, K. L. and Browning, L. (1986) "Argument and narration in organizational communication," in J. G. Hunt and J. D. Blair (eds.), *1986 Yearly Review of Management of the Journal of Management,* 12 (2): 243–59.

IV-15: Amid Crippled Rivals, Southwest Again Tries to Spread Its Wings
Low-Fare Airline Maintains Service, Mulls Expansion in Risky Bid for Traffic

Melanie Trottman

DALLAS—The tireless maverick of the airline industry is poised to pounce again.

Southwest Airlines, which has consistently pursued strategies shunned by competitors in its 30-year history, is once more heading away from the pack. Its actions during the coming weeks could reshape competition in the skies for years.

The terrorist attacks on Sept.11 shut down all airlines for two days. To stay afloat amid slack demand when they reopened, Southwest's cash-strapped rivals grounded planes and slashed their flight schedules and work forces.

Southwest is keeping all its workers and flying a full schedule. On Sunday, it even went ahead with the previously scheduled opening of a new destination, adding Norfolk, Va., to its routes. Low-fare, low-cost Southwest is the nation's most profitable airline and the only major carrier analysts expect to be profitable this year. It has lots of cash, little debt and a simple strategy. As rivals shrink, Southwest is looking to grab market share—and maybe even acquire idled airplanes—betting it can win over customers just as it has done at key moments for the industry during the past 10 years.

"They're doing what they do best, which is to shine in the hours of trouble," says Mo Garfinkle, president of GCW Consulting, an aviation consulting firm in Washington. "This, to me, is not a gamble. This is a very shrewd strategic move."

Even if they are concerned about Southwest's moves, other airlines have said repeatedly during the past few weeks that their focus is on keeping their companies afloat. "The losses we face are truly staggering.

They exceed anything we ever imagined at American," said Donald J. Carty, chairman and chief executive of AMR Corp., American Airlines' parent. "Right now, it is survival, not profitability, that is our core challenge."

For consumers, Southwest's strategy could have far-reaching impact, affecting fares and service from short hops to transcontinental routes. It's a strategy likely to appear throughout the struggling economy as strong opportunists move onto the turf of weakened rivals.

Southwest is the nation's seventh-largest airline based on annual revenue passenger miles, or traffic, which is measured as a paying passenger flown one mile. Last year, its share of traffic among the nine major U.S. airlines was 6.6%, while it generated 90% of the country's low-fare competition, according to the Department of Transportation.

It could emerge from the industry's troubles bigger and stronger. It probably will expand into more long-haul markets, even bringing lower business fares to transcontinental service. And after several years of focusing all its growth on the East Coast, Southwest may bulk up on the West Coast as UAL Corp.'s United Airlines shrinks there.

The airlines is placing a big bet that the climate for air travel will rebound in the coming months, even as its rivals plan for a long downturn. Although it has a huge

---

FIGURE 4-6 Above the Clouds

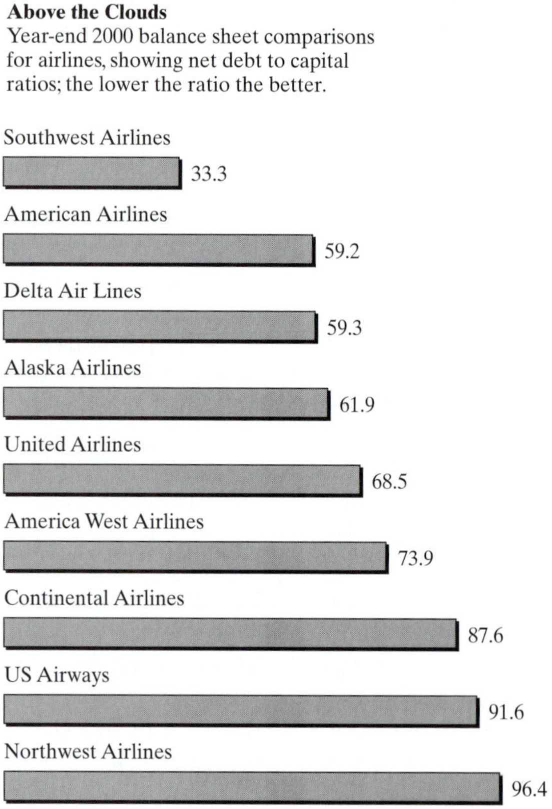

Above the Clouds

Year-end 2000 balance sheet comparisons for airlines, showing net debt to capital ratios; the lower the ratio the better.

Southwest Airlines — 33.3

American Airlines — 59.2

Delta Air Lines — 59.3

Alaska Airlines — 61.9

United Airlines — 68.5

America West Airlines — 73.9

Continental Airlines — 87.6

US Airways — 91.6

Northwest Airlines — 96.4

Source: Salomon Smith Barney.

war chest of cash on hand, Southwest is bleeding cash to keep flying while others cut back.

The Dallas-based airline started flying in June 1971, focusing on short hauls within Texas. It began interstate flights in 1979 and now serves 58 cities in 30 states, often targeting alternative, less-congested airports. Southwest's profit formula relies on keeping costs low—it skimps on meals, for instance—and squeezing the maximum profit out of its aircraft use. It does this mainly by unloading and loading planes in just 20 minutes and focusing on short-haul flights. Both tactics help Southwest get more planes, and passengers, off the ground each day.

In 1990, Southwest rapidly expanded in California when US Airways Group Inc., which had bought Pacific Southwest Airlines, pulled back. In November of that year, Southwest quickly grabbed precious territory in Chicago after Midway Airlines folded. When sagging demand and rising fuel prices forced big airlines to retrench after the Persian Gulf War, Southwest expanded rapidly to fill the void, bulking up in Nashville and San Jose, Calif., after American Airlines closed hubs there, for example. Southwest launched its East Coast campaign in Baltimore in September 1993 when it thought, mistakenly, that US Air was going to close its hub there.

Today, as financially strapped competitors eliminate their least-profitable routes, they are already reducing flights in places where they compete most heavily with Southwest. UAL said it will pull the plug on its Shuttle by United on the West-Coast. The service overlaps with Southwest in markets such as Las Vegas, Los Angeles and Oakland. US Air is eliminating its MetroJet subsidiary on the East Coast, which overlaps with Southwest's service in cities such as Providence, R.L., and Baltimore, one of Southwest's fastest-growing cities. US Air is also eliminating 51 of its 75 mainline jet routes from Baltimore,

including all nonstop flights to Florida. Delta Air Lines is cutting Delta Express in half. The service overlaps with Southwest in Florida in markets such as Orlando, Tampa and Hartford. Altogether, those three operations overlap on about 10% of Southwest's routes.

Southwest itself has put a temporary freeze on growth for the rest of this year and is negotiating with Boeing Co. to defer delivery of 11 new 737 jets scheduled to come off the assembly line by Dec.31. Southwest has tried to cut costs to ensure that losses in the current climate don't get out of hand, following the example of other airlines by cutting travel-agency commissions to 5% from 8%, for example.

At the same time, as other airlines ground Boeing 737 airplanes, Southwest says it will study whether to grab some of those jets and, perhaps as early as January, resume expansion in its fleet of 358 737s and in service. The carrier is now looking at whether to shift flights to add capacity in certain markets, depending on moves competitors make, says Chief Financial Officer Gary Kelly.

"The fact of the matter is we can be patient and we should be patient," Mr. Kelly says, "We're in the mode where we are thinking very tactically."

Southwest has already reduced flights in certain markets to provide for additional service in others, moves it made to satisfy scheduling changes planned before Sept.11, such as the opening of Norfolk. The airline had expected some of the added flights to be serviced with the Boeing jets it still hasn't taken delivery of.

Despite Southwest's financial muscle, its ambitions involve substantial risks. In 2000, the airline posted its 28th consecutive year of profitability and its ninth consecutive year of increased profits. Net income rose 31.8% from a year earlier to $625.2 million and revenue rose 19.2% to $5.65 billion. It had $1.5 billion in cash on hand early last week, and the lowest debt level by far in the industry.

But to back its bet on a rebound in air travel, Southwest tapped its full $475 million line of credit the day after the attacks. At that time, the company was losing $3 million to $4 million a day, but Mr. Kelly says the losses have narrowed since then, although he won't specify by how much.

Southwest is still primarily a short-hop airline. About 85% of its flights are less than two hours, or 750 miles, for example. If security precautions slow travelers down in terminals, driving might prove to be faster than flying for many customers. Southwest has long said its biggest competition was the automobile.

And its gambit comes at a time when the airline was already grappling with a lot of changes. In June, the carrier's legendary chairman and chief executive, Herbert D. Kelleber, stepped down as CEO to assume a more limited role, putting Jim Parker, previously the company lawyer, in the breach as the new CEO.

Mr. Parker took over an airline that was running into many of the same problems afflicting other big carriers: delays and operational snafus, labor strike, escalating costs, higher fares and questions about management.

Some veteran workers had been grumbling about staffing shortages, increased workloads and a breakdown in the company's close-knit, familial culture, which Southwest admitted it was finding harder and harder to instill into its growing workforce. Some employees who in the past agreed to lower wages to help the cause of the undergoing had begun to demand "big-airline" pay. Pilots had been gearing up for a showdown, Ramp workers went through federal mediation earlier in the year.

All that has changed since Sept.11. Workers are pitching in as before with voluntary payroll give-backs and cost-saving ideas. Some are donating a portion of their profit sharing. Others are signing over federal tax refund checks to the airline.

Management has built up goodwill with unions by avoiding layoffs. Staff shortages that looked like problems in August now seem prudent in the current climate. Moves to revamp operations, adding five minutes here and there to the schedule in order to improve on-time performance, now are paying rich dividends as the airline deals with time-consuming security procedures required at airports.

"What may have seemed like really big issues a month ago maybe aren't quite the big issues now." says Gary Shults, president of the transport workers union local 555, which represents about 5,300 camp workers and other employees.

Mr. Shults, a 21-year veteran at Southwest, also notes what many airline analysts have recalled: "When it gets bad everywhere else, it's good here."

In the early 1990s, when jet-fuel prices soared and the economy sank into recession, penny-pinching travelers turned to low-fare Southwest, and growth at the carrier continued.

Much of the growth resulted from new opportunities, even in turbulent times. When Midway Airlines announced at midnight on Nov.13, 1990, that it was out of cash and closing its doors, a Southwest team of lawyers, led by Mr. Parker, was already in place in Chicago. The team was first in line to negotiate to take over Midway's gates at the city's Midway Airport, and a slew of Southwest employees began to immediately install computers, nail Southwest signs over Midway signs and begin operations before any competitors could react. Midway became a key station for Southwest.

Southwest launched a similar biltz when US Air began reducing service on north-south routes in California, Southwest cut fares by two-thirds or more, added numerous flights to the California cities of Oakland. Burbank and Outario, and eventually became the second-biggest carrier in California behind United.

To thwart Southwest's growth, United launched its low-cost, low-fare shuttle service, mimicking Southwest by flying only Beoning 737s and loading and unloading airplanes in about half the usual time.

Southwest held its own in California, leaving the West Coast saturated with flights from the two airlines. Southwest then turned its attention to beefing up on the east coast, where incumbents US Air and Delta set up MetroJet and Delta Express as their own shuttlelike Southwest combatants.

Neither has done much to slow Southwest down. In Baltimore, Southwest had undergrown US Air two years before the latter's recently announced service cuts. In Orlando, where Southwest completes with Delta Express. Southwest has 52 daily non-stop flights to 24 cities, up from 12 nonstop daily flights to eleven cities in April 1996 when it service began. By comparison, Delta Express had 49 daily flights from Orlando prior to Sept.11, according to an airport spokeswoman.

Southwest's decision to maintain all service after Sept.11 isn't entirely bold marketing. The airline's operation is so different from other carriers that it is far more difficult to cut back. Southwest started with one of the simplest schedules to fly in the airline industry: its planes go city to city, without all feeding into one hub and out to spokes all day. Now, with its 358 planes crisscrossing

the country on a mishmash of increasing flight paths, Southwest's schedule is one of the most complex in aviation. Making changes is "very, very complicated," Mr. Kelly says, nothing that the airline has to carefully match aircraft movements to crew movements.

Jim Wimberly, the airline's executive vice president and chief of operations, has likened adding an airplane to the schedule to a jigsaw puzzle with eight billion pieces. A Southwest plane may start the day in one corner of the country, end up in another, and never fly through the same city twice. Cutting one flight from that schedule can create massive headaches.

Rather than cut back, Southwest decided early after the attacks to keep flying empty seats. To help fill them, Southwest launched a risky ad campaign, becoming the first major airline to advertise while many travelers were staying home. Other carriers were thought to be apprehensive about doing so because of fear of offending or seeming insensitive.

One-way fares as low as $34–$89 helped stimulate leisure traffic, which has been stronger than usual relative to business traffic on the airline, Mr. Kelly says.

He says he is encouraged by the recent rise in bookings and load factors. Southwest filled 38.5% of its seats for the week ended Sept. 23, and 52.4% the following week.

"Bookings over the last couple of days have been higher than normal. So the notion that you would cut flights out of certain markets based on last week would be really flawed," Mr. Kelly said last week.

Joyce Rogge, Southwest's senior vice president of marketing, says the carrier felt it was "very important" to come forward and communicate with its customers and employees to show that "America would fly again."

IV-16: Improvisation in Green

Horacio E. Schwalm

It was nearly dusk on a recent evening when a U.S. Special Forces (SF) team walked into a village northeast of Port-au- Prince (Haiti) and encountered a problem for which their training manuals had not prepared them. Several mothers were convinced that a pair of werewolves, in the form of two local women, had placed a curse on the village children and were now preparing to consume their babies' souls. As he listened, the team's warrant officer tucked his hand into his pocket, snapped open a chemical light stick that soldiers use as markers at night and announced in Creole that he would break the curse. Mumbling incantations, the officer anointed each child's forehead with a smear of the glowing green liquid. After declaring, "the spell has been lifted," he turned to the stunned werewolves and promised that if they ever pulled such a stunt again, he would put a spell on them: his magic was much more powerful than theirs.

The 9,000 American soldiers still stationed in Haiti have come to occupy two radically different worlds. The first is the world of Port-au-Prince, which belongs to conventional soldiers who patrol the streets, keep the peace and bide their time until they are scheduled to return home. The second world belongs to the 1,200 men of the Special Forces who, since the occupation began, have overseen rural Haiti. Taking on the roles of sheriff, prosecutor, judge, plumber, mayor and ghost buster, these commandos are often the only glue holding together the 5 million Haitians who live outside the capital.

From their headquarters in a former brassiere factory in Port-au-Prince, the Green Berets have fanned out to more than 500 villages. Upon arriving, they have often been forced to refashion local government after the soldiers and strongmen who terrorized the area faded away like zombies in the night, leaving behind a brutalized population. In Mirebalais, the pro-democracy deputy mayor was beheaded and his body thrown into a nearby river. At the prison in Les Cayes, inmates were treated so abominably that one man's spine was visible through the lesions on his back.

During their two months on the ground, the commandos' even-handed approach has often opened them to the charge of collaborating with the henchmen of the old regime. Yet they have also displayed a rare talent for getting things done, from powering up old electric plants and water pumps to installing mayors, protecting judges, and delivering babies. Often nine men will control a town of 20,000 people.

Their tactics, often devised on the spot, have been unusual, to say the least. To clear the streets of

---

"Improvisation in Green" by Horacio E. Schwalm. Reprinted by permission.

thugs, Green Berets on patrol took to inverting their night-vision goggles so that they glowed in the dark. In Les Cayes, the Special Forces jailed a judge overnight to teach him how inhumane prison conditions were. For Haitians traumatized by generations of dictatorship, the Americans' unconventional tactics carry a most welcome and powerful magic.*Time Magazine*, December 12, 1994)

In his book *Making Sense of the Organization,* Dr. Karl Weick discusses improvisation using the model of a jazz ensemble. He describes improvisation as a continuum that places greater demands on the abilities of the players as they move closer to true imporvisation; that is, making music that did not exist prior to it being conceived and played in front of the audience. I can think of no better model with which to juxtapose a Special Forces A-team, the 12-man group of specialists who must perform as one even in the absence of orders (or sheet music). As Dr. Weick explains, each movement along the continuum represents a greater demand on the player's imagination, concentration, and, I would add, technical competence.

Implied here are several ideas of which three are the most significant. First, the importance of the original work, the starting point for the improvisation, cannot be overstated. The musicians begin on the "same sheet of music" with the intent to finish in a new place. Second, this intent speaks to a culture of improvisation. The musicians are playing in order to improvise, to innovate, to make something that did not exist when they began playing. Additionally, the audience, too, assumes spontaneity on the part of the ensemble. A conductor standing to the front, his back to the audience, telling the saxophone player when he should be creative would be anathema to the culture of jazz. Lastly, each musician and the audi-

ence expect the band to play well. That is, the ability to produce excellent, quality music is assumed by all participants, players, and listeners. I find it difficult to imagine a more cacophonous sound than that of amateur musicians attempting to play bad instruments, poorly, and without the benefit of someone thinking for them via written musical scores. I submit, then, that those who engage in improvisation are likely to be counted among the best in their field.

Therefore, for improvisation to occur, an organization must have these three components, simultaneously: a common starting point from whence to improvise, an atmosphere that assumes and promotes improvising and spontaneity, and individuals or teams that are capable of improvising.

The starting point for the SF in Haiti during Operation Uphold Democracy in 1994 was to create a stable and secure environment for the return of democracy. This goal, I submit, is tantamount to a jazz ensemble taking the stage and hearing the audience demand to hear "some great music." What is great music? What is stable and secure? Yet, in stating the goal without telling the soldiers how to get there, the leaders of the U.S. government gave SF a mandate that allowed the full force of an improvisational culture to come to bear. The U.S. president, the Congress, and the generals said, "We want to see a stable and secure Haiti" and then sat back to see what 1,200 Green Berets might do with 5 million Haitians. The Green Berets, in turn, took to the political stage and started playing. But they played in accordance to a powerful and well- defined culture that rewards innovation. Thus, we see the second ingredient for improvisation—a culture of improvising.

The culture that spawns such thinking is taught to all members of the SF community beginning the first day that they begin their journeys as Green Berets. And the concepts of the improvisation continuum are constantly reinforced, every day, in all circumstances, starting in the selection phase. Of 1,000 or so conventional soldiers who volunteer annually for SF training, just under half will be selected. This attrition is due in great part to the stress placed upon the soldiers during the 3-week selection process. The preponderance of those who fail usually voluntarily withdraw, or VW. (*VW* has become both a noun and a verb among the members of the SF selection committee. For example, "three guys just VW'ed" would be a common phrase. "He's a VW" would be a way of denoting that someone quit. Of note, Timothy McVeigh, executed for the Oklahoma City bombing, was a VW from SF selection.)

Because the laws of the land preclude the SF selection committee from intentionally wounding SF candidates during the assessment process and then observing their behaviors while accomplishing an assigned task (say, rendering first aid to a fellow wounded teammate), the committee metes out stressful situations borne of physical exhaustion, sleep deprivation, and isolation. By the time SF candidates complete the selection phase, they will have easily walked more than 200 miles in 14 or so days with 55 pounds of rucksack strapped to each one of them. They will do most of this walking alone. The intent of such an exercise is to determine whether or not the candidates have the physical and mental endurance to operate effectively under such conditions—conditions that will stress their core beliefs about themselves and their abilities.

Although most military leaders would say that such qualities are desirable in all soldiers, not just SF, the conventional Army culture belies such claims. For example, soldiers in conventional Army units are routinely reminded to drink water when operating in hot climates. Such reminders may seem like appropriate actions for caring leaders, but an SF leader would be mocked for making such a comment to an SF soldier. That someone must be reminded to drink water infers a lack of ability to think innova-

tively in a crisis. In other words, the culture that believes a prudent leader reminds his people to drink water does not expect the people to think and lead themselves. The SF culture demands from the beginning that one be capable of leading himself—of defining reality for himself. The majority of SF operations are such that no one in the chain of command will be within miles of a team while it performs a mission. People who do not know when they should drink, or are treated like they cannot know, are not given missions by the president of the United States to operate in foreign countries in small, unsupervised groups. Once selected, soldiers advance to the SF Qualification Course and there begin their formal training, which lasts 1 to 2 years depending on the specialty. Training to be a Special Forces soldier is the longest training for combat troops in the Department of Defense. The result of such training, and the third component for improvisation, is world-class talent.

The lights are low. The music is flowing in hushed tones. The audience is tapping to the rhythm. A trumpet player steps forward on the stage. The spotlight finds him. The drummer says something like "Here we go." The anticipation is palpable. The trumpet comes up to taut lips, and the sound that emanates is reminiscent of someone stepping on a cat's tail. Everything stops. Here comes the hook from the side stage. The evening is ruined. The audience will go home remembering every detail of that moment when the trumpet player tried to improvise and failed. Intuitively, most people will come to the same conclusion: That guy had no business up there.

The ability to improvise in most fields of endeavor is directly proportional to the ability to do the tasks related to that field with processes taking a back seat to results. For example, a concert pianist makes music by not missing a note of the music that defines it. Conversely, a jazz musician may not even be able to write his name, much less read sheet music. But the ability of both artists to produce results is indisputable. For the innovator, however, the processes mean little unless they achieve desirable results. Here the concert pianist and the jazz player part company. For although both produce results, the concert performer is a slave to the sheet music. He can interpret the music, bring passion to the performance, and perform superbly, but never improvise. Nor is he expected to improvise. No matter how well the concert pianist can play, the audience expects, and rightly so, that the program for the evening's performance will be followed. Jazz players, on the other hand, train to improvise. The skills are honed, and the mind made to think forward though not anticipating the next note from the score. The mind of the innovator is looking where no one else has yet to see. He is confident of his ability to produce results. He trains to produce results. He is routinely placed, or places himself, in circumstances demanding improvisation. SF soldiers routinely conduct training around the world with militaries from cultures as varied as the world itself. They are regularly subjected to demands for excellence while not being quite clear on what standards to base excellence. Routine excellence in nonroutine circumstances constantly reinforces the SF culture of improvisation and creates world-class performers who can exploit opportunities.

Improvisation exists in industry as well as in the ranks of special operations forces and jazz bands. Those businesses that provide services are probably the best environments for creating a culture of improvisation. Training employees to deal with people can create an atmosphere where spontaneity is rooted in competence. Nordstrom comes immediately to mind. Making the customer happy is the stated goal. Only the customer knows what will make him happy. The Nordstrom representative has been given a mandate to make someone (that he has never met) happy for coming to Nordstrom (the starting point).

Nordstrom creates an environment that assumes that its employees will innovate if necessary to make the customer happy (the improvising environment). Nordstrom trains its people such that they can be of service to customers (professional excellence). Improvisation resulting in customer satisfaction is rewarded. Treating a customer in such a way as to make him unhappy is punished. Improvisation that was intended to make a customer happy but fails would require being handled on a case-by-case basis. The danger of punishing an employee who is competent and well meaning but fails to achieve results in the subjective world of customer satisfaction is to destroy the atmosphere of improvisation. Leaders who promote improvisation must be very open to new ideas and readily expect that not everything will work every time. In military parlance, leaders of improvisational organizations must avoid even the pretense of possessing a "zero defects" mentality. Such a mentality will stifle even the most creative thinkers.

Organizations that live and die on improvisation require increased demands on concentration and talent as one approaches true improvisation, especially at Nordstrom. The only thing absolute is the goal of customer satisfaction. The culture teaches and reinforces forward thinking grounded in professional competence borne of training. The stories of Nordstrom employees going beyond the call of duty are legend. The company's profile created in Collins and Porras's book *Built to Last* is one of dynamic, energetic employees focused on making people happy doing whatever it takes within the boundaries of the company's culture. That is, no one will compromise his integrity, ethics, or morals to make a sale or keep people happy.

Still, a down side exists to those organizations given to improvisation. Improvisation as a culture is not for every organization. Not every employee wants to come to work wondering what his day will be like or through which hoops he will be leaping. Businesses, like armies, need employees who are as steady and dutiful as the infantry who walked across open fields as part of Pickett's Charge at the battle of Gettysburg. Employees who thrive on a regimented life are the backbone of assembly lines and most manufacturing jobs. Industry should recognize that not everyone is equipped or desires to be an agent of innovation. In the U.S. Army, soldiers who fail to be selected for Special Forces suffer no adverse ramifications to their careers. Likewise, leaders of industry, while promoting creativity and spontaneity, must remain sensitive to those who thrive in ordered predictability and reward them for doing that for which a commando is ill suited.

Returning now to the opening vignette, the SF soldier who exorcised the children in the Haitian village did not rehearse incantations in Creole or carry a chemical light stick in his pocket for the purpose of impressing werewolves. He understood the goal of making Haiti stable and secure. Werewolves are an intuitively destabilizing factor in those countries that believe in them. He was raised in a culture that assumes improvisation. (I can easily imagine a conversation between two SF soldiers con-

taining the phrase, "Did you try conducting an exorcism?") He was trained to speak a foreign language because one cannot know a culture without knowing the language. He was conditioned through experiences in many different countries to exploit all the available resources. Because he was trained to improvise, he found the chemical light stick to be the perfect accoutrement for the impromptu exorcism. The fact is that he could have performed the same ritual without the light. But, he was in the spotlight, somebody said, "Here we go," and a village in Haiti was treated to some powerful magic.

Horacio E. Schwalm is a Lieutenant Colonel in the U.S. Army. He is stationed at MacDill Airforce Base in Florida.

Bibliography

Collins, James C., and Jerry I. Porras. *Built to Last.* New York: HarperCollins, 1997.

Fedarko, Kevin. "The power of American magic." *Time*, December 12, 1994.

Weick, Karl E. *Making Sense of the Organization.* Malden, Massachusetts: Blackwell Publishers Inc., 2001.

IV-17: Selflessness in Action

Phil Jackson and Hugh Delehanty

One finger can't fit a pebble.
– HOPI Saying

● ● ● ● ● ● ● ●
THE WAY
OF THE BULLS

When I arrived in Chicago to join the Bulls' coaching staff, I felt as if I was setting out on

a strange and wonderful adventure. No longer hampered by the responsibilities of being a head coach, I was free to become a student of the game again and explore a wide range of new ideas.

The Bulls were in a state of transition. Ever since he had taken over as vice president of basketball operations in 1985, Jerry Krause had been feverisbly rearranging the lineup, trying to find the right combination of players to complement Michael Jordan. A former NBA scout, Krause had been nick-named "the Sleuth" because of his passion-ate desire to scout a game incognito, but he has an uncanny ability to find extraordinary prospects at small, out-of-the-way colleges where nobody else had bothered to look. Among the many stars he had drafted were Earl Monroe, Wes Unseld, Alvan Adams, Jerry Sloan, and Norm Van Lier. In his first two years running the Bulls, he had drafted power forward Charles Oakley, who would later be traded to New York for center Bill Cartwright, and acquired point guard John Parson, a tough-minded clutch performer who would play a major role in the Bulls' drive for the championship. Krause's biggest coup, however, was landing Scottie Pippen and Horace Grant in the 1987 draft.

Scottie's rise to the NBA read like a fairy tale. The youngest of eleven children, he grew up in Hamburg, Arkansas, a sleepy rural town where his father worked in a paper mill. When Scottie was a teenager, his father was incapacitated by a stroke, and the family had to get by on his disability pay-ments. Scottie was a respectable point guard in high school, but at only 6'1" he didn't impress the college recruiters. But his coach believed in him and talked the athletic director at University of Central Arkansas into giving him an educational grant and a job as the basketball team's equipment manager. In his sophomore year, Scottie grew four inches and began to excel, and by his senior year had become a dynamic end-to-end player, averaging 26.3 points and 10 rebounds a game. Krause picked up on him early and tried to keep it a secret. But after Scottie excelled in a series of predraft tryout games, Krause knew he would be one of the top five prospects. So he worked out a deal to flip-flop picks with Seattle in order to acquire Scottie's draft rights.

Scottie, the fifth pick overall, was the kind of athlete Krause loves. He had long arms and big hands, and the speed and leap-ing ability to become a first-class all-around player. What impressed me about him was his natural aptitude for the game. Scottie had a near-genius basketball IQ: he read the court extremely well, knew how to make complicated adjustments on the run and, like Jordan, seemed to have a sixth sense about what was going to happen next. In practice Scottie gravitated toward Michael, eager to see what he could learn from him. While other young players shied away from covering Michael in scrimmages to avoid being humiliated, Scottie wasn't afraid to take him on, and often did a credible job guarding him.

Horace, the tenth pick overall, also came from a rural Southern town—Sparta, Georgia—but that's where his similarity to Pippen ended. Unlike Scottie, Horace, a 6'10" power forward, took a long time learn-ing the intricacies of the game. He had trou-ble concentrating at first, and often had to make up for mental lapses with his quick-ness and sheer athleticism. This made him vulnerable against teams like the Detroit Pistons, who devised subtle plays that took advantage of his defensive mistakes.

Horace has an identical twin brother, Harvey, who plays for the Portland Trail Blazers. They were close growing up—so close, in fact, they claimed to have had virtu-ally identical dreams. But their rivalry became so intense playing basketball at Clemson that Harvey decided to transfer to another school. Horace and Scottie became best friends during their rookie year, and we nicknamed them Frick and Frack because they dressed alike, drove the same model car and were rarely seen apart. As a twin, Horace expected everyone on the team to be treated equally, and later criticized man-agement publicity for giving Jordan prefer-ential treatment. Everyone liked Horace because he was guileless and unassuming, and had a generous heart. A devout born-again Christian, he was once so moved by the professed faith of a homeless man be met in front of a church in Philadelphia that he put him up in a hotel and gave him several hundred dollars in spending money.

● ● ● ● ● ● ● ● ● ● ● ●
THE JORDAN PROBLEM

The Bulls' head coach, Doug Collins, was an energetic leader brimming with ideas who worked well with young players like Horace and Scottie. Doug was a popular sports figure in Illinois. The first Illinois State player to be named an All-American, he scored what should have been the winning foul shots in the controversial final of the 1972 Olympics, before the clock was set back and the Soviet Union snatched the win in the closing seconds. A great outside shooter, Collins was drafted by the Philadelphia 76ers, the number one pick overall, and made the All-Star team four years in a row before being slowed down by injuries. Having played alongside Julius (Dr. J) Erving, the Picasso of the slam dunk, Collins had enormous respect for what Jordan could do with the ball and was reluctant to try anything that might inhibit his creative process.

Though Collins' coaching experience was limited, he had a sharp analytical mind, and Krause hoped that, with guidance from his veteran assistants, Tex Winter and Johnny Bach, he could solve the Michael Jordan problem. This was not an easy assignment. Jordan was just coming into his own as the best all-around player in the game. The year before I arrived—Collins' first season as head coach—Jordan had averaged 37.1 points a game to win his first of seven straight scoring titles, while also becoming the first player to make 200 steals and 100 blocked shots in a season. Jordan could do things with a basketball nobody had ever seen before: he seemed to defy gravity when he went up for a shot, hanging in the air for days—sometimes weeks—as he crafted his next masterpiece. Was it merely an illusion? It didn't matter. Whenever he touched the ball, everyone in the stadium became transfixed, wondering what he was going to do next.

The problem was that Jordan's teammates were often just as enchanted as the fans. Collins devised dozens of plays to get the rest of the team involved in the action; in fact, he had so many he was given the name Play-a-Day Collins. That helped, but when push came to shove, the other players usually faded into the background and waited for Michael to perform another miracle. Unfortunately, this mode of attack, which assistant coach Johnny Bach dubbed "the archangel offense," was so one-dimensional the better defensive teams had little difficulty shutting it down. Our nemesis, the Detroit Pistons, came up with an effective scheme called the Jordan Rules, which involved having three or more players switch off and close in on Michael whenever he made a move to the hoop. They could get away with it because none of the other Bulls posed much of a scoring threat.

How to open up the offense and make the other players more productive was a constant topic of conversation. Early on, I told the coaching staff about Red Holzman's axiom that the sign of a great player was not how much *he* scored, but how much he lifted his teammates' performance. Collins said excitedly, "You've got to tell that to Michael." I hesitated. "No, you've got to tell him right now," Collins insisted. So I searched the gym and found Michael in the weight room chatting with the players. Slightly embarrassed, I repeated Holzman's adage, saying "Doug thought you'd like hear this." I expected Michael, who could be sarcastic, to dismiss the remark as a product of basketball's stone age. But instead he thanked me and was genuinely curious about my experience with the championship Knicks.

The following season, 1988–89, Collins moved Jordan over to point guard in midseason and made Craig Hodges, one of the league's best three-point shooters, the shooting guard. The point guard's primary job is to move the ball upcourt and direct the offense. In that position Michael would have to focus more attention on creating scoring opportunities for his teammates. The switch worked pretty well at first: though Michael's average dropped to 32.5 points per game, the other players, especially Grant, Pippen, and the newly acquired Bill Cartwright, made up the difference. But the team struggled in the playoffs. Playing against Detroit in the Eastern Conference finals, Jordan had to expend so much energy running the offense he didn't have much firepower left at the end of the game. We lost the series, 4–2.

THE TAO OF BASKETBALL

The problem with making Jordan the point guard, as I saw it, was that it didn't address the real problem: the fact that the prevalent style of offense in the NBA reinforced a self-centered approach to the game. As I traveled around the league scouting other teams, I was amazed to discover that everybody was using essentially the same *modus operandi*—power basketball. Here's a typical sequence: the point guard brings the ball up and passes it inside to one of the big men, who will either make a power move to the hoop or kick the ball out to somebody on the wing after drawing a double team. The player on the wing, in turn, will either shoot, drive to the basket, or set up a screen-and-roll play. This style, an outgrowth of inner-city playground basketball, began to infiltrate the NBA in the late seventies with the emergence of Dr. J and other spectacular open-floor players. By the late eighties, it had taken over the league. Yet, though it can inspire breathtaking flights of creativity, the action often becomes stagnant and predictable because, at any given moment, only two or three players are involved in the play.

Not only does this make the game a mind-numbing experience for players who aren't big scorers, it also misleads everyone into thinking that basketball is nothing more than a sophisticated slam dunk competition.

The answer, in Tex Winter's mind, was a continuous-motion offense involving everybody on the floor. Tex, a white-haired "professor" of basketball who had played under legendary coach Sam Berry at the University of Southern California, had made a name for himself in the 1950s when he turned little-known Kansas State into a national powerhouse using a system he'd developed, then known as the triple-post offense. Jerry Krause, who was then a scout, considered Tex a genius and spent a lot of time hanging out at Kansas State practices trying to see what he could absorb. The day after he was put in charge of the Bulls, Jerry called Tex, who had recently retired from a consulting job at LSU, and coaxed him into moving to Chicago to help rebuild the franchise.

Collins had decided against using Tex's system because he thought it was better suited for college than the pros. He wasn't alone. Even Tex had his doubts. He had tried to implement it as head coach of the Houston Rockets in the early seventies without much luck. Nevertheless, the more I learned about Tex's system—which he now calls the triangle offense—the more convinced I became that it made sense for the Bulls. The Bulls were't a big, powerful team; nor did they have a dominant point guard like Magic Johnson or Isiah Thomas. If they were going to win the championship, it was going to be speed, quickness, and finesse. The system would allow them to do that.

Listening to Tex describe his brainchild, I realized that this was the missing link I had been searching for in the CBA. It was a more evolved version of the offense we'd run on the Knicks under Red Holzman, and, more to the point, it embodied the Zen Christian attitude of selfless awareness. In essence, the system was a vehicle for integrating mind and body, sport and spirit in a practical, down-to-earth form that anyone could learn. It was awareness in action.

The triangle offense is best described as *five-man tai chi*. The basic idea is to orchestrate the flow of movement in order to lure the defence off balance and create a myriad of openings on the floor. The system gets its name from one of the most common patterns of movement: the sideline triangle, Example: As Scottie Pippen moves the ball upcourt, he and two other players form a triangle on the right side of the floor about fifteen feet apart from each other—Steve Kerr in the corner, Luc Longley in the post and Scottie along the sideline. Meanwhile, Michael Jordan hovers around the top of the key and Toni Kukoc positions himself opposite Pippen on the other side of the floor. Next Pippen passes the ball into Longley, and everybody goes into a series of complex coordinated moves, depending on how the defense responds.

The point is not go head-to-head with the defence, but to toy with the defenders and trick them into overextending themselves. That means thinking and moving in unison as a group and being acutely aware, at any given moment, of what's happening on the floor. Executed properly, the system is virtually unstoppable because there are no set plays and the defense can't predict what's going to happen next. If the defense tries to prevent one move, the players will adjust instinctively and start another series of cuts and passes that often lead to better shot.

At the heart of the system are what Tex calls the seven principles of a sound offense:

1. *The offense must penetrate the defense.* In order to run the system, the first step is to break through the perimeter of the defense, usually around the three-point line, with a drive, a pass, or a shot. The number-one option is to pass the ball into the post and go for a three-point power play.

2. *The offense must involve a full-court game.* Transition offense starts on defense. The players must be able to play end-to-end and perform skills at fast-break pace.

3. *The offense must provide proper spacing.* This is critical. As they move around the court, the players should maintain a distance of fifteen to eighteen feet from one another. That gives everybody room to operate and prevents the defense from being able to cover two players with one man.

4. *The offense must ensure player and ball movement with a purpose.* All things being equal, each player will spend around eighty percent of his time *without the ball.* In the triangle offense, the players have prescribed routes to follow in those situations, so that they're all moving in harmony toward a common goal. When Toni Kukoc joined the Bulls, he tended to gravitate toward the ball when it wasn't in his hands. Now he has learned to fan away from the ball and move to the open spots—making him a much more difficult player to guard.

5. *The offense must provide strong rebounding position and good defensive balance on all shots.* With the triangle offense, everyone knows where to go when a shot goes up to put themselves in a position to pick off the rebound or protect against the fast break. Location is everything, especially when playing the boards.

6. *The offense must give the player with the ball an opportunity to pass the ball to any of his teammates.* The players move in such a way so that the ballhandler can see them and hit them with a pass. That sets up the counterpoint effect. As the defense increases the pressure on one point on the floor, an opening is inevitably created somewhere else that the defenders can't see. If the players are lined up properly, the ballhandler should be able to find someone in that spot.

7. *The offense must utilize the players' individual stills.* The system requires everybody to become an offensive threat. That means they have to find what they do best within the context of the team. As John Parson puts it, "You can find a way to fit into the offense, no matter what your strengths are. I wasn't a creative player. I wasn't going to take the ball and beat the other guys to the basket. But I was a good shooter, and the system played to my strength. It helped me understand what I did well and find the areas on the court where I could thrive."

. . . .

SURRENDERING THE "ME" FOR THE "WE"

What appealed to me about the system was that it empowered everybody on the team by making them more involved in the offense, and demanded that they put their individual needs second to those of the group. This is the struggle every leader faces: how to get members of the team who are driven by the quest for individual glory to give themselves over wholeheartedly to the group effort. In other words, how to teach them selflessness.

In basketball, this is an especially tricky problem. Today's NBA players have a dazzling array of individual moves, most of which they've learned from coaches who encourage one-on-one play. In an effort to become "stars," young players will do almost anything to draw attention to themselves, to say "This is me" with the ball, rather than share the limelight with others. The skewed reward system in the NBA only makes matters worse. Superstars with dramatic, eye-catching moves are paid vast sums of money, while players who contribute to the team effort in less flamboyant ways often make close to the minimum salary. As a result, few players come to the NBA dreaming of becoming good team players. Even players who weren't standouts in college believe that once they hit the pros somehow the butterfly will emerge from the chrysalis. This is a hard one to refute because there are several players around the league who've come out of nowhere to find stardom.

The battle for players' minds begins at an early age. Most talented players start getting special treatment in junior high school, and by the time they reach the pros, they've had eight years or more of being coddled. They have NBA general managers, sporting goods manufactures, and assorted hucksters dangling money in front of them and an encourage of agents, lawyers, friends, and family members vying for their favor. Then there's the media, which can be the most alluring temptress of all. With so many people telling them how great they are, it's difficult, and, in some cases, impossible, for coaches to get players to check their inflated egos at the gym door.

Tex's system helps undo some of this conditioning by getting players to play basketball with a capital B instead of including their self-interest. The principles of the system are the code of honor that everybody on the team has to live by. We put them on the chalkboard and talk about them almost every day. The principles serve as a mirror that shows each players how well they're doing with respect to the team mission.

The relationship between a coach and his players is often fraught with tension because the coach is constantly critiquing each player's performance and trying to get him to change his behavior. Having a clearly defined set of principles to work with reduces conflict because it depersonalizes the critcism. The players understand that you're not attacking them personally when you correct a mistake, but only trying to improve their knowledge of the system.

Learning that system is a demanding, often tedious process that takes years to master. The key is a repetitive series of drills that train the players, on an experiential level as well as an intellectual one, to move, as Tex puts it, "like five fingers on a hand." In that respect, the drills resemble Zen practice. After months of focusing intently on performing the drills in practice, the players begin to see—Aha! This is how all the pieces fit together. They develop an intuitive feel for how their movements and those of everyone else on the floor are interconnected.

Not everyone reaches this point. Some players' self-centered conditioning is so deeply rooted they can't make that leap. But for those who can, a subtle shift in consciousness occurs. The beauty of the system is that it allows players to experience another, more powerful form of motivation than ego-gratification. Most rookies arrive in the NBA thinking that what will make them happy is having unlimited freedom to strut their egos on national TV. But that approach to the game is an inherently empty experience. What makes basketball so exhilarating is the joy of losing yourself completely in the dance, even if it's just for one beautiful transcendent moment. That's what the system teaches players. There's a lot of freedom built into the process, but it's the freedom that John Parson talks about, the freedom of shaping a role for yourself and using all of your creative resources to work in unison with others.

When I started coaching, Dick Motta, a veteran NBA coach, told me that the most important part of the job takes place on the practice floor, not during the game. After a certain point you have to trust the players to translate into action what they've learned in practice. Using a comprehensive system of basketball makes it easier for me to detach myself in that way. Once the players have mastered the system, a powerful group intelligence emerges that is greater than the coach's ideas or those of any individual on the team. When a team reaches that state, the coach can step back and let the game itself

"motivate" the players. You don't have to give them any "win one for the Gipper" pep talks; you just have to turn them loose and let them immerse themselves in the action.

During my playing days, the Knicks had that kind of feeling. Everyone loved playing with each other so much, we had an unspoken rule among ourselves about not skipping games, no matter what your excuse. Some players—Willis Reed was the most famous example—refused to sit out even when they could barely walk. What did pain matter? We didn't want to miss the dance.

● ● ● ● ● ● ● ● ● ● ●
EASY RIDER

As it turned out, I got a chance to experiment with the triangle offense sooner than I expected. Toward the end of the 1988–89 season, the team went into a slide, and even though we made it to the conference finals, Jerry Krause lost faith in Doug Collins' ability to push the team to the next level and decided to let him go.

The portrait the press has painted of Jerry over the years is not very flattering. He is extremely distrustful of reporters, having been burned by them in the past, and is so secretive that distortions inevitably occur. (In 1991, when *The Jordan Rules*—a book by Chicago *Tribune* writer Sam Smith that portrayed Krause as hard-headed, insensitive, and a bit of a schlemiel—came out, Jerry called me into his office and pointed out 176 "lies" he'd discovered in it.)

Jerry and I are bipolar opposites. He's circumspect with the press; I'm overly trusting. He's nervous and compulsive; I'm laid-back to the point of being almost comatose. We are both strong-willed and have had several flaming arguments over what to do with the team. Jerry encourages dissent, not just from me, but from everybody on the staff. But when he finally sits down to make a decision, he keeps his own counsel, a habit he developed as a scout.

Jerry loves to tell the story of Joe Mason, a former scout for the New York Mets. Several years ago, when Jerry was director of scouting for the Chicago White Sox, he noticed that Mason had a knack for finding great prospects that nobody else knew about. When Jerry asked his scouts what Mason's secret was, they said he always ate alone and never shared information with anybody else. In other words, he was like Jerry Krause.

Jerry's unorthodox style of management worked to my advantage. The NBA is a small exclusive club that's extremely difficult to break into as a coach unless you're connected with one of its four or five major cliques. Even though I had won a championship and been named Coach of the Year in the CBA, nobody was willing to take a chance on me except Krause. He didn't care about my overblown reputation as a sixties flower child. All he wanted to know was whether I could help turn his team into a champion.

I must have passed the test. Jerry and I had worked together on the Bill Cartwright–Charles Oakley trade, and he was impressed by my ability to judge character. He also liked the fact that I had taken such a keen interest in the triangle offense, though he assured me that implementing it wouldn't be a job requirement. Several days after he dismissed Collins, Jerry called me in Montana to offer me the head coaching job.

We had a party line then, and, in true Krausian fashion, he asked me to go to a more secure phone, at a gas station six miles away. After we finished talking, I jumped on my BMW motorcycle and headed back to the lake. My mind was racing as fast as the engine as I sped down the road. "Now that I'm a head coach," I said to myself, easing off the throttle, "I guess I can't take risks and be so outrageous."

I thought that one over for a second and laughed. Then I gunned the bike all the way home.

IV-18: Code of Ethics

Kenneth L. Lay

. . . .

FOREWORD

As officers and employees of Enron Corp., its subsidiaries, and its affiliated companies, we are responsible for conducting the business affairs of the companies in accordance with all applicable laws and in a moral and honest manner.

To be sure that we understand what is expected of us, Enron has adopted certain policies, with the approval of the Board of Directors, which are set forth in this booklet. I ask that you read them carefully and com-

pletely and that, as you do, you reflect on your past actions to make certain that you have complied with the policies. It is absolutely essential that you fully comply with these policies in the future. If you have any questions, talk them over with your supervisor, manager, or Enron legal counsel.

We want to be proud of Enron and to know that it enjoys a reputation for fairness and honesty and that it is respected. Gaining such respect is one aim of our advertising and public relations activities, but no matter how effective they may be, Enron's reputation finally depends on its people, on you and me. Let's keep that reputation high.

IV-19: Invitations to Jeopardy

Robert Jackall

1

The ethic that emerges in bureaucratic contexts contrasts sharply in many respects with the original Protestant ethic. The protestant ethic was a social construction of reality of a self-confident and independent propertied social class. It was an ideology that extolled the virtues of accumulating and reinvesting wealth in a society organized around property and that accepted the stewardship responsibilities entailed by property. It was an ideology where a person's word was his bond and where the integrity of the handshake was crucial to the maintenance of good business relationships. Perhaps most important, it was connected to a predictable economy of salvation—that is, hard work will lead to success, which is a sign of election by God, a taken for granted notion also containing its own theodicy to explain the misery of those who do not make it in this world. This economy of salvation was, in my view, the decisive conscious meaning of the ideology, a meaning that linked even antagonistic segments of the old middle class. At the core of the middle class's righteous, some would say smug, faith in itself, of its inexhaustible drive, of its unremitting pragmatism, was the conviction that hard work necessarily had its just rewards here and now as a token of divine favor in the hereafter. This conviction was also the bedrock of a profound guilt mechanism that impelled one to fulfill personal and social obligations; failure to do so, like a failure to work hard, was thought to be a sin against both God and self.

From *Moral Mazes: The World of Corporate Managers* by Robert Jackall, copyright 1989 by Oxford University Press, Inc. Used by permission of Oxford University Press, Inc.

Bureaucracy and the ethic it generates undercuts the crucial premises of this classic ideology and strips it of the powerful religious and symbolic meaning it once had. Bureaucracy breaks apart the ownership of property from its control, social independence from occupation, substance from appearances, action from responsibility, obligation from guilt, language from meaning, and notions of truth from reality. Most important, and at the bottom of all of these fractures, it breaks apart the older connection between the meaning of work and salvation. In the bureaucratic world, one's success, one's sign of election, no longer depends on an inscrutable God, but on the capriciousness of one's superiors and the market; and one achieves economic salvation to the extent that one pleases and submits to new gods, that is, one's bosses and the exigencies of an impersonal market.

In this way, because moral choices are inextricably tied to personal fates, bureaucracy erodes internal and even external standards of morality not only in matters of individual success and failure but in all the issues that managers face in their daily work. Bureaucracy makes its own internal rules and social context the principal moral gauges for action.

Formerly, the businessmen of the old independent middle class turned to the Protestant sects in their communities for moral certification. A sect's acceptance of a person testified to his ethical probity, vouched to others that he was honest and, more to the point, credit-worthy. One can still see the cultural vestiges of this crucial mechanism of social and moral approbation through religious affiliation on Sunday mornings in the small southern community where Weft Corporation has its headquarters. The front pews of the local Presbyterian church are always crowded with local businessmen, corporate managers, and their families. Some Weft managers still insist, in fact, that one's prospects in the corporate hierarchy depend on one's membership and, more exactly, on one's standing in that congregation.

But the probationary crucibles that managers face in their bureaucratic milieux are much more ambiguous and demanding. Instead of relatively stable councils of elders who guard doctrine and dictate behavioral norms, the basic framework of managerial work is formed by structures of personalized authority in formally impersonal contexts, fealty with bosses and patrons, and alliances shaped through networks, coteries, cliques, and work groups that struggle through hard times together. It is always subject to upheaval and the consequent formation of new ties and alliances. Each circle of affiliation in this world, while it lasts, develops its own criteria of admission, its own standards of trustworthiness, its own gauges of emotional comfort, and even its own etiquette, all within the general structure and ethos of a particular corporation. The dominant clique in a hierarchy at any given time establishes the general tone for other groups.

Of course, the segmented work patterns of bureaucracy underlie these larger structures. Managers' cognitive maps to the thickets of their world contain sharp, sometimes absurd, caricatures of the style and ethos of different occupational groups. These suggest some of the ways in which managers appraise the myriad of character types whom they see peopling their world. Production types, for instance, are said to be hard-drinking, raucous, good-time charlies: engineers, always distinguishable by the plastic pen containers in their shirt pockets, are hostages to an outdated belief in a pristine mathematical rationality; accountants are bean counters who know how to play the shell game; lawyers are legal eagles or legal beagles in wool pinstripes who, if they had their way, would tie managers' hands completely; corporate staff are the king's spies, always ready to do his bidding and his dirty work; marketing guys are cheerful, smooth-talking, upbeat fashion plates who must nonetheless keep salesmen under their thumbs; salesmen are aggressive loudmouths who feel that they can sell freezers to penguins in Antarctica and who would sell their grandmothers just to make a deal. Salesmen hate the restraints that marketers put on their work and on their ego gratification. Financial wizards, on the ascendancy everywhere, are tight-mouthed, close-to-the-vest poker players who think that a social order can be built on paper deals. And outside consultants are men and women who borrow one's watch and then charge for telling the time. Different occupational groups meld with each other through regular work assignments, or special task forces, or through the vagaries of power shifts that subordinate one group to another. Within each group, whether based strictly on occupational expertise or emerging as the result of other melding, more general patterns of personalized authority, fealty, alliances, conflict, and power seeking prevail. Managers thus experience the corporation as an intricate matrix of rival and often intersecting managerial circles. The principal goal of each group is its own survival, of each person his own advancement. As one rises in the organization, one necessarily spends more and more time maintaining networks and alliances precisely in order to survive and flourish, a skill that, when well-developed, is usually called leadership. The unintended social consequence of this maelstrom of competition and ambition is the public social order that the corporation presents to the world.

Within such crucibles, managers are continually tested even as they continually test others. They turn to each other for moral cues for behavior and come to fashion specific situational moralities for specific significant others in their world. But the guidance that they receive from each other is as profoundly ambiguous as the social structure of the corporation. What matters in the bureaucratic world is not what a person is but how closely his many personae mesh with the organizational ideal; not his willingness to stand by his actions but his agility in avoiding blame; not his acuity in perceiving falsity or errors but his adeptness at protecting others; not his talent, his abilities, or his hard work, but how these are harnessed with the proper protocol to address the particular exigencies that face his organization; not what he believes or says but how well he has mastered the ideologies and rhetories that serve his corporation; not what he stands for but whom he stands with in the labyrinths of his organization.

In short, bureaucracy creates for managers a Calvinist world without a Calvinist God, a world marked with the same profound anxiety that characterized the old Protestant ethic but one stripped of that ideology's comforting illusions. Bureaucracy poses for managers an intricate set of moral mazes that are paradigmatic of the quandaries of public life in our social order. Within this framework, the puzzle for many individual managers becomes: How does one act in such a world and maintain a sense of personal integrity?

II

Bureaucratic work itself, of course, provides powerful frameworks that can and often do obscure tensions between requisite actions and idealized self-images, sometimes even for considerable periods. In particular, the continuous, standardized regularity of bureaucratic work tends to routinize personal experiences and helps shape taken for granted frameworks even on issues that out-

siders might find unsettling. Managers at Alchemy Inc., for instance, simply shrug at many of the widely trumpeted hazards of toxic waste; here, one person's hysteria and cause for moral outrage is another's familiar and somewhat dull routine. Moreover, bureaucratic compartmentalization, with its concomitant secrecy and fragmentation of consciousness, often prevents the passing from one level of an organization to the next, indeed from one managerial circle to another, of the actual knowledge of troublesome issues—say, the burial of important data, or the double-crossing of an associate, or payoffs to officials or to employees who threaten to "sing about where the bodies are buried," or the outright theft of ideas or strategies. At the least, compartmentalization provides wholly acceptable rationales for not knowing about problems or for not trying to find out. It also seems to be a structural inducement to private irrationalities, generating, for instance, suspicions, wild rumors, and even attributions of calculated malevolence that often, given the public roles that managers must play, get projected into the public arena in disguised forms. In this sense, the very rationality of bureaucracy may stimulate remarkable patterns of irrationality. Finally, despite the organizational premium on symbolic dexterity, some managers often come to believe, as noted earlier, their own public relations about their organizations and about themselves. The attainment of such a degree of sincerity inhibits critical reflection, especially about moral dilemmas.

Sooner or later, however, almost all managers experience clashes between the requirements of their world and aspects of their valued self-images. Such tensions arise most predictably when organizational upheavals cause an unraveling of the social and moral ties that secure one's status and social identity or when public attacks on one's organization call one's organizational morality into question. But even the everyday ambiguities and compromises of managerial work often pose invitations to jeopardy. Some of the recurring dilemmas that managers face test their own preferred self-definitions. All of these revolve in one way or another around the meaning of work. Those managers who respond fully to the organizational premiums on success are especially important here because their ambition not only drives themselves but continually regenerates the structure of their world.

First, some of the fundamental requirements of managerial work clash with the normal ethics governing interpersonal behavior, let alone friendship in our society. Our egalitarian ideology couples here with remnants of Judeo-Christian beliefs counseling honesty, loyalty, and compassion toward other people. But at bottom, a great deal of managerial work consists of onging struggles for dominance and status. Real administrative effectiveness flows, in fact, from the prestige that one establishes with other managers. Prestige in managerial hierarchies depends not only on position as determined by the crucial indices of rank, grade, title, and salary, and the external accoutrements that symbolize power. Even more fundamentally, it consists of the socially recognized ability to work one's will, to get one's way, to have the say-so when one chooses in both the petty and large choices of organizational life. At one level, the superordination and subordination of bureaucratic hierarchies guarantee clashes between the egos of men and women who—"like to control things," whose choice of occupation, in fact, has been at least partly shaped by their orientation and habituation to control. For instance, an administrative coordinator describes the daily battles between Beach, the president of one of Weft's divisions, and Schultz, his talented vice-president:

I feel every knife turn between [Beach] and [Schultz]. [Beach]

enjoys lording it over [Schultz]. For instance, in a dispute, [Beach} will says: "I'll make the final choices." And this drives [Schultz] crazy. And then the whole department is drawn up on either side of the battle. . . . [I]n the morning, I'll come in and try to cope with the latest issue. I'll be thinking: "What did [one] mean about this? How will the other guy react when he finds out?" The way things are now is that [Schultz] can work heavily toward influencing things, but if [Beach] felt that he could make some decision which would turn out well and would at the same time be against [Schultz], he would make it in a minute.

At another level, the struggle for dominance is an inevitable by-product of the pyramidal construction of bureaucracies that fuels managers' driving competitiveness. A divisional vice-president at Weft comments:

There just aren't that many places to go when you get up as high as I am. . . . [T]he competition that does occur is within the division. You're not competing for jobs with another division.

Now within the division, there's a limited number of positions, of spots, and after you're here for awhile and know the score, you don't have three guys after one spot. . . . [T]he competition is not necessarily for the jobs that open up, since they are so few. Rather the ongoing competition is *for your way of doing things*. We all want things to go our way and the competition, dilemmas, and problems are when it doesn't go my way but somebody else's. I've competed and lost on that issue. . . . That's where there is real pressure. It's in the competitiveness in trying to have it your way. You have to be able to swallow the defeat.

Defeat at the middle and upper-middle levels produces in the losers feelings of frustration and of being "boxed in." Such disappointments must be concealed, and the ideology of team play often affords a convenient cover for defeat, one that might even be translated later into organizational credit. But one cannot, of course, lose too often without risking permanent anonymity. At the top of an organization, the loss of prestige occasioned by a major policy defeat leaves the loser with the hard choice between resignation or the daily humiliation of cheerfully doing something someone else's way. Defeat in such circumstances seems especially difficult when the victor insists on being magnanimous. In such a case, the victor enjoys plaudits for big-hearted sensitivity while his defeated opponent often finds such generosity more oppressive than vindictiveness. On the other hand, winning carries with it the knowledge of others' envy and the fear that one's defeated opponents are lying in wait for an opportunity to turn the tables. One adopts then a stance of public humility, of self-effacing modesty that helps disguise whatever sense of triumph one might feel. Moreover, winning, say, on a policy dispute, carries the burden of implementation, sometimes involving those whom one has defeated. One must then simultaneously protect one's flanks and employ whatever wiles are necessary to secure requisite cooperation. Here the disarming social grace that is a principal aspect of desirable managerial style can be particularly useful in making disingenuousness seem like "straight arrow" behavior. Finally, winning sometimes requires the willingness to move decisively against others, even though this might mean undermining

their organizational careers. These may be neighbors on the same block, members of the same religious communion, longtime work colleagues, or, more rarely, members of the same club. They may be good, even excellent, employees. In short, managerial effectiveness and others' perceptions of one's leadership depend on the willingness to battle for the prestige that comes from dominance and to make whatever moral accommodations such struggles demand. In the work world, those who adhere either to secular democratic precepts as guides rather than guises or, even more, to an ethic of brotherly love, run the risk of faltering in those struggles. But those who abandon the ethics of *caritas* and hone themselves to do what has to be done must accept the peculiar emotional aridity that is one price of organizational striving and, especially, of victory.

Second, managers at the middle levels in particular also have to come to grips with the peculiar inequities of the corporate world that call the meaning, purpose, and value of their work into question. they take for granted, of course, the material and symbolic inequities embedded in their bureaucratic hierarchies, hoping as they do that they themselves will one day benefit from the opportunities to appropriate credit from subordinates, command others' deference, and enjoy the generous salaries, company cars, year-end bonuses, big offices, attractive secretaries, and golden parachutes and golden handcuffs (financial ties that bind) that are seen to be the prerogatives of high rank, prestige, and power. However, the institutionalized inequities that result from what managers see as a pervasive mediocrity in big organizations do pose dilemmas. One measure of the troublesome character of such mediocrity is the widespread emotional resonance tapped by the recent widely heralded managerial consultant slogan of "excellence in management."[1]

As managers see it, mediocrity emerges out of the lack of fixed criteria within an organization to measure quality, whether of products or performance. In a world where criteria depend entirely on the interpretive judgments of shifting groups in an ever-changing social structure, where everyone's eyes are fixed on each other and on market exigencies, the construction of notions of quality becomes highly political since individual fates depend on the outcome. Clearly, skillful leadership and mobilization of organizational resources can impose a consensus about appropriate standards. However, to do so, one has to: resist pressures for short-term expedient solutions to problems that compromise one's notion of desirable standards, be willing to confront others, both in private and in public, who espouse or embody in some way variant, undesirable standards; and enforce one's judgment with organizationally approved sanctions. But given the bureaucratic ethos, such insistence on standards of excellence can quickly earn one enemies and the feared label of being "inflexible." As it happens, when it is socially difficult to extol or uphold high standards, a kind of leveling process occurs that produces a comfortable mediocrity, a willingness to settle for, say, whatever the market will bear, or tolerate shoddiness of products or performance, provided there is no undue social disruption. In such situations, among those managers who wish for clearer, higher standards, quasifictional images of the supposed superiority of different organizations or of the purported technical and managerial prowess of the Japanese often abound, usually invoked with wistful longing and sometimes with rueful envy.

Perceptions of pervasive mediocrity breed an endless quest for social distinctions even of a minor sort that might give one an "edge," enable one to "stepout of the crowd," or at least serve as a basis for individual claims to privilege. More specifically, an atmosphere of mediocrity erodes the hope of meaningful collective achievement

and encourages, at least among more aggressive managers, a predatory stance toward their organizations, that is, a search for private deals, a working of the system for one's own personal advantage. This may mean, variously, winning the assignment of a valued account, product, or client; wrangling one of the coveted discretionary places on a bonus scheme; or getting the inside track on promotions through the exposure gained by chairing a crucial committee or task force. A system of deal making places a premium on maximizing one's organizational leverage in order to make claims on those with power to dispense perquisites. In such a system, "big numbers" may help reduce organizational vulnerability but do not necessarily help maximize leverage. Rather, the social factors that bind managers to one another, whether in conflict or in harmony, are the chief sources of deals. Such a system is thus principally characterized by the exchange of personal favors and the dispensation of patronage to seal the alliances that give one "clout;" by the systematic collection of information damaging to others and particularly about deals struck and favors won in order to argue more effectively the propriety and legitimacy of one's own claims; and, on the part of those in power, by pervasive secrecy, called confidentiality, that attempts to cordon off the knowledge of deals already made lest the demands on the system escalate unduly. It is worth noting that most middle managers' general detestation of affirmative action programs, apart from their resentment at yet another wild card in the corporate deck and at being asked to bear cheerfully the burdens of others' neglect and mistakes, is rooted in the perception that such arrangements symbolically legitimate the perceived inequities of their world, cloaking simply a new kind of expedient favoritism with self-righteous ideologies. Seen from this perspective, the corporation resembles for many a jerry-built structure, like a boardwalk erected on pilings of different heights, that, when viewed from a distance over sandy stretches in baking summer heat, shimmers rickety and swaying to the eye.

In such a world, notions of fairness or equity that managers might privately hold, as measures of gauging the worth of their own work, become merely quaint. One fluctuates between a frustrated resentment at what seems to be a kind of institutionalized corruption and systematic attempts to make onself a beneficiary of the system. Being a "good soldier" may carry for some the private satisfactions of work well done, of bargains kept, or of organizational goals attained through one's best efforts. But such dedication may also make one unfit for the maneuvers that can bring organizational privilege and reward.

Third, managers at every level face puzzles about the overall meaning of their work in a business civilization in which the old notion of stewardship has been lost and in which work in business is alternately regarded with at times adulation, at times tolerant condescension, and at times outright suspicion. Sooner or later, most managers realize, as Thorstein Veblen did many years ago, that there are no intrinsic connections between the good of a particular corporation, the good of an individual manager, and the common weal. Stories are legion among managers about corporations that "devour" individuals, "plunder" the public, and succeed extravagantly; about individual managers whose predatory stances toward their fellows, their organizations, and society itself only further propel their skyrocketing careers; about individual managers desiring to harness the great resources of private enterprise and address social ills only to end up disillusioned by their colleagues' attention to exigencies; and about corporations that have espoused noble public goals only to founder in competitive markets and endanger the occupational security of their employees by failing to concentrate on the bottom line.

Meaningful connections between organizational well-being, individual fates, and the common weal can, of course, be forged both by individual managers and by organizations at the level of policy. But, where they exist, such connections proceed from some ideological standpoint backed by institutional mechanisms. Law and regulation usually shape only the broad parameters of action and allowable public discourse in such matters. As I have suggested earlier, law and regulation can be quite important in providing requisite appeals to inevitability on controversial issues that break political deadlocks within organizations. But typically such external compulsions cannot offer the meaningful rationales that sustain the hard organizational work of coordinating diverse, sometimes opposing, managerial interests. Properly enforced, assertions of values by top management can do this, at least for periods of time until organizational reshuffling alters organizational premiums. Some corporations, for instance, espouse policies of product responsibility, tying organizational rewards to sustained vigilance over the uses and possible uses to which a product might be put. Such programs thus try to link individual success, reduction of corporate liability, and consumer safety. These programs can, of course, never be wholly successful. As the several poisonings of over-the-counter drugs in early 1986 suggest, even relatively farsighted product safety policies cannot anticipate the potential depth of individual irrationalities, whether these proceed from psychopathology or, perhaps more disturbing, from the didactic self-righteousness of those privileged to receive some ideological enlightenment. Moreover, to sustain the links between the corporation, the individual, and the common good over the long haul, important conditions must obtain within an organization. Specifically, the ideology incorporating certain values must be continuously and forcefully articulated by key authorities who are ostensibly committed to its premises, and, at the same time, the ideological links between the good of the corporation and the common weal in particular must be plausible both to managers and to important external publics. As it happens, both conditions are difficult to meet. Day to-day exigencies, the personnel transitions of large organizations, the endless circulation of new rhetorics of innovation among top managers, the entrenched cynicism of middle managers on whose backs the burdens for any such policies will fall, and of course, the "take the money and run" ethos, make it difficult to sustain organizational commitment to goals defined as socially important.

Even more difficult is fashioning some working consensus about the meaning of "corporate social responsibility," a consensus that includes top management, external publics that top management is trying to appease, and middle management, that must implement a policy. Here the precariousness of ideological bridges over the chasm between the interests of a corporation, individual managers, and the public are most apparent. Some years ago, for example, Alchemy Inc. was producing a food-grade chemical used principally as a meat preservative. The company was, in fact, one of the chief suppliers of the chemical to the processed food industry. Although the business was small in comparison to other company operations, its oligopolistic position in this particular market made the preservative a very lucrative commodity. Suddenly, a newly released government study fingered the food preservative as carcinogenic. The report received great and widespread publicity, coinciding as it did with a public debate about carcinogens in food and with a nationwide health food fad that stressed, among other things, natural diets uncontaminated with artificial ingredients. Moreover, Covenant Corporation was recovering at the time from the bad publicity of an environmental catastrophe. In light of both

developments, the CEO of Covenant, who was nearing retirement, ordered the immediate sale of the preservative business, arguing that the recent scientific evidence made such a divestiture an act of corporate social responsibility. This position earned him plaudits from several environmental and health groups.

Alchemy managers, by contrast, argued privately that the CEO's real motivation was simply the avoidance of any further public relations hassles at that stage of his career. After the managers in charge of the preservative business had divested, they had more material grounds for their skepticism as they watched the company that bought the operation "make money hand over fist." They wondered whether the CEO had not simply "caved in." Is, they asked, "supine acquiescence" to special-interest groups or to suspect or perhaps even bogus government research the meaning of corporate responsibility? Of course, they discounted the animal tests that suggested the preservative's carcinogenicity. But so what, they argued, if the preservative did in fact pose some risk of cancer? Better, they said, the risk of a slight long-run increase in the rate of stomach and intestinal cancer than the certainty of a precipitous spurt in the incidence of botulism, particularly in the lower-income black and Hispanic groups that typically consume large amounts of processed meat and, both because of poverty and cultural practices, often leave food uncovered and unrefrigerated for considerable periods. Is corporate social responsibility, they asked, maintaining a private sense and public image of moral purity while someone else does necessary but tainted work? Or is real social responsibility the willingness to get one's hands dirty, to make whatever compromises have to be made to produce a product with some utility, to achieve therefore some social good, even though one knows that one's accomplishments and motives will inevitably be misinterpreted by others for their own ends, usually by those with the least reason to complain? Besides, they pointed out, consumers continue to purchase artifically preserved meats in large quantities. Is not the proper role of business "to give the public what it wants," adopting the market as its polar star, as the only reliable guide in a pluralistic society to "the greatest good for the greatest number," as the final arbiter not of values, which are always arguable, but, more, importantly, of tastes, about which there can be no reasonable dispute?

In short, managers' occupational roles are such that they simply cannot please everybody, even fellow managers. What seems socially responsible from one perspective may seem irresponsible or just plain venal from another angle. In fact, exercises in substantive rationality—the critical, reflective use of reason—are not only subject to infinite interpretations and counterinterpretations but also invite fantastic constructions of reality, including attributions of conspiracy. Thus a major corporation provides a gift of $10 million to establish new foundations that will materially aid South African blacks and is promptly accused by a black American leader of bolstering apartheid.[2] Weft managers create an elaborate recreational complex for Weft employees in the corporation's southern community and are charged with perpetuating traditional textile company paternalism. Some executives at Images Inc. donate their time to bring together several institutional sectors of a local town in which they live for community betterment and are charged with trying to grab headlines and line up future business. Managers often feel that, however genuine it may be, altruism is a motive that is always denied them by others. To complicate matters still further, the necessary self-promotional work of presenting private goals as public goods or the self-defensive work within the corporation of

presenting public goods as hardheaded business decisions, or managers' knowledge that bureaucracy insulates them from the real consequences of their actual choices, often make their protestations of socially responsible actions suspect even to themselves.

This context helps one understand why many managers feel, particularly as they grow older, that much of the actual work of management is senseless. Of course, big victories, pleasing deals, the seizure of capricious opportunities to accomplish something one thinks is worthwhile, the intrinsic pleasure, when it occurs, of harmonious orchestration, and, with personal success, the opportunity for leading roles in philanthropic, artistic, or social organizations of various sorts, trusteeships at elite colleges and universities, directorships in other corporations and the concomitant opportunity to mingle with other powerful peers, and the respectability that money and status afford, all punctuate and mitigate such senselessness. But the anonymity that is the lot of most corporate managers exacerbates it. Moreover, the successful propagation of professional ideologies of service or truthseeking by occupations like medicine or the professoriate often make businessmen view their own attention to the material world as base or crass.

Yet attention to the material world can anchor one's sense of self. In fact, the problem of the senselessness of managerial work increases as the work itself becomes more abstract, typically as one advances. With increasing seniority, one retreats from concrete tasks, say, overseeing the manufacture of sheets or shirting material or running the production of hydrofluoric acid. One thus loses immediate connections to tangible human or industrial needs. For those who came up through the plants, one also loses regular contact with the renewing drama of industrial work. A plant manager at one of Alchemy's largest and most troublesome operations, a man who regularly goes in at all hours "to fight the dragons," tells how often he does not even wait for trouble:

> Sometimes I'll wake up in the middle of the night thinking about the plant. And if I can't get back to sleep, I'll slip out of bed and walk over to the plant and just walk around the machinery and talk to the guys. I love the smell of the oil and the grease and the sound of the machines. For me, that's what life is all about.

But to advance, one must leave behind such a comforting concreteness, indeed the visible enactment of one's rational schemes, where materials, labor, and machinery are brought together to produce value.[3] One leaves behind as well the technical knowledge or scientific expertise of one's younger years, lore now more suited for the narrower roles of technicians or junior managers. One must, in fact, put distance between oneself and technical details of every sort or risk the inevitable entrapment of the particular. Salesmen too must leave their bags and regular customers and long boisterous evenings that seal measurable deals behind them and turn to marketing strategies. Work becomes more ambiguous, directed as it is toward maneuvering money, symbols, organizational structures, and especially people. The CEO at Weft Corporation, it is said, "doesn't know a loom from a car." And the higher one goes, the more managers find that "the essence of managerial work is cronyism, covering your ass, [and] pyramiding to protect your buddies."

The more abstract work becomes, that is, the less one actually does or oversees concrete tasks, the greater the likelihood that one's rational efforts to improve an organization will meet with and even beget various kinds of irrationality. One's rational systems, say, in Weft Corporation for mea-suring loom efficiency, or in Covenant for designing a grid appraising the relative strategic potentials of a cluster of businesses, fall to others for implementation and become hostage to their own private and organizational agendas, or become the cross hairs of others' gunsights. One's best laid plans are always subject to ambush by random events, fickle markets, recalcitrant or, worse, well-intentioned but incompetent subordinates, rival managers, or simply the weariness that work produces. One's best-intentioned schemes sometimes produce exactly the opposite of what one wanted to achieve. One's best efforts at being fair, equitable, and generous with subordinates clash both with a logic that demands choices between people, inevitably producing hatred, envy and animosity, and with the plain fact that, despite protestations to the contrary, many people do not want to be treated fairly. In short, the increasingly abstract quality of managerial work as one advances both symbolizes and exacerbates the structual fragmentation of corporate, individual, and common goods. Such conundrums often produce nostalgic yearnings for simpler times, for the concrete work of one's younger years, even for fabled crisis periods when "everyone pulled together and got the job done," and perhaps especially for a society that unambiguously, it is thought, extolled work in business as socially honorable and personally salvific.

III

For most managers, especially for those who are ambitious, the real meaning of work — the basis of social identity and valued self-image — becomes keeping one's eye on the main chance, maintaining and furthering one's own position and career. This task requires, of course, unrelenting attentiveness to the social initricacies of one's organization. One gains dominance or fails depending on one's access to key managerial circles where prestige is gauged precisely by the relationships that one establishes with powerful managers and by the demonstrated favour such relationships bring. Even beyond their practical and crucial importance in furthering careers, the social psychological lure of entrance into such select groups is, of course, powerful and layers the drive to get ahead with complicated overtones. Such acceptance means, variously, no longer being relegated to marginality; having one's voice heard and opinion count in matters small and weighty; experiencing the peculiar bonds with one's fellows produced by shared secrecy, hard decisions and hard times, a sense of shared emotional aridity, and competition with rival cliques; penetrating the many layers of consciousness in the corporation that baffle outsiders and marginal mangers alike; and being able to dispense at times, ususally in the heat of battle and only within one's tried and trusted circle, with the gentlemanly politesse and requisite public advocacy of high-minded beliefs and, always with relief and sometimes with comic vulgarity, to get down to brass tacks. What one manager calls "our surrender of ourselves to groups" has its emotional touchstone in the sense of professional intimacy that acceptance into a managerial circle affords. Group intimacy, especially with powerful others, rewards and seals the self-directed transformation of self that makes one come to accept the ethos of an organization as one's own. But the process is rarely simple, precisely because such accpetance depends on developing and maintaining personal relationships with powerful others. Mastering the subtle but necessary arts of deference without seeming to be deferential, of "brown nosing" without fawning, of simultaneous self-promotion and self-effacement, and occasionally of outright self-abasement that such relationships require is a taxing endeavor that demands continual compromises with conventional and popular notions of integrity. Only those with an inexhaustible capacity for self-rationalization, fueled by boundless ambition, can escape the discomfort such compromises produce.

But self-rationalization, even for those willing to open themselves up fully to institutional demands, produces its own discomforts and discontents. As in all professional careers, particularly those dependent on large organizations, managerial work requires a psychic asceticism of a high degree, a willingness to discipline the self, to thwart one's impulses, to stifle spontaneity in favor of control, to conceal emotion and intent, and to objectify the self with the same kind of calculating functional rationality that one brings to the packaging of any commodity. Moreover, such dispassionate objectification of the self frames and paces the rational objectification of circumstances and people that alertness to expediency demands. In its asceticism, self-rationalization curiously parallels the methodical subjection to God's will that the old Proestant ethic counseled. But instead of the satisfaction of believing that one is acquiring old-time moral virtues, one becomes a master at manipulating personae; instead of making oneself into an instrument of God's will to accomplish His work in this world, one becomes, variously, a boss's "hammer," a tough guy who never blinks at hard decisions, or perhaps, if all goes very well, an "industrial statesman," a leader with vision.

On one hand, such psychic asceticism is connnected to the narcissim that one sees in executives of high rank. The simulatneous need for self-abnegation, self-promotion, and self-display, as managers work their way through the probationary crucibles of big organizational life, fosters an absorption with self and specifically with self-improvement. Managers become continually and self-consciously aware of their public performances; they measure themselves constantly against others; and they plot out whatever self-transformations will help them achieve desired goals.

On the other hand, over a period of time, psychic asceticism creates a curious sense of guilt, heightened as it happens by narcissistic self-preoccupation. Such guilt, a regret at sustained self-abnegation and deprivation, finds expression principally in one's private emotional life. One drinks too much; one is subject to pencil-snapping fits of alternating anxiety, depression, rage, and self-disgust for willingly submitting oneself to the knowing and not knowing, to the constant containment of anger, to the keeping quiet, to the knuckling under that are all inevitable in bureaucratic life. One experiences great tensions at home because one's spouse is unable to grasp or unable to tolerate the endless review of the social world of the workplace, the rehearsals of upcoming conversations, or the agonizing over real or imagined social slights or perceptions of shifts in power alignments. One wishes that one had spent more time with one's children when they were small so that one could grasp the meanings of their adolescent traumas. Or one withdraws emotionally from one's family and, with alternating fascination and regret, plunges ever deeper into the dense and intimate relationships of organizational circles where emotional aridity signals a kind of fraternity of expediency. Many try at times to escape the guilt with Walter Mitty-like fantasies of insouciant rebellion and vengeful retaliation; but one knows that only if and when one rises to high position in a bureaucratic hierarchy does one have the opportunity to turn the pain of self-repression against one's fellows.

However, for those with the requisite discipline, sheer dogged perseverance, the agile flexibility, the tolernce for extreme ambiguity, the casuistic discernment that allows one to dispense with shopworn pieties, the habit of mind that perceives opportunities in others' and even one's own own misfortunes, the brazen nerve that allows one to pretend that nothing is wrong even when the world is crumbling, and, above all, the ability to read the inner logic of events, to see and do what has to be done, the rewards of corporate success can be very great. And, of course, those who do succeed, those who find their way out of the crowded, twisting corridors and into the back rooms where the real action is, where the big games take place, and where everyone present is a player, shape, in a decisive way, the moral rules-in-use that filter down through their organizations. The ethos that they fashion turns principles into guidelines, ethics into etiquette, values into tastes, personal responsibility into an adroitness at public relations, and notions of truth into credibility. Corporate managers who become imbued with this ethos pragmatically take their world as they find it and try to make that world work according to its own institutional logic. They pursue their own careers and good fortune as best they can within the rules of their world. As it happens, given their pivotal institutional role in our epoch, they help create and re-create, as one unintended consequence of their personal striving, a society where morality becomes indistinguishable from the quest for one's own survival and advantage.

Notes

1. The stress on excellence in management boomed with the publication of Thomas J. Peters and Robert H. Waterman, Jr., *In Search of Excellence: Lessons from America's Best-Run Companies* (New York: Warner Books, 1982), a book that is another classic paradigm of managerial consultant writing, complete with a handy list of eight attributes of excellence. Two years later, a follow-up study by *Business Week*, November 5, 1984, pp. 76–83, argues that at least fourteen of the forty-three corporations cited by Peters and Waterman as excellent had "lost their luster." The article notes

that Peters at least is undeterred by such troubling news and is planning other works showing managers how to implement the attributes of excellence.

2. See Kathleen Telsch, "Coca Cola Giving $10 Million To Help South Africa Blacks," *The New York Times*, March 24, 1986, A13, col.2.

3. Take, for instance, the scene that one encounters on the main floor of Weft's large finishing plant, called "The Bleachery." The cloth from the greige mills comes to loading docks at the rear of the building in huge rolls, tinted different colors to distinguish different weights—for instance, white for shirting material and pink for heavy trouser cloth. All of the cloth contains polyvinyl alcohol(pva), one agent that facilitates the weaving process. The first operation is to remove the pva by washing the cloth in "rope" form—that is, twisted into long strands. The cloth is then untwisted and run at incredibly high speeds in flat form through gas flames on both sides. This helps remove other impurities still left in the cotton part of the cloth. Then the cloth is put back into rope form and whipped by ropes and pulleys through holes in the wall into an adjacent room where it is put into huge vats with a biologically active enzyme that removes the "sizing," the starch that gives the yarn requisite tensile strength for weaving. After the cloth sits in the vats for four hours, it is once again pulled up in rope form into a series of baths, for instance, of hot water and of caustic soda, and at each stage is dried over drying cans. After this, the cloth is often mercerized, that is, put again in a caustic soda bath to heighten its receptivity to dyes. After drying, it then goes to the dyeing ranges, and perhaps later, to the printing ranges.

All of this is an astonishing sight. At any given moment, thousands and thousands of yards of cloth in rope form swirl overhead on pulleys moving from one operation to another; here cloth is racing through flames, here over drying cans, there entering the finishing ranges a dull gray and emerging any of a series of muted or brilliant colors. At one level of their consciousness, those who work in the plant come to take for granted what seems extraordinary to an outsider. At another level, they make connections between product and process— say, the shirt that one wears and how it was made—generally unavailable to those outside a particular occupational community. Even after years of work in such a setting, some managers still find their daily exposure to the drama of coordinating human toil with technology an exhilarating experience.

IV-20: After Enron
The Ideal Corporation

John A. Byrne

Following the abuses of the '90s, executives are learning that trust, integrity, and fairness do matter— and are crucial to the bottom line.

Every summer for the past 10 years, Jack Stack has been going to Massachusetts Institute of Technology's Sloan School of Management to speak with young chief executives about the ideals and values of the engine manufacturing company he helped to make a management paragon. In the late 1980s, Stack's Springfield ReManufacturing Corp. emerged as a model for how management and labor could successfully work together in a culture of trust and ownership. Thousands of managers flocked to his company to hear his ideas while others gathered to hear him during his annual trek to MIT

Reprinted from August 26, 2002 issue of *Business Week* by special permission, copyright © 2002 by The McGraw Hill Companies, Inc.

for its Birthing of Giants program for new CEOs.

But as the dot-com era took hold in the late 1990s, Stack saw a change in the attitudes of the business leaders who showed up at MIT. They seemed far more ambitious for themselves than for their companies. They were building organizations to flip, not to last. They were more interested in the value of their stock-holdings than the profits of their companies. They told him his ideas for tapping into the enthusiasm, intelligence, and creativity of working people were antiquated. And they said he was out of touch.

Stack says that even he began to think of himself as a dinosaur. "So many young CEOs were mesmerized by getting a $1 million or $2 million pop, selling out, and then getting out of town." he says. "They forgot that business is all about values."

Suddenly, leaders like Stack — people who take concepts like ethics and fairness seriously — are back in vogue in a big way. In the post-Enron, post-bubble world, there's a yearning for corporate values that reach higher than the size of the chief executive's paycheck or even the latest stock price. Trust, integrity, and fairness do matter, and they are crucial to the bottom line. The corporate leaders and entrepreneurs who somehow forgot that are now paying the price in a downward market roiled by a loss of investor confidence.

"The chasm that separates individuals and organizations is marked by frustration, mistrust, disappointment, and even rage," says Shoshana Zuboff, a Harvard Business School professor and co-author of a new book called *The Support Economy*.

The realization that many companies played fast and loose with accounting rules and ethical standards in the 1990s is leading to a reevaluation of corporate goals and purpose. Zuboff and many other business observers are optimistic that the abuses now dominating the headlines may result in healthy changes in the post-Enron modern corporation. What's emerging is a new model of the ideal corporation.

TRUST *Giving employees an ownership stake can build an unusual level of mutual respect.*

Business leaders say corporations will likely become far more transparent — not only for investors, but also for employees, customers, and suppliers. The single-minded focus on "share-holder value," which measured performance on the sole basis of stock price, will diminish. Instead, companies will elevate the interests of employees, customers, and their communities. Executive pay, which clearly soared out of control in the past two decades, is already undergoing a reassessment and will likely fall back in an effort to create a sense of fairness. And corporate cultures will change in a way that puts greater emphasis on integrity and trust.

TRANSPARENCY *Making the inner workings visible to all will put pressure on companies to clean up their acts.*

The new agenda, say management observers, will require greater investment in financial systems, ethics training, and corporate governance. It may also demand a resetting of expectations so that investors are more realistic about the returns a company can legitimately and consistently achieve in highly competitive markets. Growth rates of 20% and up, even in technologically-driven industries, are likely to be a thing of the past.

In the anything-goes 1990s, too many companies allowed performance to be disconnected from meaningful corporate values. "A lot of companies simply looked at performance in assessing their leaders," says Larry Johnston, CEO of Albertson's Inc., the food retailer. "There have to be two dimensions to leadership; performance and values. You can't have one without the other."

This and other changes will be driven less by the threat of government intervention and more by the stigma of being branded an unethical enterprise. That's why the government's newfound zeal to indict individuals and even companies carries such power, regardless of how the cases are resolved. "Social sanctions may eclipse the law in imposing penalties for misconduct and mischief," says Richard T. Pascale, a management authority and author of *Surfing the Edge of Chaos.* "The corporation of the future has to think about this new development as an increasingly formidable factor to be reckoned with."

That's a change from the 1990s, when pressure from Wall Street and the dot-com mania led to much of the corporate excess. During those years, when Stack found his ideas decidedly out of favor, he stuck with the "open-book management" culture that had made him something of a celebrity years earlier. By sharing all of the company's financials with all employees and giving them an ownership stake in the company, Stack had built a level of mutual trust and respect unusual in business.

There were other organizations that clung to similar beliefs, from Southwest Airlines Co. to Harley-Davidson. "We all stayed close together because we knew the dot-com model didn't have legs," says Stack. "But many of us wondered if the world would get back to companies with real values." Right now, Stack's ideas about leadership and management are resonating with many who feel disillusioned about business.

If there's one change that nearly everyone foresees today, it's a move to make the corporation far more transparent. That's obvious when it comes to investors, who are demanding truth in the numbers and clarity in disclosure. But it's also important for employees if they're to have a true sense of ownership in their company's affairs. At Stack's company, there are weekly huddles with workers and managers, prominent scorecards on factory walls charting work progress, and on-going emphasis by managers on building a company and not just a product. Workers undergo training so they can understand the numbers on a balance sheet and an income statement.

That need to make the inner workings of the corporation visible to all constituencies is expected to drive lots of change. "In some sense, there aren't going to be many secrets in business anymore," believes consultant James A. Champy, chairman of Perot Systems Corp.'s consulting practice. "Even customers are calling for it today. Wal-Mart Stores Inc. wants to know what the costs of its suppliers are." The end result: It will put greater pressure on companies to clean up their management processes and become more efficient, and it will cause yet another reexamination of less-profitable businesses.

ACCOUNTABILITY An open culture will enable employees to more easily report ethical lapses and unfair practices.

Corporate cultures, which in many cases veered out of control in the 1990s by emphasizing profit at any cost, are also in for an overhaul. More than anything else, those beliefs and attitudes are set by the top execs. The values they espouse, the incentives they put in place, and their own behavior provide the cues for the rest of the organization. "The CEO sets the tone for an organization's culture, says Alfred P. West Jr., founder and CEO of financial-services firm SEI Investments Co., which operates the back-office services for mutual funds and bank trust departments.

Like Stack, West is a rather uncommon CEO. As the company's founder, he does not take stock options and pays himself a sober $660,000 a year. Rather than a spacious corner office, he has the same open-plan office space and desk as anyone else at company headquarters in Oaks, Pa., and he shuns the perks that are commonly demanded in the executive contract. Why? "If you separate yourself from everybody else with corporate aircraft and enormous stock options, your employees are going to get the wrong message," says West.

> **PAY** *Executive compensation, clearly out of control, is likely to fall back in an effort to create a sense of fairness.*

To make sure they get the right message, West spends a lot of time banging home his vision of the company to the people who work there. His goal of building an open culture of integrity, ownership, and accountability is a harbinger for what organizations will look like in the future. "We tell our employees a lot about where the company is going. We overcommunicate the vision and the strategy and continually reinforce the culture." Companies are also using that kind of openness to make it easier for their employees to report ethical lapses and unfair practices with whistle-blower hotlines and open procedures for airing grievances. And to give employees an incentive to use all that newly available information, many companies will help them acquire stakes through discounted stock plans. And even stock options are in for a revamping—with longer vesting periods and perhaps mandatory holding periods as well.

Through the current dark period, there's reason for optimism. Harvard's Zuboff notes that capitalism has avoided devastating crises because it is a robust economic system that changes and adapts. The unprecedented economic expansion of the 1990s was widely seen as the triumph of managerial capitalism. Highly motivated business people used public capital to bring to life creative ideas and concepts for new companies and products. Corporate ownership was dispersed among many shareholders, but control and the lion's share of rewards were concentrated at the top of the managerial hierarchy—whether the company was a startup or an incumbent.

The next stage, believes Zuboff, will be something she calls "distributed capitalism," in which ownership will be more widely spread and organizations will be as responsive to their employees and communities as they have been to their shareholders in the past decade.

Wishful thinking? Perhaps. But the first task of the post-Enron corporation is to acknowledge that a company's viability now depends less on making the numbers at any cost and more on the integrity and trustworthiness of its practices. In the future, leadership that preaches this new ethos and reinforces it through value-driven cultures will be far more likely to reap the rewards of the changing marketplace.

IV-21: Wal Around the World

> *The world's largest retailer still thinks of itself as a small-town outfit. That may be its greatest strength.*

THERE is no shortage of statistics describing Wal-Mart's size. With $216 billion in sales, it has bypassed General Electric to

become the world's second-largest company after ExxonMobil. With 1.2 m staff, it is the biggest private-sector employer in the world. It broadcasts more live television than any network. The computer controlling its logistics is the world's most powerful after the Pentagon's. Six years ago it sold almost no food, yet today it is America's biggest grocery retailer.

To appreciate fully how big Wal-Mart is, however, you have to travel to its headquarters in tiny Bentonville, Arkansas, a state where chickens outnumber people. A building the size of 24 football fields, carrying a giant Wal-Mart logo, looms out of the barren landscape. Yet this massive warehouse also offers a clue that size is not the main reason for Wal-Mart's success. Under the logo, in equally large letters, it says:"Our people make the difference."

Despite its size, the world's largest retailer has stuck to its small-town roots. Its founder, Sam Walton, set up shop in a hamlet near Bentonville in 1962 because retailers such as Kmart and Sears dominated large towns. That decision shaped Wal-Mart's success. "Being founded in Bentonville was a coup," argues Richard Church, an analyst at Salomon Smith Barney. Lacking customers, staff and suppliers, Walton had to do things differently. He offered incentives: profit-sharing for the staff, partnerships for suppliers. And customers got friendly service and "everyday low prices," which meant that Wal-Mart had to keep costs minimal.

Frugality came naturally to Walton, who was a country boy. He made executives sleep eight to a room on trips. Once America's richest man, he drove an old pick-up truck and flew economy class. "Every time Wal-Mart spends one dollar foolishly," he wrote, "it comes out of our customers' pockets." A decade after his death, this is still ingrained in Wal-Mart's culture.

Thus, although its soaring market capitalisation—now $252 billion—has made millionaires of executives and hourly workers alike, there are no signs of opulence or ego at the company's austere headquarters. Lee Scott, the chief executive, drives a VW Beetle and as recently as August shared a hotel room to save money. John Menzer, head of Wal-Mart International, sits in a tiny

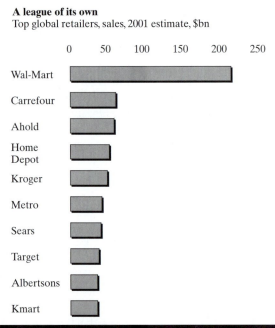

A league of its own
Top global retailers, sales, 2001 estimate, $bn

| | 0 | 50 | 100 | 150 | 200 | 250 |

Wal-Mart
Carrefour
Ahold
Home Depot
Kroger
Metro
Sears
Target
Albertsons
Kmart

FIGURE 4-7 A League of Its Own

Source: Salomon Smith Barney.

office on the same floor as his staff. Executives take out their own rubbish, pay for their coffee and are told to bring back pens from conferences.

The company's small-town values drive its relationship with staff and suppliers. Despite its enormous workforce, there is a paternal feel to Wal-Mart. It is as if everybody were still working for some strict, though ultimately benign, uncle. Employees are called "associates." Most own shares and are on profit-share.

They also enjoy a large degree of autonomy. Ken Schroader, store manager at Wal-Mart's Supercenter in Siloam Springs, Arkansas, proudly demonstrates the scanners that tell his department managers precisely how well products are selling—sales compared with last year, mark-ups, how much is in stock or in transit. Such details allow a department head to become a small shopkeeper, running his section like an independent store and moving stock faster (Wal-Mart shifts inventory twice as fast as the industry average). Every humble store worker has the power to lower the price on any Wal-Mart product if he spots it cheaper elsewhere.

That sort of delegation is apparent outside the stores too. Michael Duke, head of logistics, uses his 6,000 truck drivers (most of whom own Wal-Mart shares) to keep tabs on inventory problems at stores. Involvement breeds loyalty: driver turnover is only 5% a year, compared with an industry average of 125%. George Tracy, head of personnel at a Bentonville distribution centre, cracks down on whatever raises costs and rewards whatever lowers them.

This month, for instance, Laura Blumenstein, one of his workers, will get dinner for two and a parking spot near the entrance (this is Wal-Mart, after all) for logging inventory fast and accurately. To raise flagging spirits, weird stunts—such as pig-kissing contests and quasi-evangelical weekend get-togethers—are laid on. In America, at least, this works.

Suppliers are treated as part of the family, once they have proved their worth. Nervous newcomers are shown to "the row," a long corridor of drab rooms, each adorned with a notice explaining that Wal-Mart's buyers do not accept bribes. It is like a scene from a bazaar: sweaters spill out of suitcases and haggling over prices continues all day. Angel Burgos, from Puerto Rico, wants to sell computers to Wal-Mart: "We were grapes," he sighs, "but now we are raisins. They suck you dry."

Proven suppliers, though, feel differently. Through Wal-Mart's proprietary systems, they are given full and free access to real-time data on how their products are selling, store by store. By sharing information that other retailers jealously guard, Wal-Mart allows suppliers to plan production runs earlier and so offer better prices. Procter&Gamble's $6 billion-a-year business with Wal-Mart is so important that the maker of Crest toothpaste has a 150-strong Bentonville office dedicated to it. Andy Jett, a director there, says Europe's retailers are still blind to the competitive edge that partnering with suppliers gives Wal-Mart. "Wal-Mart treats suppliers as an extension of its company. All retailers will eventually work this way," he predicts.

All this effort has produced sparkling results. In less than four decades, Wal-Mart has come to account for 60% of America's retail sales and 7–8% of total consumer spending (excluding cars and white goods). Its same-store sales growth is running at five times the industry average and its pre-tax profits have grown by 15% a year over the past decade, to $9.3 billion in 2000. No other global retailer comes close when measured by sales. Mr.Scott says future growth will come from aggressive new store openings, plus a move into food and into such services as banking (though Wal-Mart's foray into Internet retailing has not been entirely successful). "Is there some reason we couldn't be three times this size?" he asks. However, analysts worry about saturation in America and expect domestic profit growth to slow to 9% within five years—not bad for a normal company, but disappointing for the supercharged Wal-Mart.

No other global retailer comes close when measured by sales

Wall Street is pinning its hopes instead on Wal-Mart's overseas efforts. Founded only a decade ago, the international division already accounts for 17% of sales and 11% of profits. Mr. Menzer says that the operation will contribute a third of Wal-Mart's profits growth within five years. Linda Kristiansen, an analyst at UBS Warburg, an investment bank, forecasts that profits outside America will grow by 21% a year on average until 2006. CSFB, another bank, puts the figure at 26%.

Are these predictions too bold? Wal-Mart is already the biggest retailer in Canada and Mexico. It bought itself the number three position in Britain with its £6.7 billion ($11 billion)acquisition of Asda in 1999, and it is now pushing into China. But its ventures in Argentina, Indonesia and Germany have been flops, accompanied by heavy losses. With a presence in nine countries, Wal-Mart is in fact less international than other aspiring global retailers such as France's Carrefour, which has stores in 31 countries.

Most of Wal-Mart's overseas problems were avoidable. In the 1990s it made the mistake of exporting its culture wholesale, rather than adapting to local markets. When it moved into Indonesia, it shipped in an entire warehouse on a barge. In Germany, its biggest headache, Wal-Mart was ready neither for the entrenched position of such discounters as Aldi, nor for the inflexibility of suppliers and the strength of trade unions. It had little feel for German shoppers, who care more about price than having their bags packed, or German staff, who hid in the toilets to escape the morning Wal-Mart cheer.

"We screwed up in Germany," admits Mr. Menzer. "Our biggest mistake was putting our name up before we had the service and low prices. People were disappointed." Mr. Scott is blunter, blaming the cock-up on "incompetent management." Just as well that Wal-Mart can afford such mistakes. "Who else can lose $300 m a year in Germany and barely notice?" asks CSFB's Michael Exstein.

Wal-Mart is at least learning from its experience. Unlike its small, nervous steps into some foreign markets, the acquisition of Asda was bold, providing crucial expertise in selling food. Wal-Mart is also becoming more culturally astute, even importing good ideas from overseas into its domestic business. And things are looking up in Germany. Employees like being asked what they think and shoppers, used to surly staff and dingy stores, are slowly warming to service with a smile.

But Wal-Mart's biggest problem is its lack of "human capital," says Coleman Peterson, head of personnel. The group has been at pains to replace expatriates with locals, and every overseas country team except China's is now led by a non-American. Yet it is expanding faster than it can train people internally, and has lost high-quality local managers to rivals.

Wal-Mart's biggest problem is is lack of "human capital."

This leads to another problem: that the international division still lacks scale. To exploit savings from sourcing globally, Wal-Mart needs to make more acquisitions. Buying Carrefour would be the boldest move. However, Wal-Mart is more likely to buy the hypermarket businesses of Germany's Metro, worth $ 4 billion. The two sides talked last year, and insiders say that Metro, controlled by three families, is ready to sell. Buying even part of Metro, which controls a third of Germany's retail space, would bring Wal-Mart huge clout with

European suppliers, and also some more experienced European managers.

But Wal-Mart has another problem: its image. In America, its giant stores are symbols of "big retail," blamed for the destruction of entire communities. To avoid future growth being constrained by political barriers, Wal-Mart may have to raise its head from Bentonville and worry more about how it is perceived. Unpopularity is hard for Wal-Mart executives to understand. After all, everyday low prices have been good for consumers. And a recent study by McKinsey, a consultancy, credited efficiencies in retailing (mainly Wal-Mart's) for

more of America's recent productivity spurt than technology investment.

Ultimately, few doubt that Wal-Mart has both the patience and the resources to stay on top. "Never underestimate them," advises Richard Hyman of Verdict, a consultancy. "They foster an image as country hicks. It makes the kill more of a surprise." Certainly, Wal-Mart has made mistakes, but it has also got more things right than its rivals, who mistake its small-town simplicity for naivety at their peril. As Mr.Scott puts it:"Just because we are simple, doesn't mean we are unintelligent."

IV-22: Revisiting "Dangerous Liaisons"
or Does the "Feminine-In-Management"Still Meet "Globalization"?

Marta Calas and Linda Smircich

OUR ORIGINAL PAPER

In 1993, we published an article, *Dangerous Liaisons: The "Feminine-in-Management" Meets "Globalization,"*[1] which was later reproduced in the previous edition of this book. At the time of its writing, during the summer and fall of 1992, certain claims were being made in the United States regarding the need to transform practices and discourses of management and organizations as required by globalization processes. As interested observers of the managerial and business scenes, we were mostly uneasy with such claims. In fact, in our view "globalization" had become a mantra invoked more to protect certain interests than to promote positive changes in the face of wider social transformations. Our paper attempted to

create a space for thinking about how managerial policy strengthened the less benevolent aspects of globalization. We did so through a feminist structural analysis.

From our perspective, this type of analysis would make it possible to foreground a more complex picture of globalization processes. It would facilitate showing how apparently positive managerial discourses and policies regarding women and women's characteristics as beneficial to organizations, which were also going on at the time, might be intimately connected to very negative aspects of globalization. It would also facilitate showing how "gender" used as a conceptual lens, rather than as merely a biological or social characteristic of human beings, could bring forth, beyond critique and analysis, other ways of considering the world we inhabit.

That was what we were thinking and observing nearly 10 years ago, and it was

---

[1]*Business Horizons,* March–April 1993, vol. 36, no. 2, pp. 71–81.

what we thought we were doing by writing and publishing the article. Since then, the paper—as is the case with any other publication—has taken on a life of its own. Sometimes it has been cited in support of arguments similar to ours, and at other times to support exactly the opposite view. Today, we think it is time to reflect on this publication. What has happened since? What is different now? Where do we stand?

First, we provide an abbreviated version of the original paper. Afterwards, we offer additional thoughts and reflections from today's perspective. We don't think of ourselves as "prophets," thus we had no expectation of being right. Our intentions, rather, were to provoke some resistance to powerful actors who trade in determinist thoughts to maintain their own privilege, those who claim to know exactly what is happening and to know the few possible solutions. We wanted to emphasize our belief in human agency and collective action for changing the lot of those less powerful, who can see and want things to be different but may not think them possible. These are still our thoughts, and that's the sentiment that impels us now to revisit our work. As you proceed, please keep in mind that the original paper was written much before the now common (from Seattle onwards) anti-globalization protests, as well as before the stock market's rise, and eventual fall, from the mid-1990s. Rather, when we were writing, the United States was in the midst of an economic downturn.

A DIGEST OF OUR "ORIGINAL"

HELP WANTED

Seeking transforming manager. Impatient with rituals and symbols of hierarchy. Favors strengthening networks and interrelationships, connecting with coworkers, customers, suppliers. Not afraid to draw on personal, private experience when dealing in the public realm. Not hung up by a "What's in it for me?" attitude. Focuses on the whole, not only the bot-

tom line; shows concern for the wider needs of the community. If "managing by caring and nurturing" is your credo, you may be exactly what we need. Excellent salary and benefits, including child care and parental leaves.

Contact CORPORATE AMERICA
FAX: 1-800-INTRUBL
An Equal Opportunity Employer.
We do not discriminate on the basis of sex, race, age, disabilities, or sexual orientation.

How soon can we expect to see such a want ad? Soon, no doubt, if recent literature is to be believed. Since the mid-1980s, books and articles have appeared that, like our fictitious advertisement, support approaches to management based on traits and orientations traditionally associated with women, the female, and the feminine. A common story runs through these examples: Currently, business firms in the United States are suffering countless setbacks. Changes are needed. Therefore, if women and women-oriented qualities are brought into organizations and allowed to exert influence, it is likely that changes in the right direction will occur.[2]

In principle, we cannot do other than share these sentiments, for they seem to argue for more managerial opportunities for women. But it is also important to approach this discussion cautiously. As we point out below, the current appearance of what we call here "the feminine-in-management" positions in the popular and the academic management press is not arbitrary, nor does it represent a natural pro-

---

[2]For example, Tom Peters observed in 1990 that "It's perfectly obvious that women should be better managers than men in today's topsy-turvy business environment. As we rush into the 90s, there is little disagreement about what business must become: less hierarchical, more flexible and team-oriented, faster and more fluid. In many opinion, one group of people has an enormous advantage in realizing this necessary new vision: women." T. Peters, "The Best New Managers Will Listen, Motivate, Support—Isn't That Just Like a Woman?" *Working Woman,* September 1990, pp. 216–217.

gression toward more advanced organizational knowledge. Rather, we see a repetition of a cycle common in both academic and managerial circles when a need for change appears. On those occasions there is a tendency to obscure the need for fundamental change—which would alter the established balance of power—with a surface change that maintains that same balance while creating the appearance of a radical rethinking of what is. Women have been used for this purpose on more than one occasion. Therefore, if such is the case with the feminine-in-management, what is the "essential female" obscuring? What else is happening that propels managers and management theorists to "cherchez la femme"?

Other writings that call attention to the contemporary economic scene faced by American corporations have been appearing concurrently.[3] In these writings the corporate actor is discussed within the wider environmental context of a "global reality." Different from earlier times, the arguments go, American corporations are no longer competing on familiar grounds. Contemporary managers face a more complicated competitive global field where not all actors play by the same rules. Like the feminine-in-management literature, these writings announce changes, both behaviorally and structurally, for America's corporate ways.

But why these parallel discourses now? We argue that there is, in fact, a close relationship between them. If approached separately, each of these managerial discourses appears to bring about fundamental changes in corporate America. However, when taken together, one—the feminine-in-management—maintains the domestic balance of power that allows for the other—globalization—to fight for continuing that same balance in the international arena. Together they keep in place America's traditional social, cultural, and economic values, not effecting any transformational changes.

A Brief History of the "Feminine-in-Management" Rhetoric

For about 20 years, literature on women and management emphasized that women's abilities as managers are equivalent to those of men. But in the mid-1980s, general discussions about the place of women in management took a turn. Besides talk about how women could perform managerial roles as well as men (the equality discussion), a case was now being made that women's unique "feminine skills" could make important contributions to organizational management (the difference discussion), on which the feminine-in-management rhetoric is based.

Clearly, the appeal of these ideas stems from their implications for revaluing women and feminine qualities in various kinds of activities, including approaches to management. For instance, Marilyn Loden was one of the first to argue, under the women's difference umbrella, that women's managerial styles could be what was needed for solving American productivity problems.[4] Similar arguments followed in other periodicals and books.[5] In these writings, what was once

---

[3]See, for example, R. Kuttner, *The End of Laissez-Faire: National Purpose and the Global Economy After the Cold War* (New York: Alfred A. Knopf, 1991); K. Ohmae, *The Borderless World: Power and Strategy in the Interlinked Economy* (New York: Harper, 1990); M. E. Porter, *The Competitive Advantage of Nations* (New York: Free Press, 1990); R. B. Reich, *The Work of Nations* (New York: Knopf, 1991); L. Thurow, *Head to Head: The Coming Economic Battle Among Japan, Europe and America* (New York: Morrow, 1992).

[4]M. Loden, *Feminine Leadership—or—How to Succeed Without Being One of the Boys* (New York: Times Books, 1985).
[5]See, for example, R. Eisler, "Women, Men and Management: Redesigning Our Future," *Futures,* January–February 1991, pp. 318; J. Grant, "Women as Manager: What They Can Offer to Organizations," *Organizational Dynamics,* Spring 1988, pp. 56–63; J. F. Rosener, "Ways Women Lead," *Harvard Business Review,* November–December 1990, pp. 119–125.

disparaged as female patterns that needed to be overcome to achieve success in management were now positioned as special and useful for organizations.

Perhaps the best representative of these ideas in the popular business literature has been Sally Helgesen's close-up study of four female executives, whose images of organizational structure were more similar to a web or circle than a hierarchy or pyramid.[6] From this, Helgesen articulates a notion of authority not at the head of an organization, but at its heart, as "authority comes from connection to the people around rather than distance from those below." Helgesen, like others, argues that the "integration of the feminine principles into the public realm offers hope for healing" the conditions of modern life, pervaded by "feelings of pointlessness, sterility and the separation from nature."

As these writings are gaining an important status as new representations of good management, they deserve analysis that goes beyond the question of their scientific adequacy—are they true?—in favor of asking, "Why are they being spoken?" and "Why are they being spoken now?" Our argument is this: The appropriation of the "women's difference" discourse by management writers is merely another episode in a long history of economic reasoning that ends up valuing women out of instrumental necessity. From the girls of the Lowell mills in the 1800s to Rosie the Riveter in World War II, we have seen the ebb and flow of cultural discourses that support the movement of women from the domestic to the public sphere and back again.

In our view, this recent turn toward "women's ways of leadership" is nothing other than a 1990s version of the "conquest" by women of the American business office in the 1930s. At a time when sexism did not need to be covered up with a veneer of civil-

ity, a *Fortune* magazine writer candidly accounted for the then-recent transformation of American business offices by observing that women make the office "a more pleasant, peaceful, and homelike place":

> The whole point of the whole problem is merely that the modern office necessitates a daily, intimate, and continuing relation which is much more possible between a man and a number of women than between a man and a number of men. . . . It is, if you will, a relation based upon sex. . . . It is marriage— or rather its imitation—which, as we have seen, explains and justifies the existence of the lady at the secretary's desk.[7]

The current feminine-in-management discourse parallels this earlier discourse. It maintains intact—even strengthens—traditional managerial ideologies, because it is the "female" constructed under patriarchy who is given voice and presence, extending the patriarchal family's female role from the private to the public domain.[8] As we shall see, this is the primary role that the feminine-in-management performs in the discourses of globalization.

EXTENDING THE HOUSEHOLD TO THE NATIONAL BORDER

Consider the following scenario: Some years have passed and most organizations are "globalized." Decisions are no longer made at the national level under national premises.

---

[6]S. Helgesen, *The Female Advantage: Women's Ways of Leadership* (New York: Doubleday/Currency, 1990).

[7]"Women in Business: II Being a Commentary upon the Great American Office and the Distinction Between the Girl Who Works to Marry and the Girl Who Marries to Work," *Fortune*, August 1935, pp. 50–86.
[8]Although the notion of "patriarchy" varies somewhat in different feminist theories, here we mean sex/gender relations that naturalize and universalize social practices wherein men/masculine values dominate over women/feminine values. This form of domination is

Globalization means a trans- or supranationally coordinated decision-making system that feeds from a network of national organizations, both large and small. Who are the players in this situation, and how are they positioned?

The rhetoric enabled by the feminine "web-and-connection" metaphor plays very well here. Web-and-connection brings to mind dual images: those of good, caring interpersonal communication and, at the same time, closer interorganizational relations. The first image supports changes toward "flatter" national organizations, where team-based groups would reduce hierarchy; the second image supports strong network structures and new, more powerful transnational organizations at the global level.

In this order of things, nonhierarachical ("feminized") national organizations would be the equivalent of the feminized 1930's offices, because the feminine-in-management would bring the traditional values of the American household to the national border. That is, the private/public divide (women in the household, men out in the world) will not have disappeared. It will have been displaced and re-created on a larger scale, as the hierarchy and authority system are reenacted beyond the "national household" in the global arena. Said differently, the national organization—as feminine as it might become—would be a powerless pawn in a globalized organizational world.

More than international imperatives drive this turn of events. Demographically, it is evident that America's labor force is becoming increasingly diverse. Many have praised these demographic changes as a guarantee that the "diverse," including women, will occupy better organizational positions denied them in the past. It is seldom

particularly pervasive when women uncritically assume stereotypical feminine patterns within traditional structural arrangements.

acknowledged that the trends toward flatter organizations (that is, more team based and with fewer middle-management layers) may eliminate many of these opportunities.

In this situation, the "web-and-connection" metaphor plays a fundamental role. At the domestic level, reducing the organizational hierarchy reduces the number of the "diverse" who will be appointed to managerial positions. Meanwhile, the feminine-in-management would help in converting "diversity" into homogeneous "team players" under a caring, motherly gaze. Yet who is the "good mother" portrayed by the feminine-in-management? One cannot fail to observe that the values represented by this literature are those of white, formally educated, middle- to upper-middle-class American women, and that it is their mothering styles, family values, and relationship to children that are represented in the "authority through connection" metaphors.

In short, by focusing only at the microorganizational level, the feminine-in-management creates an illusion of opportunity and change. But when placed at the larger macro-societal level, it becomes a major support for the discourses of globalization, which benefit only a selected few. The feminine-in-management arguments distract us from observing their dire consequences: It extends the established power structure by moving only the values of those who are "second best" (white women) into the vacated domestic (national) managerial spaces while true decision-making power has been moved away into the global arena.

TO SERVE WITH PRIDE AND DISTINCTION

The discourses of globalization create awareness of another national reality: America is not a high-wage manufacturing economy anymore, and manufacturing's replacement, the service economy, will not bring about high-wage jobs.[9] One of the marks of globalization is the movement of labor-intensive operations toward low-wage world regions coupled with the concomitant displacement of national workers from manufacturing jobs. Even manufacturing firms maintaining national operations often restructure into workplaces with lower wages (or fewer jobs). In the meantime, most new jobs in the service sector are in lower-paying occupations. Is it accidental that the rank-and-file jobs for "the new labor force"—comprising a higher proportion of women and minorities—are not the same high-paid, "making-things" jobs of a past American economy?

Beyond the rank-and-file level, global competitiveness has also brought about the age of the lean-and-mean organization.[10] Regardless of the causes (takeover events and associated reorganizations, added control capabilities "at a distance" with sophisticated management information systems), the very material consequence of these organizational activities is the elimination of middle-management layers, resulting in a large number of mostly white males being "outplaced" by their organizations. Under these conditions, cheaper managers are needed and, from our viewpoint, the feminine-in-management rhetoric provides precisely the low-cost answer for national restructuring toward global competitiveness.

U.S. organizations, Lester Thurow reminds us, would require "a boss to do less bossing," something that he believes American executives are incapable of doing because they covet power too much.[11] His prescribed ideological changes for solving this problem are perfectly matched by Grant's version of the feminine-in-management, in which

women's transforming and liberating force works toward public purposes rather than for personal ambition and power over others. But what Grant does not say and Thurow does is that bosses should not only boss less but also "reduce their own salaries and employment opportunities."[12]

Under these circumstances, the feminine-in-management rhetoric can contribute several other images that eventually naturalize the further exploitation of labor rather than improving managerial opportunities for women. Think, for example, of the following cliches associated with women: "A woman's work is never done," which is equivalent to extended hours for the same pay and "she did it as a labor of love," which is equivalent to unpaid work. As has been well documented, occupations that become "feminized"—including managerial and professional positions—experience declines in salaries and wages.[13] Whereas explanations for this fact vary, the condition remains. Such a situation, however, provides the ideal context for the globalized firm, which would encounter equally ready and willing "affordable labor" on any side of the border. The feminine-in-management, as it extends the values of the household to the workplace, would provide the ideal metaphor for carefully done, high-quality, cheap work, performed by docile workers, regardless of the worker's sex: "housework."[14]

TRAINING THE DOER FOR FEELINGS, NOT THINKING

Another aspect of the globalization rhetoric that has acquired prominent coverage refers to education. The typical storyline in this

---

[9]See, for example, "The Global Economy: Who Gets Hurt?" *Business Week*, August 10, 1992, pp. 48–53.

[10]"America Isn't Creating Enough Jobs, and No One Seems to Know Why," *The New York Times*, September 6, 1992, Section 4, pp. 1, 3.

[11]Turow, op cit., p. 174.

[12]Ibid.

[13]See, for example, B. F. Reskin and P. Roos, eds., *Job Queues, Gender Queues: Explaining Women's Inroads into Male Occupations* (Philadelphia: Temple University Press, 1990).

[14]N. Folbre, "The Unproductive Housewife: Her Evolution in Nineteenth-Century Economic Thought," *Signs*, 1991, vol. 16, no. 3, pp. 463–484.

respect emphasizes American students' lack of general education and the cost of such a lack because of competition with better-educated workers from other nations (mostly Japan and Germany). The problem is frequently stated as one in which the United States is falling behind in technological innovation; the solution is usually stated in terms of more general training in science and mathematics. Behind this story also lies a promise: more and better (high-paying) jobs for better-educated people.

Various elements are problematic in this story. For example, there is no acknowledgment that very well-educated people (people with college degrees) have trouble finding jobs, or that there is a difference between training and education—between being a doer and being a thinker, between technological competence and knowledge. Unfortunately, in the American context, education for globalization translates into higher education for a few elite thinkers—the "smartest" 25 percent of the population, according to Thurow—while the rest would require no more than basic "doer"training.

The turn toward "vocational training" for the majority of the population under the guise of "better education" may be supported by various aspects of the feminine-in-management rhetoric. Rarely, we observe, has the feminine-in-management rhetoric argued for women's superior intellectual capabilities. Rather, it emphasizes the traditional oppositions of "thinking/feeling" and "abstract/concrete" by focusing on women's better interpersonal relations and trustworthiness, their care-and-connection practices that would humanize the workplace, the healing processes they could contribute for the wellness of an alienated workforce, and their concrete, no-nonsense attitude and practical orientation toward everyday problems.

These abilities, we agree, are probably going to be very much in demand for managing the large percentage of "educated" American workers who will not find high-wage jobs, regardless of their diplomas. They would be particularly useful as ways to pacify emotionally the vast majority of these workers (euphemistically,"human capital") who will have to adjust downward their expectations of better pay under globalization. In the meantime, the truly educated few—the abstract thinkers, or "symbolic analysts" as Robert Reich would call them—will reap the fruits of this situation from the distance of their own very well-paid, cosmopolitan global spaces.

HEART-TO-HEART OR HEAD-TO-HEAD?

In the rhetoric of globalization, there is little that is not written in the language of warfare. For example, Thurow's book subtitle is *The Coming Economic Battle Among Japan, Europe, and America;* Ohmae's is *Power and Strategy in the Interlinked Economy.* References are constantly made to "winners and losers"in the global economy, where the world is a battleground, and where the United States should be able to outsmart everyone else. Predictably, the imagery also refers to intellectual prowess in which one would strategize a better game than one's opponent ("war games").

It would appear that this discourse offers little space for Helgesen's "female advantage" to reduce—as she urges us to do—the Warrior values of our dominant culture. Yet for all her talk about women's more holistic view of the world and greater social consciousness, at the end the "female advantage"offers no more than the ability to "master the Warrior skills of discipline, will and struggle necessary to achieve success in the public realm,"[15] even if eventually moving beyond them.

Thus, another way to understand the feminine-in-management rhetoric is as a

---

[15]Helgesen, op. cit, p. 258.

cover-up for the usual way managerial activities have been portrayed from time immemorial in the United States as a fight and struggle among enemies (labor and management, business and government, local and international competitors). The words *competitive advantage* and *female advantage* seem to be used unselfconsciously in the same paragraphs that claim some kind of unique "all heart, all peace" managerial goodness assumed to come from women's qualities. More problematic is the way they objectify women managers into convenient weapons for the international fight, as when women are a "powerful resource for sustainable competitive advantage,"[16] or when "treating women as a business imperative is the equivalent of a unique R&D product for which there is a huge demand."[17]

IMPLICATIONS: OTHER IMAGES OF WOMEN FOR RETHINKING GLOBALIZATION

In summary, we want to call attention to the relationships that may exist between two currently popular managerial discourses—the feminine-in-management and globalization—both of which claim to be bringing much needed changes to the managerial field. We argue that these assumed changes are only a surface rhetoric. Analyzed together, they cancel each other as they maintain existing power relations that benefit only a few.

For example, these discourses speak of better opportunities for all but hold onto the established order when facing the reality of an increasingly diverse workforce. They speak of growing productivity and wealth while making acceptable the lowered expectations brought about by a service economy. They speak of the importance of education and human capital while fostering little more than technical competencies for narrow thinkers. They bring in an emblematic sign of peace to soften the rough edges of a rhetoric that bespeaks of war.

We believe that analyses such as this, that cut through the rhetoric of the latest managerial quick fix, help us understand the connections that exist between the activities of any particular organization when following these popularized prescriptions and the perhaps unintended consequences those same activities may bring to the greater society to which we all belong. The feminine-in-management and their counterpart discourses of globalization are short-sighted, elitist palliatives for the realities of the contemporary world. Thus, it may be possible that in a few years we will look back and view our business organizations—those "feminine"and "globalized" American corporations—as the main perpetrators of a situation from which there is no return: bringing the capabilities of our nation to its lowest common denominator in the name of doing just the opposite.

Thus, in these last paragraphs we offer a different way of thinking "feminine": a way that would bring a different set of images of "women" into a globalized economy. Yet this time, they are images that call for effecting a radical change in the way we think about management and the way we would design our organizations for a better society. Unfortunately, these more critical inspirations from feminist theories have been absent in the feminine-in-management literature because the latter, as it stands now, is just another form of women pleasing men—of making sure it says what is acceptable to say in management now, by maintaining privileges for a few even if the rest of society is worse off.

For example, conventional managerial wisdom considers that, in a global economy,

[16]M. Jelinek and N. J. Adler, "Women: World Class Managers for Global Competition," *Academy of Management Executive,* February 1988, pp. 7–19.
[17]F. N Schwartz, "Women as a Business Imperative," *Harvard Business Review,* March–April 1992, pp. 105–113.

good management creates opportunities to produce and sell an abundance of goods in foreign markets, keep jobs at home, and keep the home population's ability to consume ("the good standard of living") alive and well. This ideal situation is supported by exporting both the goods and the values of a consumer society so the rest of the world will live (consume) as we do while supporting our "democratic values." Yet shouldn't we be wary of managerial strategies that promote consumerism both at home and abroad while pretending this is what we should call "a good standard of living" for the whole world?

The imagery that sustains these strategies is actually a feminine one of "the consumer as impulse shopper"[18] of the "buy-now-and-pay-later" variety. This is an imagery that the feminine-in-management promotes as much as any other managerial approach because what it promotes are the same old goals: more sales, better market share, and to take away from competitors, particularly those from other nations.[19] In contrast, we want to offer the imagery of "the frugal housewife," who can do with consuming less and saving for "a rainy day"; who is able to improve what she already has by conserving and preserving; who shares scarce resources with her neighbors (baby clothes) to be able to produce a "common

wealth." Such imagery may be able to bring about a form of management that not only avoids exploitation of both people and resources, but that is more likely to effect a true cooperation among nations—a better life for all, yet a better life that doesn't hinge on incremental consumption of disposable "goods."

Perhaps the "world-class standards" we export to other nations could be a concept of the good life in which people would better appreciate their own abilities and endowments; where good health and good education—not training—are the primary goods to be had for everybody in every society; where decent food and living conditions would be basic human rights and the basis for a pact among nations—a pact under the premises of "sustainable growth"; where growth is meaningful insofar as it contributes to sustaining "the global family."

We could play with many more images. What about redefining "innovation" through the imagery of "female ingenuity"(being able to do anything with a hairpin)? Such imagery would help us appreciate the talents of many different peoples—particularly those who, because of scarcity, have been able to make do with much less—while helping us learn from them (remember that old phrase about necessity being the mother of invention?). Or what about fully embracing "mother nature" as a female who hasn't yet been offered "equal opportunity," or who hasn't been covered by "affirmative action," or who has been blatantly "sexually harassed"? Would it help in giving the environment a better chance?

What about the image of the "hysterical woman"? The hysterical woman releases her emotions to cry and scream in moral indignation for the crimes against humanity that are constantly committed in the name of economic rationality. She would denounce, time and again, the illogic and the irrationality of a world in which millions of people die of hunger while productive lands are kept barren to maintain a reasonable price for

[18]E. Fischer, J. B. Ristor, "A Poststructuralist Feminist Poststructural Analysis of the Rhetoric of Marketing Relationships," *International Journal of Research in Marketing,* Amsterdam; Sept. 1994; Vol. 11, Issue 4; p. 317.

[19]Popularized "managerial wisdom" explains the global economy as one that produces opportunities to sell an abundance of goods in foreign markets, keeping jobs and a high standard of living at home. Seldom is it explained that such is only one side of the story. The true ideal of a globalized free market economy means that no country will import more than it is able to export, and that the end value of such transactions should equal zero at both the individual country and aggregate global level. Otherwise, globalization translates into exploitation of other nations through consumerism.

food in the market. Perhaps the day that we, who are in business professions in capitalist societies, allow this image of the "hysterical woman"to overcome us as an inspiration for a management theory will be the day that, paradoxically, we will come back to our senses.

That will be the day when we will define "the good economy"as the positive results of having complied with worldwide social imperatives, rather than the other way around. Otherwise, we will have to confess that the logic of democracy and capitalism, of our organizations, and of our governments, would all have failed miserably. So, perhaps we need to place another advertisement:

HELP WANTED

Seeking hysterical person. Willing to become enraged when observing worldwide exploitation, esp. when done in the name of free market economy. Ready to act in world forums to denounce such conditions. Ready to help others develop their critical voices to create a global network of well-informed peoples, who won't accept being called "less developed"or be undervalued for their own local talents and capabilities. Not afraid to call attention to the travesty of conspicuous consumption in the name of progress and demonstrate the negative long-term consequences of a "First World standard of living." If you are willing to create new forms of business organizations ready to promote sane globalization for a sustainable planet.

Contact THE WORLD
FAX: 1-800-IS-READY

We are the best in the business of Thinking and Acting Globally and Locally.

● ● ● ● ● ● ● ● ●

BACK TO
THE FUTURE?

As writers of the paper that you just read, it has been difficult for us to abbreviate the original version. It is hoped that this bare-

bone rendition of our original—moored in social and managerial discourse of the times—would still make sense to a contemporary reader. Personally, in evaluating the paper from today's perspective, we had two different reactions: How right we were! and How wrong we were! In the first instance, unfortunately, we were right about several areas that we called attention to and that have become worse than we expected. In the second instance, we were fortunate to be wrong about certain issues that were perhaps most important. We were both right and wrong on the "feminine-in-management" for "globalization."

What has happened with the "feminine-in management"?Such rhetoric has all but disappeared. It is now taken for granted that "the women's difference makes a difference," and such beliefs have been incorporated instrumentally into the managerial "tool-kit."[20] Any possible critical edge of this rhetoric has thus been silenced. We were right insofar as we saw this literature as another instance in a historical cycle in the United State where women are mobilized into the public arena to serve the interests of certain powerful actors, but then returned to their proper (private) spaces once they have served their purposes. The feminine-in-management rhetoric may have served its purpose then by calling attention to specific ways in which American corporations could be restructured. Yet, this discourse about soft values and human caring lost currency when other more "manly" discourses, such as reengineering, were mobilized to achieve the same purpose or better when it came down to downsizing. Specifically, the discourses of reengineering also appeared in the early 1990s but had the

---

[20]There are still a few instances in which they get invoked in the popular press. See, for instance, J. Macdonald, *Calling a Halt to Mindless Change: A Plea for Commonsense Management* (AMACOM: American Management Association 1998).

additional attraction of the technological, which made them irresistible.[21] In a patriarchal world, what is a guy to do when presented with the choice between woman and machine! Today, you can find ample evidence that "reengineering"is still positively voiced, and in some instances it is back with a vengeance.[22]

MORE "RIGHTS" AND "WRONGS"

We were also right when thinking that the "feminine-in-management" would contribute to limiting the access of minorities to managerial positions in deference to white women. Indeed, there is a fairly clear trend that in the United States during the 1990s, white women benefited more than women and men of color in regards to occupying managerial positions. Yet, we were wrong in imagining that managerial opportunities for white, educated, middle-class women would really improve. Despite a few visible cases, both in terms of occupations and salaries, most women still fare poorly in comparison to white men, and in particular at high-level managerial positions.[23] The feminine-in-management did not make much of a dent there. When it comes to top managerial positions, globalization simply benefits the selected few, *both* at home and abroad.[24]

Beyond managerial jobs, there were two areas in which we thought that imagery concealed within the feminine-in-management would serve to naturalize the further exploitation of U. S. labor under globalization: more service jobs that were not high-paying jobs ("labor of love"), and a higher number of work hours for the same pay ("a woman's work is never done"). Today, both of those trends are well established and even considered by managerial elites as a positive sign of globalization; thus, we were not wrong in expecting so.[25] Yet, we did not foresee at the time, perhaps because it was not as blatant as it is today, that certain other phrases also easily attached to the feminine-in-management would be particularly effective in naturalizing the exploitation of labor. We are referring to terms such as "volunteerism," so much in vogue today in the United State,[26] and more directly to "privatization" and "flexibility," which anchor the neoliberal regimes on which the claims to fame of "globalization" have come to rest.[27]

On the question of vocational training passing as education, we think we were right on the sentiment but somewhat wrong in foreseeing the actual turn of events. Our sentiment was that as more of the United State population was given an instrumental, more vocational-like education, there would be less critical awareness about how the majority of students could be subject to labor exploitation. From this perspective,

---

[21]R. Heygate and G. Brebach, "Corporate Reengineering" "Rethinking the Corporation" *The McKinsey Quarterly,* Spring 1991, no. 2, pp. 44–55; M. Hammer and J. Champy, *Re-engineering the Corporation* (NY: Harper Collins, 1993).
[22]"Re-engineering in Real Time; Information Technology Will Transform the Company As We Know It," *The Economist* (U.S.), February 2, 2002.
[23]See, for instance, Catalyst's ongoing research on these topics www. bpwusa.org/content/FairPay/Wage Gap Analysis/WageGap.htm (accessed February 2002) on the gender wage gap in the United States. Some have noticed that reductions in the wage gap between men and women may be more a function of men's wages becoming lower than of women's wages becoming higher.
[24]*Breaking Through the Glass Ceiling: Women in Management* (International Labor Organization, 2001).

[25]See P. L. Jones, R. E. Ilg, and J. M. Gradner, "Trends in Hours of Work Since the Mid-1970," *Monthly Labor Review,* April 1997, vol. 120, no. 4, pp. 3–14; also, J. Challenge, "Workplace Trends for the 21st Century," *USA Today Magazine,* September 2000, vol. 129 issue 2664, pp. 20–26.
[26]A. B. Krueger, "The President Wants Americans to Volunteer to Pick Up the Slack in Social Services. But Will That Be Enough?" *The New York Times,* February 7, 2002, p. C2(N), p. C2(L), col. 1.
[27]P. Bourdieu, "The Essence of Neoliberalism," *Le Monde diplomatique,* December 1998, www.en. monde-diplomatique.fr/1998/12/08bourdieu (accessed February 2002).

"caring" rather than "thinking" was to become the valuable skill, quite attuned to the low-paying jobs of the service society. However, we did not foresee that education would become such a commodity to be sold in the global market, and even at a distance. We pause on this issue now because we will take it up again later.

Finally, what to say of the instrumentalization of "the feminine" in order to wage a war? Although we were then reflecting mostly on the paradoxes of a managerial discourse that decries "warrior values" while objectifying women as instruments for economic warfare, we could not imagine that things would come to be where they are today.[28] We are referring, of course, to the central role that the "women of the Taliban" who "couldn't be educated" came to play when the United State decided to declare war on Afghanistan. We don't want to engage here in a discussion about justification or not for this war, regardless of our opinion on the matter. Rather, we want to point to the effects that discourses such as these have in the disempowering of women the world over, as they become instrumental in further empowering the powerful through discourses that render women without agency "as damsels in distress" to be "saved" by others.

We think this argument is particularly important today because of the way it works in the context of actual women in the world, whose capabilities to fend for themselves and do something about their lot in life become easily ignored or dismissed if by any chance they oppose the "wishes and knowledge" of the powerful. It is further important because it also mobilizes certain images about the global relationships among nations, and the positions that countries may end up occupying in these relation-

ships. Transnational and supranational organizations are core players in these events. Thus, it is at this point that we need to reflect on our alternative images for rethinking globalization.

Both Right and Wrong on "Other Images of Women for Rethinking Globalization"

For as much as we wanted to address globalization in 1992, perhaps our most glaring mistake was that we were still quite clearly located in a U.S. world view of "the global" and focused on a very U.S.-based conversation about "the feminine" and "management." It was from that position that we wanted to offer other images of women for rethinking globalization. Yet, what we forgot to say, which would also apply to our thinking at the time, was that the first and most necessary step for bringing to life those alternative images was to get out into the world and observe what others were already doing.

As we stated in the introduction to this paper, what compelled us to write in 1992 was "our belief in human agency and collective action for changing the lot of those less powerful, who could see and want things to be different but may not think them possible." These are still our sentiments. In 1992, we were convinced that there were people in the world wishing for and doing for themselves in ways that those in more privileged positions would not even care to know about. But the fact is that neither did we, for we were simply imagining a possible future for others without checking to see what was already going on. Now we are starting from a location that is not just in the United State and that provides a different view of "the global." How do our 1992 ideas compare with the realities of today's world?

---

[28]The reader may want to see the original version of our paper because we did address there the role of women as "weapons."

First, there is more agency among those "less privileged" than what most stories about globalization in the U.S. mainstream managerial texts would lead us to believe. Contemporary U.S. management texts (and much of U.S. politics and media), in their limited understanding of globalization, have become very much like the U.S. liberal feminists of the past (of which the "feminine-in-management" was also part) who believed themselves to be the model for "freedom, well-being, and democracy" the world over. Still cocooned in these beliefs, our management texts are missing much of the action.

There are countless of examples to draw from, but some are particularly indicative of the important public roles played by poorer women in the Third World. For instance, the World Bank has found that in many of these countries, women are strong economic participants, and that in these same countries the trend is toward better health and education and less public corruption.[29] Other literature shows that women home workers in several countries have organized in union-like associations as a way to overcome labor exploitation.[30] Further, it is well known that successful microfinance and microenterprise activities have been attained mostly by women.[31] Thus, it is important to recognize that many of these women are more empowered than their First World "sisters"and are quite capable of making a difference in the world. They know what they are doing, and they have something to teach to the rest of us.

Now, that is good news. The bad news is that no matter which way they are measured, wages and salaries are depressed the world over, not just now under recessionary conditions but incrementally since at least the mid-1980s. Labor restructuring and flexible working conditions, considered necessary under globalization, have changed the global equation in the distribution of income. The poor are indeed getting poorer and the rich richer.[32]

POWERFUL ACTORS

But even from these perspectives, things may be taking a turn for the better, because many powerful actors may now be caring. The version of "globalization" that required neoliberal prescriptives is today very much in question. Analyses such as Hirst and Thompson's [33] that counteract ideas about the nation-state becoming irrelevant also contribute to rethinking the position of nations in relationship to their specific needs—including social needs better served by public policy and programs—and their common global interests.[34] For instance, a recent survey of globalized nations shows that "globalization"does not necessarily require lowering of taxes and reduction of the public safety net (i.e., the race to the bottom). Highly globalized countries, more so than the United States, have been able to maintain both with no negative economic consequences.[35] In

---

[29]*Engendering Development; Through Gender Equality in Right, Resources, and Voice* (Oxford University Press–World Bank, January 2001); see also *Wedo primer: Women & Trade,* www.Wedo.org/global/wedo primer.htm (accessed February 2002).

[30]See, for example, S. Feldman, "Exploring Theories of Patriarchy: A Perspective from Contemporary Bangladesh," *Signs,* 2001, vol. 26, no. 4, pp. 1097–1127.

[31]There are a good number of example but perhaps the Graemeen Bank projects are best known.

[32]A recent report from the World Bank refined the measurements of income distribution by focusing on households and found that the world income inequality has been rising faster than previously thought. econ.worldbank.org/files/978_wps2244.pdf (accessed February 2002).

[33]P. Hirst, and G. Thompson, *Globalization in Question* 2d ed. (London: Polity, 1999). More recently, Argentina has become the "poster child" for arguing that "neoliberal" prescriptions, including structural adjustment policies, are merely the product of armchair economists, particularly in the IMF. To be fair, the IMF is becoming more accepting of these critiques despite the U.S. reluctance to accept them.

[34]For example, the Kyoto protocol on global warming.

[35]"Globalization's Last Hurrah?" *Foreign Policy,* January–February 2002, pp. 38–51.

this study, U.S. policies established to maintain competitiveness under globalization—lowering its tax base while eroding public funding for social programs and education—is shown to be more the exception than the rule among major global players.

Further, a number of nations in the world today are eager and willing to put a more humane face to globalization without needing to follow any single prescription to achieve such purpose. Also, there is greater skepticism about the rhetoric of free trade as the global palliative to all economic ills. This more humane face goes along well with our 1992 images about basic human rights, sustainable growth, the global family, health, education, and the environment. In most cases, the United State has become an outlier in these discussions, albeit unfortunately a powerful one.

Still, we are particularly saddened by the educational scene. The commondification of education appears to be a global phenomenon, but its primary perpetrators are located in the United States and the UK. This new educational ideology, delineated along neoliberal prescriptions, fosters the race to the bottom in public education as privatization and for-profit initiatives are touted as necessary for educational improvements. In many ways, the commodification of education achieves what Lester Thurow had hoped for many years before, in which real education for globalization would only be had by the elite few, while the rest would make do with a more vocational training.[36] Unfortunately, distance education has further accelerated this prescriptive into a global initiative, in which the sellers may be dominated by Anglo-American interests and the buyers are the rest of the world.[37]

Aside from all other critiques that could be leveled to this argument, one ties in directly with our hopes in 1992. At the time, we wanted to forward the image of "female ingenuity" as a way to appreciate and learn from the many talents of many different people, especially those who could make do with less and become innovative in their efforts. We are afraid that commodified Anglo-American "education," as it passes itself off as global, would not only forfeit the chances to learn from others, but also ruin the opportunities of others to continue valuing and developing their own talents in the future. A good example of this is the so-called "best practices" of transnational corporations. In general, they have decreased (along the lines of those who decide what "knowledge" is) the diversity of what can be thought and done, probably curtailing innovation. But perhaps we also will be wrong on this account, given the resilience that we have already observed in even the most dispossessed of global actors and their ability to transform the symbols and meanings of globalization.[38]

HYSTERICAL WOMEN

It is on this almost optimistic note that we want to finish these reflections, for perhaps our most cherished wish did indeed come true. We refer to our wish for the "hysterical woman" as the mobilizing symbol to stop the most negative aspects of globalization. In our view, much of what we have observed as a turn of events toward saner globalization has come from the "hysterical" anti-

---

[36]For a recent example, see "Teenagers Offered Flexible Curriculum" (news.bbc.co.uk/hi/english/education/newsid_1816000/1816258.stm, accessed February 2002).
[37]There is an abundant body of literature on this topic, but see, for example, "Global University Alliance Will

Promote Own Course" '*The Chronicle of Higher Education:*' March 16, 2001, p. A39. Some of the debates appear in "Developing Countries Turn to Distance Education: Enrollments Can Increase Quickly with Online Programs, but So Do Quality-Control Issues," *The Chronicle of Higher Education,* June 15, 2001, p. A29.
[38]See, for instance, J. Rivero, 1999 "Education and Poverty: Policies, Strategies, and Challenges" (www.worldbank.org/education/globaleducationreform/pdf/Jose%20Rivero.pdf, accessed February 2002).

globalization movements of recent years. There is no mystery about this. Recent events at the Global Economy Forum in New York City and the concurrent Global Social Forum in Brazil showed clear signs of coming to terms with a notion of globalization in which the interests of many more people are taken into account.[39] Other meetings of supranational actors, such as the WTO one in Doha, Qatar, in November 2001, also addressed the question of globalization considering broader social issues and not just economic ones.[40]

Thus, our hope for the future is that the tone and actions brought about by these conversations will continue. In particular, we hope that our U.S. fellow-people, rather than looking at the rest of the world from a distance and imagining that "they want to be like us," will be willing to engage more closely with the world and learn about reality. At a minimum, our management texts should be able to tell a more global story, for currently they are mostly preaching to the world their "wishful thinking" as if it were "knowledge," as they further promote these ideologies through the use of force. Most unfortunate indeed! But then, what do we know? We are just hysterical women!

[39]*For example,* "Unlikely Note Is Struck on World Finance Stage: Bill Gates and Bono Challenge the Treasury Chief and the U.S. to Boost Foreign Aid," *The Los Angeles Times,* February 3, 2002.
[40]See, for example, "Globalization Marches On, as U.S. Eases Up on the Reins," *The New York Times,* December 17, 2001

IV-23: Remarks by AFL-CIO Secretary-Treasurer
Before the Academy of Managements Critical Management Studies Workshop

Richard Trumka

Thank you very much for that kind introduction. I'm delighted to join you and bring you warm greetings from the AFL-CIO and the 13 million working men and women of the unions that are affiliated with our federation.

I am doubly delighted because I know I am addressing a distinguished audience here this evening of some of our country's leading business professors and academicians and respected experts in management theory and practice.

By passing along to you a few of the union movement's concerns and goals in this new global economy, maybe some of those concerns will give you a new or unexpected perspective and will find their way into your research and courses, and into the studies of your students.

As you know from your schedule, I am to speak on "Labor, Democracy, and Globalization," and with the recently held G-8 summit in Genoa and the debates on Capitol Hill over fast-track authority and truck safety under NAFTA, it is a timely topic.

It also is an enormously broad topic, so I'm going to limit my focus to a few central connections between democracy and global capitalism and the rights of workers.

. . . If you are a regular consumer of the elite media commentary in this country, you'll be surprised that there are differing views on global trade.

For the most part, America's pundits have been singing from the same hymnal.

Their refrain goes like this: The global economy is a fact of life, so get used to it . . . unfettered trade treaties are not just good but crucial for growth and jobs . . . that democratic institutions will flourish in today's repressive regimes when their economies are opened up to multinational corporation . . . and concerns for workplace conditions and workers rights are really only the camouflage of old-time, threadbare, antibusiness protectionism.

Yes, I'm probably overstating their case somewhat, but frankly not by much. Go back and revisit the commentary columns before and after the G-8 meeting a few days ago or around the time of the summit in Quebec this past spring or during the World Bank meeting here in Washington last year and you find pretty much that type of logic.

The majority of the demonstrators at those gatherings, however, have a view that's not reflected in the mainstream commentary.

Many of them are trade unionists . . . many are environmentalists and religious leaders and local community leaders . . . and many are also young . . . and they come from all around the world and most all behave peaceably.

What they've been asking for are guarantees that people and workers will be given the same degree of protection as capital and profit . . . they want safeguards to make sure that the world's air is kept clear and the waters clear . . . and they want the shroud of secrecy lifted from the trade talks, so the people can hear and see what's being proposed and what's being sacrificed in their name.

Those principles really don't strike most people as all that revolutionary, but they appall the opinion-writing community.

Tom Friedman at the *New York Times* has derided the demonstrators as "clowns." They really should be called "The Coalition to Keep Poor People Poor," says Friedman, because they really are just trying to keep the world's impoverished countries from climbing out of poverty.

Friedman's fellow columnist, Paul Krugman, paints with an even broader brush, charging that opponents of free trade—that is, union supporters who want workers' rights written into trade pacts—really are just, and these are his words, "doing their best to make the poor even poorer."

The tenor of the criticism is always intense, but for many commentators and a good part of the public discourse, workers' rights and global capitalism have become almost an intellectual hobbyhorse or a theoretical parlor game for conjuring what Adam Smith would have thought . . . as if only political points and not real lives were at stake.

The truth is that the real lives are at stake . . . the real lives of workers and trade unionists around the world . . . real people, often heroic people, who every day are accepting risks and dangers in order to secure their basic rights . . . the right to work free from discrimination, to refuse forced labor, to reject child labor.

Workers' rights are not an idle notion for workers . . . many are being persecuted, brutalized, and murdered because they've had the courage to stand up for liberty and the right to organize and bargain collectively.

A few weeks ago in Thailand, more than 100 women garment workers peacefully protesting for something more than poverty wages outside that country's Parliament House were set up, attacked, and beaten by the police.

On any day in Burma, several hundred thousand men, women, and children are forced at gunpoint by the country's military to build roads and bridges and railroads . . . and those who refuse have been jailed, tortured, raped, or murdered.

For his efforts at organizing, the president of the All Burma Workers Union has been sentenced to 17 years in prison. The executive officer of Burma's Federation of Trade Unions was given a life sentence for sending information to pro-democracy groups in exile.

On the island of Fiji, trade unionists are harassed by the military and threatened and attacked by gangs of racist thugs connected to the instigators of this past spring's coup.

In Belarus, the new president has arrested and jailed union members for taking part in demonstrations and with a unilateral decree has essentially banned any new, independent trade unions from forming.

In Cameroon, workers who want to organize a union are intimidated and arrested at the behest of employers.

In China, hundreds of workers are languishing in prisons with no hope of parole or escape for the "crime" of advocating and fighting for internationally recognized labor rights.

And in Colombia, 1500 trade unionists have been assassinated since 1990 in one of the world's longest and most vicious campaigns against the rights of workers.

There is nothing theoretical or academic about the need for basic protections of workers and basic guarantees of their rights. It's a real-life, deadly struggle going on every day, but unfortunately too often out of sight of the media and those who frame our view of the new global economy.

According to the International Confederation of Free Trade Unions, each year several hundred trade unionists are murdered.

Several thousand more are beaten in demonstrations, tortured by security forces, and sentenced to long prison terms.

Meanwhile, hundreds of thousands of workers lose their jobs merely for attempting to organize a trade union.

Their passionate drive to form and join a union is borne of the same reasons that drive American workers to become union members— they want to improve their lives and better care for their families.

They want a voice in their workplace— whether it is fair and safe and healthy— whether the wages they receive for their work will lift them out of the grinding poverty of the developing world.

And joining a union can make an enormous difference.

Here in America, union workers earn 28 percent more than nonunion workers, and the wage benefits are even more substantial for women and minorities.

Eighty-six percent of American union workers receive health benefits on the job, compared to only 74 percent of nonunion workers.

Seventy-nine percent of union workers here are also covered by guaranteed, defined-benefit pensions, compared to just 42 percent of workers who are not union members.

And union workers enjoy more secure jobs, even in today's volatile economy, and contract protections against discrimination, unjust discharge, and arbitrary firing.

Ironically, the freedom of association in the world's workplace and the freedom of workers to unionize and bargain collectively are widely recognized as fundamental human rights.

They are deeply rooted in international human rights law. The freedom of association, and by extension the freedom to join a union, was recognized as a human right in the 1947 Universal Declaration of Human Rights.

Provisions on freedom of association are a part as well of the International Covenant on Economic, Social, and Cultural Rights and the International Covenant on Civil and Political Rights.

And in the International Labor Organization's Conventions 87 and 98, the freedom of association and the right to organize and bargain collectively are specifically guaranteed.

Now, given our status as the world's dominant economic force and our stature as the world's oldest democracy, the United States should be the unchallenged leader in championing the rights of workers abroad.

But our credibility is compromised by what has become a dismal and indefensible record of failing to protect workers' rights here at home.

The realtiy is that we have an escalating war being waged in our workplaces to block the freedom of workers to choose a union.

Employers are spending more than $300 million a year on consultants specializing in tactics to stop employees from organizing, and in one third of the cases where workers vote for a union, employers never agree to a first contract.

Nine out of 10 employers force workers to attend anti-union meetings to sway or intimidate them into changing their mind about joining a union, and three out of every four employers use supervisors to pressure workers in one-on-one meetings not to organize.

And workers have reason to feel intimated. In one of every three organizing campaigns, employers illegally fire workers for supporting a union.

It was last year, after an exhaustive study of violations of workers' rights here in the United States, that Human Rights Watch warned that, and I quote, "workers' freedom of association is under sustained attack in the United States, and the government is often failing in its responsibility under international human rights standards to deter such attacks and protect workers' rights."

The report was authored by Lance Compa of Cornell University and, if you haven't seen it, I'd urge you to get a copy and read it.

It is an extremely well-researched indictment of a system of labor laws riddled with loopholes and halfhearted enforcement that too often is ignoring the mounting abuses American workers confront as they try to exercise their rights.

Illegal reprisals by employers against workers numbered in the few hundreds a year in the 1950s. Today, as Human Rights Watch reveals, cases of employer retribution number more than 23,000 every year.

Other research is also documenting how this country's embrace of no-holds-barred, free-trade policies has given employers the ability to greet and defeat union-organizing campaigns in their workplace with threats of shutting down their plants and moving abroad.

Some of you may be familiar with a study last year of more than 400 NLRB-certified union elections by Dr. Kate Bronfenbrenner, also of Cornell University.

She found such threats have become pervasive, with more than half of the employers she examined [having] tried to defeat a union drive by pledging to pick up and move their company.

In captive meetings with employers, workers were given specific and unambiguous verbal threats that if they voted for union representation, the plant might shut down.

In some cases management supervisors pointedly asked individual workers whether their families were ready to move to Mexico.

The fact that the public and our policy makers haven't been paying attention to this record of abuses really shouldn't be surprising.

For at least the last decade, and actually much longer, our national attention has been on the soaring Dow Jones and high-flying mutual funds. We've been preoccupied and enthralled with the dot.com economy, and plucky entrepreneurs, savvy CEOs, dogged day traders, and the overnight investor millionaires who now grace the covers of our business magazines.

In short, we've been swept up in New Markets mania, and the view from the workers' perspective and our appreciation of labor's concerns and the union movement too often has slipped into the recesses.

More than a few colleges and universities, as some of you can attest, that once offered courses on labor history or integrated union studies in their business schools have shifted priorities and changed their focus.

The premise of the new globalism, though, says "not to worry." It is free trade and open markets, after all, that will open up closed foreign societies and repressive regimes, and democratic institutions will take root, the economies will be lifted up, and the masses now mired in poverty will be turned into tomorrow's wage-earning workers.

Workers' rights and decent working conditions, so the logic goes, will be brought along after the developing economies have their feet on the ground and begin to prosper.

Again, I've crystallized greatly the general free-trade argument, but I don't believe unfairly so. That is the essential premise, and it is also dead wrong.

Worker rights aren't a by-product of democratization. They're the key building blocks for democratic civil societies.

Having a voice in the workplace has been essential to tempering the harsh extremes of capitalism and building the solid, broad middle class that successful modern democracies depend upon.

The crucial protections and safeguards we now accept as so routine in America . . . laws for safety in our workplaces, prohibitions on child labor, disability insurance for injured workers, the minimum wage, the 40-hour workweek, overtime pay, retirement pensions, the right to bargain collectively . . . these were not the products of enlightened Gilded Age capitalism.

They were a necessary response to the excesses and exploitation of free-market economics, and they were finally enacted at the insistence of workers and trade unionists and an American public a century ago that had become increasingly appalled at the economic brutality it witnessed all around it.

The core, fundamental right of free association, of the freedom to organize a union in the workplace and to have a voice in the workplace, might be the single most essential catalyst for the thriving economy of this past century.

Putting the cart before the horse, as free-trade enthusiasts insist upon . . . that is, capital first, workers' rights later on . . . is now driving the world in a horrific race to the bottom.

In all too many cases, the jobs created by free trade in the developing world are giving a few people work but still with wages at or below poverty.

In El Salvador, where many brand-label U.S. clothing makers now go to have their goods produced, 8 of every 10 of the country's garment workers are women and, yes, they have jobs because of U.S. trade, but few earn enough to feed their children or take care of their families, and they labor in unsafe workplaces where unions are not allowed.

We finally got a clear look inside El Salvador's garment industry when a report that had been suppressed for months by that country's government was released. The report was funded in part by the U.S. Agency for International Development.

Today, the United States now imports nearly $1.6 billion worth of clothing manufactured in El Salvador— in fact, we now get more of our clothing from El Salvador than all but seven other countries.

But according to the report, many of El Salvador's 229 apparel factories do not provide basic safety equipment, and threats to fire workers unless they agreed to work long hours of overtime are routine.

Many factories, the report found, knowingly impose unrealistic production quotas and force workers to put in extra hours with no pay when they fall behind the quotas.

And the report documented what it described as the "systematic violation" of workers' efforts to form unions.

Not one of the 229 so-called "maquiladora," or free-trade zone factories, has a union contract, and that's not surprising, since it's common practice by the companies to threaten to fire workers who belong to a union or try to organize one.

Such free-trade, or so-called export-processing, zones have become a driving engine of the new global economy.

In 1995, there were more than 230 export-processing zones, spread across nearly 70 countries, including more than 100 in Latin America and the Caribbean, 64 in Asia, and 31 in Africa.

They also have become a device for unscrupulous employers and pliant local governments to exclude union organizers and deny workers their basic right to freedom of association.

Eighty percent of the workers in the zones are young and unorganized women who earn barely poverty-level wages.

The prosperity of the new globalism isn't likely to trickle down to them until they have a voice in their workplace and the right to bargain collectively, to work free from discrimination, to refuse forced labor, and to reject child labor.

The demand for that right and for consumer and environmental protections isn't a flash-in-the-pan cause. This is a long, deeply felt, and tenaciously embraced struggle.

Congress's reluctance to give the president fast-track authority for a hemisphere-wide, free-trade accord and the recent votes to impose safety standards under NAFTA on Mexican trucks are signs that lawmakers in this capitol are starting to hear the concerns of workers.

At the AFL-CIO, we've mounted a "Voice at Work" campaign to defend the rights of workers to choose a union and combat the tactics of employers who try to thwart those rights.

We've also started a Campaign for Global Fairness to build international solidarity with workers abroad and incorporate workers' rights into trade and investment agreements and to hold corporations accountable when they deny workers their rights.

This year, we're joining our affiliated unions, the International Trade Secretariats, and the International Confederation of Free Trade Unions to make sure that all workers in this new global economy understand their rights.

We're doing so by posting in workplaces and union halls and government buildings around the world the International Labor Organization's Declaration on Fundamental Principles and Rights at Work—the freedom of association and right to organize and bargain collectively, the right to be free from child labor, the freedom from forced labor, and the freedom from employment discrimination.

Let me close by urging you to consider the arena of workers' rights in this new economy as subject matter for your academic research and course studies.

. . . But for starters, I'd suggest as an interesting research topic to shift from the normal focus of many business schools on the "best practices" in business and instead spotlight the "despotic" forms of management that also operate in our economy.

There is also a burgeoning industry of scab-labor providers and union-busting consultants that's ripe for a close examination.

And not enough has been done to really explore the outlandish corporate compensation of many U.S. CEOs that's routinely out of whack with the wages of workers and with what foreign CEOs receive.

But most importantly, you can help instill in the students you have, who will be the next managers of this economy, an appreciation of the right of workers to join a union and of the long, hard struggle required to win that right.

If you can provide a lesson in the value of the ability and the right of workers to bargain collectively, you will have served your students and all of us quite well.

Thank you very much.

SECTION V

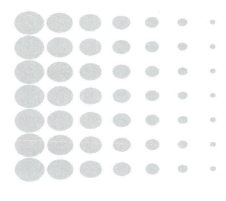

CONVERSATIONS INTO THE TWENTY-FIRST CENTURY

We have had the first major jolts of the twenty-first century: the terrorist attacks on the World Trade Center on September 11, 2001; the bursting of the high-tech bubble; and the financial and leadership scandals of Enron, WorldCom, and many others, which have shaken the trust of investors in many countries. We have had floods and famines; we have witnessed the tragedies of wars, rebellions, and harsh dictatorships. We also have the ongoing revolution of technology and of global issues (despite protectionist acts in some countries). What might be the conversations about organizations and those who lead and work in them into this still-new century? We present a collage of opinions and ideas from several different sources. Doubtless, the future will turn out differently from what we expect, but we think the issues we include in this section will remain important regardless of the circumstances.

Who will be the future leaders of our major corporations, and how will they fare? Many of the heroes of the turn of the century are no longer in charge of these companies, and some of them have fallen from grace along the way. In *Fallen Idols*, the argument is advanced that the business media made the leaders of many corporations into celebrities or that they became celebrities without substance, puffed up by a strong economy and an uncritical press. Once the markets declined and it was discovered that companies like Enron had inflated profits and applied faulty, even unethical, accounting practices, these same heroic leaders took the fall for the failures of their companies.

This interpretation of events and actions is probably true to an extent, and one useful conversation could focus on how to prevent this false appreciation of companies and their leaders in the future. For this conversation to go beyond sensational and relatively superficial proposals, however, it is worth wondering, as Peter Drucker does, in *Will the Corporation Survive?* whether leading the corporation of today (and tomorrow) is an impossible job. The leaders of many of the companies who fell in the early twenty-first century were chosen for their competence in their previous jobs, yet they failed quickly in these most challenging top jobs. Drucker suggests that the problem is systemic, not about human failings, and that we need a new model for the role. One possible model he describes comes from the Jack Welch era. Welch, says Drucker, had built a top-management team in which "the company's chief financial officer and its chief human resources manager are near equals to the chief executive, and both are excluded from the succession to the top job." This arrangement spreads the load and eliminates dysfunctional jockeying and competition. Drucker adds some other intriguing notions about the shape of things to come for the corporation: "In the next society's corporation," he writes, "top management will, in fact, be the company. Everything else can be outsourced." This serves as food for thought and conversation.

When Jack Welch retired, the reins of GE passed of Jeff Immelt. (See *A Talk with Jeff Immelt.*) The interview with Immelt is an instructive read. It sheds light on some of the personal demands and organizational challenges that faced a leader at a time when external conditions had changed dramatically from Welch's era. It would seem from his vantage point and early experience in the role that the company was left in good shape by its predecessor and that the changes that he envisages for this diversified company will prove successful.

One aspect of Drucker's analysis of the next society that rang true for us was the growth and influence of the knowledge worker class and the increasing importance these workers attach to personal achievement and responsibility. Self-leadership in this case refers to being able to manage oneself as a viable portfolio of skills and interests. It is also about the worker being willing and able to take on the role of responsible leadership in projects and changing organizational ventures, whether or not he or she is a designated leader. Poet David Whyte *(At the Cliff Edge of Life)* writes powerfully about the role of work in shaping an individual's identity. People live and work to different rhythms from one another, and his stories and metaphors provide useful messages about how to forge a path that has authenticity and vitality in the unfolding world of work. "Whether it is a place like Galápagos (Where he had his first job as a biologist) or a place like our office, if we are serious about our work we tend to find ourselves apprenticed to something much larger than we expected, something that calls on more of our essence than we previously imagined, something seemingly raw and overpowering." This offers the chance for a conversation about a much more engaging and passionate future than many that posit a rather impersonal and technology-dominated future. It is one that deserves attention and discussion in business school classrooms, in corporate boardrooms, and in other centers of learning.

Our final piece, *The Child and the Starfish*, is one of our favorites because it speaks of actions of optimism and of hope and of the power of individuals to make a difference, however small. When such individual acts of positive deviance (as our colleague Bob Quinn describes them) are aggregated, they can become a force for change that is constructive and humane. Whatever lies ahead, we need to honor this possibility in ourselves and in those we teach, manage, and support.

V-1: Fallen Idols
The Overthrow of Celebrity CEOs

THE WORLD IS FALLING OUT OF LOVE WITH CELEBRITY CHIEF EXECUTIVES

BUSINESS leaders are being knocked off their pedestals faster than Communist heroes after the fall of the Berlin Wall. Bernie Ebbers, a deal maker from Mississippi whose creation, WorldCom, was the epitome of telecoms excitement, was forced out this week. Diana "DeDe" Brooks, a forceful former chief executive of Sotheby's, was sentenced to house arrest and narrowly missed jail—the fate handed out to her former chairman, Alfred Taubman. Even Jack Welch, the former boss of General Electric who was perhaps the best-known celebrity chief executive of all, has seen his reputation dive.

The vehemence of today's reaction against business leaders is partly a reflection of how far their companies' shares have fallen, and also of the extent of their personal greed. But it is also a reaction against the worship heaped on them in the 1990s. Revolutions devour their children, and the impact of new technology and the bull market on business was little short of a revolution. Now for the devouring.

ENRON THE CATALYST

The cult of the all-powerful chief executive was fostered by the fact that investors found themselves lost in the maths of e-business. Company accounts, once a trusty guide, were ill-equipped to measure the strange things going on in the new economy. Investors reverted to familiar faces and seductive speeches. In their search for winners, it was easier to follow the jockeys than the form.

Disillusionment often follows when first-time investors are seduced en masse to a stockmarket, as they were in the late 1990s. It happened in Britain in the 1980s, when privatisation set out to show that equities need not be just for toffs. Naive investors then chose to follow stars—such as Anita Roddick of Body Shop and Asil Nadir of Polly Peck—without looking too closely at the numbers. Then, as now, it often ended in tears. Polly Peck, for example, went spectacularly bust.

This time the catalyst was Enron. Few understood its accounts. But they trusted Kenneth Lay and Jeffrey Skilling when they said that their company was in a totally new Internet game, a game that was going to lead to undreamed-of riches. Likewise, they loved and trusted tough Mr. Welch when he produced uncannily smooth earnings growth at GE, the company Americans most admire.

Once started, this process is self-perpetuating. Stars become chief executives, not the other way round. "If you were making a movie and said 'Get me a CEO' to the casting director, he'd give you Michael Armstrong," wrote Jeffrey Garten, the dean of the Yale School of Management, in his book, "The Mind of the CEO." Mr. Armstrong had a "vision" to take an old telecoms company, in the shape of AT&T, to the heart of the new-economy revolution. The vision destroyed $140 billion of shareholder value and brought AT&T to its knees, a feat that few from central casting could ever hope to achieve.

Americans are not alone in turning against their former heroes. Europe is at it too. Jean-Marie Messier, the chauffeur's grandson who tamed a French utility into Vivendi Universal, a global media empire, was once adored for having planted the French flag near the summit of Hollywood. But last week he was heckled at the company's four-hour annual meeting and is now fighting for his business life. Lousy results, much publicised infighting and a 40% fall in the share price this year have turned investors against him.

Then there is Percy Barnevik, a soft-spoken Swede once described by Fortune as "Europe's answer to Jack Welch." Mr. Barnevik was perceived as having single-handedly turned ABB into Europe's greatest transnational corporation. But that was before ABB announced massive losses last year and disclosed retirement benefits of $136 m arranged by Mr. Barnevik for himself and his successor. The erstwhile hero is now being vilified for his greed.

Yet nowhere raises their corporate heroes as high as America; and nowhere are they knocked down so low. The hero worship has this time been vastly encouraged by the growth of new media. A new breed of television channel devoted to business and finance—CNBC, Bloomberg and CNN Money—needed faces to put on their screens. And there were new business magazines with covers to fill. "Mugs sell mags" is a tenet of cover designers, and the likes of Jack Welch, Jeff Bezos, Larry Ellison and even Bernie Ebbers were favourite fillers. One piece of research actually found a correlation between the number of times that chief executives appeared on magazine covers and the excessive amount they had paid for their acquisitions. Call it the cost of hubris.

It took Enron's demise to shatter completely investors' illusion that backing the jockeys was a good idea. The greed and deceit of its bosses have tarred everybody. Mr. Welch is now widely portrayed not as a star chief executive but as an ageing philanderer; business journalists in America yearn to be the first to reveal the accounting tricks that made GE's earnings levitate for so long.

● ● ● ● ● ● ● ● ● ● ● ● ● ● ● ● ● ● ● ●
A CALL TO ACCOUNT

Now that they no longer trust the man, investors (and others) need to put more faith in the figures. It is for those who set accounting standards the world over to ensure that the numbers improve. That will involve at least three things. Investors must learn to live with figures that are more volatile, but more truly reflect the shifting risks of the real world. Accounts should become less focused on a single "bottom line" number, such as "profits." When undue attention is focused on a single figure, undue effort is devoted to manipulating it. Finally, there needs to be a return to the practice whereby accounts (always to some extent subjective) are judged "fair" by an independent and trustworthy outsider.

Academics and consultants are trying to prove that modest, unassuming folk are the ideal chief executives for the 21st century. But big business today has too much in common with show business. When there are no stars, they tend to be created. By all means tear the statues down, but don't destroy them. The faces can be rechiselled next time round.

V-2: Will the Corporation Survive?

Peter Drucker

● ● ● ● ● ● ● ● ●

THE NEW WORKFORCE: KNOWLEDGE WORKERS ARE THE NEW CAPITALISTS

A century ago, the overwhelming majority of people in developed countries worked with their hands: on farms, in domestic service, in small craft shops and (at that time still a small minority) in factories. Fifty years later, the proportion of manual workers in the American labour force had dropped to around half, and factory workers had become the largest single section of the workforce, making up 35% of the total. Now, another 50 years later, fewer than a quarter of American workers make their living from manual jobs. Factory workers still account for the majority of the manual workers, but their share of the total workforce is down to around 15% — more or less back to what it had been 100 years earlier.

Of all the big developed countries, America now has the smallest proportion of factory workers in its labour force. Britain is not far behind. In Japan and Germany, their share is still around a quarter, but it is shrinking steadily. To some extent this is a matter of definition. Data-processing employees of a manufacturing firm, such as

"Will the Corporation Survive?" by Peter Drucker. *The Economist*, May 4, 2002.

the Ford Motor Company, are counted as employed in manufacturing, but when Ford outsources its data processing, the same people doing exactly the same work are instantly redefined as service workers. However, too much should not be made of this. Many studies in manufacturing businesses have shown that the decline in the number of people who actually work in the plant is roughly the same as the shrinkage reported in the national figures.

Before the first world war there was not even a word for people who made their living other than by manual work. The term "service worker" was coined around 1920, but it has turned out to be rather misleading. These days, fewer than half of all non-manual workers are actually service workers. The only fast-growing group in the workforce, in America and in every other developed country, are "knowledge workers"-people whose jobs require formal and advanced schooling. They now account for a full third of the American workforce, outnumbering factory workers by two to one. In another 10 years or so, they are likely to make up close to two-fifths of the workforce of all rich countries.

The terms "knowledge industries," "knowledge work" and "knowledge worker" are only 40 years old. They were coined around 1960, simultaneously but independently; the first by a Princeton economist, Fritz Machlup, the second and third by this writer. Now everyone uses them, but as yet hardly anyone understands their implications for human values and human behaviour, for managing people and making them productive, for economics and for politics. What is already clear, however, is that the emerging knowledge society and knowledge economy will be radically different from the society and economy of the late 20th century, in the following ways.

First, the knowledge workers, collectively, are the new capitalists. Knowledge has become the key resource, and the only scarce one. This means that knowledge workers collectively own the means of production. But as a group, they are also capitalists in the old sense: through their stakes in pension funds and mutual funds, they have become majority shareholders and owners of many large businesses in the knowledge society.

Effective knowledge is specialised. That means knowledge workers need access to an organisation—a collective that brings together an array of knowledge workers and applies their specialisms to a common end-product. The most gifted mathematics teacher in a secondary school is effective only as a member of the faculty. The most brilliant consultant on product development is effective only if there is an organised and competent business to convert her advice into action. The greatest software designer needs a hardware producer. But in turn the high school needs the mathematics teacher, the business needs the expert on product development, and the PC manufacturer needs the software programmer. Knowledge workers therefore see themselves as equal to those who retain their services, as "professionals" rather than as "employees." The knowledge society is a society of seniors and juniors rather than of bosses and subordinates.

HIS AND HERS

All this has important implications for the role of women in the labour force. Historically women's participation in the world of work has always equalled men's. The lady of leisure sitting in her parlour was the rarest of exceptions even in a wealthy 19th-century society. A farm, a craftsman's business or a small shop had to be run by a couple to be viable. As late as the beginning of the 20th century, a doctor could not start a practice until he had got married; he needed a wife to make appointments, open the door, take patients' histories and send out the bills.

But although women have always worked, since time immemorial the jobs they have done have been different from men's. There was men's work and there was women's work. Countless women in the Bible go to the well to fetch water, but not one man. There never was a male spinster. Knowledge work, on the other hand, is "unisex", not because of feminist pressure but because it can be done equally well by both sexes. That said, the first modern knowledge jobs were designed for only one or the other sex. Teaching as a profession was invented in 1794, the year the Ecole Normale was founded in Paris, and was seen strictly as a man's job. Sixty years later, during the Crimean war of 1853–56, Florence Nightingale founded the second new knowledge profession, nursing. This was considered as exclusively women's work. But by 1850 teaching everywhere had become unisex, and in 2000 two-fifths of America's students at nursing school were men.

There were no women doctors in Europe until the 1890s. But one of the earliest European women to get a medical doctorate, the great Italian educator Maria Montessori, reportedly said: "I am not a woman doctor; I am a doctor who happens to be a woman." The same logic applies to all knowledge work. Knowledge workers, whatever their sex, are professionals, applying the same knowledge, doing the same work, governed by the same standards and judged by the same results.

High-knowledge workers such as doctors, lawyers, scientists, clerics and teachers have been around for a long time, although their number has increased exponentially in the past 100 years. The largest group of knowledge workers, however, barely existed until the start of the 20ᵗʰ century, and took off only after the second world war. They are knowledge technologists—people who do much of their work with their hands (and to that extent are the successors to skilled workers), but whose pay is determined by the knowledge between their ears, acquired in formal education rather than through apprenticeship. They include X-ray technicians, physiotherapists, ultrasound specialists, psychiatric case workers, dental technicians and scores of others. In the past 30 years, medical technologists have been the fastest-growing segment of the labour force in America, and probably in Britain as well.

In the next 20 or 30 years the number of knowledge technologists in computers, manufacturing and education is likely to grow even faster. Office technologists such as paralegals are also proliferating. And it is no accident that yesterday's "secretary" is rapidly turning into an "assistant," having become the manager of the boss's office and of his work. Within two or three decades, knowledge technologists will become the dominant group in the workforce in all developed countries, occupying the same position that unionised factory workers held at the peak of their power in the 1950s and 60s.

The most important thing about these knowledge workers is that they do not identify themselves as "workers" but as "professionals." Many of them spend a good deal of their time doing largely unskilled work, e.g., straightening out patients' beds, answering the telephone or filing. However, what identifies them in their own and in the public's mind is that part of their job involves putting their formal knowledge to work. That makes them full-fledged knowledge workers.

Such workers have two main needs: formal education that enables them to enter knowledge work in the first place, and continuing education throughout their working lives to keep their knowledge up to date. For the old high-knowledge professionals such as doctors, clerics and lawyers, formal education has been available for many centuries. But for knowledge technologists, only a few countries so far provide systematic and organised preparation. Over the next few decades, educational institutions to prepare knowledge technologists will grow rapidly in all developed and emerging countries, just as new institutions to meet new requirements have always appeared in the past. What is different this time is the need for the continuing education of already well-trained and highly knowledgeable adults. Schooling traditionally stopped when work began. In the knowledge society it never stops.

Knowledge is unlike traditional skills, which change very slowly. A museum near Barcelona in Spain contains a vast number of the hand tools used by the skilled craftsmen of the late Roman empire which any craftsman today would instantly recognise, because they are very similar to the tools still in use. For the purposes of skill training, therefore, it was reasonable to assume that whatever had been learned by age 17 or 18 would last for a lifetime.

Conversely, knowledge rapidly becomes obsolete, and knowledge workers regularly have to go back to school. Continuing education of already highly educated adults will therefore become a big growth area in the next society. But most of it will be delivered in non-traditional ways, ranging from weekend seminars to online training programmes, and in any number of places, from a traditional university to the student's home. The information revolution, which is expected to have an enormous impact on education and on traditional schools and universities, will probably have an even greater effect on the continuing education of knowledge workers.

Knowledge workers of all kinds tend to identify themselves with their knowledge.

They introduce themselves by saying "I am an anthropologist" or "I am a physiotherapist." They may be proud of the organisation they work for, be it a company, a university or a government agency, but they "work at the organisation"; they do not "belong to it." Most of them probably feel that they have more in common with someone who practices the same specialism in another institution than with their colleagues at their own institution who work in a different knowledge area.

Although the emergence of knowledge as an important resource increasingly means specialisation, knowledge workers are highly mobile within their specialism. They think nothing of moving from one university, one company or one country to another, as long as they stay within the same field of knowledge. There is a lot of talk about trying to restore knowledge workers' loyalty to their employing organisation, but such efforts will get nowhere. Knowledge workers may have an attachment to an organisation and feel comfortable with it, but their primary allegiance is likely to be their specialised branch of knowledge.

Knowledge is non-hierarchial. Either it is relevant in a given situation, or it is not. An open-heart surgeon may be much better paid than, say a speech therapist, and enjoy a much higher social status, yet if a particular situation requires the rehabilitation of a stroke victim, then in that instance the speech therapist's knowledge is greatly superior to that of the surgeon. This is why knowledge workers of all kinds see themselves not as subordinates but as professionals, and expect to be treated as such.

Money is as important to knowledge workers as to anybody else, but they do not accept it as the ultimate yardstick, nor do they consider money as a substitute for professional performance and achievement. In sharp contrast to yesterday's workers, to whom a job was first of all a living, most knowledge workers see their job as a life.

EVER UPWARDS

The knowledge society is the first human society where upward mobility is potentially unlimited. Knowledge differs from all other means of production in that it cannot be inherited or bequeathed. It has to be acquired anew by every individual, and everyone starts out with the same total ignorance.

Knowledge has to be put in a form in which it can be taught, which means it has to become public. It is always universally accessible, or quickly becomes so. All this makes the knowledge society a highly mobile one. Anyone can acquire any knowledge at a school, through a codified learning process, rather than by serving as an apprentice to a master.

Until 1850 or perhaps even 1900, there was little mobility in any society. The Indian caste system, in which birth determines not only an individual's status in society but his occupation as well, was only an extreme case. In most other societies too, if the father was a peasant, the son was a peasant, and the daughters married peasants. By and large, the only mobility was downward, caused by war or disease, personal misfortune or bad habits such as drinking or gambling.

Even in America, the land of unlimited opportunities, there was far less upward mobility than is commonly believed. The great majority of professionals and managers in America in the first half of the 20th century were still the children of professionals and managers rather than the children of farmers, small shopkeepers or factory workers. What distinguished America was not the amount of upward mobility but, in sharp contrast to most European countries, the way it was welcomed, encouraged and cherished.

The knowledge society takes this approval of upward mobility much further: it considers every impediment to such mobility a form of discrimination. This implies that everybody is now expected to be a "success"—an idea that would have seemed ludicrous to earlier generations. Naturally, only a tiny number of people can be outstanding successes; but a very large number are expected to be adequately successful.

In 1958 John Kenneth Galbraith first wrote about "The Affluent Society." This was not a society with many more rich people, or in which the rich were richer, but one in which the majority could feel financially secure. In the knowledge society, a large number of people, perhaps even a majority, have something even more important than financial security: social standing, or "social affluence."

THE PRICE OF SUCCESS

The upward mobility of the knowledge society, however, comes at a high price: the psychological pressures and emotional traumas of the rat race. There can be winners only if there are losers. This was not true of earlier societies. The son of the landless labourer who became a landless labourer himself was not a failure. In the knowledge society, however, he is not only a personal failure but a failure of society as well.

Japanese youngsters suffer sleep deprivation because they spend their evenings at a crammer to help them pass their exams. Otherwise they will not get into the prestige university of their choice, and thus into a good job. These pressures create hostility to learning. They also threaten to undermine Japan's prized economic equality and turn the country into a plutocracy, because only well-off parents can afford the prohibitive cost of preparing their youngsters for university. Other countries, such as America, Britain and France, are also allowing their schools to become viciously competitive. That this has happened over such a

short time—no more than 30 or 40 years—indicates how much the fear of failure has already permeated the knowledge society.

Given this competitive struggle, a growing number of highly successful knowledge workers of both sexes—business managers, university teachers, museum directors, doctors—"plateau" in their 40s. They know they have achieved all they will achieve. If their work is all they have, they are in trouble. Knowledge workers therefore need to develop, preferably while they are still young, a non-competitive life and community of their own, and some serious outside interest—be it working as a volunteer in the community, playing in a local orchestra or taking an active part in a small town's local government. This outside interest will give them the opportunity for personal contribution and achievement.

WILL THE CORPORATION SURVIVE?: YES, BUT NOT AS WE KNOW IT

For most of the time since the corporation was invented around 1870, the following five basic points have been assumed to apply:

•   The corporation is the "master," the employee is the "servant," Because the corporation owns the means of production without which the employee could not make a living, the employee needs the corporation more than vice versa.

•   The great majority of employees work full time for the corporation. The pay they get for the job is their only income and provides their livelihood.

•   The most efficient way to produce anything is to bring together under one management as many as possible of the activities needed to turn out the product.

The theory underlying this was not developed until after the second world war, by Ronald Coase, an Anglo-American economist, who argued that bringing together activities into one company lowers "transactional costs," and especially the cost of communications (for which theory he received the 1991 Nobel prize in economics). But the concept itself was discovered and put into practice 70 or 80 years earlier by John D. Rockefeller. He saw that to put exploration, production, transport, refining and selling into one corporate structure resulted in the most efficient and lowest-cost petroleum operation. On this insight he built the Standard Oil Trust, probably the most profitable large enterprise in business history. The concept was carried to an extreme by Henry Ford in the early 1920s. The Ford Motor Company not only produced all parts of the automobile and assembled it, but it also made its own steel, its own glass and its own tyres. It owned the plantations in the Amazon that grew the rubber trees, owned and ran the railroad that carried supplies to the plant and carried the finished cars from it, and planned eventually to sell and service Ford cars too (though it never did).

• Suppliers and especially manufactures have market power because they have information about a product or a service that the customer does not and cannot have, and does not need if he can trust the brand. This explains the profitability of brands.

• To any one particular technology pertains one and only one industry, and conversely, to any one particular industry pertains one and only one technology. This means that all technology needed to make steel is peculiar to the steel industry; and conversely, that whatever technology is being used to make steel comes out of the steel industry itself. The same applies to the paper industry, to agriculture or to banking and commerce.

On this assumption were founded the industrial research labs, beginning with Siemens's, started in Germany in 1869, and ending with IBM's, the last of the great traditional labs, founded in America in 1952. Each of them concentrated on the technology needed for a single industry, and each assumed that its discoveries would be applied only in that industry.

EVERYTHING IN ITS PLACE

Similarly, everybody took it for granted that every product or service had a specific application, and that for every application there was a specific product or material. So beer and milk were sold only in glass bottles; car bodies were made only from steel; working capital for a business was supplied by a commercial bank through a commercial loan; and so on. Competition therefore took place mainly within an industry. By and large, it was obvious what the business of a given company was and what its markets were.

Every one of these assumptions remained valid for a whole century, but from 1970 onwards every one of them has been turned upside down. The list now reads as follows:

• The means of production is knowledge, which is owned by knowledge workers and is highly portable. This applies equally to high-knowledge workers such as research scientists and to knowledge technologists such as physiotherapists, computer technicians and paralegals. Knowledge workers provide "capital" just as much as does the provider of money. The two are dependent on each other. This makes the knowledge worker an equal—an associate or a partner.

• Many employees, perhaps a majority, will still have full-time jobs with a salary that provides their only or main income. But a growing number of people who work for an organisation will not be full-time employees but part-timers, temporaries, consultants or contractors. Even of those who do have a full-time job, a large and growing number may not be employees of the organisation for which they work, but employees of, e.g., an outsourcing contractor.

- There always were limits to the importance of transactional costs. Henry Ford's all-inclusive Ford Motor Company proved unmanageable and became a disaster. But now the traditional axiom that an enterprise should aim for maximum integration has become almost entirely invalidated. One reason is that the knowledge needed for any activity has become highly specialised. It is therefore increasingly expensive, and also increasingly difficult, to maintain enough critical mass for every major task within an enterprise. And because knowledge rapidly deteriorates unless it is used constantly, maintaining within an organisation an activity that is used only intermittently guarantees incompetence.

The second reason why maximum integration is no longer needed is that communications costs have come down so fast as to become insignificant. This decline began well before the information revolution. Perhaps its biggest cause has been the growth and spread of business literacy. When Rockefeller built his Standard Oil Trust, he had great difficulty finding people who knew even the most elementary book-keeping or had heard of the most common business terms. At the time there were no business textbooks or business courses, so the transactional costs of making oneself understood were extremely high. Sixty years later, by 1950 or 1960, the large oil companies that succeeded the Standard Oil Trust could confidently assume that their more senior employees were business literate.

By now the new information technology—Internet and e-mail—have practically eliminated the physical costs of communications. This has meant that the most productive and most profitable way to organise is to disintegrate. This is being extended to more and more activities. Outsourcing the management of an institution's information

technology, data processing and computer system has become routine. In the early 1990s most American computer firms, e.g., Apple, even outsourced the production of their hardware to manufacturers in Japan or Singapore. In the late 1990s practically every Japanese consumer-electronics company repaid the compliment by outsourcing the manufacturing of its products for the American market to American contract manufactures.

In the past few years the entire human-resources management of more than 2 m American workers—hiring, firing, training, benefits and so on—has been outsourced to professional employee organisations. This sector, which ten years ago barely existed, is now growing at a rate of 30% a year. It originally concentrated on small and medium-sized companies, but the biggest of the firms, Exult, founded only in 1998, now manages employment issues for a number of fortune 500 companies, including BP, a British-American oil giant, and Unisys, a computer maker. According to a study by McKinsey, a consultancy, outsourcing human-relations management in this way can save up to 30% of the cost, and increase employee satisfaction as well.

- The customer now has the information. As yet, the Internet lacks the equivalent of a telephone book that would make it easy for users to find what they are looking for. It still requires pecking and hunting. But the information is somewhere on a website, and search firms to find it for a fee are rapidly developing. Whoever has the information has the power. Power is thus shifting to the customer, be it another business or the ultimate consumer, Specifically, that means the supplier, e.g., the manufacturer, will cease to be a seller and instead become a buyer for the customer. This is already happening.

General Motors (GM), still the world's largest manufacturer and for many years its most successful selling organisation, last year announced the creation of a major business that will buy for the ultimate car consumer. Although wholly owned by GM, the business will be autonomous, and will buy not only General Motors Cars, but whatever car and model most closely fits the individual customer's preferences, values and wallet.

- Lastly, there are few unique technologies any more. Increasingly, the knowledge needed in a given industry comes out of some totally different technology with which, very often, the people in the industry are unfamiliar. No one in the telephone industry knew anything about fiberglass cables. They were developed by a glass company, Corning, Conversely, more than half the important inventions developed since the second world war by the most productive of the great research labs, the Bell Laboratory, have been applied mainly outside the telephone industry.

The Bell Lab's most significant invention of the past 50 years was the transistor, which created the modern electronics industry. But the telephone company saw so little use for this revolutionary new device that it practically gave it away to anybody who asked for it—which is what put Sony, and with it the Japanese, into the consumer-electronics business.

WHO NEEDS A RESEARCH LAB?

Research directors, as well as high-tech industrialists, now tend to believe that the company-owned research lab, that proud 19th-century invention, has become obsolete. This explains why, increasingly, development and growth of a business is taking place not inside the corporation itself but through partnerships, joint ventures, alliances, minority participation and know-how agreements with institutions in different industries and with a different technology. Something that only 50 years ago would have been unthinkable is becoming common: alliances between institutions of a totally different character, say a profit-making company and university department, or a city or state government and a business that contracts for a specific service such as cleaning the streets or running prisons.

Practically no product or service any longer has either a single specific end-use or application, or its own market. Commercial paper competes with the banks' commercial loans. Cardboard, plastic and aluminium compete with glass for the bottle market. Glass is replacing copper in cables. Steel is competing with wood and plastic in providing the studs around which the American one-family home is constructed. The deferred annuity is pushing aside traditional life insurance—but, in turn, insurance companies rather than financial-service institutions are becoming the managers of commercial risks.

A "glass company" may therefore have to redefine itself by what it is good at doing rather than by the material in which it has specialised in the past. One of the world's largest glass makers, Corning, sold its profitable business making traditional glass products to become the number one producer and supplier of high-tech materials. Merck, America's largest pharmaceutical company, diversified from making drugs into wholesaling every kind of pharmacy product, most of them not even made by Merck, and a good many by competitors.

The same sort of thing is happening in the non-business sectors of the economy. One example is the free-standing "birthing centre" run by a group of obstetricians that competes with the American hospital's maternity ward. And Britain, long before the Internet, created the "Open University," which allowed people to get a university education and obtain a degree without ever setting foot in a classroom or attending a lecture.

THE NEXT COMPANY

One thing is almost certain: in future there will be not one kind of corporation but several different ones. The modern company was invented simultaneously but independently in three countries: America, Germany and Japan. It was a complete novelty and bore no resemblance to the economic organisation that had been the "economic enterprise" for millennia: the small, privately owned and personally run firm. As late as 1832, England's McLane Report—the first statistical survey of business—found that nearly all firms were privately owned and had fewer than ten employees. The only exceptions were quasi-governmental organisations such as the Bank of England or the East India Company. Forty years later a new kind of organisation with thousands of employees had appeared on the scene, e.g., the American railroads, built with federal and state support, and Germany's Deutsche Bank.

Wherever the corporation went, it acquired some national characteristics and adapted to different legal rules in each country. Moreover, very large corporations everywhere are being run quite differently from the small owner-managed kind. And there are substantial internal differences in culture, values and rhetoric between corporations in different industries, Banks everywhere are very much alike, and so are retailers or manufactures. But banks everywhere are different from retailers or manufacturers. Otherwise, however, the differences between corporations everywhere are more of style than of substance. The same is true of all other organisations in modern society: government agencies, armed forces, hospitals, universities and so on.

The tide turned around 1970, first with the emergence of new institutional investors such as pension funds and mutual trusts as the new owners, then—more decisively—with the emergence of knowledge workers as the economy's big new resource and the society's representative class. The result has been a fundamental change in the corporation.

A bank in the next society will still not look like a hospital, nor be run like one. But different banks may be quite different from one another, depending on how each of them responds to the changes in its work force, technology and markets. A number of different models is likely to emerge, especially of organisation and structure, but perhaps also of recognitions and rewards.

The same legal entity—e.g., a business, a government agency or a large not-for-profit organisation—may well contain several different human organisations that interlock, but are managed separately and differently. One of these is likely to be traditionally organisation of full-time employees. Yet there may also be a closely linked but separately managed human organisation made up mainly of older people who are not employees but associates or affiliates. And there are likely to be "perimeter" groups such as the people who work for the organisation, even fulltime, but as employees of an outsourcing contractor or of a contract manufacturer. These people have no contractual relationship with the business they work for, which in turn has no control over them. They may not have to be "managed," but they have to be made productive. They will therefore have to be deployed where their specialised knowledge can make the greatest contribution. Despite all the present talk of "knowledge management," no one yet really knows how to do it.

Just as important, the people in every one of these organisational categories will have to be satisfied. Attracting them and holding them will become the central task of people management. We already know what does not work; bribery. In the past ten or 25 years many business in America have used bonuses or stock options to attract and keep knowledge workers. It always fails.

According to an old saying, you cannot hire a hand; the whole man always comes with it. But you cannot hire a man either; the spouse almost always comes with it. And the spouse has already spent the money when falling profits eliminate the bonus or falling stock prices make the option worthless. Then both the employee and the spouse feel bitter and betrayed.

Of course knowledge workers need to be satisfied with their pay, because dissatisfaction with income and benefits is a powerful disincentive. The incentives, however, are different. The management of knowledge workers should be based on the assumption that the corporation needs them more than they need the corporation. They know they can leave. They have both mobility and self-confidence. This means they have to be treated and managed as volunteers, in the same way as volunteers who work for not-for-profit organisations. The first thing such people want to know is what the company is trying to do and where it is going. Next, they are interested in personal achievement and personal responsibility—Which means they have to be put in the right job. Knowledge workers expect continuous learning and continuous training. Above all, they want respect, not so much for themselves but for their area of knowledge. In that regard, they have moved several steps beyond traditional workers, who used to expect to be told what to do, although later they were increasingly expected to "participate." Knowledge workers, by contrast, expect to make the decisions in their own area.

FROM CORPORATION
TO CONFEDERATION

Eighty years ago, GM first developed both the organisational concepts and the organisational structure on which today's large corporations everywhere are based. It also invented the idea of a distinct top management. Now it is experimenting with a range of new organisational models. It has been changing itself from a unitary corporation held together by control through ownership into a group held together by management control, with GM often holding only a minority stake. GM now controls but does not own Fiat, itself one of the oldest and largest car makers. It also controls Saab in Sweden and two smaller Japanese car makers, Suzuki and Isuzu.

At the same time GM has divested itself of much of its manufacturing by spinning off into a separate company, called Delphi, the making of parts and accessories that together account for 60–70% of the cost of producing a car. Instead of owning—or at least controlling—the suppliers of parts and accessories, GM will in future buy them at auction and on the Internet. It has joined up with its American competitors Ford and DaimlerChrysler, to create an independent purchasing co-operative that will buy for its members from whatever source offers the best deal. All the other car makers have been invited to join.

GM will still design its cars, it will still make engines, and it will still assemble. It will also still sell its cars through its dealer network. But in addition to selling its own cars, GM intends to become a car merchant and a buyer for the ultimate consumer, finding the right car for the buyer no matter who makes it.

THE TOYOTA WAY

GM is still the world's largest car manufacturer, but for the past 20 years Toyota has been the most successful one. Like GM Toyota is building a worldwide group, but unlike GM, Toyota has organised its group round its core competence in manufacturing. The company is moving away from having multiple suppliers of parts and accessories, ultimately aiming for no more than two suppliers for any one part. These suppliers will be separate and independent companies, owned locally, but Toyota will in effect run their manufacturing operation for them. They will get the Toyota business only if they agree to being inspected and "advised" by a special Toyota manufacturing consulting organisation. And Toyota will also do most of the design work for the suppliers.

This is not a new idea. Sears Roebuck did the same for its suppliers in the 1920s and 1930s. Britain's Marks & Spencer, although in deep trouble now, was the world's most successful retailer for 50 years, maintaining its pre-eminence largely by keeping an iron grip on its suppliers. It is rumoured in Japan that Toyota intends ultimately to market its manufacturing consultancy, to non-car companies, turning its manufacturing core competence into a separate big business.

Yet another approach is being explored by a large manufacturer of branded and packaged consumer goods. Some 60% of the company's products are sold in the developed countries through some 150 retail chains. The company plans to create a worldwide website that will take orders direct from customers in all countries, either to be picked up in the retail store nearest to them or to be delivered by that store to their home. But — and this is the true innovation — the website will also take orders for non-competing packaged and branded consumer products made by other, and especially smaller, firms. Such firms have great difficulty in getting their wares on to increasingly crowded supermarket shelves. The multinational's website could offer them direct access to customers and delivery through an established large retailer. The pay-off for the multinational and the retailer would be that both get a decent commission without having to invest any money of their own, without risk and without sacrificing shelf space to slow-moving items.

There are already a good many variations on this theme: the American contract manufacturers, already mentioned, who now make the products for half a dozen competing Japanese consumer-electronics firms; a few independent specialists who design software for competing information-hardware makers; the independent specialists who design credit cards for competing American banks and also often market and

clear the cards for the bank. All the bank does is the financing.

These approaches, however different, still all take the traditional corporation as their point of departure. But there are also some new ideas that do away with the corporate model altogether. One example is a "syndicate" being tested by several non-competing manufacturers in the European Union. Each of the constituent companies is medium-sized, family-owned and owner managed. Each is a leader in a narrow, highly engineered product line. Each is heavily export-dependent. The individual companies intend to remain independent, and to continue to design their products separately. They will also continue to make them in their own plants for their main markets, and to sell them in these markets. But for other markets, and especially for emerging or less developed countries, the syndicate will arrange for the making of the products, either in syndicate-owned plants producing for several of the members or by local contract manufacturers. The syndicate will handle the delivery of all members' products and service them in all markets. Each member will own a share of the syndicate, and the syndicate, in turn, will own a small share of each members' capital. If this sounds familiar, it is because the model is the 19th century farmers' co-operative.

As the corporation moves towards a confederation or a syndicate, it will increasingly need a top management that is separate, powerful and accountable. This top management's responsibilities will cover the entire organisation's direction, planning, strategy, values and principles; its structure and its relationship between its various members: its alliances, partnerships and joint ventures; and its research, design and innovation. It will have to take charge of the management of the two resources common to all units of the organisation: key people and money. It will represent the corporation to the outside world and maintain relationships with governments, the public, the media and organised labour.

LIFE AT THE TOP

An equally important task for top management in the next society's corporation will be to balance the three dimensions of the corporation: as an economic organisation, as a human organisation and as an increasingly important social organisation. Each of the three models of the corporation developed in the past half-century stressed one of these dimensions and subordinated the other two. The German model of the "social market economy" put the emphasis on the social dimension, the Japanese one on the human dimension and the American one ("shareholder sovereignty") on the economic dimension.

None of the three is adequate on its own. The German model achieved both economic success and social stability, but at the price of high unemployment and dangerous labour-market rigidity. The Japanese model was strikingly successful for 20 years, but faltered at the first serious challenge; indeed it has become a major obstacle to recovery from Japan's present recession. Shareholder sovereignty is also bound to flounder. It is a fair-weather model that works well only in times of prosperity. Obviously the enterprise can fulfill its human and social functions only if it prospers as a business. But now that knowledge workers are becoming the key employees, a company also needs to be a desirable employer to be successful.

Crucially, the claim to the absolute primacy of business gains that made shareholder sovereignty possible has also highlighted the importance of the corporation's social function. The new shareholders whose emergence since 1960 or 1970 produced shareholder sovereignty are not "capitalists." They are employees who own a stake in the business through their retirement and pension funds. By 2000, pension funds and mutual funds had come to own the majority of the share capital of America's large companies. This has given shareholders the power to demand short-term rewards. But the need for a secure retirement income will increasingly focus people's minds on the future value of the investment. Corporations, therefore, will have to pay attention both to their short-term business results and to their long-term performance as providers of retirement benefits. The two are not irreconcilable, but they are different, and they will have to be balanced.

Over the past decade or two, managing a large corporation has changed out of all recognition. That explains the emergence of the "CEO superman," such as Jack Welch of GE, Andy Grove of Intel or Sanford Weill of Citigroup. But organisations cannot rely on finding supermen to run them; the supply is both unpredictable and far too limited. Organisations survive only if they can be run by competent people who take their job seriously. That it takes genius today to be the boss of a big organisation clearly indicates that top management is in crisis.

IMPOSSIBLE JOBS

The recent failure rate of chief executives in big American companies points in the same direction. A large proportion of CEOs of such companies appointed in the past ten years were fired as failures within a year or two. But each of these people had been picked for his proven competence, and each and been highly successful in his previous jobs. This suggests that the jobs they took on had become undoable. The American record suggests not human failure but systems failure. Top management in big organisation needs a new concept.

Some elements of such a concept are beginning to emerge. For instance, Jack Welch at GE has built a top-management team in which the company's chief financial officer and its chief human-resources officer are near-equals to the chief executive, and are both excluded from the succession to the top job. He has also given himself and his team a clear and publicly announced priority task on which to concentrate. During his 20 years in the top job, Mr. Welch has had three such priorities, each occupying him for five years or more. Each time he has delegated everything else to the top managements of the operating businesses within the GE confederation.

A different approach has been taken by Asea Brown Boveri (ABB), huge Swedish-Swiss engineering multinational. Goran Lindahl, who retired as chief executive earlier this year, went even further than GE in making the individual units within the company into separate worldwide businesses and building up a strong top management team of a few non-operating people. But he also defined for himself a new role as a one-man information system for the company, traveling incessantly to get to know all the senior managers personally, listening to them and telling them what went on within the organisation.

A largish financial-services company tried another idea: appointing not one CEO but six. The head of each of the five operating businesses is also CEO for the whole company in one top management area, such as corporate planning and strategy or human resources. The company's chairman represents the company to the outside world and is also directly concerned with obtaining, allocating and managing capital.

All six people meet twice a week as the top management committee. This seems to work well, but only because none of the five operating CBOs wants the chairman's job; each prefers to stay in operations. Even the man who designed the system, and then himself took the chairman's job, doubts that the system will survive once he is gone.

In their different ways, the top people at all of these companies were trying to do the same thing: to establish their organisation's unique personality. And that may well be the most important task for top management in the next society's big organisations. In the half-century after the second world war, the business corporation has brilliantly proved itself as an economic organisation i.e., a creator of wealth and jobs. In the next society; the biggest challenge for the large company—especially for the multinational—may be its social legitimacy: its values, its mission, its vision. Increasingly, in the next society's corporation, top management will, in fact, be the company. Everything else can be outsourced.

Will the corporation survive? Yes, after a fashion. Something akin to corporation will have to co-ordinate the next society's economic resources. Legally and perhaps financially, it may even look much the same as today's corporation. But instead of there being a single model adopted by everyone, there will be a range of models to choose from.

V-3: A Talk with Jeff Immelt
Jack Welch's Successor Charts a Course for GE in the Twenty-first Century

Stephen B. Shepard

After winning the highest-prized succession race in corporate history, filling Jack Welch's

Reprinted from January 28, 2002 issue of *Business Week* by special permission, copyright © 2002 by The McGraw Hill Companies, Inc.

seat as CEO and chairman of General Electric Co., Jeffrey R. Immelt now finds himself charged with delivering double-digit growth amid war and a nasty downturn. *Business Week* Editor-in-Chief Stephen B. Shepard spoke with Immelt on Jan. 15 as part of the magazine's Captains of Industry series at Mankallan's 92nd Street. Y. Here are excerpts from their conversations:

It's fascinating to me that your father worked 38 years for GE and then you ended up running the joint. When you told your father, what did he say?

IT WAS THE FIRST CALL I MADE AND ONE OF THOSE MOMENTS I'LL ALWAYS REMEMBER. HE SAID HOW PROUD HE WAS. HE SAID CONGRATULATIONS. AND HE SAID, "NOW YOU CAN DO SOMETHING ABOUT THE PENSION."

What would have happened if you hadn't gotten the job?

IN ABOUT SEPTEMBER OF 2000, JACK TOLD ALL THREE OF US THAT IF WE DIDN'T GET THE JOB, HE WANTED US TO LEAVE. I KNEW I COULD FIND A JOB SOMEWHERE. PROBABLY, AT THE END OF THE DAY, I WOULD HAVE GONE TO SM WHERE JIM MCNERNEY ENDED UP. THE THREE OF US GOT EMBROLLED IN SOMETHING THAT WAS CAST AS THE RACE OF THE CENTURY. BUT WE'VE REMAINED GOOD FRIENDS BECAUSE WE RESPECT ONE ANOTHER.

I'm told you work seven days a week and sleep five hours a night.

I THINK ABOUT THE COMPANY ALL THE TIME, AND I DON'T NEED MUCH SLEEP.

It's also true that you read a book a week?

JUST ABOUT. YEAH.

What kind do you read?

I DO A LOT OF A BIOGRAPHIES, A FAIR AMOUNT OF HISTORY, AND SOME NOVELS. I DON'T READ MANY BUSINESS BOOKS. I JUST READ THE [EDMUND MORRIE] BOOK ON THEODORE ROOSEVELT.

You and George Bush.

I WASN'T EATING PRETZELS AT THE TIME, THOUGH, SO IT'S LITTLE SAFER.

What CEOs in America do you admire or respect?

I'VE HAD A LONG-TERM RELATIONSHIP WITH STEVE BALLMER [AT MICROSOFT CORP.]. I THINK [VIVENDI UNIVERSAL'S] JEAN-MARIE MENAIER IS BUILDING A HECK OF A COMPANY IN THAT BUSINESS. RICK WAGONER IS DOING A GOOD JOB AT GM. THERE'S [SUN MICROSYSTEMS INC.'S] SCOTT MCNEALY, WHO IS ON OUR BOARD. I'VE ALWAYS ADMIRED SCOTT'S SENSE OF HUMOR, HIS VISION, HIS ABILITY TO STICK WITH A VISION. GLOBALLY, I HAVE A LOT OF RESPECT FOR JOHN BROWNE AT BP AND FOR [NOBUYUKI] IDEI-SAN AT SONY.

What do you want to accomplish in your first few years?

I WANT TO TAKE THE POWER OF DIGITIZATION AND, LIKE WE'VE DONE WITH SIX SIGMA, TRANSFORM THE WAY THE COMPANY IS RUN. ABOUT 40% OF THE COMPANY IS NOW ADMINISTRATION, FINANCE, AND BACKROOM FUNCTIONS. OVER THE NEXT THREE YEARS, I WANT TO SHRINK THAT BY 75%. ON TOP OF THAT, THE MOST IMPORTANT THING IS TO GROW. WE'RE A $130 BILLION GROWTH BUSINESS BECAUSE WE DON'T RUN IT AS A $130 BILLION BLOB. WE RUN IT AS A $10 BILLION MEDICAL BUSINESS, A $1 BILLION ULTRASOUND BUSINESS. WE KNOW HOW TO GET DOUBLE-DIGIT GROWTH IN THIS ENVIRONMENT.

How did September 11 make things more difficult for the company and for you personally?

LET'S CATEGORIZE SEPTEMBER 11 AS AN AMAZING TRAGEDY, JUST AN UNBELIEVABLE, UNSPEAKABLE TRAGEDY. IT HAD AN IMPACT ON THE AIRLINE INDUSTRY AND THE TOURISM INDUSTRY AND THE INSURANCE INDUSTRY. BUT THIS ECONOMY WAS IN RECESSION ON SEPT. 10. THIS ECONOMY STARTED GETTING WORSE IN AUGUST OF 2000. IT WAS ACCELERATING IN TERMS OF GETTING IN RECES-

SIONARY MODE. AND SEPTEMBER 11 JUST MADE IT TOUGHER.

I LOOK AT THIS ENVIRONMENT AS A TREMENDOUS CHANCE TO PLAY OFFENSE AT GE. THE STRENGTH OF GE IS OUR DIVERSITY. SO WHILE 30% OF OUR COMPANY GETS HIT IN AN ECONOMY LIKE THIS, 70% IS STILL FLOURISHING. WE'LL GENERATE $17 BILLION IN CASH IN 2001, SO WE'LL HAVE LOTS OF CAPABILITY TO DO ACQUISITIONS. YOU KNOW, I HATE WHERE MY STOCK PRICE IS TODAY, BUT I LOVE WHERE EVERYBODY ELSE'S IS. SO IT'S A GREAT TIME TO DO ACQUISITIONS AND PLAY OFFENSE.

WE'RE LOOKING AT THIS TIME AS THE DEFINITIVE TIME FOR GE. QUITE HONESTLY, IT WAS TOUGHER TO RUN THE COMPANY IN 1999. WE WERE GROWING. THE MARKETS WERE GREAT; THE EQUITY MARKETS WERE GREAT. BUT EVERYBODY HATED A 120-YEAR-OLD COMPANY. YOU KNOW, ANYTHING THAT WASN'T NEW WAS TERRIBLE. NOW WE LOOK SEXY AGAIN.

Do you object when people use the word conglomerate to describe GE?

HATE IT. I WENT TO BUSINESS SCHOOL LEARNING HOW COMPANIES LIKE GE COULDN'T EXIST. WE RUN A MULTIBUSINESS COMPANY WITH COMMON CULTURES, WITH COMMON MANAGEMENT. . . WHERE THE WHOLE IS ALWAYS GREATER THAN THE SUM OF ITS PARTS. CULTURE COUNTS.

Is there any company anywhere in the world that is remotely close to the way you do it?

MY ASSUMPTION IS YES. I VIEW SIEMENS AS A VERY STRONG COMPETITOR; FROM GERMANY. I THINK DENNIS KOZLOWSKI AT TYCO IS ATTEMPTING TO DO THE SAME THING. SO WE NEVER TAKE FOR GRANTED THAT WE'VE GOT THE ONLY MODEL THAT WORKS AND THAT THERE AREN'T PEOPLE OUT THERE TRYING TO COMPETE WITH US. I JUST THINK THAT WE'VE GOT A COMPANY THAT CAN RUN IN THIS WAY.

GE Capital accounts for 40% to 45% of your earnings. Do you think that's too high?

MY PREFERENCE WOULD BE TO KEEP IT IN THAT RANGE. BUT I HEDGE THAT IT'S AN EXCEPTIONALLY GOOD TIME TO BE ACQUIRING FINANCIAL ASSETS TODAY. IF WE HAVE THE OPPORTUNITY TO MAKE GE CAPITAL BIGGER IN THE SHORT TERM, WE'LL PROBABLY TAKE THAT OPPORTUNITY.

What about the lower-margin businesses, like lighting and appliances? What happens to them?

IF WE WERE BUILDING A PORTFOLIO TODAY, WE WOULDN'T START WITH LIGHTING AND APPLIANCES, THAT IS FOR SURE. WE'RE LIMITED BY THE GROWTH, AND WE'RE LIMITED BY THE POSITIONS THEY HAVE IN TERMS OF BEING ABLE TO GLOBALIZE AND THINGS LIKE THAT. NEITHER BUSINESS IS ON FIRE. WE'RE NO. 1 IN BOTH. THEY BOTH RETURN THEIR COST IN CAPITAL. THEY'RE GOOD FOR THE BRAND.

AND THE WAY THAT WE USE A BUSINESS LIKE APPLIANCES IS, IT'S A GREAT PLACE TO TRAIN PEOPLE. IT'S A GREAT WAY FOR MANAGERS TO GO THERE AND LEARN WHAT A RECESSION IS LIKE. BECAUSE THOSE BUSINESSES ARE IN RECESSION ALMOST ALL THE TIME. EVEN THE GOOD YEARS ARE TOUGH. SO YOU LEARN UNBELIEVABLE MANAGEMENT SKILLS AT BUSINESSES LIKE THAT.

Let's talk about globalization, one of your big initiatives. I'm going to name countries, and I want you to tell me what you think the opportunities are. Let's start with Japan.

VERY BLEAK. MOST OF THE GLOBAL COMPANIES ARE MOVING MANUFACTURING FACILITIES OUTSIDE OF JAPAN. MY FEAR IS THAT IT'S IN A PERMANENT STATE OF SIDEWAYS MOVEMENT. YOU'D ALMOST RATHER SEE AN IMPETUS OF A SHARP DECLINE THAT WOULD DRIVE STRUCTURAL CHANGE. UNFORTUNATELY, WHAT WE HAVE IS CONSTANT ZERO. I

THINK IT'S DEMORALIZING TO THE PEOPLE IN JAPAN.

China?

CHINA IS GOING TO BE THE SECOND-BIGGEST ECONOMY IN THE WORLD. THE POLITICAL LEADERSHIP OF THE COUNTRY REALLY DOES UNDERSTAND THE PEOPLE. I'M NOT HERE TO MAKE A POLITICAL STATEMENT. NONE OF US AGREES WITH EVERYTHING THEY DO, BUT I THINK THERE'S AN INEXTRICABLE MOVEMENT TO THE FUTURE. THERE'S JUST NO STOPPING THAT COUNTRY.

India?

INDIA IS A GREAT PLACE. THEY GRADUATE 30,000 ELECTRICAL ENGINEERS EVERY YEAR. FROM THE STANDPOINT OF HUMAN CAPITAL AND FROM THE STANDPOINT OF EDUCATION AND SMART PEOPLE, THEY ARE FABULOUS. THE INFRASTRUCTURE OF INDIA KEEPS IT FROM BEING A GREAT GLOBAL MARKET. THE POWER STILL GOES OUT WHEN YOU'RE SHAVING EVERY MORNING AT 6. BUT IT HAS PROBABLY GOT THE BEST INTELLECTUAL DEPTH IN THE WORLD.

Europe?

I REALLY DO BELIEVE THAT THE EUROPEAN UNION AND EUROPEAN UNITY IS GOING TO CHANGE THE WAY EUROPE DOES BUSINESS. HAVING ONE CURRENCY, HAVING ONE MARKET IS GOING TO BE A GOOD DEAL. OUR MARGIN RATES ARE HALF WHAT THEY ARE IN THE U.S., SO THERE ARE GREAT OPPORTUNITIES TO IMPROVE.

BEYOND THAT, I HATE THE WAY THE HONEYWELL ACQUISITION ENDED IN EUROPE. AND I HATE THE WAY IT CAST OUR COMPANY. SO EUROPE IS VERY BIG ON MY AGENDA LIST. WE GOT PAINTED WITH A BRUSH THAT WAS UNFAIR: OF BEING TOO BIG, OF NOT BEING FOCUSED ON CUSTOMERS IN THE MARKETPLACE. I'M REALLY DEDICATED TO PROVING THAT WRONG. WE'RE GOING TO

BE A GREAT EUROPEAN COUNTRY—I MEAN COMPANY.

So you do have some politician in you. Latin America?

NAFTA REALLY DID WORK FROM BOTH A MEXICAN AND U.S. STANDPOINT. BUT SOUTH AMERICA IS VERY TOUGH. IT'S NEVER BEEN A PLACE WHERE GE INVESTED A LOT BECAUSE OF CURRENCY INSTABILITY AND A LACK OF TRANSPARENCY. UNFORTUNATELY, ARGENTINA ONLY SERVES TO REINFORCE THAT.

Let's turn to Enron. It's a mess. What are the lessons of this?

EITHER PEOPLE IN LEADERSHIP MISLED FOLKS, OR THERE'S SOMETHING WRONG WITH THE SYSTEM, AND THE SYSTEM HAS TO BE CHANGED. THAT'S WHAT WE'RE GOING TO LEARN OVER THE NEXT FEW MONTHS.

TWO YEARS AGO, EVERY BUSINESS LEADER ON EARTH GOT THE BENEFIT OF THE DOUBT. BECAUSE OF THE RECESSION, BECAUSE OF ENRON, THAT TRUST HAS EVAPORATED. SO IT'S INCUMBENT ON ME NOT JUST TO DESCRIBE MY COMPANY. I NOW TELL PEOPLE, LOOK, I REVIEW EVERY BUSINESS IN GE SIX TIMES A YEAR. I HAVE 500 INTERNAL AUDITORS; WE DO THOUSANDS OF AUDITS EVERY YEAR. WE ALL HAVE ONE CURRENCY AT GE—THAT'S GE STOCK. WE'RE TOTALLY ALIGNED WITH SHAREHOLDERS. I DON'T WANT MY COMPANY TO BE PAINTED WITH THAT BRUSH.

But you worry a little bit that there might be backlash?

THE BACKLASH IS BEGINNING. WHEN THE SEVENTH-LARGEST COMPANY IN THE WORLD GOES BANKRUPT IN SIX MONTHS, SOMETHING HAPPENED. SOMETHING HAPPENED THAT'S WRONG, AND THAT'S BAD. BUT ONE OF THE THINGS THAT I'M GOING TO STAND UP FOR EACH AND EVERY DAY IS THE INTEGRITY OF THE COMPANY I WORK FOR.

When do you think the recession will end, or when will we have a turnaround?

The two factors I watch, Steve, are what's happening with the consumer and when will technology reinvestment occur. There is massive excess capacity in technology today. And I think when you add all those things up, we're doing all our business planning assuming that 2002 stays as tough as it is right now. A zero-growth economy. If we get a second-half rebound, all the better. By 2003, we see the economy getting better.

Just about two years ago, Jack Welch was here on this stage. We asked him why there were so few women in the top management ranks at GE. And his answer was, "Shame on us." What is it about GE that there aren't more women in the top ranks, and are you going to do anything about it?

You know, Steve, if you look at the last 12 months, 50% of our appointees of the top 500 people are women and African Americans. So we're moving the needle very quickly. About 20% of the leadership today is diverse. We've got a great pipeline of women in place to be able to fill those jobs. I think it's a leadership prerogative, and it's a leadership objective, to be a more diverse company.

I've told people that one of the things that I'm going to be accountable to the organization in is the percentage of women and African Americans that are in the top 175 in the company and the top 500 in the company. Again, it all has to do with remaining a modern company. And 21st century companies are going to have more diversity throughout their leadership.

So there was nothing about the company's culture that made it more difficult for women?

This is a performance culture. And I just refuse to believe that there's something about the culture that makes it unattractive for anybody to work. It's a meritocracy. People like meritocracy. And they like knowing that they get ahead based on the merits of their ideas. I don't think that's sex-based.

What keeps you up at night?

It's always an integrity issue of some kind. With 300,000 people, you always worry that somebody doesn't get it. We can survive bad markets. What you can't live through is anybody who takes from the company or does something wrong in the community.

At a recent *Business-Week* event, Jack Welch said that Walter Hewlett's opposition to the Compaq/Hewlett-Packard merger was "a sin." What are your thoughts on Walter's standoff with the Hewlett-Packard board?

I am firmly on [HP CEO Carleton S. Fiorina's] side with respect to her right to do it, the process she used to do it, and the fact that a board can't work that way. There's a time and a place for a board to make a decision and to make its feelings known. To break ranks and to come out and question publicly is wrong.

Do you send handwritten memos to your top staff, similar to Jack's memos to you?

No, my handwriting is terrible. Jack had the luxury of not only running the company but he had the best penmanship. I send e-mails.

V-4: At the Cliff Edge of Life
From Powerlessness to Participation

David Whyte

I awoke to a different rhythm, a recognizably changed sway and catch of the boat's movement. As I opened my eyes, I felt a sudden subliminal terror. I knew immediately that the boat was moving free, at the mercy of the waves, under no human control. I felt instinctively the spectral loom of the land very near to us, and I heard a deep, muffled, booming sound which set my blood to freeze. I looked across and saw our new replacement captain asleep. I leapt out of my bunk and ran in a frenzy up the ladder to the cockpit. My first view was of last night's anchorage, two good sea miles to the stern and a vast gulf of choppy water between us and it. I looked quickly over my shoulder and swore out loud; the lava cliff shadowed everything, the tip of the waves were sounding off the rock and throwing spray over the boat. Even as I looked, the boat was beginning to turn sideways on, the mast rising toward the curving roof of the cliff.

A moment later we were front on again, the bow lifting toward the rock. I looked madly for the lay of the trailing anchor line and saw it mercifully free of the propeller. A quick twist of the oil key, a stab of the button, and the engine coughed into life; then a mist of diesel fumes, a moment of unspeakable fear beneath the unholy roof of the cliff as the bow reared toward that implacable

solidity, and I flattened the lever back into reverse. The bow rail seemed to freeze forever on its rise, then it dropped, fell off, and retreated from the cliff; the stern shot suddenly backwards, the deathly cliff receded, the world returned swiftly to sanity again, and the captain bounded from below.

A mere eighteen months had passed since my encounter with the stranger high on a Welsh mountain and already I was on the far side of the world, farther than my imagination could have carried me that gray morning as I had looked out over the Irish Sea. The determination forged by my encounter with the stranger in the farmhouse seemed to have shifted the wind round in my favor, and I had graduated, weathered the gloomy job prospects, and with good fortune favoring the newly brave, landed myself a plumb job as a naturalist guide in the Galápagos islands.

I was right bang on the equator, in the Pacific Ocean, 700 miles from the South American coast, in the Mecca of biologists, living and working aboard the *Bronzewing,* a handsome forty-eight-foot sloop that had become my very movable home. Galápagos was everything a naturalist might dream of: exotic one-of-a-kind species above and below water, and the lingering glamour of Darwin's brief passage still shimmering in the air despite the 140 years since his going. Like the young Darwin who had arrived here electric with excitement, I felt I had my work now, my direction; but no work or career can be a steady, laid-out progression.

All in this garden was not completely rosy, and it was certainly no paradise familiar to the human eye.

THE SHOCK
OF THE REAL

Though I had a dream job, I was suffering a kind of culture shock. Not the shock of encountering an unfamiliar human culture but the profound, shattering impact of looking nature straight in the face. I had encountered in Galápagos a culture that did not seem to include the human at all. For most of human history, these islands have remained undiscovered, and we are but recent visitors to Galápagos. As a species, we are youngsters in this very old world, and I was young, too, just in my early twenties. I found myself prone to the loneliness of this new world of ocean rocks and strange animals. I had come to study nature in all its glory, yet a secret portion of me found Galápagos in its raw form intensely frightening. Everywhere I went, I saw animals living and dying according to some other mercy than my human mind could stand. It all seemed to paint a world in which there was no immunity or hiding place for anything from the great cycles of life and death. This incident beneath the lava cliff was everything I had been anticipating for months in my secret fears.

Though we profess to love nature, we like it packaged according to our human desires. We do not look too hard at the world for fear of what we will find there. On the threshold of this new world, I was no exception. I found Galápagos intensely disturbing. The natural world unmediated by society is no picturesque, environmental idea but a raw force in which human beings often seem to participate on sufferance. Young as I was in Galápagos, I began to touch an exposed nerve in human experience: the sense that there is something larger in the world than mere human priorities. Whatever work I was doing, something larger, more frightening, with a different order of priorities was moving in parallel. Something that encompassed a grander and more difficult universe than my career goals.

NATURE, FORTUNE,
AND FEAR

There is a long connection between the way we stand in fear of the natural world and the way we have used work as a bastion against the wilder, nonhuman forces of existence. Societally and individually, whatever we say on the surface, we are afraid of nature, and rightly so. Humans work hard and build imaginatively, generation after generation. Then, as Camille Paglia says, "Let nature shrug, and all is in ruin." Venezuelan shorelines disintegrate in torrential downpours. Industrious Kobe's concrete overpasses fall in a tremor as if pushed by a petulant child, and even now, vast shelves of Antarctic ice threaten to float off and melt in our warming seas. We hear the news and ignore it all, but underneath, some old human imagination is stirred. "Get a good job," a parent says, meaning "Get a safe job." As if, over the years they have learned the wicked, veering manner of the winds that blow through life in their unmerciful ways; but also, they are passing on, parent to child, a fear bred into our human bones of that dark outer wind's howling, pushing presence. The same wind that howled outside the farmhouse that night in Wales. The same winds that blew us onto the lava cliff from our anchorage. Work provides safety. To define work in other ways than safety is to risk our illusions of immunity in the one organized area of life where we seem to keep nature and the world at bay.

● ● ● ● ● ● ● ● ●
THE EDGE OF NECESSITY

In work, it has always taken courage to follow a unique and individual path exactly, because making our own path takes us off the path, in directions which seem profoundly unsafe. A pilgrimage into the night and the night wind. The territory through which we must travel to make a life for ourselves is always more difficult than we could first imagine; it takes us to the cliff edges of life. The amusing part is that you can spend years preparing for the possibility of falling *off* the cliff and then find yourself suddenly *under* the cliff, approaching it from another, equally terrifying direction.

Finding a work to which we can dedicate ourselves always calls for some kind of courage, some form of heartfelt participation. It needs courage because the intrinsic worth of work lies in the fact that it connects us to larger, fiercer worlds where we are forced to remember first priorities. The farm laborer knows the toil that literally puts bread on the table. The police officer knows firsthand the invisible line between order and disorder in society. I remember a recent dinner conversation with a water utility executive who had been in the midst of a massive Turkish earthquake. Awake night after night, doing work that was not part of his official job description, be and his team brought water, medicines, and supplies to bereft, panicking communities. Once the crisis was past, he wondered if he would ever feel that aliveness and urgency again the rest of his days, He was wistful for the fron-

tier encounter, the cliff edge. This cliff edge is a frontier where passion, belonging, and need call for our presence, our powers, and our absolute commitment.

To approach work in this manner is not merely to look for constant excitement but to join a conversation with the great cycles of existence, cycles that often terrify us even as they call on the best of us. I think of my sisters, hospital nurses, intimately familiar with the once great, now fallen and achingly vulnerable: the former CEO wandering the hospital corridors in a dreamlike dementia, calling, "John . . . John . . . John"; the track athlete slowly moving his legs after the car smash, his triumph now confined to the slightest increase in their arc of movement. It is astonishing how much of our everyday work has powerful life-or-death consequences: the firefighter on the fragile roof, the policeman on the street, the electrical engineer bringing power back to a darkened neighborhood. The teacher curses his way to school and then says exactly the right thing at the right time to the vulnerable, listening adolescent. All good work should have an edge of life and death to it, if not immediately apparent, then to be found by ardently exploring its greater context. Absent the edge, we drown in numbness.

In Galápagos, I felt the presence of that cliff edge, almost every day and night—particularly in the night, when we navigated the reef-strewn islands without beacons, lights, or electronic instruments. All we had was the faint illuminationes of a compass and dead reckoning, Meanwhile, my own inner compass was pointing in a direction I didn't want to go. After years of distant biological conceptualization, I was being given a personal introduction to the 800-pound gorilla called nature. Whatever it wanted, in the end, nature seemed to get. The enormous power and reach of natural work in Galápagos stirred me to search for whatever courage I could muster to face life in a way that was not based at its root on dread.

The closest I had come to this raw power in my own growing had been the fierce moorland winds of my native Yorkshire. As I looked into the wave forms cresting past the boat at night, I remembered the North Country fogs, the winter blizzards, the unending bogs. My mind roved back over the austere beauty of those seas of moss and peat. I couldn't help but think of an equally fierce young woman who lived on the shoreline of those moors.

> No coward soul is mine,
> No trembler in the world's storm-
> troubled sphere:
> I see Heaven's glories shine,
> And faith shines equal, arming me
> from fear.

That was Emily Brontë, author of *Wuthering Heights,* at her own cliff edge, in defiance of all the fearful dangers standing between her and her work. She had to find a way across a very storm-troubled sphere. She spoke not only of the tearing elemental nature of that North Country wind but also of the forces she fought against in her own lifetime as a writer and a women; a woman very visible to herself but barely visible to the masculine Victorian world into which she was born. What was the faith that armed her from fear? Fear of the wind and fear of societal displeasure? To my mind, it was some kind of intimate conversation that Emily was able to sustain, along with her sisters, Charlotte and Anne, with the more frightening, often hidden forces of life.

Emily Brontë lived at the cliff edge of life from a very early age. She and her sisters, along with their brother, Branwell, lost their mother as young children. Her father, though present in the house, lived mostly in his study and his church and left them to parent themselves. There were no real adult voices advising imaginative caution. For most of us, an inner parental voice continually keeps the world at bay. It says, "Life is precarious; you young cannot know how precarious, Don't add to the sum total of difficulty that awaits you: Stay off the moors: stay off the ocean, stay away from the edge, don't follow the intensity of your more passionate dreams, find safe work, and adventure not into your own nature lest it lead you directly into nature itself. Adventure only on the weekends of life and not in the working week."

These wary voices are deep inside us, whispering into our ears on the edge of decision or as a background chorus as we walk into the office every day, even as we grow into our own middle age. Despite the lineaments of our streamlined organizations, the flow charts and the carefully calculated retirement, when we neglect this more forceful conversation with the edges of existence, a great part of us feels entirely subject to the mercies of the windblown world that has now become a stranger to us.

THE EDGE OF THE UNKNOWN

Stories of near disaster on dangerous shores are not so far, then, from the dynamics that underlie a normal workday. Without the presence of an edge in our lives, much of our work is bent toward keeping chaos at bay, staving off financial disaster, or integrating the differing wave forms of dozens of unpredictable people in a given organization. In the midst of it all, like a child determined to be noticed above the surrounding din, we have to keep up the noisy drumroll of results. Wave against wave, work is an uncharted sea. Any difficult conversation, any sudden change of career, we feel, may lead to a possible shipwreck. Yet increasingly now, despite our wish for safety, there is less that resembles a steady career or a straight career path. This moment of reckoning under the lava cliff speaks to the many dangerous arrivals in a life of work and to the way we must continually forge our identities through our endeavors.

● ● ● ● ● ● ● ● ● ● ● ●
A NECESSARY SIMPLICITY

Whether it is a place like Galápagos or a place like our office, if we are serious about our work we tend to find ourselves apprenticed to something much larger than we expected, something that calls on more of our essence than we previously imagined, something seemingly raw and overpowering. The young, exhausted lawyer glimpses, late one evening, the enormous commitment needed for her future partnership; the apprentice violin maker can only marvel at the older man's simultaneous ease and absolute precision with the tiny wood plane. Seemingly superhuman forces always call on individual human beings to simplify themselves. A kind of simplification, achieved day by day, hour by hour, in our given work, right into the essence of what needs to be done. That simplified essence can terrify us, as I found in Galápagos. And that simplified essence is not to be found so easily, as T.S. Eliot indicated, using the metaphor of the sea so brilliantly. It seems to be hidden, between the waves themselves, because indeed, newly arrived at the edge, we have not yet developed the faculties that will allow us to see the pattern in full.

Our drama aboard the *Bronzewing*, adrift beneath the lava cliff, almost cost us everything, but our collective response to the near disaster was anything but simple. I will never forget the pale distress of the captain as he first appeared and looked quickly from the cliff to me. In an instant, everything was said. Under the stricken white parchment of his face, I could see the sense of guilt plainly written for the world. He didn't see it in mine because I was not yet fully aware of my part in the drama and I had hidden my contribution to the disas-

ter at the bottom of a chasm yet to be explored I could afford to be smug and artificially generous on the surface though secretly hold him to blame, even while my smugness slowly began to unravel from within.

● ● ● ● ● ● ● ● ● ● ● ●
LOOKING INTO THE ABYSS

My first reaction was the easy one. I could see only his neglect—his almost criminal neglect, to our seagoing minds—as *captain*. He had slept through not only the anchor dragging but our long, long, nighttime drift. I saw his painful humiliation too, because I, the mere naturalist on board, had discovered our plight. But there was a rising disquiet beginning to beat in my own chest. I and my fellow crew member Carlos, really knew our boat better than this new captain, and we were definitely more familiar with the particular anchorage from which we had drifted. We should we have persisted in our shared opinion the previous night about our need to put out a second anchor line. We should have dropped another anchor without consultation, as crews are wont to do when they do not want to argue with their captain. We should have woken too.

No matter that the inherited world of the sea told us that the captain is the be-all and end-all of all responsibility, we had all contributed to the lapse, the inexcusable lapse. The edge is no place for apportioning blame. If we had merely touched that cliff, we would have been for the briny deep, crew and passengers alike. The under-tow and the huge waves lacerating against that undercut, barnacle-encrusted fortress would have killed us all.

Nothing was said; Carlos had appeared in the cockpit as we left the shadow of the cliff, knew all instantly, and disappeared just as quickly. We motored away, back toward the anchorage, the sleeping passengers blissfully unaware of how close they had been to a sudden, shocked and very violent end. I could hear Carlos starting on the breakfast. Nothing could be said—there was nothing to be said. The near-disaster seemed beyond any post-mortem, but my mind swung back and forth, unable to rest. There was nothing criminal in dragging our single line; we had gone to sleep in a flat calm, with the wind coming up suddenly in the night. Rabida Island has a notorious, difficult, sloping beach, unable to hold an anchor in any kind of blow.

It was the captain's sleeping through it all that had been so shocking. Captains do not sleep when wind or weather changes, they wake up. More secretly Carlos and I were shocked that we had slept on, too, but the captain was there in all his inherited and burdened glory and thus convenient for the blame. Historically, *captaincy* is not just a post, it is an inhabitation, the boat a second skin. It is parenthood, and even in your sleep an invisible monitoring consciousness should wake to the least whimper, to the most minute change in motion, never mind a dragged anchor and a two-mile rocking drift on a rough night sea.

It was all the more disturbing when Carlos and I thought of our previous captain. A robust, strapping man, bred to the sea, Raphael had always been preternaturally alert and omnipresent, appearing on deck at the least sign of trouble. Raphael had been someone in the midst of the main event at all times and out of that example galvanized us to the same pitch of attention. We had made a tight, mutually trusting crew on board the *Bronzewing*. Raphael ran a *very* tight ship, but we also laughed, fished, and dove for lobster together. Raphael had guided my Spanish, and I had taught him the rudiments of English. He was good, very good for my first real apprenticeship to the sea, and then suddenly he was gone, promoted away from us. We had privately mourned Raphael's rise to one of the larger yachts and the breaking up of our little team, though we had said little to one another at the time. Now, it was easy to feel an outer confirmation of our inner sense that there was a stranger in our midst. We were surrounded by the far-stretching, changing ocean every day; trust in one another in the midst of this unknown, ever-shifting immensity was unspoken but incredibly important. The new captain had let us down. No matter that the *Bronzewing* was now forging purposefully back to Rabida Island, we were all in our hearts and minds temporarily adrift.

CAPTAINS COURAGEOUS

The great irony was that in his all-knowing alertness, we had allowed Raphael to lull us subtly into a lack of responsibility at the very core; we were alert as crew members, but Raphael had so filled his role of captain to capacity that we ourselves had become incapacitated in one crucial area: We had given up our own inner sense of captaincy. Somewhere inside us we had come to the decision that ultimate responsibility lay elsewhere. I told this story of near disaster to a recently retired admiral from the U.S. Navy. He listened with a lifetime's experience at sea, looked me straight in the eye, and summed it all up: "A good crew doesn't let a new captain fail."

A six-month-old child is admitted to the hospital with early congestive heart failure. The doctor prescribes *Rogoxin* which steadies the heart rate but can be lethal above a certain level. The doctor places the decimal point in the wrong place and prescribes 0.9 mg instead of 0.09. An experienced nurse catches the error and consults with another nurse. They both say it is too high; they take it to a second doctor for a second opinion; he does the recalculation and says the first doctor was right. They give the

Rogoxin at the higher dose and the child dies. Who had the captaincy? Somewhere inside themselves the nurses thought the doctor was the real captain no matter the outward circumstances and that they were powerless. They were not; they had the captaincy, but not the courage of a captain's convictions.

- - - - - - - - - - - - - - - -
THE LOST LEADER

Sailing back to our anchorage in the midst of that silence set me to thinking of the edges and boundaries of everyday identity and especially the way that we live at the edges of our identity in work. Beyond the edge we have established for ourselves lies the unknown, where we often feel powerless and ready to blame. Above the throb of the engine, I was desperate to blame someone, crying out for someplace to lodge an ultimate sense of responsibility, and panicking a little because it came to rest nowhere but on my own shoulders. But how we long for that parental image of a captain or leader to carry the burden.

"O Captain! my Captain!"

Walt Whitman cried out to Lincoln, seeing in his president a stabilizing, organizing force, that could guide him, not only through a terrible Civil War, but through the generous, untidy sea of Whitman's own life. Whitman's lines of poetry are generally long, marvelous, out-of-control wave-forms. You see the great outlines of life through the way his poetry crashes and froths on the headlands and reefs of whatever he was attempting to describe. But in Lincoln, Whitman intuited someone who was neither claimed by the chaos of the waves nor chained by the stability of dry land, someone living right at the conversational cliff edge of a whole nation. In the bloody American Civil War, Whitman worked in frontline hospitals tending the wounded and the soon to be dead; he must have seen Lincoln as the great survivor, a man who lived through a whole series of near shipwrecks—in those perilous times, a true captain. Lincoln seemed to be steering the country even as it was convulsed by civil war, guiding a vessel that seemed to be coming apart in the bitterness of slavery. Even in difficulty, the president seemed awake, present, alert to the veering winds of conflict, trimming a way through the elements.

> "O Captain! my Captain! Our fearful
>   trip is done,
> The ship has weathered every rack, the
>   prize we sought is won,
> The port is near, the bells I hear, the
>   people all exulting . . ."

How desperately we need that captain. Someone to rely on, someone who will awaken when we are asleep, someone to take care of us without making it too obvious, but someone obviously to blame when everything goes wrong. We love a captain in our personal kingdom, our politics, our country, our workplace, and especially in the reflection of our own mirror. All or nothing. I am the captain, or someone else is. *The Boss.* We say, all our resentments held in suspension while the word soaks up our sense of responsibility. In the image of that all-knowing presence is everything we think we need.

Until, that is, Lincoln is suddenly assassinated and we find ourselves immediately orphaned in the world. In the all-powerful presence of a great leader, it is easy to remain unaware of our own personal compass, a direction, a willingness to meet life unmediated by any cushioning parental presence. Whitman's cry for Lincoln is the cry for those selfsame qualities brought to life in the heart of every individual. The shock of Lincoln's death was the shock of living without his outer image, of having to live out that legacy firsthand.

What do you see Walt Whitman?
Who are they you salute, and that one
    after another salute you?
                    —WALT WHITMAN
                    "Salut au Monde!"

The death of anyone close to us is always a form of salutation, a simultaneous good-bye to their physical presence and a deep hello to a more intimate imaginal relationship now beginning to form in their absence. My captain in the outer world had essentially been killed, he had let me down, and I was struggling to salute and recognize a personal sense of captaincy that lived in everyone. It seems emblematic to me also of the times in which we live—when, for many, all of the outer captains have been done away with; by their own actions, by our cynicism, or perhaps more truly because we no longer want captaincy to be static and concentrated in single personalities but movable and available, a provenance of our own.

WAKING THE CAPTAIN

In the moment that I had woken in a panic and seen the captain still asleep in his bunk, simply for the sake of sheer survival I had not had time to wake him and was forced to rouse an equivalent responsibility in myself. It may be that we all come to this threshold at one time or another in our lives when suddenly the person on whom we have conferred captaincy is no longer present or available. It may be their literal absence or a sudden insight in a meeting room that the man or woman at the end of the table cannot be relied on. We look and look and finally realize they are not available, they are deep inside some insulation which cannot be engaged and therefore cannot be trusted. Not because they are bad people but because they are not awake people. At that moment, whatever their outer title, to us they are no longer the captain. At that moment

we are orphaned from a familiar parent-child relationship but we are also, if we can rise to the occasion, thankfully emancipated. We are ushered into an adult-adult conversation with our own powers. Something must be done: We must speak out, take the wheel, call the rest of the crew ourselves, or, if all of these avenues are blocked, abandon ship, resign, and go elsewhere.

Whenever we attempt something difficult there is always a sense that we have to wake some giant slumbering inside ourselves, some greater force as yet hidden from us. We look for better work by first looking for a better image of ourselves. We stir this inner giant to life in order to find the strength to live out the life we want for ourselves. We want to live that image not for abstract heroic reasons but because we are desperate for more presence, more responsiveness, more alertness in our work. But first we must be able to recognize the image.

WAKING THE GIANT

What do we look for in the hidden giant, the captain that is living inside us, as yet asleep? The same qualities we admire in good leaders we see in the outside world. What are the qualities that make us love the good captains, the good leaders, the good bosses of this world? What is it about them that brings out the best in us and makes us want to shine not only for them but for something we seem to be discovering simultaneously in ourselves? What is it about a great leader that allows us to be ourselves despite or even because of our faults and difficulties? Why are we so existentially disappointed when someone in a responsible position fails in that responsibility, when the captain fails to be a captain? Is it because, like Whitman, we feel without them we are losing a little of the color and texture of life, that when we lose them we also lose a little faith in our own calling?

One of the outer qualities of great captains, great leaders, great bosses is that they are unutterably themselves. This is what makes their stature so gigantic in our imaginations. They are living at a frontier, a cliff edge, in a kind of exhilaration that we want to touch in our own lives. The best stay true to a conversation that is the sum of their own strange natures and the world they inhabit, and do not attempt to mimic others in order to get on. Though they may try sincerely to communicate with others, these giants will not make themselves like everyone else in order to do it. These is no replacing a Mandela, the present Dalai Lama, a Rose Parks, a Martin Luther King, a Churchill, a Susan B. Anthony, not because there are no more great leaders like them to come but because there are no more of those particular individuals.

Rosa Parks was tired, not heroic, when she refused to move to the back of the bus; it was her own tiredness and she stood by it, as if she was reclaiming an edge of exhaustion she hadn't allowed herself to feel until then. It was the tiredness of work but also the utter exhaustion of being invisible, of not being seen. It was as if the true inner reality of her tiredness suddenly became the only thing visible to her, and having touched it, she was damned if she was going to let anyone take even that away from her. She took an element of her nature normally seen in a bad light and by inhabiting if fully turned a form of extreme tiredness that we normally consider as lead, into gold. She was a tiny individual who, because of her intense refusal to be anyone but her tired self, looms in giant fashion over our historical perspective of the sixties.

At the other end of the spectrum, when we come to the image of a classic war leader, I think of Churchill, no bland product of strategizing spin doctors, but a cigar-chomping, brick-laying eccentric of the first order. No Puritan either, Churchill did all of his morning work while comfortable in bed

and, during a long life, drank his own very substantial weight in Champagne and brandy many times over. He had suffered satire, discouragement, near bankruptcy and political exile, yet when Britain was drifting onto the rocks of defeat in May 1940, he was awake and ready to face the shadows of Nazi Germany. He offered to the British people not the need to please, but "blood, sweat and tears," the will to survive, and a glimmering hope of future triumph. Britain had a giant to wake because Churchill was a giant self, independent of any outer recognition.

I think also, against all my better instincts, of Margaret Thatcher, much loved in the United States but mostly disliked now in the Britain that elected her to power throughout the eighties. Her great triumph was to smash an old complacent political order that was doing no one any good, but to do it in a way which disenfranchised many and set people at each other's throats. That being said, it took a certain species of obnoxious self-righteousness peculiar only to herself to be able to do it. I vividly remember being backstage at an international event in San Francisco with the former Soviet Leader Mikhail Gorbachev and former U.S. president George Bush, waiting for the proceedings to begin. All at once, the door seemed to blow open, and from the outer world, Margaret swept in with all the impact on our quiet backwater of a tropical cyclone. In moments she had roiled the calm backstage ambiance and bent everything and everyone to her enormous will.

Firstly, she told the former president of the Soviet empire to sit down and rest because he looked exhausted, then she turned upon the former leader of the free world and told him in no uncertain terms that he looked piqued and must immediately get something from the buffet. George went with the tide and complied. Finally she pinned Bernard Shaw of CNN up against the wall and insisted that he reveal the questions she was to be asked that evening in front of the television cameras. All protestations of journalistic freedom were batted aside and Bernard was worn down and snapped at like a sheepdog with an errant ewe until he surrendered up at least a tiny morsel of information. This done, he was released and allowed to assume an upright position.

I couldn't help but marvel at the sheer bloody-minded willfulness of the woman. No matter my prejudices against her, she was unutterably herself, a force of nature. I thought to myself that there was nothing essentially wrong with her; whatever the negative fallout of her political reign, it was the fault of those of us, her ministers, her political opposition, the voting population, who could not stand up to her and be just as robust in our ability to say *no*. There had been almost no one who had had enough confidence in themselves to meet her on equal terms. When in the presence of that kind of power we give up on our own powers, we allow for a kind of despotism. We allow an individual to be themselves in isolation from all other individuality, which is good for neither the Margaret Thatchers of this world nor the world on which they leave their mark.

To wake the giant inside ourselves, we have to be faithful to our own eccentric nature, and bring it out into conversation with the world. We can rely on the conversation itself to iron out the selfish aspects of our nature. In baseball parlance, we have to step up to the plate; in the parlance of the soul's exploration, we must step to the frontier of the unknown where there are great possibilities at play, where we do not know where our courageous speech might lead us. We have to say *no* just as firmly as we say *yes*. Yes, we want the attributes of leadership but often falter in the presence of the real thing.

We love a strong captain, but how do we live out our own captaincy in the shadow of those who seem to overwhelm our own nursling qualities by the overpowering nature of their character or competency? Is it because we have no equivalent image inside ourselves to match the outer image which is trampling over our world? Margaret Thatcher was famous for her tyrannical hold over her ministers—almost all of them men, almost all of them products of Britain's traditional public schools. They had absolutely no experience of powerful women behaving in this fashion. Perhaps they had read about certain Greek goddesses in their classical studies, but the only woman they would have had any daily contact with through their schooling would have been the matron; the school nurse. They had absolutely no inner image of a wilder, more willful femininity to correspond to this outer political fury, and they were almost all helpless before her. Orbiting her central sun, they became a bland circle of yes-men caught in the grip of her gravitational influence.

In order to stand up against a force of nature, we often have to find that same elemental nature inside ourselves. Many times in our work lives we walk through the office door with our shoulders hunched to our necks, feeling powerless and bullied by those who hold power over us. Our refusal to stand up to those who harass us on a daily basis becomes, in effect, a lack of faith in our own voice, and the nature that that voice bestows on us. A vicious circle begins in which our refusal to speak out confirms our vulnerability and increases our invisibility. We feel certain that we will lose our job, our position, our career, and no one will ever look at us again. Or, like the ministers who surrounded Margaret Thatcher, we may not even know how to begin a conversation with that kind of irrational power. Sometimes we are rightly quiet in the face of dire consequences for our career or our families, but more often than not we are simply living in the shadow of our own fears.

I remember Joel, a consultant friend of mine, telling me of his failure to stand up to one bullying CEO early in his career. Joel recounts with some wonder how he had collapsed completely at a crucial moment of confrontation because there was no inner giant to wake inside him. Quite the contrary, not only did Joel see himself being fired if he stood up to the CEO, but he had the incredible and irrational image of himself living out the rest of his existence as a bag lady on the streets of Berkeley, his then home in California. The prospect of being fired was not irrational to Joel, the image of himself as a bag lady was. What Joel had stumbled into was an unspoken fear which he had not yet explored, and which hid from him the deeper strengths of his own nature. As soon as he found himself in that unspeakable territory, his will collapsed. The fact is that whatever Joel was most afraid of he would surely become if he confronted the angry CEO, no matter that it involved the little imaginative matter of a sex change. Joel was sure that the CEO would talk to every other CEO in his native California and bar him from a fruitful career. But Joel went on to say that whatever courage he had learned now as a consultant in his organizational work came from that moment. Joel realized that in order to be effective he had to take an inventory of his own fears; whatever he did not know of his own fears would blind him at the moments when he was faced with an unknown. Joel made a further crucial distinction: He did not have to overcome his fears, he simply had to know *what* he was afraid of.

Almost always when we ask hard questions about leaders and leadership, we have to ask hard questions of ourselves, too. We have to take an inventory not only of the gifts we have to give but of the gifts we are afraid of receiving. What are we afraid of, what stops us from speaking out and claiming the life we want for ourselves? Quite often it is a sudden horrific understanding of the intimate and extremely personal nature of the exploration. What we

ask in a serious manner for those marvellous outer abstracts of courage, captaincy, and greatness, we set in motion an exploration that tests us to the very core. We suddenly realize the intensely personal nature of all these attributes. Stephen Spender has it very well in his poem, The Truly Great.

Spender talks of hoarding from the spring branches the desires falling across our bodies like blossoms. A simultaneous harvest and fading away, growth and disappearance, that involves an exploration of both sides of life's equation, our continual appearance and disappearance as if rehearsing for the ultimate disappearance in death. Is there any other real source of courage? At the end is left only a vivid signature in the air, an echo of Keats's epitaph, "Here lies one whose name was writ in water." Not a testament to loss but a courageous acceptance that we make our mark and then move on, but it is the making that makes the meaning.

· · · · · · · · · · · · · · · · · · ·

PERSONALITY AND PASSION

The great question about leadership, about taking real steps on the pilgrim's path, is the great question of any individual life: how to make everything more personal. How to understand life or leadership not as an abstract path involving devious strategies but more like an inhabitation, a *way* of life, a conversation, a captaincy; an expression of individual nature and gifts and a familiarity with the specific nature of your own desires and fears. In a conversation there is always more than one voice, and one of the voices must be our own or it is no conversation at all. We do not try to overpower others at work with our voice in order to have a conversation, nor do we substitute someone else's for our own, but we are there, we are present, we are heard. We play the tension like a violin string at concert pitch. We stop looking for heroes to come and show us the path to glory, but we do not ignore the courageous example of others. In their presence, or under the influence of their reputation, we attempt to find the same inner correspondences in our own bodies that will allow us to take the next courageous step that we can also call our own.

In order to assume our captaincy, we should not genuflect before the imposing array of other captains. We must stop indulging in worshipful idolatry of Bill Gates or Jack Welch (in their wiser moments, they surely wish to escape from that idolatry), and put our energies toward taking the short but difficult next step on our own pilgrim's path to self-knowledge. So long as this path is a real conversation with the greater world, it will lead us right to the frontier of presence we desire. Taking any step that is courageous, however small, is a way of bringing any gifts we have to a surface, where they can be received. For that we have to come out of hiding, out from behind the insulation. In a way, we come to an understanding of ourselves in our work according to where we have established our edge. Wherever our edge of understanding has been established is the very place we should look more intently, but it is also the very place that fills us most with fear. In my own captain's failure I had come to an edge that I had previously refused.

COMING OUT OF HIDING: BEING THE CAPTAIN

After our near disaster beneath the cliff face, how did I see the captain's failure? It had everything to do with being in hiding. Somehow this new captain, whose professional world was made up of his maritime experience, the boat, its itinerary, its crew, its passengers and the wild elements that surrounded it, had allowed his attention to retreat into an insulated room inside himself that had no connection with the immediacy of his outer world. In the rough territory of the Galápagos, washed by the restless Pacific, the result was a neglect and forgetfulness, a sleep in which others could die.

There is a marvelous relationship between the living body of a sailing vessel and the actual human body we try to inhabit every day in the workplace. Our attempt to convey an idea to others in the office, or our attempt to show others that we are useful and have something to give, is a way of feeling physically present in the world. Our bodies and our personalities are vessels, and leadership, like captaincy, is a full inhabitation of the vessel. Having the powerful characteristics of captaincy or leadership of any form is almost always an outward sign of a person inhabiting their physical body and the deeper elements of their own nature. In the same way, to sleep through crucial moments of our work life is to eventually find ourselves on the rocks, to put ourselves or our organizations in danger.

It is not that a captain cannot sleep, but even in sleep theirs should be a cultivated attentiveness, which is essential at sea. It is something akin to the way we can wake ourselves at a specific time for an important occasion even if we have forgotten to set the bedside alarm, except this is a continuous alertness—accessible even in the deepest modes of sleep. Every turn of the tide or the weather is important. A good captain wakes as soon as the wind veers or the rhythm of the waves lapping at the hull increases.

Waking in response to change is, in effect, a litmus test of identity for a leader or a captain, because the ability to know even in unconscious modes what is occurring at the surface speaks to the way that the attributes of seamanship have soaked right through to the core of the captain's identity. Even when a captain rests, he or she does it in conversation with the rhythm of the ocean. The life of the edge is perceived right through to the interior, even in darkness, even in sleep. At sea, this edge is the skin of the boat and the way that edge responds to the living commands of the ocean and the moving air. This edge is more often than not represented by all the courageous conversations we must continually have to keep in touch with the dynamics affecting work; by staying aware of this elemental edge, we can more readily keep to the bearing indicated by our inner compass.

Once we begin to engage those elemental edges through daily courageous speech, we start to build a living picture of our own nature, exactly the same way a captain gets to know her vessel and the particular way it reacts to the elements that surround it. As captain of our soul's journey, we feel the angle of the sails, the creak and strain of the ropes, the lean of the tiller, and learn the particular hum and song of our conversation with the elements. It is this conversation that gives us not only our powers of survival but a music of exhilaration for our journey and arrival.

It seems to me that every human life has the elements of a sea voyage, of a journey and an arrival. That every human life is also like a vessel that contains innumerable other lives for which we have a deep responsibility. That this vessel journeys from one unknown sea to another as we go through important epochs of our lives, and that every soul's journey in the world is like a captaincy—that is, an identity which is necessarily attentive, powerful, and responsible, but not fixed, more like a meeting place of the elements in which the known vessel and the unknown sea must join in vital conversation. Out of this conversation we create a directional movement in the world that not only ensures our survival but creates exhilaration, the wind on our face, an immersion in the present whilst we simultaneously experience the joy of speeding toward our destination.

To my mind, this captaincy, this responsible and responsive presence, this creation of an elemental meeting place inside oneself or in one's organization or society, is not just an individual dynamic, but one in which the whole of humanity is collectively engaged. We are living at a time when much of the way we see and describe ourselves is under immense strain from the currents of change that swirl around us. Our old fixed, terrestrial ideas and the language to describe those ideas do not seem terribly well adapted to the fluidity of our new ocean world. We are each being impacted in enormous, far-reaching ways by the tides of ecological and technological change and the sudden realization that we inhabit a much more complex, intimate universe than we imagined. We intuit that we are about to cross a great expanse to a new place, but our maritime abilities, our sense of captaincy, our courage, our responsiveness—individually and collectively—are under severe test.

IMAGINATION AMID COMPLEXITY

The severest test of work today is not of our strategies but of our imaginations and identities. For a human being, finding good work and doing good work is one of the ultimate ways of making a break for freedom. In order to find that freedom in the midst of the complex world of work, we need to cultivate simpler, more elemental identities truer to the template of our own natures. We must understand that we carry enough burdens in the outer world not to want to replicate that same sense of burden in our inner selves. We need a sense of spaciousness and freedom, but find we can claim that freedom only by living out a radical, courageous simplicity—a simplicity based on the particular way we belong to the world we inhabit. If we ignore our simpler necessities, the attempt to create a complex professional identity most often buries us in layers of insulation through which it is impossible to touch our best gifts. Our lives take the form of absence. Like the captain asleep below, we become exhausted from the effort needed to sustain our waking identities. The day may be full, we may be incredibly busy, but we have forgotten who is busy and why we are busy. We lose the conversation, we lose our calling, we lose our sense of captaincy. To wake up and assume the captaincy no matter the perceived outer hierarchy, we have to realize that our lives are at stake; the one unique life, entirely our own, it is possible for each of us to live. Death is much closer to each of us then we will admit; we must not postpone that living as if we will last forever.

We speak of genius when we speak of leadership, hoping for some of that elusive genius in ourselves, but the word *genius* in its Latin originality means simply, *the spirit of a place*. The genius of Galápagos lies in its being unutterably itself; the genius of an individual lies in the inhabitation of their peculiar and particular spirit in conversa-

tion with the world. Genius is something that is itself and no other thing.

The task is simple and takes a life pilgrimage to attain, to inhabit our life fully, just as we find it, and in that inhabitation, let everything ripen to the next stage of the conversation. We do this because that is how we make meaning and how we make everything real. The core act of leadership must be the act of making conversations real. The conversations of captaincy and leadership are the conversations that forge real relationships between the inside of a human being and their outer world, or between an organization and the world it serves. All around these conversations, the world is still proceeding according to mercies other than our own. This is the ultimate context to our work. The cliff edge of mortality is very near. We must know how easy it is to forget, how easy it is to drift onto the rocks and put our lives to hazard. Everything is at stake, and everything in creation, if we are listening, is in conversation with us to tell us so.

V-5: The Star Thrower

Loren C. Eiseley

I awoke early, as I often did, just before sunrise to walk by the ocean's edge and greet the new day. As I moved through the misty dawn, I focused on a faint, far away motion. I saw a youth, bending and reaching and flailing arms, dancing on the beach, no doubt in celebration of the perfect day soon to begin.

As I approached, I sadly realized that the youth was not dancing to the bay, but rather bending to sift through the debris left

by the night's tide, stopping now and then to pick up a starfish and then standing, to heave it back into the sea. I asked the youth the purpose of the effort. "The tide has washed the starfish onto the beach and they cannot return to the sea by themselves," the youth replied. "When the sun rises, they will die, unless I throw them back to the sea."

As the youth explained, I surveyed the vast expanse of beach, stretching in both directions beyond my sight. Starfish littered the shore in numbers beyond calculation. The hopelessness of the youth's plan became clear to me and I countered, "But there are more starfish on this beach than you can

From the book, *The Star Thrower* by Loren C. Eiseley. Harvest Publishers, 1979.

ever save before the sun is up. Surely you cannot expect to make a difference."

The youth paused briefly to consider my words, bent to pick up a starfish and threw it as far as possible. Turning to me he simply said, "I made a difference to that one."

I left the boy and went home, deep in thought of what the boy had said. I returned to the beach and spent the rest of the day helping the boy throw starfish in to the sea.